METAPHOR
AND
THOUGHT

METAPHOR
AND
THOUGHT

SECOND EDITION

edited by
Andrew Ortony

School of Education and Social Policy
and
Institute for the Learning Sciences
Northwestern University

CAMBRIDGE
UNIVERSITY PRESS

Published by the Press Syndicate of the University of Cambridge
The Pitt Building, Trumpington Street, Cambridge CB2 1RP
40 West 20th Street, New York, NY 10011-4211, USA
10 Stamford Road, Oakleigh, Melbourne 3166, Australia

First published 1979
Second edition 1993

Printed in the United States of America

Library of Congress Cataloging-in-Publication Data
Metaphor and thought / edited by Andrew Ortony. – 2nd ed.
p.   cm.
Includes bibliographical references and index.
ISBN 0–521–40547–5. – ISBN 0–521–40561–0 (pbk.)
1. Thought and thinking.   2. Metaphor.   I. Ortony, Andrew,
1942–   .
BF455.M47   1993
169–dc20   92–37625
                                                      CIP

A catalog record for this book is available from the British Library.

ISBN 0–521–40547–5 hardback
ISBN 0–521–40561–0 paperback

TO LAURA

Contents

Contents

METAPHOR AND EDUCATION

Contributors

MAX BLACK
Department of Philosophy
Cornell University

RICHARD BOYD
Department of Philosophy
Cornell University

L. JONATHAN COHEN
The Queen's College
Oxford University

BRUCE FRASER
Department of Special
Education
Boston University

HOWARD GARDNER
Project Zero
Harvard Graduate School of
Education

DEDRE GENTNER
Department of Psychology and
The Institute for the Learning
Sciences
Northwestern University

RAYMOND W. GIBBS, JR.
Program in Experimental
Psychology
University of California, Santa
Cruz

SAM GLUCKSBERG
Department of Psychology
Princeton University

THOMAS F. GREEN
Department of Foundations of
Education
Syracuse University

MICHAEL JEZIORSKI
Department of Psychology
Wayne State University

BOAZ KEYSAR
Department of Psychology
University of Chicago

THOMAS S. KUHN
Department of Linguistics and
Philosophy
Massachusetts Institute of
Technology

GEORGE LAKOFF
Department of Linguistics and Program in Cognitive Science University of California, Berkeley

SAMUEL R. LEVIN
Department of English The Graduate School and University Center City University of New York

RICHARD E. MAYER
Department of Psychology University of California, Santa Barbara

GEORGE A. MILLER
Department of Psychology Princeton University

JERRY L. MORGAN
Department of Linguistics and The Beckman Institute University of Illinois at Urbana–Champaign

GEORGIA NIGRO
Department of Psychology Cornell University

ANDREW ORTONY
School of Education and Social Policy and The Institute for the Learning Sciences Northwestern University

REBECCA S. OSHLAG
Graduate School of Education State University of New York at Buffalo

ALLAN PAIVIO
Department of Psychology University of Western Ontario

HUGH G. PETRIE
Graduate School of Education State University of New York at Buffalo

ZENON W. PYLYSHYN
Center for Cognitive Science Rutgers University

MICHAEL J. REDDY
Department of Linguistics Columbia University

DAVID E. RUMELHART
Department of Psychology Stanford University

JERROLD M. SADOCK
Department of Linguistics University of Chicago

DONALD A. SCHÖN
Department of Urban Studies and Planning Massachusetts Institute of Technology

JOHN R. SEARLE
Department of Philosophy University of California, Berkeley

ROBERT J. STERNBERG
Department of Psychology Yale University

THOMAS G. STICHT
Applied Behavioral and Cognitive Sciences Inc. El Cajon, California

ROGER TOURANGEAU
National Opinion Research Center

MARY WALSH
Department of Psychology University of Western Ontario

ELLEN WINNER
Department of Psychology Boston College, and Project Zero Harvard Graduate School of Education

Preface to the second edition

The publication of the first edition of *Metaphor and Thought* in the fall of 1979 coincided with, and to some degree contributed to, a rapid burgeoning of interest in and research into the nature and function of metaphor in language and thought. This interest has shown itself in a number of different disciplines – including the philosophy of language and the philosophy of science, linguistics, cognitive and clinical psychology, education, and artificial intelligence – with the result that during the last decade or so some important and influential new ideas have appeared. In addition, a new journal, *Metaphor and Symbolic Activity,* was launched in 1986 and continues to thrive as a major outlet for research ideas. Finally, 1990 saw the publication of *METAPHOR II – A Classified Bibliography of Publications from 1985–1990,* a volume containing some three and a half thousand references (Van Noppen & Hols, 1990).

In view of developments such as these, it seemed appropriate to prepare a second edition of *Metaphor and Thought,* in which all the authors of chapters appearing in the first edition (with the exception of Max Black, who, sadly, died in 1988) would have the opportunity to update their original contributions to reflect any changes in their thinking. Of the twenty-one chapters in the first edition, eight have been revised, some extensively. The eight revised chapters have an asterisk preceding their titles in this edition. In two cases, Paivio and Petrie, the revisions were done in collaboration with a new coauthor. In addition, six new chapters have been added in an attempt to sample the new ideas in the field. These are by Gentner and Jeziorski, Gibbs, Glucksberg and Keysar, Lakoff, Mayer, and Winner and Gardner.

The inclusion of these new chapters, along with shifts in the theoretical issues now considered to be central to the cognitive and related sciences, made it prudent to reconsider the organization of the book as a whole. Accordingly, this edition is organized somewhat differently from the first edition. There are now five sections. The chapters in the first section, Metaphor and Meaning, tend to view metaphors as forms of language, whereas those in the second section, Metaphor and Representation, tend to view them as forms of mental representation. The section Metaphor and Understanding deals with the psychological processes involved in understanding metaphors and other tropes. Finally, the last two sections deal with the role of metaphors and analogies in science and their role in teaching and learning, respectively.

Putting this second edition together turned out to be a much more onerous task than I had originally envisaged. My main debt in accomplishing this task is to Laura Monti, not only for her love, but also for her helpful comments on some of the new writing, and for her help in getting the everswelling manuscript in order. I would also like to express my gratitude to Teri Lehmann for her cheerful and efficient administrative help, to Sharon Lewis for the wonderful job she did in compiling the new and much expanded list of references, and to Katharita Lamoza of Cambridge University Press for doing her usual excellent job as production editor.

It is my hope that this new edition will better reflect the state of thinking on the topic of metaphor as it is in the 1990s.

Andrew Ortony

Evanston, Illinois
December 1992

Preface to the first edition

In September 1977, a group of leading philosophers, psychologists, linguists, and educators gathered at the University of Illinois at Urbana–Champaign to participate in a multidisciplinary conference on metaphor and thought which was attended by nearly a thousand people. Most of the essays in this volume are substantially revised versions of papers presented at that conference. The conference was structured around a number of topics, and some of that structure has survived the transition to book form. Specifically, in both parts of the book there are three topics, each addressed by three papers. The second and third papers of these triplets are frequently devoted, at least in part, to a discussion of the first paper. The first part of the book contains two additional chapters: an opening one by Max Black that might be regarded as "scene setting," and a closing one by George Miller that might be regarded as a bridge between the two parts.

Because the conference constituted the genesis of this book, it is appropriate to acknowledge those groups and individuals whose help made it the success that it was. The principal source of funding for the conference was a contract from the National Institute of Education. Supplementary financial support was generously provided by a variety of sources within the University of Illinois. These included: the Advisory Committee to the Council of Academic Deans and Directors, the Center for Advanced Study, the College of Education, the College of Liberal Arts and Sciences, and the Office of the Chancellor. To all of these I should like to express my thanks. I should also like to express my appreciation to the National Academy of Education, whose award to me of a Spencer Fellowship helped in many concrete ways.

No large conference can function without a group of key people. In this case, Daniel Alpert, Jerry Morgan, and Hugh Petrie worked with me for nearly a year on the planning. Surprisingly, our frequent meetings often resulted in decisions, and the implementation of these decisions was largely effected through the dedicated efforts of Peggy Harris and Paula Sherman. To them, I owe a special word of thanks, for the doing is always so much more difficult than the talking.

The preparation of the final manuscript that resulted from all these efforts was no less onerous a task than the organization of the conference itself, partly because it was necessary to try to ensure that successive revisions of papers were not made totally in ignorance of revisions of related papers. (Readers should be cautioned that this undertaking may not have been in every case successful.) Apart from my gratitude to the authors for an unusually high level of cooperation in producing legible manuscripts within a reasonable time, my principal debt is to Michael Nivens, who was chiefly responsible for entering almost the entire manuscript onto computer files to facilitate editing, indexing, and general manuscript management. I also wish to thank Bonnie Anderson, who drew many of the illustrations.

With so diverse an array of topics there seemed little hope of achieving a coherent integration in an introductory chapter. It seemed more appropriate to attempt to identify the major questions, to highlight recurring themes, and to try to show how the individual chapters related to them. The constructive comments on various aspects of the introductory chapter made by William Alston, Janet Dougherty, Peter Haidu, Walter Kintsch, George Lakoff, and George Miller were very much appreciated. Thanks are also due to Eric Wanner.

Andrew Ortony

Urbana, Illinois
December 1978

1

*Metaphor, language, and thought

ANDREW ORTONY

A central presupposition of our culture is that the description and explanation of physical reality is a respectable and worthwhile enterprise – an enterprise that we call "science." Science is supposed to be characterized by precision and the absence of ambiguity, and the language of science is assumed to be correspondingly precise and unambiguous – in short, literal. For this reason, literal language has often been thought the most appropriate tool for the objective characterization of reality. For example, in early twentieth-century Western philosophy a tacit belief in the privileged status of literal language was an important underlying assumption of picture theories of meaning (e.g., Russell, 1956; Wittgenstein, 1921/1961). This belief reached a peak in the doctrine of logical positivism, so pervasive amongst philosophers and scientists sixty years ago. A basic notion of positivism was that reality could be precisely described through the medium of language in a manner that was clear, unambiguous, and, in principle, testable – reality could, and should, be literally describable. Other uses of language were meaningless for they violated this empiricist criterion of meaning. During the heyday of logical positivism, literal language reigned supreme.

A different approach is possible, however, an approach in which any truly veridical epistemological access to reality is denied. The central idea of this approach is that cognition is the result of mental *construction*. Knowledge of reality, whether occasioned by perception, language, or memory, necessitates going beyond the information given. It arises through the interaction of that information with the context in which it is presented and with the knower's preexisting knowledge. This general orientation is the hallmark of the relativist view (E. Sapir, 1921; Whorf, 1956) that the objective world is not directly accessible but is constructed on the basis of the constraining influences of human knowledge and language. In this kind of view – which provides no basis for a rigid differentiation between scientific language and other kinds – language, perception, and knowledge are inextricably intertwined.

Opposing beliefs along the lines of these two views find their expression in a number of different areas. They can be found in anthropology, in sociology, in linguistics, in cognitive psychology, in epistemology and the philosophy of science, and even in literary theory (e.g., Bartlett, 1932; Berger & Luckmann, 1966; Blumer, 1969; Brooks & Warren, 1938; Chomsky, 1965; Greimas, 1970; Hanson, 1958; Hempel, 1965; Kant, 1787/ 1963; J. J. Katz, 1966; Lévi-Strauss, 1963; Neisser, 1967; Price, 1950; Sperber, 1975). I shall refer to these opposing conceptions as "constructivism" and "nonconstructivism," fully recognizing that this terminology is far from ideal. Different scholars subscribe to these opposing beliefs to different degrees, and in different ways. Few subscribe to them in the extreme forms in which I have presented them and few will agree with the labels I attach to them. Nevertheless, it seems useful to attempt to relate two alternative approaches to metaphor – metaphor as an essential characteristic of the creativity of language, and metaphor as deviant and parasitic upon normal usage – to a more fundamental and pervasive difference of opinion about the relationship between language and the world.

The constructivist/nonconstructivist distinction provides an interesting perspective from which to view the essays in this collection. The constructivist approach seems to entail an important role for metaphor in both language and thought, but it also tends to undermine the distinction between the metaphorical and literal. Because, for the constructivist, meaning has to be constructed rather than directly perceived, the meaning of nonliteral uses of language does not constitute a special problem. The use of language is an essentially creative activity, as is its comprehension. Metaphors and other figures of speech may sometimes require a little more creativity than literal language, but the difference is quantitative, not qualitative. By contrast, the nonconstructivist position treats metaphors as rather unimportant, deviant, and parasitic on "normal usage." If metaphors need explaining at all, their explanation will be in terms of violations of linguistic rules. Metaphors characterize rhetoric, not scientific discourse. They are vague, inessential frills, appropriate for the purposes of politicians and poets, but not for those of scientists because the goal of science is to furnish an accurate (i.e., literal) description of physical reality.

As the various disciplines of human enquiry gained their independence over the centuries, adopting their own domains, techniques, and metalanguages, the study of metaphor survived as a curiosity in some and disappeared as irrelevant in others. There was but one discipline in which the study of metaphor was central – rhetoric. The area of literary theory called rhetoric was for centuries chiefly concerned with figurative language, especially tropes (see Preminger, 1974, for a detailed account of such troublesome terms as "literature," "rhetoric," "poetics," "figurative language," "trope," etc.). What for others was but an occasional means of communication, for the rhetorician became the principal object of study. Contemporary scholars of literature vary in their theoretical persuasions almost along constructivist/nonconstructivist lines. Some literary theorists, for example, semioticians, challenge the literal/figurative distinction, whereas others, for example, the New Critics and some structuralists, accept it almost without question. Thus, literary scholars vary in the extent to which the study of metaphors and other tropes is central to their enterprise. Even so, until recently, few would have denied that tropes (of which metaphor is the archetype) are in some way special to literature. In many of the chapters that follow, however, it is implied that all language, including scientific language, is tropological. Again, the constructivist approach, with which this conclusion is principally associated, seems to threaten the distinction between the language of the poet and that of the scientist by repudiating the distinction between the metaphorical and the literal on which it is usually based.

Because rhetoric has been a field of human enquiry for over two millennia, it is not surprising that any serious study of metaphor is almost obliged to start with the works of Aristotle. Aristotle was interested in the relationship of metaphor to language and the role of metaphor in communication. His discussion of the issues, principally in the *Poetics* and in the *Rhetoric,* have remained influential to this day. He believed metaphors to be implicit comparisons, based on the principles of analogy, a view that translates into what, in modern terms, is generally called the *comparison* theory of metaphor. As to their use, he believed that it was primarily ornamental. In the *Topica* he argued that it is necessary to be wary of the ambiguity and obscurity inherent in metaphors, which often masquerade as definitions. He urged that a clear distinction be made between genuine definitions and metaphors.

A more contemporary influence on the theoretical study of metaphor was that of Richards (e.g., 1936b). Richards not only proposed a set of useful terms for talking about metaphors (the "topic" or "tenor," the "vehicle," and the "ground"), he also proposed a theory about how they function. This theory, called the "tensive" view, emphasized the conceptual incompatibility, the "tension," between the terms (the topic and the vehicle) in a metaphor.

More recently, there has been a growing interest in metaphor in a number of other disciplines. In linguistics, for example, an increasing concern with linguistic performance and pragmatics (in contrast to the emphasis on linguistic competence so characteristic of the Chomskian revolution), and an increasing interest in the nature of text, have resulted in more attention being given to nonliteral uses of language. In psychology, especially cognitive psychology, characterizing the processes involved in the comprehension of metaphors is not only an interesting challenge in its own right, but the specification of those processes also constitutes a good test of the power of theories of language comprehension in general. There are other disciplines in which metaphor is of interest, some of which are represented in this book. The chapters that follow deal primarily with a variety of philosophical, linguistic, psychological, and educational issues pertinent to the study of metaphor. Thus, the focus is mainly on metaphor from nonliterary perspectives, not because literary perspectives are unimportant, but because they have been extensively dealt with elsewhere. It is to be hoped that literary theorists will see some virtue in these new disciplinary perspectives on old problems.

The chapters in this book could be organized and classified in many ways. For example, they could be classified on the basis of whether they take a microscopic or macroscopic approach to metaphors. In the microscopic approach, the arguments and analyses tend to be based on examples in which the metaphors (and in some cases other tropes) are of words or (sometimes) sentences. By contrast, the macroscopic approach is more concerned with systems of metaphors, or metaphoric or analogical models (Geertz, 1974). In such cases there may be a sentence level, or "root metaphor" (V. W. Turner, 1974), but the emphasis tends to be on the larger system that emanates from it.

A second, and more fundamental way in which to classify the chapters is in terms of which of two major questions they address, even though these questions are not always addressed explicitly. One of these questions – *What are metaphors?* – has to do with the *nature* of metaphor, and the other – *What are metaphors for?* – is concerned with the *uses* of metaphor. The first question is the primary, but by no means the only concern of the chapters in the first three sections, namely, those on Metaphor and Meaning, Metaphor and Representation, and Metaphor and Understanding. The second question is more central to the last two sections of the book, which deal with Metaphor and Science, and Metaphor and Education.

The issues raised in the first section, Metaphor and Meaning, tend to presuppose that metaphors are primarily *linguistic* phenomena. For the most part, the examples used are of metaphors as words, and the approaches taken are somewhat traditional. The presuppositions that underlie many of these chapters are that metaphors are somehow "deviant," that they need to be explained in terms of "normal" or "literal" uses of language, and that their main function is to provide an alternative linguistic mechanism for expressing ideas – a communicative function. This can be seen clearly in Chapter 2, by Black.

One of Black's purposes is to further develop his *interaction* theory of metaphor, a theory whose origins can be found in the work of Richards

(1936a), but which was first articulated in detail by Black (1962b). Black now seeks to specify the theory in terms that are not themselves metaphorical. He restricts his discussion to metaphors that he considers to be theoretically interesting, "vital" metaphors. In addressing the question of how to distinguish metaphors from other forms of language (the central "What are metaphors?" question), he suggests that any search for an infallible criterion of "metaphorhood" is doomed to failure. Any criterion one cares to suggest, says Black, can be shown to break down under certain circumstances.

Black believes that metaphors sometimes function as "cognitive instruments," a view that foreshadows Boyd's on their role in scientific discourse. Just as Boyd argues that some metaphors actually constitute scientific theories, so Black argues that some metaphors permit us to see aspects of reality that they themselves help to constitute. This claim is related to two themes that surface repeatedly throughout the book. The first is the idea that something new is created when a metaphor is understood. The second is that metaphors afford different ways of viewing the world. The question of whether metaphors give rise to something new when they are understood is only partly an empirical question. Clearly, with respect to an individual, new knowledge can result from the comprehension of language in general, and to that extent at least, it can result from the comprehension of metaphors in particular. But whether, for example, metaphors in some special way create new similarities by changes in word meanings, as Black (1962b) implied, depends, as Black now points out, on how one construes notions such as "creating similarities" and "changes in word meanings." Certainly one can come to see relationships that one did not see before, but whether exclusively by metaphor is doubtful. Certainly, in some sense, the interpretations of some words in metaphors are different from their interpretations in literal contexts, but whether that constitutes a change in word meanings is also doubtful. It is clear, however, that the emergence of "something new" is a pivotal concept in Black's interaction theory of metaphor. If Black is right, then the idea needs to receive the kind of elaboration that he offers, at least as a first step.

The idea that metaphors afford different ways of perceiving the world is central to the chapters of Schön and of Reddy. Schön proposes that in social contexts, "generative" metaphors may result in a sort of cognitive myopia wherein some aspects of a situation are unwittingly (or not) emphasized at the expense of other, possibly equally important aspects. If one believes that important social problems can be viewed from "correct" and "incorrect" (or "healthy" and "unhealthy") perspectives (see Geertz, 1974), then the possibility exists that metaphors may sometimes lead to an incorrect (and consequently, a socially harmful or undesirable) view. Schön is concerned with social policy planning, especially urban planning. He describes how society's ills receive conflicting descriptions, often couched as metaphors. These descriptions, these "stories people tell" carry with

them, often covertly and insidiously, natural "solutions." Thus the way in
which a social situation is viewed constrains the set of problem solutions in
a sometimes wrong or inappropriate way. Schön calls this dilemma "frame
conflict," and the solution to it "frame restructuring." Frame restructuring
involves the coordination and reconciliation of the conflicting descriptions.
Conflicts of frames, he argues, cannot be resolved by appeal to the facts,
because all the "relevant" facts are already embedded in the metaphor.
Thus, Schön's chapter emphasizes the extent to which metaphors can constrain and sometimes dangerously control the way in which we construct
the world in which we live. It is a warning to be wary of such "generative"
metaphors, metaphors that generate their own solutions, because more
often than not they will fail to present an objective characterization of the
problem situation.

Reddy, applying Schön's notion to language itself, argues that the metaphors we use to talk about human communication encourage us to view
communication in the wrong way – they encourage us to see it from a
nonconstructivist rather than from a constructivist perspective. In talking
about English, the metalinguistic resources available and normally used are
the result of what he calls the "conduit metaphor." This metaphor for
communication in natural language is based on the idea that language is a
carrier of ideas, thoughts, aspirations, and so on, so that all a hearer needs
to do is to *unpack* the message and *take out* what was *in* it. Reddy argues
that the conduit metaphor falsely presupposes a certain objectivity – an
objectivity that ignores the contribution of the hearer's or reader's own
knowledge and experience. He observes that it leads to erroneous attempts
to solve various kinds of communication problems, and, one might add,
until a few years ago, to erroneous attempts to uncover the psychological
processes involved in language comprehension. Reddy's chapter contains
an appendix of examples of the conduit metaphor in action. This appendix
is in itself a major piece of work, providing linguistics with an unusual
corpus, as well as substantiating Reddy's claims about the pervasiveness of
the root metaphor. The conduit metaphor that Reddy sees as being so
misleading, turns out to be isomorphic with the nonconstructivist approach
to language and cognition. The alternative analogy that he proposes (the
"toolmaker's paradigm") is an attempt to sketch a constructivist alternative. Reddy's main point, however, is fundamentally the same as Schön's,
namely, that the way we talk about things (in Reddy's case, human communication, and in Schön's case, social problems) often depends on root
metaphors that are essentially misleading and inaccurate.

As we shall see later, toward the end of the book Petrie and Oshlang
redress the balance somewhat by arguing that metaphor does not have to
be the villain; the alternative ways of seeing that it affords are not only an
advantage in educational contexts, but a necessary feature of them.

The constructivist claims of Schön and Reddy find their most thorough and explicit treatment in Lakoff's chapter. Lakoff, acknowledging his intellectual debt to Reddy, presents a detailed account of a theory of mental representation firmly rooted in the idea that metaphor plays a central role in the way in which we think and talk about the world. Many of our most mundane concepts, such as those of time, states, change, causation, and purpose are, Lakoff argues, represented metaphorically, that is, in terms of other concepts. Lakoff repudiates a number of cherished assumptions that he considers as underlying not only many approaches to metaphor, but more generally entire domains of inquiry – domains such as the philosophy of language, symbolic approaches to artificial intelligence, and information processing psychology.

The macroscopic views of Schön, Reddy, Lakoff, and others contrast quite sharply with some of the more microscopic views. For example, Sternberg, Tourangeau, and Nigro, in their chapter, share most of Schön's conclusions, but they arrive at them from their own microscopic approach. They propose a theory of the processes involved in the generation and comprehension of metaphors, as well as a characterization of the representation of knowledge consistent with the operation of those processes. The basic construct that they employ is that of "semantic feature spaces." The idea is that a good metaphor utilizes regions in two remote conceptual spaces that occupy similar positions within each space. An important issue that they address is that of the "goodness" or "success" of a metaphor which, they claim, depends on maximizing the distance between the different domains (feature spaces) involved, while minimizing the difference between the positions occupied by each term within each domain. This conception of the goodness or "aesthetic pleasingness" of a metaphor they contrast with a notion of the "comprehensibility" of a metaphor, which is enhanced by minimizing the distance between the domains themselves. From this it follows that the better the metaphor, the less comprehensible it is (up to some limit). The analysis that Sternberg et al. offer is consistent with the belief that metaphors are an important means of expressing ideas for which the language may not have any literal terms. This is because, in their view, a function of metaphors can be to identify a point in the topic feature space such that the corresponding point in a different, vehicle, feature space has no lexical items associated with it.

Sadock, Rumelhart, and others raise challenging questions about the distinction between literal and metaphorical meaning, sharing Black's doubts about the possibility of a valid criterion for "metaphorhood." Sadock believes that if linguistics is conceived of in a strict, traditional manner, then the study of metaphor does not constitute a proper part of it because metaphors are features of language use rather than of language per se. He argues that there seems to be no rational basis for distinguishing literal from metaphorical language at all. Where are we to draw the line? Why could it not be argued that the use of the word "lion" to refer to both

the species in general, and male members of that species in particular, is a
kind of semantic or metaphorical extension to both? Who is to say which is
the "core" meaning, and which is the extended meaning? Even at this
simple level, there are questions about how the metaphorical can be distinguished from the literal. Although those, like Searle, who advocate more
extreme positions are willing to agree that the notion of literal meaning is
not without its problems, still that notion has to be presupposed in order
for their accounts to get off the ground.

Rumelhart comes to a similar conclusion from a rather different starting
point. His position is that the distinction between metaphorical and literal
language does not have any psychological correlate in the underlying processes involved in their comprehension. The processes required to understand the one are the same as those required to understand the other.
According to Rumelhart, metaphor plays a crucial role in language acquisition. In applying old words to new objects or situations, children engage in
a kind of metaphorical extension. Sometimes these extensions are consistent with conventional uses of the word, and we perceive the child as
having learned something more about the word's applications. Sometimes
they are not consistent with conventional uses, and adults, in their wisdom,
are quick to attribute an error to the child. Thus, when a child, having first
learned to use the word "open" in the context of opening his or her mouth,
"correctly" uses the same word in the context of opening a door or a
window, he or she is doing exactly the same thing as when "incorrectly"
using it in the context of "opening" a light switch or a faucet. In the former
case the new use is conventional (in English) whereas in the latter case it is
not (but interestingly it is, for example, in French). On this view, metaphor
cannot be regarded as some kind of linguistic aberration that requires an
extraordinary explanation. Rather, it has to be regarded as an essential
ingredient of language acquisition, and consequently a natural and normal
linguistic phenomenon. From Rumelhart's perspective, metaphor is still
immensely important, but its role in language is now viewed quite differently. It is viewed from a constructivist position.

The approach advocated by Black is probably not a typical pragmatic
account, as is the one proposed by Searle in his chapter. It is pragmatic in
its reliance on context, but it does not follow the familiar Gricean tack (see
Grice, 1975; Searle, 1969). Both pragmatic accounts, however, are in sharp
contrast to the semantic approach advocated by Cohen. For Cohen, metaphors can be accounted for solely within a theory of semantics – itself part
of a general theory of language, rather than a theory of language use. Thus,
Cohen attempts to characterize the kinds of systematic violations of semantic rules that would be needed to explain the basis of metaphors. In particular, he examines rules that specify the cancellation of semantic features as a
means of arriving at metaphorical meaning directly from literal meaning.
His chapter is interesting and provocative, representing, as it does, a well

worked out account based on a now unfashionable approach to meaning. Cohen's position is that all that is required to account for metaphors is a set of (essentially) linguistic rules.

On the other hand, Searle sees the fundamentally important question as being much the same as for indirect speech acts, namely, What are the mechanisms whereby a sentence meaning can be related to the speaker's meaning? Searle discusses some candidate mechanisms, including the proposal that the link between the two could be achieved by the hearer "calling to mind" appropriate relating elements. Searle distinguishes metaphors from indirect speech acts by suggesting that whereas in indirect speech acts the speaker intends to convey both the sentence meaning and the indirect meaning, in metaphors the intention can only be to convey the latter. Morgan's chapter questions the power of Searle's notion of "calling to mind." Searle casts the net too wide, Morgan claims. Thus, while generally sympathetic to Searle's approach, Morgan is nevertheless unhappy with the details. Searle argues that if a literal interpretation is rejected, a metaphorical interpretation must be sought. Morgan objects that such an account is too vague because it fails to distinguish between metaphors, mistakes, irony, and a host of other indirect speech acts.

Morgan's call for a need to distinguish the principles underlying different kinds of tropes is answered, albeit indirectly and in different ways, in two of the new chapters included in this second edition, the one by Gibbs, and the one by Winner and Gardner. Gibbs takes as his starting point Lakoff's "Contemporary Theory" and presents some empirical results designed to support the contention that metaphors and various other kinds of tropes are understood effortlessly because experience is conceptualized in the kinds of metaphorical ways that Lakoff describes. Naturally, with this orientation, Gibbs rejects Searle's pragmatic account, based as it is on a sharp distinction between literal and metaphorical uses of language. On the other hand, Winner and Gardner in their chapter accept the distinction between literal and nonliteral language, and offer data from comprehension studies with young children to illuminate the difference between metaphor and irony. In doing so, they examine the relative roles in the understanding process of domain knowledge, metalinguistic knowledge, and children's emerging theories of mind.

A semantic account of metaphor, epitomized by Cohen's chapter, locates metaphors primarily at the level of word meanings, so that augmented metaphorical word meanings contribute to a different sentence meaning. The pragmatic account, exemplified in Searle's chapter, moves up a level and locates metaphors at the level of different uses of sentences by speakers: speaker meaning can be the same as sentence meaning, or it can require a metaphorical reinterpretation of sentence meaning. As we have already seen, however, some authors reject both these accounts, although not necessarily for the same reasons (compare, for example, the reasons of

Rumelhart with those of Lakoff). Glucksberg and Keysar also flatly reject
the kind of pragmatic approach advocated by Searle, but their view is also
at odds with Lakoff's. Glucksberg and Keysar propose that metaphors are
class inclusion statements and are understood as such in the normal course
of language comprehension.

Levin, on the other hand, is willing to accept the general thrust of Searle's
approach, especially the separation of sentence meaning and speaker
meaning – a separation that he sees as being of theoretical utility. Levin
argues, however, that the mechanisms whereby metaphors are understood
are more complex, and he advances two reasons for believing this. First, he
suggests that the metaphorical transfer is artificially made unidirectional by
the use of examples that introduce the predicate through the copula (X is a
Y). This, he says, makes it difficult to conceive of a metaphorical transfer
going from X to Y, rather than from Y to X. He argues, however, that if we
take a sentence like "the brook smiled," we can see there is a choice as to
whether to attribute characteristics of smiling to the brook, or characteristics of brooks to smiling. His second reservation is more radical. The kind of
approach advocated by Searle, he suggests, may be suited to metaphors
that arise in everyday language, but another approach might be more appropriate for literary metaphors. In literary metaphors, linguistic construal –
whereby the language is reinterpreted to fit the world – might better be
replaced by phenomenalistic construal, wherein a reader's model of the
world is changed to accommodate a literal interpretation of the metaphor.
This approach, suggests Levin, may provide a better basis for understanding what it is that poets are doing. What is defective, on this account, is not
the use of language, but the model of the world that is being built up. The
notion of phenomenalistic construal fits rather well with the discussion of
the reading process presented by Miller in his chapter – what it requires in
literature is a suspension of disbelief, rather than a reinterpretation of the
language.

Perhaps the semantic and pragmatic views of metaphor need not be quite
so antithetical as their strongest proponents imply. The radical pragmatics
position accepts a notion of "literal meaning" (sentence meaning), that is
alleged to deviate from the speaker's meaning. It would thus be possible, at
least in principle, to conceive of the transformation mechanisms from the
one to the other as involving precisely the kinds of rules that the radical
semantics position claims are required to account for metaphor. To be sure,
the pragmatic approach is going to want more than that, but it is doubtful it
can get away with less. Not all positions on this issue are amenable to such a
rapprochement, however. Lakoff, Rumelhart, and to a lesser extent Miller,
believe that there is no cognitive basis for a sharp distinction between the
literal and the nonliteral. Rather, metaphoricity is a dimension along which
statements can vary. Rumelhart clearly thinks that no special mechanisms
need be postulated to account for the comprehension of metaphors –

neither a pragmatically nor a semantically motivated reinterpretation is required. And if no reinterpretation is required the rules of the radical semanticists would appear to be left without any cognitive counterparts.

The controversy over whether metaphor can be dealt with purely within semantics is a reflection of the broader question: "What are metaphors?" The dispute concerns how metaphors should be categorized – as a purely linguistic phenomenon, as a more general, communication phenomenon, or even more radically, à la Lakoff and Gibbs, as a phenomenon of thought and mental representation. If metaphors can be handled by a purely linguistic theory, there is no need to invoke extralinguistic knowledge to account for them. The extreme alternatives seem to map quite directly onto the nonconstructivist and the constructivist approaches respectively. Black's chapter urges us to consider genuine cases of nontrivial metaphors. But such "naturally occurring" metaphors are frequently incomprehensible if one does not consider the contexts in which they occur. If we have to refer to a context of use in order to know if something is a metaphor, it would seem that a purely semantic account is too restrictive. Such an account cannot accommodate the observations of Black and Searle that in some contexts a speaker may intend to convey both the literal meaning of an utterance and a metaphorical meaning. Furthermore, it cannot even begin to explain that level of the comprehension of metaphors that Black calls "interaction." It is by no means clear, however, that the kind of approach advocated by Searle would be any better suited to the explanation of interaction. Indeed, it could be argued that the three traditional theories of metaphor – the substitution view, the comparison view, and the interaction view – are all equally compatible, or incompatible, with the semantics and the pragmatics approaches. Both approaches seem primarily concerned with the nature of the relationship between metaphor meaning and surface meaning. Of course, Black is not really interested in what particular metaphors mean. As indicated above, he is concerned with giving an account of metaphor that satisfies an intuition that he and many others have, namely, that there is some special, emergent "new thing" that is created when a novel metaphor is understood – something new that is attributable to the metaphor rather than to its novelty.

The emergence of something new is considered by Paivio and Walsh to be one of the central problems surrounding the comprehension of metaphors. They see as a tool for its explanation the notion of integration, whereby disparate elements in the utterance are combined to yield something greater than the sum of their parts. They see the concepts of similarity and relation as also being implicated, and their chapter discusses these three central concepts and their relationship to metaphor. Paivio and Walsh make a number of suggestions about the way in which knowledge is represented in interacting visual and verbal modes – suggestions that relate to the role of imagery in metaphor. Coupled with these suggestions are some empirical predictions about the relative effectiveness of concrete versus abstract metaphorical vehicles.

Fraser describes some systematically collected interpretive responses to a set of sentences. The sentences were constructed to be semantically anomalous, but Fraser's subjects were called on to give them metaphorical interpretations, which they apparently did very willingly. Fraser found little consistency among the various interpretations offered, suggesting that in their interpretations, subjects were drawing heavily on their own associations to, and knowledge about the predicates requiring metaphorical interpretations. Fraser concludes that there is little agreement among people about the interpretation of metaphors. It ought to be noted, perhaps, that the subjects in Fraser's study might have been straining to make metaphorical interpretations of contextually unsupported sentences with no specific referents ("She is an octopus"). In more naturalistic cases, there might be more agreement. This is an outcome that seems to be demanded by the fact that people can and do communicate successfully using metaphors.

A question explicitly raised in the chapter by Paivio and Walsh and in many of the other chapters concerns the role of similarity in metaphors. This question is discussed in my own chapter. Although the emphasis is primarily on the role of similarity in similes, some attention is devoted to the relationship between similes and metaphors. One of the more controversial claims made is that similes cannot be construed as literal comparisons, a claim apparently also made by Searle. Although no answer to the basic question "What are metaphors?" appears, one candidate solution – that metaphors are implicit comparisons – is rejected. It is argued that the comparisons that underlie metaphors must themselves be regarded as nonliteral, or metaphorical. Consequently, there is no explanatory value in asserting that metaphors are comparisons unless one then goes on to explain the difference between literal comparisons and metaphorical ones.

There can be other reasons for rejecting the view that metaphors are implicit comparisons, Glucksberg and Keysar, for example, reject it because they believe that metaphors are not comparisons at all; they are just what they seem on the surface – class-inclusion statements. Glucksberg and Keysar turn the traditional comparison view on its head, arguing that when metaphors are expressed as comparisons (i.e., similes) they are understood as implicit class-inclusion statements.

The question of the role of comparisons in metaphors is one of the major foci of Miller's chapter. Recognizing that a persistent criticism of the comparison theory of metaphor is its vagueness, Miller presents a detailed formal treatment of the various ways in which similarity statements can underlie metaphors. He also touches on a number of other important issues, including the recognition of metaphors, the interpretation of metaphors, the construction of a world model to "fit" a metaphor, and the fundamental uniformity of the comprehension processes for literal and nonliteral language alike. These and many other issues, are brought together in Miller's attempt to find a place for the comprehension of metaphors within a more general framework for the comprehension of text.

It might be argued that if the strongly constructivist views of Schön, Reddy, Lakoff, and others can be upheld, there would be important implications for theories of language, be they philosophical, linguistic, or psychological. Indeed, this claim is made explicitly by Lakoff. The argument would be that constructivist claims are quite inconsistent with a sharp distinction between semantics and pragmatics, or even between language and knowledge. They are inconsistent with approaches based on formal logic, or with semantic systems such as interpretive semantics (e.g., J. J. Katz & Fodor, 1963) or generative semantics (e.g., Lakoff, 1971). Such approaches seem ill equipped to deal with what many view as a central aspect of human thought and cognition, namely the ability to understand things from different points of view. The extreme nonconstructivist position is that cognition is understanding things in the way they are, whereas the extreme constructivist position is that the notion of alternative ways of seeing things is fundamental to cognition. Therefore, if metaphors are important because of their ability to provide alternative or new ways of viewing the world, then so-called literal language may be too restrictive because of its inability to provide those perspectives. Consequently, approaches that attribute to literal language a privileged status vis-à-vis its access to reality will have to be regarded as fundamentally incorrect. This issue is central to Boyd's chapter, a large part of which is concerned with the nature of our access to "objective reality." It also impinges on more general questions in the history and philosophy of science, as evidenced by Gentner and Jeziorski's chapter.

Gentner and Jeziorski examine the role of metaphor and analogy in the history of Western science as a vehicle for exploring the question of whether analogical reasoning (which together with the perception of similarity, they take to underlie both) is an innate cognitive capacity. Their conclusion is that whereas the drawing of comparisons is universal at least in the sense that it has been a major demonstrable component of scientific thought for centuries, the use to which comparisons have been put and the implicit criteria for their legitimate use have changed dramatically. One point that emerges clearly from their discussion is that historically metaphors and analogies have played an important role in the formulation and transmission of new theories – a function of metaphors that Boyd concentrates on in his chapter.

Boyd argues that sometimes metaphors are essential to the statement of novel scientific theories. Such metaphors he refers to as "theory-constitutive" metaphors. He concedes that they may lack the linguistic precision many have taken to be important in scientific discourse, but this imprecision, he argues, is a referential one. It is not a special feature of metaphors in scientific discourse, but of referring terms in general. Thus, Boyd sees the role of metaphors in the transmission of novel scientific conceptions as an essential part of a more general theory of reference. He goes on to propose a theory of reference that not only addresses many of the standard problems in epistemology associated with such theories, but also offers a comfortable home for metaphors. His theory is cast in terms of the ability of general terms to provide "epistemic access" to important and interesting aspects of reality. Boyd's chapter offers, therefore, one answer to the question: "What are metaphors for?" They permit the articulation of new ideas, of which scientific theories are but a special case. It is a function that cannot always be fulfilled using literal language.

Kuhn for the most part accepts Boyd's position, but he sees the role of metaphors as being more extensive than does Boyd. Boyd limits his account to his theory-constitutive metaphors, arguing that some uses of metaphors in science are purely exegetic (for example, the metaphor of atomic structure as a miniature solar system). Kuhn believes that even metaphors like this – where it is alleged that we know exactly the basis of similarity – require the employment of metaphorlike processes. He argues that we must still distinguish between those aspects that are similar and those that are not. Thus, Kuhn wants to extend an interactive account of metaphor to the use of models in general; they are not merely heuristic, pedagogical devices, they lie at the heart of theory change and transmission. For both Boyd and Kuhn, the necessity of metaphor lies in its role in establishing links between the language of science and the world it purports to describe and explain. They agree in their unwillingness to restrict that function, as the nonconstructivist would, solely to literal language.

Pylyshyn, although finding the general thrust of Boyd's arguments attractive, poses a question raised earlier by Sadock and others about how one can decide whether something is a metaphorical or literal description. He argues that many of the examples that Boyd gives of metaphorical terms in cognitive psychology are really examples of literal uses – particularly the concept of computation. Furthermore, Pylyshyn is concerned that it should be possible to distinguish between metaphors that are powerful and those that are impotent. In other words, he wants to distinguish those that carry with them explanations as well as descriptions from those that have no explanatory potential, even though they might leave their protagonists with an unwarranted and unhelpful "comfortable feeling" that something has been explained. Thus, two important points emerge from Pylyshyn's chapter. First, again, the point that distinguishing metaphors from literal uses of language is by no means an easy task, and, second, that the careless use of metaphors may do more harm than good.

It is interesting to note that whereas the debate as to whether it is possible or even meaningful to distinguish between the literal and the metaphorical is one of the most clear-cut issues in the theoretical chapters, the more practically oriented chapters, especially those in the section on Metaphor and Education implicitly accept the distinction as useful and focus on how metaphors can be and are used effectively to facilitate learning. Mayer, for example, shows how effective metaphorical models can be as a means of inducing qualitative, conceptual knowledge about new domains. Focusing on science education, Mayer notes the tendency of textbooks to concentrate on quantitative, formulaic information, but argues that there is much evidence to show that scientific problem solving requires a prior ability to engage in qualitative reasoning. For Mayer, an instructive metaphor is one which successfully induces representations that can form the basis of such reasoning.

The transmission of new scientific ideas and theories is but a special case of purveying ideas that are new (for the intended audience). If one takes this line, then the role of metaphors in human thought and communication suddenly seems to blossom, as can be seen in Mayer's chapter. Metaphor becomes ubiquitous, an everyday phenomenon in the lives of ordinary men, women, and perhaps especially, children. This is the position taken by Petrie and Oshlag, who argue that a principal function of metaphor is to permit the understanding of new concepts by an iterative process of successive approximations from the more familiar metaphorical vehicle. They see this process as being analogous to the account of the change of paradigms involved in scientific revolutions (Kuhn, 1970a). Whereas Petrie and Oshlag argue that metaphors, or something like them, are necessary as the bridges between the known and the unknown, Green argues that they are not. Green maintains that reason and inference are normally quite sufficient to permit the learning of something radically new if, indeed, such learning ever takes place at all. This seems to be the conclusion Sticht reaches as well, although he goes on to discuss other uses of metaphors in education. He discusses the role of metaphors as indicators of comprehension, as frames of reference for producing text coherence, and as tools for creative problem solving. Thus, in Sticht's chapter, we find more proposals for answering the second major question, "What are metaphors for?"

The contribution of this book does not lie in the provision of definitive answers to the important questions; rather, it lies in the identification of these questions. Two central ones are: "What are metaphors?" (basically a theoretical issue), and "What are metaphors for?" (a more practical issue). These subsume a host of others raised at various places in this book. How can metaphorical language be distinguished from literal language? How literal is literal language? Should the problem of metaphor be handled by a theory of language, a theory of language use, or a theory of mental representation? Are the comprehension processes for metaphorical uses of language the same as those for literal uses? Can metaphors be reduced to comparisons? Is the reduction of metaphors to comparisons a fruitful approach to understanding the nature of metaphor? Are the comparisons to which one might attempt to reduce metaphors themselves in need of explanation? Are metaphors necessary for the transmission of new scientific concepts? Are metaphors necessary for the transmission of new ideas in general? What are the dangers associated with the use of metaphors to describe new or problematical situations? These are but some of the questions discussed in the chapters that follow.

NOTE

This introductory chapter is a revision of the one that appeared in the first edition under the title *Metaphor: A multidimensional problem.*

METAPHOR
AND
MEANING

2

More about metaphor

MAX BLACK

This paper is intended to supplement the earlier study in which I introduced and defended an "interaction view of metaphor" (namely, Black, 1962b, referred to hereafter as *Metaphor*). A reader unfamiliar with that study will find a summary in the section entitled "The Interaction View Revisited."

I shall try here to amplify my original formulation by explicating the grounds of the metaphors of "interaction," "filtering," and "screening," which I used in trying to understand how metaphorical statements work. I shall add some suggestions about the relations of a metaphor to its grounding resemblances and analogies (somewhat neglected in *Metaphor*), with the hope of also shedding some further light on the connections between metaphors and models (for which, see Black, 1962c).

This occasion gives me an opportunity to take some notice of the numerous criticisms, mostly friendly, which *Metaphor* has received since its original publication. Pleased though I am at the widespread acceptance of the *interaction view,* I agree with Monroe Beardsley, Ted Cohen, Paul Ricœur, and others that more work will be needed before the power and limitations of this approach to the subject can be fully appreciated.

Reasons for current interest in metaphor

John Middleton Murry's essay, "Metaphor" (Murry, 1931), opens with the remark that, "Discussions of metaphor – there are not many of them – often strike us at first as superficial." Today both comments would be inappropriate. The extraordinary volume of papers and books on the subject produced during the past forty years might suggest that the subject is inexhaustible.[1]

Warren Shibles's useful bibliography (Shibles, 1971) has entries running to nearly three hundred pages and contains perhaps as many as four thousand titles. As for these discussions being superficial, one might rather complain today of ungrounded profundity, because so many writers, agreeing with Murry that "metaphor is as ultimate as speech itself and speech as ultimate as thought" (p. 1), rapidly draw ontological morals, while leaving the nature of metaphorical speech and thought tantalizingly obscure.

In the inconclusive debate between the appreciators and depreciators of metaphor, the former nowadays score most points. But they are characteristically prone to inflation. As Nowottny (1962, p. 89) puts it:

Current criticism often takes metaphor *au grand sérieux*, as a peephole on the nature of transcendental reality, a prime means by which the imagination can see into the life of things.

She adds:

This attitude makes it difficult to see the workings of those metaphors which deliberately emphasize the frame, offering themselves as deliberate fabrications, as a prime means of seeing into the life not of things but of the creative human consciousness, framer of its own world.

Enthusiastic friends of metaphor are indeed prone to various kinds of inflation, ready to see metaphor everywhere, in the spirit of Carlyle, who said:

Examine language; what, if you except some primitive elements of natural sound, what is it all but metaphors, recognized as such or no longer recognized; still fluid and florid or now solid-grown and colourless? If these same primitive garments are the osseous fixtures in the Flesh-Garment Language then are metaphors its muscle and living integuments. (From S. J. Brown, 1927, p. 41)

This quotation illustrates a pervasive tendency for writers, including myself in *Metaphor,* to frame their basic insights in metaphorical terms.

A related inflationary thrust is shown in a persistent tendency, found in Aristotle's still influential treatment, and manifest in as recent a discussion as Nelson Goodnan's *Languages of Art* (Goodman, 1968), to regard all figurative uses of language as metaphorical, and in this way to ignore the important distinctions between metaphor and such other figures of speech as simile, metonymy, and synecdoche.

To make a sufficiently intricate topic still harder to handle, the depreciators tend to focus upon relatively trivial examples ("Man is a wolf') that conform to the traditional "substitution view," and the special form of it that I called the "comparison view" (see Black, 1962b, especially pp. 30–37), whereas appreciators, in their zeal to establish "that metaphor is the omnipresent principle of language" (Richards, 1936b, p. 92),[2] tend to dwell upon excitingly suggestive but obscure examples from Shakespeare, Donne, Hopkins, or Dylan Thomas, to the neglect of simpler instances that also require attention in a comprehensive theory.

Although I am on the side of the appreciators, who dwell upon what Empson and Ricœur call "vital" metaphors, I think their opponents (typically philosophers, scientists, mathematicians, and logicians) are right in asking for less "vital" or less "creative" metaphors to be considered. It may well be a mistaken strategy to treat profound metaphors as paradigms.

In what follows, I shall steer a middle course, taking as points of departure metaphors complex enough to invite analysis, yet sufficiently transparent for such analysis to be reasonably uncontroversial. My interest in this paper is particularly directed toward the "cognitive aspects" of certain metaphors, whether in science, philosophy, theology, or ordinary life, and their power to present in a distinctive and irreplaceable way, insight into "how things are" (for which, see the section entitled "Can a Metaphorical Statement Ever Reveal 'How Things Are'?"). I shall leave the "poetic metaphors" invoked by Nowottny for another occasion.

What is the "mystery" of metaphor?

One writer, who might be speaking for many, says, "Among the mysteries of human speech, metaphor has remained one of the most baffling" (Boyle, 1954, p. 257). But what is this supposed mystery? Given the prevalence or, if we are to trust Richards and many other thinkers, the ubiquity of metaphor, metaphorical discourse might well seem no more mysterious than singing or dancing – and, one might add, no more improper or deviant.

In the sentence following the one I have quoted, Father Boyle refers to the "odd predilection for asserting a thing to be what it is not." So perhaps the "mystery" is simply that, *taken as literal,* a metaphorical statement appears to be perversely asserting something to be what it is plainly known not to be. (And that makes the metaphor user look like a liar or a deceiver.) When Juliet says to Romeo, "The light that shines comes from thine eyes," she surely cannot *really mean* that his eyeballs are lighting up the chamber; when Wallace Stevens says, "A poem is a pheasant," he cannot *really* mean that it flaps its wings and has a long tail – for such things are plainly false and absurd. But such "absurdity" and "falsity" are of the essence: in their absence, we should have no metaphor but merely a literal utterance. So a metaphor user, unless he is merely babbling, would seem, according to the ancient formula, to "say one thing and mean another." But why?

An intelligent child, hearing his scientist father refer to a "field of force," might ask – but with a twinkle in his eye, one hopes – "And who ploughs it?" In order to feel the supposed "mystery," one needs to recapture the naiveté of somebody who takes metaphorical utterances to be literal or the false naiveté of someone who pretends to do so. But to assume that a metaphorical utterance presents something as what it is plainly not – or to assume that its producer really does intend to say one thing while meaning something else – is to beg disastrously a prime question by accepting the misleading view of a metaphor as some kind of deviation or aberration from proper usage.

Somebody seriously making a metaphorical statement – say, "The Lord is my Shepherd" – might reasonably claim that he meant just what he said, having chosen the words most apt to express his thought, attitudes, and feelings, and was by no means guilty of uttering a crass absurdity. Such a position cannot be rejected out of hand.

The danger of an approach that treats literal utterance as an un-problematic standard, while regarding metaphorical utterance as problem-atic or mysterious by contrast, is that it tends to encourage reductionist theories: As the plain man might say, "If the metaphor producer didn't mean what he said, why didn't he say something else?" We are headed for the blind alley taken by those innumerable followers of Aristotle who have supposed metaphors to be replaceable by literal translations.

A sympathetic way of following Father Boyle's lead might be to start by asking what distinguishes a metaphorical statement from a literal one. That, of course, assumes that there is at least a prima facie and observable difference between metaphorical and literal statements – a donnée that seems to me initially less problematic than it does to some theorists. When a writer says, "Men are verbs, not nouns," a reader untrammeled by theo-retical preconceptions about the ubiquity of metaphor will immediately recognize that "verbs" and "nouns" are not being used literally. Dictionar-ies do not include men as a special case of verbs, and a competent speaker will not list them as paradigm cases of the application of that word. And so in general, it would be relatively easy to devise tests, for those who want them, of the literal meaning of the word that is the metaphorical "focus" of a metaphorical utterance. Tacit knowledge of such literal meaning induces the characteristic feeling of dissonance or "tension" between the focus and its literal "frame."

Starting so, and acknowledging a clear prima facie difference between literal and metaphorical uses of expressions, need not, however, prejudge the validity of some "deeper" insight that might eventually reject the com-monsensical distinction between the literal and the metaphorical as superfi-cial and ultimately indefensible. But such a revisionist view needs the sup-port of a thorough exploration of the implicit rationale of the common-sense distinction. An effort to do so will naturally concern itself with crucial supple-mentary questions about the point of using metaphors and, more generally, about the distinctive powers of metaphorical discourse.

Some writers, notably Coleridge, but not he alone, have imputed a peculiarly "creative" role to metaphor (for which, see the section entitled "Are Metaphors Ever 'Creative'?"). That a puzzle or mystery might be perceived in this connection can be supported by the following train of thought. A successful metaphor is *realized* in discourse, is embodied in the given "text," and need not be treated as a riddle. So the writer or speaker is employing conventional means to produce a nonstandard effect, while using only the standard syntactic and semantic resources of his speech community. Yet the meaning of an interesting metaphor is typically new or "creative," not inferable from the standard lexicon. A major task for theorists of metaphor, then, is to explain how such an outcome – striking for all its familiarity – is brought about.

We may usefully consider, for the sake of contrast, the situation of a participant in a rule-governed practice more tightly constrained than speech – say the game of chess. There, too, a creative aspect is readily discernible, because even if all the mistakes are waiting to be discovered (as a master once said) a player must still search for and ultimately *choose* his move: In most chess positions, there is no decision procedure and no demonstrably "correct" move. Yet the player's scope for creativity is sharply limited by the game's inflexible rules, which provide him always with a finite and well-defined set of options.

Imagine now a variation, say "epichess," in which a player would have the right to move any piece as if it were another of equal or inferior value (a bishop moving for once like a knight, say, or a pawn) *provided the opponent accepted such a move.* There we have a primitive model of conversation and discourse, where almost any "move" is acceptable if one can get away with it; that is, if a competent receiver will accept it. But even here there are *some* constraints upon creativity: one cannot couple any two nouns at random and be sure to produce an effective metaphor. (If the reader doubts this, let him try to make sense of "a chair is a syllogism." In the absence of some specially constructed context, this must surely count as a failed metaphor.)

But what is a "creative," rule-violating metaphor producer really trying to do? And what is a competent hearer expected to do in response to such a move?

In *Metaphor,* I suggested that such questions, and most of the others posed by theorists of metaphor, might be regarded as concerned with "the 'logical grammar' of 'metaphor' and words having related meaning"; or as expressing "attempts to become clearer about some uses of the word 'metaphor' " (p. 25); or as the start of an effort "to analyze the notion of metaphor" (p. 26). Although this semantic emphasis has alienated some of my critics, I see no particular harm in it. There would be no substantial difference in an approach that was conceived, in a more ontological idiom, as an effort to "become clearer about the nature of metaphor." Indeed, I would regard the two formulas as equivalent.

Identifying the targets

The reader will have noticed my references to metaphorical statements. Indeed, my standing concern is with full metaphorical statements and, derivatively, with "statement-ingredients" (words or phrases used metaphorically) only as they occur in *specific* and relatively complete acts of expression and communication. (Hereafter, "metaphor" is usually short for "metaphorical statement.") A "statement," in my intended sense, will be identified by quoting a whole sentence, or a set of sentences, together with as much of the relevant verbal context, or the nonverbal setting, as may be needed for an adequate grasp of the actual or imputed speaker's meaning. I use "meaning" here for whatever a competent hearer may be said to have grasped when he succeeds in responding adequately to the actual or hypothetical verbal action consisting in the serious utterance of the sentence(s) in question.

As examples of such identifications of metaphorical statements, I offer:
(1) "L'homme n'est qu'un roseau, le plus faible de la nature, mais c'est un roseau pensant" (Pascal in the *Pensées*) – or, more briefly, Pascal's metaphor of man as a thinking reed.
(2) "You are a metaphor and they are lies/Or there true least where their knot chance unfurls." (William Empson, *Letter I'*)
(3) Ezra Pound's metaphor of education as sheepherding (in his *ABC of Reading,* passim).

Of these metaphors, the last is relatively the most independent of its context and might be sufficiently identified, with suppression of Pound's name, as "the metaphor of education as sheepherding." Yet, justice to Pound's view might demand citation of relevant passages in his tract. Textual elaboration is more obviously needed to appreciate Pascal's deceptively simple metaphor or Empson's characteristically obscure one.

I propose to distinguish what is identified merely by a formula like "the metaphor of A as B," without further specification of its contextual use, as a metaphor-*theme,* regarded as an abstraction from the metaphorical statements in which it does or might occur. A metaphor-theme is available for repeated use, adaptation, and modification by a variety of speakers or thinkers on any number of specific occasions.[3]

One danger in attending mainly to what I have called metaphor-themes is that of postulating a standard response to a given metaphorical statement – a response determined by linguistic, conceptual, cultural, or other conventions. Such a view is untenable because a metaphorical statement involves a rule violation: There can be no rules for "creatively" violating rules.[4] And that is why there can be no *dictionary* (though there might be a thesaurus) of metaphors.

Any attempt to be more precise about the identifying and individuating criteria for metaphorical statements will be embarrassed by the following difficulty. The *very same* metaphorical statement, as I wish to use that expression, may appropriately receive a number of different and even partially conflicting readings. Thus Empson's metaphor, reproduced above, might be taken by one reader, but not another, as imputing falsity to the person addressed. We might choose to say that both were right about two different metaphors expressed in Empson's words; or, less plausibly, that one reader must have been mistaken. There is an inescapable indeterminacy in the notion of a *given* metaphorical statement, so long as we count its import as part of its essence.

I hope these brief terminological remarks will serve for the present occasion. In what follows, I shall not insist pedantically upon using the qualifiers "-statement" or "-theme," usually leaving the context to resolve any possible ambiguity.

On classifying metaphors; and the importance of emphasis and resonance

Given the prevalence of metaphorical statements and their manifest versatility, a student of the subject would find some generally accepted classification helpful in making even the simplest distinctions: But at present, he is in an even worse situation than a biologist before Linnaeus. For the only entrenched classification is grounded in the trite opposition (itself expressed metaphorically) between "dead" and "live" metaphors. This is no more helpful than, say, treating a corpse as a special case of a person: A so-called dead metaphor is not a metaphor at all, but merely an expression that no longer has a pregnant metaphorical use.

A competent reader is not expected to recognize such a familiar expression as "falling in love" as a metaphor, to be taken *au grand sérieux.* Indeed, it is doubtful whether that expression was ever more than a case of catachresis (using an idiom to fill a gap in the lexicon).

If the "actuality" of a metaphor, its possessing the distinctive characteristics, whatever they may be, of genuine metaphorical efficacy, is important enough to be marked, one might consider replacing the dead and alive contrast by a set of finer discriminations: distinguishing perhaps between expressions whose etymologies, genuine or fancied, suggest a metaphor beyond resuscitation (a muscle as a little mouse, *musculus*); those where the original, now usually unnoticed, metaphor can be usefully restored (obligation as involving some kind of *bondage*); and those, the objects of my present interest, that are, and are perceived to be, actively metaphoric. Appropriate labels might be: "extinct," "dormant," and "active" metaphors. But not much is to be expected of this schema or any more finely tuned substitute. (I shall be concerned hereafter only with metaphors needing no artificial respiration, recognized by speaker and hearer as authentically "vital" or active.)

Given an active metaphorical statement, it would be useful to discriminate two aspects, which I shall call *emphasis* and *resonance.* A metaphorical utterance is *emphatic,* in my intended sense, to the degree that its producer will allow no variation upon or substitute for the words used – and especially not for what in *Metaphor* I called the "focus," the salient word or expression, whose occurrence in the literal frame invests the utterance with metaphorical force. Plausible opposites to "emphatic" might include: "expendable," "optional," "decorative," and "ornamental." (Relatively dispensable metaphors are often no more than literary or rhetorical flourishes that deserve no more serious attention than musical grace notes.) Emphatic metaphors are intended to be dwelt upon for the sake of their unstated implications: Their producers need the receiver's cooperation in perceiving what lies *behind* the words used.

How far such interpretative response can reach will depend upon the complexity and power of the metaphor-theme in question: Some metaphors, even famous ones, barely lend themselves to implicative elaboration, while others, perhaps less interesting, prove relatively rich in background implications. For want of a better label, I shall call metaphorical utterances that support a high degree of implicative elaboration *resonant.*

Resonance and emphasis are matters of degree. They are not independent: Highly emphatic metaphors tend to be highly resonant (though there are exceptions), while the unemphatic occurrence of a markedly resonant metaphor is apt to produce a dissonance, sustained by irony or some similarly distancing operation.

Finally, I propose to call a metaphor that is both markedly emphatic and resonant a *strong metaphor.* My purpose in the remainder of this paper is to analyze the raison d'être and the mode of operation of strong metaphors, treating those that are relatively "weak" on account of relatively low emphasis or resonance as etiolated specimens.

A weak metaphor might be compared to an unfunny joke, or an unilluminating philosophical epigram: One understands the unsuccessful or failed verbal actions in the light of what *would be* funny, illuminating, or what have you. Yet if all jokes are intended to be funny, and fail to the degree that they are not, not all metaphors aim at strength, and some may be none the worse for that.

Consider the following example from a letter of Virginia Woolf to Lytton Strachey:

How you weave in every scrap – my god what scraps! – of interest to be had, like (you must pardon the metaphor) a snake insinuating himself through innumerable golden rings – (Do snakes? – I hope so). (Nicolson & Trautmann, 1976, p. 205)

The snake metaphor used here should certainly count as weak in my terminology, because Strachey was intended to take the rich implicative background lightly.

The interaction view revisited

The interaction view which I presented in *Metaphor* was there character-ized as an attempt "to become clearer about some uses of the word 'metaphor' – or, if one prefers the material model, to analyze the notion of metaphor" (pp. 25–6). In retrospect, I would prefer to think of my position as a help to understanding how strong metaphorical statements *work*. But this shift of formulation from conceptual analysis to a functional analysis, though potentially important, need not detain us.

The merits of the interaction view, a development and modification of I. A. Richards's valuable insights, should be weighed against those of its only available alternatives – the traditional "substitution view" and "comparison view" (a special case of the former). Briefly stated, the substitution view regards "the entire sentence that is the locus of the metaphor as replacing some set of literal sentences" (p. 31); while the comparison view takes the imputed literal paraphrase to be a statement of some similarity or analogy, and so takes every metaphor to be a condensed or elliptic simile (pp. 35–6).

The reader will notice that both of these views treat metaphors as unem-phatic, in my terminology – in principle, expendable if one disregards the incidental pleasures of stating figuratively what might just as well have been said literally.

A brief summary of the preferred interaction view might consist of the following claims, based upon the concluding summary of *Metaphor* (pp. 44–5). I reproduce the original formulations, with minor improvements, appending afterthoughts in each case.

    1. A metaphorical statement has two distinct subjects, to be identified as the "primary" subject and the "secondary" one.

        In *Metaphor,* I spoke instead of the "principal" and "subsidiary" subjects. The duality of reference is marked by the contrast between the metaphorical statement's *focus* (the word or words used non-literally) and the surrounding literal *frame.*

    2. The secondary subject is to be regarded as a system rather than an individual thing.

        Thus, I think of Wallace Stevens's remark that "Society is a sea" as being not so much about the sea (considered as a thing) as about a system of relationships (the "implicative complex" discussed below) signaled by the presence of the word "sea" in the sentence in question. (In *Metaphor,* I proposed that the primary subject, also, be taken as a system. But it seems in retrospect needlessly paradoxical, though not plainly mistaken, to say that Stevens was viewing society, too, as a system of social relationships.) In retrospect, the intended emphasis upon "systems," rather than upon "things" or "ideas" (as in Richards) looks like one of the chief novelties in the earlier study.

3. The metaphorical utterance works by "projecting upon" the primary subject a set of "associated implications," comprised in the implicative complex, that are predicable of the secondary subject.

   The label "implicative complex" is new. "Projection" is, of course, a metaphor, that will need further discussion. In the earlier study, I spoke of a "system of associated commonplaces" (which later provoked some pointed criticisms by Paul Ricœur). My notion was that the secondary subject, in a way partly depending upon the context of metaphorical use, determines a set of what Aristotle called *endoxa*, current opinions shared by members of a certain speech-community. But I also emphasized, as I should certainly wish to do now, that a metaphor producer may introduce a novel and nonplatitudinous "implication-complex."

4. The maker of a metaphorical statement selects, emphasizes, suppresses, and organizes features of the primary subject by applying to it statements isomorphic with the members of the secondary subject's implicative complex.

   The mechanisms of such "projection" (a still serviceable metaphor) are discussed and illustrated in the next section.

5. In the context of a particular metaphorical statement, the two subjects "interact" in the following ways: (a) the presence of the primary subject incites the hearer to select some of the secondary subject's properties; and (b) invites him to construct a parallel implication-complex that can fit the primary subject; and (c) reciprocally induces parallel changes in the secondary subject.

   This may be considered a crux for the interaction view (an attempted explication of Richards's striking image of the "interanimation of words"). Although I speak figuratively here of the *subjects* interacting, such an outcome is of course produced in the minds of the speaker and hearer: It is they who are led to engage in selecting, organizing, and projecting. I think of a metaphorical statement (even a weak one) as a verbal action essentially demanding *uptake*, a creative response from a competent reader. In *Metaphor*, I said – scandalizing some of my subsequent critics – that the imputed interaction involves "shifts in meaning of words belonging to the same family or system as the metaphorical expression" (p. 45). I meant, of course, a shift in the *speaker's* meaning – and the corresponding *hearer's* meaning – what both of them understand by words, as used on the particular occasion.

How metaphorical statements work

Consider "Marriage is a zero-sum game." In this relatively "active" metaphor the implication-complex might be spelled out somewhat as follows:

(G1) A "game" is a *contest;*
(G2) between two opponents;
(G3) in which one player can win only at the expense of the other.

The corresponding system of imputed claims about marriage depends crucially upon the interpretations given to "contest," "opponents," and especially to "winning." One might try:

(M1) A marriage is a sustained struggle;
(M2) between two contestants;
(M3) in which the rewards (power? money? satisfaction?) of one contestant are gained only at the other's expense.[5]

Here, the "projected" propositions can be taken literally – or almost so, no matter what one thinks of their plausibility (the metaphor's aptness not being here in question).

Such a heavy-handed analysis of course neglects the ambiance of the secondary subject, the suggestions and valuations that necessarily attach themselves to a game-theory view of marriage, and thereby suffuse the receiver's perception of it: A marriage that can be seen as a competitive "game" of skill and calculation is not the kind made in heaven.

The relations between the three members of the implication complex (G1–3) in this relatively simple example and their correlated statements about marriage (M1–3) are a mixed lot. M2 might be said to predicate of marriage precisely what G2 does of a two-person game (with some hesitation about the matching of "opponents" and "contestants"); but in the shift from G1 to M1 it seems more plausible to discern some similarity rather than strict identity; and in M3, finally, "gain" must surely have an extended sense, by contrast with its sense in G3, since marital struggles usually do not end in clear-cut conventional victories. The difficulty in making firm and decisive judgments on such points is, I think, present in *all* cases of metaphorical statement. Since we must necessarily read "behind the words," we cannot set firm bounds to the admissible interpretations: Ambiguity is a necessary by-product of the metaphor's suggestiveness.

So far as I can see, after scrutinizing many examples, the relations between the meanings of the corresponding key words of the two implication complexes can be classified as (a) identity, (b) extension, typically ad hoc, (c) similarity, (d) analogy, or (e) what might be called "metaphorical coupling" (where, as often happens, the original metaphor implicates subordinate metaphors).

Let us now idealize the connection between the two implication-complexes (G and M) in the following way: G consists of certain statements, say Pa, Qb, . . . , and aRb, cSd, . . . , while M comprises corresponding statements Pa', $Q'b'$, . . . , and $a'R'b'$, $c'S'd'$, . . . , where P is uniquely correlated with P', a with a', R with R', and so on. Then the two systems have, as mathematicians say, the same "structure"; they are isomorphic (see Eberle, 1970, for a lucid exposition of this notion). One important deviation from the mathematical conception is that G is linked with M by a "mixed lot" of projective relations, as we saw in the game-marriage example, and not (as typically in mathematical contexts) by a single projective relation.

With such conceptions to hand, we need not speak metaphorically about "projecting" the secondary system. Viewed in this way (and neglecting the important suggestions and connotations – the ambience, tone, and attitudes that are also projected upon M) G is precisely what I have called in the past an "analog-model" (cf. Black, 1962c).[6] I am now impressed, as I was insufficiently so when composing *Metaphor,* by the tight connections between the notions of models and metaphors. Every implication-complex supported by a metaphor's secondary subject, I now think, is a *model* of the ascriptions imputed to the primary subject: Every metaphor is the tip of a submerged model.

Metaphors and similes

I have said that there is a similarity, analogy or, more generally, an identity of structure between the secondary implication-complex of a metaphor and the set of assertions – the primary implication-complex – that it maps. In "Poverty is a crime," "crime" and "poverty" are nodes of isomorphic networks, in which assertions about crime are correlated one-to-one with corresponding statements about poverty.

Hence, every metaphor may be said to mediate an analogy or structural correspondence. (That is the correct insight behind the classical comparison view of metaphor as elliptical or truncated simile.) Hence, also, every metaphorical statement may be said to implicate a likeness-statement and a comparison-statement, each weaker than the original metaphorical statement. ("I didn't say that he is *like* an echo; I said and meant that he *is* an echo!") But to perceive that a metaphor is grounded in similarity and analogy is not to agree with Whatley (1961) that "the simile or comparison may be considered as differing *in form only* from a metaphor" or with Bain (1888) that "the metaphor *is* a comparison implied in the use of a term" (cf. *Metaphor,* p. 36). Implication is not the same as covert identity: Looking at a scene through blue spectacles is different from *comparing* that scene with something else.

To call, "Poverty is a crime," a simile or comparison is either to say too little or too much. In a given context of utterance, "Poverty is like a crime" may still be figurative, and hardly more than a stylistic variant upon the original metaphorical statement. Burns might have said, "My Love is a red, red rose," instead of "My Love is like a red, red rose," if the meter had permitted, with little semantic difference, if any. But to suppose that the metaphorical statement is an abstract or précis of a literal point-by-point comparison, in which the primary and secondary subjects are juxtaposed for the sake of noting dissimilarities as well as similarities, is to misconstrue the function of a metaphor. In discursively comparing one subject *with* another, we sacrifice the distinctive power and effectiveness of a good metaphor. The literal comparison lacks the ambience and suggestiveness, and the imposed "view" of the primary subject, upon which a metaphor's power to illuminate depends. In a metaphor as powerful as Pascal's, of man as a "thinking reed" (*un roseau pensant*), the supporting ground is disconcertingly simple, being intended chiefly to highlight human frailty and weakness (*faiblesse*). The figure's effect depends, in this instance, very much on the ambience.

It is helpful to remind oneself that "is like" has many uses, among them: to point to some obvious, striking, or salient resemblance as in, "Doesn't he look like Mussolini?" (where some such qualification as *"looks* like" or *"sounds* like" is needed); in an "open comparison," to mark the start of a detailed, literal point-by-point comparison; or as a mere stylistic variation upon the metaphorical form (which raises nearly all the questions I am here trying to answer).

Thinking in metaphors

The foregoing account, which treats a metaphor, roughly speaking, as an instrument for drawing implications grounded in perceived analogies of structure between two subjects belonging to different domains, has paid no attention to the state of mind of somebody who *affirms* a metaphorical statement. A good metaphor sometimes *impresses,* strikes, or seizes its producer: We want to say we had a "flash of insight," not merely that we were comparing A with B, or even that we were thinking of A as if it were B. But to say seriously, emphatically, that, "Life *is* the receipt and transmission of information," is at least to be thinking of life *as* the passage of information (but not that, merely). Similarly for all metaphorical utterances that are asserted and not merely entertained.

It might, therefore, be a large step forward in becoming clearer about what might be called *metaphorical thought* (a neglected topic of major importance) if we had a better grasp on what it is to think of something (*A*) *as* something else (*B*). What, then, is it to think of *A* as *B*?

Consider the relatively simple case of thinking of the geometrical figure sometimes called the "Star of David" in the following different ways:

(1) as an equilateral triangle set upon another of the same size (Figure 2.1);

(2) as a regular hexagon, bearing an equilateral triangle upon each of its edges (Figure 2.2);

(3) as three superimposed congruent parallelograms (Figure 2.3);

(4) as the trace left by a point moving continuously around the perimeter of the Star and then around the interior hexagon;

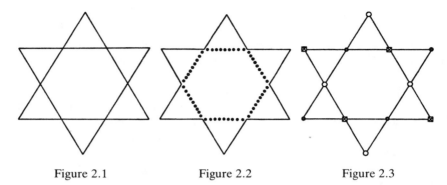

Figure 2.1   Figure 2.2   Figure 2.3

(5) as in (4), but with the point tracing out the hexagon before moving to the outside.

One might ask a child to think of the figure in each of these ways in turn. In the difficult third case of the three parallelograms, he would probably need some help, so there is something that he can be taught to do. But what?

The images one forms in trying to obey instructions corresponding to these five aspects of the Star are heuristically essential. A slow learner might be helped by having the different geometrical forms outlined in contrasting colors or, in cases (4) and (5), by watching a moving pencil point actually produce the figure. But the comprehension could not consist merely in possessing such images, important as they may be: Any competent teacher would ask the learner such questions as whether the moving point could trace the whole figure continuously – or, in the simpler cases, whether the triangles in question had the same size and shape. A test of mastery is the ability to tease out the implications of the intended perceptual analysis.

So far, the case somewhat resembles what happens when we see some *A* as metaphorically *B*: The child sees the Star *as* superimposed parallelograms; a metaphor thinker sees life as a flow of information; both apply concepts that yield discovery; both manifest skills shown in ability to tease out suitable implications of their respective insights. But this comparison is somewhat lame, because the child learner, unlike the metaphor thinker, has not yet been required to make *conceptual innovations,* the parallelograms he perceives being just those he had antecedently learned to draw and recognize.

So let us vary the illustration. One might ask a child to think of each of the following figures as a triangle: one composed of three *curved* segments; a straight line segment (viewed as a collapsed triangle, with its vertex on the base); two parallel lines issuing from a base segment (with the vertex "gone to infinity"); and so on. The imaginative effort demanded in such exercises (familiar to any student of mathematics) is not a bad model for what is needed in producing, handling, and understanding all but the most trivial of metaphors. That the use of the relevant concepts employed should *change* (so that "game" is *made* to apply to marriage; "information" to life; "reed" to man; and so on) seems essential to the operation.

Why stretch and twist, press and expand, concepts in this way – Why try to see *A* as metaphorically *B,* when it literally is not *B*? Well, because we *can* do so, conceptual boundaries not being rigid, but elastic and permeable; and because we often need to do so, the available literal resources of the language being insufficient to express our sense of the rich correspondences, interrelations, and analogies of domains conventionally separated; and because metaphorical thought and utterance sometimes embody insight expressible in no other fashion.

How do we recognize metaphors?

While praising the interaction theory, Monroe C. Beardsley has urged that it is:

. . . incomplete is not explaining what it is about the metaphorical attribution that *informs* us that the modifier is metaphorical rather than literal. (Beardsley, 1958, p. 161, italics added)

Elsewhere, Beardsley (1967) states the tasks of a theory of metaphor as follows:

The problem is to understand how that radical shift of intension [how the metaphorical modifer acquires a special sense in its particular context] comes about; *how we know that the modifier is to be taken metaphorically;* and how we construe or explicate its meaning correctly. (p. 285, italics added)

The supplement that Beardsley desires, therefore, seems to be some *diagnostic criterion,* as it might be called, for the occurrence of a metaphorical statement, some mark or indication that will allow its presence and metaphorical character to be detected. I use "diagnostic criterion" here to suggest a bodily symptom, such as a rash, that serves as a reliable sign of some abnormal state though not necessarily qualifying as a defining condition. But Beardsley may, after all, be seeking more ambitiously an observable and *necessary condition* for a statement to be metaphorical.

The need for some such identification criterion, essential or merely diagnostic, has been forcibly urged by other writers. Ina Loewenberg says:

Any satisfactory formulation of the principle of metaphor requires the identifiability of metaphors since they cannot be understood or produced unless recognized as such. (Loewenberg, 1973, p. 316)

Here "*the* principle of a metaphor" alludes to her contention that metaphors "exemplify a single principle of semantic change." If "identifiability" is taken in a broad sense, I could agree with Loewenberg's requirement, with a possible reservation about a "producer" being necessarily aware of using a metaphor. But the rest of her valuable essay shows that she, like Beardsley at least part of the time, is demanding what I have called a "diagnostic criterion" for a statement to be metaphorical.

Beardsley proceeds to offer such a diagnostic criterion as the cornerstone of his "controversion theory."[7] According to him, the recognizable mark of a metaphorical statement is that *taken literally* it would have to count as a logical contradiction or an absurdity, in either case something patently *false*.

An obvious objection is that this test, so far as it fits, will apply equally to such other tropes as oxymoron or hyperbole, so that it would at best certify the presence of some figurative statement, but not necessarily a metaphor. A more serious objection is that authentic metaphors need not manifest the invoked controversion, though many of them do. Suppose I counter the conversational remark, "As we know, man is a wolf – *homo homini lupus*" – by saying, "Oh, no, man is not a wolf but an ostrich."[8] In context, "Man is not a wolf" is as metaphorical as its opposite, yet it clearly fails the controversion test. The point is easy to generalize: The negation of any metaphorical statement can itself be a metaphorical statement and hence possibly true if taken literally. Nor need the examples be confined to such negatives. When we say, "He does indeed live in a glass house," of a man who actually lives in a house made of glass, nothing prevents us from using the sentence to make a metaphorical statement.

Our recognition of a metaphorical statement depends essentially upon two things: Our general knowledge of what it is *to be* a metaphorical statement, and our specific judgment that a metaphorical reading of a given statement is here preferable to a literal one. The decisive reason for the choice of interpretation may be, as it often is, the patent falsity or incoherence of the literal reading – but it might equally be the banality of that reading's truth, its pointlessness, or its lack of congruence with the surrounding text and nonverbal setting. The situation in cases of doubt as to how a statement is best taken is basically the same as that in other cases of ambiguity. And just as there is no infallible test for resolving ambiguity, so there is none to be expected in discriminating the metaphorical from the literal.

There is an important mistake of method in seeking an infallible mark of the presence of metaphors. The problem seems to me analogous to that of distinguishing a joke from a nonjoke. If a philosopher, whose children have trouble in deciding when he is joking, introduces the convention that a raised thumb indicates seriousness, he might sometimes be joking in raising his thumb! An explicit assertion that a remark is being made metaphorically (perhaps the best candidate for a reliable diagnostic sign) cannot guarantee that a metaphor is in question, for that does not depend simply upon its producer's intentions, and the sign might itself be used metaphorically. Every criterion for a metaphor's presence, however plausible, is defeasible in special circumstances.

If Beardsley and other critics of the interaction view are, after all, not looking for a diagnostic criterion but rather something essential to a metaphor's *being* a metaphor, my above rebuttals will miss that mark. But then the tension of which Beardsley and others speak seems to be only one feature of that peculiar mode of language use in which metaphor's focus induces a "projection" of a "secondary system," as already explained in this paper. "Tension" seems to me somewhat less suggestive than "interaction," but there is no point in quarrelling over labels.

Are metaphors ever "creative"?

The production of a new metaphorical statement obviously introduces some small change into a world that includes statements and the thoughts they express, as well as clouds and rocks. Even the reaffirmation of an old metaphor can be viewed as a trivial insertion into the world of a new token of a known statement-type. That metaphors should be creative in this boring way is hardly worth mentioning except for the sake of contrast.

Emphasis upon the alleged creativity of metaphors becomes more interesting when they are viewed as miniature poems or poem fragments. But the production of a work of art would interest me here, given the general thrust of this essay, only if such a work "tells us something about the world." Indeed, I intend to defend the implausible contention that a metaphorical statement can sometimes generate new knowledge and insight by *changing* relationships between the things designated (the principal and subsidiary subjects). To agree would be to assign a strong cognitive function to certain metaphors; but to disagree is not necessarily to relegate them entirely to some realm of fiction.[9] For it may be held that such metaphors reveal connections without *making* them. (Would it not be unsettling to suppose that a metaphor might be self-certifying, by generating the very reality to which it seems to draw attention?)

In my earlier essay, I stated one form of what might be called the "strong creativity thesis" in this way:

It would be more illuminating in some of these cases [i.e., of metaphors imputing similarities difficult to discern otherwise] to say that the metaphor creates the similarity than to say that it formulates some similarity antecedently existing. (*Metaphor,* p. 37)

It will be noticed that the claim was explicitly hedged: to say, "it would be more illuminating," to view some metaphors as ontologically creative falls short of claiming that they *are* creative. Yet no remark in *Metaphor* has provoked stronger dissent.

Khatchadourian (1968), in the course of a generally approving account of the interaction view, thinks the thesis cannot be right. He asks rhetorically, "How can one, anyway, literally create a feature or a similarity by means of a metaphor?" (p. 235). Granting that a metaphor user "can bring into prominence *known* features . . . which he thinks deserve special attention" (ibid., my italics) and thereby "give us a new vision or a new insight," Khatchadourian concludes that, "The creation of some effect in the hearer or reader [does not involve] *the creation of a similarity* between the principal and the subsidiary subject" (p. 236).

Long ago, S. J. Brown (1927) summarily dismissed a related contention (on the part of Gustave Lanson) that, by means of metaphor, "Our mind, perceiving a common quality in two different objects, or *creating between them a relation which assimilates them to one another,* names one of them by a term which suits, or belongs to, the other" (p. 47; emphasis added). Brown says: "How the mind can create a relation which does not previously exist, M. Lanson does not explain, nor ought such explanation be expected of a writer on literary theory" (ibid.). Such offhand rejection is clearly motivated by a picture of the "relation" in question as being "objective" or "out there" – existing quite as independently as the relation of "having-the-same-height-as": One rightly wants to deny that cubits can be added to stature by saying or thinking so. But this conception of some objective relation as antecedently existing is question-begging when applied to that variegated set of relations that we bundle together as "similarity."[10] When applied to the explication of metaphors, "is like" is not as sharply contrasted with "*looks* like" as "is taller than" is with "*looks* taller than." The imputed relations in a generative metaphor, one might say, must have a subjective as well as an objective aspect, but each may contribute to the other, as I hope to show. I shall try to make the strong creativity thesis at least plausible by considering a series of five answers to questions having the form, "Did X exist before it was perceived?"

(1) Did the other side of the moon exist before it was seen?

It would take a fanatical idealist to say no. We think, of course, of the rocks, plains, and mountains as having been there all the time, prior to observation. It is crucial to this conception – as contrasted with some of the following examples – that the existence of the physical objects and configurations in question is held to depend in no way upon the existence of human or other sentient beings, or upon their contingent possession and use of thought and language.

(2) Did genes exist before their existence was recognized by biologists?

The question might be rephrased as, "Did things properly *called* 'genes' exist before they were admitted into accepted biological theory?" An affirmative answer is no doubt used to contrast this case with those in which the "objects" in question were *synthesized* by human agency. *Qua* things found but not made, "natural" and not "artificial," genes – it must be agreed – were "there all the time," even before their existence was discovered. But it is less obvious that *genes* "were there all the time, waiting to be discovered." The term "gene" has its place within a man-made theory, in whose absence it would have no intelligible use: The relation between "gene" and what that term designates is more like that of a dot on a map and the city it represents than like that of a personal name and the person it designates. So the proper answer to this second question should be, "Yes and no."

(3) "Were there bankrupts before the financial institutions of the Western world were developed?"

If the question is taken in a literal sense, the only acceptable answer must be no. For here the allusion to man-made constructions (institutions rather than developed theory) is uncontroversial: "Bankrupt" (applied to someone judged insolvent on petition to a court of law) had no application before the requisite legal procedures had come into existence. A positive answer to the question would need to take the tortuously counterfactual form of: "If there had been the corresponding legal institutions (say in 1066), such-and-such a person would have been judged a bankrupt if the requisite petitions had been lodged."

(4) "Did the view of Mount Everest from a point one hundred feet above its summit exist before anybody had seen that view?"

An affirmative answer can be accepted only in the counterfactual sense proposed in the last paragraph: "If anybody had been in a position to view the mountain from the point specified, it *would* have looked as it does now from a plane flying overhead (i.e., the view has not changed)." But if we agree, we should reject the reifying mythology of the *unseen* view, "there all the time" and available for inspection like some ethereal emanation. The notion of a "view" implicates human beings as possible perceivers (though not as the creators and subjects of legal institutions, as in the last case): It is logically necessary that a view can be *seen* (viewed). Now, when a certain view is actually seen, that is a fact about the mountain as well as about the viewer – about a world that includes both. It is objectively true, not a matter of mere convention or whim, that the view of Everest from such-and-such a point has such-and-such features.

(5) Did the slow-motion appearance of a galloping horse exist before the invention of cinematography?

Here the "view" is necessarily mediated by a man-made instrument (though this might cease to be true if some mutant children were born with the power to see "slow motion" with one eye). And yet what is seen in a slow-motion film becomes a part of the world once it is seen.

The last example comes the closest to what I originally had in mind by the strong creativity thesis. If some metaphors are what might be called "cognitive instruments," indispensable for perceiving connections that, once perceived, are *then* truly present, the case for the thesis would be made out. Do metaphors ever function as such cognitive instruments? I believe so. When I first thought of Nixon as "an image surrounding a vacuum," the verbal formulation was necessary to my seeing him in this way. Subsequently, certain kinetic and visual images have come to serve as surrogates for the original verbal formulation, which still controls the sensory imagery and remains available for ready reaffirmation.

For such reasons as this, I still wish to contend that some metaphors enable us to see aspects of reality that the metaphor's production helps to constitute. But that is no longer surprising if one believes that the world is necessarily a world *under a certain description* – or a world seen from a certain perspective. Some metaphors can create such a perspective.

Can a metaphorical statement ever reveal "how things are"?

In the last section, my attention was fixed upon the creative or productive aspects of generative metaphors, in virtue of which they can sometimes function as cognitive instruments through which their users can achieve novel views of a domain of reference. But a view, however mediated, must be a view of *something:* My task here is to make some suggestions about what that "something" is and how far its possession can yield insight about "how things are."

I have chosen the unpretentious formula, "how things are," in order to avoid the fixation of a number of writers who discuss the same topic under the rubric, "Can metaphorical statements be true?"[11] Their strategy seems to me misguided and liable to induce distortion by focusing exclusively upon that special connection between statement and reality that we signal by the attribution of truth value. In ordinary language, the epithet "true" has more restricted uses than philosophers usually recognize. It is most uncontroversially appropriate in situations where the prime purpose is to state a "fact," that is, where the fact-stating statement in question is associated with some accepted procedure for verification or confirmation: A witness who swears to "tell the truth and nothing but the truth" is expected to "speak plainly," that is, to eschew figurative language, and commits himself not only to refrain from lying, but also to abstain from producing probability statements, generalizations, explanations, and interpretations of actions (though some of these excluded types of statements may in other contexts, for example, those of scientific inquiry, be properly judged true or false). In such fact-stating uses, the concepts of truth and falsity are closely associated with such semantic paronyms as "lying," "believing," "knowing," "evidence," "contradiction," and others. The relevant linguistic subpractice (or *Sprachspiel,* as Wittgenstein would call it) characteristically assumes agreement about ways of checking upon what is being said, and about ways of contesting or qualifying such sayings.

Hence, one way to recognize that we are in *this* domain of language use is to consider whether supplementary questions such as, "Are you perhaps lying?", "What's the evidence?", "How do you know?", "Aren't you contradicting what you said a moment ago?", and the like are in order. With such considerations in mind, we can readily dismiss the question about whether metaphorical statements have truth values. If somebody urges that, "Nixon is an image surrounding a vacuum," it would be inept to ask soberly whether the speaker *knew* that to be so, or how he came to know it, or how we could check on the allegation, or whether he was saying something consistent with his previous assertion that Nixon was a shopkeeper. Such supplementary moves are never appropriate to any metaphorical statements except those degenerately "decorative" or expendable ones in which the metaphorical focus can be replaced by some literal equivalence. It is a violation of philosophical grammar to assign either truth or falsity to strong metaphors.

What lies behind the desire to stretch "true" to fit some such cases (as when somebody might quite intelligibly respond to the Nixon metaphor by saying, "How true!") is a recognition that an emphatic, indispensable metaphor does not belong to the realm of fiction, and is not merely being used, as some writers allege, for some mysterious aesthetic effect, but really does say something (Nixon, if we are not mistaken, is indeed what he is metaphorically said to be).

Such recognition of what might be called the representational aspect of a strong metaphor can be accommodated by recalling other familiar devices for representing "how things are" that cannot be assimilated to "statements of fact." Charts and maps, graphs and pictorial diagrams, photographs and "realistic" paintings, and above all models, are familiar cognitive devices for *showing* "how things are," devices that need not be perceived as mere substitutes for bundles of statement of fact. In such cases we speak of correctness and incorrectness, without needing to rely upon those overworked epithets, "true" and "false."

This is the clue we need in order to do justice to the cognitive, informative, and ontologically illuminating aspects of strong metaphors. I have been presenting in this essay a conception of metaphors which postulates interactions between two systems, grounded in analogies of structure (partly created, partly discovered). The imputed isomorphisms can, as we have seen, be rendered explicit and are then proper subjects for the determination of appropriateness, faithfulness, partiality, superficiality, and the like. Metaphors that survive such critical examination can properly be held to convey, in indispensable fashion, insight into the systems to which they refer. In this way, they can, and sometimes do, generate insight about "how things are" in reality.

NOTES

The present paper is a slightly modified version of one appearing under the same title in *Dialectica*, Vol. 31, Fasc. 3–4. 1977, pp. 43–57. I wish to thank the publishers of *Dialectica* for granting permission to reprint it.

1 This suggestion is sometimes attributed to Michel Bréal (1899). See his *Essai,* p. 115. But the subject he called "infini" was the special one of the influence of metaphors upon the extension and renewal of a standard lexicon, of which he provides numerous illustrations.

2 Richards says that this "can be shown by mere observation."

3 It might be thought puzzling that while the act of producing a metaphorical statement is a datable event, its semantic content can be described, referred to, and discussed at any time: consequently, what by definition seems to be subjective, as produced by a particular speaker or thinker, has an *import,* as one might say, that is sufficiently stable or objective – in spite of violating the background linguistic conventions to be available for subsequent analysis, interpretation, and criticism. But is this really more puzzling than the fact that what a tennis player did in his last serve can be talked about (more or less) at any subsequent time?

4 For this reason, my analogy of "epicness" may be somewhat misleading. For in that game, there was a "super-rule" of sorts that determined *how* and *when* the rules of ordinary chess might be violated. In view of what looks like the essential lawlessness of metaphorical transgression, I am less sanguine than other writers about the prospects of treating the production of a metaphorical statement as a speech act in Austin's sense. I, too, wish to attend particularly to what a metaphor user is doing and what he expects his auditor to do. But I see little profit in modeling this primal situation on that of a promise giver (Austin's paradigm case), where the consequences of the performative statement are determined by a speech community's *conventions.*

5 To these might be added the following optional implications, that would readily occur to somebody familiar with game theory, though not to a layman:
   (G4) There is no rational procedure for winning in a single play.
   (G5) A "maximin" strategy (playing to minimize possible losses) may, though controversially, be considered rational.
   (G6) Playing a long-run "mixed strategy" (alternating available moves randomly but in a predetermined frequency) is (again, controversially) a "solution."
   These further implications would, of course, strengthen the metaphor and heighten its interest.

6 This conception might, accordingly, be regarded as a generalization of S. J. Brown's view of metaphor as an "analogy between . . . two relations" (p. 71). I differ from him in admitting any number of predicates and relations in isomorphic correlation – and in laying less stress than he does upon analogy, that tantalizingly suggestive but obscure notion.

7 In later writing, he called his view the "Revised Verbal Opposition Theory" (Beardsley, 1962, passim). The preferred later title indicates his interest in explaining the supposed "tension between the subject and the modifier by which we are alerted to something special, odd and startling in the combination" (p. 285). Here, he has in mind what would be an essential and not merely a diagnostic feature of metaphor.

8 This is an adaptation of an example used by Binkley (1974). See also Ted Cohen (1976) which also contains many counterexamples to Beardsley's thesis.

9 According to Oakeshott (1959), all "poetic imagining" (as in the use of indispensable metaphors) is concerned with "fictions," which would be radically misconstrued as "contributions to an enquiry into the nature of the real world." He adds: "When it is said that poetic imagining is 'seeing things as they really are' . . . we seem to have been inveigled back into a world composed, not of images but of cows and cornfields" (pp. 45–6). Contrast with this Wallace Stevens's (1957) dictum: "Metaphor creates a new reality from which the original appears to be unreal" (p. 169).

10 For which, see John Whatley's (1961) illuminating essay. I agree with him that, "To say, as philosophers sometimes at least imply, that 'A is like B' designates a 'similarity relation' tends to group like-statements to statements of physical, temporal and other purely objective relationships" (p. 112). On the whole, Whatley tends to stress nonobjective uses of "like"; but he also says of some uses that, "There is, in all but peculiar circumstances, some very definite sense in which these resemblances must correspond to fact" (p. 113).

11 Unsurprisingly, a notable exception is Austin (1961), who says: "We become obsessed with 'truth' when discussing statements, just as we become obsessed with 'freedom' when discussing conduct . . . Not merely is it jejune to suppose that all a statement aims to be is 'true', but it may further be questioned whether every 'statement' does aim to be true at all. The principle of Logic, that 'Every proposition must be true or false', has too long operated as the simplest, most persuasive and most pervasive form of the descriptive fallacy" (pp. 98–9).

3

Figurative speech and linguistics

JERROLD M. SADOCK

Introduction

I take synchronic linguistics to be the study of those aspects of human communication that are unique to natural language, no matter whether they are principled and inhere specifically in the nature of human language or are arbitrary features of particular languages. All nonliteral speech, then, including metaphor, falls outside the domain of synchronic linguistics, for nonliteral acts having nothing to do with natural language occur and parallel those that we perform by using language.

The study of metaphor, specifically, would not be a proper subject for synchronic linguistics for the reason that the basis of metaphor is a kind of indirection that is shared with nonlanguage behavior. Whatever might be unclear about the way metaphor is used and understood, I take it for granted that the underlying principles governing metaphor are of a general psychological sort and are thus not specifically linguistic. While the intellectual faculties that are involved might be *prerequisites* to speech, they are independent of it. The fact that a certain group of stars in the night sky reminded someone of a bull and the fact that a lion on a warrior's shield suggests that its bearer is brave are, I think, nonlinguistic instances of the same analogical urge that functions in the issuance and apprehension of metaphor.

Other figures of speech, from anacoluthon to zeugma, have counterparts in realms of behavior other than speaking, but here I am interested particularly in the nonliteral figures of speech, of which metaphor is one. Metonymy, synecdoche, hyperbole, understatement, irony, and euphemism (especially the sort that have been labeled "indirect speech acts") are the most important nonliteral figures of speech, besides, of course, meta-phor. They all rest their success upon an apparent clash between what is done (i.e., what is *said*) and what is intended. They therefore comprise an important natural class of speech acts.

Nonliteral figures differ from one another in the way in which what is said is connected with what is intended. In irony, what is said is (roughly) the opposite of what is intended. Overstatement and understatement are either more or less (in senses along the lines of Horn, 1976, or Gazdar, 1976) than what is intended. Euphemism is the saying of something innocu-ous that either hints at, or establishes a precondition of, some possibly offensive intended act.

In metaphor, the locus of the indirection is one part of an utterance, namely a predication. The predication may be buried inside a noun phrase, as in Aristotle's example "the sunset of life," or it may be overt, as in the sentence, "Life has a sunrise and a sunset." But all of these types of figures are alike in that they communicate in an indirect way what might have been communicated directly in terms of the conventions of a language. For this reason, they have an effect over and above what would accompany the direct accomplishment of the intended effect. As I shall argue, the fact of nonliteralness is crucially important to our understanding of the way that language functions as an integrated communicative system. Therefore in what follows, I will not restrict my attention to metaphor, but will freely examine other sorts of linguistic indirection in an effort to explicate what I consider to be the most important property of metaphor as far as linguistic pursuits go, namely its nonliteralness.

Now, linguistic figuration does differ from the general psychological ten-dencies to analogize and generalize, in that it is an aspect of social behav-ior. For this reason it is governed by whatever natural or arbitrary princi-ples govern other aspects of social interaction. Paramount among these are the sorts of rules that Grice (1975) has called cooperative maxims, rules that govern our interactions for our mutual benefit, which are, ceteris paribus, always assumed to be in force. Because linguistic figuration is ordinarily voluntary social action, it has been assumed by Grice to be subject to all general conditions on such activities. Grice would trace the recognition of figurative, or nonliteral language use, to apparent violations of one or another of these principles. I am convinced that he is right and that his treatment is superior in all respects to others, such as that of Reddy (1969). When the literal sense of an uttered monologue, sentence, phrase, or word is in apparent conflict with the cooperative principle – by seeming to be irrelevant, false, or lacking in justification – the hearer is forced to seek a figurative, but cooperative, intent behind the utterance. The produc-tion of figurative speech is then reflexively governed by the speaker's awareness of the hearer's expectation of cooperative behavior on his (the speaker's) part.

Thus, the abilities that allow and control the nonliteral use of natural language expressions are not specifically linguistic faculties and hence figuration does not fall within the domain of linguistics, at least under the narrow definition that I suggested above. But that is not to say that the phenomenon of figurative speech is of no interest to the linguist. On the contrary, there are at least two ways in which a proper understanding of metaphor and other tropes is critical to the linguist.

Figuration and semantic change

First, there is the indisputable fact that figurative language is one of the most productive sources of linguistic change. In particular, reanalysis of figures of speech as literal signs is clearly the most important source of semantic change. It is a commonplace that most lexical items prove to be dead metaphors that were alive and kicking at some time in the past. (In a similar fashion, essentially nonlinguistic articulatory and perceptual facts are the source for first phonetic, and then phonological, changes in language.)

Therefore, if the mechanism of metaphor were better understood, we would have a better grasp of the principles of semantic change and this, in turn, would yield a better understanding of synchronic grammar and grammars. Languages are the way they are in part because of historical accident, because of common psychology and experience, but also in part because of constraints peculiar to language. Not knowing a great deal about the way languages change, one may mistake basically diachronic facts for synchronic facts, and basically psychological or sociological facts for linguistic facts.

To make matters worse, the essentially nonliguistic forces behind language change are mostly constant across time, culture, and language. We find that the same sorts of semantic shifts crop up over and over. (Similarly, the same sorts of phonological changes are attested in language after language.) Lacking detailed knowledge of what produces these changes, the error of labeling such cross-language facts "language universals" is easy to commit.

It is probably the case that, in any language, vowels will be nasalized before nasal consonants at a sufficiently rapid rate of speech. It happens, of course, that this phonetic phenomenon gets incorporated into the grammars of individual languages, but the tendency toward nasalization is universal. But is it a *linguistic* universal? I think not. An accurate ballistic description of the organs of speech, and particularly of the tongue and velum, would predict allegro nasalization *whether there was speech or not.* It seems, therefore, to be a grave error to write a specifically linguistic universal nasalization rule or rule schema, as Chomsky and Halle (1968) do. There is, to be sure, a universal tendency toward vowel nasalization, but it is no more a reflection of our specifically linguistic makeup than the fact that people will stumble if they dance the polka too fast is a fact about our specifically terpsichorean abilities. True, this universal phonetic tendency has insinuated itself into the grammars of numerous languages (usually due to other changes in the linguistic system that have nothing to do with nasalization) but this is mere historical accident. Now I am *not* saying that all phonological universals are nonlinguistic in origin, nor am I saying that all phonological change has its roots in phonetics. But some universals are surely to be explained by reference to principles that impinge on language, rather than to principles that constitute language.

Analogously, much semantic change has its origin in metaphor, or some other figure of speech, and in some cases the metaphor is so obvious that it shows up in numerous languages and therefore might be misdescribed as a universal tendency of language rather than a natural tendency of thought. One case in point is the widespread occurrence of spatial metaphors for temporal relations. In English we say "at 3:00," just as we say "at the corner of Fourth and Green," we say "within an hour," "throughout the year," "before Monday," "toward the end of the month," and so on. Even the otherwise locative deictics "here" and "there" pop up in temporal usages in the forms "heretofore" and "thereafter." Facts like these are by no means unique to English. Eskimo has four suffixes that represent the spatial relations "*X* is located at *Y*," "*X* (moves) toward *Y*," "*X* (moves) away from *Y*," and "*X* (moves) from one end of *Y* to the other." Some of these same suffixes are used in the temporal mode as well and very little needs to be said about their meaning, since the metaphor of space for time is so readily understood. Compare, for example, Greenlandic "ukiume" (in the winter) with "igdlume" (in the house); and "ukiukut" (throughout the winter) with "nunakut" (across the land).

Facts like these could prompt linguists to suggest a language universal to the effect that the same morphemes express both spatial and temporal relations. But it seems to me that this is rather a fact that owes its existence to universal human psychology, perception, and experience and is quite independent of language. Accidents of history do often elevate this metaphor to the status of a grammatical fact. The metaphor in English (and Eskimo) is imperfect in that, for example, words like "during" and "previously" refer only to time, while "in front of" and "in back of" refer only to space. Closely related languages can differ in the use of relational elements in the spatial and temporal modes. For example, German "um" translates English "around" when it refers to space but "um 8 Uhr" means "at 8:00," and not "around 8:00." Thus it is clear that the underlying metaphor has been conventionalized, to a certain extent, in English and German, and I suspect that this is true in most other languages as well. Nevertheless, there is no need to postulate a *linguistic* universal to explain this cross-linguistic syncretism: It is due to the inevitable freezing of a metaphor so natural that it has occurred to people of nearly all cultures.

Figuration and synchronic grammar

As I stated earlier, and as many before me have pointed out, frequent figurative phrases can come to be directly associated with the senses that they previously conveyed only indirectly. That is, metaphors and other figures of speech can become idioms.

Pure idioms convey what they do entirely conventionally, whereas figures of speech achieve their effect for principled reasons having to do in part with some conventional meaning – the so-called literal meaning. Individual lexical items with their ordinary senses are thus idioms of a kind since there is no principled basis for their meaning what they do. Now the problem that the existence of figurative speech poses for the synchronic description of language is this: Which effects of the use of chunks of the language are purely conventional (arbitrary, idiomatic) and which effects follow from extralinguistic principles? What, in other words, do the morphemes of a language mean and what can these meanings be used to convey?

One manifestation of this problem is in the difficulty that a careful linguist encounters in trying to decide whether a lexical item, construction, or sentence is gramatically ambiguous or whether it is univocal but allows, besides the literal interpretation, a figurative understanding. That true ambiguities exist in natural languages seems undeniable. There is no conceivable reason why the word "swallow" should designate a particular sort of bird and an action of the throat – but it does. Similarly the fact that a sentence like, "He found her home" can be taken in two very different ways, one parallel to "He found me home" and the other parallel to "He found my home" seems inexplicable on natural grounds and must be relegated to the grammar of English – the repository of arbitrary, conventional facts of the language.

At the same time, it is indisputable that certain univocal words, phrases, and so on, have two or more effects for natural reasons. In such cases, one use is literal and the rest are figuratively based upon it. One clear set of examples is discussed by L. J. Cohen (1971). Should we treat the noun "flower" as lexically ambiguous because it can be used to refer to the sexual organs of plants as well as likenesses of them in paint or plastic? Such a treatment is quite implausible because it would require us to treat every concrete noun in the language as similarly ambiguous. The theory that "flower," "rabbit," and "cyclotron," for example, are all homonyms would also not explain why it is that any new noun that comes into the language would admit of both understandings. If I announce that I have just invented an electric dinner fork and if I dub it a "flibbus," no one needs to consult a lexicographer to find out whether it would be acceptable to refer to the likeness of this technological miracle as a "flibbus" as well.

By far the more pleasing account of these facts would be just the one suggested by Cohen, namely that "flower," "flibbus," and so on, have only one sense each, a literal sense, but that we may metonymically speak of any semblance of a thing by using the name of the thing itself. Thus a sentence such as, "This is a flower," said while pointing to a conglomeration of pigment on canvas would be, strictly speaking, false. But its metonymical intent is plain enough. The utterance is perfectly acceptable under the circumstances, although it is literally false.

Indirect speech acts provide examples of syntactic configurations that might be analyzed as ambiguous or as having one true sense and a parasitic figurative use. In some cases, the double understanding should be branded as an arbitrary, grammatically specified fact of the language (which might well have had a principled historical origin), but in other cases, the proper analysis would treat the indirect effect as a sort of figuration.

A more subtle version of the same problem has to do with the proper specification of the synchronic meaning of morphemes, or concatenations of them, regardless of whether they are ambiguous. The problem involves linguistic material which is semantically complex in the sense that its meaning seems to involve a conjunction of terms. Thus the meaning of "bachelor" somehow involves the notions male and unmarried. Most often, of course, there does not seem to be any necessary connection between the various components of the meaning of such items. But it sometimes happens that one aspect of the meaning of a lexical item is figuratively dependent on the rest of the meaning. Uncontroversial examples are hard to find, but the following cases strike me as having some plausibility.

The infinitive-taking verb "fail" appears to have two components to its meaning. "Alfred failed to finish the exam" indicates not only that Alfred did not finish the exam, but moreover that he tried. Now the standard analysis of this lexical item (as represented, for example, in the work of Karttunen & Peters, 1975); treats both aspects of the import of "fail" as completely conventional. But it can also be suggested that the only conventional import of "fail" is that of the negative. The implication that some effort was made would be merely a suggestion or, in Grice's terms, a conversational "implicature" that rests on the literal sense per se. The implicature would be triggered in part because of the additional syntactic baggage that sentences with "fail" require as compared to simple negative sentences. I shall not attempt a lengthy account of the nonconventional treatment of certain parts of the effect of lexical items like "fail" here, because I am only trying to illustrate a sort of analysis and not (necessarily) trying to produce a correct one.

A slightly different example is provided by sets of lexical items for approximately the same thing. Most if not all members of such sets will differ from one another in connotation if not denotation. Thus, a light current of air through a house is called "a breeze" if we like it and "a draft" if we don't. The former term might be claimed to encompass (among other

things) the specification "pleasant," and the latter the specification "unpleasant." But it seems more plausible to say that one of these terms is
neutral (or unmarked) with respect to the speaker's attitude and only
figuratively acquires an additional force in virtue of the fact that it stands in
contrast to some connotatively nonneutral (or marked) lexical item.

The importance of the problem

The stated goal of one major brand of modern linguistics is to make explicit
the relationship between form and meaning. One group of modern philosophers sees as its goal the construction of a truth definition for the sentences
of a natural language. Neither of these objectives is achievable unless we
first understand, at least intuitively, what the sentences of a language
mean – as opposed to what they can be used to convey. Stated differently,
we must know which aspects of the communication achieved by an utterance are achieved solely through the agency of meaning conventions of the
linguistic system, and which are achieved indirectly through figuration of
one sort or another.

We cannot hope to provide a semantic representation for sentences of
English unless we are able to determine whether a sentence such as "John is
the Rock of Gibraltar" is ambiguous and should be grammatically associated with separate meanings, or not. Put in terms of formal logic, we must
have grounds for saying whether this sort of sentence is true or false in the
state of affairs where John is, in fact, an unfailing friend, but not a geologi-
cal formation at the entrance to the Mediterranean, if a complete truth
definition for the sentences of English is to be constructed.

There are innumerable examples, both in syntax and lexicography,
where the choice between ascribing what an utterance conveys to conventional meaning or to figurative import is not at all easy to make. I shall list
here a few such cases. While we might be prejudiced toward one or the
other treatment, I must stress that both possibilities are open.

Consider the words "lion," "goose," and "newt." The first two of these
allow two interpretations each. "Lion" can be used to refer to any member
of the species *Leo leonis,* or more specifically, to a male of that species.
"Goose" can indicate a particular sort of fowl, or particularly the females of
that kind. "Newt," by contrast to the previous two words, cannot be used in
a sex-specific way. Now these facts seem accidental enough to warrant
separating the more inclusive and more specific uses of "lion" and "goose"
into two separate, but related lexical entries, one a semantic extension of
the other. On the other hand, this lexical complication could be avoided by
claiming that the words "lion" and "goose" are univocal, but allow a *figurative* extension. And here there are two further choices. Either we could say
that "lion," for example, properly refers only to the male of the species and
that through a kind of synecdoche it can be used to refer to the whole

species, or we could say that "lion" has only a generic sense but through metonymy can be used in an apparently more specific way.

This second type of figurative account resembles Grice's mode of explanation in that it postulates a weak sense that takes on greater specificity when it is invoked in a particular context. The argument may be supported by claiming that it is the existence of a word "lioness" (which does specifically indicate the female) that bolsters the more specific suggestion of maleness that surrounds the use of "lion." The first kind of explanation, while also tantamount to the claim that figurative, or nonliteral, use is involved, is like L. J. Cohen's in that the basic sense is claimed to be rather strong, but that it may, under appropriate circumstances, be used loosely. At any rate, it is not clear whether any use of "lion" involves figuration. The word might still be lexically ambiguous.

There is only one way to understand the expression, "a likely story." It signifies something on the order of "an unlikely story." Now are we to take this as an idiom in English or should we rather treat this as an instance of irony? There is evidence on both sides.

First, on the side of irony, is the fact that the expression indicates just what an ironical interpretation of the apparent literal sense would be expected to be. "A plausible story" suggests just the same thing, when used ironically. Also on the side of a figurative treatment is the fact that it is difficult to disagree with a statement like, "That's a likely story." Neither "No, it's not" nor "Yes, it is" seems like the appropriate way to indicate that one thinks that the story in question is plausible. The same holds for clear cases of irony and, in fact, most examples of nonliteral speech. Since they are not intended to be taken literally, they are not as open to rebuttal as literal utterances. This immunity to contradiction may, in fact, be one of the purposes of figuration. Indubitable idioms, on the other hand, can readily be denied. The response, "No, he didn't," to the statement, "Bill kicked the bucket," straightforwardly means, "Bill didn't die."

On the side of "idiomaticity" is, principally, the fact that the import of the expression is quite rigidly fixed. It never conveys what its component words would suggest that it should.

There is a discrepancy between the most natural effects of the following sentences and the meanings they ought to have in virtue of the meanings of their parts: "Uncle Scrooge has money"; "A fraction of the people voted Libertarian"; "Tiny Tim was a man of stature"; "Be a man"; "A number of my friends are literate." The ordinary understanding involves what appears to be a variety of understatement: "to have money" ("nerve," "muscles," "brains," etc.) indicates having a great deal of that commodity. "A number of X" usually indicates "a large number." (Conversely, "a fraction" indicates "a small fraction.") Now in these cases, the figurative source of the use of these locutions is obvious and fairly plausible.

But if the assumption of univocality plus figuration is the correct account in these cases, why not in the following case as well? The words "tall," "big," "heavy," "intelligent," "wide," and so on, indicate something on the order of "more (adj.) than average," when used in the formula "X is (adj.)." Further, as has often been pointed out, a different use is found in expressions like, "X is as (adj.) as Y," "X is N units (adj.)," "X is more (adj.) than Y." Here the adjective simply means that the entity of which it is predicated has the property to some degree, namely the degree specified in the sentence. Thus arises the famous fact that sentence (1) does not seem to entail (2).

(1) Bolivar is five feet tall.

(2) Bolivar is tall.

The parallel with the case of expressions like "to have money," "a number," and so on, should be obvious. It is also the case that (3) does not entail (the ordinary understanding of) (4).

(3) The number of my friends that are literate is two.

(4) A number of my friends are literate.

Thus, by parity of reasoning, it should be possible, perhaps desirable, to treat "tall" and other basic graded adjectives as having only one sense wherever they occur, but as allowing a use as a kind of understatement. "John is tall" would be taken as meaning (strictly) that John has height to some extent. But – because of its obviously trivial sense – it will ordinarily be used figuratively to indicate much more. While this treatment is possible, it is disturbing. But, if it is wrong, how do we know it is?

"Some X" almost always indicates, among other things, "not all X." Horn (1976) very convincingly argued that it does not *mean* this, but only suggests it. He proposed a mechanism along the following lines as giving rise to the conversational implicature (that is, to the additional figurative understanding): "all" is a "stronger" quantifier than "some." Speakers are constrained to say as much as is required. Therefore in using any quantifier, a speaker implicates that no stronger quantifier could have been used.

Now consider the way we understand a sentence such as (5):

(5) Bill has written almost twenty articles.

We will usually (maybe always) take an utterance of this sentence as indicating that the number of articles Bill has written is not much less than twenty. "Almost" in this use seems to have a compound significance: "almost N" indicates "not much less than N but not N." The question thus arises as to whether both parts of the understanding of "almost" are independent, conventional aspects of its meaning. It is possible, at least in principle, to treat one of these as figuratively dependent on the other. Note that the expression "not much less than N" usually indicates "not N," without apparently meaning it. Therefore it is not implausible to treat "almost" as meaning *only* something like "not much less than N," and figuratively, albeit invariably. suggesting in addition "not N." But is this the right analysis? Is

(5) true, false, or neither, if Bill happens to have written exactly twenty articles?

Thus there appear to be many cases where it is difficult to determine where meaning leaves off and figuration begins. Each such case is a stumbling block in the path of the linguist whose goal is the formalization of the principles linking meaning and form. Likewise, these are examples that will prevent the construction of formal truth definitions for natural languages until the issue of conventionality versus figurative effect is resolved.

Testing for convention and figuration

If the distinction between figurative, nonconventional effect and literal conventional meaning is real, it ought to correlate with properties that could serve as touchstones for distinguishing them in the difficult cases. Indeed, several such tests have been suggested, principally by Grice (1975). I have criticized these tests at length elsewhere (Sadock, 1976, 1978) and shown, to my satisfaction at least, that in the truly intractable cases, the tests do not give reliable results. I would like to give a brief indication here of what I found wrong with these tests: I shall leave out a few which are quite patently circular: tests that require that we know beforehand what an expression means in order to gain results as to what that expression conveys figuratively, that is, as to what it does not mean.

1. *Calculability:* If C is figuratively conveyed by an utterance of an expression E, then there should be some rational scheme for figuring out that the speaker intended to convey C based on whatever else E *conventionally* means.

Criticisms:

a. Almost any effect is calculable, starting from almost any utterance.
b. If E in fact *means C, C* might still be calculable.
c. One needs to know (at least part of) the conventional meaning beforehand. How is this knowledge gained?

2. *Context dependence:* Whether an uttered expression is taken figuratively will depend on context. Further, the speaker's knowledge will play a role in deciding whether a particular utterance will be interpreted as having been intended to have a particular figurative intent.

Criticism:

a. This cannot serve to distinguish figuration from genuine ambiguity. Context plays a role in determining which of two senses of an uttered expression must have been intended, and the utterer is aware of this and uses his knowledge to help insure that his intentions are properly grasped. Worse, the mechanisms of disambiguation and the apprehension of figurative intent are similar. The principal logical tool, I believe, is elimination of alternatives. Given the choice between intention *A* and *B, B* is favored if *A* is false, irrelevant, unjustified, and so on. The only difference is that in the case of disambiguation, both *A* and *B* are literal senses, but in the cases of apprehension of figuration, *A* is a literal sense and *B* a figurative intent.

3. *Translatability:* Figures of speech translate well into other languages. Idioms (i.e., noncompositional, but literal, collocations) do not.

Criticisms:

a. Some idioms, namely those that have arisen from "natural" figures of speech, will also translate well (see discussion of the space-for-time metaphor.)

b. Some figures of speech may differ in popularity from one culture to another. It is said that irony is rarely used in the Southern United States. Such a difference could make translation of a genuine figure of speech difficult.

4. *Paraphrasability:* Figures of speech are paraphrasable *salva sensu*. Idioms generally are not. (This is Grice's nondetachability criterion.)

Criticisms:

a. This begs the question to a certain extent. Paraphrase involves substitution of one expression for another *with the same meaning*. But this test is supposed to tell us what the literal meaning of an expression is. It could be claimed (rather implausibly) that "boot the pail" does not replace "kick the bucket" without important changes in significance, because "boot" does not mean quite the same thing as "kick" and because "pail" does not mean quite the same thing as "bucket." It *has* been claimed (somewhat more plausibly) that "Are you able to close the door?" does not have the same effect as, "Can you close the door?" because "be able" is not identical in meaning to "can."

b. Certain figures depend for their effect not just on what is said, but *how* it is said. Litotes, or double negation, ought to be logically equivalent to a simple positive, but it has a different effect be cause of its form. In such cases (i.e., where Grice would say that the maxim of manner has been flouted) paraphrase does not work.

5. *Commitment:* A speaker is held responsible for the literal content of his utterance, but he may without oddity, deny – or otherwise behave as if he did not intend – any figurative significance that might be attached to his utterance. (This is Grice's cancellability test.)

Criticism:

a. This holds just as much for cases of genuine ambiguity. A speaker can always deny one proper sense of a strictly ambiguous utterance, or behave as if he does not hold to that sense, without giving the appearance of holding contradictory beliefs.

6. *Reiterability:* Since figurative effect is not literal content, a possibly figurative expression, *E*, may be conjoined with an expression whose literal

content is similar to the potential figurative effect of E and no redundancy should result.

Criticisms:

a. As above.

b. Some redundancy is tolerated in natural language, for example, "He entered into an agreement," or, in some varieties of English, "He repeated the process again" (i.e., "He did it a second time").

7. *Incontrovertibility:* Figurative effects are nonpolemical. They have a rather personal, emotive character, and thus are difficult to contest. Literal senses, including those that are idiomatic, are, on the other hand, easy to deny. When I respond, "No, he didn't," to the statement, "Bill kicked the bucket," I obviously mean that Bill did not die.

Criticisms:

a. The test applies only to declarative sentences, but the phenomenon of nonliteral speech is not limited to these.

b. No theory backs up this test. It seems to work in the clearer cases, but it is not clear why.

8. *Interaction with grammar:* Conventional content often suffers grammatical idiosyncrasies; figurative effects do not.

Criticisms:

a. It is often difficult to say what is a grammatical fact and what is not.

b. Some parts of the grammar will be regular enough that nothing will be grammatically peculiar.

9. *Normality:* Figurative language is superficially odd; literal language is not. (A version of a test suggested by Abraham, 1975.)

Criticisms:

a. The criterion is vague, at best.

b. Idioms are also odd, at least from a very superficial point of view.

10. *Appropriate responses:* One responds to the literal content of a figurative utterance rather than to its intended significance. (A version of a test used by Searle, 1975).

Criticisms:

a. Almost any response is, on occasion, appropriate to almost any utterance. Thus sequences such as, "Is today Monday?" "Well, this is Paris," are perfectly fine dialogues. Much research indicates that this criterion is simply false.

b. The criterion conflicts with criterion 6.

I consider the criticisms offered here to be serious enough that these tests, singly or in combination, can at most be taken as suggestive. None of them provides a sufficient criterion for convention or its absence nor, as far as I can see, does any conjunction of them. Therefore, the important question of defining the boundary between literally and nonliterally conveyed communication is not answered. The problem that verbal figuration poses for the linguist (and the logician) thus remains unsolved.

Variability of the results

When it comes to applying these tests, it appears clearly that they have to do not with properties that utterance/understanding pairs either have or do not have, but rather with properties that such pairs possess in varying degrees. If, indeed, these are criteria that distinguish between conventional meaning and figurative effect, then we are faced with a situation that mainstream formal linguistics is not equipped to deal with. American linguistic theory, at least, pretty much without regard to whether it is practiced in Massachusetts, Illinois, or California, assumes that each sentence of a natural language is mapped onto a finite number of distinct meanings (semantic representations, readings, etc.). That is, a sentence either does or does not have any particular meaning, a sentence either is or is not ambiguous, two sentences either are or are not paraphrases, and so on. But the tests appear to indicate that a particular aspect of the understanding of a given utterance may be more-or-less conventional, and more-or-less figurative.

Calculability not only turns out to be a variable property – it would seem it would have to be. Given enough steps, just about any effect could be worked out on the basis of the utterance of nearly any sentence. Put differently, there is no limit to the possible figurative significances of any given utterance.

Let us say that E is some expression in a natural language and that U_c (E) is the utterance of E on some occasion c. Further, let us say that U_c(E) conveys P (where P is a proposition, or something like that). Now either $U_c(E)$ conveys P in virtue of the fact that E *means P,* or the intent to convey P is calculated on the basis of the fact that E (with its meaning, whatever it is) has been uttered on occasion c. If the calculation is short and obvious, then it is quite plausible that U_c(E) only figuratively conveys P, whereas if the required calculations are cumbersome and farfetched, then it is easier to believe that U_c(E) conveys P because E conventionally means P. Thus the calculability criterion gives us hierarchical results ranking examples in terms of the likelihood of their being instances of figuration.

It should be apparent that context dependence is also a matter of degree. Whether U_c(E) conveys P will always depend to a certain extent on the nature of c, *even when E means P.* Namely, U_c(E) will *not* convey P, even if E means P, in just those contexts where E is taken as figurative. When I say, "John is a genius," and intend it ironically – and am taken as having intended it ironically – I convey my feeling that John is not very clever, but I do not simultaneously convey my feeling that he is extremely smart. So it is not just a matter of whether the conveying of P depends on context or not that indicates that an effect is figurative or literal. Rather, it is a matter of *how much* the success of the effect depends on context. The more reference to context is required in the account of how P is conveyed, the more it seems that E does not mean P and conversely, the weaker the role of context in the success of $U_c(E)$ conveying P, the more it seems that E must have P as part of its conventional meaning.

Translatability is also a matter of degree. We cannot expect that all idioms are such that they have no counterparts in any other language. Particularly in the case of idioms based historically upon very natural metaphors, or other figures of speech, translatability might well be rather good. Such idioms will appear to be closer to figuration than those that are grounded in more implausible or unique images. On the other hand, figures of speech that require reference to some very specific unusual cultural fact for their interpretation will translate more poorly than figures that rest only on common human experience. Such figures have some of the character of idioms — at least according to the translatability test.

The other tests also give variable results, as the reader may determine for himself. It appears, then, that $U_c(E)$ can in principle convey P not just figuratively or conventionally, but often to some extent in both ways.

Variable conventionality and linguistic theory

One way of allowing for degrees of conventionality in communication would simply be to rewrite the theory. Consider the case of a putatively ambiguous expression that could also be considered to be univocal but to allow, on occasion, a figurative interpretation.

Indirect speech acts are a much-discussed case in point. Disputed examples have been analyzed as ambiguous between a straightforward compositional sense and an idiomatic (noncompositional) sense by some researchers, and, by others, as unambiguous but capable of producing a figurative effect when they are put to use in conversation. The figure of speech that would seem to play a role in the production and comprehension of the most popular varieties of indirect speech acts is euphemism; indirect means are chosen because the intended action is too offensive, prying, pushy, or embarrassing, to approach directly. An act that in and of itself is less of an affont, but which hints at the true intent of the utterance, is therefore resorted to.

Let us say that it has been decided, according to the criteria above, that the sentence, "Can you close the door?" is exactly fifty percent conventionalized as a request to close the door. Now instead of the grammar just spewing out meaning/form pairs, as in the older conception, let us say that the grammar produces ordered triples, where the first element is a meaning, the second a syntactic form, and the third a number n, $0 > n > 1$, which is an index of conventionality. In the case at hand, the index would be 0.5. But what do we gain from such a description? What interpretation are we to give it? What shall we say about the truth value of declarative sentences with indexes of conventionality less than 1? It seems to me that this brute-force description is almost totally unenlightening. At best it is a means of acknowledging the fact that conventionality is not an off-on switch, but in no sense can it be looked upon as an account, let alone an explanation, of the phenomenon.

One novel and promising suggestion has recently been made by Morgan (1978). He distinguishes between conventions of usage and conventions of language. An ordinary meaning convention (e.g., that the word "dog" in English designates members of the set of dogs) is a convention of language. Conventions of usage concern appropriate linguistic means for accomplishing specified purposes (possibly on specified occasions).

Morgan's idea is that the more specific the conventional means, the more the convention comes to resemble a convention of language, that is, a meaning. He also notes that there is a qualitative difference between conventional means that make no reference to expressions in a natural language and those that do. The former kind might more appropriately be called conventional "methods" (my term), while the word "means" might better be reserved for conventionally specified expressions.

It can be seen that these distinctions provide four qualitatively different degrees of conventionalization:

1. The totally nonconventional. The purpose is accomplished by whatever linguistic methods and means the speaker feels will be effective. True figures of speech belong in this category, because the methods of accomplishing the purpose are presumably not culture, or language, specific.

2. Conventional methods, but no conventional means. Morgan cites several examples in indirect speech acts. Irony might be an example from among the more traditional varieties of figures of speech since (as I mentioned earlier) irony barely exists in some cultures, such as that of the Southern United States, whereas its use is endemic in others – for instance, the Yiddish-speaking cultures of Eastern Europe. The kennings of old Germanic poetry are also examples. While these are generally just metaphors (albeit rather obscure ones), there is an element of the conventional in their use, because (a) they are restricted to a certain kind of poetry, and (b) certain notions (ships, swords, the sea, death) are almost obligatorily communicated in this indirect fashion.

3. Conventional methods and conventional means. Most of the sticky examples come under this heading. Most proverbs, I would think, are like this, too. Here one idea is expressed figuratively by reference to another conventionally specified idea. In addition, the very words to be used in expressing this second idea are conventionally established. We say, "Too many cooks spoil the broth," not "A superabundance of

chefs ruins the consommé," to get across the notion that someone's help is not desired.

4. No conventional methods but conventional means. These are Morgan's conventions of language. The difference between this class of examples and the previous two classes is that there is no rationale for the fact that particular forms in the language can be used to accomplish certain ends. True idioms, as well as lexical items (mini-idioms) and arbitrary, but functional, syntactic patterns belong here.

By providing two intermediate levels of conventionality, Morgan's ideas hold out the hope of resolving the dilemma that figurative speech creates for linguistic theory. I find this prospect exciting.

Conclusions

In summary, I see the importance of metaphor to linguistics as twofold. First, metaphor and other varieties of nonliteral figures of speech are the locus of semantic change in natural language. The facts of semantic change and their implications for universal grammar can only be grasped if we have a thorough understanding of the principles of linguistic figuration.

Second, I have argued that a large part of English (and presumably of other natural languages as well) is in flux; the pragmatic effects of numerous figures of speech are on the way to becoming part of the conventional content of the expressions that are used to convey them. But this process occurs by stages so that in most cases the communicative value of an expression that began life as a metaphor or as some other trope is partially conventional and partially not. This fact makes untenable one of the most cherished assumptions of modern formal linguistics, namely the assumption that conventional content and linguistic form are connected by a discrete function. Thus, while figuration in general, and metaphor in particular, are not specifically linguistic phenomena, their study is of the utmost importance to an understanding of the part that grammar itself plays in natural language communication.

4

The semantics of metaphor

L. JONATHAN COHEN

Metaphor as a feature of sentence-readings

Professor Sadock's position is that metaphor is not a linguistic problem at all, because the mechanisms underlying metaphor exist independently of language. The use of "a lion on a warrior's shield," he says, manifests "the same analogical urge that functions in the issuance and apprehension of verbal metaphors." But it is vital here to distinguish metaphor, on the one hand, from similes and other nonmetaphorical analogies, on the other. There is certainly no special linguistic problem about such explicitly figurative sentences as (1) or (2):

(1) He is as brave as a lion.
(2) He is like a father to her.

The linguistic problem arises instead because of implicit figuration, as in (3) or (4):

(3) He is a lion in battle.
(4) The child is father to the man.

The problem is to explain how such sentences can have the meaning they do, when they are false or nonsensical if taken literally. In other words, the analogical urge operates sometimes in literal speech, sometimes in metaphorical. It can produce both and so cannot explain the difference between the two.

My own position, as against Sadock's, is that the fundamental problem about metaphor is a problem for our theory of *langue,* not for our theory of *parole.* But I speak here only about metaphor, and not about other figures such as irony, litotes, allegory, or simile.

Various considerations operate in favor of this position, although they neither severally nor jointly entail it.

First, if the synchronic description of a language takes no account of metaphor, it provides an inadequate basis for diachronic explanations of semantic innovation. Language is full of dead metaphors like "inflamed passion," "feeble argument," or "rain of blows": How have they got there?

Again, it is clearly characteristic of certain categories of artificial languages that they must lack any possibility of metaphor. Programming-languages for computers, like Fortran, or interpreted formal systems, like Carnap's, would be very seriously flawed in the performance of the tasks for which they are severally designed if they allowed their component words or symbols to be attributed new and unstipulated meanings in certain contexts. It is arguable, therefore, that we radically blur the difference between these kinds of artificial languages on the one side, and ordinary natural languages, like English (or artificial languages for everyday use, like Esperanto), on the other, if we do not allow essentially for the possibility of metaphor in our analysis of the latter. For example, it is characteristic of a natural language sentence like (5)

(5) He is a lion

that it is indefinitely rich in possible meaning. Alongside one or more literal readings it admits also an indefinite variety of metaphorical ones. A theory that does not allow this will never satisfy the intuitions of people who are expert in the use of language, like the best creative writers. (The French classical tradition was an exception, but a self-conscious and theoretically motivated one.)

Thirdly, metaphor cannot be explained within a theory of speech acts, because a supposed speech act of metaphorizing would differ from standard types of speech act in an important respect. If Tom utters the sentence

(6) I am sorry,

he may well be apologizing. But, if I utter the sentence

(7) Tom said that he was sorry,

I am not apologizing myself; I am just reporting Tom's apology. The original speech act is overridden by the passage from oratio recta to oratio obliqua. Now metaphor behaves quite differently. When Tom describes his friend by saying

(8) The boy next door is a ball of fire,

Tom's description can be fully understood only by someone who understands the metaphor. But equally, if I myself report later

(9) Tom said that the boy next door is a ball of fire,

my report of Tom's utterance can also be fully understood only by someone who understands the metaphor. The metaphor is not overridden by the passage from oratio recta to oratio obliqua: the oratio obliqua sentence contains the same element of metaphorical meaning that the oratio recta contained. Arguably, therefore, metaphorical meaning inheres in sentences, not just in speech acts. We should be perfectly happy to say here, "What Tom said is true," not just, "What Tom meant is true."

This point is a very serious difficulty for anyone, like Searle (cf. his paper in the present volume), who wants to construe metaphor solely in terms of speaker's meaning – the meaning of the utterance rather than of the sentence uttered. The metaphoricalness, or special character, of (8) is preserved under transformation into indirect discourse: The apology-making character of (6) is not. Why is this? The simplest explanation seems to be that metaphoricalness is a property of sentences. Those, like Searle, who wish to reject such an explanation bear the onus of presenting a convincing alternative one. Otherwise their theory limps.

No doubt the linguistic context of utterance often fails to provide sufficient cues for us to disambiguate a metaphorical sentence. We must turn then to whatever features of the nonlinguistic setting are relevant. But just the same is true of nonmetaphorical sentences, as with the meaning of "unsatisfactory," say, in

(10) He's unsatisfactory.

It would be a mistake to suppose that this familiar component of communicational situations provides any special support for a speech-act theory of metaphor.

Fourthly, if our linguistic theory gives no account of metaphor, it may well make so much the poorer a contribution to the framework within which psycholinguistic investigations are carried on. Language-learning infants often speak in metaphors without knowing the literal meanings of the sentences they utter (Cohen & Margalit, 1972, p. 470).

But there is another reason why the stock attitude of linguistic theorists to metaphor is incorrect; and this reason is an intrinsically stronger one, because it looks inwardly to the structure of synchronic semantics, rather than outwardly to the use of semantic analyses in etymological explanations, in comparisons between natural and artificial languages, in speech-act theory, or in psychological inquiry. I have in mind a certain choice that exists in the methodology of natural language semantics, which I shall refer to as the choice between the method of cancellation and the method of multiplication. This choice arises in relation to quite a range of other problems besides that of metaphor; and my argument will be that whatever choice of method is made to deal with metaphor both reinforces, and is reinforced by, the choice of the same method in the other cases. In particular, if we need to introduce the method of cancellation into our semantics in order to deal with certain kinds of nonmetaphorical sentences, we might just as well exploit its potential for the analysis of metaphor.

Let us turn briefly from metaphor to examine these other, nonmetaphorical cases. Consider the differences between

(11) It wasn't an insult because it was not intended as such

and

(12) It was an unintentional insult.

Clearly the word "insult" might be described by a compositional semantics as occurring in a sense that is +INTENTIONAL in (11), but not in (12). But such a description chooses what I have called the method of cancellation. It supposes that the occurrence of the adjective "unintentional" in (12) has cancelled the +INTENTIONAL feature in this occurrence of the word "insult," (because the retention of that feature would render the sentence self-contradictory). We need then, for the description of (11) and (12), just one lexical entry for "insult," alongside some general set of rules for semantic feature-cancellation in the process of composing sentential meaning. Correspondingly both (11) and (12) are unambiguous.

Alternatively, however, we could employ the method of multiplication. We could have two lexical entries: "insult$_1$" which is +INTENTIONAL, and "insult$_2$" which is $+/-$INTENTIONAL. We would then dispense here with the use of any rules for semantic cancellation, and both (11) and (12) would now be ambiguous. One of the two underlying sentences for (11) would have the same meaning as on our previous interpretation of (11), the other would be rather a non sequitur. Similarly, one of the two underlying sentences for (12) would be self-contradictory, the other would have the same meaning as our previous interpretation. But what is crucial here is that the alternative to the method of cancellation is a method that doubles the number of relevant lexical entries.

Perhaps I should add here that there is not a third – quasi-Gricean – possibility. It will not do to say that "insult" never has the feature +INTENTIONAL but carries with it, in normal contexts, a conversational implicature of intentionality, which happens to be cancelled in (12). The reason why this possibility is not available is because it cannot explain the force of the "because . . ." clause in (11). (In regard to the logical particles of natural language, Grice's theory of implicatures does afford an alternative approach to the method of cancellation, but arguably an inferior one. See L. J. Cohen, 1971, 1977a.[1])

It would be easy to give many more examples of the issue about +INTENTIONAL, which is a particularly familiar hazard in the register of jurisprudence. But other kinds of example are also frequent. Consider

(13) I tried to warn him but he didn't hear me

and

(14) I warned him, but he didn't hear me.

The method of cancellation would describe the word "warn" as occurring in a sense that is +UPTAKE in (13) but not in (14). But the method of multiplication would generate two correspondingly different lexical entries for the word "warn."

Another familiar feature in relation to which we are faced with a choice between the method of cancellation and the method of multiplication is the feature +ANIMATE. Consider the difference between

(15) A lion eats ten pounds of meat a day

and

(16) A stone lion needs no feeding.

According to the method of cancellation, the feature +ANIMATE is present in the occurrence of "lion" in (15), but is cancelled in (16): according to the method of multiplication the lexeme "lion$_1$" occurs in (15) and a different lexeme, "lion$_2$," occurs in (16). A vast number of analogous examples can be given, like "china dog," "plastic flower," and so on. The method of cancellation avoids the need to multiply lexical entries in order to deal with such phrases. But the method of multiplication promotes a second lexical entry, with the sense "replica of a lion," "replica of a dog," "replica of a flower." Of course, one could hope to avoid cancelling or multiplying anything in relation to "lion" if one supposed that "stone" in (16) meant "stone replica of a." But the focus of methodological choice – choice between the method of cancellation and the method of multiplication – has now just shifted to "stone." The contrast is now between the occurrence of "stone" in (16) and its occurrence in

(17) A stone wall surrounds the garden.

Again the feature for mode of functioning, or mode of operation, would be at issue for a word like "car" in such sentence pairs as

(18) We will pack the luggage into the car

and

(19) We will pack the car into the luggage.

The method of cancellation allows us to suppose the same lexeme occurs in the composition of both (18) and (19). The method of multiplication requires us to suppose two lexical entries in relation to every inanimate object as well as in relation to every plant or animal: one for the name of the original, and a second for the name of its replica.

If we are always to prefer the method of multiplication wherever possible, our linguistic theory can hardly have anything of interest to say about metaphor. Consider, for example

(20) Their legislative program is a rocket to the moon.

The method of multiplication can either treat (20) as involving some neologism that could, if it becomes established in the language, figure as "rocket$_2$" in a listing of English lexemes. Metaphor is then reduced to polysemy. Or alternatively the method of multiplication could reduce metaphor to simile by adding to the ordinary copula a second lexeme "is$_2$," in the sense of "is like," and making similar additions for other predicative morphemes. In neither case will metaphor appear as anything other than a rather peripheral or superficial item in the immense motley of lexical variety. Its existence will have no particularly close dependence on certain special modes of sentential composition, and those linguists who have postponed its treatment until they have an adequate semantics for nonmetaphorical sentences will be immune to any charge of methodological hysteron proteron.

But is it right to adopt the method of multiplication in cases like (12), (14), (16), and (19)? Scientific inquiry tends to make more progress if it avoids unnecessary multiplications of entities, and it is this Ockhamian policy that the method of cancellation pursues. If we could formulate principles controlling feature-cancellation in the composition of sentence meanings we should gain a powerful, general insight into the semantics of natural language, which will be forever denied us if we are content to follow the method of multiplication and merely list or catalogue its proliferation of lexical entries. No doubt there are some points at which the method of cancellation ceases to pay dividends. Where the meanings of a polyseme have grown apart and taken on different positive features, like "funny" meaning "comic" and "funny" meaning "strange," the best procedure may well be to follow the method of multiplication and treat the word semantically just as if it were a homonym. Where a particular combination of words, like "kick the bucket," has lost all touch with the component words' meanings in other combinations, the phrase may need to be listed as an idiom alongside single words and have its own lexical entry. But the fact that in such circumstances we are forced into falling back on the method of multiplication constitutes no argument against pursuing, wherever possible, the economies and insights that are afforded by the method of cancellation. The method of multiplication merely records what meanings exist, without explaining how they are generated. It lists elements but does not explore relations.

The problem of feature-cancellation

What then should be said about metaphor in a componential semantics if our policy in analysing the composition of sentence meanings is to be the Ockhamian one of preferring, wherever possible, the method of cancellation to the method of multiplication? Clearly we have to regard metaphorical meaning as being put together by a different kind of cancellation from that which appears in nonmetaphorical cases like (12), (14), (16), and (19). But what is the nature of the difference?

Let us distinguish broadly between those semantical features that represent attributes which are empirical, immediately evident, or relatively obvious, and those which are inferential, intellectually appreciated, or relatively latent. It will be convenient to refer to these groups of features as "empirical" and "inferential," respectively, though determinate classification will often be difficult and there are bound to be many borderline issues. Then a tempting hypothesis is that in the normal, literal cases it tends to be inferential features (though not necessarily all of them) that are cancelled, whereas in metaphorical sentences it is empirical features (though again not necessarily all of them) that tend to be cancelled. Thus in the examples considered earlier the cancelled features +INTENTIONAL,

+ANIMATE and +UPTAKE are all inferential ones. But in the metaphorical sentence (20), the legislative program is presumably said to be a rocket only in a sense that has shed such empirical features as +MATERIAL, +AIRCLEAVING, +CYLINDRICAL, and so on, which are incompatible with the features of "legislative program," while retaining such features as +FAST-MOVING, +FAR-AIMING.

Such a hypothesis seems to jibe well with the common use of metaphor to enliven discussion of an abstract subject with concrete imagery. And it would be no objection to this hypothesis that even the uncancelled features in a word's metaphorical occurrence may also sometimes be empirical ones, as in

(21) Jane has the face of a wild rose

or

(22) The clouds are made of pure gold.

For, though a woman's face may share the color of a wild rose blossom, or even have a similar shape, it certainly lacks other empirical properties associated with wild roses, such as their spiky stems; and though sunset clouds share the color of pure gold, they certainly lack its tangibility.

Nevertheless, there are at least two reasons why this hypothesis is unsatisfactory.

First, even nonmetaphorical cancellation sometimes removes empirical features, as in

(23) They have produced a new breed of animal – a hornless cow.

The feature +HORNED is certainly an empirical one, but it is cancelled from the sense of "cow" in (23) without any intuitable semblance of metaphor. We need a hypothesis that will explain why an empirical description in which one or more of a lexeme's empirical features have been cancelled is metaphorical in (21) and (22) but not in (23).

Secondly, in some cases of metaphorical cancellation there seem to be no empirical features available for removal. Consider, for example,

(24) The troop movements ordered by Wellington were logarithmic in their strategy: By adding complementary units to one another in a particular location, he obtained the same effect as if he had multiplied the number of mutually ill-assorted units in that location.

Here we have an image taken from the highly abstract subject matter of mathematics and applied to the somewhat less abstract topic of military strategy.

It would appear that a more satisfactory hypothesis might be one which exploited the concept of a semantic category. On this view, cancellation would be metaphorical, if and only if, the features cancelled were intrinsic to the lexeme's superordinate semantic category. Thus in (12), (14), (16), and (19), it might be argued, the category remains essentially unaltered. We are still dealing with a name for a type of speech act in (12) as in (11), and in (14) as in (12): we are still dealing with a name for a type of physical object in (16) as in (15), and in (19) as in (18). On the other hand in (20) we are dealing with a name for something – a legislative program – that does not belong in the same semantic category as "rocket," and in (24) we have a shift from the name of a mathematical operation to the description of a military one. So far so good.

But the trouble here is that what we should need to count as a semantic category for dealing with some sentences cuts across what we should need to count as a semantic category for dealing with others. Thus to maintain the nonmetaphoricalness of (16) we need to think of both lion and stone lion as belonging in a single category, that of PHYSICAL OBJECT. Yet "face" and "rose" also seem to belong in this category, though we should need to think of them as belonging in different categories in order to explain the metaphoricalness of (21) by the proposed hypothesis. If criteria for sameness and difference of semantic category in a natural language have to be systematically adapted to native-speakers' intuitions of metaphoricalness, we can no longer appeal to categorical structure for an explanation of the differences between metaphorical and nonmetaphorical cancellation. The description of categorical structure would be just a restatement of this difference.

I was once inclined therefore (Cohen & Margalit, 1972) to favor a third hypothesis, which relies neither on the "empirical–inferential" distinction nor on the concept of a semantic category. The assumption that lies behind this third hypothesis is that, for theoretical purposes, semantic features should not be classified dichotomously, whether as empirical or inferential, or as categorical or noncategorical or in any other way, but should rather be arranged in an order of decreasing semantic importance. Then a cancellation would be metaphorical if and only if it removes the most important feature or features. For example, *gold* would be said to have a metaphorical occurrence in (22) because its most important feature +METALLIC would be cancelled.

Now there are several good reasons, quite apart from this issue of metaphorical and nonmetaphorical cancellation, why a semantic theory for natural language should assume the semantic features appropriate in this or that area of a language's vocabulary to be at least partially ordered in importance, rather than merely coordinate with one another. One reason is that we need such an assumption in diachronic semantics. It explains why in borderline cases, where there is a choice between either modifying one word to fit a novel or unusual situation or modifying another, we may be inclined to choose the modification that makes less of an inroad into the core of a word's meaning. For example, the verb naming the action of a hang-glider is "to glide," not "to parachute." A second reason is that to suppose an ordering of this kind provides a certain room for maneuver in the philosophical analysis of a concept. The claim to be concerned only with the nuclear sense of a concept may provide a valid excuse for not pursuing the analysis of the concept into those thickets of refinement where the argument gets bogged down in dealing with ingenious but far-fetched counterexamples. Thirdly, it can be shown (L. J. Cohen, 1970, p. 35ff.; 1977b, p. 129ff.) that any inductive processing mechanism, like a vocabulary-learning infant, which seeks to learn from the variety of its experiences rather than from the mere multiplicity of experiences of one particular kind, must impose some importance-ordering on the relevant patterns of variation.

However, I do not want to digress here into issues that belong more properly to other inquiries than to linguistic theory. Suffice it to say that the most serious mistake in the Wittgensteinian family-resemblance theory about the meanings of certain descriptive terms is its incompatibility with the assumption of some kind of importance-ordering for semantic features. And any theory of metaphor must operate within the framework of this assumption. Nevertheless, it will not do at all to say, as I once said (Cohen & Margalit, 1972, p. 484), that metaphorical cancellation is distinguished by its always being the cancellation of semantically important features. After all +ANIMATE hardly seems much less important a feature than +ME-TALLIC. Yet its cancellation in (16) does not render the sentence's meaning metaphorical. Moreover, importance is a matter of degree, but though metaphors may be better or worse, a phrase's or sentence's meaning seems to be *either* literal *or* metaphorical.

How in any case is semantical importance to be graded? We must certainly distinguish carefully here between semantical and practical importance – between what is relevant for the applicability of a generic name, and what is relevant for attitudes towards things of the kind named. It may be highly relevant to your mobility whether you have a drivable car or only a toy one, and highly relevant to your safety whether a cow has horns or not. But what counts for semantical importance is the capacity to falsify propositions about the applicability of terms, not the capacity to falsify propositions about what practical course of action is possible or desirable. Hence the features that are relatively more important from a semantical point of view are those that are relatively more distinctive and specific. Because they are less probable (that is, have greater prior improbability in the universe of feature-instantiations), they carry more information. And if that is how semantic importance is to be graded, I suspect that most metaphorical cancellation, like all nonmetaphorical cancellation, begins at the lower end of the scale. Rather general features like +ANIMATE or +METALLIC are highly eligible for cancellation because they are semantically unimportant; whereas features representing specific peculiarities of appearance or behavior are considerably less eligible for cancellation because they are semantically much more important.

The relevance of the topic–comment distinction

So, though it is quite clear that some metaphorical cancellation occurs at the upper end of the scale, as in, for example,

(25) The poor used to be the blacks of Europe,

the difference between metaphorical and nonmetaphorical cancellation cannot depend on either the nature or the semantic importance of the feature cancelled. But if this difference does not depend on which kinds of elements are connected by the cancellation-relation, and if feature-cancellation itself is a uniform operation, then perhaps we shall get a clue to what the difference does depend on from the direction of the cancellation-relation, as determined by the grammatical functions of the expressions related. If we can distinguish within any phrase or sentence in which cancellation occurs, between the topic-expression – the expression that would normally be isolated by the particle "wa" in Japanese – and the comment-expression, or between the head and the modifier, then metaphorical cancellation seems normally (exceptions are considered below) to be imposed by the topic-expression on the comment-expression, or part of it, or by the head on the modifier, whereas nonmetaphorical cancellation is imposed by the comment-expression on the topic-expression, or part of it, or by the modifier on the head. Thus cancellation runs from "legislative program" to "rocket" in (20), from "clouds" to "gold" in (22), from the second sentence in (24) to "logarithmic," and from "Europe" to "blacks" in (25). But it runs from "unintentional" to "insult" in (12), from "but he didn't hear me" to "warned" in (14), from "stone" to "lion" in (16), from "into the luggage" to "car" in (19), and from "hornless" to "cow" in (23).

We have still to explain, however, just why it is that the direction of feature-cancellation normally varies thus from sentence to sentence or sentence-sequence to sentence-sequence. One might perhaps have expected, prior to examining instances, that an operation of this kind would always run in the same direction. Why does that not happen? I suggest that the explanation lies in the overriding linguistic need to make the topic of a sentence or sentence-sequence easily identifiable. Ease of topic-identification must be conserved under variations in the amount of feature-cancellation. If the extent of cancellation (considered as a function of the number and importance of features cancelled) is relatively small, as in (12), (14), (16), (19) or (23), cancellation runs naturally from comment-expression to topic-expression – parallel to the normal direction of modification. But when cancellation is relatively extensive, as in (20), (21), (24), (26), and (27), easy identification of the topic is preserved by the cancellation's running from the topic-expression to the comment-expression; and it is thus, in the grammatically well-formed sentences of a language, that what we commonly call metaphors arise. Of course, a good or apt metaphor will not involve too much cancellation, because then it will have too few points of similarity with that for which it is a metaphor. But if there is too little cancellation in a word or phrase it will not be a metaphor at all. An expression has a metaphorical occurrence in a sentence-sequence if and only if the extent of cancellation (from the expression's semantic features) is so great as to exclude it from identifying a topic independently of some special circumstance (such as an ad hoc convention, a relevant previous sentence in the sequence, a familiar linguistic practice, and so on).

If we consider apparent exceptions to this principle, they will all be found, I suspect, to rely on certain special circumstances for their feasibility. For example,

(26) The brightest star in my sky has just run off with the milkman

is obviously a sentence in which the topic is identified by a metaphorical expression. But this is possible just because the metaphor is a trite one.[2] An original or unfamiliar metaphor, unaided by context, would not identify a topic with any clarity. For example, the sentence "The sparkle on summer dew has just run off with the milkman" is a kind of nonsense if considered as an isolated unit. But its topic would become quite apparent if it occurred in some suitable sequence of sentences that contained

(27) My wife is the sparkle on summer dew

as an earlier element. Somehow or other, whether by being more readily intelligible, or by being present at least in the first occurrence of metaphor, the comment-making use of a metaphor is primary and any topic-identifying use is secondary and derivative.

A number of amplificatory points need to be made in conclusion.

First, I take it that lexical entries for a natural language can draw no clear distinction between features that are supposed to be "purely linguistic" and features that are supposed to represent common knowledge or commonly accepted beliefs. The *Concise Oxford Dictionary* (6th ed., 1976) tells us quite appropriately that lions are found in Africa and South Asia and that privet is much used for hedging. There is no confusion here between the function of a dictionary and the function of an encyclopedia. We need encyclopedias to tell us things that are not common knowledge, not things that are. Of course, all a word's semantic features have to be ordered for importance, and the type of feature that we are inclined to call "common knowledge" is normally a relatively unimportant one. Because it is less important it is less insisted upon, and sentences articulating it are more easily treated as synthetic propositions. However, such features frequently provide a vital part of the residual analogy that a metaphorical sentence seeks to convey.

Secondly, I am not claiming that the same order of importance for semantic features extends throughout a language's vocabulary. For example, while the features determining visible appearance are highly relevant for animal names, they are clearly not so relevant for the lexemes that name social roles, such as "policeman," "president," or "banker." The main differences between such lexemes are revealed by inferential rather than empirical features. A plain-clothes policeman is still a policeman, and a water-skiing banker is still a banker.

Thirdly, each of the sentences that I have discussed so far is either obviously literal or obviously metaphorical. Many others are ambiguous between these two possibilities. For example, the sentence

(28) It will never get off its launching pad

has not only a (familiar) literal meaning but also a metaphorical one – in which it might be uttered as a reply to the utterance of (20). The sentences that are normally called metaphorical ones, like (20), (21), (22), (24), (25), (26), or (27), are sentences that appear absurd or flagrantly false if we try to give them a literal reading. But to know how we should understand an utterance of (20) we need to know its topic. Or we could say, in general, that though there is normally a presumption in favor of a literal interpretation, this presumption can be rebutted by suitable contextual cues.[3] Correspondingly in *langue,* if we always consider not just isolated sentences but sufficiently long sentence-sequences, we can take any such sequence to be a literal one throughout, unless this involves an absurdity that would disappear on a metaphorical interpretation.

Fourthly, I have assumed throughout that we cannot dispense with some kind of compositional approach to the semantics of natural language if we are to achieve any determinate progress – anything more than pious generalities – in this area of inquiry. An analytic-resolutive methodology, as so many other sciences can testify, leads us naturally into a deeper understanding of richly structured wholes, and the meaning of a natural language sentence, whether literal or metaphorical, is certainly such a whole. But once a compositional approach is accepted we can scarcely avoid being led, for the reasons already canvassed, to prefer what I have called the method of cancellation to the method of multiplication, to recognize the significance of the direction in which feature-cancellation operates, and to explain the choice of this direction by reference to the extent of the cancellation and the need to conserve ease of topic-identification. I do not underestimate the immense difficulty and complexity of the task that anyone would undertake who sought to construct a rigorously adequate theory of cancellation. But in the present paper I have been concerned rather to argue the more general issue: How intrinsic to linguistic theory is the problem of metaphor and what, in general, is the best solution for it? I have also not been concerned at all with the corresponding psychological problem: How are metaphors invented and comprehended? But it is reasonable to suppose that until the linguistic problem has a definitive solution, the psychological one cannot be adequately articulated.

Postscript (added January 1991)

I still think that the issue about the direction of cancellation is important. It creates a natural space in semantic theory within which metaphor may be treated coordinately with polysemy. But if a philosopher does not even recognize the role of cancellation in relation to the problem of polysemy, it is unlikely that he will wish to develop a semantical treatment for metaphor. In this connection I have Donald Davidson particularly in mind (see Davidson, 1984, and L. J. Cohen, 1985).

NOTES

I am grateful to Dr. Gillian Cohen for some very helpful comments on an earlier draft of the present paper.

1 The discussion of proposition-compounding particles, like "or" and "if," in these papers could be extended to quantifiers like "some." For example, either "some" has a cancelable semantic feature that implies "not all" or its use normally carries a conversational implicature "not all." A Gricean treatment would begin to run into difficulties with sentences like: "If some of the money has already been found, the rest will be found quite soon." Note that it would be unreasonable to expect that semantic cancelability will be preserved when such a word is disambiguated by compound phrases like "a part but only a part" and "a part or even the whole," respectively.

2 It is tempting to think that some proverbs claim a certain kind of metaphorical truth alongside their literal truth, as in "A stitch in time saves nine." If this is the correct way to regard such proverbs, the metaphor will be as trite as the proverb is familiar.

3 For example, where cancellation of some kind is necessary, but its direction is underdetermined by the sentence itself, the appropriate direction of cancellation on a particular occasion of the sentence's utterance, and thus the literalness or metaphoricalness of the appropriate reading, may be determined by contextual cues to the topic. Compare an utterance of "That lion is made of stone" in Trafalgar Square with an utterance of the same sentence in a typical safari park. (I owe this example to Mr. Peter Lamarque.) In Trafalgar Square cancellation would normally run from comment to topic and the appropriate reading would be a literal one, but the opposite is true of the safari park.

5

Some problems with the notion of literal meanings

DAVID E. RUMELHART

In his paper, Professor Sadock brings to the fore a fundamental dilemma of semantic analysis as practiced by many linguists and modern philosophers. The approach adopted by these workers is committed to the existence of a sharp distinction between what an utterance might *mean* (that is, its literal meaning) and what that utterance is, or can be, used to *convey*. (See, for example, Searle's chapter [this volume] which emphasizes the distinction between "sentence meaning" and "utterance meaning.") To a linguist interested in form-meaning pairs, or to a philosopher interested in truth conditions on expressions, this distinction might be crucial. In these cases, the concern is to build a theory of literal meaning and to assign conveyed meanings to the application of unspecified psychological processes not specific to language. As a psychologist I find myself primarily interested in the mechanisms whereby meanings are conveyed. Whatever role "literal meanings" (as defined by these linguists and philosophers) might play in the comprehension of language (that is, in the determination of what some utterance conveys), psychological theory must concern itself with conveyed meanings.

Sadock, arguing from a linguistic perspective, makes an interesting comparison between what he calls *figurative* and what he calls *conventional* language use. His analysis leads him to conclude that "conventional" and "figurative" do not form two well-defined categories of utterances as implied by most theories of language. Rather a particular utterance may be more-or-less figurative and more-or-less conventional. Conventionality and figurativeness are at two ends of a scale. Purely figurative and purely conventional utterances are, at best, rare. Moreover, he points out that the classic approaches to semantics require such a distinction; yet they are incapable of providing a rational basis for it. Hence, a new approach is clearly required.

Interestingly, looking at language from a psychological point of view, one can be led to a somewhat similar conclusion. I shall argue that the distinction between literal and metaphorical language is rarely, if ever, reflected in a qualitative change in the psychological processes involved in the processing of that language.[1] I argue that the classification of an utterance as to whether it involves literal or metaphorical meanings is analogous to our judgment as to whether a bit of language is formal or informal. It is a judgment that can be reliably made, but not one which signals fundamentally different comprehension processes.

I have been led to these conclusions through two sorts of considerations. First, in attempting to develop psychologically plausible models of *literal* language comprehension, I have been forced to consider comprehension mechanisms with enough power to interpret literal and metaphorical language alike. Second, both theoretical considerations of the language-acquisition process and empirical observations of the language of children suggest that far from being a special aspect of language, which perhaps develops only after children have full control of literal language, figurative language appears in children's speech from the very beginning.

Language comprehension and metaphor

First, I want to discuss a fairly typical observation on the child's use of language. Consider the following observation of one of my children making a perfectly ordinary remark. One day I was driving down a freeway with my wife and two children when one of my sons, age eight, remarked: "Hey, Mom, my sock has a hangnail." My wife, quietly, and without special note, responded: "Don't worry about it, I'll fix it when we get home," and the topic was dropped. I was the only one of the four who even noticed anything unusual in this interchange. Here, a new metaphor was created, produced, and comprehended without the slightest awareness by either of the primary participants.

This free and easy use of words in a "nonliteral" fashion is, I believe, not at all unusual. It does not require special note because it is not special. Children and adults alike produce and understand metaphorical utterances constantly. A logical consideration of some of the problems of language acquisition and the production of so-called semantic errors by children offers, I believe, some insight into the naturalness of this process. To begin, of course, children are unaware of the "correct" domain of application for a particular lexical item. Presumably, a child learns a lexical item with respect to some particular domain of reference that in no way exhausts the set of situations to which the word can be correctly applied. In this domain of original use, some of the features of the use situation presumably are relevant, and others presumably are not. Normally speaking, the process of language comprehension and production for a young child not fully familiar with the conventional range of application of a term must proceed through a process of fitting the aspects of the current situation into the closest lexical concept already available. Often this will conform with the conventional application of the term and it will therefore appear that the child is using the bit of language "literally." Just as often, the child will apply the concepts in a nonstandard way and appear to generate "nonliteral" or "metaphorical" speech. Thus, for example, if the term "open" is learned in the context of (say) a child's mouth being open, and then it is applied to a door or a window, the child will appear merely to be demonstrating an understanding of the term. On the other hand, if the child uses the term "open" to mean "turn on" (as with a television set or a light) the child will be perceived as having produced a metaphor. Yet the process of applying words to situations is much the same in the two cases – namely that of finding the best word or concept to communicate the idea in mind. For the child the production of literal and nonliteral speech may involve *exactly* the same processes.

The same arguments just made for production apply equally well for comprehension. When trying to understand an utterance, the child must make use of the situations associated with the various lexical items at hand and try, as well as possible, to construct a cogent interpretation of the utterance (in light of the current context). As a rule, this will involve the extension of concepts from one domain to another. Those extensions may or may not correspond to the intentions of the speaker and the utterance may or may not contain words used in a nonliteral way, but the child's process is the same in either case. If a child has difficulty understanding metaphorical language (as judged by an adult), this is presumably due to the child's difficulty in making the connection between his or her conception of the situation underlying the lexical items used and the situation at hand, not because of any inherent inability to apply terms learned in one context to another. This process must be the only way a child can learn to comprehend language at all.

Thus, the child's language-acquisition process should not be construed, as it often seems to be, as a process of first learning literal language and then, after that is thoroughly mastered, moving on into nonliteral language. Rather, it would appear that the child's early comprehension and production processes involve the production and comprehension of what is for the child *nonconventional* (and probably) nonliteral language. Thus, I believe that the processes involved in the comprehension of nonliteral speech are part of our language production and comprehension equipment from the very start, and that far from being a special aspect of linguistic or pragmatic competence, it is the very basis for this competence.

At first blush, this fact – that metaphor is natural and widespread in our speech, not having any apparent special status – is remarkable. How is it that falsehoods such as my son's comment can pass for normal speech? The answer I think, arises not so much through a careful analysis of metaphor as through a careful analysis of so-called literal language. Before pressing this issue, however, let me turn to the traditional view of meaning and metaphor to see why this fact should be so remarkable.

The traditional program of semantic analysis (cf. Katz & Fodor, 1963) provides a set of *meanings* for the individual lexemes of the language and then provides a set of *rules of composition* whereby the individual meanings of the lexemes are *combined* to form the *meaning of the sentence*. Likewise, for any discourse, the meanings of the individual sentences of the discourse can be combined to form the meaning of the discourse. Meanings built up in this way are the *literal meanings* of the sentence or discourse. Arguably, this program of semantic analysis can provide a reasonable account of the *conveyed meanings* (that is, what the listener understands upon hearing the sentence uttered in some context) of many sentences in English. However, as Sadock has pointed out, this is not always the case. Sometimes, as in the case of my son's comment, such an analysis simply does not work. We cannot suppose that there was an *actual* hangnail on my son's sock. Yet, unless we assume that the lexical entry for "hangnail" includes provision for a thread hanging from something (an after-the-fact interview held later the same day indicated that my son knew that the thread hanging from his sock was not a *real* hangnail), we are forced to the conclusion that the literal meaning of such an utterance offers no account of its conveyed meaning. At this point, there are four possible moves that can be made.

1. We could reject the traditional program of semantics and try to formulate a new account of both literal and conveyed meanings.
2. We could retain the traditional program, but assume that metaphor and other cases of figurative language represent mere curiosities to be accounted for by some other theory entirely.
3. We could assume that the traditional theory works correctly for most cases and that some additional processing is required when the literal meaning is nonsensical or violates some rule of conversation.
4. We could modify the traditional theory to make it work for metaphor as well as literal language.

Sadock has opted for alternative (3) and Cohen for option (4). I believe that neither of these alternatives will work, and that (1) will be necessary. For the most part, options (2) and (3) have been the most popular and, in fact, accounts along these lines have been mildly successful. This success has had a number of unfortunate (in my view) effects on the development of theories of language comprehension.

First, for example, it has led to the view that language is *actually understood* by the individual's looking up the meanings of the lexemes in some "internal lexicon" and then putting them together to form the meaning of the entire sentence. Second, it has led to the supposition, for literal sentences, that the literal meaning (as derived from the appropriate rules of concatenation) and the conveyed meaning are often identical. Third, it has led to the view that the conveyed meaning of a discourse consists of a simple concatenation of the meanings of the individual sentences of the discourse. Finally, it has tended to put metaphor and other similar cases of nonliteral speech into a special category. Related to this is the idea that we use special mechanisms to deal with nonliteral language, mechanisms that are different from those employed in processing literal speech.

In my view, each of these positions is suspect. But they have so dominated thought about semantics and meaning that psychologists interested in meaning have often accepted them without adequate analysis. They therefore warrant serious scrutiny, and I shall devote the remainder of this paper to a more detailed discussion of their defects and their repair.

Is literal meaning necessary to get the conveyed meaning?

The first supposition, namely, that language is comprehended by first computing the literal meaning and then, if it violates some rule of conversation (e.g., Grice's, 1975, maxim of relevance), somehow calculating the conveyed meaning, has already developed a strong hold in psychology. Clark and Lucy (1975), for example, have proposed the following three-stage model for the comprehension of indirect requests. They argue that in order to comprehend such a request (e.g., "Must you do x," meaning "Do not do x"), a person must: (a) determine the literal meaning of the utterance (presumably by a simple composition of lexeme meanings); (b) compare the literal meaning so determined with various contextual and conversational rules to decide if the literal meaning could also be the intended meaning; (c) if the literal meaning is determined inappropriate, apply additional rules to determine the indirect, or conveyed, meaning.

Here we have a model which takes very seriously the distinction between literal and conveyed meaning, and which assumes that the determination of literal meaning is a necessary step on the way toward finding the conveyed meaning – at least of an indirect request. In a recent study, a student of mine, Ray Gibbs, set out to test this model. The critical sentences of his study were sentences like "Must you open the window," which can function either as indirect requests meaning something like "Don't open the window!" or literally with an interpretation of the form "Is it necessary that you open the window?" In his experiment, these sentences could either appear out of context with the subject judging whether one or the other of these paraphrases was the correct one, or they appeared in the context of one of two stories, in which one or the other of these two interpretations was clearly demanded. In both cases, the sentence was immediately followed by one or the other of the two paraphrases and the subjects had to judge whether or not the paraphrase was correct. The results showed that whereas out of context it took longer to determine that the indirect-request paraphrase could be true of the statement – thereby confirming the sequential model for out-of-context sentences – it took no longer to verify the correct indirect request paraphrase when the sentence occurred in context. Thus, when indirect requests occur in an appropriate context, they can be understood as quickly as when the literal interpretation of the same statement is required. However, with no supporting context, the indirect-request reading of the statements takes longer to verify. So, whereas the sequential model may be correct for sentences occurring out of context, we cannot be determining the literal readings first in context, since in context the two sentence-types are processed and verified equally quickly.

Are conveyed meanings ever literal meanings?

It is often claimed that although figurative language is problematic for the sort of semantic theories under discussion, *normally* the conveyed meaning and the literal meanings are the same. The problems only arise for these special cases. I suspect that, on the contrary, the same problems arise for literal language as for figurative language. In both cases, what is conveyed is not easily determined from the meanings of the individual lexical items of the utterance; and in both cases, the interpretation seems to depend on knowledge well beyond definitions of the terms involved. There are no rules whereby lexical meanings can be combined to generate conveyed meanings. I believe that the processes involved in the comprehension of nonfigurative language are no less dependent on knowledge of the world than those involved in figurative language. Any theory rich enough to generate the meanings people actually assign to nonfigurative language is rich enough to deal with figurative language as well. In this section I look at a few cases of nonfigurative language in order to illustrate some of the problems a theory of "literal" speech must face and then suggest a mechanism that I believe is rich enough to deal with nonfigurative speech In the following sections I indicate how this same mechanism can be employed for figurative language.

Linguistic utterances are always interpreted in some context. The context of utterance, along with any knowledge available to the listener, may potentially be employed in the process of constructing an interpretation of the utterance. Moreover, I suspect that this knowledge is not employed in any ad hoc way, say simply as a filter in choosing among the various possible readings a sentence might have. Rather, these elements play a central role in determining what interpretations are possible for a given utterance. Consider the following two examples:

(1) If you mow the lawn, I'll pay you $5;

(2) If you are a senator, you are over thirty-five.

People seem to interpret the "if" in these two sentences in rather different ways. In the first case, the "if" is normally interpreted to mean "if and only if," whereas, in the second, a simple implication reading is obtained. If we were to take the concatenation view of meaning construction, we would be led to suggest one of three possible explanations for this phenomenon: First, perhaps "if" is ambiguous between the simple implication and bi-conditional readings. The bi-conditional is selected in (1) and the simple implication in (2). Second, perhaps "if" is univocal, and people simply misunderstand (1). Third, perhaps the true meaning of "if" is the conditional reading, but through some conversational implicature or another, in (1) it is interpreted to mean "if an only if."

I find none of these explanations very convincing. It seems unlikely that the first is the case since both sentences should exhibit the same ambiguity and they seem not to do so. The second merely denies the claim that (1) *conveys* the bi-conditional. The third, while the most plausible of the three, offers no clue as to what maxims are violated or how the respective readings are settled upon.

There is, however, an explanation rather more obvious than these. Namely, the claim that the difference in interpretation has nothing at all to do with the word "if," nor with the meaning of any of the individual lexemes. Rather it depends on our *real world knowledge,* of business contracts, of senators, of payments, and so on. In the case of (1), we know that we get paid only if we do the work we contract to do. No work, no pay. Hence the conveyed meaning is a product of our social knowledge. In (2), we know that senators are rather few and far between and that they tend to need quite a lot of political experience. Knowing that someone is over thirty-five provides very little evidence that a person is a senator. This and numerous other similar examples lead me to posit the following very general account of the comprehension process – which, as I hope to show, is applicable to literal and figurative language alike. The process of comprehension is identical to the process of selecting and verifying conceptual schemata to account for the situation (including its linguistic components) to be understood. Having selected and verified that some configuration of schemata offers a sufficient account for the situation, it is said to be understood. As I use the term, a "schema" is taken to be an abstract representation of a generalized concept or situation, and a schema is said to "account for a situation" whenever that situation can be taken as an instance of the general class of concepts represented by the schema. Thus, in the case of (1), a listener presumably brings to mind schemata involving the formation of business contracts in which one works in exchange for pay. The sentence is then presumably understood *as a case of this general schema,* and the biconditional interpretation is a natural consequence of this interpretation.

This approach is, I believe, quite different from the "standard" approach. The standard view emphasizes the "bottom up" processes of constructing meaning from smaller component meanings. Nonlinguistic knowledge comes into play only *after* the set of possible meanings has been selected. My approach suggests that comprehension, like perception, should be likened to Hebb's paleontologist (Hebb, 1949) who uses his beliefs and knowledge about dinosaurs in conjunction with the clues provided by the bone fragments available to construct a full-fledged model of the original. In this case, the words spoken and the actions taken by the speaker are likened to the clues of the paleontologist, and the dinosaur, to the meaning conveyed through those clues. On this view, the processing is much more "top down" in that internal hypotheses are actively imposed on the observed utterances.

Now consider how this general framework would deal with the following:

(3) The policeman raised his hand and stopped the car.

The comprehension of this utterance through the mechanisms I envision would involve searching memory for a schema to account for the described event. There are probably many possible accounts of this event, but perhaps the most likely is one involving a traffic cop who is signalling to a driver to stop his car. Note that this brings under consideration a number of concepts that are not mentioned in the sentence itself. For example, this interpretation requires that the car has a *driver* and that the policeman stopped the car by signaling with his hand to the driver, who then most likely puts his *foot* on the *brake* of the car causing it finally to halt. It is difficult to imagine how the meanings of the individual lexemes could be put together in such a way as to generate such an interpretation. Moreover, it seems unlikely that the example is in any way an instance of figurative language. Here we have the literal interpretation of an utterance clearly dependent on our knowledge of policemen, cars, how policemen are known to signal to drivers, and so forth. It would seem that no model can account for the interpretation of this sentence without itself incorporating all of this rather general knowledge. The situation is even more complicated than this. Suppose that we had been given the knowledge that there was no driver in the car and that the policeman in question was really Superman in disguise. We would then get a very different interpretation. We would probably understand that Superman had *physically* stopped the car by bracing his legs and putting his hand on the car thus preventing further forward motion. Clearly, our knowledge of the nature of cars, people, and Superman, and of the conventions whereby policemen signal drivers, are all essential in making these interpretations.

In summary then, the supposition that conveyed meanings are ever identical to *literal meanings* (where literal meanings are assumed to be those given by a compositional semantic theory) is surely suspect. The problems of determining conveyed meanings of literal sentences are no less difficult (I believe) than finding those of figurative ones.

The meaning of discourses

I have, over the past several years, been involved in a study of the processes whereby people interpret stories. It was here that it became clearest to me that literal meanings – in the sense implied by the advocates of compositional theories – and conveyed meanings deviated in even the most mundane cases. It also became clear to me that a schema-based notion of the comprehension process is the most viable alternative account. A careful look at almost any story and the interpretations given to it makes this abundantly clear. Consider the following brief passage:

Business had been slow since the oil crisis. Nobody seemed to want anything really elegant anymore. Suddenly the door opened and a well-dressed man entered the showroom. John put on his friendliest and most sincere expression and walked toward the man.

Although the example is merely a fragment, most people generate a rather clear interpretation of this story. Apparently, John is a car salesman fallen on hard times. He probably sells rather large elegant cars – most likely Cadillacs. Suddenly a good prospect enters the showroom where John works. John wants to make a sale. To do that, he must make a good impression on the man. Therefore he tries to appear friendly and sincere. He also wants to talk to the man to deliver his sales pitch. Thus, he makes his way over to the man. Presumably, had the story continued, John would have made the sales pitch and, if all went well, sold the man a car.

How do people arrive at such an interpretation? Clearly, people do not arrive at it all at once. As the sentences are read, schemata are activated, evaluated, and refined or discarded. When people are asked to describe their various hypotheses as they read the story, a remarkably consistent pattern of hypothesis generation and evaluation emerges. The first sentence is usually interpreted to mean that business is slow *because* of the oil crisis. Thus, people are led to see the story as about a business which is somehow dependent on oil and, consequently, suffering. Frequent hypotheses involve either the selling of cars, or of gasoline. A few interpret the sentence as being about the economy in general. The second sentence, about people not wanting elegant things anymore, leads readers with the gas-station hypothesis into a quandary. Elegance just does not fit with gas stations. The gas station hypothesis is weakened, but not always rejected. On the other hand, people with hypotheses about the general economy or about cars have no trouble incorporating this sentence into their emerging interpretation. In the former case, they conclude that it means that people do not buy luxury items, and in the latter, they assume it means that people tend not to buy large elegant cars – Cadillacs – anymore. The third sentence clinches the car interpretation for nearly all readers. They are already looking for a business interpretation – that most probably means a selling interpretation – and

when a *well-dressed man* enters the door he is immediately labeled as someone with money – a prospective buyer. The word *showroom* clearly invali-
dates the gas-station interpretation and strongly implicates automobiles,
which are often sold from a showroom. Moreover, the reference to a specific
event does not fit at all well with the view that the passage is a general
discussion of the state of the economy. Finally, with the introduction of *John,*
we have an ideal candidate for the seller. John's actions are clearly those
stereotypic of a salesman. John wants to make a sale and his *putting on* is
clearly an attempt on his part to "make a good impression." His movement
toward the man fits nicely into this interpretation. If he is a salesman, he
must make contact with the man and deliver the stereotypic pitch.

The process outlined here is, I believe, typical of the processes involved
in understanding language. There is no sense in which the meanings of
sentences are simply compounded to derive the meanings of discourses.
Again, although this story fragment contained no metaphorical statements,
the processes of active hypothesis testing and evaluation employed in deriving an interpretation of such a passage is also required for deriving an
interpretation of metaphorical material. There is no reason to suppose that
metaphorical understanding is in any way an extension beyond normal
understanding. As I will discuss, I believe that it is an aspect of the quality
of the account, rather than the processes whereby an account is reached,
that distinguishes metaphorical from literal language.

Are metaphorical uses of language special?

As I have indicated previously, it is perhaps an unfortunate consequence of
accepting the strong distinction between literal language and metaphorical
language that we tend to miss the strong similarities between the comprehension processes employed in the two cases. There is a tendency to miss
the lessons that I believe metaphorical language has for models of literal-
language comprehension and thought. A large portion of the language that
we ordinarily use is based on metaphor. Perhaps one of the best examples
of this is in the so-called dual-function adjective.

Although we often have strong intuitions about what is *literally* true and
what is only *metaphorically* true, the judgments are not always easy and,
more importantly, they often have substantial implications about the nature of metaphor. Consider, as an example, the sentence
(4) John is a cold person,
when uttered in a context in which it is interpreted to mean that John is
unemotional. Is this sentence *literally* true? There are three possible answers to this question.

    1. No, it is not literally true, John is not actually *cold,* the sense in which
       he is cold is metaphorical, not literal.
    2. Yes, cold is a word with several senses: one of these senses involves

being unemotional, and in that sense of cold it is literally the case that John is cold.

3. Well yes and no. The use of cold to mean unemotional was originally metaphorical, but is now conventional. It is now merely an idiom. There is a sense in which idioms are *never* literally true, but it is not a figurative use either. Perhaps it is better to say that in our idiom John is literally a cold person, but were the words used according to their normal meanings, we would not say that he was cold, but that he was unemotional.

I think it is important to get clear in our minds which one of these three answers we believe to be best. I suspect that, depending on which it is, we get a substantially different notion about how language-comprehension processes operate. If we choose the first alternative, metaphor in language is absolutely ubiquitous and the existence of nonmetaphorical language is questionable. Nearly always, when we talk about abstract concepts, we choose language drawn from one or another concrete domain. A good example of this is our talk about the mind. Here we use a spatial model to talk about things that are clearly nonspatial in character. We have things "in" our minds, "on" our minds, "in the back corners of" our minds. We "put things out" of our minds, things "pass through" our minds, we "call things to mind," and so on. It is quite possible that our primary method of understanding nonsensory concepts is through analogy with concrete experiential situations.

I believe that alternative (2) will never work. It is clearly not the word "cold" that has two meanings. We could also have said: John is a cool person, or John is a warm person, or even John is a block of ice. In all of these cases, it would seem much more economical to say, not that the word has two meanings, but rather that temperature and emotional states are analogous to one another in a certain way. The meanings of the terms "cold" and "warm" presumably do not have to be learned independently; rather, the learning of one clearly reinforces and modifies the use of the other. Surely, the learner of the language just learns the general model and can *productively* derive these and other cases of applying temperature words to emotional states.

In many ways, (3) is the most pleasing of the three answers. It would be nice if we could discount these troublesome cases and concentrate on cases of "real" metaphor. However, I suspect that to include these as cases of idioms is to strain the concept of idiom beyond its breaking point. Clearly, unlike idioms such as "kick the bucket" or "pull my leg," these idioms are very productive. We can always generate new cases based on the "conventional" analogy. It, therefore, seems to me that we are left with (1). Moreover, I believe that most metaphor works in just the same way, by reference to analogies that are known to relate the two domains. Consider, as an example, the metaphor discussed in Ortony's chapter in this volume.

(5) Encyclopedias are gold mines.

How are we to understand it? According to the schema theory of comprehension suggested above, the task for the comprehender is to find a schema
within which this utterance is coherent. Here we have a case of predication,
the process of interpretation presumably involves applying the schemata
suggested by the predicate term to the subject term. Thus, the interpretation that the speaker is asserting that we should view an encyclopedia as a
gold mine is entertained. In general, predication suggests that the characteristic properties of the predicate concept are to be applied to the subject
concept. In this case, we find that the "gold mine" schema fits only partially, although certain of the primary characteristics of gold mines can be
shown to be true of encyclopedias (such as the characteristic of containing
something of value – if only you look for it), other characteristics (such as
being underground) do not hold. I suspect that it is the unevenness of
account – certain primary features of the gold mine schema fit very well,
others not at all – that leads to the metaphorical flavor of statements such
as this. The interpretation process, I believe, is no different here than for a
literal predication, the outcome is simply different. We say that a statement
is literally true when we find an existing schema that accounts fully for the
data in question. We say that a statement is metaphorically true when we
find that although certain primary aspects of the schema hold, others
equally primary do not hold. When no schema can be found which allows
for a good fit between any important aspects of the schema and the object
for which it is said to account, we are simply unable to interpret the input at
all.

NOTE

1　I except here particularly obscure cases in which the interpretation of a piece of
language is not immediately given in our awareness, but instead requires a
lengthy reasoning process – extending from several seconds to several years.
Still, this process, which is sometimes required for particularly obscure figurative
uses, has its counterpart in nonfigurative uses such as mathematics and scientific
discourse. The full understanding of such discourse can often require rather
lengthy reasoning processes and thus may well employ qualitatively different
comprehension strategies.

6

Metaphor

JOHN R. SEARLE

Formulating the problem

If you hear somebody say, "Sally is a block of ice," or "Sam is a pig," you are likely to assume that the speaker does not mean what he says literally but that he is speaking metaphorically. Furthermore, you are not likely to have very much trouble figuring out what he means. If he says, "Sally is a prime number between 17 and 23," or "Bill is a barn door," you might still assume he is speaking metaphorically, but it is much harder to figure out what he means. The existence of such utterances – utterances in which the speaker means metaphorically something different from what the sentence means literally – poses a series of questions for any theory of language and communication: What is metaphor, and how does it differ from both literal and other forms of figurative utterances? Why do we use expressions metaphorically instead of saying exactly and literally what we mean? How do metaphorical utterances work, that is, how is it possible for speakers to communicate to hearers when speaking metaphorically inasmuch as they do not say what they mean? And why do some metaphors work and others not?

In my discussion, I propose to tackle this latter set of questions – those centering around the problem of how metaphors work – both because of its intrinsic interest, and because it does not seem to me that we shall get an answer to the others until this fundamental question has been answered. Before we can begin to understand it, however, we need to formulate the question more precisely.

The problem of explaining how metaphors work is a special case of the general problem of explaining how speaker meaning and sentence or word meaning come apart. It is a special case, that is, of the problem of how it is possible to say one thing and mean something else, where one succeeds in communicating what one means even though both the speaker and the hearer know that the meanings of the words uttered by the speaker do not exactly and literally express what the speaker meant. Some other instances of the break between speaker's utterance meaning and literal sentence meaning are irony and indirect speech acts. In each of these cases, what the speaker means is not identical with what the sentence means, and yet what he means is in various ways dependent on what the sentence means.

It is essential to emphasize at the very beginning that the problem of metaphor concerns the relations between word and sentence meaning, on the one hand, and speaker's meaning or utterance meaning, on the other. Many writers on the subject try to locate the metaphorical element of a metaphorical utterance in the sentence or expressions uttered. They think there are two kinds of sentence meaning, literal and metaphorical. However, sentences and words have only the meanings that they have. Strictly speaking, whenever we talk about the metaphorical meaning of a word, expression, or sentence, we are talking about what a speaker might utter it to mean, in a way that departs from what the word, expression, or sentence actually means. We are, therefore, talking about possible speaker's intentions. Even when we discuss how a nonsense sentence, such as Chomsky's example, "Colorless green ideas sleep furiously," could be given a metaphorical interpretation, what we are talking about is how a speaker could utter the sentence and mean something by it metaphorically, even though it is literally nonsensical. To have a brief way of distinguishing what a speaker means by uttering words, sentences, and expressions, on the one hand, and what the words, sentences, and expressions mean, on the other, I shall call the former *speaker's utterance meaning,* and the latter, *word,* or *sentence meaning.* Metaphorical meaning is always speaker's utterance meaning.

In order that the speaker can communicate using metaphorical utterances, ironical utterances, and indirect speech acts, there must be some principles according to which he is able to mean more than, or something different from, what he says, whereby the hearer, using his knowledge of them, can understand what the speaker means. The relation between the sentence meaning and the metaphorical utterance meaning is systematic rather than random or ad hoc. Our task in constructing a theory of metaphor is to try to state the principles which relate literal sentence meaning to metaphorical utterance meaning. Because the knowledge that enables people to use and understand metaphorical utterances goes beyond their knowledge of the literal meanings of words and sentences, the principles we seek are not included, or at least not entirely included, within a theory of semantic competence as traditionally conceived. From the point of view of the hearer, the problem of a theory of metaphor is to explain how he can understand the speaker's utterance meaning given that all he hears is a sentence with its word and sentence meaning. From the point of view of the speaker, the problem is to explain how he can mean something different from the word and sentence meaning of the sentence he utters. In light of these reflections, our original question, How do metaphors work? can be recast as follows: What are the principles that enable speakers to formulate, and hearers to understand, metaphorical utterances? and How can we state these principles in a way that makes it clear how metaphorical utterances differ from other sorts of utterances in which speaker meaning does not coincide with literal meaning?

Because part of our task is to explain how metaphorical utterances differ from literal utterances, to start with we must arrive at a characterization of literal utterances. Most – indeed all – of the authors I have read on the subject of metaphor assume that we know how literal utterances work; they do not think that the problem of literal utterances is worth discussing in their account of metaphor. The price they pay for this is that their accounts often describe metaphorical utterances in ways that fail to distinguish them from literal ones.

In fact, to give an accurate account of literal predication is an extremely difficult, complex, and subtle problem. I shall not attempt anything like a thorough summary of the principles of literal utterance but shall remark on only those features which are essential for a comparison of literal utterance with metaphorical utterance. Also, for the sake of simplicity, I shall confine most of my discussion of both literal and metaphorical utterance to very simple cases, and to sentences used for the speech act of assertion.

Imagine that a speaker makes a literal utterance of a sentence such as

(1) Sally is tall
(2) The cat is on the mat
(3) It's getting hot in here.

Now notice that in each of these cases, the literal meaning of the sentence determines, at least in part, a set of truth conditions; and because the only illocutionary force indicating devices (see Searle, 1969) in the sentences are assertive, the literal and serious utterance of one of these sentences will commit the speaker to the existence of the set of truth conditions determined by the meaning of that sentence, together with the other determinants of truth conditions. Notice, furthermore, that in each case the sentence only determines a definite set of truth conditions relative to a particular context. That is because each of these examples has some indexical element, such as the present tense, or the demonstrative "here," or the occurrence of contextually dependent definite descriptions, such as "the cat" and "the mat."

In these examples, the contextually dependent elements of the sentence are explicitly realized in the semantic structure of the sentence: One can see and hear the indexical expressions. But these sentences, like most sentences, only determine a set of truth conditions against a background of assumptions that are not explicitly realized in the semantic structure of the sentence. This is most obvious for (1) and (3), because they contain the relative terms "tall" and "hot." These are what old-fashioned grammarians called "attributive" terms, and they only determine a definite set of truth conditions against a background of factual assumptions about the sort of things referred to by the speaker in the rest of the sentence. Moreover, these assumptions are not explicitly realized in the semantic structure of the sentence. Thus, a woman can be correctly described as "tall" even though she is shorter than a giraffe that could correctly be described as "short."

Though this dependence of the application of the literal meaning of the sentence on certain factual background assumptions that are not part of the literal meaning is most obvious for sentences containing attributive terms, the phenomenon is quite general. Sentence (2) only determines a definite set of truth conditions given certain assumptions about cats, mats, and the relation of being on. However, these assumptions are not part of the semantic content of the sentence. Suppose, for example, that the cat and mat are in the usual cat-on-mat spatial configuration, only both cat and mat are in outer space, outside any gravitational field relative to which one could be said to be "above" or "over" the other. Is the cat still *on* the mat? Without some further assumptions, the sentence does not determine a definite set of truth conditions in this context. Or suppose all cats suddenly became lighter than air, and the cat went flying about with the mat stuck to its belly. Is the cat still on the mat?

We know without hesitation what are the truth conditions of "The fly is on the ceiling," but not of "The cat is on the ceiling," and this difference is not a matter of meaning, but a matter of how our factual background information enables us to apply the meanings of sentences. In general, one can say that in most cases a sentence only determines a set of truth conditions relative to a set of assumptions that are not realized in the semantic content of the sentence. Thus, even in literal utterances, where speaker's meaning coincides with sentence meaning, the speaker must contribute more to the literal utterance than just the semantic content of the sentence, because that semantic content only determines a set of truth conditions relative to a set of assumptions made by the speaker, and if communication is to be successful, his assumptions must be shared by the hearer (for further discussion of this point, see Searle, 1978).

Notice finally that the notion of similarity plays a crucial role in any account of literal utterance. This is because the literal meaning of any general term, by determining a set of truth conditions, also determines a criterion of similarity between objects. To know that a general term is true of a set of objects is to know that they are similar with respect to the property specified by that term. All tall women are similar with respect to being tall, all hot rooms similar with respect to being hot, all square objects similar with respect to being square, and so on.

To summarize this brief discussion of some aspects of literal utterance, there are three features we shall need to keep in mind in our account of metaphorical utterance. First, in literal utterance the speaker means what he says; that is, literal sentence meaning and speaker's utterance meaning are the same; second, in general the literal meaning of a sentence only determines a set of truth conditions relative to a set of background assumptions which are not part of the semantic content of the sentence; and third, the notion of similarity plays an essential role in any account of literal predication.

When we turn to cases where utterance meaning and sentence meaning are different, we find them quite various. Thus, for example, (3) could be uttered not only to tell somebody that it is getting hot in the place of utterance (literal utterance), but it could also be used to request somebody to open a window (indirect speech act), to complain about how cold it is (ironical utterance), or to remark on the increasing vituperation of an argument that is in progress (metaphorical utterance). In our account of metaphorical utterance, we shall need to distinguish it not only from literal utterance, but also from these other forms in which literal utterance is departed from, or exceeded, in some way.

Because in metaphorical utterances what the speaker means differs from what he says (in one sense of "say"), in general we shall need two sentences for our examples of metaphor – first the sentence uttered metaphorically, and second a sentence that expresses literally what the speaker means when he utters the first sentence and means it metaphorically. Thus (3), the metaphor (MET):

(3) (MET) It's getting hot in here.

corresponds to (3), the paraphrase (PAR):

(3) (PAR) The argument that is going on is becoming more vituperative

and similarly with the pairs:

(4) (MET) Sally is a block of ice
(4) (PAR) Sally is an extremely unemotional and unresponsive person
(5) (MET) I have climbed to the top of the greasy pole (Disraeli)
(5) (PAR) I have after great difficulty become prime minister
(6) (MET) Richard is a gorilla
(6) (PAR) Richard is fierce, nasty, and prone to violence.

Notice that in each case we feel that the paraphrase is somehow inadequate, that something is lost. One of our tasks will be to explain this sense of dissatisfaction that we have with paraphrases of even feeble metaphors. Still, in some sense, the paraphrases must approximate what the speaker meant, because in each case the speaker's metaphorical assertion will be true if, and only if, the corresponding assertion using PAR sentence is true. When we get to more elaborate examples, our sense of the inadequacy of the paraphrase becomes more acute. How would we paraphrase

(7) (MET) My Life had stood – a Loaded Gun –
            In Corners – till a Day
            The Owner passes – identified
            And carried Me away – (Emily Dickinson)?

Clearly a good deal is lost by

(7) (PAR) My life was one of unrealized but readily realizable potential (a
            loaded gun) in mediocre surroundings (corners) until such time (a
            day) when my destined lover (the owner) came (passed), recognized
            my potential (identified), and took (carried) me away.

Yet, even in this case, the paraphrase or something like it must express a
large part of speaker's utturance meaning, because the truth conditions are
the same.

Sometimes we feel that we know exactly what the metaphor means and
yet would not be able to formulate a literal PAR sentence because there are
no literal expressions that convey what it means. Thus even for such a
simple case as

(8) (MET) The ship ploughed the sea,

we may not be able to construct a simple paraphrase sentence even though
there is no obscurity in the metaphorical utterance. And indeed metaphors
often serve to plug such semantic gaps as this. In other cases, there may be
an indefinite range of paraphrases. For example, when Romeo says:

(9) (MET) Juliet is the sun,

there may be a range of things he might mean. But while lamenting the
inadequacy of paraphrases, let us also recall that paraphrase is symmetrical
relation. To say that the paraphrase is a poor paraphrase of the metaphor is
also to say that the metaphor is a poor paraphrase of its paraphrase. Furthermore, we should not feel apologetic about the fact that some of our
examples are trite or dead metaphors. Dead metaphors are especially interesting for our study, because, to speak oxymoronically, dead metaphors
have lived on. They have become dead through continual use, but their
continual use is a clue that they satisfy some semantic need.

Confining ourselves to the simplest subject-predicate cases, we can say
that the general form of the metaphorical utterance is that a speaker utters
a sentence of the form "S is P" and means metaphorically that S is R. In
analyzing metaphorical predication, we need to distinguish, therefore, between three sets of elements. Firstly, there is the subject expression "S"
and the object or objects it is used to refer to. Secondly, there is the
predicate expression "P" that is uttered and the literal meaning of that
expression with its corresponding truth conditions, plus the denotation if
there is any. And thirdly, there is the speaker's utterance meaning "S is R"
and the truth conditions determined by that meaning. In its simplest form,
the problem of metaphor is to try to get a characterization of the relations
between the three sets, S, P, and R,[1] together with a specification of other
information and principles used by speakers and hearers, so as to explain

how it is possible to utter "*S* is *P*" and mean "*S* is *R*," and how it is possible to communicate that meaning from speaker to hearer. Now, obviously, that is not all there is to understand about metaphorical utterances; the speaker does more than just assert that *S* is *R*, and the peculiar effectiveness of metaphor will have to be explained in terms of how he does more than just assert that *S* is *R* and why he should choose this roundabout way of asserting that *S* is *R* in the first place. But at this stage we are starting at the beginning. At the very minimum, a theory of metaphor must explain how it is possible to utter "*S* is *P*" and both mean and communicate that *S* is *R*.

We can now state one of the differences between literal and metaphorical utterances as applied to these simple examples: In the case of literal utterance, speaker's meaning and sentence meaning are the same; therefore the assertion made about the object referred to will be true if and only if it satisfies the truth conditions determined by the meaning of the general term as applied against a set of shared background assumptions. In order to understand the utterance, the hearer does not require any extra knowledge beyond his knowledge of the rules of language, his awareness of the conditions of utterance, and a set of shared background assumptions. But, in the case of the metaphorical utterance, the truth conditions of the assertion are not determined by the truth conditions of the sentence and its general term. In order to understand the metaphorical utterance, the hearer requires something more than his knowledge of the language, his awareness of the conditions of the utterance, and background assumptions that he shares with the speaker. He must have some other principles, or some other factual information, or some combination of principles and information that enables him to figure out that when the speaker says, "*S* is *P*," he means "*S* is *R*." What is this extra element?

I believe that at the most general level, the question has a fairly simple answer, but it will take me much of the rest of this discussion to work it out in any detail. The basic principle on which all metaphor works is that the utterance of an expression with its literal meaning and corresponding truth conditions can, in various ways that are specific to metaphor, call to mind another meaning and corresponding set of truth conditions. The hard problem of the theory of metaphor is to explain what exactly are the principles according to which the utterance of an expression can metaphorically call to mind a different set of truth conditions from the one determined by its literal meaning, and to state those principles precisely and without using metaphorical expressions like "call to mind."

Some common mistakes about metaphor

Before attempting to sketch a theory of metaphor, I want in this section and the next to backtrack a bit and examine some existing theories. Roughly speaking, theories of metaphor from Aristotle to the present can be divided into two types.² Comparison theories assert that metaphorical utterances involve a *comparison* or *similarity* between two or more *objects* (e.g., Aristotle, 1952a, 1952b; Henle, 1965), and semantic interaction theories claim that metaphor involves a *verbal opposition* (Beardsley, 1962) or *interaction* (Black, 1962b) between two *semantic contents,* that of the expression used metaphorically, and that of the surrounding literal context. I think that both of these theories, if one tries to take them quite literally, are in various ways inadequate; nonetheless, they are both trying to say something true, and we ought to try to extract what is true in them. But first I want to show some of the common mistakes they contain and some further common mistakes made in discussions of metaphor. My aim here is not polemical; rather, I am trying to clear the ground for the development of a theory of metaphor. One might say the endemic vice of the comparison theories is that they fail to distinguish between the claim that the statement of the comparison is part of the *meaning,* and hence the *truth conditions,* of the metaphorical statement, and the claim that the statement of the similarity is the *principle of inference,* or a step in the process of *comprehending,* on the basis of which speakers produce and hearers understand metaphor. (More about this distinction later.) The semantic interaction theories were developed in response to the weaknesses of the comparison theories, and they have little independent argument to recommend them other than the weakness of their rivals: Their endemic vice is the failure to appreciate the distinction between sentence or word meaning, which is never metaphorical, and speaker or utterance meaning, which can be metaphorical. They usually try to locate metaphorical meaning in the sentence or some set of associations with the sentence. In any event, here are half a dozen mistakes, which I believe should be noted:

It is often said that in metaphorical utterances there is a change in meaning of at least one expression. I wish to say that on the contrary, strictly speaking, in metaphor there is never a change of meaning; diachronically speaking, metaphors do indeed initiate semantic changes, but to the extent that there has been a genuine change in meaning, so that a word or expression no longer means what it previously did, to precisely that extent the locution is no longer metaphorical. We are all familiar with the processes whereby an expression becomes a dead metaphor, and then finally becomes an idiom or acquires a new meaning different from the original meaning. But in a genuine metaphorical utterance, it is only because the expressions have not changed their meaning that there is a metaphorical utterance at all. The people who make this claim seem to be confusing *sentence* meaning with *speaker's* meaning. The metaphorical utterance does indeed mean something different from the meaning of the words and sentences, but that is not because there has been any change in the meanings of the lexical elements, but because the speaker means something different by them; speaker meaning does not coincide with sentence or word meaning. It is essential to see this point, because the main problem of metaphor is to explain how speaker meaning and sentence meaning are different and how they are, nevertheless, related. Such an explanation is impossible if we suppose that sentence or word meaning has changed in the metaphorical utterance.

The simplest way to show that the crude versions of the comparison view are false is to show that, in the production and understanding of metaphorical utterances, there need not be any two objects for comparison. When I say metaphorically

(4) (MET) Sally is a block of ice,

I am not necessarily quantifying over blocks of ice at all. My utterance does not entail literally that

(10) $(\exists x)$ (x is a block of ice),

and such that I am comparing Sally to x. This point is even more obvious if we take expressions used as metaphors which have a null extension. If I say

(11) Sally is a dragon

that does not entail literally

(12) $(\exists x)$ (x is a dragon).

Or, another way to see the same thing is to note that the negative sentence is just as metaphorical as the affirmative. If I say

(13) Sally is not a block of ice,

that, I take it, does not invite the absurd question: Which block of ice is it that you are comparing Sally with, in order to say that she is not like it? At its *crudest,* the comparison theory is just muddled about the referential character of expressions used metaphorically.

Now, this might seem a somewhat minor objection to the comparison theorists, but it paves the way for a much more radical objection. Comparison theories which are explicit on the point at all, generally treat the statement of the comparison as part of the meaning and hence as part of the truth conditions of the metaphorical statement. For example, Miller (this volume) is quite explicit in regarding metaphorical statements as statements of similarity, and indeed for such theorists the meaning of a *metaphorical* statement is always given by an explicit *statement* of similarity. Thus, in their view, I have not even formulated the problem correctly. According to me, the problem of explaining (simple subject-predicate) metaphors is to explain how the speaker and hearer go from the literal sentence meaning "*S* is *P*" to the metaphorical utterance meaning "*S* is *R.*" But, according to them, that is not the utterance meaning; rather the utterance meaning must be expressible by an explicit statement of similarity, such as "*S* is like *P* with respect to *R*," or in Miller's case, the metaphorical statement "*S* is *P*" is to be analyzed as, "There is some property *F* and some property *G* such that *S*'s being *F* is similar to *P*'s being *G*." I will have more to say about this thesis and its exact formulation later, but at present I want to claim that though similarity often plays a role in the *comprehension of* metaphor, the metaphorical assertion is not necessarily an assertion of similarity. The simplest argument that metaphorical assertions are not always assertions of similarity is that there are true metaphorical assertions for which there are no objects to be designated by the *P* term, hence the true metaphorical statement cannot possibly presuppose the existence of an object of comparison. But even where there are objects of comparison, the metaphorical assertion is not necessarily an assertion of similarity. Similarity, I shall argue, has to do with the production and understanding of metaphor, not with its meaning.

A second simple argument to show that metaphorical assertions are not necessarily assertions of similarity is that often the metaphorical assertion can remain true even though it turns out that the statement of similarity on which the inference to the metaphorical meaning is based is false. Thus, suppose I say,

(6) (MET) Richard is a gorilla

meaning

(6) (PAR) Richard is fierce, nasty, prone to violence, and so forth.

And suppose the hearer's inference to (6 PAR) is based on the belief that

(14) Gorillas are fierce, nasty, prone to violence, and so forth,

and hence (6 MET) and (14), on the comparison view, would justify the inference to

(15) Richard and gorillas are similar in several respects; *viz.,* they are fierce, nasty, prone to violence, and so forth,

and this in turn would be part of the inference pattern that enabled the hearer to conclude that when I uttered (6 MET) I meant (6 PAR). But suppose ethological investigation shows, as I am told it has, that gorillas are not at all fierce and nasty, but are in fact shy, sensitive creatures, given to bouts of sentimentality. This would definitely show that (15) is false, for (15) is as much an assertion about gorillas as about Richard. But would it show that when I uttered (6 MET), what I said was false? Clearly not, for what I meant was (6 PAR), and (6 PAR) is an assertion about Richard. It can remain true regardless of the actual facts about gorillas; though, of course, what expressions we use to convey metaphorically certain semantic contents will normally depend on what we take the facts to be.

To put it crudely, "Richard is a gorilla" is just about Richard; it is not literally about gorillas at all. The word "gorilla" here serves to convey a certain semantic content other than its own meaning by a set of principles I have yet to state. But (15) is literally about both Richard and gorillas, and it is true if and only if they both share the properties it claims they do. Now, it may well be true that the hearer employs something like (15) as a step in the procedures that get him from (6 MET) to (6 PAR), but it does not follow from this fact about his *procedures of comprehension* that this is part of the *speaker's utterance meaning* of (6 MET); and, indeed, that it is not part of the utterance meaning is shown by the fact that the metaphorical statement can be *true* even if it turns out that gorillas do not have the traits that the metaphorical occurrence of "gorilla" served to convey. I am not saying that a metaphorical assertion can *never* be equivalent in meaning to a statement of similarity – whether or not it is would depend on the intentions of the speaker; but I am saying that it is not a necessary feature of metaphor – and is certainly not the point of having metaphor – that metaphorical assertions are equivalent in meaning to statements of similarity. My argument is starkly simple: In many cases the metaphorical statement and the corresponding similarity statement cannot be equivalent in meaning because they have different truth conditions. The difference between the view I am attacking and the one I shall espouse is this. According to the view I am attacking, (6 MET) *means* Richard and gorillas are similar in certain respects. According to the view I shall espouse, similarity functions as a comprehension strategy, not as a component of meaning: (6 MET) says that Richard has certain traits (and to figure out what they are, look for features associated with gorillas). On my account the *P* term need not figure literally in the statement of the truth conditions of the metaphorical statement at all.

Similar remarks apply incidentally to similes. If I say,

(16) Sam acts like a gorilla

that need not commit me to the truth of

(17) Gorillas are such that their behavior resembles Sam's.

For (16) need not be about gorillas at all, and we might say that "gorilla" in (16) has a metaphorical occurrence. Perhaps this is one way we might distinguish between figurative similes and literal statements of similarity. Figurative similes need not necessarily commit the speaker to a literal statement of similarity.

The semantic interaction view, it seems to me, is equally defective. One of the assumptions behind the view that metaphorical meaning is a result of an interaction between an expression used metaphorically and other expressions used literally, is that all metaphorical uses of expressions must occur in sentences containing literal uses of expressions, and that assumption seems to me plainly false. It is, incidentally, the assumption behind the terminology of many of the contemporary discussions of metaphor. We are told, for example, that every metaphorical sentence contains a "tenor" and a "vehicle" (Richards, 1936a) or a "frame" and a "focus" (Black, 1962b). But it is not the case that every metaphorical use of an expression is surrounded by literal uses of other expressions. Consider again our example (4): In uttering "Sally is a block of ice," we referred to Sally using her proper name literally, but we need not have. Suppose, to use a mixed metaphor, we refer to Sally as "the bad news." We would then say, using a mixed metaphor,

(18) The bad news is a block of ice.

If you insist that the "is" is still literal, it is easy enough to construct examples of a dramatic change on Sally's part where we would be inclined, in another mixed metaphor, to say

(19) The bad news congealed into a block of ice.

Mixed metaphors may be stylistically objectionable, but I cannot see that they are necessarily logically incoherent. Of course, most metaphors do occur in contexts of expressions used literally. It would be very hard to understand them if they did not. But it is not a logical necessity that every metaphorical use of an expression occurs surrounded by literal occurrences of other expressions and, indeed, many famous examples of metaphor are not. Thus Russell's example of a completely nonsensical sentence, "Quadrilaterality drinks procrastination," is often given a metaphorical interpretation as a description of any postwar four-power disarmament conference, but none of the words, so interpreted, has a literal occurrence; that is, for every word the speaker's utterance meaning differs from the literal word meaning.

However, the most serious objection to the semantic interaction view is not that it falsely presupposes that all metaphorical occurrences of words must be surrounded by literal occurrence of other words, but rather, that even where the metaphorical occurrence is within the context of literal occurrences, it is not in general the case that the metaphorical speaker's meaning is a result of any interaction among the elements of the sentence in any literal sense of "interaction." Consider again our example (4). In its metaphorical utterances, there is no question of any interaction between the meaning of the "principal subject" ("Sally") and the "subsidiary subject" ("block of ice"). "Sally" is a proper name; it does not have a meaning in quite the way in which "block of ice" has a meaning. Indeed, other expressions could have been used to produce the same metaphorical predication. Thus,

(20) Miss Jones is a block of ice

or

(21) That girl over there in the corner is a block of ice

could have been uttered with the same metaphorical utterance meaning.

I conclude that, as general theories, both the object comparison view and the semantic interaction view are inadequate. If we were to diagnose their failure in Fregean terms, we might say that the comparison view tries to explain metaphor as a relation between references, and the interaction view tries to explain it as a relation between senses and beliefs associated with references. The proponents of the interaction view see correctly that the mental processes and the semantic processes involved in producing and understanding metaphorical utterances cannot involve references themselves, but must be at the level of intentionality, that is, they must involve relations at the level of beliefs, meanings, associations, and so on. However, they then say incorrectly that the relations in question must be some unexplained, but metaphorically described, relations of "interaction"[3] between a literal frame and a metaphorical focus.

Two final mistakes I wish to note are not cases of saying something false about metaphors but of saying something true which fails to distinguish metaphor from literal utterance. Thus it is sometimes said that the notion of similarity plays a crucial role in the analysis of metaphor, or that metaphorical utterances are dependent on the context for their interpretation. But, as we saw earlier, both of these features are true of literal utterances as well. An analysis of metaphor must show how similarity and context play a role in metaphor different from their role in literal utterance.

A further examination of the comparison theory

One way to work up to a theory of metaphor would be to examine the strengths and weaknesses of one of the existing theories. The obvious candidate for this role of stalking horse is a version of the comparison theory that goes back to Aristotle and can, indeed, probably be considered the common-sense view – the theory that says all metaphor is really literal simile with the "like" or "as" deleted and the respect of the similarity left unspecified. Thus, according to this view, the metaphorical utterance, "Man is a wolf," means "Man is like a wolf in certain unspecified ways"; the utterance, "You are my sunshine," means "You are like sunshine to me in certain respects," and "Sally is a block of ice," means "Sally is like a block of ice in certain but so far unspecified ways."

The principles on which metaphors function, then, according to this theory are the same as those for literal statements of similarity together with the principle of ellipsis. We understand the metaphor as a shortened version of the literal simile.[4] Since literal simile requires no special extralinguistic knowledge for its comprehension, most of the knowledge necessary for the comprehension of metaphor is already contained in the speaker's and hearer's semantic competence, together with the general background knowledge of the world that makes literal meaning comprehensible.

We have already seen certain defects of this view, most notably that metaphorical statements cannot be equivalent in meaning to literal statements of similarity because the truth conditions of the two sorts of statements are frequently different. Furthermore, we must emphasize that even as a theory of metaphorical comprehension – as opposed to a theory of metaphorical meaning – it is important for the simile theory that the alleged underlying similes be literal statements of similarity. If the simile statements which are supposed to explain metaphor are themselves metaphorical or otherwise figurative, our explanation will be circular.

Still, treated as theory of comprehension, there does seem to be a large number of cases where for the metaphorical utterance we can construct a simile sentence that does seem in some way to explain how its metaphorical meaning is comprehended. And, indeed, the fact that the specification of the values of R is left vague by the simile statement may, in fact, be an advantage of the theory, inasmuch as metaphorical utterances are often vague in precisely that way: it is not made *exactly* clear what the R is supposed to be when we say that S is P, meaning metaphorically that S is R. Thus, for example, in analyzing Romeo's metaphorical statement, "Juliet is the sun," Cavell (1976, pp. 78–9) gives as part of its explanation that Romeo means that his day begins with Juliet. Now, apart from the special context of the play, that reading would never occur to me. I would look for other properties of the sun to fill in the values of R in the formula. In saying this I am not objecting to either Shakespeare or Cavell, because the metaphor in question, like most metaphors, is open-ended in precisely that way.

Nonetheless, the simile theory, in spite of its attractiveness, has serious difficulties. First, the theory does more – or rather, less – than fail to tell us how to compute the value of R exactly: So far it fails to tell us how to compute it at all. That is, the theory still has almost no explanatory power, because the task of a theory of metaphor is to explain how the speaker and hearer are able to go from "S is P" to "S is R," and it does not explain that process to tell us that they go from "S is P" to "S is R" by first going through the stage "S is like P with respect to R" because we are not told how we are supposed to figure out which values to assign to R. Similarity is a vacuous predicate: any two things are similar in some respect or other. Saying that the metaphorical "S is P" implies the literal "S is like P" does not solve our problem. It only pushes it back a step. The problem of understanding literal similes with the respect of the similarity left unspecified is only a part of the problem of understanding metaphor. How are we supposed to know, for example, that the utterance, "Juliet is the sun," does not mean "Juliet is for the most part gaseous," or "Juliet is 90 million miles from the earth," both of which properties are salient and well-known features of the sun.

Yet another objection is this: It is crucial to the simile thesis that the simile be taken literally; yet there seem to be a great many metaphorical utterances where there is no relevant literal corresponding similarity between S and P. If we insist that there are always such similes, it looks as if we would have to interpret them metaphorically, and thus our account would be circular. Consider our example (4), "Sally is a block of ice." If we were to enumerate quite literally the various distinctive qualities of blocks of ice, none of them would be true of Sally. Even if we were to throw in the various beliefs that people have about blocks of ice, they still would not be literally true of Sally. There simply is no class of predicates, R, such that Sally is literally like a block of ice with respect to R where R is what we intended to predicate metaphorically of Sally when we said she was a block of ice. Being unemotional is not a feature of blocks of ice because blocks of ice are not in that line of business at all, and if one wants to insist that blocks of ice are literally unresponsive, then we need only point out that

that feature is still insufficient to explain the metaphorical utterance meaning of (4), because in that sense bonfires are "unresponsive" as well, but

(22) Sally is a bonfire

has a quite different metaphorical utterance meaning from (4). Furthermore, there are many similes that are not intended literally. For example, an utterance of "My love is like a red, red rose" does not mean that there is a class of literal predicates that are true both of my love and red, red roses and that express what the speaker was driving at when he said his love was like a red, red rose.

The defender of the simile thesis, however, need not give up so easily. He might say that many metaphors are also examples of other figures as well. Thus, "Sally is a block of ice" is not only an example of metaphor, but of hyperbole as well.[5] The metaphorical utterance meaning is indeed derived from the simile, "Sally is like a block of ice," but then both the metaphor and the simile are cases of *hyperbole;* they are exaggerations, and indeed, many metaphors are exaggerations. According to this reply, if we interpret both the metaphor and the simile hyperbolically, they are equivalent.

Furthermore, the defender of the simile thesis might add that it is not an objection to the simile account to say that some of the respects in which Sally is like a block of ice will be specified metaphorically, because for each of these metaphorical similes we can specify another underlying simile until eventually we reach the rock bottom of literal similes on which the whole edifice rests. Thus "Sally is a block of ice" means "Sally is like a block of ice," which means "She shares certain traits with a block of ice, in particular she is very cold." But since "cold" in "Sally is very cold" is also metaphorical, there must be an underlying similarity in which Sally's emotional state is like coldness, and when we finally specify these respects, the metaphor will be completely analyzed.

There are really two stages to this reply: First, it points out that other figures such as hyperbole sometimes combine with metaphor, and, secondly, it concedes that some of the similes that we can offer as translations of the metaphor are still metaphorical, but insists that some recursive procedure of analyzing metaphorical similes will eventually lead us to literal similes.

Is this reply really adequate? I think not. The trouble is that there do not seem to be any literal similarities between objects which are cold and people who are unemotional that would justify the view that when we say metaphorically that someone is cold what we mean is that he or she is unemotional. In what respects exactly are unemotional people like cold objects? Well, there are some things that one can say in answer to this, but they all leave us feeling somewhat dissatisfied.

We can say, for example, that when someone is physically cold it places severe restrictions on their emotions. But even if that is true, it is not what we meant by the metaphorical utterance. I think the only answer to the question, "What is the relation between cold things and unemotional people?" that would justify the use of "cold" as a metaphor for lack of emotion is simply that as a matter of perceptions, sensibilities, and linguistic practices, people find the notion of coldness associated in their minds with lack of emotion. The notion of being cold just is associated with being unemotional.

There is some evidence, incidentally, that this metaphor works across several different cultures: It is not confined to English speakers (cf. Asch, 1958). Moreover, it is even becoming, or has become, a dead metaphor. Some dictionaries (for example, the *O.E.D.*) list lack of emotion as one of the meanings of "cold." Temperature metaphors for emotional and personal traits are in fact quite common and they are not derived from any literal underlying similarities. Thus we speak of a "heated argument," "a warm welcome," "a lukewarm friendship," and "sexual frigidity." Such metaphors are fatal for the simile thesis, unless the defenders can produce a literal *R* which *S* and *P* have in common, and which is sufficient to explain the precise metaphorical meaning which is conveyed.

Because this point is bound to be contested, it is well to emphasize exactly what is at stake. In claiming that there are no sufficient similarities to explain utterance meaning, I am making a negative existential claim, and thus not one which is demonstrable from an examination of a finite number of instances. The onus is rather on the similarity theorist to state the similarities and show how they exhaust utterance meaning. But it is not at all easy to see how he could do that in a way that would satisfy the constraints of his own theory.

Of course, one can think of lots of ways in which any *S* is like any *P*, for example, ways in which Sally is like a block of ice, and one can think of lots of *F*'s and *G*'s such that Sally's being *F* is like a block of ice's being *G*. But that is not enough. Such similarities as one can name do not exhaust utterance meaning and if there are others that do, they are certainly not obvious.

But suppose with some ingenuity one could think up a similarity that would exhaust utterance meaning. The very fact that it takes so much ingenuity to think it up makes it unlikely that it is the underlying principle of the metaphorical interpretation, inasmuch as the metaphor is obvious: There is no difficulty for any native speaker to explain what it means. In "Sam is a pig," both utterance meaning and similarities are obvious, but in "Sally is a block of ice," only the utterance meaning is obvious. The simpler hypothesis, then, is that this metaphor, like several others I shall now discuss, functions on principles other than similarity.

Once we start looking for them, this class of metaphors turns out to be quite large. For example, the numerous spatial metaphors for temporal duration are not based on literal similarities. In "time flies," or "the hours crawled by," what is it that time does and the hours did which is literally like flying or crawling? We are tempted to say they went rapidly or slowly respectively, but of course "went rapidly" and "went slowly" are further spatial metaphors. Similarly, taste metaphors for personal traits are not based on properties in common. We speak of a "sweet disposition" or a "bitter person," without implying that the sweet disposition and the bitter person have literal traits in common with sweet and bitter tastes which exhaust the utterance meaning of the metaphorical utterance. Of course, sweet dispositions and sweet things are both pleasant, but much more is conveyed by the metaphor than mere pleasantness.

So deeply embedded in our whole mode of sensibility are certain meta-phorical associations that we tend to think there must be a similarity, or even that the association itself is a form of similarity. Thus, we feel inclined to say that the passage of time *just is like* spatial movement, but when we say this we forget that "passage" is only yet another spatial metaphor for time and that the bald assertion of similarity, with no specification of the respect of similarity, is without content.

The most sophisticated version of the simile thesis I have seen is by George Miller (this volume), and I shall digress briefly to consider some of its special features. Miller, like other simile theorists, believes that the meanings of metaphorical statements can be expressed as statements of similarity, but he offers a special kind of similarity statement (rather like one of Aristotle's formulations, by the way) as the form of "reconstruc-tion" of metaphorical statements. According to Miller, metaphors of the form "S is P," where both S and P are noun phrases, are equivalent to sentences of the form

(23) $(\exists F)(\exists G)\{\text{SIM }[F(S), G(P)]\}$.

Thus, for example, "Man is a wolf," according to Miller would be ana-lyzed as

(24) There is some property F and some property G such that man's being F is similar to a wolf's being G.

And when we have metaphors where a verb or predicate adjective F is used metaphorically in a sentence of the form "x is F" or "xF's," the analysis is of the form

(25) $(\exists G)(\exists y)\{\text{SIM }[G(x), F(y)]\}$.

Thus, for example, "The problem is thorny" would be analyzed as

(26) There is some property G and some object y such that the problem's being G is similar to y's being thorny.

I believe this account has all the difficulties of the other simile theories – namely, it mistakenly supposes that the use of a metaphorical predicate commits the speaker to the existence of objects of which that predicate is literally true; it confuses the truth conditions of the metaphorical statement with the principles under which it is comprehended; it fails to tell us how to compute the values of the variables (Miller is aware of this problem, he calls it the problem of "interpretation" and sees it as different from the problem of "reconstruction"); and it is refuted by the fact that not all metaphors have literal statements of similarity underlying them. But it has some additional problems of its own. In my view, the most serious weakness of Miller's account is that according to it the semantic contents of most metaphorical utterances have too many predicates, and, in fact, rather few metaphors really satisfy the formal structure he provides us with. Consider, for example, "Man is a wolf." On what I believe is the most plausible version of the simile thesis, it means something of the form

(27) Man is like a wolf in certain respects, R.

We could represent this as

(28) SIM_R (man, wolf).

The hearer is required to compute only one set of predicates, the values for R. But according to Miller's account, the hearer is required to compute no less than three sets of predicates. Inasmuch as similarity is a vacuous predicate, we need to be told in which respect two things are similar for the statement that they are similar to have any informative content. His formalization of the above metaphorical utterance is

(29) $(\exists F)\,(\exists G)\,\{\text{SIM}\,[F\,(\text{man}),\,G\,(\text{wolf})]\}$.

In order to complete this formula in a way that would specify the respect of the similarity we would have to rewrite it as

(30) $(\exists F)\,(\exists G)\,(\exists H)\,\{\text{SIM}_H\,[F\,(\text{man}),\,G\,(\text{wolf})]\}$.

But both the reformulation (30), and Miller's original (29), contain too many predicate variables: When I say "Man is a wolf," I am not saying that there are some *different* sets of properties that men have from those that wolves have, I am saying they have the *same* set of properties (at least on a sympathetic construal of the simile thesis, that is what I am saying). But according to Miller's account, I am saying that man has one set of properties F, wolves have a different set of properties G, and man's having F is similar to wolves having G with respect to some other properties H. I argue that this "reconstruction" is (a) counterintuitive, (b) unmotivated, and (c) assigns an impossible computing task to the speaker and hearer. What are these F's, G's and H's supposed to be? and, How is the hearer supposed to figure them out? It is not surprising that his treatment of the interpretation problem is very sketchy. Similar objections apply to his accounts of other syntactical forms of metaphorical utterances.

There is a class of metaphors, that I shall call "relational metaphors," for which something like his analysis might be more appropriate. Thus, if I say

(8) The ship ploughed the sea

or

(31) Washington is the father of his country,

these might be interpreted using something like his forms. We might treat (8) as equivalent to

(32) There is some relation R which the ship has to the sea and which is similar to the relation that ploughs have to fields when they plough fields;

and (31) as

(33) There is some relation R which Washington has to his country and
   which is like the relation that fathers have to their offspring.

And (32) and (33) are fairly easily formalized *à la* Miller. However, even
these analyses seem to me to concede too much to his approach: (8) makes
no reference either implicitly or explicitly to fields and makes no reference
to offspring. On the simplest and most plausible version of the simile thesis
(8) and (31) are equivalent to:

(34) The ship does something to the sea which is like ploughing

and

(35) Washington stands in a relation to his country which is like the
   relation of being a father.

And the hearer's task is simply to compute the intended relations in the two
cases. By my account, which I shall develop in the next section, similarity
does not, in general, function as part of the truth conditions either in
Miller's manner or in the simpler version; rather, when it functions, it
functions as a strategy for interpretation. Thus, very crudely, the way that
similarity figures in the interpretation of (8) and (31) is given by

(36) The ship does something to the sea (to figure out what it is, find a
   relationship like ploughing)

and

(37) Washington stands in a certain relationship to his country (to figure
   out what it is, find a relationship like that of being a father).

But the hearer does not have to compute any respects in which these
relations are similar, inasmuch as that is not what is being asserted. Rather,
what is being asserted is that the ship is doing something to the sea and that
Washington stands in a certain set of relations to his country, and the
hearer is to figure out what it is that the ship does and what the relations are
that Washington stands in by looking for relations similar to ploughing and
being a father of.

To conclude this section: The problem of metaphor is either very difficult
or very easy. If the simile theory were true, it would be very easy, because
there would be no separate semantic category of *metaphors* – only a category of *elliptical utterances* where "like" or "as" had been deleted from the
uttered sentence. But alas, the simile theory is not right. and the problem
of metaphor remains very difficult. I hope our rather lengthy discussion of
the simile theory has been illuminating in at least these respects. First,
there are many metaphors in which there is no underlying literal similarity
adequate to explain the metaphorical utterance meaning. Second, even
where there is a correlated literal statement of similarity, the truth conditions, and hence the meaning of the metaphorical statement and the similarity statement, are not, in general, the same. Third, what we should salvage
from the simile theory is a set of strategies for producing and understanding
metaphorical utterances, using similarity. And fourth, even so construed,

that is, construed as a theory of interpretation rather than of meaning, the simile theory does not tell us how to compute the respects of similarity or which similarities are metaphorically intended by the speaker.

The principles of metaphorical interpretation

The time has now come to try to state the principles according to which metaphors are produced and understood. To reiterate, in its simplest form, the question we are trying to answer is, How is it possible for the speaker to say metaphorically "S is P" and mean "S is R," when P plainly does not mean R; furthermore, How is it possible for the hearer who hears the utterance "S is P" to know that the speaker means "S is R"? The short and uninformative answer is that the utterance of P calls to mind the meaning and, hence, truth conditions associated with R, in the special ways that metaphorical utterances have of calling other things to mind. But that answer remains uninformative until we know what are the principles according to which the utterance calls the metaphorical meaning to mind, and until we can state these principles in a way which does not rely on metaphorical expressions like "calls to mind." I believe that there is no single principle on which metaphor works.

The question, "How do metaphors work?" is a bit like the question, "How does one thing remind us of another thing?" There is no single answer to either question, though similarity obviously plays a major role in answering both. Two important differences between them are that metaphors are both restricted and systematic; restricted in the sense that not every way that one thing can remind us of something else will provide a basis for metaphor, and systematic in the sense that metaphors must be communicable from speaker to hearer in virtue of a shared system of principles.

Let us approach the problem from the hearer's point of view. If we can figure out the principles according to which hearers understand metaphorical utterances, we shall be a long way toward understanding how it is possible for speakers to make metaphorical utterances, because for communication to be possible, speaker and hearer must share a common set of principles. Suppose a hearer hears an utterance such as "Sally is a block of ice," or "Richard is a gorilla," or "Bill is a barn door." What are the steps he must go through in order to comprehend the metaphorical meaning of such utterances? Obviously an answer to that question need not specify a set of steps that he goes through consciously; instead it must provide a rational reconstruction of the inference patterns that underlie our ability to understand such metaphors. Furthermore, not all metaphors will be as simple as the cases we shall be discussing; nonetheless, a model designed to account for the simple cases should prove to be of more general application.

I believe that for the simple sorts of cases we have been discussing, the hearer must go through at least three sets of steps. First, he must have some strategy for determining whether or not he has to seek a metaphorical interpretation of the utterance in the first place. Secondly, when he has decided to look for a metaphorical interpretation, he must have some set of strategies, or principles, for computing possible values of *R,* and third, he must have a set of strategies, or principles, for restricting the range of *R*'s – for deciding which *R*'s are likely to be the ones the speaker is asserting of *S.*

Suppose he hears the utterance "Sam is a pig." He knows that that cannot be literally true, that the utterance, if he tries to take it literally, is radically defective. And, indeed, such defectiveness is a feature of nearly all of the examples that we have considered so far. The defects which cue the hearer may be obvious falsehood, semantic nonsense, violations of the rules of speech acts, or violations of conversational principles of communication. This suggests a strategy that underlies the first step: *Where the utterance is defective if taken literally, look for an utterance meaning that differs from sentence meaning.*

This is not the only strategy on which a hearer can tell that an utterance probably has a metaphorical meaning, but it is by far the most common. (It is also common to the interpretation of poetry. If I hear a figure on a Grecian Urn being addressed as a "still unravish'd bride of quietness," I know I had better look for alternative meanings.) But it is certainly not a necessary condition of a metaphorical utterance that it be in any way defective if construed literally. Disraeli might have said metaphorically

(5) (MET) I have climbed to the top of the greasy pole,

though he had in fact climbed to the top of a greasy pole. There are various other cues that we employ to spot metaphorical utterances. For example, when reading Romantic poets, we are on the lookout for metaphors, and some people we know are simply more prone to metaphorical utterances than others.

Once our hearer has established that he is to look for an alternative meaning, he has a number of principles by which he can compute possible values of *R.* I will give a list of these shortly, but one of them is this: *When you hear* "S *is* P" *to find possible values of* R *look for ways in which* S *might be like* P, *and to fill in the respect in which* S *might be like* P, *look for salient, well known, and distinctive features of* P *things.*

In this case, the hearer might invoke his factual knowledge to come up with such features as that pigs are fat, gluttonous, slovenly, filthy, and so on. This indefinite range of features provides possible values of *R.* However, lots of other features of pigs are equally distinctive and well known; for example, pigs have a distinctive shape and distinctive bristles. So, in order to understand the utterance, the hearer needs to go through the third step where he restricts the range of possible *R*'s. Here again the hearer may employ various strategies for doing that but the one that is most commonly used is this: *Go back to the S term and see which of the many candidates for the values of R are likely or even possible properties of S.*

Thus, if the hearer is told, "Sam's car is a pig," he will interpret that metaphor differently from the utterance, "Sam is a pig." The former, he might take to mean that Sam's car consumes gas the way pigs consume food, or that Sam's car is shaped like a pig. Though, in one sense, the metaphor is the same in the two cases, in each case it is restricted by the *S* term in a different way. The hearer has to use his knowledge of *S* things and *P* things to know which of the possible values of *R* are plausible candidates for metaphorical predication.

Now, much of the dispute between the interaction theories and the object comparison theories derives from the fact that they can be construed as answers to different questions. The object comparison theories are best construed as attempts to answer the question of stage two: "How do we compute the possible values of *R*?" The interaction theories are best construed as answers to the question of stage three: "Given a range of possible values of *R*, how does the relationship between the *S* term and the *P* term restrict that range?" I think it is misleading to describe these relations as "interactions," but it seems correct to suppose that the *S* term must play a role in metaphors of the sort we have been considering. In order to show that the interaction theory was also an answer to the question of stage two, we would have to show that there are values of *R* that are specifiable, given *S* and *P* together, that are not specifiable given *P* alone; one would have to show that *S* does not *restrict* the range of *R*'s but in fact, creates new *R*'s. I do not believe that can be shown, but I shall mention some possibilities later.

I said that there was a variety of principles for computing *R*, given *P* – that is, a variety of principles according to which the utterance of *P* can call to mind the meaning *R* in ways that are peculiar to metaphor. I am sure I do not know all of the principles that do this, but here are several (not necessarily independent) for a start.

Principle I

Things which are *P* are by definition *R*. Usually, if the metaphor works, *R* will be one of the salient defining characteristics of *P*. Thus, for example,

(38) (MET) Sam is a giant

will be taken to mean

(38) (PAR) Sam is big,

because giants are by definition big. That is what is special about them.

Principle 2

Things which are *P* are contingently *R*. Again, if the metaphor works, the property *R* should be a salient or well known property of *P* things.

(39) (MET) Sam is a pig

will be taken to mean

(39) (PAR) Sam is filthy, gluttonous, sloppy, and so on.

Both principles 1 and 2 correlate metaphorical utterances with literal similes, "Sam is like a giant," "Sam is like a pig," and so on. Notice in connection with this principle and the next that small variations in the *P* term can create big differences in the *R* terms. Consider the differences between "Sam is a pig," "Sam is a hog," and "Sam is a swine."

Principle 3

Things which are *P* are often said or believed to be *R*, even though both speaker and hearer may know that *R* is false of *P*. Thus,

(6) (MET) Richard is a gorilla

can be uttered to mean

(6) (PAR) Richard is mean, nasty, prone to violence, and so on,

even though both speaker and hearer know that in fact gorillas are shy, timid, and sensitive creatures, but generations of gorilla mythology have set up associations that will enable the metaphor to work even though both speaker and hearer know these beliefs to be false.

Principle 4

Things which are *P* are not *R*, nor are they like *R* things, nor are they believed to be *R*, nonetheless it is a fact about our sensibility, whether culturally or naturally determined, that we just do perceive a connection, so that utterance of *P* is associated in our minds with *R* properties. Thus,

(4) (MET) Sally is a block of ice

(40) (MET) I am in a black mood

(41) (MET) Mary is sweet

(42) (MET) John is bitter

(43) (MET) The hours $\left\{ \begin{array}{l} \text{crept} \\ \text{crawled} \\ \text{dragged} \\ \text{sped} \\ \text{whizzed} \end{array} \right\}$ by as we waited for the plane

are sentences that could be uttered to mean metaphorically that: Sally is unemotional; I am angry and depressed; Mary is gentle, kind, pleasant, and so on; John is resentful; and the hours seemed (of varying degrees of duration) as we waited for the plane; even though there are no literal similarities on which these metaphors are based. Notice that the associations tend to be scalar: degrees of temperature with ranges of emotion, degrees of speed with temporal duration, and so forth.

Principle 5

P things are not like *R* things, and are not believed to be like *R* things, nonetheless the condition of being *P* is like the condition of being *R*. Thus, I might say to someone who has just received a huge promotion
    (44) You have become an aristocrat,
meaning not that he has personally become *like* an aristocrat, but that his new status or condition is like that of being an aristocrat.

Principle 6

There are cases where *P* and *R* are the same or similar in meaning, but where one, usually *P,* is restricted in its application, and does not literally apply to *S*. Thus, "addled" is only said literally of eggs, but we can metaphorically say
    (45) This soufflé is addled
    (46) That parliament was addled
and
    (47) His brain is addled.

Principle 7

This is not a separate principle but a way of applying principles 1 through 6 to simple cases which are not of the form "*S* is *P*" but relational metaphors, and metaphors of other syntactical forms such as those involving verbs and predicate adjectives. Consider such relational metaphors as
    (48) Sam devours books
    (8) The ship ploughs the sea
    (31) Washington was the father of his country.
In each case, we have a literal utterance of two noun phrases surrounding a metaphorical utterance of a relational term (it can be a transitive verb, as in (48) and (8) but it need not be, as in (31)). The hearer's task is not to go from "*S* is *P*" to "*S* is *R*" but to go from "*S P*-relation *S'*" to "*S R*-relation *S'*" and the latter task is formally rather different from the former because, for example, our similarity principles in the former case will enable him to find a property that *S* and *P* things have in common, namely, *R*. But in the latter, he cannot find a relation in common, instead he has to find a relation *R* which is different from relation *P* but similar to it in some respect. So, as applied to these cases, principle 1, for example, would read
    P-relations are by definition *R*-relations.
For example, *ploughing* is by definition partly a matter of moving a substance to either side of a pointed object while the object moves forward; and though this definitional similarity between the *P*-relation and the *R*-relation would provide the principle that enables the hearer to infer

the *R*-relation, the respect of similarity does not exhaust the context of the *R*-relation, as the similarity exhausts the content of the *R* term in the simplest of the "*S* is *P*" cases. In these cases, the hearer's job is to find a relation (or property) that is similar to, or otherwise associated with, the relation or property literally expressed by the metaphorical expression *P;* and the principles function to enable him to select that relation or property by giving him a respect in which the *P*-relation and the *R*-relation might be similar or otherwise associated.

Principle 8

According to my account of metaphor, it becomes a matter of terminology whether we want to construe metonymy and synecdoche as special cases of metaphor or as independent tropes. When one says, "*S* is *P*," and means that "*S* is *R*," *P* and *R* may be associated by such relations as the part-whole relation, the container-contained relation, or even the clothing and wearer relation. In each case, as in metaphor proper, the semantic content of the *P* term conveys the semantic content of the *R* term by some principle of association. Since the principles of metaphor are rather various anyway, I am inclined to treat metonymy and synecdoche as special cases of metaphor and add their principles to my list of metaphorical principles. I can, for example, refer to the British monarch as "the Crown," and the executive branch of the U.S. government as "the White House" by exploiting systematic principles of association. However, as I said, the claim that these are special cases of metaphor seems to me purely a matter of terminology, and if purists insist that the principles of metaphor be kept separate from those of metonymy and synecdoche, I can have no non-taxonomical objections.

In addition to these eight principles, one might wonder if there is a ninth. Are there cases where an association between *P* and *R* that did not previously exist can be created by the juxtaposition of *S* and *P* in the original sentence? This, I take it, is the thesis of the interaction theorists. However, I have never seen any convincing examples, nor any even halfway clear account, of what "interaction" is supposed to mean. Let us try to construct some examples. Consider the differences between

(49) Sam's voice is $\begin{cases} \text{mud} \\ \text{gravel} \\ \text{sandpaper} \end{cases}$

and

(50) Kant's second argument for the transcendental deduction is so

much $\begin{cases} \text{mud} \\ \text{gravel} \\ \text{sandpaper} \end{cases}$

The second set clearly gives us different metaphorical meanings – different values for R – than the first trio, and one might argue that this is due not to the fact that the different S terms restrict the range of possible R's generated by the P terms, but to the fact that the different combinations of S and P create new R's. But that explanation seems implausible. The more plausible explanation is this. One has a set of associations with the P terms, "mud," "gravel," and "sandpaper." The principles of these associations are those of principles 1 through 7. The different S terms restrict the values of R differently, because different R's can be true of voices than can be true of arguments for transcendental deductions. Where is the interaction?

Because this section contains my account of metaphorical predication, it may be well to summarzie its main points. Given that a speaker and a hearer have shared linguistic and factual knowledge sufficient to enable them to communicate literal utterance, the following principles are individually necessary and collectively sufficient to enable speaker and hearer to form and comprehend utterances of the form "S is P," where the speaker means metaphorically that S is R (where $P \neq R$).

First, there must be some shared strategies on the basis of which the hearer can recognize that the utterance is not intended literally. The most common, but not the only strategy, is based on the fact that the utterance is obviously defective if taken literally.

Second, there must be some shared principles that associate the P term (whether the meaning, the truth conditions, or the denotation if there is any) with a set of possible values of R. The heart of the problem of metaphor is to state these principles. I have tried to state several of them, but I feel confident that there must be more.

Third, there must be some shared strategies that enable the speaker and the hearer, given their knowledge of the S term (whether the meaning of the expression, or the nature of the referent, or both), to restrict the range of possible values of R to the actual value of R. The basic principle of this step is that only those possible values of R which determine possible properties of S can be actual values of R.

Metaphor, irony, and indirect speech acts

To conclude, I wish to compare briefly the principles on which metaphor works with those on which irony and indirect speech acts work. Consider first a case of irony. Suppose you have just broken a priceless K'ang Hsi vase and I say ironically, "That was a brilliant thing to do." Here, as in metaphor, the speaker's meaning and sentence meaning are different. What are the principles by which the hearer is able to infer that the speaker meant "That was a stupid thing to do," when what he heard was the sentence "That was a brilliant thing to do"? Stated very crudely, the mechanism by which irony works is that the utterance, if taken literally, is obviously inappropriate to the situation. Since it is grossly inappropriate, the hearer is compelled to reinterpret it in such a way as to render it appropriate, and the most natural way to interpret it is as meaning the *opposite* of its literal form.

I am not suggesting that this is by any means the whole story about irony. Cultures and subcultures vary enormously in the extent and degree of the linguistic and extralinguistic cues provided for ironical utterances. In English, in fact, there are certain characteristic intonational contours that go with ironical utterances. However, it is important to see that irony, like metaphor, does not require any conventions, extralinguistic or otherwise. The principles of conversation and the general rules for performing speech acts are sufficient to provide the basic principles of irony.

Now consider a case of an indirect speech act. Suppose that in the usual dinner-table situation, I say to you "Can you pass the salt?" In this situation you will normally take that as meaning "Please pass the salt." That is, you will take the question about your ability as a request to perform an action. What are the principles on which this inference works? There is a radical difference between indirect speech acts, on the one hand, and irony and metaphor, on the other. In the indirect speech act, the speaker means what he says. However, in addition, he means something more. Sentence meaning is part of utterance meaning, but it does not exhaust utterance meaning In a very simplified form (for a more detailed account, see Searle, 1975), the principles on which the inference works in this case are: First, the hearer must have some device for recognizing that the utterance might be an indirect speech act. This requirement is satisfied by the fact that in the context, a question about the hearer's ability lacks any conversational point. The hearer, therefore, is led to seek an alternative meaning. Second, since the hearer knows the rules of speech acts, he knows that the ability to pass the salt is a preparatory condition on the speech act of requesting him to do so. Therefore, he is able to infer that the question about his ability is likely to be a polite request to perform the act. The differences and similarities between literal utterances, metaphorical utterances, ironical utterances, and indirect speech acts are illustrated in Figure 6.1.

The question of whether all metaphorical utterances can be given a literal paraphrase is one that must have a trivial answer. Interpreted one way, the answer is trivially yes; interpreted another way, it is trivially no. If we interpret the question as "Is it possible to find or to invent an expression that will exactly express the intended metaphorical meaning R, in the sense of the truth conditions of R, for any metaphorical utterance of 'S is P,' where what is meant is that S is R?" the answer to that question must surely be yes. It follows trivially from the Principle of Expressibility (see Searle, 1969) that any meaning whatever can be given an exact expression in the language.

If the question is interpreted as meaning "Does every existing language

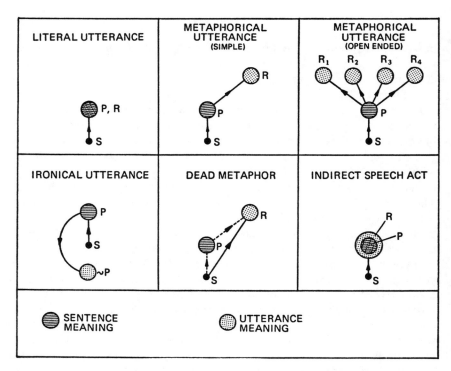

LITERAL UTTERANCE	METAPHORICAL UTTERANCE (SIMPLE)	METAPHORICAL UTTERANCE (OPEN ENDED)
P, R ← S	R ↗ P ← S	R_1 R_2 R_3 R_4 ↖↑↗ P ← S

IRONICAL UTTERANCE	DEAD METAPHOR	INDIRECT SPEECH ACT
P ← S ↷ ~P	R ↗ P ← S	R P ← S

⊖ SENTENCE MEANING   ● UTTERANCE MEANING

Figure 6.1. A graphical comparison of the relations between sentence meaning and utterance meaning where the sentence meaning is S is P and the utterance meaning is S is R, that is, where the speaker utters a sentence that means literally that the object S falls under the concept P, but where the speaker means by his utterance that the object S falls under the concept R.

a. *Literal Utterance.* A speaker says S is P and he means S is P. Thus the speaker places object S under the concept P, where P = R. Sentence meaning and utterance meaning coincide.

b. *Metaphorical Utterance (simple).* A speaker says S is P but means metaphorically that S is R. Utterance meaning is arrived at by going through literal sentence meaning.

c. *Metaphorical Utterance (open ended).* A speaker says S is P, but means metaphorically an indefinite range of meanings, S is R_1, S is R_2, etc. As in the simple case, utterance meaning is arrived at by going through literal meaning.

d. *Ironical Utterance.* A speaker means the opposite of what he says. Utterance meaning is arrived at by going through sentence meaning and then doubling back to the opposite of sentence meaning.

e. *Dead Metaphor.* The original sentence meaning is bypassed and the sentence acquires a new literal meaning identical with the former metaphorical utterance meaning. This is a shift from the metaphorical utterance (simple), *b* above, to the literal utterance, diagram *a*.

f. *Indirect Speech Act.* A speaker means what he says, but he means something more as well. Thus utterance meaning includes sentence meaning but extends beyond it.

provide us exact devices for expressing literally whatever we wish to express in any given metaphor?" then the answer is obviously no. It is often the case that we use metaphor precisely because there is no literal expression that expresses exactly what we mean. Furthermore, in metaphorical utterances, we do more than just state that S is R; as Figure 6.1 shows, we state that S is R by way of going through the meaning of "S is P." It is in this sense that we feel that metaphors somehow are intrinsically not paraphrasable. They are not paraphrasable, because without using the metaphorical expression, we will not reproduce the semantic content which occurred in the hearer's comprehension of the utterance.

The best we can do in the paraphrase is reproduce the truth conditions of the metaphorical utterance, but the metaphorical utterance does more than just convey its truth conditions. It conveys its truth conditions by way of another semantic content, whose truth conditions are not part of the truth conditions of the utterance. The expressive power that we feel is part of good metaphors is largely a matter of two features. The hearer has to figure out what the speaker means – he has to contribute more to the communication than just passive uptake – and he has to do that by going through another and related semantic content from the one which is communicated. And that, I take it, is what Dr. Johnson meant when he said metaphor gives us two ideas for one.

NOTES

I am indebted to several people for helpful comments on earlier drafts of this article, and I especially want to thank Jerry Morgan, Andrew Ortony, Paul Rauber, and Dagmar Searle.

1 It is essential to avoid any use-mention confusions when talking about these sets. Sometimes we will be talking about the words, other times about meanings, other times about references and denotations, and still other times about truth conditions.

2 I follow Beardsley (1962) in this classification.

3 Even in Black's clarification (this volume) of interaction in terms of "implication-complexes" there still does not seem to be any precise statement of the principles on which interaction works. And the actual example he gives, "Marriage is a zero-sum game," looks distressingly like a comparison metaphor: "Marriage is *like* a zero-sum game in that it is an adversary relationship between two parties in which one side can benefit only at the expense of the other." It is hard to see what the talk about interaction is supposed to add to this analysis.

4 By "literal simile," I mean literal statement of similarity. It is arguable that one should confine "simile" to nonliteral comparisons, but that is not the usage I follow here.

5 Furthermore, it is at least arguable that "block of ice" functions metonymously in this example.

7

*Language, concepts, and worlds: Three domains of metaphor

SAMUEL R. LEVIN

According to Searle (this volume), metaphors represent a class of linguistic expression that says one thing and means another. In this respect, he points out, they resemble cases of irony and indirect speech acts. A characteristic of all such types of linguistic expressions is that the literal utterance – what in fact is said – is in some sense "defective," taking the form of "obvious falsehood, semantic nonsense, violation of the rules of speech acts, or violations of conversational principles of communication." The problem posed by such expressions is therefore to determine where, if not in the utterance itself, one should look to ascertain what they in fact mean. In this connection, Searle has introduced the distinction between (literal) sentence meaning and (speaker's) utterance meaning, and he has suggested that one should look to the latter for true meaning. In other words, the sentence may say one thing, but the speaker may intend (by it) something else, and the meaning to be inferred from the sentence must be attributed to and read off that intention. In saying, for example, "Sally is a block of ice," the speaker may intend to convey that Sally is a cold and unresponsive person, and the hearer, to properly interpret that utterance, must read off that intended meaning.

There is much in Searle's account that is extremely beneficial to the study of metaphor, and if I differ from his views it is not so much that I disagree with his conclusions as that I envisage in my approach a different role to be played by metaphor.

To begin with, I think it is necessary in developing accounts of metaphor to make clear whether the account is designed to apply to metaphoric language in general, to metaphors as they occur in everyday language, or to metaphors as they occur in literature, particularly poetry. Although here and there in Searle's discussion there appears a metaphor that comes from poetry, I think it is fair to say that most of his examples are of the sort that one would encounter in everyday speech, that is, they are prosaic rather than poetic metaphors. There is no reason why Searle's account should not have application to metaphor in general, to literary as well as ordinary language metaphors. In fact, such is probably Searle's intention. Nevertheless, if our purpose is to develop a theory of metaphor applicable to poetic metaphors, perhaps a different approach to the general problem may be needed.

The comparison theory and the interaction theory

Before entering into an exposition of my own views on the subject, it might be useful to recall the theoretical situation in 1979 when Searle's article originally appeared. In particular, I want to focus on Searle's discussion of what he regarded as the shortcomings of two differing fundamental approaches to the interpretation of metaphor – one that posits a comparison or similarity between two objects, and the other that involves a verbal opposition or interaction between two semantic contents.

In keeping with the pragmatic orientation of his own theory of metaphor, Searle locates the deficiencies of these two approaches in their focus on fundamentally semantic aspects of the metaphoric utterance. As Searle has it, according to the one theory, the metaphoric utterance, in asserting a relation of similarity as obtaining between two objects, defines a set of truth conditions which entail the existence of the objects between which the relation is purported to hold; moreover, the claim of similarity made by the metaphoric utterance is assumed to be true. Searle disputes these two requirements of the comparison theory by means, respectively, of examples like "Sally is a dragon" and "Richard is a gorilla."

Against the comparison theory Searle argues that it assumes existence for the objects being compared and that because existence is not a necessary requirement for successful metaphor, the claim must be false. This strikes me as an arbitrary criticism. Any theory of metaphor, Searle's included, must deal with the assertions made in metaphoric expressions. Whether we concern ourselves with the assertions made in the metaphoric utterance itself, or with those assumed to constitute the speaker's intention in producing that utterance, we confront an implicit claim for the existence of certain states of affairs. And to the extent that truth conditions are implicit in those claims, it would appear that existence is entailed for any objects referred to. But these logical considerations obviously play no critical role in the formation and production of metaphors. Nor need they play any role in assessing theories of metaphor. Thus, it is just as open to a comparison theory to dispose of properties in the absence of the objects presumed to be the bearers of those properties as it is to any other theory of metaphor. It should not be reckoned fatal to a comparison theory that for its analysis of "Sally is a dragon," it is not able to produce a dragon.

When Searle comes to criticize the semantic interaction theory, he cites as one of its assumptions the requirement that in a metaphoric utterance one element in that utterance must be literal – to function as the "vehicle" or "frame" – and he says of that assumption that it is plainly false. As far as I know, however, proponents of the semantic interaction theory nowhere claim it to be *necessary* that one of the elements in a metaphoric utterance be literal. In any case, as Searle's example ("The bad news is a block of ice") shows, any departure from that requirement will have a strained and affected air.

Searle's other objection to the semantic interaction theory is that "it is not in general the case that the metaphorical speaker's meaning is the result of any interaction among the elements of the sentence in any literal sense of 'interaction.' " His argument is based on the assumption that the meaning of certain types of noun phrases – primarily proper names and indexical expressions – is exhausted in their referring function, and that there is little or no semantic residue left over to engage in "interaction." This is a substantive argument, but here again, it can be turned against Searle's own theory. Searle allows himself considerable latitude where "semantics" is concerned; he includes factual knowledge, speakers' beliefs, associations, perceptions, attitudes, and so forth. If this range of possibilities were to be applied in determining the signification of a proper name or indexical expression, the upshot would be more than simple reference to an individual. Thus, if provision is made for the employment of all these features in the interaction theory, Searle could not cite proper names and indexicals as invalidating that theory. Conversely, if one were to disallow these features in Searle's account of metaphor, it would suffer the same handicap where such expressions are concerned that he alleges against the interaction theory.

Davidson on metaphor

At roughly the same time as the original, 1979, publication of Searle's article, there appeared an article by Donald Davidson on the problem of metaphor (D. Davidson, 1978). Despite significant differences in their respective approaches, the two essays resemble each other in certain critical respects. Both assert that in metaphoric utterances there is no modification of meaning in any of the elements of the metaphoric expression – like literal utterances, metaphoric utterances mean simply what they say, their composite elements bearing only the meanings that they have in literal utterances. In other words, both theories deny the central claim of the semantic interaction theory, that as a consequence of the "interaction" the meaning of one or more of the elements in the metaphoric utterance is somehow modified. At the same time, however, given that metaphoric utterances mean simply and only what they say, it remains necessary for a theory of metaphor somehow to rationalize the fact that such utterances require for the registration of their metaphoric significance or purport a special or characteristic type of linguistic processing. For Searle this processing involves an inference to the meaning intended by the speaker, a meaning which in these cases differs from the meaning of the sentence as uttered; for Davidson it involves a special exercise of the hearer's interpretive activity, an exercise in which *uncodified* resemblances or similarities play a significant role.

It is understood that Searle's theory, exploiting as it does the critical role played by speaker's meaning, has a pronounced pragmatic dimension. The same claim can be made for Davidson's theory. At one point he writes, "I depend on the distinction between what words mean and what they are used to do. I think metaphor belongs exclusively to the domain of use" (D. Davidson, 1978, p. 33). Several aspects of this "use" function can be distinguished in Davidson's essay. Thus, at one point he compares metaphors with lies and points to their similarity in that "lying, like making a metaphor, concerns not the meaning of words, but their use" (1978, p. 42). In telling a lie the speaker knows that what he says is false, but he intends that the hearer take it as true; similarly, when a speaker makes a metaphor, he knows that what he says is false; in this case, however, says Davidson, he intends that the hearer take it as metaphoric. All this, with a significant shift in focus, can be cast in terms of Searle's speech act analysis.

In Searle's treatment of metaphor, the sentence means one thing ("S is P"), but the speaker's meaning is something different ("S is R"), where "S is R," the meaning the speaker has in mind, is the metaphoric meaning, and thus has a definite cognitive content; moreover, and most important, the interpreter of the metaphor must somehow recover this content. Thus Searle writes at one point: "In its simplest form, the question we are trying to answer is How is it possible for the speaker to say metaphorically 'S is P' and mean 'S is R', when P plainly does not mean R?"; Searle continues, with what is relevant in the present context, "furthermore, How is it possible for the hearer who hears the utterance 'S is P' to know that the speaker means 'S is R'?". With regard to the latter point, Davidson's position is significantly different. As with Searle, on Davidson's analysis the sentence means one thing but the speaker uses it to convey something else (or at least something more). In this process, however, there is no requirement or implication that the meaning induced by the sentence, that is, the interpretation the hearer imposes on it, need correspond with a meaning intended by the speaker. Indeed, Davidson explicitly denies any such correlation. He writes, "The central error about metaphor is most easily attacked when it takes the form of a theory of metaphorical meaning, but behind that theory, and statable independently, is the thesis that associated with a metaphor is a cognitive content that its author wishes to convey and that the interpreter must grasp if he is to get the message. This theory is false, whether or not we call the purported cognitive content a meaning" (1978, p. 46). For Davidson the significant work in the metaphoric enterprise takes place at the "receiving" end of the transaction. Whatever the author of the metaphor may have intended to communicate, the utterance itself has only its literal meaning; as a reaction to this meaning, however, the hearer is stimulated to entertain and process a series of novel relationships.

It is possible to claim a further pragmatic dimension for Davidson's theory. As we have seen, where for Searle there exists a problematic space between what the sentence means and what the speaker intends it to mean, for Davidson such a space exists between what the sentence means and what the hearer or reader interprets it to mean. He writes, "A metaphor makes us see one thing as another by making some literal statement that prompts or inspires the insight" (1978, p. 47). The literal statement that prompts us to the insight has, typically, a characteristic property, that of being *patently* false (1978, p. 42). The fact that the falsity is patent will then lead the reader of the metaphor to discount the truth claims that the sentence may be making and, according good faith to the author of the sentence, attempt to construe a meaning for the sentence – to seek out its "hidden implication." In this process the reader will be led to consider new possibilities of relationship between the world's objects: "A metaphor makes us attend to some likeness, often a novel or surprising likeness, between two or more things" (1978, p. 33). What this means is that in construing a metaphor we must bring to bear our knowledge of the world (encyclopedic knowledge); that is, the implicated likeness being novel, the knowledge here in question will not be codified knowledge, the kind implicitly incorporated in words as used with their normal extensions and sentences with their normal predications. Instead, metaphors require us to think of the world's objects in unprecedented, hence nonsemantically codified relations. One may or may not consider that the use of encyclopedic knowledge in our interpretation of sentences constitutes a dimension of pragmatics; in the process of metaphoric construal as described above, however, in which the normal semantic function of linguistic elements is effectively superseded and where it is our knowledge of the world's objects that functions critically – in such a process, it seems to me, one can reasonably claim a pragmatic dimension.

Davidson's approach to semantics is rigorously extensional. Thus, of the four types of "defectiveness" listed by Searle as setting in motion the process of metaphoric construal ("obvious falsehood, semantic nonsense, violation of the rules of speech acts, or violation of the conversational principles of communication"), Davidson deems as operative only the first (and its polar complement, obvious truth). In including what he calls "semantic nonsense" as one of the conditions triggering metaphoric construal, Searle, it seems to me, makes the better case. Metaphors come in all kinds of syntactic arrangements. To reduce the meaning quotients of all these different arrangements to the single semantic category of patent (obvious) falsity appears unsound from both an empirical and a theoretical point of view. Apparently motivating Searle to include "semantic nonsense" in his set of triggering mechanisms are metaphors of the type represented by "The ship ploughs the sea" (the type represented by "Sally is a block of ice" motivating obvious falsehood). For Davidson both these sentences, and the types they represent, would be patently false. Taken literally, both these sentences are false: no person is a block of ice and a ship does not plough the sea. But we arrive at this conclusion not by checking the facts; we read it off the sentences themselves. Perhaps this is what Davidson means by calling such sentences *patently* false, that is, the truth conditions they implicate are such that empirical investigation is not needed to adjudge them false. One need not, however, approach the analysis of such sentences in terms of the treatment they would receive in a truth-theoretic semantics; they can be approached against the background of how a speaker involved in an actual speech situation would respond to them on the basis of his linguistic competence. If one takes this approach – and one needs to seriously consider this approach if one is concerned not merely with the critic's analysis of metaphor but also with the hearer or reader's experience of it – one must include semantic nonsense (what I would prefer to call "semantic deviance") in the set of conditions that trigger metaphoric construal.

At a certain stage in our linguistic development, perhaps on the basis of earlier having compared factual conditions with the truth claims made by sentences, we codify the relations into which the syntactic and semantic categories of our language can enter. Codification of these relations is what intuitive knowledge of a grammar amounts to. Against a grammar so internalized, a sentence must pass muster both as to its syntactic well-formedness and its semantic consistency; metaphors typically pass the first of these tests and fail the second, and they fail the second immediately and intuitively, on a purely grammatical basis, recourse to truth tests being at this stage of our linguistic development no longer necessary.

This fact is largely lost sight of if our focus is on run-of-the-mill examples of metaphor like "Man is a wolf," "Sam is a pig," "Sally is a block of ice," copulative sentences in which a subject noun phrase is subsumed by a sortally inconsistent predicate. For metaphors of this type, patent falsity may with some plausibility be nominated as the mechanism that triggers construal. But where the metaphoric sentence is not of the copulative type, as in "The ship ploughs the sea" – not to mention examples from poetry like "My life stood – a loaded gun" – it becomes more and more doubtful that our immediate response is referential in nature; it is much more likely that we respond on the basis of our ingrained linguistic competence, by an intuitive sense that the components of the metaphoric sentence violate the rules that define the permitted relations among semantic elements.

Let us consider in this connection the following lines from Yeats' "Sailing to Byzantium":

> An aged man is but a paltry thing,
> A tattered coat upon a stick, unless
> Soul clap its hands and sing,

If we analyze the major metaphors in this passage, we could argue that the two primary assertions that men are coats (upon a stick) and that souls clap their hands and sing, are both patently false, in that men are not coats and souls neither have hands nor sing. But this analysis would disregard an important distinction: men *are* not coats, whereas souls are not the *kinds of things* that have hands or sing. In the first metaphor the predicate assigns the subject to an improper category, in the second it attributes to it an inapplicable property or characteristic. In grammatical terms this means that both metaphors violate the rules for semantic consistency. As indicated above, the violations take different forms. Now I think that our response to the "defectiveness" in metaphors operates in the first instance always as a function of our internalized grammars.[1] It may be, however, that where copulative metaphors are concerned, the response to a violation of a subsumption (class membership) rule is one with our recognition that the claim made by the metaphoric assertion is false. I leave this question open. When, however, we encounter a metaphor that involves not an improper subsumption but an improper attribution, then, I would argue, our immediate response is purely linguistic, deriving from our tacit understanding of the constraints on the rules for semantic combination, and not from our knowledge of how the world is constituted.

The actuation problem

It might be worthwhile at this point to say a bit more about the "actuation" problem, to consider in a more general context what it is that causes a hearer or reader to infer that the expression he encounters requires to be construed (cf. note 1). I have indicated above why I think that for literary metaphors the process is entrained by an intuitive recognition that the elements in the utterance are semantically incompatible with one another. In this regard, cases of irony and indirect speech acts differ fundamentally, in that, unlike metaphor, where the actuation is based on semantic characteristics, for irony and indirect speech acts it derives from pragmatic considerations. This is a corollary of the fact that ironic utterances and indirect speech acts make perfect sense semantically. There is no semantic incompatibility among the words in "That was a most intelligent remark" or

"Your radio is making a lot of noise." Both these sentences could be uttered in circumstances such that sentence meaning and speaker's meaning would be coincident, with no indication that they invited other than normal apprehension. For the former sentence to function ironically there must be an incompatibility between what the sentence says and features of the nonlinguistic context; for the latter to function as an indirect speech act something about the context must indicate that the sentence is being used to do more than merely assert a fact. Seen in this way, irony and indirect speech acts are crucially pragmatic in nature.

In this connection we may take up another expression type that frequently figures in discussions of metaphor. Thus, the claim sometimes made that semantic deviance is a necessary condition for metaphor is usually countered by adducing examples in which there is no such deviance. In his discussion Searle mentions as such an example Disraeli's remark when he became Prime Minister: "I have climbed to the top of the greasy pole." In the present discussion the important fact about this and similar examples is that for them to be taken metaphorically they must be used in an incompatible (nonlinguistic) context – for example, where there is no greasy pole and where no act of climbing has occurred. If these conditions should in fact be present and if the speaker intends to refer to them, the sentence will not then function metaphorically. We might term such sentences *equivocal* metaphors. The recourse in such metaphors to the speaker's utterance meaning – as also in irony and indirect speech acts – must be induced by the incompatibility of the sentence meaning with the environment in which it is uttered. Only in this way can we determine the speaker's proper intention. The situation is quite otherwise with poetic or literary metaphors where that intention, in Searle's terms, is read off the utterance itself.

Lakoff and Johnson on metaphor

In the theory of metaphor presented by Lakoff and Johnson (1980), the separation of what is said from what is intended plays a significant role, although in a manner quite different from the way it plays that role in Searle's theory. Like Searle, Lakoff and Johnson contend that lying behind metaphoric utterances there is a speaker's mental construct, but whereas for Searle that construct generally represents a nonmetaphoric notion (in many cases a literal paraphrase), this construct is for Lakoff and Johnson itself metaphoric. Our language is peppered with expressions like "I demolished his argument," "I attacked his major thesis," "He mustered many facts to support his position." Such expressions, according to Lakoff and Johnson, derive from and reflect the presence in our minds of a metaphorical *concept* which holds that *Argument is War*. Conceptual metaphors need not, as such, be expressed. Evidence for their existence is provided by, and inferred from, those linguistic metaphors, like the ones listed above, which occur commonly and consistently in the everyday speech of most speakers (see also Lakoff, this volume).

Although the two theories correspond in that to arrive at some rationalization for what is said one must recur to what is in the speaker's mind, this is about as far as the similarity extends. For Searle, the recourse is an outcome of his speech-act approach to the analysis of language, and thus a function of pragmatics. For Lakoff and Johnson the recourse grows out of a conviction that conceptual metaphors, in their aggregate, define an outlook on "truth" and reality; they are thus making a metaphysical argument. In this respect their position bears a certain affinity with that represented by the Sapir-Whorf hypothesis. The difference is that whereas in the latter the registration of the grammatical categories of the language in a speaker's mind purportedly determined the speaker's world view, for Lakoff and Johnson that function is performed by the speaker's having had impressed on his mind a body of conceptual metaphors.

Granting that these mental impressions are indeed metaphoric in nature, the question arises as to the status of those expressions that occur in speech and presumably derive from and reflect the existence of the conceptual metaphors. In most theories of metaphor, Searle's included, there is no question as to the metaphoric status of the linguistically occurrent expressions that are cited by way of exemplification. Here and there a stock example may be introduced whose metaphoric function has been somewhat attenuated ("Sam is a pig," "The argument became heated," etc.), but in essence the focus in these studies is on linguistic expressions whose metaphoric status is not in doubt. The case is otherwise with the linguistic expressions that figure in the theory of Lakoff and Johnson. Among the examples that they adduce are "wasting time," "attacking positions," "going our separate ways." These expressions, they say, "are reflections of systematic metaphorical concepts that structure our actions and thoughts. They are 'alive' in the most fundamental sense: they are metaphors we live by. The fact that they are conventionally fixed within the lexicon of English makes them no less alive" (1980, p. 55).

This last statement has about it an air of paradox, if not indeed inconsistency. One normally assumes that to the extent that items are conventionally fixed within the lexicon their meanings are normalized, and thus rendered stable. And metaphors that have undergone this process are standardly referred to as "dead," not "alive." Now Lakoff and Johnson do discuss a type of metaphor that counts for them as dead, "foot of the mountain." Metaphors of this type ("head of cabbage," "leg of a table," etc.), they say, are "idiosyncratic" because they "do not interact with other metaphors" and they "play no particularly interesting role in our conceptual system" (1980, p. 55).

These conclusions highlight the strongly conceptual nature of Lakoff and Johnson's theory of metaphor. For them the "vitality" of a linguistic expression is not determined by the status of its elements in the lexicon and the role played by those elements in grammatical arrangements; it is determined, rather, by the role those elements play in our conceptual system and by the significance of their function in the conduct of and talk about our daily lives.

A proposal for literary metaphor

Implicit in Searle's account of metaphor (and in other accounts as well) is the assumption that, given an incompatibility between the utterance and conditions in the world, the conditions are to be taken as fixed, and it is the utterance that must be construed. Now this is not a logically necessary position. We may, if we like, in the face of an incompatibility between what is asserted in an utterance and conditions as they obtain in the world, regard the utterance as fixed and construe the world. Instead, that is, of construing the utterance so that it makes sense in the world, we construe the world so as to make sense of the utterance. On this account, "defectiveness" is located in the world (i.e., the actual world), not in the utterance. "Deviant" utterances are taken literally; they mean what they say – what gives is the world.

In employing this conception of metaphor, the states of affairs depicted by the linguistic expressions (taken at face value) have somehow to be rationalized. Inasmuch as those states will be preternatural, ontologically bizarre, their rationalization cannot actually be brought off; the concept expressed by the utterance cannot really be brought to mental representation. As I have argued elsewhere, however, although preternatural states of affairs cannot be conceived as actually existing, the possibility of their existing can be conceived *of*: we can form a *conception* of what a world would have to be like were it in fact to comprise such states of affairs (see Levin, 1988, pp. 65–73). In conceiving of such a world, we do not project the actuality of preternatural states, but we lend credence to their possibility. If we read in a poem "the sky is angry," we conceive of a world in which the sky might be angry; in the same way, the wind might be hungry, the stars happy, and so on. The usual process of construal is simply inverted; instead of constructing an interpretation that consists with conditions in the actual world, we construct one that conforms to the actual language of the utterance. In consequence what emerges as metaphoric is not the language in which the poem is expressed, but the world that language has caused us to project. We have projected ourselves into a metaphoric world.

That we take the language of metaphoric utterances literally is the recommendation also of Searle and Davidson; the two differ only in what they claim the construal process to consist in. For Searle construal takes the form of an inference to the speaker's meaning, whereas for Davidson construal is a process in which the reader or analyst entertains an open-ended series of novel relationships which the literal meaning stimulates. For both Searle and Davidson taking the metaphor literally is a stage in the development of an interpretation that departs from the meaning comprised by the actual utterance. As I have described the process, the language of the metaphor is also to be taken literally. On my account, however, there is no semantic displacement from or amplification of the literal meaning; the metaphor is assumed to mean nothing different from or more than what it says. Inasmuch, however, as metaphor expressions (in poetry) typically are semantically deviant, this means that the burden of construal falls on conceiving preternatural states of affairs – metaphoric worlds.

In the context of the preceding remarks, let us consider the following poem by Emily Dickinson:

> The mountain sat upon the plain
> In his eternal chair,
> His observation manifold,
> His inquest everywhere.
> The seasons prayed around his knees,
> Like children round a sire:
> Grandfather of the days is he,
> Of dawn the ancestor.

A standard type of interpretation might include observations like the following: in the first two lines the mountain's location in a certain place is expressed by "sat . . . in his eternal chair"; that it rises higher than its surroundings is expressed metaphorically in lines 3 and 4; line 5, "the seasons prayed around his knees" is a metaphor for the mountain's steadfastness throughout the years; lines 7 and 8 contain metaphors for its extreme age. Assuming that the preceding observations generally reflect a standard approach to metaphoric analysis, we would conclude that Emily Dickinson experienced a rather ordinary poetic insight – that of a mountain being high, old, and physically impressive – and proceeded to make an interesting if unspectacular poem out of that insight by contriving to express it in an extraordinary arrangement of language. If we now invert the approach, we countenance a world in which the mountain has the properties the language of the poem attributes to it: it actually sits on an eternal chair, looks everywhere, has knees around which the seasons pray, and so on. On this view it is not the language that is remarkable, it is the conception; that language is simply a faithful description of that conception.

The question might be raised whether in writing her poem Emily Dickinson really intended to project such a version of reality as the one I have proposed. I'm not sure that this is a necessarily relevant question. In the case of certain poets (and novelists) we may, on the basis of what we have learned about their world views, have a fair degree of confidence that a "conceptionalist" reading of the sort I have proposed above is well motivated.[2] Thus, in dealing with William Wordsworth, a case can be made for his having held a view of the universe in which a single, undifferentiated spirit coursed through all of nature, uniting human beings and the objects of their natural surroundings. A literal reading of the metaphors in his poetry (compare, as representative of a consistent class of metaphors, "the calm which Nature breathes among the hills and groves," *Prelude,* I.280–1) would then generate a conception of the universe consistent with such a world view (see Levin, 1988, pp. 227–37). Even in the absence of any specific knowledge about an author's general outlook, however, it remains open to us to impose a conceptionalist interpretation on a work. Some of the stories of Jorge Luis Borges, as well as the novels of so-called "fabulous realism" lend themselves to and, in my opinion, reward such a reading. The poetry of William Blake is similarly susceptible. In the final analysis, whether we decide to take – *and interpret* – the metaphors in the work literally may depend simply on whether or not we wish to bring the outlook of that work into conformity with *our own* conception of how the work might be ordered. And this decision may derive contingently from the particular work that is being analyzed, or it may derive from one's general aesthetic, cultural, or philosophical principles.

NOTES

This chapter is a revision of the one that appeared in the first edition under the title *Some observations on the pragmatics of metaphor.*

1 It is necessary to understand as distinct the process of construing a metaphor and the response to an utterance that it requires construal. The latter is a spontaneous reaction that *triggers* the construal process. As to the construal process itself, that process, I claim, is characteristic; a different order of semantic circumstances is involved in the processing of a metaphor than is involved in the processing of a literal utterance. Davidson in a footnote (1978, p. 46) avers that for any use of language the range of what it may cause us to notice is endless, so that in this respect metaphor does not differ from literal language. I do not find it necessary to disagree with this claim. My focus, however, is on the difference between the *sorts* of things that are brought to our notice. What is significant for me is the fact that, on Davidson's own account, metaphors bring *novel* things and relations to our notice. This fact makes the construal process for metaphors different from that for literal utterances. In fact, I would not say for the latter type of utterance that we construe them; we simply understand them.

2 The contrast implicit between what I am calling a "conceptionalist" approach to metaphor and the conceptualist approach of Lakoff and Johnson amounts to more than merely a difference in terminology. Their primary concern is with our ordinary language, whereas mine is with literary language. For them concepts determine the form the language takes; for me the language (of the poem or novel) determines the form a conception will take. There are other differences as well, but this is not the place to go into them.

8

Observations on the pragmatics of metaphor

JERRY L. MORGAN

Introduction

I am persuaded that the main points in Professor Searle's paper are correct, but there are a few arguments which leave me unsatisfied. I agree with his point that metaphor can only be understood by close attention to the distinction between "sentence meaning" and "utterance meaning," and that metaphor must be considered a case of the latter, not the former. But I find some aspects of his proposal for a proper treatment of metaphor tantalizingly vague or incomplete. In particular, it seems to me that his discussion of "call to mind" casts the net too wide, capturing some things that are not in the same boat as clear cases of metaphor. Moreover, there are some difficult leaps in his three-step analysis of metaphor, and I think that his proposal avoids dealing with an important question about its nature. I have a few other quibbles that I shall mention along the way, though I do not think they are a serious threat to Searle's analysis, with which, as I have said, I generally agree.

The proper domain of the analysis of metaphor

The distinction Searle makes between sentence meaning and utterance meaning is a crucial one, not only for metaphor, but for the study of meaning in general. The mistake of overlooking this distinction has constantly plagued work on meaning by linguists, and I think recognition of the importance of the distinction is a real advance.

Searle argues that metaphor is a matter of utterance meaning, hence a pragmatic problem, rather than a semantic one. This is a point worth dwelling on, because there have been proposals made for accounts of metaphor that could be construed as semantic treatments. For example, one well-known position on metaphor (Matthews, 1971) is that it always involves violation of "selection restrictions," rendering metaphor a kind of semantic deviance. At its simplest, this approach is no more than a putative method for detecting metaphors. It says nothing about how language users are able to make sense of supposedly deviant sentences. But a more serious objection is that this characterization of metaphor is just plain wrong, a point made forcefully by Reddy (1969), and Ortony, Schallert, Reynolds, and Antos (1978). Reddy points out that perfectly sensible sentences can be used metaphorically. He makes this point with some thoroughly convincing examples, including the following:

(1) He suspected that most of his listeners were sympathetic to the position that selection restrictions were totally inadequate. But he attacked the sputtering tyrant once again, if only to place his little penknife alongside the daggers of his companions. (p. 242)

And he observes that

(2) The rock is becoming brittle with age

could be used either literally or metaphorically; it could be used literally in the context of a group of people on a geology expedition, metaphorically in the context of a group of students walking out of the office of some staunch old professor emeritus (p. 242). So the theory that all metaphors are semantically anomalous in some way cannot stand.

Another approach to metaphor that could be construed as semantic is one involving a meaning change of some sort, wherein a "semantic feature" of some element in the sentence is changed, or some kind of operation results in a change in the meaning of the sentence. Searle rejects this approach out of hand, but I think it is worth a closer look, in part because it is a sidelight on the need for more precise language in discussion of metaphor.

There are a number of senses in which we might take the term "change in meaning" as a description of the interpretation of metaphor. I shall try to show that on close examination the only sense that makes sense is one that is indistinguishable from Searle's position.

First, I must sort out what one might mean by "meaning" in the phrase, "change of meaning." As far as I can see, there are only two possibilities. One might mean the meaning that is assigned to the sentence by the compositional rules of the language being used. But on this interpretation, metaphor as change of meaning is clearly incoherent. Taken literally, a claim that an instance of metaphor involves a change in meaning in this sense can only mean that the meaning is not what it used to be; either the original meaning has been replaced by a new meaning – the metaphorical one – or the new meaning has been added beside the old (literal) one. Any other construal of "change" would be metaphorical. Thus the claim that interpretation of metaphor involves a change in meaning would imply that by using a sentence metaphorically, one somehow changes the compositional rules of the language so that that sentence henceforth has a different, or an additional, literal meaning. Clearly this is not what is meant by the phrase "change of meaning" as applied to metaphor. While it is logically possible, I suppose, for there to be a language community so insane that the rules of the language are changed every time some speaker produces a metaphor, it seems to me that this is not in general the case. If I say "John is a wall," meaning thereby to convey that he is immovable, the rules of English remain intact, including those that assign conventional meaning to the word "wall."

Then we might take "meaning" in another sense, that is, in the sense of Searle's speaker meaning – whatever it is that the speaker has in mind to convey by his utterance. But obviously this kind of meaning is not subject to change in the comprehension process. The speaker means whatever he means, something it makes no sense to speak of changing.

But there is a way to make sense of "changing" the sentence meaning. Namely, that starting with the literal meaning, one constructs a modified version that differs in some way from the original literal meaning. But this is not in any literal sense a "change" in sentence meaning. It is no more accurate to call this process "change in meaning" than it is to say that constructing a slightly modified version of the Louvre in Peoria constitutes a "change" in the Louvre. The case of metaphor is parallel. There is no sense in which meaning is, strictly speaking, changed. Rather, one starts with a meaning, then performs some operation that produces a second thing that could be called a meaning, which is related in some way to the first meaning. We have as a result two different meanings, one in some way derivative of the other, but it is not accurate to say that anything has been changed.

The next question is, What sort of operation is it that is involved in this so-called change? Searle proposes that it is a matter of utterance meaning, of figuring out by inference in context what the speaker intends to convey by saying what he says. But an advocate of a semantic treatment of metaphor might reply that the involvement of inference and context is not sufficient grounds for concluding that the matter is pragmatic. For inference and context are also involved in matters of literal meaning – in resolving ambiguity, for example. If I say to somebody, "The chicken is ready to eat," one could plausibly argue that the hearer must use knowledge of context, rules of conversation, and so forth, to infer which of the two literal meanings of the sentence I intended to convey. Just so with metaphor: there are two meanings, a literal one and a metaphoric one, and the hearer is required to infer which one was intended. Then metaphor is no different from any other kind of duality of meaning.

But, in fact, there is an important difference. In the case of ambiguity, the relation between the two meanings is a coincidence of the language, so that the same two meanings might well be translated into separate sentences in another language. But in the case of metaphor one of the meanings is derivative in some way from the other. If I say "John is a wall," the metaphorical reading is not a coincidental second meaning, but *derivative* of the literal meaning. Moreover, the number of metaphorical readings a sentence can have is not some small number (as in the case of multiple literal meanings), but an open set. "John is a wall" can have any number of metaphorical interpretations, depending on context – whether it is said, for example, by a teacher about a student, by a football coach about an offensive lineman, by anybody about a fat person, and so on. Furthermore, the process by which the metaphorical interpretation is derived from the literal meaning, whatever that process is, cannot be just some kind of formal linguistic operation on literal meaning, because as Searle points out, metaphor can be based not only on properties involved in literal meaning, but on associations, myths, and things we happen to know about the things referred to in the literal meaning. It is not really from the literal meaning that the metaphor is calculated, but from a complete understanding, an enriched sort of meaning with all the pragmatic gaps filled in. This is most clearly demonstrated by the fact that one can make metaphors indirectly, by using a nonmetaphorical sentence to conversationally implicate something that can only be understood as metaphor, as in something like

(3) A: How can I make John feel at home?

B: Buy him some Purina Hog Chow,

an example of an indirect conveyance of a frozen metaphor. Or, if asked about John's level of enthusiasm, I might say the following literally impeccable sentence:

(4) Somebody should set a match to him on the Fourth of July,

meaning thereby to convey indirectly that John is a firecracker, itself a metaphor.

My claim is, then, that when the phrase "change of meaning" is closely examined, it turns out to make no sense if taken literally; and if one seeks for the spirit of the phrase by taking it metaphorically, then it leads to the same conclusions Searle reaches in his paper – that metaphor is a matter of utterance meaning, and that the proper domain for an account of metaphor is pragmatics, not semantics. Moreover, I think talking of metaphor as a kind of meaning is a mistake itself, in that it naturally leads to thinking of metaphor as a property of sentences. But I think it is not a property of the sentence, but a matter of what one *does* in saying the sentence. To make clearer what I mean, let me compare metaphors with indirect speech acts. Although I do not mean to say that metaphor is just another kind of indirect speech act, there is an important similarity.

If I say to someone who is sitting on my hat,

(5) You're sitting on my hat,

as an indirect way of getting him off it, it is not my *sentence that* informs him that I wish he would get off my hat, but what I have *done* by saying the sentence. I have informed my interlocutor that he is sitting on my hat. If I could inform him in some nonlinguistic manner, the effect would be the same. It is clear to him that I want him to know he is sitting on my hat, for why else would I say it? Then for what purpose would I want him to know it? My purpose is obvious, given the right context. My interlocutor will infer that my reason for informing him was that if he were aware of his position, he would change it. Moreover, he would rightfully infer that it was my intention that he make this inference from my informing him. Now, clearly it is a grave mistake to try to attach this hint to the meaning of the sentence. It is an inference one might reasonably make about what I intend in *doing* what I do, informing being just one of those things one can do by linguistic means. So a proper treatment of this kind of indirect meaning belongs not in a theory of sentence meanings, but in a theory of acts, in particular in that subpart of a theory of acts that deals with the special case of communicative acts. Just so with metaphor. I think Black (this volume) puts his finger on an important point in saying that when Stevens writes, "A poem is a pheasant," he means not that a poem is *like* a pheasant, but that it is a pheasant. One might draw the same conclusion from the fact that (6) could be used metaphorically:

(6) John's not just *like* a tree, he *is* a tree.

If I am right that it can be used metaphorically, then it would appear that no simple simile theory can deal with this case, since it asserts the metaphor but denies the simile. Metaphors are *not* just grammatical variants of similes. When one says

(7) John's mind is a meadow in winter,

one takes a position on the truth of this very sentence, just as one always does in asserting. And it is by so *doing* that metaphor is conveyed, not by the sentence as a semantic object. The hearer does not just carry out some operation on the semantics of the sentence: he must picture what the world would be like if the sentence were true, or he could never know that I do not mean to be taken literally. Then he must figure out what the world could be like to lead me to make such an outrageously false assertion. He constructs a picture of the world that is as close as relevantly and sensibly possible to the world that corresponds to the literal meaning of the sentence.

I suppose that the interpretation of metaphor I am arguing for is one of overstatement. But clearly there is more to it than that. The interpretation of metaphor is not, as one might conclude, just a matter of getting rid of it, by turning it back into literal meaning; it is not just literal meaning in disguise.

Some criticisms of Searle

First, some minor criticisms concerning Searle's arguments against simile theory. To begin with, I think it is necessary to make a distinction between clear cases of metaphor and cases that have become conventional in one way or another, yet are not idioms. A clear case of metaphor is one not previously encountered, which one must really figure out. The second kind, which I shall call a "stored metaphor," just to have a way of talking about it, is a metaphor with which everybody is familiar, on its way to becoming an idiom, but still, in fact, understood figuratively. Several of Searle's examples are clearly of this kind. On being told, for example, that one is a pig, one does not greet it as a new metaphoric problem, to be figured out afresh via Searle's rules. One already has the knowledge that the phrase is used metaphorically to say something about personal habits, and recalls this information immediately. Recognizing the phrase, one knows immediately what is intended. It is an institutionalized metaphor, and knowledge that the phrase "a pig" is used this way short circuits the process of figuring out the metaphor from literal meaning (for a discussion of "short-circuited" indirect speech acts, see Morgan, 1978). Surely, it is obvious that one does not process "John is a pig" in the same way that one processes "John is a kangaroo." One knows immediately what is meant in the former case; the latter takes a little figuring. These stored metaphors are different from fresh metaphors in that they are *not* processed by first trying to make sense of the literal meaning, then, failing, trying to construe it as a figure of speech. This can be seen in that in a context where both the literal and the figurative senses are appropriate, the effect is of a pun. For example, if a lamp fetishist had a special passion for a certain lamp and kept it lit constantly, he could say,

(8) This lamp is the light of my life,

and have it work as a pun (albeit a feeble one). Or one could say of the comic-book character, the Flame, that he is a "ball of fire," and achieve the same punlike effect. Now, if the figurative sense were calculated only as a default reading when the literal reading was rejected, we should expect such puns to be impossible. The figurative reading would never be reached, since the literal one is sensible and relevant. This is, in fact, the case with genuine metaphor: Trying to make such puns with a fresh metaphor does not work. If one said

(9) The King Tut exhibit is a pharaoh's burial treasure,

intending to convey that the exhibit was worth a lot of money, there is little chance that the metaphor would be conveyed, since the literal meaning makes sense and is in fact true. On the other hand,

(10) John's bank account is a pharaoh's burial treasure,

is more likely to work as metaphor, because the literal reading is likely to be rejected.

The upshot of this is that some apparent metaphors are fresh and must be calculated or figured out, others are stored, labeled as figures of speech, a kind of instant metaphor – just add water and stir – and are recognized as such and understood immediately, probably because of some look-up strategy like "Try the largest chunk first." This class of institutionalized metaphors, which I call "stored metaphors," is quite different from the class of fresh metaphors – and therefore dubious as a test case for an understanding of metaphor – if I am right in assuming that it is fresh metaphor that is the central problem for a theory of metaphor, with stored metaphor to be treated derivatively. And I think at least some of Searle's examples are of this kind. If so, they are not useful ammunition in an attack on a simile theory of metaphor.

In fact, as Searle himself acknowledges, some of them might not even be metaphors at all, but idioms, such that the expression is now truly ambiguous, assigned two *literal* meanings by the rules of English. And an odd kind of nonliteral use (I hesitate to call it metaphor) can be built on idioms. For example, it is clear that the phrase "kick the bucket" is an idiom, having as a second literal meaning the meaning of "die," so that

(11) John kicked the bucket

is truly ambiguous. Speakers can exploit this special kind of ambiguity in a creative way, as in,

(12) When John kicked the bucket, he knocked it into the next county

used to describe a particularly spectacular death; likewise,

(13) John put his foot in his mouth and most of his leg as well,

used to convey that John really said the wrong thing, or similar wordplay on ambiguity like

(14) I'm so low I have to look up to tie my shoelaces.

One might propose, then, that the word "cold" is a kind of idiom for having "unresponsive," and similar attributes, as a second literal meaning, and that, "Sally is a block of ice," is an exploitation of this ambiguity, in a way similar to the examples above.

Finally, another way to save simile theory from Searle's claim that "Sally is a block of ice" has no meaning as a literal simile is to deny his premise that there is no similarity between cold things and unresponsive people. In fact, some of his later examples indirectly raise this possibility for escape. It is clear that metaphor can be built on *mythical* similarities that everybody knows are not really true. Searle cites the case of gorillas and their image: concerning owls there is a shared myth that they are wise. Foxes are clever, snakes sneaky, and so on. Metaphors, or at least stored metaphors, can be built on such myths, inasmuch as everybody knows that everybody knows the myths, even though everybody knows, further, that nobody *believes* the myths. One might propose, then, that "cold" is such a myth – that there is a shared myth that unresponsive people are cold, and that metaphor or figures of speech can exploit that myth, even though nobody really believes the myth is literally true.

It seems to me that these various possibilities for reinterpreting Searle's examples weaken his case against simile theory, insofar as his case depends on those examples.

As an aside, I should say that I do not share Searle's confidence about the cross-cultural validity of his examples. Figurative usage differs cross-culturally according to differences in shared beliefs, including the sort of myths that I have discussed. In fact, it seems to me to follow from Searle's point that metaphor can be constructed on myths, that we should find cross-cultural differences in metaphor corresponding to differences in such connotations and myths. Out of curiosity, I checked with some friends from abroad on the figurative uses of Searle's examples and a few others. The consultants were Nepali, Arab, and Chinese. I checked for figurative use of "blue," "yellow," "green," "cold," "warm," "square," "bad news," "sunset," "dawn," "moon," "sun," "wolf," "pig," "fox," and "dirt." I found as many differences as similarities. None accepted "warm" as a figurative counterpart of "cold." I was told that in Arabic, there are two words for "cold," only one of which has Searle's figurative use. One could conclude from this that one has to *learn* that "warm" is used figuratively to mean friendly, responsive, and so on.

Regarding Searle's proposal, my most serious complaint is not that it is wrong, but that it leaves some important questions unanswered. The first of these has to do with the nature of metaphor. In Searle's schema, if literal meaning is found to violate rules of conversation – by being nonsensical, obviously false, or merely irrelevant – the next step is to infer that a metaphor (or one of a few other things) is intended.

One can see how to get part way to this inference. If the sentence meaning is deviant, and the speaker is rational, then the speaker cannot intend (just) the sentence meaning. Then, assuming that the speaker means to convey anything at all, it must be different from sentence meaning. But if the speaker is rational, then there was some purpose in uttering the sentence he did. Therefore, there must be some connection between the meaning of the sentence and the meaning the speaker intends to convey.

This far one can get. But it is not clear how to get to the inferred conclusion that the connection of sentence meaning to speaker meaning is a metaphoric one. Is this a natural inference that could be made by any reasoning being? Or does it depend on prior knowledge that there is such a thing as metaphor that people use occasionally for certain purposes? If some rational being from another galaxy could be imbued with a grammar of English and enough knowledge of the world to get along, but no exposure to either the concept of metaphor or any example of metaphor, would he instantly recognize a metaphor for what it was the first time he encountered one? Or would he have to be told, or learn by example, what a metaphor is and its rules and purpose? Is metaphor a natural function of the mind, or a concept that must be learned? This is an empirical question, but I speculate that metaphor is a natural function of the mind.

The second step, the method of determining the possible (set of) properties that are being metaphorically predicated, Searle characterizes with the phrase, "call to mind," and gives a taxonomy of subcases, remarking that there are surely more subtypes. The question here is, Is it possible to replace this list with one or two generalizations from which the list can be derived as a consequence, or are we stuck with an arbitrary list of unknown length? The phrase, "call to mind," is surely too general. First of all, and obviously, there must be some condition to the effect that the thing "called to mind" was intended by the speaker. This avoids labeling as metaphor all sorts of random, private associations in the hearer's mind that the speaker does not intend to provoke, and may not even know about. I think this kind of condition is implicit in Searle's schema.

Second, there are things that are intuitively different from metaphor, though perhaps a subtype of figurative speech, that could be characterized as calling to mind a second meaning, due to rejection of the literal meaning. But before I give an example of this kind, I must establish that there are cases where an entire sentence is used metaphorically, without any particular part of the sentence corresponding to any particular part of what is metaphorically described. For example, if somebody is asked about the status of his tenure case and replies with (15) or (16),

(15) The sky is darkening

(16) It's clouding up,

there is no particular thing "the sky" or "it" refers to; the whole sentence serves as a metaphor, and somehow calls to mind an unpleasant state of affairs that can be applied to his tenure case. Now to the troublesome case. What is there that sets cases like (15) and (16) apart from cases like (17):

(17) Q: How do you like the soufflé?

A: On the whole, I'd rather be in Philadelphia.

Given the right set of beliefs, one can convey by saying the latter sentence that the soufflé is as bad as death. The inference that this is the intended meaning rests on knowledge that it is said (and it does not matter whether it is true or not) that this sentence is the epitaph on W. C. Fields' headstone. The intended meaning there, of course, is, "better in Philadelphia than dead." If the hearer knows this story, the response will call to mind what Fields supposedly meant by it, and by inferential steps I will not go into, the hearer will infer that a parallelism is intended wherein the soufflé is like death. Perhaps this kind of thing ought to be included in the general category of metaphor. I am not sure how to decide whether it should or not, save by arbitrary definition. At any rate, it is clearly different from, "Juliet is the sun."

Some further indications that "call to mind" is too general: My wife's most vivid memory of a certain village in the Balkans (I shall call it Pazari, though that is not its name) is of a certain official who was an obnoxious sexist. Any mention of Pazari immediately calls to mind this unpleasant man. Knowing this, why can I not, when speaking to my wife, use (18)

(18) John is Pazari,

to convey metaphorically that John is an obnoxious sexist? Or again, everybody who knows my father knows that he is a machinist; it is an important part of his life, and a salient property for people who know him. But I cannot imagine any circumstances under which (19)

(19) John is my father,

could be used to convey metaphorically to anybody that John is a machinist.

In the same way, Searle's inclusion of metonymy and synecdoche lets in some things that seem intuitively to deserve separate status. If "call to mind" includes the part–whole, container–contained, clothing–wearer, and similar associational relationships, then the following, consistency dictates, all qualify as metaphors:

(20) The kettle is boiling (i.e., its contents)

(21) IBM dropped 30 points (i.e., its stock)

(22) Read Chapter 3 of Chomsky for tomorrow (i.e., the book he wrote)

(23) Turn on the fish (i.e., the burner of the stove on which the pan containing the fish is located, in order to cook the fish).

It is not clear to me what senses of the word "Washington" are literal, but I suspect at least two of the following four sentences would probably count as metaphor in Searle's system:

(24) Washington covers a lot of land (that is, the physical structure, or the abstract plot of land)

(25) Washington elected a new mayor (that is, the people who live there)

(26) Washington rejected the Albanian proposal (that is, the executives of the government whose capital is there)

(27) Washington was founded in 1942 (that is, the abstract legal entity).

These strike me as unlike central cases of metaphor in being prosaic and unexciting, lacking the quasi-magical properties one usually thinks of metaphor as having. The difference is not merely the difference between predicating and referring expressions; one can get the central kind of metaphor in referring expressions as well, as in (28) and (29).

(28) My tender rosebud has left me

(29) The brightest star in my sky has run off with the milkman.

The difference between these and (20),

(20) The kettle is boiling,

resides in the *purpose* of choosing an expression that refers only indirectly to the object in question. The reason for choosing "the kettle" to refer to the contents of the kettle is mere convenience, as far as I can see. It serves to call to mind for the hearer the intended referent, and that is all there is to it. But in the other example, there is a purpose beyond this – to inform or remind the hearer, by choice of referring expression, of the emotional role and importance of the referent.

This relates to my final point of the "call to mind" relation. It seems to me that the most common type of "call to mind" connection in metaphors of the street, that is, in ordinary conversation, have a common property: The salient properties involved in the metaphor tend to be those with "affective" value (in the sense of Osgood et al., 1957); that is, some emotional or evaluative aspect. This relates, no doubt, to an important question that goes unanswered in Searle's system: What is the purpose of metaphor? Why does a speaker choose to use metaphor at all, instead of literal language? Searle apparently assumes that the fundamental questions of metaphor can be dealt with and understood without worrying about its purpose. I am suspicious of this assumption. In the case of indirect speech acts, the usual purpose of indirectness is just that: indirectness. The hearer's observation that the speaker is choosing to do things indirectly has important consequences for matters of politeness and other aspects of social interaction. To overlook this fact is to miss a potential source of explanation of difficult facts. For example, taking into account the purpose of indirectness provides a potential explanation for the fact that the oddness of preverbal "please" increases with indirectness: Preverbal "please" is a fairly direct indication of a request; thus to put it in a sentence intended to convey a request very indirectly is self-defeating, hence strange, as in

(30) *I wonder if anybody's going to please bring me a drink.

The answer to the question of the purpose of metaphor is surely not a simple one. It is not indirectness in the same sense as in indirect speech acts. And it is not mere convenience, a lazy inclination to use metaphor because an equally effective literal utterance would be too much work. Surely its purpose is more than the enjoyment of puzzle solving. There is something special about metaphor and its purpose that goes beyond the purpose of other kinds of indirect speech. The picture of metaphor one often gets, as I mentioned earlier, is of something to be eliminated as quickly as possible, to get down to the literal meaning that the metaphor covers up. If this were all there were to it, then the real question about metaphor would be, "Why bother?" Until we get at the question of why metaphor is used, I doubt that we will ever understand what it is.

METAPHOR
AND
REPRESENTATION

9

Generative metaphor: A perspective on problem-setting in social policy

DONALD A. SCHÖN

Introduction

Much of the interest in metaphor on the part of linguists and philosophers of language has had to do with metaphor as a species of figurative language which needs explaining, or explaining away. (See, for a notable example, Searle, this volume. Two classic articles, Black, 1962b, and Beardsley, 1967, are also in this vein.) Metaphor, in this tradition, is a kind of anomaly of language, one which must be dispelled in order to clear the path for a general theory of reference or meaning. There is a very different tradition associated with the notion of metaphor, however – one which treats metaphor as central to the task of accounting for our perspectives on the world: how we think about things, make sense of reality, and set the problems we later try to solve.[1] In this second sense, "metaphor" refers both to a certain kind of product – a perspective or frame, a way of looking at things – and to a certain kind of process – a process by which new perspectives on the world come into existence. In this tradition, metaphorical utterances – "Man is a wolf" along with the rest of the rather dreary repertoire of hallowed examples – are significant only as symptoms of a particular kind of SEEING-AS, the "meta-pherein" or "carrying over" of frames or perspectives from one domain of experience to another. This is the process which, in the remainder of this paper, I shall call generative metaphor.[2]

In the second tradition, there are two central puzzles. The first has to do with interpretation. From what people say and do, especially in problematic situations, how ought we to infer how they are *thinking* about those situations, whether their thinking involves a generative metaphor and, if so, what it is. This is the hermeneutic problem,[3] the problem of the interpretation of texts in a very broad sense, the problem of literary criticism. The concern here is to understand the kinds of inferences by which such interpretations are made, the sorts of evidence pertinent to them, and the criteria by which they should be judged and tested.

The second puzzle has to do with generativity. It is nothing less than the question of how we come to see things in new ways. Conceiving of generative metaphor as a special case – a special version of SEEING-AS by which we gain new perspectives on the world – we ask how the process of generative metaphor works. What is the anatomy of the making of generative metaphor?

In this paper, I shall be considering aspects of both of these puzzles as they crop up in a particular domain, that of social policy.

For some twenty years, it has been a powerful, indeed a dominant, view that the development of social policy ought to be considered as a problem-solving enterprise. In opposition to this view, I have become persuaded that the essential difficulties in social policy have more to do with problem setting than with problem solving, more to do with ways in which we frame the purposes to be achieved than with the selection of optimal means for achieving them. It becomes critically important, then, to learn how social policy problems are actually set and to discover what it means to set them well or badly.[4]

Problem settings are mediated, I believe, by the "stories" people tell about troublesome situations – stories in which they describe what is wrong and what needs fixing. When we examine the problem-setting stories told by the analysts and practitioners of social policy, it becomes apparent that the framing of problems often depends upon metaphors underlying the stories which generate problem setting and set the directions of problem solving. One of the most pervasive stories about social services, for example, diagnoses the problem as "fragmentation" and prescribes "coordination" as the remedy. But services seen as fragmented might be seen, alternatively, as autonomous. Fragmented services become problematic when they are seen as the shattering of a prior integration. The services are seen as something like a vase that was once whole and now is broken.

Under the spell of metaphor, it appears obvious that fragmentation is bad and coordination, good. But this sense of obviousness depends very much on the metaphor remaining tacit. Once we have constructed the metaphor which generates the problem-setting story, we can ask, for example, whether the services appropriate to the present situation are just those which used to be integrated, and whether there may not be benefits as well as costs associated with the lack of integration. In short, we can spell out the metaphor, elaborate the assumptions which flow from it, and examine their appropriateness in the present situation.

The notion of generative metaphor then becomes an interpretive tool for the critical analysis of social policy. My point here is not that we *ought* to think metaphorically about social policy problems, but that we *do* already think about them in terms of certain pervasive, tacit generative metaphors; and that we ought to become critically aware of these generative metaphors, to increase the rigor and precision of our analysis of social policy problems by examining the analogies and "disanalogies" between the familiar descriptions – embodied in metaphors like "fragmented services" – and the actual problematic situations that confront us.

The train of thought which leads me to argue for greater awareness of the metaphors which generate our setting of social policy problems also leads me to propose an argument about the making of generative metaphor.

When we become attentive to the framing of social problems, we thereby become aware of conflicting frames. Our debates over social policy turn often not on problems but on dilemmas. The participants in the debate bring different and conflicting frames, generated by different and conflicting metaphors. Such conflicts are often not resolvable by recourse to the facts – by technological fixes, by trade-off analyses, or by reliance on institutionalized forms of social choice. Indeed, these stubborn conflicts of perspective, full of potential for violent contention, have become in their own right issues of social policy. The question then arises as to whether it is possible by *inquiry* to achieve the restructuring, coordination, reconciliation, or integration of conflicting frames for the construction of social problems. If so, what is the nature of this inquiry?

I shall argue that we are sometimes intuitively able to engage in reciprocal inquiry by which conflicting frames are reconstructed and coordinated. And I shall propose that "frame restructuring" is in several crucial respects similar to the making of generative metaphor. These two kinds of processes seem to me to have a family resemblance, and our efforts to account for them can be mutually illuminating.

I shall pursue this line of thought by considering two examples – the first drawn from the domain of technology, and the second, from the field of housing policy. I shall consider in the first example the making of a generative metaphor, and in the second, a conflict of two ways of setting a social policy problem (each generated by a metaphor of its own) – a conflict which is resolved in a particular context through a process of frame restructuring and coordination, which resembles in several important respects the cognitive work involved in the making of generative metaphor.

The making of generative metaphor: A technological example

Some years ago, a group of product-development researchers was considering how to improve the performance of a new paintbrush made with synthetic bristles.[5] Compared to the old natural-bristle brush, the new one delivered paint to a surface in a discontinuous, "gloppy" way. The researchers had tried a number of different improvements. They had noticed, for example, that natural bristles had split ends, whereas the synthetic bristles did not, and they tried (without significant improvement resulting) to split the ends of the synthetic bristles. They experimented with bristles of different diameters. Nothing seemed to help.

Then someone observed, *"You know, a paintbrush is a kind of pump!"* He pointed out that when a paintbrush is pressed against a surface, paint is forced through the *spaces between bristles* onto the surface. The paint is made to flow through the "channels" formed by the bristles when the channels are deformed by the bending of the brush. He noted that painters will sometimes *vibrate a* brush when applying it to a surface, so as to facilitate the flow of paint.

The researchers tried out the natural and synthetic bristle brushes, thinking of them as pumps. They noticed that the natural brush formed a *gradual curve* when it was pressed against a surface whereas the synthetic brush formed a shape more nearly an angle. They speculated that this difference might account for the "gloppy" performance of the bristle brush. How then might they make the bending shape of the synthetic brush into a gentle curve?

This line of thought led them to a variety of inventions. Perhaps fibers could be varied so as to create greater density in that zone. Perhaps fibers could be bonded together in that zone. Some of these inventions were reduced to practice and did, indeed, produce a smoother flow of paint.

Paintbrush-as-pump is an example of what I mean by a generative metaphor.

In ordinary discourse, we call a paintbrush "paintbrush" and we call a pump, "pump." Paintbrushes and pumps are two quite different things and it is not appropriate to call one thing by the other's name. It is true that we can subsume both paintbrushes and pumps under a more general category; for example, they are both examples of tools. But when we think of the two things as tools, we also recognize that they are designed and used for different purposes, and that they operate according to different mechanisms. Hence, we would describe them differently. We might say, for example, that paintbrushes serve to "spread paint on a surface" whereas pumps serve to "move a quantity of liquid from one place to another." We might say that a pump works by "pushing or sucking liquid through a channel" whereas one makes a paintbrush work by "dipping it in paint and then transferring the paint to a surface by wiping the brush across that surface."

When one of the researchers said, "You know, a paintbrush is a kind of pump!" he was himself thinking of the paintbrush as a pump, seeing it as a pump, and he was inviting the other researchers to do likewise. In the language of description, we might say that he was taking the ordinary description of "pump" – something on the order of "an instrument that moves liquid from one place to another by pushing or sucking it through a channel" – as a putative description of "paintbrush." It is as though he were posing a kind of riddle ("How is a paintbrush a pump?") which, once entertained, led him and the other researchers to notice new features of the brush and of the painting process. The constellation of notions familiarly associated with pumping (what Black, 1962b, calls the "associated common-places") the researchers project onto the painting situation, transforming their perception of pumping. They notice the spaces *between* the bristles, for example, rather than just the bristles; and they think of these spaces as channels through which paint can flow. One might say that the spaces which had been background become foreground elements, objects of attention in their own right, as in a pump the contained space called a "channel" is a foreground element with a special name of its own. Rather than perceiving the paint as adhering to the surface of the bristles (later scraped off onto a surface), they now see the paint as flowing through the channels formed by the bristles. They can then pay attention to the different bending angles of the natural and synthetic brushes, noting how these different angles make for different ways of compressing channels and thereby affecting the pumping of liquid through the channels; and they can incorporate this observation into a new explanation of the differences in the brushes' performance. They invent ways to smooth out the bending angle of the synthetic brush in order to make it pump (not wipe) paint more evenly onto the surface.

Paintbrush-as-pump became a *metaphor* for the researchers.[6] One can characterize the metaphor-making process by saying that the researchers, who had begun by describing painting in a familiar way, entertained the description of a different, already-named process (pumping) as an alternative description of painting and that in their redescription of painting, both their perception of the phenomenon and the previous description of pumping were transformed. What makes the process one of metaphor making, rather than simply of redescribing, is that the new putative description already belongs to what is initially perceived as a different, albeit familiar thing; hence, everything one knows about pumping has the potential of being brought into play in this redescription of painting. There is, in this sense, great economy and high leverage in this particular kind of re-description.[7] To use the language of "seeing" rather than "describing,"[8] we can also say that the researchers were engaged in seeing A as B, where A and B had previously seemed to them to be different things. Every instance of metaphor making is an instance of SEEING-AS, though not every instance of SEEING-AS involves metaphor making. (For example, someone might see □ as a box.) In metaphor making, A and B are initially perceived, named, and understood as very different things – so different that it would ordinarily pass as a mistake to describe one as the other. It is the restructuring of the perception of the phenomena named by "A" and "B" which enables us to call "metaphor" what we might otherwise have called "mistake."

Not all metaphors are generative. In the researchers' talk about the paintbrush problem, for example, they also spoke of painting as "masking a surface." But this metaphor did not generate perceptions of new features of the paintbrush nor did it give rise to a new view of the problem. Paintbrush-as-pump was a *generative* metaphor for the researchers in the sense that it generated new perceptions, explanations, and inventions.

It is possible in this account to notice several important features of the process of making a generative metaphor. The researchers had, to begin with, certain ways of describing the brush and the painting process, but these descriptions were unsatisfactory. They did not lead to a setting of the technological problem that enabled it to be solved; they did not provoke invention. The triggering of the generative metaphor ("A paintbrush is a kind of pump!") occurred while the researchers were involved in the concrete, sensory experience of using the brushes and feeling how the brushes worked with the paint. The researchers used words like "gloppy" and "smooth" to convey some of the qualities of the phenomena they were experiencing. It seems to me very likely that the triggering of the metaphor occurred because the researchers were immersed in experience of the phenomena.

Once the metaphor had been triggered, one might say that the researchers *mapped* their descriptions of "pump" and "pumping" onto their initial descriptions of "paintbrush" and "painting." But this would be at least partly incorrect. For in the first instance, the two descriptions resisted mapping. It was only after elements and relations of the brush and the painting had been regrouped and renamed (spaces between bristles made into foreground elements and called "channels," for example) that the paintbrush could be seen as a pump.

It is important to note that the researchers were able to see painting as similar to pumping before they were able to say "similar with respect to what."[9] At first, they had only an unarticulated perception of similarity which they could express by doing the painting and inviting others to see it as they did, or by using terms like "squeezing" or "forcing" to convey the pumplike quality of the action. Only later, and in an effort to account for their earlier perception of similarity, did they develop an explicit account of the similarity, an account which later still became part of the general theory of "pumpoids," according to which they could regard paintbrushes and pumps, along with washcloths and mops, as instances of a single technological category.

It would be seriously misleading, then, to say that, in making their generative metaphor, the researchers first "noticed certain similarities between paintbrushes and pumps." For the making of generative metaphor involves a developmental process. It has a life cycle. In the earlier stages of the life cycle, one notices or feels that A and B are similar, without being able to say similar with respect to what. Later on, one may come to be able to describe relations of elements present in a restructured perception of both *A* and *B* which account for the preanalytic detection of similarity between *A* and *B,* that is, one can formulate an *analogy* between *A* and *B.* Later still, one may construct a general model for which a redescribed *A* and a redescribed *B* can be identified as instances. To read the later model back onto the beginning of the process would be to engage in a kind of historical revisionism.

Problem setting in social policy

My second example of generative metaphor will be drawn from a very different field, that of social policy; and here I shall pay particular attention to the issue of housing.

In introducing this field, I should like first to observe that it has come to be dominated, at least in the United States over the last twenty or thirty years, by a particular perspective – a perspective under which inquiry into social policy is regarded as a form of problem solving.

The problem-solving perspective contains three central components. It directs our attention, first of all, to the search for solutions. The problems themselves are generally assumed to be given. Thus, it is assumed that we know, or can easily voice, the problems of cities, the problems of the economy, the problems of population control, but that we cannot yet solve them. The task is to find solutions to known problems.

If problems are assumed to be given, this is in part because they are taken always to have the same form. Problem solving consists in the effort to find means for the achievement of our objectives in the face of the constraints that make such achievement difficult. According to this *instrumentalist* position, there are always objectives, goals, or purposes; these are rooted in human values and are, in a sense, arbitrary, inasmuch as they depend on what we (or others) want to achieve. There are also constraints to the achievement of these objectives, always including the constraint of limited resources. And finally, there are the various available means, the optional courses of action from which we may select the best (or at least an acceptable) path to our objectives. The problem solver, as Simon (1969) has said, is always engaged in searching some problem-space in order to find means well-suited, in the face of constraints, to the achievement of some objective function.

The problem-solving perspective has been very generally adopted by those in our society who, by profession and position, are most powerfully involved in the analysis, design, implementation, and criticism of social policy. Whatever the significant differences may be among economists, administrators, engineers, policy analysts, and planners, in recent years they have all come to regard themselves as problem solvers, in the sense described above. Indeed, the public view of government has come increasingly to include the notion of government as a solver of social problems.[10] In spite of this evolving consensus, however, there are great difficulties with the problem-solving perspective. A sense of its inadequacy has begun to spread among practitioners of social policy and among the public at large. Let me summarize briefly here criticisms which have been made at length elsewhere.

Problems are not given. They are constructed by human beings in their attempts to make sense of complex and troubling situations. Ways of describing problems move into and out of good currency (as the urban problem, for example, tended to be defined in the 1950s as "congestion"; in the 1960s as "poverty"; and in the 1970s as "fiscal insolvency"). New descriptions of problems tend not to spring from the solutions of the problem earlier set, but to evolve independently as new features of situations come into prominence. Indeed, societal problem solving has often created unintended consequences, which come to be perceived as problems in their own right (as public housing, conceived initially as a solution to the problem of housing the temporarily poor, came later to be perceived as a concentration of social pathology). This pattern of solutions creating unanticipated problems casts doubt upon the tenets of instrumentalism. Our efforts to correct errors have not converged upon solutions that are relatively free of error. On the contrary, the iterative cycles of problem setting and problem solving seem to diverge. The social situations confronting us have turned out to be far more complex than we had supposed, and it becomes increasingly doubtful that in the domain of social policy, we can make accurate temporal predictions, design models which converge upon a true description of reality, and carry out experiments which yield unambiguous results. Moreover, the unexpected problems created by our search for acceptable means to the ends we have chosen reveal (as in the cases of health and welfare policies) a stubborn conflict of ends traceable to the problem setting itself. Hence, in the domain of social policy, it has become clear that we ought no longer to avoid the problem of setting the problem.

How, then, are social problems set?

The domain of urban housing is a good one in which to pursue this question. Over the last thirty or forty years, people have told some very different stories about urban housing, and there have been some very dramatic shifts in ideas in good currency about the problem. We shall consider two of these stories, each of which sets out a view of what is wrong and what needs fixing.[11]

Blight and renewal

The first is a story out of the fifties. It is drawn from Justice Douglas's opinion on the constitutionality of the Federal Urban Renewal Program in the District of Columbia.

The experts concluded that if the community were to be healthy, if it were not to revert again to a blighted or slum area, as though possessed of a congenital disease, the area must be planned as a whole. It was not enough, they believed, to remove existing buildings that were unsanitary or unsightly. It was important to redesign the whole area so as to eliminate the conditions that cause slums – the overcrowding of dwellings, the lack of parks, the lack of adequate streets and alleys, the absence of recreational areas, the lack of light and air, the presence of outmoded street patterns. It was believed that the piecemeal approach, the removal of individual structures that were offensive, would be only a palliative. The entire area needed redesigning so that a balanced, integrated plan could be developed for the region including not only new homes, but also schools, churches, parks, streets, and shopping centers. In this way it was hoped that the cycle of decay of the area could be controlled and the birth of future slums prevented. (quoted in Bellush & Hausknecht, 1967, p. 62)

In this story, the community itself is one main character, and the planner, or "expert," is another. The community, once healthy, has become blighted and diseased. The planner, beholding it in its decayed condition, conceives the image of the community become healthy once again, with "new homes . . . schools, churches, parks, streets and shopping centers." But this can be achieved only through redesign of the whole area, under a balanced and integrated plan. Otherwise the area will "revert again to a . . . slum area, as though possessed of a congenital disease."

The slum as natural community

According to the second story, the places called "slums" are not all the same. Some of them are, indeed, decadent and impoverished, the victims of cycles of decay exacerbated by federal policies of "immuring" and of "urban renewal." Others, such as the West End and the North End in Boston, or the East Village in New York City, are true low income communities which offer to their residents the formal services and informal supports which evoke feelings of comfort and belonging. The task is not to redesign and rebuild these communities, much less to destroy buildings and dislocate residents, but to reinforce and rehabilitate them, drawing on the forces for "unslumming" that are already inherent in them.

This story can be made out in Peggy Gleicher and Mark Fried's summary of their study of West End residents.

In summary, then, we observe that a number of factors contribute to the special importance that the West End seemed to bear for the large majority of its inhabitants:
. . . Residence in the West End was highly stable, with relatively little movement from one dwelling unit to another and with minimal transience into and out of the area. Although residential stability is a fact of importance in itself, it does not wholly account for commitment to the area.
. . . For the great majority of the people, the local area was a focus for strongly

positive sentiments and was perceived, probably in its multiple meanings, as home. The critical significance of belonging in or to an area has been one of the most consistent findings in working-class communities both in the U.S. and in England.

. . . patterns of social interaction were of great importance in the West End. Certainly for a great number of people, local space . . . served as a locus for social relationships . . . In this respect, the urban slum community also has much in common with the communities so frequently observed in folk cultures.

. . . These observations led us to question the extent to which through urban renewal we relieve a situation of stress or create further damage. If the local spatial area and orientation toward localism provide the core of social organization and integration for a large proportion of the working class and if, as current behavioral theories would suggest, social organization and integration are primary factors in providing a base for effective social functioning, what are the consequences of dislocating people from their local areas? Or, assuming that the potentialities of people for adaptation to crisis are great, what deeper damage occurs in the process? (Gleicher & Fried, 1967, pp. 126–35)

These are powerful stories, powerful in the sense that they have shaped public consciousness about the issues of housing. Each in its time guided the writing of legislation, the formation of policy, the design of programs, the diligence of planners, the allocation of funds, the conduct of evaluation. Each, moreover, has had its period of dominance. The story of "blight and renewal" shaped public policy in the 1950s when the idea of urban renewal was at its height. In the 1960s, the story of the "natural community and its dislocation" expressed the negative reactions to urban renewal.

Each story conveys a very different view of reality and represents a special way of seeing. From a situation that is vague, ambiguous, and indeterminate (or rich and complex, depending on one's frame of mind), each story selects and names different features and relations which become the "things" of the story – what the story is about: in the first, for example, "community," "blight," "health," "renewal," "cycle of decay," "integrated plan"; in the second, "home," "spatial identity," "patterns of interaction," "informal networks," "dislocation." Each story places the features it has selected within the frame of a particular context – for example, of blight and the removal of blight; of natural communities, their threatened dissolution, and their preservation.

Each story constructs its view of social reality through a complementary process of *naming* and *framing*. Things are selected for attention and named in such a way as to fit the frame constructed for the situation. Together, the two processes construct a problem out of the vague and indeterminate reality which John Dewey (1938) called the "problematic situation." They carry out the essential problem-setting functions. They select for attention a few salient features and relations from what would otherwise be an overwhelmingly complex reality. They give these elements a coherent organization, and they describe what is wrong with the present situation in such a way as to set the direction for its future transformation. Through the processes of naming and framing, the stories make what Rein and Schön (1974) have called the "normative leap from data to recommendations, from fact to values, from 'is' to 'ought'." It is typical of diagnostic/ prescriptive stories such as these that they execute the normative leap in such a way as to make it seem graceful, compelling, even obvious.

How are these functions carried out?

In our two stories, the naming and framing of the urban housing situation proceeds via generative metaphor. Just as a paintbrush was seen, in our previous example, as a pump, so here the urban-housing situation is seen first as a disease which must be cured and then as the threatened disruption of a natural community which must be protected or restored. Here, too, the researcher sees A and B; he takes an existing description of B as a putative redescription of A. In this case, however, the constellation of ideas associated with B is inherently normative. In our ideas about disease and about natural community, there is already an evaluation – a sense of the good which is to be sought and the evil which is to be avoided. When we see A as B, we carry over to A the evaluation implicit in B.

Once we are able to see a slum as a blighted area, we know that blight must be removed ("unsanitary and unsightly" buildings must be torn down) and the area must be returned to its former state ("redesigned" and "rebuilt"). The metaphor is one of disease and cure. Moreover, the cure must not be a "mere palliative"; a particular, holistic view of medicine is involved in this metaphor. It would not be enough, the experts said, to remove offensive structures piecemeal.

The entire area needed redesigning so that a balanced, integrated plan could be developed for the region . . . In this way it was hoped that the cycle of decay of the area could be controlled and the birth of future slums prevented.

Effective prophylaxis requires an "integrated and balanced" plan. Just as in medicine one must treat the whole man, so one must "treat" the whole community.

Once we are able to see the slum as a "natural community" (Gleicher and Fried's, 1967, "folk community" or Herbert Gans's, 1962, "urban village"), then it is also clear what is wrong and what needs doing. What is wrong is that the natural community, with its homelike stability and its informal networks of mutual support, is threatened with destruction – indeed, by the very prophylaxis undertaken in the name of "urban renewal." We should think twice about "dislocating people from their local areas"; "natural communities" should be preserved.

Each of these generative metaphors derives its normative force from certain purposes and values, certain normative images, which have long been powerful in our culture. We abhor disease and strive for health.

Indeed, popular culture seems often to identify the good life with the healthy life and to make progress synonymous with the eradication of disease (although it may give us pause that "social prophylaxis" has had so strong an appeal for Fascist regimes – such as those of Stalin, Hitler, and the rightist dictatorships of the Third World). We also have a strong affinity for the "natural" and a deep distrust of the "artificial." The idea of Nature, with its Romantic origins in the writings of Rousseau and its deeper sources in pantheism, still works its magical appeal.

A situation may begin by seeming complex, uncertain, and indeterminate. If we can once see it, however, in terms of a normative dualism such as health/disease or nature/artifice, then we shall know in what direction to move. Indeed, the diagnosis and the prescription will seem obvious. This sense of the obviousness of what is wrong and what needs fixing is the hallmark of generative metaphor in the field of social policy.

But that which seems obvious to the unreflecting mind may upon reflection seem utterly mistaken. In so far as generative metaphor leads to a sense of the obvious, its consequences may be negative as well as positive. In the pump-paintbrush example, we emphasized the positive contribution of generative metaphor to the construction of explanations and inventions; but when we see *A* as *B*, we do not necessarily understand *A* any better than before, although we understand it differently than before. How well we understand it has something to do with how well we understand *B* to begin with, something to do with the ways in which seeing *A* and *B* leads us to restructure our perceptions of *A*, and something to do with the developmental process by which we pass from a pre-analytic detection of similarity between *A* and *B* to the construction of a model under which we are able to treat *A* and *B* (redescribed) as instances. At any stage of the life cycle of generative metaphor, we may, in seeing *A* as *B*, ignore or distort what we would take, upon reflection, to be important features of *A*. We need, then, to become aware of the generative metaphors which shape our perceptions of phenomena. We need to be able to attend to and describe the dissimilarities as well as the similarities between *A* and *B*.

In order to dissolve the obviousness of diagnosis and prescription in the field of social policy, we need to become aware of, and to focus attention upon, the generative metaphors which underlie our problem-setting stories.[12] However, this is not as easy as it sounds, for generative metaphors are ordinarily tacit. Often we are unaware of the metaphors that shape our perception and understanding of social situations.

We may be helped, in attending to underlying generative metaphors, by the presence of several different and conflicting stories about the situation. As in the Japanese film *Rashomon,* one is apt to be puzzled, disturbed, and stimulated to reflection by the telling of several different stories about the same situation, when each story is internally coherent and compelling in its own terms but different from, and perhaps incompatible with, all the others. Such a multiplicity of conflicting stories about the situation makes it dramatically apparent that we are dealing not with "reality" but with various ways of making sense of a reality. Then we may turn our attention to the stories themselves.

In order to bring generative metaphors to reflective and critical awareness, we must construct them, through a kind of policy-analytic literary criticism, from the givens of the problem-setting stories we tell. Indeed, it is through storytelling that we can best discover our frames and the generative metaphors implicit in our frames.

In this process, it is important to distinguish between what one might call "surface" and "deep" metaphors. The language in which the story is told may, as in the two cases we have considered, offer clues to the generative metaphors which set the problem of the story. Justice Douglas, for example, makes explicit reference to health and disease. But the surface language of the story need *not* contain the words "health" and "disease," even though health/disease is the generative metaphor which underlies the story. The deep metaphor, in this sense, is the metaphor which accounts for centrally important features of the story – which makes it understandable that certain elements of the situation are included in the story while others are omitted; that certain assumptions are taken as true although there is evidence that would appear to disconfirm them; and, especially, that the normative conclusions are found to follow so obviously from the facts. Given a problem-setting story, we must construct the deep metaphor which is generative of it. In making such a construction, we interpret the story. We give it a "reading," in a sense very much like the one employed in literary criticism. And our interpretation is, to a very considerable extent, testable against the givens of the story.

Once we have constructed a generative metaphor, once we have concluded that in this story we are seeing *A* as *B*, then we can explore and reflect upon similarities and differences between *A* and *B*. In doing so, we draw upon a repertoire of additional ways of perceiving and understanding both *A* and *B*. Thus, when we are presented with the two housing stories, we may wish to ask the following kinds of questions:

–What does it mean to say that an area is "blighted," when one man's blight may be another man's folk community? What one person sees as "unsanitary and unsightly," another may find comfortable, homelike, or even picturesque. On what criteria of "disease," then, is it appropriate to say that the North End of Boston is diseased?

–What is it that makes communities such as Boston's North and West Ends "natural," whereas the replacement of the old West End is described as "artificial"? Both are man-made and both involve social networks of human interactions. Further, the dislocation of the immigrant from his "natural community" may in some instances (as Gleicher and Fried have suggested) actually contribute to his subsequent achievement of increased autonomy and integration in a different community. Under what conditions, then, is "dislocation" harmful?

Questions such as these call attention to what is metaphorical about generative metaphors. It is precisely because neighborhoods are not literally diseased that one can *see* them *as* diseased. It is because urban communities are not literally natural that one can see them as natural. When in these examples of SEEING-AS we carry over to urban neighborhoods the familiar ideas of disease/health and artifice/nature, we find and construct in the context of these neighborhoods (as they are, as they once were, and as they might be) features and relations organized and evaluated as they are organized and evaluated in the familiar contexts of health and disease, nature and artifice. In this SEEING-AS we construct what is wrong and what needs fixing.

But when we interpret our problem-setting stories so as to bring their generative metaphors to awareness and reflection, then our diagnoses and prescriptions cease to appear obvious and we find ourselves involved, instead, in critical inquiry. We become aware of differences as well as of similarities between the new problematic situation and the familiar situation whose description we have projected upon the new. The glide from facts to recommendations no longer seems graceful or obvious. Attention to generative metaphor then becomes a tool for critical reflection on our construction of the problems of social policy.

Frame awareness, frame conflict, and frame restructuring

From all this, it follows that problem setting matters. The ways in which we set social problems determine both the kinds of purposes and values we seek to realize, and the directions in which we seek solutions. Contrary to the problem-solving perspective, problems are not given, nor are they reducible to arbitrary choices which lie beyond inquiry. We set social problems through the stories we tell – stories whose problem-setting potency derives at least in some cases from their generative metaphors.

It follows, too, that we should become aware of the ways in which we set social problems. We should reflect on the problem-setting processes which are usually kept tacit, so that we may consciously select and criticize the frames which shape our responses.

But what will frame awareness bring? It is likely to bring us into sharper and more explicit confrontation with frame conflict. As we become aware that our social policy debates reflect multiple, conflicting stories about social phenomena stories which embody different generative metaphors, different frames for making sense of experience, different meanings and values – then we also become aware that frame conflicts are not problems. They do not lend themselves to problem-solving inquiry, in the sense earlier described, because frame conflicts are often unresolvable by appeal to facts. In the case of the two housing stories, for example, the adversaries do not disagree about the facts; they simply turn their attention to *different* facts. Further, when one is committed to a problem frame, it is almost always possible to reject facts, to question data (usually fuzzy, in any case), or to patch up one's story so as to take account of new data without fundamental alteration of the story.

The method of iterative convergent sequences of model building and model testing cannot resolve conflicting frames which are attentive to different features of reality and are able to assimilate new versions of the facts.

I have argued elsewhere (Rein & Schön, 1974, 1977), that, in social policy debates, frame conflicts often take the form of dilemmas – that is, they are situations in which no available choice is a good one, because we are involved in a conflict of *ends* which are incommensurable. Ends are incommensurable because they are embedded in conflicting frames that lead us to construct incompatible meanings for the situation.

What, then, are the possible responses to frame conflicts and to dilemmas? This question is of the utmost importance to us, not only because of the inherent importance of the policy dilemmas themselves, but because these dilemmas often find their social expressions in societal divisions that are sources of anguish in their own right. When frame conflict takes the form of regional, ethnic, and class divisions, it becomes in itself a superordinate policy question.

The question is not, of course, a new one, and various researchers have offered responses to it – responses which take the form of *relativism,* or of an extended instrumentalism (which would resolve dilemmas by means of technological "fixes" or by the application of tradeoff analysis), or of recourse to types of institutionalized competition (the voting booth, the bargaining table, and the marketplace). Each of these responses seems to me to be radically unsatisfactory. I have argued this case elsewhere, and I do not propose to repeat this argument here. What I do want to emphasize is that each of these responses is presented by its protagonists as an alternative to a certain kind of inquiry. It is because it is thought to be impossible, or unfeasible, to *inquire* into conflicting ends – to subject frame conflict to shared inquiry – that we are thought to have to manage such intractable conflicts by institutionalized competition.

The two-pronged question I should like to ask here is whether frame conflict lends itself to inquiry and, if so, to inquiry of what kind? This is the question which points to the link between the making of generative metaphor and the resolution of conflicting frames.

We do, at least on some occasions, inquire into dilemmas and we do so intuitively in ways that involve cognitive work, occasionally yield insight, and may be judged as more or less well done. Yet, because this sort of inquiry does not fit the dominant model of problem solving, we lack a name for it. We risk denying our intuitive capacity because we cannot describe it.

In this sort of inquiry – which I shall call *frame restructuring* – we respond to frame conflict by constructing a new problem-setting story, one in which we attempt to integrate conflicting frames by including features and relations drawn from earlier stories, yet without sacrificing internal coherence or the degree of simplicity required for action. We do this best, I believe, in the context of particular situations whose information-richness gives us access to many different combinations of features and relations, countering our Procrustean tendency to notice only what fits our ready-made category schemes.

I should like to offer an example of frame restructuring in the domain of housing policy, drawn this time from the experience of developing countries.

Squatter settlements are the shantytowns, the vast spread-out communities in which the poor live in shacks they have built themselves, in the major cities in developing countries throughout the world. In *Housing by People,* J. Turner (1976) estimates that about one-third of the population of Caracas, one-half the population of Ankara, between one-third and one-half the population of Lusaka, Zambia, and one-third the population of Manila, live in squatter settlements. Such massive phenomena can hardly avoid being seen, but they are seen and interpreted in very different ways.

For the officials of municipal governments and housing agencies, and for many of the well-to-do residents of these cities, the settlements are an eyesore, a mass of debris which has been established by illegal, indeed criminal, action, in violation of property rights, housing codes, and zoning laws. The squatter settlements are, from this perspective, a blight upon the land and a spoiling of the planned city. Public housing projects, on the other hand, are clean, standard, and decent dwellings constructed on land set aside for low-income housing, and built according to regulations for adequate construction. It is true that many low-income persons cannot afford this sort of housing, and that there is too little of it to go around. But there are, in any case, too many poor people in cities who ought to have remained in their villages.

For the partisans of squatter settlements (such as Turner) public housing does not serve those most in need, and produces environments that are often dysfunctional in the extreme.

In the case of the *superbloque* in Caracas . . . built by the Perez Jiminez regime in the 1960's, if it had not been for the very costly programme of community development carried out after the fall of the regime, perhaps all 115 of these monstrous 14-storey buildings would also have had to be pulled down. Before the development of an adequate community infrastructure, they had become scenarios for pitched battles between armed gangs that had taken over the buildings and armoured army units . . . [these cases] highlight the well-known problems of management and maintenance of large schemes, structurally sound but where so many residents become alienated. (J. Turner, 1976, p. 59)

On the contrary, self-help construction, in the context of squatter settlements, provides an environment of amenity, community, and economic viability.

Thanks to its rent-free accommodation, the family has a small surplus for saving toward its anticipated move, perhaps towards the purchase of a plot of land and construction of its own permanent dwelling. The family pays its share of the utilities . . . the shack is not too great a hardship as long as the roof keeps the rain out – which it does adequately thanks to the use of plastic and other materials culled from the dump. Together with the use of the enclosed and private backyard, the family has plenty of personal space for its domestic life. (J. Turner & Fichter, 1972, pp. 241–2)

It is true that squatter settlements are sometimes sites for malnutrition, unsanitary conditions, disease. But these are defects in an otherwise natural, user governed system that meets the actual needs of its inhabitants far better than the public housing created by formal governmental programs.

The two perspectives on squatter settlements are comparable to the perspectives of the partisans and critics of "urban renewal" in the United States, and it is not difficult to detect their resemblance to our familiar housing stories. On the one hand, there is "blight" and the need for its removal through integrated redesign of whole areas. On the other, there are natural communities which provide their members with informal supports, stability, and a sense of home. On the one hand, there is a belief in the efficacy of formal services, professional expertise, governmental programs administered by large bureaucracies. On the other, there is distrust of formal, professional bureaucratized services and a belief in informal practices and informal networks of people who create communities and control environments through their own initiatives.

Considered together, these opposing views evoke a number of policy dilemmas. How is one both to protect property rights, maintain standards of construction and sanitation, and keep total costs within bounds, while at the same time providing housing services to those who need them, allowing people to get shelter at prices they can afford, accommodating the changing needs and capacities of families, and leaving initiative and control in the hands of the users?

Is it possible to integrate these conflicting frames?

Over the last fifteen years or so, a movement has grown up which has tried to do so. The programmatic slogan for this effort is "sites and services." In some cities (Lima, Peru, is an example), some people have considered how squatter settlements might be supported, rather than disrupted, by government action. Confronted with the failures of public-housing programs and with the persistence of squatter invasions, government officials and their advisors have explored what they might design in the way of a mix of formal supports and informal action, of government investment and user initiative.

Turner describes one such venture:

The *barriada* of Huascaran contained an area that was large enough for some twenty single-family dwellings, which the settlement association had acquired and wished to distribute to member families who for lack of their own plots had been living doubled up with relatives or friends in the settlement. When the association approached our agency for funds and technical assistance, Marcial and I suggested to the chief executive . . . that the agency simply lend the plot recipients the cash and let them get on with it under a minimum of supervision . . . The procedure was extremely simple. The local association allocated the plots to bona fide families who had no other urban properties and who contracted to build the minimum units specified within six months of receiving the first of five staged payments. The local recipients also undertook to repay the debt within a fifteen year period on very easy, subsidized interest rate terms. If the property were to be transferred, the debt would also be transferred . . . A new dwelling . . . would . . . be built at far less cost to the public than those built by commercial contractors . . . The total loans were small, just enough for the materials and skilled labor (bricklayer, roofer, electrician, plumber). (J. Turner & Fichter, 1972, p. 140)

In other, larger projects the government agency provided more than low-interest construction loans:

In one major new settlement, with a site assigned by the central government, well over 100,000 inhabitants were served with graded streets, electric light and power and water mains serving public standpipes in the initial stages of settlement and in consultation with the settlers' association which formed an effective provisional local government. The costs of such simple and basic installations can generally be borne either by the inhabitants or by the government or by a combination of public subsidies and local contributions. (J. Turner, 1976, p. 157)

Such a program grows out of a complex coordination of the two perspectives held by municipal officials and by partisans of squatter settlement. The squatters' behavior is seen neither as criminality nor as self-sufficiency, but as initiative that may be both supported and controlled within the constraints of a government program. Individual settlers are seen neither as passive recipients of government services nor as independent violators of governmental regulations, but as responsible participants who can be trusted both to repay loans and avoid being cheated on the purchase of materials. Indeed, Turner reports that

. . . the Huascaran project participants had gotten their bricks with little or no delay. Another participant, a truck driver, took care of deliveries. One of them had a brother in a brick factory who negotiated such a good bargain with his employer that the project participants managed to get themselves a 5 percent better discount than the materials loan program. (J. Turner & Fichter, 1972, p. 142)

The competitive game formerly played between municipal officials, in which officials seek to control and punish while squatters seek to evade control, gives way here to a collaborative game in which officials and settlers *both* win when houses are built and loans repaid.[13] The choice is no longer conceived of as one between formal governmental interventions, such as public housing, and informal networks of squatters. Rather, a new question is raised as to the ways in which formal governmental interventions can best complement the informal support system that grows up in squatter settlements. The new question leads to a reframing of the roles of the various parties. Government provides the large-scale infrastructure and the construction loans, while individual squatter families construct their own dwellings, and local associations organize the processes of supply and distribution of resources. As for the role of large industry:

What is being argued is that large organizations should have little or no business building or managing the dwelling environments. Instead, they should be doing a great deal more business installing infrastructure and manufacturing and supplying tools and materials that people and their own small enterprises can use locally. There is plenty of room for debate over the extent to which central administrations are in fact necessary for specific components of infrastructure. (J. Turner, 1976, p. 129)

Sites-and-services has become an idea in good currency in its own right. The World Bank, for example, has now established loans in many parts of the developing world for sites-and-services programs. The point is not that sites-and-services is a panacea for the problem of housing in the Third World, or even for the problems posed by squatter settlements. Predictably, as the scale of the program has increased, difficulties of organization and management have arisen, which manifested themselves in minor ways, if at all, in the early exploratory programs. Nevertheless, the emergence of this idea, out of the conflicting perspectives associated with municipal housing and with squatter settlements, suggests how social policy dilemmas may yield to frame restructuring.

One may argue, of course, that a dilemma, if it can be resolved, is not a dilemma at all! But what we call a dilemma hinges on the strategies we have for describing the problematic situation and the purposes at stake in it. We can know purposes only as descriptions. If conflicting purposes are redescribed so that they no longer conflict, then we may properly say that the dilemma has been dissolved. By "frame restructuring," however, I do not mean the mere recasting of a problem-setting story so as to escape a dilemma. People do sometimes respond to dilemmas by a kind of surgery, simply leaving out of account values which in an earlier formulation entered into conflict. In such cases the protagonist learns nothing from the dilemma except that it made life difficult. In the sites-and-services example, however, we have what I believe to be an instance of a very different kind of process. Here, two different ways of seeing the housing problem are made to come together to form a new integrating image; it is as though, in the familiar gestalt figure, one managed to find a way to see both vase and profiles at once![14]

It is quite consistent to say both that we are sometimes able to carry out such processes, and that we are usually unable to say how we do it. I believe that the problem-solving perspective blinds us to the few examples in which some of us, at some times, engage intuitively in the restructuring and coordination of conflicting frames. Hence, we lose the few resources available to us for learning how to carry out such processes where we need most desperately to do so. Starting with reflection on these rare intuitive processes, we need to build a full and explicit understanding of them.

It is here that the link between frame restructuring and the making of generative metaphor seems to me to be most critical. Certainly, it would not be surprising, seeing that we often frame social policy problems through generative metaphor, if frame restructuring and coordination strongly resembled the making of generative metaphor. We can explore this possibility by comparing the two examples which have been central to this paper.

In the pump–paintbrush example, we begin with one way of seeing the situation (the brush, the performance gap between the two brushes). Then it is proposed to look at the brush as a pump. The process can be illustrated as in Figure 9.1. In the housing example, we have two ways of seeing squatter settlements (versions of the "disease" and "natural community" frames) which are held by persons who contend with one another over the fate of squatter settlements. Site and services is an integration of these conflicting perspectives, one which reflects a restructuring and coordination of the two frames (see Figure 9.2).

The two cases are quite symmetrical. In both examples, we have the construction of a new description of the phenomenon, one in which the previously conflicting descriptions are restructured and coordinated. In the housing case, however, the two descriptions are initially advanced as conflicting descriptions of the same thing; in the pump–paintbrush example, an existing description of one thing is advanced as a putative description of another.

In both cases, there is a social context in which individuals engage with one another in a kind of reciprocal inquiry through which they reset the problem of their problematic situation. By recapitulating and comparing features of the cognitive work involved in the making of generative metaphor and in the restructuring and coordination of conflicting frames, we can gauge the degree to which these two processes share a family resemblance.

The participants try initially to intermap two different descriptions of a situation, but the descriptions initially resist mapping. The researchers cannot at first map the elements and relations in "pump" and "paintbrush" onto one another; they cannot see paintbrush as pump. No more can municipal officials in Peru map their descriptions of formal governmental

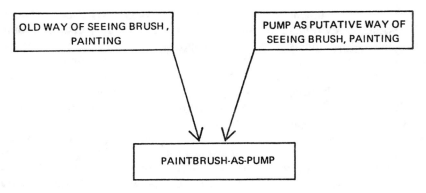

Figure 9.1

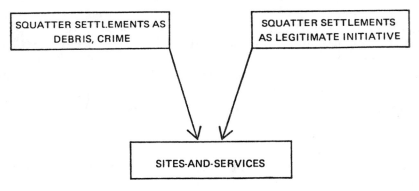

Figure 9.2

housing programs onto the informal, self-help activities of the squatters; they cannot see the squatter settlement as a housing program. Yet in both cases the two conflicting descriptions are available, and there is energy devoted to considering each in the context of the other. From the moment one of the researchers says, "A paintbrush is a kind of pump!" the others try to discover how this may be so. In the context of squatter settlements, different individuals representing different interests and social groups, contend with one another on the basis of their different descriptions of the situation.

In each case, the cognitive work involves the participants in attending to new features and relations of the phenomena, and in renaming, regrouping, and reordering those features and relations. As the researchers explore the paintbrush in the light of the possibility of its being a kind of pump, they focus on new features of the brush (the spaces between bristles, for example); they regroup and reorder features in relation to one another (perceiving the paint as a liquid that flows through the spaces between bristles); and they rename the new groupings of elements (bristles become the "walls" of "channels"). As the partisans of self-help and the municipal officials contend over the proper response to squatter settlements, some of them begin to regroup housing activities which had been lumped together either as "public housing" or as "squatting." They now decompose "housing development" into the purchasing and distribution of materials, into the construction of individual dwellings, into unskilled and skilled tasks, and into the provision of infrastructure. They now distinguish three kinds of groups as participants in the housing process: individual families, settlers' associations, and municipal agencies. In the new program description, sites-and-services, the newly named components of housing activity are linked with elements in the new grouping of participants: individual families, with construction of dwellings; settlers' associations, with purchasing and distribution of land and materials; municipal agencies, with provision of infrastructure. The participants themselves are also redescribed in ways that capture different features and relations to one another. Settlers are no longer "scavengers" or "passive recipients of service" but become parties to a contract with government, trusted to use cash wisely for the purposes intended. The municipal agency, no longer a policeman or a provider of housing, becomes a lender and builder of roads and sewage lines. The two parties are no longer related as regulator/regulatee but as contractor/contractee. And the housing program becomes a mix of formal and informal services.

In both cases, it is significant that the participants are involved in a particular concrete situation; at the same time that they are reflecting on the problem, they are experiencing the phenomena of the problem. In the pump–paintbrush case, the researchers experimented with what it felt like actually to use the brush. In the housing case, municipal officials were involved with settlers in a particular *barriada*. It is as though the effort to map onto one another descriptions which initially resist mapping causes the participants to immerse themselves, in reality or in imagination, in concrete situations which are information-rich.

The cognitive work of restructuring draws upon the richness of features and relations which are to be found in the concrete situation. There, one can notice the gentle curve of the natural brush and the sharp angle of the synthetic one. One can observe how settlers go about purchasing bricks, how somebody's brother-in-law has a truck that is used to deliver them. These new features can then be incorporated in the new descriptions of the situations. One is not limited to the features captured by the category-schemes with which one began.

The information-richness of particular situations poses a difficulty, however. Although the inquirer has suspended the earlier conflicting descriptions (he is now thinking *about* them rather than seeing the situation in terms of them), he has not yet achieved the restructuring that will enable him to make a new description. In this intermediate state, he needs a way of representing to himself the particularity of the situation in which he is involved – one which is dominated by neither of the descriptions with which he began. At this point, story telling can play an important part.[15] The inquirer can tell the story of his experience of the situation (can tell it, that is, both to others and to himself) and he can do this before he has constructed a new, coordinated description of the situation. Considered as a strategy for representing the situation, his story captures the juxtaposition of events in time, the "next-next-next" of temporal experience. This strategy of representation permits the inquirer to convey much of the richness of the situation without being constrained by either of the category-schemes with which he begins. The researcher can tell what it feels like to paint with the two brushes. The municipal officials can tell the story of their response to the settlers' association. Subsequently, the inquirers may construct new models of the situation from the stories they have told. Their new, coordinated descriptions may then select out fixed properties which this particular situation shares with others, as in the researchers' model of pumpoids or the planners' model of sites-and-services. But in the midst of the process, when earlier descriptions have been suspended and coordinated descriptions have not yet been developed, the inquirers need strategies of representation which enable them to hang onto and convey the richness of their experience of the events themselves.

From this account, it is reasonable to conclude, I believe, that frame restructuring and the making of generative metaphor are closely related processes. In both kinds of processes, participants bring to a situation different and conflicting ways of seeing – different and conflicting descriptions. There is an impetus to map the descriptions onto one another, but the descriptions resist mapping. In the context of a particular concrete situation, the participants work at the restructuring of their initial descriptions – regrouping, reordering, and renaming elements and relations; selecting new features and relations from their observations of the situation. As this work proceeds, they represent their experience of the situation through strategies which capture the "next-next-next" of temporal experience of events: and from such representations, of which storytelling is a prime example, they draw the restructured groupings and relations of elements which they are able to embed in a new, coordinated description.

It is important also to notice what does *not* happen. The old descriptions are not mapped onto one another by matching corresponding elements in each, for the old descriptions resist such a mapping. Rather, the *restructured* descriptions are coordinated with one another, which is to say that some pairs of restructured elements now match one another, and others are juxtaposed in the new description as components of larger elements. The new description is also not a "compromise," an average or balance of values implicit in the earlier descriptions. One cannot say, for example, that site-and-services strikes a balance between values attached to "government control" and to "settler initiative"; rather, in the new description, there is a shift in the meanings of these terms, and along with this, a shift in the distribution of the redescribed functions of initiative and control. Finally, we cannot say that the two descriptions are "fused," for the restructuring they undergo is not characterized by the joining of elements and the blurring of boundaries connoted by "fusion."

There is a kind of cognitive work common to the integration of conflicting frames and to the making of generative metaphor, and to this shared process I have given the name "frame restructuring and frame coordination." We find closely related versions of this process in the problem-setting inquiries central to technological invention and to social-policy debate. We are sometimes able to perform such processes intuitively, but our ability to describe and model them is severely limited. I have tried only to describe some of their principal components. Even from these meager beginnings, it is clear that frame restructuring and coordination differs greatly from the processes suggested by such terms as "correspondence mapping," "compromise" and "fusion." The study of frame restructuring and coordination can, and must, be empirically grounded, starting with the careful description and analysis of particular instances of intuitive inquiry.

Two orders of questions seem to me to be critically important for the direction of this research. First, with respect to the workings of the process itself, we need much better descriptions of the component activities which I have called "restructuring" and "coordination." Particular attention ought to be paid to the functions of renaming, regrouping, and reordering, and to the resetting of boundaries, all of which give rise to new perceptions of the elements we call "things" and of the organization of foreground and background. It will be important to characterize the particular kind of *stance* toward the process which enables us to recognize descriptions as descriptions rather than as "reality," and to entertain and juxtapose conflicting descriptions. It will be important to examine the functions of immersion in the concrete experience of the phenomena of the situation, and to explore the strategies of representation which enable us to capture the experienced richness of the situation (its "phenomenology") without forcing it into existing formal categories. And it will be important to inquire into the processes by which we are able to construct new category-schemes, new models, from the information-rich stories we tell.

In all of this, we need to ask what is involved in learning to do this kind of cognitive work? What is its relation, on the one hand, to domain-specific knowledge and, on the other hand, to very general sorts of competence in the use of language? How does the process of frame restructuring and coordination resemble and differ from changes in strategies of representation which occur in the course of cognitive development?

A second group of questions has to do with the conditions favorable to the practice of frame restructuring. In the context of social policy dilemmas, where we most need to learn how to integrate conflicting frames, it is most unlikely that a better understanding of these processes will be sufficient to lead us to undertake them. On the contrary, it is already remarkable how little we draw upon existing cognitive capacity in situations of difficulty and stress. What, then, are the configurations of personal stance toward inquiry, of interpersonal process, and of institutional design, which will be conducive to the use of our understandings of frame restructuring? (For a discussion of some of these conditions, see Schön & Argyris, 1978.)

These two very different lines of inquiry are critical to the improvement of our capacity for engaging social policy dilemmas. If we are to coordinate them, then we must engage in the very process we are studying.

NOTES

1 Ernst Cassirer's work – in particular, his *Language and Myth* (1946) – is central to this tradition.

2 The term was first used in Schön and Bamberger (1976). Schön (1963) was an earlier treatment of this topic.

3 The hermeneutic tradition, developed in late nineteenth-century Germany by the philosopher Dilthey, has been taken up again in recent years by continental philosophers such as Paul Ricoeur (see, e.g., Ricoeur, 1970).

4 My interest in problem setting in social policy has been developed through my collaboration with Martin Rein. (See Rein, 1976; and Rein & Schön, 1977.) Others who have written on this topic, with close attention to functions of metaphor, are Nisbet (1969), and R. H. Brown (1976).

5 This example was first described in Schön (1963).

6 There is, of course, the critically important question of the evidence for this assertion. Although I am not primarily concerned here with the problem of interpretation, I have tried to suggest that my construction of the metaphor which informed the work of the researchers may be treated against the data provided by my description of what they actually said and did. My attribution to them of a particular generative metaphor is, I believe, a falsifiable proposition. I shall take up this question again in the discussion of problem setting in social policy.

7 Many authors have noted the economic functions of metaphor conceived both as a kind of utterance and as a way of thinking. See, for example, Cassirer (1946).

8 The notion of SEEING-AS, its relation to "thinking as" and to literal seeing, and its relevance to an understanding of description, have all been set forth by Wittgenstein (1953, especially pp. 193–216).

9 The phrase is Thomas Kuhn's. See Kuhn (1970b).

10 For reference to those who take such a view, and for criticisms of it, see Vickers (1973), Rein (1976), and Schön (1971).

11 For a fuller treatment of this use of "story," see Rein and Schön (1977). Here, I

shall simply note that in my usage, "story" does not necessarily connote a narrative of the "Once upon a time . . ." variety. Yet it is a narrative account of some phenomenon, an account in which temporal sequence is central. Explanatory stories are those in which the author, seeking to account for some puzzling phenomenon, narrates a sequence of temporal events wherein, starting from some set of initial conditions, events unfold in such a way as to lead up to and produce the phenomenon in question. A diagnostic/prescriptive story gives an explanatory, narrative account of some phenomenon in such a way as to show what is wrong with it and what needs fixing.

Justice Douglas, in the example that follows, tells a diagnostic/prescriptive story about urban neighborhoods, one framed by the notion of "blight" and "renewal." If Justice Douglas were to *describe* an actual urban neighborhood, I suspect that the things he would say about it, the things he would notice, the features he would select for attention, the ways in which he would group and bound phenomena would all reflect the fundamental story he had learned to tell about this sort of neighborhood.

12 It is worth pointing out here that although I believe that all problem-setting stories have frames which enable their authors to select out features for attention, it is not necessarily true that all of these frames are metaphorical in nature. The health/disease and nature/artifice frames are generative metaphors for the two stories under consideration here. But many problem-setting stories are framed, for example, by the notion of "mismatch of services to needs" and this is not so obviously an example of generative metaphor.

13 Max Wertheimer (1959) gives a very nice example of the invention of a new game which converts competition to collaboration: He watched two boys playing badminton, one of them very much superior to the other. As the game progressed, each trying to win, the older boy won easily, the younger played worse and worse, until one of the boys then proposed a new game whose objective would be to keep the bird in the air as long as possible. Wertheimer reports that in the course of *this,* while both had to work as hard as they could, the efforts of the older boy were complementary to those of the younger one; both began to feel good about the game, and the younger boy's playing improved.

Not all frame restructuring takes the form of converting games of competition to games of collaboration, however. Wilson (1975) notes the fundamental conflict, in criminal justice policy, between punishment and rehabilitation. But he considers it in the light of the difficulty in drawing conclusions from experimental approaches to the treatment of criminals. After reviewing the evidence, he argues that we know nothing at all about the comparative effectiveness of programs in probation, incarceration, and community care. He finds not only that we do not know but that, in the nature of the case, we cannot know. From this conclusion he moves not to a position of relativism or fatalism but to a reframing of the problem. Emphasis should be placed upon such knowable variables as consistency of sentencing, and the comparative costs of treatment. In short, he argues that because we cannot know what we need to know in order to make the policy choices we have framed, then we must reframe the policy choices so as to make them depend upon what we can know.

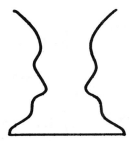

Figure 9.3

14 The gestalt figures are used ordinarily to show how "the same figure" may be seen in very different, incompatible ways. For example, in the well-known figure shown here (Figure 9.3) some people see the two profiles, others the vase. Usually, one can manage (after learning what is there to be seen) to move rapidly from one way of seeing the figure to the other. It is unusual to find someone who claims to be able to see both at once. Yet this, too, can be managed if one thinks of the figure as two profiles pressing their noses into a vase! It is this integrating image (dreamed up by Seymour Papert) which makes it possible to bring together the two different ways of seeing the figure.

15 Storytelling is employed here as a special case of the use of strategies of representation which Bamberger and I have called "figural." In Schön and Bamberger (1976) we have argued that figural strategies, which group features on the basis of their temporal and/or spatial juxtaposition in a situation, rather than on the basis of fixed properties which they share, play a crucially important role in many kinds of generative processes.

10

The conduit metaphor: A case of frame conflict in our language about language

MICHAEL J. REDDY

I should like to respond to Professor Schön's chapter by replaying his theme several octaves lower. In my opinion, he has struck exactly the right set of notes. "Problem setting" should indeed be considered the crucial process, as opposed to "problem solving." And the "stories that people tell about troublesome situations" do set up or "mediate" the problem. And "frame conflict" between various stories should be studied in detail, precisely because it is quite often "immune to resolution by appeal to the facts." It is hard to think of a better overture to genuine advance in the social and behavioral sciences than this. At the same time, it seems to me that Schön has managed to sound these excellent notes only in their overtones, so that the fundamental frequency is barely to be heard – even though, to my ears at least, Schön's kind of thinking is real and long awaited music.

Quite simply, what I believe is missing is the application of Schön's wisdom – this paradigm-consciousness – to human communication itself. It may seem predictable that I, a linguist, would take such a position. But, if I do, it is hardly disciplinary narrow-mindedness that motivates me. In 1954, Norbert Wiener, one of the originators of information theory, and the "father of cybernetics," stated quite flatly: "Society can only be understood through a study of the messages and communications facilities which belong to it" (Wiener, 1954, p. 16). I have never thought of this statement as referring to things like the size and adequacy of the telephone system. Wiener was talking primarily about the basic processes of human communication – how they work, what sort of wrinkles there are in them, when and why they are likely to succeed or fail. The problems of society, government, and culture depend ultimately on something like the daily box score of such successes or failures to communicate. If there are too many failures, or systematic types of failure, troubles will multiply. A society of near-perfect communicators, though it would no doubt still face conflicts of interest, might well be able to avoid many of the destructive, divisive effects of these inevitable conflicts.

What lies behind Schön's term "frame restructuring," and Kuhn's term "translation" (Kuhn, 1970a) seems to be just this much: better communication. Alleviating social and cultural difficulties requires better communication. And the problem that faces us is, how do we improve our communication? But, if we come around to saying this, then it is high time that we listened to Schön's good advice. It will not do to set out posthaste to "solve the problem" of inadequate communication. The most pressing task is rather to start inquiring immediately about *how that problem presents itself to us.* For problem setting, not problem solving is the crucial process. What kinds of stories do people tell about their acts of communication? When these acts go astray, how do they describe "what is wrong and what needs fixing"?

In this chapter, I am going to present evidence that the stories English speakers tell about communication are largely determined by semantic structures of the language itself. This evidence suggests that English has a preferred framework for conceptualizing communication, and can bias thought process toward this framework, even though nothing more than common sense is necessary to devise a different, more accurate framework. I shall thus be trying to convince you of what may be a disturbing premise: that merely by opening our mouths and speaking English we can be drawn into a very real and serious frame conflict. My own belief is that this frame conflict has considerable impact on our social and cultural problems. If we are largely unable, despite the vast array of communications technologies available to us today, to bring about substantive improvements in human communication, it may well be because this frame conflict has led us to attempt faulty solutions to the problem.

It is, of course, impossible to make such assertions without calling to mind the speculations and arguments of many twentieth-century figures – notably those of Whorf (1956) and of Max Black's (1962d) reluctant but thorough refutation of Whorf. There is an old joke about the Whorf hypothesis to the effect that, if it should be true, then it would be by definition unprovable. For if two human beings not only spoke radically different languages, but also thought and perceived the world differently, well then they would be far too busy throwing rocks and spears at one another to ever sit down and establish this as a fact. The grain of truth in this facetiousness can be found in Schön's dictum that frame conflicts are "immune to resolution by appeal to the facts." As he says, "New facts have a way of being either absorbed or disregarded by those who see problematic situations under conflicting frames." Now, for the past several years, I have been collecting some new facts and talking about them with many different people. Very slowly, during this period of time, these new facts initiated a frame change in my own thinking about language. I had always been interested in Uriel Weinreich's observation that "Language is its own metalanguage." But after the frame change, I knew that, as a metalanguage, English, at least, was its own worst enemy. And I knew that there was something more than mysticism to Whorf's ideas. At this point, curiously enough, when everything seemed to fall into place for me, it became much harder to talk to others about the new facts. For now I was speaking across the chasm of frame conflict.

I mention these things because I want to suggest at the outset that the discussion that follows is a marvelous opportunity for one of those failures to communicate which we are concerned to prevent. It is a little bit like the joke about Whorf. If I am right in what I believe about frames, then it may well be difficult to convince you, because the frames I am talking about exist in you and will resist the change. For my part, in writing this, I have made strenuous efforts to remember what it was like before I shifted frames, and how long it took before the "new facts" made sense to me. At the same time, I should like to request that you, on your side, make yourselves receptive to what may be a serious alteration of consciousness. To use Schön's terminology, we are engaged perforce in frame restructuring, and special effort is called for.

The conduit metaphor

What do speakers of English say when communication fails or goes astray? Let us consider (1) through (3), some very typical examples,

(1) Try to *get* your *thoughts across* better
(2) None of Mary's *feelings came through to* me with any clarity
(3) You still haven't *given me* any *idea* of what you mean,

and do as Schön has suggested – take them as problem-setting stories, as descriptions of "what is wrong and what needs fixing." Are there metaphors in the examples? Do these metaphors set the directions for possible problem-solving techniques? Although (1) through (3) contain no fresh metaphors, there is in each case a dead metaphor. After all, we do not literally "get thoughts across" when we talk, do we? This sounds like mental telepathy or clairvoyance, and suggests that communication transfers thought processes somehow bodily. Actually, no one *receives* anyone else's thoughts directly in their minds when they are using language. Mary's feelings, in example (2), can be perceived directly only by Mary; they do not really "come through to us" when she talks. Nor can anyone literally "give you an idea" – since these are locked within the skull and life process of each of us. Surely, then, none of these three expressions is to be taken completely at face value. Language seems rather to help one person to construct out of his own stock of mental stuff something like a replica, or copy, of someone else's thoughts – a replica which can be more or less accurate, depending on many factors. If we could indeed send thoughts to one another, we would have little need for a communications system.

If there are dead metaphors in (1) through (3), then they all seem to involve the figurative assertion that language *transfers* human thoughts and feelings. Notice that this assertion, even in its present, very general form, leads already to a distinct viewpoint on communications problems. A person who speaks poorly does not know how to use language to send people his thoughts; and, conversely, a good speaker knows how to transfer his thoughts perfectly via language. If we were to follow this viewpoint, the next question would be: What must the poor speaker do with his thoughts if he is to transfer them more accurately by means of language? The surprising thing is that, whether we like it or not, the English language does follow this veiwpoint. It provides, in the form of a wealth of metaphorical expressions, answers to this and other questions, all of which answers are perfectly coherent with the assumption that human communication achieves the physical transfer of thoughts and feelings. If there were only a few such expressions involved, or if they were random, incoherent figures of speech arising from different paradigms – or if they were abstract, not particularly graphic images – then one might just succeed in dismissing them as harmless analogies. But in fact, none of these mitigating circumstances comes into play.

Typical solutions to the unskilled speaker's communications problems are illustrated by (4) through (8).

(4) Whenever you have a good *idea* practice *capturing it in words*

(5) You have to *put* each *concept into words* very carefully

(6) Try to *pack* more *thoughts into* fewer *words*

(7) Insert those *ideas* elsewhere *in* the *paragraph*

(8) Don't *force* your *meanings into* the wrong *words*.

Naturally, if language transfers thought to others, then the logical container, or conveyer, for this thought is words, or word-groupings like phrases, sentences, paragraphs, and so on. One area of possible difficulty is then the insertion process. The speaker might be generally unpracticed or careless about this, and so be admonished with (4) or (5). As (6) shows, he could fail to put enough meaning in. Or, according to (7), he could put the right meanings in, but put them in the wrong place. Example (8), which stretches common sense most seriously, indicates that he might put meanings into the words which somehow do not fit in them, thus presumably deforming these meanings. It might also be, of course, that the speaker puts too much meaning into words. And there are expressions for this as well.

(9) Never *load* a *sentence with* more *thoughts* than it can hold.

In general, this class of examples implies that, in speaking or writing, humans place their internal thoughts and feelings within the external signals of the language. A more complete listing may be found in the Appendix.

The logic of the framework we are considering – a logic which will henceforth be called the *conduit* metaphor – would now lead us to the bizarre assertion that words have "insides" and "outsides." After all, if thoughts can be "inserted," there must be a space "inside" wherein the meaning can reside. But surely the English language, whatever metaphysical meanderings it may have been guilty of thus far, cannot have involved us in this kind of patent nonsense. Well, a moment's reflection should nudge anyone into remembering that "content" is a term used almost synonymously with "ideas" and "meaning" And that recollection is quite meaning-full (sic) in the present context. Numerous expressions make it clear that English does view words as containing or failing to contain thoughts, depending on the success or failure of the speaker's "insertion" process.

(10) That *thought is in* practically every other *word*

(11) The *sentence was filled with emotion*

(12) The *lines* may rhyme, but *they are empty* of both *meaning* and *feeling*

(13) Your *words are hollow* – you don't mean them.

Or, in general, there is another class of examples that imply that words contain or convey thoughts and feelings when communication is successful. We assert, without batting an eyelash, that "the meaning is right there in the words." Further instances are to be found in the Appendix.

It may be that the fault in a communication failure does not lie with the speaker. Perhaps, somehow, the listener has erred. In the framework of the conduit metaphor, the listener's task must be one of extraction. He must find the meaning "in the words" and take it out of them, so that it gets "into his head." Many expressions show that English does view the matter in this way.

(14) Can you actually *extract* coherent *ideas from* that *prose*?

(15) Let me know if you *find* any good *ideas in* the *essay*

(16) I don't *get* any *feelings* of anger *out of* his *words*.

Curiously, my initial work on these expressions suggests that it is easier, when speaking and thinking in terms of the conduit metaphor, to blame the speaker for failures. After all, receiving and unwrapping a package is so passive and so simple – what can go wrong? A package can be difficult or impossible to open. But, if it is undamaged, and successfully opened, who can fail to find the right things in it? Thus, there are graphic and powerful expressions which blame particularly writers for making the package hard to open, as in (17) through (19).

(17) That *remark is* completely *impenetrable*

(18) Whatever *Emily meant, it's* likely to be *locked up* in that cryptic little *verse* forever

(19) He writes *sentences* in such a way as to *seal up* the *meaning in them*.

But, apart from readers and listeners "not paying attention to what's there in the words," the conduit metaphor offers little explanation for failing to "find" enough thoughts or the right thoughts in "what someone says." Should someone discover too many thoughts, however, we have a wonderfully absurd expression faulting him for this.

(20) You're *reading things into* the poem.

The power of the framework to enforce consistency of rationale even when the results are inane should be apparent here. We must see the reader as having surreptitiously made use of his power to insert thoughts into words when he should have restricted himself purely to extraction. He sneaked those thoughts into the words himself and then turned around and pretended that he found them there. Perhaps because the problem of too much meaning occurs more often in reading, we have never developed the corresponding expression for speaking – "hearing things into the poem." Instead, we use "reading things into" for both modalities. Once again, further examples appear in the Appendix.

Perhaps we should pause at this point and set up some apparatus for generalizing what we have seen so far. It is not the numbered sentences above that are important, but rather the expressions in italics. These expressions could appear in many different utterances and take many different forms, and we have as yet no way of isolating what is crucial to them. Notice, for instance, that in every example there has been one word, such as "ideas," or "thoughts," or "meanings," or "feeling," which denotes internal conceptual or emotional material. Apart from what seem to be minor stylistic co-occurence restrictions, these and other terms like them can be substituted freely for one another. Thus, it is irrelevant to an example which one of these is present, and it would be helpful to have some abbreviation for the entire group. Let us picture each person as having a "repertoire" of mental and emotional material. This will allow us to say that any term denoting a *repertoire member,* abbreviated "RM," will fit, say, as object in (1) and produce an example utterance. Underlying (1), (2), and (3), then, are what we shall call "core expressions," which can be written as follows.

(21) get RM *across* [underlying (1)]

(22) RM *comes through* (to someone) [underlying (2)]

(23) give (someone) RM [underlying (3)].

The parentheses in (22) and (23) indicate optional complements. Examples (4) through (20), in addition to a term from the RM group, all contain another term, such as "word," "phrase," "sentence," or "poem." These words, in their basic senses at least, designate the external physical patterns of marks or sounds that do pass between speakers. Such energies, unlike the thoughts themselves, are received bodily, and are what information theorists would have called "signals." If we adopt this generic name for the second group, and abbreviate it as "s," then the core expressions for (4) through (6) are,

(24) capture RM in s [underlying (4)];
(25) put RM *into* s [underlying (5)];
(26) pack RM *into* s [underlying (6)].

In the Appendix, the core expression is always given first, and is then followed by one or two examples. Obviously, each core expression can be responsible for a very large number of different sentences.

The conduit metaphor, and the core expressions which embody it, deserve a great deal more investigation and analysis. My listing of the core expressions is most likely far from complete, and the logical reverberations of this paradigm affect both the syntax and the semantics of many words which are not themselves part of the core expressions. Later on, we shall focus on one such reverberation, which affects the entire s group. Apart from this, however, we shall have to be content to close the present discussion with a brief characterization of some further types of core expression.

Our examples thus far have been drawn from the four categories which constitute the "major framework" of the conduit metaphor. The core expressions in these categories imply, respectively, that: (1) language functions like a conduit, transferring thoughts bodily from one person to another; (2) in writing and speaking, people insert their thoughts or feelings in the words; (3) words accomplish the transfer by containing the thoughts or feelings and conveying them to others; and (4) in listening or reading, people extract the thoughts and feelings once again from the words. Beyond these four classes of expressions, there are a good many examples which have different, though clearly related, implications. The fact that it is quite foreign to common sense to think of words as having "insides" makes it quite easy for us to abstract from the strict, "major" version of the metaphor, in which thoughts and emotions are always contained in something. That is, the major framework sees ideas as existing either within human heads or, at least, within words uttered by humans. The "minor" framework overlooks words as containers and allows ideas and feelings to flow, unfettered and completely disembodied, into a kind of ambient space between human heads. In this case, the conduit of language becomes, not sealed pipelines from person to person, but rather individual pipes which allow mental content to escape into, or enter from, this ambient space. Again, it seems that this extension of the metaphor is aided by the fact that, somewhere, we are peripherally aware that words do not really have insides.

In any case, whatever the cause of the extension, there are three categories of expressions in the minor framework. The categories imply, respectively, that: (1) thoughts and feelings are ejected by speaking or writing into an external "idea space": (2) thoughts and feelings are reified in this external space, so that they exist independent of any need for living human beings to think or feel them; (3) these reified thoughts and feelings may, or may not, find their way back into the heads of living humans. Some outstanding examples of minor framework expressions are, for the first category,

> *put* RM *down on paper*

(27) Put those thoughts down on paper before you lose them!

> *pour* RM *out*

(28) Mary poured out all of the sorrow she had been holding in for so long.

> *get* RM *out*

(29) You should get those ideas out where they can do some good.

And for the second category,

> RM *float around*

(30) That concept has been floating around for decades.

> RM *find way*

(31) Somehow, these hostile feelings found their way to the ghettos of Rome.

> *find* RM EX LOC

(32) You'll find better ideas than that in the library.

(33) John found those ideas in the jungles of the Amazon, not in some classroom.

> (EX LOC here stands for any locative expression designating a place other than within human beings, that is, an *external locative*.)

And for the third category,

> *absorb* RM

(34) You have to "absorb" Aristotle's ideas a little at a time.

> RM *go over someone's head*

(35) Her delicate emotions went right over his head.

> *get* RM *into someone's head*

(36) How many different concepts can you get into your head in one evening?

For further examples, see the Appendix.

The toolmakers paradigm

In order to investigate the effect of the conduit metaphor on the thought processes of speakers of English, we need some alternate way of conceiving of human communication. We require another story to tell, another model, so that the deeper implications of the conduit metaphor can be drawn out by means of contrast. Simply speaking, in order to engage in frame restructuring about human communication, we need first an opposing frame.

To begin this other story, I should like to suggest that, in talking to one another, we are like people isolated in slightly different environments. Imagine, if you will, for sake of the story, a huge compound, shaped like a

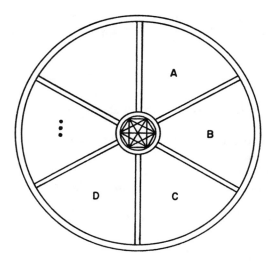

Figure 10.1. The toolmakers paradigm.

wagon wheel (see Figure 10.1). Each pie-shaped sector of the wheel is an environment, with two spokes and part of the circumference forming the walls. The environments all have much in common with one another – water, trees, small plants, rocks, and the like – yet no two are exactly alike. They contain different kinds of trees, plants, terrain, and so on. Dwelling in each sector is one person who must survive in his own special environment. At the hub of the wheel there is some machinery which can deliver small sheets of paper from one environment to another. Let us suppose that the people in these environments have learned how to use this machinery to exchange crude sets of instructions with one another – instructions for making things helpful in surviving, such as tools, perhaps, or shelters, or foods, and the like. But there is, in this story, absolutely no way for the people to visit each other's environments, or even to exchange samples of the things they construct. This is crucial. The people can only exchange these crude sets of instructions – odd looking blueprints scratched on special sheets of paper that appear from a slot in the hub and can be deposited in another slot – and nothing more. Indeed, since there is no way to shout across the walls of the sectors, the people only know of one another's existence indirectly, by a cumulative series of inferences. This part of the story, the no visiting and no exchange of indigenous materials rule, we shall call the postulate of "radical subjectivity."

In the analogy, the contents of each environment, the "indigenous materials," represent a person's repertoire. They stand for the internal thoughts, feelings, and perceptions which cannot themselves be sent to anyone by any means that we know of. These are the unique material with which each person must work if he is to survive. The blueprints represent the signals of human communication, the marks and sounds that we can actually send to one another. We shall have to ignore the question of how the system of instructions became established, even though this is an interesting part of the story. We shall simply assume that it has reached some sort of steady state, and shall watch how it functions.

Suppose that person *A* has discovered an implement that is very useful to him. Say he has learned to build a rake and finds he can use it to clear dead leaves and other debris without damaging the living plants. One day person *A* goes to the hub and draws as best he can three identical sets of instructions for fashioning this rake and drops these sets in the slots for persons *B*, *C*, and *D*. As a result, three people struggling along in slightly different environments now receive these curious sheets of paper, and each one goes to work to try to construct what he can from them. Person *A*'s environment has a lot of wood in it, which is probably why he has leaves to rake in the first place. Sector *B*, on the other hand, runs more to rock, and person *B* uses a lot of rock in his constructions. He finds a piece of wood for the handle, but begins to make the head of the rake out of stone. *A*'s original rake head was wood. But since it never occurred to him that anything but wood would be available or appropriate, he did not try to specify wood for the head in his instructions. When *B* is about halfway finished with the stone rake head, he connects it experimentally to the handle and realizes with a jolt that this thing, whatever it is, is certainly going to be heavy and unwieldy. He ponders its possible uses for a time, and then decides that it must be a tool for digging up small rocks when you clear a field for planting. He marvels at how large and strong person *A* must be, and also at what small rocks *A* has to deal with. *B* then decides that two large prongs will make the rake both lighter and better suited to unearthing large rocks.

Quite happy with both his double-bladed rock-pick and his new ideas about what this fellow *A* must be like, person *B* makes three identical sets of instructions himself, for his rock-pick, and inserts them in the slots for *A*, *C*, and *D*. Person *A*, of course, now assembles a rockpick following *B*'s instructions, except that he makes it entirely of wood and has to change the design a little if a wooden, two-pronged head is to be strong enough. Still, in his largely rockless environment, he cannot see much use for the thing, and worries that person *B* has misunderstood his rake. So he draws a second set of more detailed instructions for the rake head, and sends them out to everyone. Meanwhile, over in another sector, person *C*, who is particularly interested in clearing out a certain swamp, has created, on the basis of these multiple sets of instructions – the hoe. After all, when you are dealing with swamp grass and muck, you need something that will slice cleanly through the roots. And person *D*, from the same sets of instructions, has come up with a gaff. He has a small lake and fishes quite a bit.

Although it would be interesting to get to know *C* and *D*, the primary heroes of this story are persons *A* and *B*. We return now to them for the climax of the great rake conversation, in which, to everyone's surprise, some real communication takes place. *A* and *B*, who have had profitable interchanges in the past, and thus do not mind working quite hard at their communications, have been caught up in this rake problem for some time now. Their instructions simply will not agree. *B* has even had to abandon his original hypothesis that *A* is a huge man who has only small rocks to deal with. It just does not fit the instructions he is getting. *A*, on his side, is getting so frustrated that he is ready to quit. He sits down near the hub and, in a kind of absent-minded display of anger, grinds two pebbles together. Suddenly he stops. He holds these rocks up in front of his eyes and seems to be thinking furiously. Then he runs to the hub and starts scribbling new instructions as fast as he can, this time using clever iconic symbols for rock and wood, which he hopes *B* will understand. Soon *A* and *B* are both ecstatic. All sorts of previous sets of instructions, not just about rakes, but about other things as well, now make perfect sense. They have raised themselves to a new plateau of inference about each other and each other's environments.

For purposes of comparison, let us now view this same situation once again, as the conduit metaphor would see it. In terms of the radical subjectivist paradigm for human communication, what the conduit metaphor does is permit the exchange of materials from the environments, including the actual constructs themselves. In our story, we would have to imagine a marvelous technological duplicating machine located in the hub. Person *A* puts his rake in a special chamber, pushes a button, and instantly precise replicas of the rake appear in similar chambers for *B*, *C*, and *D* to make use of. *B*, *C*, and *D* do not have to construct anything or guess about anything. Should person *B* want to communicate with *C* and *D* about *A*'s rake, there is no excuse for him sending anything except an exact replica of that rake to these people. There will still be differences in environments, but learning about these is now a trivial matter. Everything *B* has ever sent to *A* has been constructed largely of rock, and *A* is thus perfectly aware of his neighbor's predicament. Even if the marvelous machine should falter now and again, so that artifacts arrive damaged, still, damaged objects look like damaged objects. A damaged rake does not become a hoe. One can simply send the damaged object back, and wait for the other person to send another replica. It should be clear that the overwhelming tendency of the system, as viewed by the conduit metaphor, will always be: success without effort. At the same time, it should be similarly obvious that, in terms of the *toolmakers paradigm,* and the postulate of radical subjectivity, we come to just the opposite conclusion. Human communication will almost always go astray unless real energy is expended.

This comparison, then, brings to light a basic conflict between the conduit metaphor and the toolmakers paradigm. Both models offer an explana-

tion of the phenomenon of communication. But they come to totally different conclusions about what, in that phenomenon, are more natural states of
affairs, and what are less natural, or constrained, states. In terms of the
conduit metaphor, what requires explanation is failure to communicate.
Success appears to be automatic. But if we think in terms of the toolmakers
paradigm, our expectation is precisely the opposite. Partial miscommunica-
tion, or divergence of readings from a single text, are not aberrations. They
are tendencies inherent in the system, which can only be counteracted by
continuous effort and by large amounts of verbal interaction. In this view,
things will naturally be scattered, unless we expend the energy to gather
them. They are not, as the conduit metaphor would have it, naturally
gathered, with a frightening population of wrong-headed fools working to
scatter them.

As many scholars have pointed out (Kuhn, 1970a; Butterfield, 1965),
such shifts in the notion of what a thing does "naturally," that is, if left to its
own devices, are the stuff of which scientific revolutions are made. If the
earth holds still at some center point, then it is the motions of celestial
bodies that must be theorized about and predicted. But if the sun is at that
center point, then we must theorize about the motion of the earth. In this
regard, the present situation is a little curious. The toolmakers paradigm is
very much in accord with the long-postulated connection between information, in the mathematical sense, and the entropy expression of the second
law of thermodynamics (Cherry, 1966, pp. 214–17). The second law states
that if left to their own devices, all forms of organization always decrease in
time. Successful human communication involves an increase in organization, which cannot happen spontaneously or of its own accord. Thus, the
shift in viewpoint of the toolmakers paradigm merely seems to bring the
model of human communication into line with a previously extant paradigm from the physical sciences. But even though, mathematically, information is expressed as negative entropy, debate and confusion have always
surrounded this connection. And it may be that this confusion springs, in
part at least, from the dominant position occupied by the conduit metaphor
in our language. For the conduit metaphor is definitely in conflict with the
second law.

But I do not want to argue too strongly either for or against either of
these models in this paper. I do not want to attempt any "appeal to the
facts" at this point. For the real question here is to what extent language
can influence thought processes. To me, from my vantage point now, it
seems that the toolmakers paradigm and radical subjectivism simply form a
coherent, common-sense view of what happens when we talk – a common-
sense view which finds support in everything from this second law of thermodynamics to recent work in artificial intelligence or cognitive psychology. But if my major claim is true – that the conduit metaphor is a real and
powerful semantic structure in English, which can influence our thinking –

then it follows that "common sense" about language may be confused. I confess that it took nearly five years for me to come around to radical subjectivism as "common sense." What stood in the way was never a counter-argument, but rather the simple inability to think clearly about the matter. My mind would seem to go to sleep at crucial moments, and it was only the mounting weight of more and more evidence that finally forced it to stay awake. Thus, there is the likelihood that arguments about these models either will not be needed, or alternatively, if they are needed, will fall on deaf ears until the biasing effect of the conduit metaphor has been dealt with. Most important, then, is some survey of the evidence that the conduit metaphor can and does influence our thinking.

Semantic pathology

Let us assume now, for the sake of argument, that it is agreed that communication functions as the toolmakers paradigm suggests, and not as the conduit metaphor would have it. And let us assume further that the conflicting implications of the two frames are theoretically interesting or even important. You may well grant me these things and still hold that the conduit metaphor expressions in everyday language do not really influence, or confuse, our thought processes. After all, all of us succeeded in shifting mental gears and thinking about language in terms of the toolmakers paradigm right here in the present discussion. The conduit metaphor did not prevent us from doing this. Where really is the problem? How can anything troublesome arise from a conceptual frame that we were able to discard so easily? This is the question to which we shall address ourselves now. Can the conduit metaphor really bias our thinking? And if so, how?

To begin with, it must be made clear that no speaker of English, not even your author, has discarded the conduit metaphor. Thinking in terms of the toolmakers paradigm briefly may, perhaps, have made us aware of the conduit metaphor. But none of us will discard it until we succeed in bringing about an entire series of linked changes in the English language. The logic of the framework runs like threads in many directions through the syntactic and semantic fabric of our speech habits. Merely becoming cognizant of this in no way alters the situation. Nor does it appear that one can adopt a new framework and develop it while ignoring the cloth of the language. For everywhere one runs into the old threads, and each one pushes conversation and thought back a little way toward the established pattern. No matter how otherworldly this may seem, there is some exceedingly poignant evidence that it has occurred and continues to occur.

The precise claim being made here is important. It has to do, I think, with one of the ways in which people commonly misunderstand the Whorf hypothesis. I do not claim that we cannot think momentarily in terms of another model of the communication process. I argue, rather, that that thinking will remain brief, isolated, and fragmentary in the face of an entrenched system of opposing attitudes and assumptions.

I have not been able to gather hard statistics about the number of core expressions arising from the conduit metaphor. Indeed, inasmuch as the concept of a "core expression" is itself somewhat loose, and inasmuch as it is difficult in some cases to decide whether an expression should or should not be listed, I am not sure whether hard statistics can ever be assembled. Nevertheless, the present tally of conduit metaphor expressions is about 140. If one looks about for alternative ways of speaking about communication – ways which are either metaphorically neutral, or metaphorically opposed to the conduit framework – the list of expressions numbers between 30 and 40. A conservative estimate would thus be that, of the entire metalingual apparatus of the English language, at least seventy percent is directly, visibly, and graphically based on the conduit metaphor.

Whatever influence the remaining thirty percent might have appears to be weakened beyond this direct proportionality by several factors. First, these expressions tend to be the multisyllabic, latinate abstractions ("communicate," "disseminate," "notify," "disclose," and so on) which are neither graphic nor metaphorically coherent. Thus, they do not present an alternative model of the communication process, which leaves the notion of "putting ideas into words" as the sole available conception. Second, most of them can be used with the adjunct "in words" ("in s," more generally), thereby losing their neutrality and lending added support to the conduit metaphor. "Communicate your feelings using simpler words," for example, succeeds in avoiding the conduit metaphor, whereas, "Communicate your feelings in simpler words," does not. And finally, to the extent that etymologies are relevant, many of these expressions have roots which spring directly from the conduit framework ("express," "disclose," etc). See Part Two of the Appendix for this listing.

The simplest, and perhaps most convincing illustration of our dependence on the conduit metaphor core expressions is a test that can be performed by anyone. Familiarize yourself with the listings in the Appendix. Then begin to become aware of, and try to avoid, conduit metaphors. Every time you find yourself using one, see if you can replace it with a neutral expression, or some circumlocution. My experience in teaching classes which dealt with this subject has been that I am constantly called to account by my students for using the expressions I am lecturing about. If I speak very carefully, with constant attention, I can do fairly well at avoiding them. But the result is hardly idiomatic English. Instead of walking into a classroom and asking "Did you get anything out of that article?" I have to say, "Were you able to construct anything of interest on the basis of the assigned text?" If one should look, I daresay even the present article is not free from conduit metaphor expressions. I ended the preceding section with a minor framework, category three example, (141) in the Appendix, when I wrote: "The arguments will fall on deaf ears." Practically speaking, if you try to avoid all obvious conduit metaphor expressions in your usage, you are nearly struck dumb when communication becomes the topic. You can say to your wayward student, "Try to communicate more effectively, Reginald," but it will not have nearly the impact of, "Reginald, you've got to learn how to put your thoughts into words."

But even if you could avoid all such obvious conduit "metaphorisms," this would still not free you from the framework. The threads, as I said, are nearly everywhere. To see that they go much deeper than just a list of expressions, I should like to resurrect a concept from pretransformational semantics. In his *Principles of Semantics,* Stephen Ullmann (1957, p. 122) makes use of the term *semantic pathology.* A semantic pathology arises "whenever two or more incompatible senses capable of figuring meaningfully in the same context develop around the same name." For some time, my favorite English illustration of this was the delicate and difficult problem of distinguishing sympathy from apology. That is, "I'm sorry" can mean either "I empathize with your suffering," or "I admit fault and apologize." Sometimes people expect apologies from us when we only wish to sympathize, in which case saying, "I'm sorry," is either the perfect hedge or the opening line of a fight. Other times, people think we are apologizing when they see no need for us to apologize and respond with, "That's alright, it wasn't your fault."

As I studied the conduit metaphor, however, I came to rely on this example less and less. I kept coming across terms which were ambiguous between what we have here called "repertoire members" and what we have called "signals." I would find a word which, in its basic sense, referred to some grouping of the marks or sounds which we do exchange with one another. But then I would use it in sentences and realize that it could refer just as easily and just as often to segments of human thought or emotions. Consider the word "poem," for example. In (37) through (39),

(37) The poem was almost illegible
(38) The poem has five lines and forty words
(39) The poem is unrhymed,

this word clearly refers to a text, some signals involving either marks or sounds. For sake of clarity, let us call the *word-sense* operating here POEM₁ (for an operational definition of "word-sense," see Reddy, 1973). Now notice that, in (40) through (42),

(40) Donne's poem is very logical
(41) That poem was so completely depressing
(42) You know his poem is too obscene for children,

the most probable referent of the work is not a text, but rather the concepts and emotions assembled in the reading of a text. I say "most probable" here because it is possible to imagine contexts in which the referent is actually once again a text. Suppose, for instance, (41) is uttered by a teacher of penmanship about a child's hasty copy of some poem. Barring such unusual contexts, however, "poem" in these examples refers to conceptual and emotional material. The word-sense functioning here we shall call POEM$_2$. Example (43) can be read with either POEM$_1$ or POEM$_2$.

(43) Martha's poem is so sloppy!

It is easy to see that this ambiguity of the term "poem" is intimately related to the conduit metaphor. If the words in language contain the ideas, then POEM$_1$ contains POEM$_2$, and metonymy, a process of meaning extension second in importance only to metaphor, takes over. That is, when two entities are always found together in our experience, the name of one of them – usually the more concrete – will develop a new sense which refers to the other. Just as ROSE$_1$ (= the blossom) developed ROSE$_2$ (= the shade of pinkish red) by metonymy, so POEM$_1$ gave rise to POEM$_2$. For, in terms of the conduit metaphor, the two are seen as existing together, the second within the first, and all the conditions for metonymy are met. As long as we are happy with the conduit metaphor, then this ambiguity is in no way problematic, and is certainly not a semantic pathology.

But now consider what happens to the linguistic idealist who wants to think about communication in terms of the toolmakers paradigm and radical subjectivism without making any changes in the English language. In this new model, the words do not contain the ideas, and so POEM$_1$ does not contain POEM$_2$. Instead, it is of greatest importance to preserve a principled distinction between POEM$_1$ and POEM$_2$. There is in most cases only one POEM$_1$, one text, to worry about. But because of the differences in repertoires from one person to the next, and because of the difficult task of assembling these mental and emotional materials on the basis of the instructions in the text, it is obvious to our theorist that there will be as many POEM$_2$'s in existence as there are readers or listeners. These internal POEM$_2$'s will only come to resemble one another after the people expend some energy talking with one another and comparing notes. There is now not the slightest basis for a metonymical extension of POEM$_1$ to POEM$_2$. If we had viewed language in terms of the toolmakers paradigm historically, these two profoundly different concepts would never have been accessed by the same word. Talking about an entire series of slightly, or even terribly, different entities as if there were only one would obviously have led to communicative disaster.

We see, then, that things have taken a troublesome turn for our linguistic idealist. This ambiguity of the word "poem" is for him a real and severe semantic pathology. Other speakers, who accept the conduit metaphor, can be perfectly blasé about it. But he cannot. It befuddles the very distinction he is most concerned to make and bring others to make. More troublesome still is the fact that this pathology is global. It is not an isolated development in the language, involving only the word "poem." I have discussed "poem" here as a paradigm case for the entire class of words in English which denote signals. Analogous examples are available for all of the s words discussed on page 169 – "word," "phrase," "sentence," "essay," "novel," and so on. Even the word "text" has the two senses, as evidenced by (44) and (45):

(44) I am tired of illegible texts

(45) The text is logically incoherent.

In addition, all the proper names of texts, poems, plays, novels, speeches, and the like share this ambiguity. Notice,

(46) The *Old Man and the Sea* is 112 pages long

(47) The *Old Man and the Sea* is deeply symbolic.

As I became aware of this systematic, widespread semantic pathology, I was, of course, far less impressed with the difficulties caused by, "I'm sorry." For here was a case that involved more words than any pathology I had ever heard of. Furthermore, this case showed that semantic structures could be completely normal with respect to one view of reality, and at the same time, pathological with respect to another view. Or in other words, here was some strong evidence that language and views about reality have to develop hand in hand. Finally, I also noticed that this new, potential pathology affected what might be called the "morphosemantics" of the words involved. Suppose, for example, we pluralize the word "poem." As shown in (48),

(48) We have several poems to deal with today,

this produces a form whose most natural referents are a number of POEM$_1$'s, that is, a series of different texts. It would be quite unnatural to utter (48) and mean that there were several internal POEM$_2$'s, Michael's POEM$_2$, Mary's POEM$_2$, Alex's POEM$_2$, and so on, all constructed from the same POEM$_1$, which were to be discussed on a given day. What this means is that, although POEM$_1$, pluralizes with the change in morphology, the other sense, POEM$_2$, is lost in this change. In the case of proper names, pluralization is even more problematic. For most names of texts, there is no morphology defined for the plural. How should our budding radical subjectivist pluralize *The Old Man and the Sea*? Does he say, "Our internal *The Old Man and the Sea-s*"? Or should it be, "Our internal *Old Man and the Sea*"? And notice that it will not help him very much to use (49), or (50).

(49) Our versions of the poem

(50) Our versions of *The Old Man and the Sea*.

For if, in (49), the word "poem" means POEM$_1$, then this phrase applies to variants of the text – which is not what he wants to say. On the other hand, if "poem" means POEM$_2$, then he is still in trouble. Now it sounds like there is one proper and correct POEM$_2$, available to us all, which we may however, for reasons of taste, alter slightly. The radical subjectivism, the absolute nontransferability of any "correct" POEM$_2$, is muddied completely by (49) and (50). This most important fact, that there is one POEM$_1$ but necessarily many POEM$_2$'s, cannot be expressed easily, consistently, or at all naturally.

This discussion, though it says by no means all that could be said, provides an initial illustration of what would happen to someone who really tried to discard the conduit metaphor and think seriously and coherently in terms of the toolmakers paradigm. He would face serious linguistic difficulties, to say the least, and would quite clearly have to create new language as he restructured his thought. But, of course, he would be likely to do this *only* if he shared our present awareness of the biasing power of the conduit metaphor. So far as I know, none of the thinkers who have tried to present alternate theories of language and the nature of meaning have had this awareness. Thus, the conduit metaphor has undercut them, without any knowledge on their part of what was happening. Of course, the problems caused by this confusion in aesthetics and criticism are legion, and it is easy to document my claims by analysis of works in this area. However, a more convincing documentation – indeed, the most convincing documentation one could wish for – is to be found in the historical development of *mathematical information theory.* For here, if ever, with both a concept-free algebra of information, and working machines to use as models, the effect of the conduit metaphor should have been avoided. But, in fact, it was not. And the conceptual basis of the new mathematics, though not the mathematics itself, has been completely obscured by the semantic pathologies of the conduit metaphor.

The framework of mathematical information theory has much in common with our toolmakers paradigm. Information is defined as the ability to make nonrandom selections from some set of alternatives. Communication, which is the transfer of this ability from one place to another, is envisioned as occurring in the following manner. The set of alternatives and a *code* relating these alternatives to physical signals are established, and a copy of each is placed at both the sending and receiving ends of the system. This act creates what is known as an "a priori shared context," a prerequisite for achieving any communication whatsoever. At the transmitting end, a sequence of the alternatives, called the *message,* is chosen for communication to the other end. But this sequence of alternatives is not sent. Rather, the chosen alternatives are related systematically by the code to some form of energy patterns which can travel quickly and retain their shape while they do travel – that is, to the signals.

The whole point of the system is that the alternatives themselves are not mobile, and cannot be sent, whereas the energy patterns, the "signals" are mobile. If all goes well, the signals, when they arrive at the receiving end, are used to duplicate the original selection process and recreate the message. That is, using the relationships of the code and the copy of the original set of alternatives, the receiving end can make the same selections that were made earlier on the transmitting end when the message was generated. Quantification is possible in this framework only because one can set up measures of how much the received signals narrow down the possible choices of preexistent alternatives.

In terms of our toolmakers paradigm, the predefined set of alternatives of information theory corresponds to what we have called the "repertoire." The environments of the persons in the wagon-wheel compound all have much in common – otherwise their system of instructions would not work at all. The "signals" of the mathematical theory are exactly the same as our "signals" – the patterns that can travel, that can be exchanged. In the world of the compound, they are the sheets of paper sent back and forth. Notice, now, that in information theory, as in our paradigm, the alternatives – the "messages" – are not contained in the signals. If the signals were to arrive at the receiving end, and the set of alternatives was damaged or missing, the proper selections could not be made. The signals have no ability to bring the alternatives with them; they carry no little replica of the message. The whole notion of information as "the power to make selections" rules out the idea that signals *contain* the message.

Now, this may be abundantly clear when spelled out in this fashion. And it seems to remain clear as long as information theory is restricted to simple, technical applications. But as most of you know, this theory was hailed as a potential breakthrough for biology and the social sciences. And numerous attempts were made to extend its range of application to include human language and behavior (see Cherry, 1966). Such attempts, of course, were not simple and technical. They required a very clear understanding, not so much of the mathematics of the theory, but rather of the conceptual foundations of the theory. By and large, these attempts were all accounted to be failures. I think that the reason for these failures was the interaction of the conduit metaphor with the conceptual foundations of information theory. As soon as people ventured away from the original, well-defined area of the mathematics, and were forced to rely more on ordinary language, the essential insight of information theory was muddled beyond repair.

The destructive impact of ordinary language on any extensions of information theory begins with the very terms the originators (Shannon & Weaver, 1949) chose to name parts of the paradigm. They called the set of alternatives, which we have referred to here as the "repertoire," the *alphabet*. It is true that in telegraphy the set of alternatives is in fact the alphabet; and telegraphy was their paradigm example. But they made it quite clear that the word "alphabet" was for them a technical coinage which was supposed to refer to *any* set of alternative states, behaviors, or what have you. But this piece of nomenclature is problematic when one turns to human communication. For years I taught information theory in a nonmathematical way to future English teachers, using the term "alphabet." Always this seemed to confuse them, though I never could fathom why, until one year, a student put up her hand and said, "But you can't call the alternatives the *signals*." Now it is strange, on the face of it, that Weaver, particularly, who was very concerned about applying the theory to human communication, would have let this go unnoticed. It confuses the all-important distinction between signals and repertoire members. Substituting the present term, "repertoire," for "alphabet" made my teaching much easier.

But another mistake in terminology makes it seem probable that Shannon and Weaver were never quite clear themselves about the importance of this distinction to their own system. Consider the choice of the term "message" to represent the selection of alternatives from the repertoire. "Message," as the following examples show, partakes of the same semantic pathology as "poem."

(51) I got your message (MESSAGE₁), but had no time to read it

(52) Okay, John, I get the message (MESSAGE₂); let's leave him alone.

For information theory, this is extremely confusing, because MESSAGE₁ means literally a set of signals, whereas MESSAGE₂, means the repertoire members involved with the communication. For conduit-metaphor thinking, in which we send and receive the MESSAGE₂, within the MESSAGE₁, the ambiguity is trivial. But for a theory based totally on the notion that the "message" (MESSAGE₂) is never sent anywhere, this choice of words leads to the collapse of the paradigm. Shannon and Weaver were very careful to point out that the "received signals" were not necessarily the "transmitted signal" because of the possible intervention of distortion and noise. But they blithely wrote the word "message" on the right, or receiving side of their famous paradigm (Shannon & Weaver, 1949, p. 7). At the very least they should have written "reconstructed message" there. In their theory, something is *rebuilt* on that right side which, hopefully, resembles the original message on the left side. The ambiguity of the word "message" should have led them to regard this word as a disaster and never to consider it for use.

If they did not, I believe it is because their thought processes were responding to the biasing effect of the conduit metaphor. Weaver, it seems, could not hold the theory clearly in mind when he spoke of human communication, and used conduit metaphor expressions almost constantly. "How precisely," he asked, "do the transmitted symbols *convey* the desired meaning?" [italics mine] (p. 4). Or he compared two "messages, one of which is *heavily loaded with meaning* and the other of which is pure nonsense" (p. 8). In truth, it seems that he still thought of the MESSAGE₂, the repertoire members, as being sent across the channel, even though this destroys the notion of information as selective power. Weaver hedges significantly when he describes the action of the transmitter. It "changes" he says, "the *message* into the *signal*" [italics Weaver's] (p. 7). Really, this is a strange description. A code is a relationship between two distinct systems. It does not "change" anything into anything else. It merely preserves in the second system the pattern of organization present in the first system. Marks or sounds are not transmuted into electronic pulses. Nor are thoughts and emotions magically metamorphosed into words. Again, this is conduit-metaphor thinking. There is no justification whatsoever in information theory for talking about communication this way.

It is worth noting that Shannon, who actually originated the mathematics, may have had a more coherent understanding than Weaver. At some points in his own exposition, Shannon used exactly the right ordinary language terms. He wrote, "The *receiver* ordinarily performs the inverse operation of that done by the transmitter, reconstructing the message from the signal" (p. 34). But it still does not seem that he perceived the damage done to the paradigm by his own and Weaver's conduit metaphorisms.

Quite the same thing can be said for other ways of speaking associated with information theory. They do violence to the theory, yet support and uphold the conduit metaphor admirably. Consider "encode" and "decode." These mean to put the repertoire members "into" code, and then take them out of code, respectively. Or think about the term "information content." The theory conceives of information as the power to reproduce an organization by means of nonrandom selections. Signals *do something*. They cannot *contain* anything. If the conduit metaphor is capable of influencing thought processes, then why has an entire generation of information theorists talked in this confusing and detrimental way? One would have to suppose that Weaver and many researchers who have followed him were simply bent on professional destruction. It seems easier to believe that the English language has the power to lead them astray.

A recent anthology collecting psychological and sociological efforts to create a communication theory for human interactions points out in the introduction that "investigators have yet to establish a completely acceptable definition of communication" (Sereno & Mortensen, 1970, p. 2). Then it goes on to say,

Those models based upon a mathematical conception describe communication as analogous to the operations of an information processing machine: an event occurs in which a *source* or *sender transmits a signal* or *message* through a *channel* to some *destination* or *receiver.* [italics from anthology] (p. 71)

Notice the statement, "transmits a signal or message." Here, twenty-one years after Shannon and Weaver, the same confusion persists – can the "message" be sent, or not? And it persists in almost every article of the volume. Consider one more brief example. "The theory [of information] was concerned with the problem of defining the quantity of information contained in a message to be transmitted . . . " (p. 62). Note that here information is *contained* in a transmitted "message." If the author means MESSAGE$_1$, then he is thinking in terms of the conduit metaphor, and saying that information is contained in the signals. If he means MESSAGE$_2$, then he is saying that repertoire members, which are transmitted inside of signals, have inside of *them* something called information, which can be measured. Either way, the insight of information theory has been overwhelmed.

Social implications

I should like to conclude with some remarks on the social implications of the situation we have outlined. If the English language has a less than accurate idea of its own workings, and if it has the power to bias thought processes in the direction of this model, what practical impact does this have? We have seen evidence that the conduit metaphor can confuse serious attempts at theory building – but does it matter at all to the man on the street, to mass culture, to federal policy-making?

I must limit myself here to suggesting two ways in which the conduit metaphor does matter to all speakers of English. To discuss the first way, I would like to return to the "stories" told in an earlier section and add a final sequel.

It came to pass, one year, that an evil magician, who was an expert at hypnosis, flew over the toolmakers' compound. Looking down, he saw that, despite the formidable handicaps, *A, B, C,* and *D* were doing quite well with their system of instruction sending. They were very aware that communicating was hard work. And their successes were extremely rewarding to them, because they retained a distinct sense of awe and wonder that they could make the system work at all. It was a daily miracle, which had improved their respective standards of living immensely. The evil magician was very upset about this, and decided to do the worst thing he could think of to *A, B, C,* and *D.* What he did was this. He hypnotized them in a special way, so that, after they received a set of instructions and struggled to build something on the basis of them, they would immediately forget about this. Instead, he planted in them the false memory that the object had been sent to them directly from the other person, via a marvelous mechanism in the hub. Of course, this was not true. They still had to build the objects themselves, out of their own materials – but the magician blinded them to this.

As it turned out, the evil magician's shrewdness was profound. For even though, objectively, the communications system of the compound had not changed one bit, it nevertheless fell very quickly into disuse and decay. And as it crumbled, so did the spirit of harmony and communal progress that had always characterized the relations of *A, B, C,* and *D.* For now, since they would always forget that they had assembled an object themselves and thus bore a large share of responsibility for its shape, it was easy to ridicule the sender for any defects. They also began to spend less and less time working to assemble things, because, once the mental block descended, there was no feeling of reward for a job well done. As soon as they finished an assembly, the hypnosis would take effect, and suddenly – well, even though they were worn out, still, it was the other fellow who had done all the hard, creative work of putting it together. Any fool could take a finished product out of the chamber in the hub. So they came to resent, and therefore abandon, any assembly jobs that required real work. But this was not the worst effect foreseen by the evil magician when he cast his peculiar spell. For, indeed, it was not long before each of the persons came to entertain, privately, the idea that all the others had gone insane. One would send instructions to the others for some device of which he was particularly proud, just as he had always done. Only now of course he believed that he sent, not instructions, but the thing itself. Then, when the others would send him instructions in return, to confirm their receipt of his, he would assemble the object, forget, think that they had returned him the thing itself, and then stare in horror at what he saw. Here he had sent them a wonderful tool, and they returned to him grotesque parodies. Really, what could explain this? All they had to do was to successfully remove his object from the chamber in the hub. How could they change it so shockingly in performing an operation of such moronic simplicity? Were they imbeciles? Or was there perhaps some malice in their behavior? In the end, A, B, C, and D all came privately to the conclusion that the others had either become hostile or else gone berserk. Either way, it did not matter much. None of them took the communications system seriously any more.

Among other things, this sequel attempts to sketch some of the social and psychological effects of believing that communication is a "success without effort" system, when, in fact, it is an "energy must be expended" system. I am sure that no one has failed to realize that, to the extent that the parable applies, the evil magician is the English language, and his hypnotic spell is the bias imparted to our thought processes by the conduit metaphor. This model of communication objectifies meaning in a misleading and dehumanizing fashion. It influences us to talk and think about thoughts as if they had the same kind of external, intersubjective reality as lamps and tables. Then, when this presumption proves dramatically false in operation, there seems to be nothing to blame except our own stupidity or malice. It is as if we owned a very large, very complex computer – but had been given the wrong instruction manual for it. We believe the wrong things about it, and teach our children the wrong things about it, and simply cannot get full or even moderate usage out of the system.

Another point from the story worth emphasizing is that, to the extent that the conduit metaphor does see communication as requiring some slight expenditure of energy, it localizes this expenditure almost totally in the speaker or writer. The function of the reader or listener is trivialized. The radical subjectivist paradigm, on the other hand, makes it clear that readers and listeners face a difficult and highly creative task of reconstruction and hypothesis testing. Doing this work well probably requires considerably more energy than the conduit metaphor would lead us to expect.

But we are still a long way from government policy in these effects. Let us turn, then, to the second example of the impact of the conduit metaphor, which will help to close this gap. The expression employed in (53), number 114 in the Appendix,

(53) You'll *find* better *ideas* than that in the *library,*
is derived from the conduit metaphor by a chain of metonymies. That is, we think of the ideas as existing in the words, which are clearly there on the pages. So the ideas are "there on the pages" by metonymy. Now the pages are in the books – and again, by metonymy, so are the ideas. But the books are in the libraries, with the final result that the ideas, too, are "in the libraries." The effect of this, and the many other minor framework core expressions is to suggest that the libraries, with their books, and tapes, and films, and photographs, are the real repositories of our culture. And if this is true, then naturally we of the modern period are preserving our cultural heritage better than any other age, because we have more books, films, tapes, and so on, stored in more and bigger libraries.

Suppose now that we drop the conduit metaphor and think of this same situation in terms of the toolmakers paradigm. From this point of view, there are of course no ideas in the words, and therefore none in any books, nor on any tapes or records. There are no ideas whatsoever in any libraries. All that is stored in any of these places are odd little patterns of marks or bumps or magnetized particles capable of creating odd patterns of noise. Now, if a human being comes along who is capable of using these marks or sounds as instructions, then this human being may assemble within his head some patterns of thought or feeling or perception which resemble those of intelligent humans no longer living. But this is a difficult task, for these ones no longer living saw a different world from ours, and used slightly different language instructions. Thus, if this human who enters the library has not been schooled in the art of language, so that he is deft and precise and thorough in applying instructions, and if he does not have a rather full and flexible repertoire of thoughts and feelings to draw from, then it is not likely that he will reconstruct in his head anything that deserves to be called "his cultural heritage."

Quite obviously, the toolmakers paradigm makes it plain that there is no culture in books or libraries, that, indeed, there is no culture at all unless it is reconstructed carefully and painstakingly in the living brains of each new generation. All that is preserved in libraries is the mere opportunity to perform this reconstruction. But if the language skills and the habit of engaging in reconstruction are not similarly preserved, then there will be no culture, no matter how large and complete the libraries may become. We do not preserve ideas by building libraries and recording voices. The only way to preserve culture is to train people to rebuild it, to "regrow" it, as the word "culture" itself suggests, in the only place it can grow – within themselves.

The difference of viewpoint here between the conduit metaphor and the toolmakers paradigm is serious, if not profound. Humanists appear to be dying these days, and administrators and governments seem to feel few compunctions about letting this occur. We have the greatest, most sophisticated system for mass communication of any society that we know about, yet somehow mass communication becomes more and more synonymous with less communication. Why is this? One reason, at least, may be that we are following our instruction manual for use of the language system quite carefully – and it is the wrong manual. We have the mistaken, conduit-metaphor influenced view that the more signals we can create, and the more signals we can preserve, the more ideas we "transfer" and "store." We neglect the crucial human ability to reconstruct thought patterns on the basis of signals and this ability founders. After all, "extraction" is a trivial process, which does not require teaching past the most rudimentary level. We have therefore, in fact, less culture – or certainly no more culture – than other, less mechanically inclined, ages have had. Humanists, those traditionally charged with reconstructing culture and teaching others to reconstruct it, are not necessary in the scheme of the conduit metaphor. All the ideas are "there in the library," and anyone can go in and "get them." In the toolmakers paradigm, on the other hand, humanists themselves *are* the repositories, and the only real repositories of ideas. In the simplest of terms, the conduit metaphor lets human ideas slip out of human brains, so that, once you have recording technologies, you do not need humans any more.

I am suggesting, then, that in the same way that "urban renewal" misled the policymakers discussed in Schön's paper, the conduit metaphor is leading us down a technological and social blind alley. That blind alley is mass communications systems coupled with mass neglect of the internal, human systems responsible for nine-tenths of the work in communicating. We think we are "capturing ideas in words," and funneling them out to the greatest public in the history of the world. But if there are no ideas "within" this endless flood of words, then all we are doing is replaying the myth of Babel – centering it, this time, around a broadcasting tower.

APPENDIX

A partial listing of the metalingual resources of English

This appendix is divided into two parts. The first lists expressions arising from the logic of the conduit metaphor; the second lists expressions which are either metaphorically neutral or involve logics alternative to the conduit metaphor. Further search for expressions, along with a more elaborate means of analyzing and classifying, will be required before either collection can be termed complete. In some cases, in Part One, core expressions which I have placed in one category could with justification be placed in a different category as well. These and other niceties must await later exposition. One or two examples follow each expression.

Part One: The conduit metaphor

I. THE MAJOR FRAMEWORK

A. Implying that human language functions like a conduit enabling the transfer of repertoire members from one individual to another.
  1. get RM across (to someone)
     "You'll have to try to get your real attitudes across to her better."
     "It's very hard to get that idea across in a hostile atmosphere."
  2. put RM across (to someone)
     "If you salesmen can't put this understanding across to the clients more forcefully, our new product will fail."
  3. give RM (to someone)
     "You know very well that I gave you that idea."
  4. give RM away
     "Jane gives away all her best ideas."
  5. get RM from someone
     "Marsha got those concepts from Rudolf."
  6. RM get through (to someone)
     "Your real feelings are finally getting through to me."
  7. RM come through (to someone)
     "Apparently, your reasons came through to John quite clearly."
     "What comes through most obviously is anger."
  8. RM come across (to someone)
     "Your concepts come across beautifully."

9. RM make it across (to someone)
   "Your thoughts here don't quite make it across."
10. let someone have RM
    "Oh come on, let me have some of your great ideas about this."
11. present someone with RM
    "Well, you have presented me with some unfamiliar thoughts
    and I think I should let them settle awhile."
12. Send RM (to someone)
    "Next time you write, send better ideas."
13. language transfers RM
    "Language transfers meaning."

B. Implying that, in speaking or writing, humans place their internal reper-
    toire members within the external signals, or else fail to do so in unsuc-
    cessful communication.

14. put RM into s
    "It is very difficult to put this concept into words."
15. capture RM in s
    "When you have a good idea, try to capture it immediately in
    words."
16. fill s with RM
    "Harry always fills his paragraphs with meaning."
17. pack s with RM
    "A good poet packs his lines with beautiful feelings."
18. pack RM into s
    "If you can't pack more thought into fewer words, you will
    never pass the conciseness test."
19. load s with RM
    "Never load a sentence with more thought than it can carry."
20. load RM into s
    "John loads too much conflicting feeling into what he says."
21. insert RM in s
    "Insert that thought elsewhere in the sentence."
22. include RM in s
    "I would certainly not include that feeling in your speech."
23. burden s with RM
    "You burden your words with rather terribly complex mean-
    ings."
24. overload s with RM
    "Harry does not exactly overload his paragraphs with thought."
25. stuff RM into s
    "You cannot simply stuff ideas into a sentence any old way!"
26. stuff s with RM/full of RM
    "You have only a short time, so try to stuff the essay with all
    your best ideas."

"You can stuff the paper full of earthshaking ideas – that man still won't notice."

27. cram RM into s

"Dickinson crams incredible amounts of meaning into her poems."

28. cram with RM/full of RM

"He crammed the speech with subversive ideas."

"Harry crammed the chapter full of spurious arguments."

29. unload RM in s

"Unload your feelings in words – then your head will be clearer."

30. force RM into s

"Don't force your meanings into the wrong words."

31. get RM into s

"I can't seem to get these ideas into words."

32. shove RM into s

"Trying to shove such complicated meanings into simple sentences is exceedingly difficult."

33. fit RM into s

"This notion does not seem to fit into any words."

C. Implying that signals convey or contain the repertoire members, or else fail to do this in unsuccessful communication.

34. s carry RM

"His words carry little in the way of recognizable meaning."

35. s convey RM

"The passage conveys a feeling of excitement."

36. s transfer RM

"Your writing must transfer these ideas to those who need them."

37. s display RM

"This essay displays thoughts I did not think Marsha capable of."

38. s bring RM (with it)

"His letter brought the idea to the French pilots."

39. s contain RM

"In terms of the rest of the poem, your couplet contains the wrong kind of thoughts."

40. s have RM-content/RMa-content

"The introduction has a great deal of thought content."

"The statement appears to have little emotional content."

"The speech has too much angry content."

("RMa" stands for adjectives appropriate to repertoire members.)

41. RM be in s

"That thought is in practically every phrase!"

42. s be pregnant with RM

"His words, pregnant with meaning, fell on receptive ears."

43. s be fraught with RM
    "The poem is fraught with dire thoughts about civilization."
44. s be saturated with RM
    "The last stanza is saturated with despair."
45. s be hollow
    "Your words seem rather hollow."
46. s be full of RM
    "The oracle's words were full of meaning."
47. s be without RM
    "The sentence is without meaning."
48. s have no RM
    "Sam's words have not the slightest feeling of compassion."
49. s be empty (of RM)
    "His lines may rhyme, but they are empty of either meaning or feeling."
    "The sentences are empty; they say nothing to me."
    "What the candidates have said is so much empty sound."
50. s be void of RM
    "The entire chapter is void of all useful ideas."
51. s's RM/RM of s
    "The thought of this clause is somehow disturbing."
    "This paragraph's thought is completely garbled."
52. s be bursting with RM
    "The poem is bursting with ecstasy!"
53. s be overflowing with RM
    "The line is overflowing with pure happiness."
54. RM show up in s
    "This idea shows up in the second paragraph."
55. s hand RM (to someone)
    "But this sentence hands us a completely different idea."

D. Implying that, in listening or reading, humans find repertoire members within the signals and take them into their heads, or else fail to do so in unsuccessful communication.

56. get RM out of s/from s
    "I have to struggle to get any meaning at all out of the sentence."
    "I got the idea of patience from your statement."
57. get the RM in s into one's head
    "Everybody must get the concepts in this article into his head by tomorrow or else!"
58. extract RM from s
    "Can you really extract coherent thoughts from that incredible prose?"
59. RM arise from s
    "The feeling arises from the second paragraph."

60. see RM in s

"We will see this thought several times again in the sonnet."

61. find RM in s

"John says that he cannot find your idea anywhere in the passage."

63[*sic*]. Come upon RM in s

"I would be quite surprised if you came upon any interesting concepts in Stephen's essay."

64. uncover RM in s

"John admits that we uncovered those ideas in the ode, but still doesn't believe that Keats put them there."

65. overlook RM in s

"Don't overlook the idea of fulfilled passion later on in the passage."

66. pay attention to RM in s/what's in s

"You rarely pay enough attention to the actual meaning in the words."

"Please pay attention to what's there in the words!"

67. reveal RM in s

"Closer reading reveals altogether uncharacteristic feelings in the story."

68. miss RM in s

"I missed that idea in the sentence completely."

69. s be impenetrable

"The poem is meant to be impenetrable – after all, Blake wrote it."

70. RM be locked up in s

"Whatever she meant, it's likely to be locked up in that cryptic little verse forever."

71. RM be sealed up in s

"It's as if he wrote the sentences in such a way as to seal up the meaning in them."

72. RM be hidden (away) in s

"The attitudes I want to show you are hidden away someplace in the last chapter."

73. RM be/get lost in s

"Mary has good ideas, but they get lost in her run-on sentences."

74. RM be buried in s

"Yes, but the man's thought is buried in these terribly dense and difficult paragraphs."

75. RM be sunk in s

"The thought is there, although I grant that it's sunk pretty deep in paradoxical language."

76. lay bare RM in s
    "John's analysis really lays bare the ideas in the chapter."
77. bare RM in s
    "You have bared the hidden meanings in the sentence."
78. unseal RM in s
    "To unseal the meaning in Wittgenstein's curious phrases is no easy task."
79. expose RM in s
    "You have exposed certain feelings in the essay of which the author would not be proud."

II. THE MINOR FRAMEWORK

E. Implying that, particularly when communications are recorded or delivered in public, speakers and writers eject their repertoire members into an external "space."

80. get RM out
    "I feel some responsibility to get these ideas out where they can do some good."
81. get RM into circulation
    "Try to get your feelings about the merger into circulation among the board members."
82. put RM into circulation
    "We intend to put these new concepts into circulation among actual teachers."
83. put RM forth
    "IBM put forth the idea that they had been mistreated."
84. pour RM out
    "Mary poured out her sorrows."
85. pour RM forth
    "You come over and pour forth your anger and expect me to take it all in!"
86. bring RM out
    "Dr. Williams brings out some unusual thoughts on the matter."
87. s put RM forth
    "IBM's legal brief puts forth the idea that they have been mistreated."
88. s brings RM out
    "The essay brings out unusual thoughts on the matter."
89. bring RM forth
    "That child brought forth feelings I couldn't cope with."
90. RM leak out
    "Your thoughts will leak out anyway."
91. get RM down on paper
    "Get your insights down on paper at once."

92. put RM down on paper

"Perhaps you could put this feeling of sympathy down on paper and send it to your brother."

93. set RM down on paper

"Can you set the latest idea down on paper and let me take it?"

94. lay RM out on paper

"Lay your thoughts out on paper where you can see them."

95. let RM drop

"Someone let drop the idea of continuing anyway."

96. let RM slip out

"Who let this understanding slip out?"

97. deliver self of RM

"He delivered himself of a great deal of anger."

98. RM pour out

"Interesting ideas just seem to pour out of that man."

99. RM flow out

"Don't let your feelings flow out so freely when he's around."

100. RM gush out/forth

"Let your emotions gush right out – that's what we're here for."

"All these thoughts can't gush forth at once, you know."

101. RM ooze out

"Her sympathy just oozes out."

102. RM escape someone's lips

"That idea will never escape Mary's lips."

103. throw out RM

"I just want to throw out some new ideas for you folks to look at."

104. throw RM EX LOC

"You can't just throw ideas onto the page any old way!"

"Mary throws her ideas at the reader too fast."

(EX LOC stands for *external locative,* that is, any expression denoting a place external to the speaker or writer's head.)

105. toss out RM

"I shall begin the class by tossing out some apparently very simple thoughts."

106. blurt out RM

"You always blurt out your feelings before anyone is ready to cope with them."

F. Implying that repertoire members are reified in this external "space," independent of any need for living humans to think or feel them.

107. RM float around

"That concept has been floating around for centuries."

108. RM circulate

"Those precise thoughts began circulating shortly after your birth."

109. RM move

"In America, ideas tend to move from the coasts to the middle of the country."

110. RM make its/their way

"The concept made its way very quickly into the universities."

111. RM find its/their way

"These feelings found their way to the ghettos of Rome."

112. RM arrive

"A fantastic idea arrived in the mail this morning!"

113. RM travel

"The notion traveled from Russia to China that communism would have to be modified."

114. find RM in/at L

"You won't find that idea in any bookstore!"

(L stands for any edifice or room containing reading matter.)

115. RM be in/at L

"I'm sure those thoughts are already in the library."

116. find RM in B

"You can find that idea in several books"

(B stands for those physical objects that normally contain writing – i.e., "magazines," "newspapers," etc., and also expressions like "on microfilm.")

117. RM be in B

"I'm sure those thoughts are in some magazine."

118. RM be on radio/television/tape/records

"That kind of anger has never been on television."

119. immerse self in RM

"He immersed himself in the fresher ideas of topology."

120. bury self in RM

"Don't bury yourself in these concepts in any case."

121. lose self in/among RM

"She lost herself among her intense feelings."

"She lost herself in the feeling of grief."

122. wander among RM

"Harry was now free to wander happily among the ideas of the more learned hedonists."

123. kick RM around

"We were kicking around some of Dave's ideas."

124. toss RM back and forth

"They tossed your thoughts back and forth for over an hour, but still could not make sense of them."

125. throw RM around

"That professor throws around esoteric ideas like it was going out of style."

G. Implying that the reified repertoire members may or may not find their way once again into the heads of living humans.

126. absorb RM

"You have to absorb Plato's ideas a little at a time."

127. RM sink in

"Harry just won't let certain kinds of thoughts sink in."

128. take RM in

"You have to learn to take in your friends' emotions and react sensibly to them."

129. internalize RM

"Marsha has obviously not internalized these ideas."

130. catch RM

"It was a notion I didn't catch right away."

131. get RM

"We didn't get that idea until very late in the semester."

132. RM come to someone

"Then the thought came to me that you might have already left."

133. RM come to mind

"Different ideas come to mind in a situation like this."

134. RM come to someone's ears

"The thought of doing things differently came to my ears in a very curious fashion."

135. soak up RM

"You should see him soak up ideas!"

136. stuff someone/someone's head with/full of RM

"That have already stuffed his head full of radical ideas."

137. cram (RM)

"I'm cramming history tonight for tomorrow's exam."

"Cramming most of the major ideas of organic in a single night is impossible."

"I'm sorry, but I have to cram this afternoon."

138. shove RM into someone/someone's head

"I've shoved so many ideas into my head today I'm dizzy."

139. RM go over someone's head

"Of course, my ideas went right over his head."

140. RM go right past someone

"It seems like the argument went right past him."

141. RM fall on deaf ears

"Her unhappy feelings fell on deaf ears."

Part Two: Other metalingual resources

Many of the expressions below can be used with common adjuncts to form statements that support the conduit metaphor. Thus, it is only when they are used without these adjuncts that they can be thought of as alternatives. To make this apparent, I shall present starred examples which show how easily the neutrality of these expressions can be lost. There are also expressions which appear to involve the conduit metaphor in one reading, but not in another. These I shall flag with a question mark.

I.   Alternatives to Categories IA, IB, and IE of the Conduit Metaphor: Expressions which do not imply that language functions like a conduit, or that speaking and writing are acts of insertion into the words or ejection into an external space.

    1. speak of/about RM (to someone) (NLI s)
"please speak to me more clearly about your feelings."
(NLI stands for any *non-locative instrumental,* such as "with," "by means of," etc. To be ruled out here are the *locative instrumentals,* "through words" and "in words," which signal the conduit metaphor.)
"Speak to me of your feelings using simpler words."
*"Speak to me of your feelings in simpler words."

    2. talk of/about RM (to someone) (NLI s)
"Mary talked about her new ideas."
"Harry talked about his ideas using very complex sentences."
*"Harvey talked about his ideas through very complex sentences."

    3. write of/about RM (to someone) (NLI s)
"John can write of his feelings with real clarity."
*"Try to write about your feelings in simpler words."

    4. state RM (to someone) (NLI s)
"State your thoughts plainly."
*"State your thoughts in other words, please."

?5. communicate (of/about) RM (to someone) (NLI s)
"Is that the feeling you are trying to communicate?"
*"Why not communicate this thought in the next paragraph?"

    6. tell someone of/about RM (NLI s)
"John told you about those ideas yesterday."
*"Mary told me about her sorrow in graphic sentences."

    7. inform someone of/about RM (NLI s)
"I informed them of my changing ideas."
*"Did you inform him of your feelings through words he could understand?"

    8. mention RM (to someone) (NLI s)

"You should never have mentioned the idea to Harry."

"When I mentioned the thoughts to John, I used the same words I used with you."

*"When I mentioned the thoughts to John. I did it in the same words I used with you."

9. express RM (to someone) (NLI S)

"I cannot express these feelings accurately."

*"Perhaps you should express your concepts through other words."

10. report RM (to someone) (NLI S)

"You can report your ideas using layman's language."

*"Report your feelings in different words."

?11. desribe RM (to/for someone) (NLI S)

"Describe those concepts for me again."

*"Rich described his feelings in beautiful words."

?12. sketch RM (for someone) (NLI S)

"We only have time to sketch the ideas right now."

*"When you sketch a thought, don't do it in such complicated sentences."

?13. impart RM (to someone) (NLI S)

"It's difficult to impart ideas to a class like this."

*"I'll have to impart the idea in different words."

14. give notice of RM (to someone) (NLI S)

"What she gave notice of was her feeling of isolation."

*"You gave notice of your attitude in words you should not have used."

15. make RM known (to someone) (NLI S)

"When did you make your idea known to her?"

*"You may have tried to make your anger known to them, but you did it in words that were bound to fail."

16. advise someone of/about RM (NLI S)

"Did you advise them about your feelings?"

*"You certainly advised him of your ideas in the right phrases."

17. apprise someone of/about RM (NLI S)

"Mary did not apprise John of her thoughts."

*"John apprised the repairman of his feeling through the simplest of words."

?18. acquaint someone with RM (NLI S)

"I acquainted them with your feelings."

*"You cannot acquaint him with the idea in those words."

19. enlighten someone about RM (NLI S)

"How will you enlighten Mary about your thoughts?"

*"If you enlighten them about the concept in those words, he may never speak to you again."

?20. disclose RM (to someone) (NLI s)
   "When you get ready to disclose the ideas, let me know."
   *"I would disclose the thoughts first in German, and only later in English."
21. notify someone of/about RM (NLI s)
   "Have you notified anyone of these new feelings?"
   *"Notify your readers of this idea immediately in the first paragraph."
22. announce RM (to someone) (NLI s)
   "You should not announce these attitudes to the group."
   *"You certainly could announce these ideas in different words."
23. bring news of RM (to someone)
   "Henry brought news of Jeri's ideas."
24. bring tidings of/about RM (to someone)
   "Someone should bring tidings of these thoughts to the world at large."
25. give account of RM (to someone) (NLI s)
   "He could not give a clear account of Einstein's ideas."
(Starred examples exist for any core expression with the NLI s adjunct. But since the format of these should be clear by now, I shall cease to provide such examples at this point.)
26. discuss RM (with someone) (NLI s)
   "I have never discussed my thoughts with John."
27. converse about RM (with someone) (NLI s)
   "You should learn to converse intelligently about your feelings."
28. exchange words about RM (with someone)
   "John and I exchanged words about our feelings."
29. have verbal interchange about RM (with someone)
   "The class had several verbal interchanges about the new concepts."
?30. publish RM (NLI s)
   "When are you going to publish your ideas?"
?31. make RM public (NLI s)
   "John does not know how to make his attitudes public"
?32. disseminate RM (NLI s)
   "How can we disseminate such ideas?"
II. Alternatives to Categories IC and IF of the Conduit Metaphor: Expressions which do not imply that words contain or convey meanings, or that ideas exist independent of human beings in an abstract "space."
33. s symbolize RM
   "Words symbolize meanings."
   "Gestures can symbolize various emotions."
34. s correspond to RM
   "The sentence corresponds to my thoughts."

35. s stand for RM

   "Sentences stand for human thoughts."

?36. s represent RM

   "Language represents our thoughts and feelings."

?37. s mean/have meanings (to someone)

   "I hope my words mean something to you."

(It appears that we make up for the poverty of this category by reusing many Category I expressions with s words, as opposed to humans, as subjects. Thus, "John's words tell us of his ideas," or "This sentence states your thoughts plainly." Whether this personification of the signals is linked to the conduit metaphor or not, I have not yet determined. The conduit metaphor does view words as containing ideas just as humans do, however, which could provide motivation for the transfer. That is, the signals could be "giving us the ideas they contain," just as, in speaking, humans "give us the ideas they contain." This question will have to await deeper analysis.)

III. Alternatives to Categories ID and IG of the Conduit Metaphor: Expressions which do not imply that reading and listening are acts of extraction, or that reified ideas reenter human heads from an abstract "space."

38. understand s/RM – but not *understand RM in s

   "I have some trouble understanding the sentence."

   "I can rarely understand his thoughts."

   *"I have never understood the meaning in that essay."

39. comprehend s/RM – but not *comprehend RM in s

   "Have you comprehended the sentence?"

   "She does not comprehend my thoughts."

   *"John comprehends few of the thoughts in Mary's paper."

?40. grasp s – but not *grasp RM or *grasp RM in s

   "I have not yet grasped the sentence."

   *"I have had little time to grasp his thoughts, especially the meaning in the last chapter."

41. construct a reading for s

   "It is easy to construct a reading for that sentence."

42. build a reading for s

   "How do you build readings for sentences like that?"

?43. get reading for s

   "How did you get that reading for that phrase?"

?44. interpret s

   "I find it hard to interpret his paragraphs."

45. follow s

   "I could follow his sentences easily."

11

The contemporary theory of metaphor

GEORGE LAKOFF

Do not go gentle into that good night.
— Dylan Thomas

Death is the mother of beauty.
— Wallace Stevens, "Sunday Morning"

Introduction

These famous lines by Thomas and Stevens are examples of what classical theorists, at least since Aristotle, have referred to as metaphor: instances of novel poetic language in which words like "mother," "go," and "night" are not used in their normal everyday sense. In classical theories of language, metaphor was seen as a matter of language, not thought. Metaphorical expressions were assumed to be mutually exclusive with the realm of ordinary everday language: everyday language had no metaphor, and metaphor used mechanisms outside the realm of everyday conventional language.

The classical theory was taken so much for granted over the centuries that many people didn't realize that it was just a theory. The theory was not merely taken to be true, but came to be taken as definitional. The word "metaphor" was defined as a novel or poetic linguistic expression where one or more words for a concept are used outside of their normal conventional meaning to express a "similar" concept.

But such issues are not matters for definitions; they are empirical questions. As a cognitive scientist and a linguist, one asks: what are the generalizations governing the linguistic expressions referred to classically as "poetic metaphors"? When this question is answered rigorously, the classical theory turns out to be false. The generalizations governing poetic metaphorical expressions are not in language, but in thought: they are general mappings across conceptual domains. Moreover, these general principles which take the form of conceptual mappings, apply not just to novel poetic expressions, but to much of ordinary everyday language.

In short, the locus of metaphor is not in language at all, but in the way we conceptualize one mental domain in terms of another. The general theory of metaphor is given by characterizing such cross-domain mappings. And in the process, everyday abstract concepts like time, states, change, causation, and purpose also turn out to be metaphorical.

The result is that metaphor (that is, cross-domain mapping) is absolutely central to ordinary natural language semantics, and that the study of literary metaphor is an extension of the study of everyday metaphor. Everyday metaphor is characterized by a huge system of thousands of cross-domain mappings, and this system is made use of in novel metaphor.

Because of these empirical results, the word "metaphor" has come to be used differently in contemporary metaphor research. It has come to mean "a cross-domain mapping in the conceptual system." The term "metaphorical expression" refers to a linguistic expression (a word, phrase, or sentence) that is the surface realization of such a cross-domain mapping (this is what the word "metaphor" referred to in the old theory). I will adopt the contemporary usage throughout this chapter.

Experimental results demonstrating the cognitive reality of the extensive system of metaphorical mappings are discussed by Gibbs (this volume). Mark Turner's 1987 book, *Death Is the Mother of Beauty*, whose title comes from Stevens' great line, demonstrates in detail how that line uses the ordinary system of everyday mappings. For further examples of how literary metaphor makes use of the ordinary metaphor system, see *More Than Cool Reason: A Field Guide to Poetic Metaphor*, by Lakoff and Turner (1989) and *Reading Minds: The Study of English in the Age of Cognitive Science*, by Turner (1991).

Since the everyday metaphor system is central to the understanding of poetic metaphor, we will begin with the everyday system and then turn to poetic examples.

Homage to Reddy

The contemporary theory that metaphor is primarily conceptual, conventional, and part of the ordinary system of thought and language can be traced to Michael Reddy's (this volume) now classic essay, "The Conduit Metaphor," which first appeared in the first edition of this collection. Reddy did far more in that essay than he modestly suggested. With a single, thoroughly analyzed example, he allowed us to see, albeit in a restricted domain, that ordinary everyday English is largely metaphorical, dispelling once and for all the traditional view that metaphor is primarily in the realm of poetic or "figurative" language. Reddy showed, for a single, very significant case, that the locus of metaphor is thought, not language, that metaphor is a major and indispensable part of our ordinary, conventional way of conceptualizing the world, and that our everyday behavior reflects our metaphorical understanding of experience. Though other theorists had noticed some of these characteristics of metaphor, Reddy was the first to demonstrate them by rigorous linguistic analysis, stating generalizations over voluminous examples.

Reddy's chapter on how we conceptualize the concept of communication by metaphor gave us a tiny glimpse of an enormous system of conceptual metaphor. Since its appearance, an entire branch of linguistics and cognitive science has developed to study systems of metaphorical thought that we use to reason and base our actions on, and that underlie a great deal of the structure of language.

The bulk of the chapters in this book were written before the development of the contemporary field of metaphor research. My chapter will therefore contradict much that appears in the others, many of which make certain assumptions that were widely taken for granted in 1977. A major assumption that is challenged by contemporary research is the traditional division between literal and figurative language, with metaphor as a kind of figurative language. This entails, by definition, that: what is literal is not metaphorical. In fact, the word "literal" has traditionally been used with one or more of a set of assumptions that have since proved to be false:

Traditional false assumptions

All everyday conventional language is literal, and none is metaphorical.
All subject matter can be comprehended literally, without metaphor.
Only literal language can be contingently true or false.
All definitions given in the lexicon of a language are literal, not metaphorical.
The concepts used in the grammar of a language are all literal; none are metaphorical.

The big difference between the contemporary theory and views of metaphor prior to Reddy's work lies in this set of assumptions. The reason for the difference is that, in the intervening years, a huge system of everyday, conventional, conceptual metaphors has been discovered. It is a system of metaphor that structures our everyday conceptual system, including most abstract concepts, and that lies behind much of everyday language. The discovery of this enormous metaphor system has destroyed the traditional literal–figurative distinction, since the term "literal," as used in defining the traditional distinction, carries with it all those false assumptions.

A major difference between the contemporary theory and the classical one is based on the old literal–figurative distinction. Given that distinction, one might think that one "arrives at" a metaphorical interpretation of a sentence by "starting" with the literal meaning and applying some algorithmic process to it (see Searle, this volume). Though there do exist cases where something like this happens, this is not in general how metaphor works, as we shall see shortly.

What is not metaphorical

Although the old literal–metaphorical distinction was based on assumptions that have proved to be false, one can make a different sort of literal–metaphorical distinction: those concepts that are not comprehended via conceptual metaphor might be called "literal." Thus, although I will argue that a great many common concepts like causation and purpose are metaphorical, there is nonetheless an extensive range of non-metaphorical concepts. A sentence like "the balloon went up" is not metaphorical, nor is the old philosopher's favorite "the cat is on the mat." But as soon as one gets away from concrete physical experience and starts talking about abstractions or emotions, metaphorical understanding is the norm.

The contemporary theory: Some examples

Let us now turn to some examples that are illustrative of contemporary metaphor research. They will mostly come from the domain of everyday conventional metaphor, since that has been the main focus of the research. I will turn to the discussion of poetic metaphor only after I have discussed the conventional system, since knowledge of the conventional system is needed to make sense of most of the poetic cases.

The evidence for the existence of a system of conventional conceptual metaphors is of five types:

Generalizations governing polysemy, that is, the use of words with a number of related meanings

Generalizations governing inference patterns, that is, cases where a pattern of inferences from one conceptual domain is used in another domain

Generalizations governing novel metaphorical language (see Lakoff & Turner, 1989)

Generalizations governing patterns of semantic change (see Sweetser, 1990)

Psycholinguistic experiments (see Gibbs, 1990a; 1990b)

We will be discussing primarily the first three of these sources of evidence, since they are the most robust.

Conceptual metaphor

Imagine a love relationship described as follows:
   Our relationship has hit a *dead-end street.*
   Here love is being conceptualized as a journey, with the implication that
the relationship is *stalled,* that the lovers cannot *keep going the way they've
been going,* that they must *turn back,* or abandon the relationship altogether. This is not an isolated case. English has many everyday expressions
that are based on a conceptualization of love as a journey, and they are
used not just for talking about love, but for reasoning about it as well.
Some are necessarily about love; others can be understood that way:
   Look *how far we've come.* It's been *a long, bumpy road.* We can't *turn
back* now. We're at a *crossroads.* We may have to *go our separate ways.* The
relationship isn't *going anywhere.* We're *spinning our wheels.* Our relationship is *off the track.* The marriage is *on the rocks.* We may have to *bail out*
of this relationship.
   These are ordinary, everyday English expressions. They are not poetic,
nor are they necessarily used for special rhetorical effect. Those like *look
how far we've come,* which aren't necessarily about love, can readily be
understood as being about love.
   As a linguist and a cognitive scientist, I ask two commonplace questions:
   Is there a general principle governing how these linguistic expressions
      about journeys are used to characterize love?
   Is there a general principle governing how our patterns of inference
      about journeys are used to reason about love when expressions such as
      these are used?
   The answer to both is yes. Indeed, there is a single general principle that
answers both questions, but it is a general principle that is neither part of
the grammar of English, nor the English lexicon. Rather, it is part of the
conceptual system underlying English. It is a principle for understanding
the domain of love in terms of the domain of journeys.
   The principle can be stated informally as a metaphorical scenario:

The lovers are travelers on a journey together, with their common life goals seen as
destinations to be reached. The relationship is their vehicle, and it allows them to
pursue those common goals together. The relationship is seen as fulfilling its purpose as long as it allows them to make progress toward their common goals. The
journey isn't easy. There are impediments, and there are places (crossroads) where
a decision has to be made about which direction to go in and whether to keep
traveling together.

   The metaphor involves understanding one domain of experience, love,
in terms of a very different domain of experience, journeys. More techni-
cally, the metaphor can be understood as a mapping (in the mathematical

sense) from a source domain (in this case, journeys) to a target domain (in this case, love). The mapping is tightly structured. There are ontological correspondences, according to which entities in the domain of love (e.g., the lovers, their common goals, their difficulties, the love relationship, etc.) correspond systematically to entities in the domain of a journey (the travelers, the vehicle, destinations, etc.).

To make it easier to remember what mappings there are in the conceptual system, Johnson and I (Lakoff & Johnson, 1980) adopted a strategy for naming such mappings, using mnemonics which suggest the mapping. Mnemonic names typically (though not always) have the form: TARGET-DOMAIN IS SOURCE-DOMAIN, or alternatively, TARGET-DOMAIN AS SOURCE-DOMAIN. In this case, the name of the mapping is LOVE IS A JOURNEY. When I speak of the LOVE IS A JOURNEY metaphor, I am using a mnemonic for a set of ontological correspondences that characterize a mapping, namely:

THE LOVE-AS-JOURNEY MAPPING
The lovers correspond to travelers.
The love relationship corresponds to the vehicle.
The lovers' common goals correspond to their common destinations on the journey.
Difficulties in the relationship correspond to impediments to travel.

It is a common mistake to confuse the name of the mapping, LOVE IS A JOURNEY, for the mapping itself. The mapping is the set of correspondences. Thus, whenever I refer to a metaphor by a mnemonic like LOVE IS A JOURNEY, I will be referring to such a set of correspondences.

If mappings are confused with names of mappings, another misunderstanding can arise. Names of mappings commonly have a propositional form, for example, LOVE IS A JOURNEY. But the mappings themselves are not propositions. If mappings are confused with names for mappings, one might mistakenly think that, in this theory, metaphors are propositional. They are anything but that: metaphors are mappings, that is, sets of conceptual correspondences.

The LOVE-AS-JOURNEY mapping is a set of ontological correspondences that characterize epistemic correspondences by mapping knowledge about journeys onto knowledge about love. Such correspondences permit us to reason about love using the knowledge we use to reason about journeys. Let us take an example. Consider the expression, "we're stuck," said by one lover to another about their relationship. How is this expression about travel to be understood as being about their relationship?

"We're stuck" can be used of travel, and when it is, it evokes knowledge about travel. The exact knowledge may vary from person to person, but here is a typical example of the kind of knowledge evoked. The capitalized expressions represent entities in the ontology of travel, that is, in the source domain of the LOVE-IS-A-JOURNEY mapping given above.

Two TRAVELERS are in a VEHICLE, TRAVELING WITH COMMON DESTINATIONS. The VEHI-
CLE encounters some IMPEDIMENT and gets stuck, that is, becomes nonfunctional. If
the travelers do nothing, they will not REACH THEIR DESTINATIONS. There are a
limited number of alternatives for action:
> They can try to get the vehicle moving again, either by fixing it or getting it past
> the IMPEDIMENT that stopped it.
> They can remain in the nonfunctional VEHICLE and give up on REACHING THEIR
> DESTINATIONS.
> They can abandon the VEHICLE.
The alternative of remaining in the nonfunctional VEHICLE takes the least effort, but
does not satisfy the desire to REACH THEIR DESTINATIONS.

The ontological correspondences that constitute the LOVE IS A JOURNEY
metaphor map the ontology of travel onto the ontology of love. In doing
so, they map this scenario about travel onto a corresponding love scenario
in which the corresponding alternatives for action are seen. Here is the
corresponding love scenario that results from applying the correspondences to this knowledge structure. The target domain entities that are
mapped by the correspondences are capitalized:

Two LOVERS are in a LOVE RELATIONSHIP, PURSUING COMMON LIFE GOALS. The RELA-
TIONSHIP encounters some DIFFICULTY, which makes it nonfunctional. If they do
nothing, they will not be able to ACHIEVE THEIR LIFE GOALS. There are a limited
number of alternatives for action:
> They can try to get it moving again, either by fixing it or getting it past the
> DIFFICULTY.
> They can remain in the nonfunctional RELATIONSHIP, and give up on ACHIEVING
> THEIR LIFE GOALS.
> They can abandon the RELATIONSHIP.
The alternative of remaining in the nonfunctional RELATIONSHIP takes the least
effort, but does not satisfy the desire to ACHIEVE LIFE GOALS.

This is an example of an inference pattern that is mapped from one domain
to another. It is via such mappings that we apply knowledge about travel to
love relationships.

Metaphors are not mere words

What constitutes the LOVE AS JOURNEY metaphor is not any particular
word or expression. It is the ontological mapping across conceptual domains, from the source domain of journeys to the target domain of love.
The metaphor is not just a matter of language, but of thought and reason.
The language is secondary. The mapping is primary, in that it sanctions
the use of source domain language and inference patterns for target domain concepts. The mapping is conventional, that is, it is a fixed part of
our conceptual system, one of our conventional ways of conceptualizing
love relationships.

This view of metaphor is thoroughly at odds with the view that metaphors are just linguistic expressions. If metaphors were merely linguistic expressions, we would expect different linguistic expressions to be different metaphors. Thus, "We've hit a dead-end street" would constitute one metaphor. "We can't turn back now" would constitute another, entirely different metaphor. "Their marriage is on the rocks" would involve still a different metaphor. And so on for dozens of examples. Yet we don't seem to have dozens of different metaphors here. We have one metaphor, in which love is conceptualized as a journey. The mapping tells us precisely how love is being conceptualized as a journey. And this unified way of *conceptualizing* love metaphorically is realized in many different *linguistic* expressions.

It should be noted that contemporary metaphor theorists commonly use the term "metaphor" to refer to the conceptual mapping, and the term "metaphorical expression" to refer to an individual linguistic expression (like *dead-end street*) that is sanctioned by a mapping. We have adopted this terminology for the following reason: Metaphor, as a phenomenon, involves both conceptual mappings and individual linguistic expressions. It is important to keep them distinct. Since it is the mappings that are primary and that state the generalizations that are our principal concern, we have reserved the term "metaphor" for the mappings, rather than for the linguistic expressions.

In the literature of the field, small capitals like LOVE IS A JOURNEY are used as mnemonics to name mappings. Thus, when we refer to the LOVE IS A JOURNEY metaphor, we are referring to the set of correspondences discussed above. The English sentence "love is a journey," on the other hand, is a metaphorical expression that is understood via that set of correspondences.

Generalizations

The LOVE IS A JOURNEY metaphor is a conceptual mapping that characterizes a generalization of two kinds:

Polysemy generalization: a generalization over related senses of linguistic expressions, for example, *dead-end street, crossroads, stuck, spinning one's wheels, not going anywhere,* and so on.

Inferential generalization: a generalization over inferences across different conceptual domains.

That is, the existence of the mapping provides a general answer to two questions:

Why are words for travel used to describe love relationships?

Why are inference patterns used to reason about travel also used to reason about love relationships?

Correspondingly, from the perspective of the linguistic analyst, the existence of such cross-domain pairings of words and of inference patterns provides evidence for the existence of such mappings.

Novel extensions of conventional metaphors

The fact that the LOVE-IS-A-JOURNEY mapping is a fixed part of our conceptual system explains why new and imaginative uses of the mapping can be understood instantly, given the ontological correspondences and other knowledge about journeys. Take the song lyric, "We're driving in the fast lane on the freeway of love." The traveling knowledge called upon is this: when you drive in the fast lane, you go a long way in a short time and it can be exciting and dangerous. The general metaphorical mapping maps this knowledge about driving into knowledge about love relationships. The danger may be to the vehicle (the relationship may not last) or the passengers (the lovers may be hurt emotionally). The excitement of the love journey is sexual. Our understanding of the song lyric is a consequence of the preexisting metaphorical correspondences of the LOVE IS A JOURNEY metaphor. The song lyric is instantly comprehensible to speakers of English because those metaphorical correspondences are already part of our conceptual system.

The LOVE IS A JOURNEY metaphor and Reddy's Conduit Metaphor were the two examples that first convinced me that metaphor was not a figure of speech, but a mode of thought, defined by a systematic mapping from a source to a target domain. What convinced me were the three characteristics of metaphor that I have just discussed:

1. The systematicity in the linguistic correspondences.
2. The use of metaphor to govern reasoning and behavior based on that reasoning.
3. The possibility for understanding novel extensions in terms of the conventional correspondences.

Motivation

Each conventional metaphor, that is, each mapping, is a fixed pattern of conceptual correspondence across conceptual domains. As such, each mapping defines an open-ended class of potential correspondences across inference patterns. When activated, a mapping may apply to a novel source domain knowledge structure and characterize a corresponding target domain knowledge structure.

Mappings should not be thought of as processes, or as algorithms that mechanically take source domain inputs and produce target domain outputs. Each mapping should be seen instead as a fixed pattern of ontological correspondences across domains that may, or may not, be applied to a source domain knowledge structure or a source domain lexical item. Thus, lexical items that are conventional in the source domain are not always conventional in the target domain. Instead, each source domain lexical item may or may not make use of the static mapping pattern. If it does, it has an extended lexicalized sense in the target domain, where that sense is characterized by the mapping. If not, the source domain lexical item will not have a conventional sense in the target domain, but may still be actively mapped in the case of novel metaphor. Thus, the words *freeway* and *fast lane* are not conventionally used of love, but the knowledge structures associated with them are mapped by the LOVE IS A JOURNEY metaphor in the case of "We're driving in the fast lane on the freeway of love."

Imageable idioms

Many of the metaphorical expressions discussed in the literature on conventional metaphor are idioms. On classical views, idioms have arbitrary meanings, but within cognitive linguistics, the possibility exists that they are not arbitrary, but rather motivated. That is, they do not arise automatically by productive rules, but they fit one or more patterns present in the conceptual system. Let us look a little more closely at idioms.

An idiom like "spinning one's wheels" comes with a conventional mental image, that of the wheels of a car stuck in some substance – mud, sand, snow, or on ice – so that the car cannot move when the motor is engaged and the wheels turn. Part of our knowledge about that image is that a lot of energy is being used up (in spinning the wheels) without any progress being made, that the situation will not readily change of its own accord, that it will take a lot of effort on the part of the occupants to get the vehicle moving again – and that may not even be possible.

The LOVE IS A JOURNEY metaphor applies to this knowledge about the image. It maps this knowledge onto knowledge about love relationships: a lot of energy is being spent without any progress toward fulfilling common goals, the situation will not change of its own accord, it will take a lot of effort on the part of the lovers to make more progress, and so on. In short, when idioms have associated conventional images, it is common for an independently motivated conceptual metaphor to map that knowledge from the source to the target domain. For a survey of experiments verifying the existence of such images and such mappings, see Gibbs (1990a; 1990b).

Mappings are at the superordinate level

In the LOVE-IS-A-JOURNEY mapping, a love relationship corresponds to a vehicle. A vehicle is a superordinate category that includes such basic level categories as car, train, boat, and plane. The examples of vehicles are typically drawn from this range of basic level categories: car (*long bumpy road, spinning our wheels*), train (*off the track*), boat (*on the rocks, founder-*

ing), plane (*just taking off, bailing out*). This is not an accident: in general, we have found that mappings are at the superordinate rather than the basic level. Thus, we do not find fully general submappings like A LOVE RELATION-SHIP IS A CAR; when we find a love relationship conceptualized as a car, we also tend to find it conceptualized as a boat, a train, a plane, and so forth. It is the superordinate category VEHICLE not the basic level category CAR that is in the general mapping.

It should be no surprise that the generalization is at the superordinate level, while the special cases are at the basic level. After all, the basic level is the level of rich mental images and rich knowledge structure. (For a discussion of the properties of basic level categories, see Lakoff, 1987, pp. 31–50.) A mapping at the superordinate level maximizes the possibilities for mapping rich conceptual structures in the source domain onto the target domain, since it permits many basic level instances, each of which is information rich.

Thus, a prediction is made about conventional mappings: the categories mapped will tend to be at the superordinate rather than the basic level. One tends not to find mappings like A LOVE RELATIONSHIP IS A CAR or A LOVE RELATIONSHIP IS A BOAT. Instead, one tends to find both basic level cases (e.g., both cars and boats), which indicates that the generalization is one level higher, at the superordinate level of the vehicle. In the hundreds of cases of conventional mappings studied so far, this prediction has been borne out: it is superordinate categories that are used in mappings.

Basic semantic concepts that are metaphorical

Most people are not too surprised to discover that emotional concepts like love and anger are understood metaphorically. What is more interesting, and I think more exciting, is the realization that many of the most basic concepts in our conceptual systems are also normally comprehended via metaphor – concepts like time, quantity, state, change, action, cause, purpose, means, modality, and even the concept of a category. These are concepts that enter normally into the grammars of languages, and if they are indeed metaphorical in nature, then metaphor becomes central to grammar.

I would like to suggest that the same kinds of considerations that lead to our acceptance of the LOVE IS A JOURNEY metaphor lead inevitably to the conclusion that such basic concepts are often, and perhaps always, understood via metaphor.

Categories

Classical categories are understood metaphorically in terms of bounded regions, or "containers." Thus, something can be *in* or *out* of a category, it can be *put into* a category or *removed from* a category. The logic of classical categories is the logic of containers (see Figure 11.1).

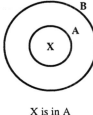

X is in A
A is in B
∴ X is in B

Figure 11.1

If X is in container A and container A is in container B, then X is in container B.

This is true not by virtue of any logical deduction, but by virtue of the topological properties of containers. Under the CLASSICAL CATEGORIES ARE CONTAINERS metaphor, the logical properties of categories are inherited from the logical properties of containers. One of the principal logical properties of classical categories is that the classical syllogism holds for them. The classical syllogism,

Socrates is a man.
All men are mortal.
Therefore, Socrates is mortal.

is of the form:

If X is in category A and category A is in category B, then X is in category B.

Thus, the logical properties of classical categories can be seen as following from the topological properties of containers plus the metaphorical mapping from containers to categories. As long as the topological properties of containers are preserved by the mapping, this result will be true.

In other words, there is a generalization to be stated here. The language of containers applies to classical categories and the logic of containers is true of classical categories. A single metaphorical mapping ought to characterize both the linguistic and logical generalizations at once. This can be done provided that the topological properties of containers are preserved in the mapping.

The joint linguistic-and-inferential relation between containers and classical categories is not an isolated case. Let us take another example.

Quantity and linear scales

The concept of quantities involves at least two metaphors. The first is the well-known MORE IS UP, LESS IS DOWN metaphor as shown by a myriad of

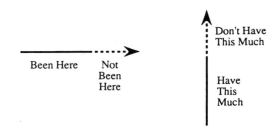

Figure 11.2

expressions like *prices rose, stocks skyrocketed, the market plummeted,* and so on. A second is that LINEAR SCALES ARE PATHS. We can see this in expressions like:

John is *far* more intelligent than Bill.
John's intelligence *goes way beyond* Bill's.
John is *way ahead of* Bill in intelligence.

The metaphor maps the starting point of the path onto the bottom of the scale and maps distance traveled onto quantity in general.

What is particularly interesting is that the logic of paths maps onto the logic of linear scale (see Figure 11.2).

Path inference: if you are going from A to C, and you are now at an intermediate point B, then you have been at all points between A and B and not at any points between B and C.

Example: If you are going from San Francisco to New York along Route 80, and you are now at Chicago, then you have been to Denver but not to Pittsburgh.

Linear scale inference: if you have exactly $50 in your bank account, then you have $40, $30, and so on, but not $60, $70, or any larger amount.

The form of these inferences is the same. The path inference is a consequence of the cognitive topology of paths. It will be true of any path image-schema. Again, there is a linguistic-and-inferential generalization to be stated. It would be stated by the metaphor LINEAR SCALES ARE PATHS, provided that metaphors in general preserve the cognitive topology (that is, the image-schematic structure) of the source domain.

Looking at the inferential structure alone, one might suggest a non-metaphorical alternative in which both linear scales and paths are instances of a more general abstract schema. But when *both* the inferential and lexical data are considered, it becomes clear that a metaphorical solution is required. An expression like "ahead of" is from the spatial domain, not the linear scale domain: "ahead" in its core sense is defined with respect to one's head – it refers to the direction in which one is facing. To say that there is no metaphorical mapping from paths to scales is to say that "ahead of" is not fundamentally spatial and characterized with respect to heads; it is to claim rather that "ahead" is very abstract, neutral between space and linear scales, and has nothing to do with heads. This would be a bizarre analysis. Similarly, for sentences like "John's intelligence goes beyond Bill's," the nonmetaphorical analysis would claim that "go" is not fundamentally a verb of motion at all, but is somehow neutral between motion and a linear relation. This would also be bizarre. In short, if one grants that "ahead of" and "go" are fundamentally spatial, then the fact that they can also be used of linear scales suggests a metaphor solution. There could be no such neutral sense of "go" for these cases, since "go beyond" in the spatial sense involves motion, while in the linear scale sense, there is no motion or change, but just a point on a scale. Here the neutral case solution is not even available.

The Invariance Principle

In the examples we have just considered, the image-schemas characterizing the source domains (containers, paths) are mapped onto the target domains (categories, linear scales). This observation leads to the following hypothesis, called "The Invariance Principle":

Metaphorical mappings preserve the cognitive topology (that is, the image-schema structure) of the source domain, in a way consistent with the inherent structure of the target domain.

What the Invariance Principle does is guarantee that, for container-schemas, interiors will be mapped onto interiors, exteriors onto exteriors, and boundaries onto boundaries; for path-schemas, sources will be mapped onto sources, goals onto goals, trajectories onto trajectories, and so on.

To understand the Invariance Principle properly, it is important not to think of mappings as algorithmic processes that "start" with source domain structure and wind up with target domain structure. Such a mistaken understanding of mappings would lead to a mistaken understanding of the Invariance Principle, namely, that one first picks all the image-schematic structure of the source domain, then one copies it onto the target domain unless the target domain interferes.

One should instead think of the Invariance Principle in terms of constraints on fixed correspondences: if one looks at the existing correspondences, one will see that the Invariance Principle holds: source domain interiors correspond to target domain interiors; source domain exteriors correspond to target domain exteriors, and so forth. As a consequence it will turn out that the image-schematic structure of the target domain cannot be violated: One cannot find cases where a source domain interior is mapped onto a target domain exterior, or where a source domain exterior is mapped onto a target domain path. This simply does not happen.

Target domain overrides

A corollary of the Invariance Principle is that image-schema structure inherent in the target domain cannot be violated, and that inherent target domain structure limits the possibilities for mappings automatically. This general principle explains a large number of previously mysterious limitations on metaphorical mappings. For example, it explains why you can give someone a kick, even if that person doesn't have it afterward, and why you can give someone information, even if you don't lose it. This is a consequence of the fact that inherent target domain structure automatically limits what can be mapped. For example, consider that part of your inherent knowledge of actions that says that actions do not continue to exist after they occur. Now consider the ACTIONS ARE TRANSFERS metaphor, in which actions are conceptualized as objects transferred from an agent to a patient, as when one gives someone a kick or a punch. We know (as part of target domain knowledge) that an action does not exist after it occurs. In the source domain, where there is a giving, the recipient possesses the object given after the giving. But this cannot be mapped onto the target domain since the inherent structure of the target domain says that no such object exists after the action is over. The target domain override in the Invariance Principle explains why you can give someone a kick without his having it afterward.

Abstract inferences as metaphorical spatial inferences

Spatial inferences are characterized by the topological structure of image-schemas. We have seen cases such as CATEGORIES ARE CONTAINERS and LINEAR SCALES ARE PATHS where image-schema structure is preserved by metaphor and where abstract inferences about categories and linear scales are metaphorical versions of spatial inferences about containers and paths. The Invariance Principle hypothesizes that image-schema structure is always preserved by metaphor.

The Invariance Principle raises the possibility that a great many, if not all, abstract inferences are actually metaphorical versions of spatial inferences that are inherent in the topological structure of image-schemas. I will now turn to other cases of basic, but abstract, concepts to see what evidence there is for the claim that such concepts are fundamentally characterized by metaphor.

Time

It has often been noted that time in English is conceptualized in terms of space. The details are rather interesting.

Ontology: Time is understood in terms of things (that is, entities and locations) and motion.

Background condition: The present time is at the same location as a canonical observer.

Mapping:

Times are things.

The passing of time is motion.

Future times are in front of the observer; past times are behind the observer.

One thing is moving, the other is stationary; the stationary entity is the deictic center.

Entailment:

Since motion is continuous and one-dimensional, the passage of time is continuous and one-dimensional.

Special case 1:

The observer is fixed; times are entities moving with respect to the observer.

Times are oriented with their fronts in their direction of motion.

Entailments:

If time 2 follows time 1, then time 2 is in the future relative to time 1.

The time passing the observer is the present time.

Time has a velocity relative to the observer.

Special case 2:

Times are fixed locations; the observer is moving with respect to time.

Entailment:

Time has extension, and can be measured.

An extended time, like a spatial area, may be conceived of as a bounded region.

This metaphor, TIME PASSING IS MOTION, with its two special cases, embodies a generalization that accounts for a wide range of cases where a spatial expression can also be used for time. Special case 1, TIME PASSING IS MOTION OF AN OBJECT, accounts for both the linguistic form and the semantic entailments of expressions like:

The time will come when . . . The time has long since gone when . . . The time for action has arrived. That time is here. In the weeks following next Tuesday . . . On the preceding day . . . I'm looking ahead to Christmas. Thanksgiving is coming up on us. Let's put all that behind us. I can't face the future. Time is flying by. The time has passed when . . .

Thus, special case 1 characterizes the general principle behind the temporal use of words like *come, go, here, follow, precede, ahead, behind, fly, pass,* accounting not only for why they are used for both space and time, but why they mean what they mean.

Special case 2, TIME PASSING IS MOTION OVER A LANDSCAPE, accounts for a different range of cases, expressions like:

There's going to be trouble down the road. He stayed there for ten years. He stayed there a long time. His stay in Russia extended over many years. He passed the time happily. He arrived on time. We're coming up on Christmas. We're getting close to Christmas. He'll have his degree within two years. I'll be there in a minute.

Special case 2 maps location expressions like *down the road, for* + location, *long, over, come, close to, within, in, pass,* onto corresponding temporal expressions with their corresponding meanings. Again, special case 2 states a general principle relating spatial terms and inference patterns to temporal terms and inference patterns.

The details of the two special cases are rather different; indeed, they are inconsistent with one another. The existence of such special cases has an especially interesting theoretical consequence: words mapped by both special cases will have inconsistent readings. Take, for example, the *come* of *Christmas is coming* (special case 1) and *We're coming up on Christmas* (special case 2). Both instances of *come* are temporal, but one takes a moving time as first argument and the other takes a moving observer as first argument. The same is true of *pass* in *The time has passed* (special case 1) and in *He passed the time* (special case 2).

These differences in the details of the mappings show that one cannot just say blithely that spatial expressions can be used to speak of time, without specifying details, as though there were only one correspondence between time and space. When we are explicit about stating the mappings, we discover that there are two different – and inconsistent – subcases.

The fact that time is understood metaphorically in terms of motion, entities, and locations accords with our biological knowledge. In our visual systems, we have detectors for motion and detectors for objects/locations. We do not have detectors for time (whatever that could mean). Thus, it makes good biological sense that time should be understood in terms of things and motion.

Duality

The two special cases (location and object) of the TIME PASSING IS MOTION metaphor are not merely an accidental feature of our understanding of time. As we shall see below, there are other metaphors that come in such location/object pairs. Such pairs are called "duals," and the general phenomenon in which metaphors come in location/object pairs is referred to as "duality."

Simultaneous mappings

It is important to recall that metaphorical mappings are fixed correspondences that can be activated, rather than algorithmic processes that take inputs and give outputs. Thus, it is *not* the case that sentences containing conventional metaphors are the products of a real-time process of conversion from literal to metaphorical readings. A sentence like *The time for action has arrived* is not understood by first trying to give a literal reading to *arrive,* and then, on failing, trying to give it a temporal reading. Instead, the metaphor TIME PASSING IS MOTION is a fixed structure of existing correspondences between the space and time domains, and *arrive* has a conventional extended meaning that makes use of that fixed structure of correspondences.

Thus, it is possible for two different parts of a sentence to make use of two distinct metaphorical mappings at once. Consider a phrase like, *within the coming weeks.* Here, *within* makes uses of the metaphor of time as a stationary landscape which has extension and bounded regions, whereas *coming* makes use of the metaphor of times as moving objects. This is possible because the two metaphors for time pick out different aspects of the target domain. *The coming weeks* conceptualizes those weeks as a whole, in motion relative to the observer. *Within* looks inside that whole, conceptualizing it as a bounded region with an interior. Each mapping is used partially. Thus, although the mappings – as wholes – are inconsistent, there are cases where parts of the mappings may be consistently superimposed. The Invariance Principle allows such parts of the mappings to be picked out and used to characterize reasoning about different aspects of the target domain.

Simultaneous mappings are very common in poetry. Take, for example, the Dylan Thomas line "Do not go gentle into that good night." Here "go" reflects DEATH IS DEPARTURE, "gentle" reflects LIFE IS A STRUGGLE, with death as defeat. "Night" reflects A LIFETIME IS A DAY, with death as night. This one line has three different metaphors for death, each mapped onto different parts of the sentence. This is possible since mappings are fixed correspondences.

There is an important lesson to be learned from this example. In mathematics, mappings are static correspondences. In computer science, it is common to represent mathematical mappings by algorithmic processes that take place in real time. Researchers in information processing psychology and cognitive science also commonly represent mappings as real-time algorithmic procedures. Some researchers from these fields have mistakenly supposed that the metaphorical mappings we are discussing should also be represented as real-time, sequential algorithmic procedures, where the input to each metaphor is a literal meaning. Any attempt to do this will fail for the simultaneous mapping cases just discussed.

Event structure

I now want to turn to some research by myself and some of my students (especially Sharon Fischler, Karin Myhre, and Jane Espenson) on the metaphorical understanding of event structure in English. What we have found is that various aspects of event structure, including notions like states, changes, processes, actions, causes, purposes, and means, are characterized cognitively via metaphor in terms of space, motion, and force.

The general mapping we have found goes as follows:

The event structure metaphor

States are locations (bounded regions in space).
Changes are movements (into or out of bounded regions).
Causes are forces.
Actions are self-propelled movements.
Purposes are destinations.
Means are paths (to destinations).
Difficulties are impediments to motion.
Expected progress is a travel schedule; a schedule is a virtual traveler, who reaches prearranged destinations at prearranged times.
External events are large, moving objects.
Long term, purposeful activities are journeys.

This mapping generalizes over an extremely wide range of expressions for one or more aspects of event structure. For example, take states and changes. We speak of being *in* or *out* of a state, of *going into* or *out of* it, of *entering* or *leaving* it, of getting *to* a state or emerging *from* it.

This is a rich and complex metaphor whose parts interact in complex ways. To get an idea of how it works, consider the submapping "Difficulties are impediments to motion." In the metaphor, purposive action is self-propelled motion toward a destination. A difficulty is something that impedes motion to such a destination. Metaphorical difficulties of this sort come in five types: blockages; features of the terrain; burdens; counterforces; lack of an energy source. Here are examples of each:

Blockages:
He got over his divorce. He's trying to get around the regulations. He went through the trial. We ran into a brick wall. We've got him boxed into a corner.

Features of the terrain:
He's between a rock and a hard place. It's been uphill all the way. We've been bogged down. We've been hacking our way through a jungle of regulations.

Burdens:
He's carrying quite a load. He's weighed down by a lot of assignments. He's been trying to shoulder all the responsibility. Get off my back!

Counterforces:
Quit pushing me around. She's leading him around by the nose. She's holding him back.

Lack of an energy source:
I'm out of gas. We're running out of steam.

To see just how rich the event structure metaphor is, consider some of its basic entailments:

Manner of action is manner of motion.

A different means for achieving a purpose is a different path.

Forces affecting action are forces affecting motion.

The inability to act is the inability to move.

Progress made is distance traveled or distance from goal.

We will consider examples of each of these one by one, including a number of special cases.

Aids to action are aids to motion:

> It is smooth sailing from here on in. It's all downhill from here. There's nothing in our way.

A different means of achieving a result is a different path:

> Do it this way. She did it the other way. Do it any way you can. However you want to go about it is fine with me.

Manner of action is manner of motion:

> We are moving/running/skipping right along. We slogged through it. He is flailing around. He is falling all over himself. We are leaping over hurdles. He is out of step. He is in step.

Careful action is careful motion:

> I'm walking on eggshells. He is treading on thin ice. He is walking a fine line.

Speed of action is speed of movement:

> He flew through his work. He is running around. It is going swimmingly. Keep things moving at a good clip. Things have slowed to a crawl. She is going by leaps and bounds. I am moving at a snail's pace.

Purposeful action is self-propelled motion to a destination; this has the following special cases:

Making progress is forward movement:

> We are moving ahead. Let's forge ahead. Let's keep moving forward. We made lots of forward movement.

Amount of progress is distance moved:

> We've come a long way. We've covered lots of ground. We've made it this far.

Undoing progress is backward movement:

> We are sliding backward. We are backsliding. We need to backtrack. It is time to turn around and retrace our steps.

Expected progress is a travel schedule; a schedule is a virtual traveler, who reaches prearranged destinations at prearranged times:

> We're behind schedule on the project. We got a head start on the project. I'm trying to catch up. I finally got a little ahead.

Starting an action is starting out on a path:

> We are just starting out. We have taken the first step.

Success is reaching the end of the path:

> We've reached the end. We are seeing the light at the end of the tunnel. We only have a short way to go. The end is in sight. The end is a long way off.

Lack of purpose is lack of direction:

> He is just floating around. He is drifting aimlessly. He needs some direction.

Lack of progress is lack of movement:

> We are at a standstill. We aren't getting any place. We aren't going anywhere. We are going nowhere with this.

External events are large moving objects:

Special case 1: Things

> How're things going? Things are going fine with me. Things are going against me these days. Things took a turn for the worse. Things are going my way.

Special case 2: Fluids

> You gotta go with the flow. I'm just trying to keep my head above water. The tide of events . . . The winds of change. . . . The flow of history . . . I'm trying to get my bearings. He's up a creek without a paddle. We're all in the same boat.

Special case 3: Horses

> Try to keep a tight rein on the situation. Keep a grip on the situation. Don't let things get out of hand. Wild horses couldn't make me go. "Whoa!" (said when things start to get out of hand).

Such examples provide overwhelming empirical support for the existence of the event structure metaphor. And the existence of that metaphor shows that the most common abstract concepts – TIME, STATE, CHANGE, CAUSATION, ACTION, PURPOSE and MEANS – are conceptualized via metaphor. Since such concepts are at the very center of our conceptual systems, the fact that they are conceptualized metaphorically shows that metaphor is central to ordinary abstract thought.

Inheritance hierarchies

Metaphorical mappings do not occur isolated from one another. They are sometimes organized in hierarchical structures, in which "lower" mappings in the hierarchy inherit the structures of the "higher" mappings. Let us consider an example of a hierarchy with three levels:

Level 1: The event structure metaphor

Level 2: A PURPOSEFUL LIFE IS A JOURNEY

Level 3: LOVE IS A JOURNEY; A CAREER IS A JOURNEY

To refresh your memory, recall:

The event structure metaphor

Target domain: Events   Source domain: Space

States are locations (bounded regions in space).

Changes are movements (into or out of bounded regions).
Causes are forces.
Actions are self-propelled movements.
Purposes are destinations.
Means are paths to destinations.
Difficulties are impediments to motion.
Expected progress is a travel schedule; a schedule is a virtual traveler,
    who reaches prearranged destinations at prearranged times.
External events are large, moving objects.
Long-term, purposeful activities are journeys.

In our culture, life is assumed to be purposeful, that is, we are expected
to have goals in life. In the event structure metaphor, purposes are destinations and purposeful action is self-propelled motion toward a destination.
A purposeful life is a long-term, purposeful activity, and hence a journey.
Goals in life are destinations on the journey. The actions one takes in life
are self-propelled movements, and the totality of one's actions form a path
one moves along. Choosing a means to achieve a goal is choosing a path to
a destination. Difficulties in life are impediments to motion. External
events are large moving objects that can impede motion toward one's life
goals. One's expected progress through life is charted in terms of a life
schedule, which is conceptualized as a virtual traveler that one is expected
to keep up with.

In short, the metaphor A PURPOSEFUL LIFE IS A JOURNEY makes use of all
the structure of the event structure metaphor, since events in a life conceptualized as purposeful are subcases of events in general.

A PURPOSEFUL LIFE IS A JOURNEY
Target domain: Life   Source domain: Space
    The person leading a life is a traveler.
Inherits event structure metaphor, with:
    Events = significant life events
    Purposes = life goals
Thus we have expressions like:

He got a head start in life. He's without direction in his life. I'm where I want to be
in life. I'm at a crossroads in my life. He'll go places in life. He's never let anyone
get in his way. He's gone through a lot in life.

Just as significant life events are special cases of events, so events in a
love relationship are special cases of life events. Thus, the LOVE IS A
JOURNEY metaphor inherits the structure of the LIFE IS A JOURNEY metaphor. What is special about the LOVE IS A JOURNEY metaphor is that there
are two lovers who are travelers and that the love relationship is a vehicle.
The rest of the mapping is a consequence of inheriting the LIFE IS A
JOURNEY metaphor. Because the lovers are in the same vehicle, they have
common destinations, that is, common life goals. Relationship difficulties
are impediments to travel.

LOVE IS A JOURNEY
Target domain: Love   Source domain: Space
   The lovers are travelers.
   The love relationship is a vehicle.
Inherits the LIFE IS A JOURNEY metaphor.

A career is another aspect of life that can be conceptualized as a journey. Here, because STATUS IS UP, a career is actually a journey upward. Career goals are special cases of life goals.

A CAREER IS A JOURNEY
Target domain: Career   Source domain: Space
   A careerist is a traveler.
   Status is up.
Inherits LIFE IS A JOURNEY, with life goals = career goals. Ideal: to go as high, far, and fast as possible.
Examples include:

He clawed his way to the top. He's over the hill. She's on the fast track. He's climbing the corporate ladder. She's moving up in the ranks quickly.

This inheritance hierarchy accounts for a range of generalizations. First, there are generalizations about lexical items. Take the word *crossroads*. Its central meaning is in the domain of space, but it can be used in a metaphorical sense to speak of any extended activity, of one's life, of a love relationship, or of a career.

I'm at a crossroads on this project. I'm at a crossroads in life. We're at a crossroads in our relationship. I'm at a crossroads in my career.

The hierarchy allows one to state a general principle: *crossroads* is extended lexically via the submetaphor of the event structure metaphor that LONG-TERM PURPOSEFUL ACTIVITIES ARE JOURNEYS. All its other uses are automatically generated via the inheritance hierarchy. Thus, separate senses for each level of the hierarchy are not needed.

The second generalization is inferential in character. Thus the understanding of difficulties as impediments to travel occurs not only in events in general, but also in a purposeful life, in a love relationship, and in a career. The inheritance hierarchy guarantees that this understanding of difficulties in life, love, and careers is a consequence of such an understanding of difficulties in events in general.

The hierarchy also allows us to characterize lexical items whose meanings are more restricted: Thus, *climbing the ladder* refers only to careers, not to love relationships or to life in general.

Such hierarchical organization is a very prominent feature of the metaphor system of English and other languages. So far we have found that the metaphors higher up in the hierarchy tend to be more widespread than those mappings at lower levels. Thus, the event structure metaphor is very widespread (and may even be universal), while the metaphors for life, love, and careers are much more restricted culturally.

Duality in the event structure system

In our discussion of time metaphors, we noted the existence of an object/ location duality. There were two related time metaphors. In both, the passage of time was understood in terms of relative motion between an observer and a time. In the object-dual, the observer is fixed and times are moving objects. In the location-dual, the opposite is true. The observer moves and times are fixed locations in a landscape.

The event structure system that we have seen so far is based wholly on location. But there is another event structure system that is the dual of the one we have just discussed – a system based on objects rather than locations. In both systems, CHANGE IS MOTION and CAUSES ARE FORCES that control motion. The difference is this:

In the location system, change is the motion of the thing-changing to a new location or from an old one.

In the object system, the thing-changing doesn't necessarily move. Change is instead the motion of an object to, or away from, the thing-changing.

In addition, the object in motion is conceptualized as a possession and the thing-changing as a possessor. Change is thus seen as the acquisition or loss of an object. Causation is seen as giving or taking. Here are some examples:

I have a headache. (The headache is a possession)

I got a headache. (Change is acquisition – motion to)

My headache went away. (Change is loss – motion from)

The noise gave me a headache. (Causation is giving – motion to)

The aspirin took away my headache. (Causation is taking – motion from)

We can see the duality somewhat more clearly with a word like "trouble":

I'm in trouble. (Trouble is a location)

I have trouble. (Trouble is an object that is possessed)

In both cases, trouble is being attributed to me, and in both cases, trouble is metaphorically conceptualized as being in the same place as me (co-location) – in one case, because I possess the trouble-object and in the other case, because I am in the trouble-location. That is, attribution in both cases is conceptualized metaphorically as co-location. In "I'm in trouble," trouble is a state. A state is an attribute conceptualized as a location. Attributes (or properties) are like states, except that they are conceptualized as possessible objects.

Thus, STATES ARE LOCATIONS and ATTRIBUTES ARE POSSESSIONS are duals, since possession and location are special cases of the same thing – co-location – and since states and attributes are also special cases of the same thing – what can be attributed to someone.

Given this, we can see that there is an object-version of the event structure metaphor:

Attributes are possessions.

Changes are movements (of possessions, namely, acquisitions or losses).

Causes are forces (controlling the movement of possessions, namely, giving or taking away).

These are the duals of:

States are locations.

Changes are movements (to or from locations).

Causes are forces (controlling movement to or from locations).

Similarly, ACTIONS ARE SELF-PROPELLED MOVEMENTS (to or from locations) has as its object-dual ACTIONS ARE SELF-CONTROLLED ACQUISITIONS OR LOSSES. Thus, there is a reason why one can "take" certain actions – one can take a shower, or take a shot at someone, or take a chance.

The submapping PURPOSES ARE DESTINATIONS also has a dual. Destinations are desired locations and so the submapping can be rephrased as PURPOSES ARE DESIRED LOCATIONS, and ACHIEVING A PURPOSE IS REACHING A DESIRED LOCATION. Replacing "location" by "object," we get the dual PURPOSES ARE DESIRED OBJECTS, and ACHIEVING A PURPOSE IS ACQUIRING A DESIRED OBJECT (or ridding oneself of an undesirable one).

Here are some examples:

ACHIEVING A PURPOSE IS ACQUIRING A DESIRED OBJECT
They just handed him the job. It's within my grasp. It eluded me. Go for it. It escaped me. It slipped through my hands. He is pursuing a goal. Reach for/grab all the gusto you can get. Latch onto a good job. Seize the opportunity. He found success.

There is also a hierarchical structure in the object-version of the event structure metaphor. A special case of getting an object is getting an object to eat. Hence:

ACHIEVING A PURPOSE IS GETTING SOMETHING TO EAT
He savored the victory. All the good jobs have been gobbled up. He's hungry for success. The opportunity has me drooling. This is a mouth-watering opportunity.

Traditional methods of getting things to eat are hunting, fishing, and agriculture. Each of these special cases can be used metaphorically to conceptualize achieving (or attempting to achieve) a purpose.

TRYING TO ACHIEVE A PURPOSE IS HUNTING
I'm hunting for a job. I bagged a promotion. The pennant is in the bag.

The typical way to hunt is to use projectiles (bullets, arrows, etc.)

I'm shooting for a promotion. I'm aiming for a career in the movies. I'm afraid I missed my chance.

TRYING TO ACHIEVE A PURPOSE IS FISHING
He's fishing for compliments. I landed a promotion. She netted a good job. I've got a line out on a good used car. It's time to fish or cut bait.

TRYING TO ACHIEVE A PURPOSE IS AGRICULTURE
It's time I reaped some rewards. That job is a plum. Those are the fruits of his labor. The contract is ripe for the picking.

I will not try to survey all the dualities in the English metaphor system, but it is worth mentioning a few to see how subtle and persuasive dualities are. Take, for example, the LIFE IS A JOURNEY metaphor, in which goals in life are destinations, that is, desired locations to be reached. Since the dual of PURPOSES ARE DESTINATIONS is PURPOSES ARE DESIRED OBJECTS, the dual of LIFE IS A JOURNEY is a metaphor in which life is an activity through which one acquires desired objects. In this culture, the principal activity of this sort is business, and hence, LIFE IS A BUSINESS is the dual of LIFE IS A JOURNEY.

A PURPOSEFUL LIFE IS A BUSINESS
He has a rich life. It's an enriching experience. I want to get a lot out of life. He's going about the business of everyday life. It's time to take stock of my life.

Recall that LOVE IS A JOURNEY is an extension of A PURPOSEFUL LIFE IS A JOURNEY. It happens that LOVE IS A JOURNEY has a dual that is an extension of the dual of A PURPOSEFUL LIFE IS A JOURNEY, which is A PURPOSEFUL LIFE IS A BUSINESS. The dual of LOVE IS A JOURNEY is LOVE IS A PARTNERSHIP, that is, a two-person business. Thus, we speak of lovers as "partners," there are marriage contracts, and in a long-term love relationship the partners are expected to do their jobs and to share in both responsibilities (what they contribute to the relationship) and benefits (what they get out of it). Long-term love relationships fail under the same conditions as businesses fail – when what the partners get out of the relationship is not worth what they put into it.

Duality is a newly discovered phenomenon. The person who first discovered it in the event structure system was Jane Espenson, a graduate student at Berkeley who stumbled upon it in the course of her research on causation metaphors. Since Espenson's discovery, other extensive dualities have been found in the English metaphor system. It is not known at present, however, just how extensive dualities are in English, or even whether they are all of the location/object type.

At this point, I will leave off discussing the metaphor system of English, although hundreds of other mappings have been described to date. The major point to take away from this discussion is that metaphor resides for the most part in this huge, highly structured, fixed system, a system anything but "dead." Because it is conventional, it is used constantly and automatically, with neither effort nor awareness. Novel metaphor uses this system, and builds on it, but only rarely occurs independently of it. It is most interesting that this system of metaphor seems to give rise to abstract reasoning, which appears to be based on spatial reasoning.

Invariance again

The metaphors I have discussed primarily map three kinds of image-schemas: containers, paths, and force-images. Because of the complexity of the subcases and interactions, the details are intricate, to say the least. However, the Invariance Principle does make claims in each case as to what image-schemas get mapped onto target domains. I will not go through most of the details here, but so far as I can see, the claims made about inferential structure are reasonable ones.

For example, the logic of force-dynamics does seem to map, via the submapping CAUSES ARE FORCES, onto the logic of causation. The following are inferences from the logic of forces inherent in force dynamics:

A stationary object will move only when force is applied to it; without force, it will not move.

The application of force requires contact; thus, the applier of the force must be in spatial contiguity with the thing it moves.

The application of force temporarily precedes motion, since inertia must be overcome before motion can take place.

These are among the classic inferential conditions on causation: spatial contiguity, temporal precedence, and that A caused B only if B wouldn't have happened without A.

At this point, I would like to take up the question of what else the Invariance Principle would buy us. I will consider two cases that arose while Mark Turner and I were writing *More Than Cool Reason* (Lakoff & Turner, 1989). The first concerns image-metaphors and the second, generic-level metaphors. But before I move on to those topics, I should mention an important consequence of invariance.

Johnson and I argued in *Metaphors We Live By* (Lakoff & Johnson, 1980) that a complex propositional structure could be mapped by metaphor onto another domain. The main example we gave was ARGUMENT IS WAR. Kövecses and I, in our analysis of anger metaphors (Lakoff, 1987, case study 1; Kövecses, 1990), also argued that metaphors could map complex propositional structures. The Invariance Principle does not deny this, but it puts those claims in a very different light. Complex propositional structures involve concepts like time, states, changes, causes, purposes, quantity scales, and categories. If all these abstract concepts are characterized metaphorically, then the Invariance Principle claims that what we had called propositional structure is really image-schematic structure. In other words:

So-called propositional inferences arise from the inherent topological structure of the image-schemas mapped by metaphor onto concepts like time, states, changes, actions, causes, purposes, means, quantity, and categories.

I have taken the trouble to discuss these abstract concepts to demonstrate this consequence of the Invariance Principle: what have been seen in the past as propositional inferences are really image-based inferences. If the Invariance Principle is correct, it has a remarkable consequence:

Abstract reasoning is a special case of image-based reasoning.

Image-based reasoning is fundamental and abstract reasoning is image-based reasoning under metaphorical projections to abstract domains.

To look for independent confirmation of the Invariance Principle, let us turn to image metaphors.

Novel metaphors

Image metaphors

There are kinds of metaphors that function to map one conventional mental image onto another. These contrast with the metaphors I have discussed so far, each of which maps one conceptual domain onto another, often with many concepts in the source domain mapped onto many corresponding concepts in the target domain. Image metaphors, by contrast, are "one-shot" metaphors: they map only one image onto one other image.

Consider, for example, this poem from the Indian tradition:

> Now women-rivers
> belted with silver fish
> move unhurried as women in love
> at dawn after a night with their lovers
> (Merwin & Masson, 1981, p. 71)

Here the image of the slow, sinuous walk of an Indian woman is mapped onto the image of the slow, sinuous, shimmering flow of a river. The shimmering of a school of fish is imagined as the shimmering of the belt.

Metaphoric image mappings work in the same way as all other metaphoric mappings: by mapping the structure of one domain onto the structure of another. But here, the domains are conventional mental images. Take, for example, this line from André Breton:

> My wife . . . whose waist is an hourglass.

This is a superimposition of the image of an hourglass onto the image of a woman's waist by virtue of their common shape. As before, the metaphor is conceptual; it is not in the words themselves, but in the mental images. Here, we have a mental image of an hourglass and of a woman, and we map the middle of the hourglass onto the waist of the woman. Note that the words do not tell us which part of the hourglass to map onto the waist, or even that only part of the hourglass shape corresponds to the waist. The words are prompts for us to map from one conventional image to another. Similarly, consider:

> His toes were like the keyboard of a spinet.
> (Rabelais, "The Descriptions of King Lent," trans. J. M. Cohen)

Here, too, the words do not tell us that an individual toe corresponds to an individual key on the keyboard. The words are prompts for us to perform a conceptual mapping between conventional mental images. In particular, we map aspects of the part-whole structure of one image onto aspects of the part-whole structure of another. Just as individual keys are parts of the whole keyboard, so individual toes are parts of the whole foot.

Image mapping can involve more than mapping physical part-whole relationships. For example, the water line of a river may drop slowly and that slowness is part of a dynamic image, which may be mapped onto the slow removal of clothing:

> Slowly slowly rivers in autumn show
> sand banks
> bashful in first love woman
> showing thighs
> (Merwin & Masson, 1981, p. 69)

Other attributes are also mapped: the color of the sand bank onto the color of flesh, the quality of light on a wet sand bank onto the reflectiveness of skin, the light grazing of the water's touch receding down the bank onto the light grazing of the clothing along the skin. Notice that the words do not tell us any clothing is involved. We get that from a conventional mental image. Part-whole structure is also mapped in this example. The water covers the hidden part of the bank just as the clothing covers the hidden part of the body. The proliferation of detail in the images limits image mappings to highly specific cases. That is what makes them one-shot mappings.

Such mappings of one image onto another can lead us to map knowledge about the first image onto knowledge about the second. Consider the following example from the Navaho:

> My horse with a mane made of short rainbows.
> ("War God's Horse Song I," words by Tall Kia ahni, interpreted by Louis Watchman)

The structure of a rainbow, its band of curved lines for example, is mapped onto an arc of curved hair, and many rainbows onto many such arcs on the horse's mane. Such image mapping allows us to map our evaluation of the source domain onto the target. We know that rainbows are beautiful, special, inspiring, larger than life, almost mystic, and that seeing them makes us happy and inspires us with awe. This knowledge is mapped onto what we know of the horse: it too is awe-inspiring, beautiful, larger than life, almost mystic. This line comes from a poem containing a series of such image mappings:

> My horse with a hoof like a striped agate,
> with his fetlock like a fine eagle plume:
> my horse whose legs are like quick lightning
> whose body is an eagle-plumed arrow:
> my horse whose tail is like a trailing black cloud.

Image metaphors raise two major issues for the general theory of metaphor:

How do they work? What constrains the mappings? What kinds of internal structures do mental images have that permit some mappings to work readily, others only with effort, and others not at all?

What is the general theory of metaphor that unifies image metaphors with all the conventional metaphors that map the propositional structure of one domain onto the propositional structure of another domain?

Turner and I (Lakoff & Turner, 1989) have suggested that the Invariance Principle could be an answer to both questions. We suggest that conventional mental images are structured by image-schemas and that image metaphors preserve image-schematic structure, mapping parts onto parts and wholes onto wholes, containers onto containers, paths onto paths, and so on. The generalization would be that all metaphors are invariant with respect to their cognitive topology, that is, each metaphorical mapping preserves image-schema structure.

Generic-level metaphors

When Turner and I were writing *More Than Cool Reason,* we hypothesized the existence of what we called "generic-level metaphors" to deal with two problems we faced – first, the problem of personification and second, the problem of proverbs, which requires an understanding of analogy. I shall discuss each in turn.

Personification. In studying a wide variety of poems about death in English, we found that, in poem after poem, death was personified in a relatively small number of ways: drivers, coachmen, footmen; reapers, devourers and destroyers, or opponents in a struggle or game (say, a knight or a chess opponent). The question we asked was: why these? Why isn't death personified as a teacher or a carpenter or an ice cream salesman? Somehow, the ones that occur repeatedly seem appropriate. Why?

In studying personifications in general, we found that the overwhelming number seem to fit a single pattern: events (like death) are understood in terms of actions by some agent (like reaping). It is that agent that is personified. We thus hypothesized a very general metaphor, EVENTS ARE ACTIONS, which combines with other, independently existing metaphors for life and death. Consider, for example, the DEATH IS DEPARTURE metaphor. Departure is an event. If we understand this event as an action on the part of some causal agent – someone who brings about, or helps to bring about, departure – then we can account for figures like drivers, coachmen, footmen, and so forth. Take the PEOPLE ARE PLANTS metaphor. In the natural course of things, plants wither and die. If we see that event as a causal action on the part of some agent, that agent is a reaper. So far, so good. But why destroyers and devourers? And what about the impossible cases?

Destroying and devouring are actions in which an entity ceases to exist. The same is true of death. The overall shape of the event of death is similar in this respect to the overall shapes of the events of destroying and devouring. Moreover, there is a causal aspect to death: the passage of time will eventually result in death. Thus, the overall shape of the event of death has an entity that over time ceases to exist as the result of some cause. Devouring and destroying have the same overall event shape. That is, it is the same with respect to causal structure and the persistence of entities over time.

Turner (1987) had noticed a similar case in *Death Is the Mother of Beauty,* his classic work on kinship metaphor. In expressions like "necessity is the mother of invention," or "Edward Teller was the father of the H-bomb," causation is understood in terms of giving birth or fathering, what Turner called the CAUSATION IS PROGENERATION metaphor. But, as he observed (pp. 145–148), this metaphor could not be used for just any instance of causation. It could only be used for cases that had the overall event shape of progeneration: something must be created out of nothing, and the thing created must persist for a long time (as if it had a life).

Thus, for example, we can speak of Saussure as the father of modern synchronic linguistics, or of New Orleans as giving birth to jazz. But we cannot use this metaphor for a single causal action with a short-lived effect. We could not speak of Jose Canseco as the father of the home run he just hit, or of that home run as giving birth to the Oakland As' victory in the game. We could, however, speak of Babe Ruth as the father of modern home-run hitting, and of home runs giving birth to the era of baseball players as superstars. The overall event shape of the target domain limits the applicability of the metaphor.

Recalling Turner's observation about CAUSATION IS PROGENERATION, we therefore hypothesized that EVENTS ARE ACTIONS is constrained in the following way: the action must have the same overall event shape as the event. What is preserved across the mapping is the causal structure, the aspectual structure, and the persistence of entities. We referred to this as "generic-level structure."

The preservation of generic-level structure explained why death is not metaphorized in terms of teaching, or filling the bathtub, or sitting on the sofa. These actions do not have the same causal and overall event structure, they do not share "generic-level structure."

Proverbs. In Asian figures – proverbs in the form of short poems – the question arises as to what the limitations are on the interpretation of a proverb. Some interpretations are natural; others seem impossible. Why? Consider the following example from *Asian Figures,* translated by William Merwin.

> Blind
> blames the ditch

To get some sense of the possible range of interpretations, consider the following application of the proverb:

Suppose a presidential candidate knowingly commits some personal impropriety (though not illegal and not related to political issues) and his candidacy is destroyed by the press's reporting of the impropriety. He blames the press for reporting it, rather than himself for committing it. We think he should have recognized the realities of political press coverage when he chose to commit the impropriety. We express our judgment by saying, "Blind / blames the ditch."

Turner and I (1989) observed that the knowledge structure used in comprehending the case of the candidate's impropriety shared certain things with knowledge structure used in comprehending the literal interpretation of "Blind / blames the ditch." That knowledge structure is the following:
  There is a person with an incapacity, namely, blindness.
  He encounters a situation, namely a ditch, in which his incapacity, namely his inability to see the ditch, results in a negative consequence, namely, his falling into the ditch.
  He blames the situation, rather than his own incapacity.
  He should have held himself responsible, not the situation.
This specific knowledge schema about the blind man and the ditch is an instance of a general knowledge schema, in which specific information about the blindness and ditch are absent. Let us refer to it as the "generic-level schema" that structures our knowledge of the proverb. That generic-level knowledge schema is:
  There is a person with an incapacity.
  He encounters a situation in which his incapacity results in a negative consequence.
  He blames the situation rather than his own incapacity.
  He should have held himself responsible, not the situation.
This is a very general schema characterizing an open-ended category of situations. We can think of it as a variable template that can be filled in in

many ways. As it happened, Turner and I were studying this at the time of the Gary Hart scandal. Hart, a presidential candidate, committed certain sexual improprieties during a campaign, had his candidacy dashed, and then blamed the press for his downfall. "Blind / blames the ditch" fits this situation. Here's how:

The person is the presidential candidate.

His incapacity is his inability to understand the consequences of his personal improprieties.

The context he encounters is his knowingly committing an impropriety and the press's reporting it.

The consequence is having his candidacy dashed.

He blames the press.

We judge him as being foolish for blaming the press instead of himself. If we view the generic-level schema as mediating between the proverb "Blind / blames the ditch" and the story of the candidate's impropriety, we get the following correspondence:

The blind person corresponds to the presidential candidate.

His blindness corresponds to his inability to understand the consequences of his personal improprieties.

Falling into the ditch corresponds to his committing the impropriety and having it reported.

Being in the ditch corresponds to being out of the running as a candidate.

Blaming the ditch corresponds to blaming the press coverage.

Judging the blind man as foolish for blaming the ditch corresponds to judging the candidate as foolish for blaming the press coverage.

This correspondence defines the metaphorical interpretation of the proverb as applied to the candidate's impropriety. Moreover, the class of possible ways of filling in the generic-level schema of the proverb corresponds to the class of possible interpretations of the proverb. Thus, we can explain why "Blind / blames the ditch" does not mean "I took a bath" or "My aunt is sitting on the sofa" or any of the myriad things the proverb cannot mean.

All the proverbs that Turner and I studied turned out to involve this sort of generic-level schema, and the kinds of things that turned up in such schemata seemed to be pretty much the same in case after case. They include:

Causal structure

Temporal structure

Event shape; that is, instantaneous or repeated, completed or open-ended, single or repeating, having fixed stages or not, preserving the existence of entities or not, and so on

Purpose structure

Modal structure

Linear scales

This is not an exhaustive list, but it includes most of the major elements of generic-level structure we discovered. What is striking to us about this list is that everything on it is, under the Invariance Principle, an aspect of image-schematic structure. In short, if the Invariance Principle is correct, the way to arrive at a generic-level schema for some knowledge structure is to extract its image-schematic structure.

The metaphoric interpretation of such discourse forms as proverbs, fables, allegories, and so on seems to depend on our ability to extract generic-level structure. Turner and I have called the relation between a specific knowledge structure and its generic-level structure the GENERIC IS SPECIFIC metaphor. It is an extremely common mechanism for comprehending the general in terms of the specific.

If the Invariance Principle is correct, then the GENERIC IS SPECIFIC metaphor is a minimal metaphor that maps what the Invariance Principle requires it to and nothing more. Should it turn out that generic-level structure is exactly image-schematic structure, then the Invariance Principle would have enormous explanatory value. It would obviate the need for a separate characterization of generic-level structure. Instead, it would itself characterize generic-level structure, explaining possible personifications and the possible interpretations for proverbs.

Analogy

The GENERIC IS SPECIFIC metaphor is used for more than just the interpretation of proverbs. Turner (1991) has suggested that it is also the general mechanism at work in analogic reasoning and that the Invariance Principle characterizes the class of possible analogies. We can see how this works with the Gary Hart example cited above. We can convert that example into an analogy with the following sentence: "Gary Hart was like a blind man who fell into a ditch and blamed the ditch." The mechanism for understanding this analogy makes use of:

A knowledge schema for the blind man and the ditch

A knowledge schema concerning Gary Hart

The GENERIC IS SPECIFIC metaphor

The GENERIC IS SPECIFIC metaphor maps the knowledge schema for the blind man and the ditch into its generic-level schema. The generic-level schema defines an open-ended category of knowledge schemata. The Gary Hart schema is a member of that category, since it fits the generic-level schema given the correspondences stated above.

It appears at present that such analogies use this metaphorical mechanism. But it is common for analogies to use other metaphorical mechanisms as well, for instance, the Great Chain Metaphor and the full range of conventional mappings in the conceptual system. Sentences like "John is a wolf" or "Harry is a pig" use the Great Chain metaphor (see Lakoff & Turner, 1989, chap. 4).

A good example of how the rest of the metaphor system interacts with GENERIC IS SPECIFIC is the well-known example of Glucksberg and Keysar (this volume), "my job is a jail." First, the knowledge schema for a jail includes the knowledge that a jail imposes extreme physical constraints on a prisoner's movements. The GENERIC IS SPECIFIC metaphor preserves the image-schematic structure of the knowledge schema, factoring out the specific details of the prisoner and the jail: X imposes extreme physical constraints on Y's movements. But now two additional conventional metaphors apply to this generic-level schema: The event structure metaphor, with the submetaphor ACTIONS ARE SELF-PROPELLED MOVEMENTS, and PSYCHO-LOGICAL FORCE IS PHYSICAL FORCE. These metaphors map "X imposes extreme physical constraints on Y's movements" into "X imposes extreme psychological constraints on Y's actions." The statement "my job is a jail" imposes an interpretation in which X = my job and Y = me, and hence yields the knowledge that "my job imposes extreme psychological constraints on my actions." Thus, the mechanism for understanding "my job is a jail" uses very common, independently existing metaphors: GENERIC IS SPECIFIC, PSYCHOLOGICAL FORCE IS PHYSICAL FORCE, and the Event Structure Metaphor.

The Glucksberg–Keysar Claim

I mention this example because of the claim by Glucksberg and Keysar (this volume) that metaphor is simply a matter of categorization. In personal correspondence, however, Glucksberg has written, "We assume that people can judge and can also infer that certain basic level entities, such as 'jails,' typify or are emblematic of a metaphoric attributive category such as 'situations that are confining, unpleasant, etc.' " Glucksberg and Keysar give no theory of how it is possible to have such a "metaphoric attributive category" – that is, how it is possible for one kind of thing (a general situation) to be metaphorically categorized in terms of a fundamentally spatial notion like "confining." Since Glucksberg is not in the business of describing the nature of conceptual systems, he does not see it as his job to give such an account. I have argued in this essay that the general principle governing such cases is the Event Structure Metaphor. If such a metaphor exists in our conceptual system, then the Glucksberg–Keysar "jail" example is accounted for automatically and their categorization theory is not needed. Indeed, the category he needs – "situations that are confining, unpleasant, etc." – is a "metaphoric attributive category." That is, to get the appropriate categories in their categorization theory of metaphor he needs an account of metaphor. But given such an account of metaphor, the metaphor-as-categorization theory becomes unnecessary.

Even worse for the Glucksberg–Keysar theory, it cannot account for either everyday conceptual metaphor of the sort we have been discussing or for really rich poetic metaphor, such as one finds in the works of, say, Dylan Thomas, or for image metaphor of the sort common in the examples cited above from the Sanskrit, Navaho, and surrealist traditions. Since it does not even attempt to deal with most of the data covered by the contemporary theory of metaphor, it cannot account for "how metaphor works."

More on novel metaphor

At the time most of the chapters in this volume were written (the late 1970s), "metaphor" was taken to mean "novel metaphor," since the huge system of conventional metaphor had barely been noticed. The authors therefore never took up the question of how the system of conventional metaphor functions in the interpretation of novel metaphor. We have just seen one such example. Let us consider some others.

As common as novel metaphor is, its occurrence is rare by comparison with conventional metaphor, which occurs in most of the sentences we utter. Our everyday metaphor system, which we use to understand concepts as commonplace as TIME, STATE, CHANGE, CAUSATION, PURPOSE, and so forth is constantly active, and is used maximally in interpreting novel metaphorical uses of language. The problem with all the older research on novel metaphor is that it completely missed the major contribution played by the conventional system.

As Turner and I discussed in detail (Lakoff & Turner, 1989), there are three basic mechanisms for interpreting linguistic expressions as novel metaphors: extensions of conventional metaphors, generic-level metaphors, and image metaphors. Most interesting poetic metaphor uses all these superimposed on one another. Let us begin with examples of extensions of conventional metaphors. Dante begins the *Divine Comedy:*

> In the middle of life's road
> I found myself in a dark wood.

"Life's road" evokes the domain of life and the domain of travel, and hence the conventional LIFE IS A JOURNEY metaphor that links them. "I found myself in a dark wood" evokes the knowledge that if it's dark you cannot see which way to go. This evokes the domain of seeing, and thus the conventional metaphor that KNOWING IS SEEING, as in "I see what you're getting at," "his claims aren't clear," "the passage is opaque," and so forth. This entails that the speaker doesn't know which way to go. Since the LIFE IS A JOURNEY metaphor specifies destinations are life goals, the speaker must not know what life goals to pursue, that is, he is without direction in his life. All this uses nothing but the system of conventional metaphor, ordinary knowledge structure evoked by the conventional meaning of the sentence, and metaphorical inferences based on that knowledge structure.

Another equally simple case of the use of the conventional system is
Robert Frost's

> Two roads diverged in a wood, and I–
> I took the one less traveled by,
> And that has made all the difference.

Since Frost's language often does not overtly signal that the poem is to be
taken metaphorically, incompetent English teachers occasionally teach
Frost as if he were a nature poet, simply describing scenes. (I have actually
had students whose high school teachers taught them that!) Thus, this
passage could be read nonmetaphorically as being just about a trip on
which one encounters a crossroads. There is nothing in the sentence itself
that forces one to a metaphorical interpretation. But, since it is about
travel and encountering crossroads, it evokes a knowledge of journeys.
This activates the system of conventional metaphor we have just discussed,
in which long-term, purposeful activities are understood as journeys, and
further, how life and careers can also be understood as one-person journeys
(love relationships, involving two travelers, are ruled out here). The poem
is typically taken as being about life and a choice of life goals, though it
might also be interpreted as being about careers and career paths, or about
some long-term, purposeful activity. All that is needed to get the requisite
range of interpretations is the structure of conventional metaphors discussed above, and the knowledge structure evoked by the poem. The conventional mapping will apply to the knowledge structure yielding the appropriate inferences. No special mechanisms are needed.

Searle's theory

I will not pursue discussion of other more complex poetic examples, since
they require lengthy treatment which can be found in Lakoff and Turner
(1989), Turner (1987), and Turner (1991). Instead, I will confine myself to
discussing three examples from John Searle's chapter in this volume. Consider first Disraeli's remark, "I have climbed to the top of the greasy
pole."

This could be taken nonmetaphorically, but its most likely metaphorical
interpretation is via the CAREER IS A JOURNEY metaphor. This metaphor is
evoked jointly by source domain knowledge about pole climbing, which is
effortful, self-propelled, destination-oriented motion upward, and knowledge that the metaphor involves effortful, self-propelled, destination-
oriented motion upward. Part of the knowledge evoked is that the speaker
is as high as he can get on that particular pole, that the pole was difficult to
climb, that the climb probably involved backward motion, that it is difficult
for someone to stay at the top of a greasy pole, and that he will most likely
slide down again. The CAREER IS A JOURNEY metaphor maps this knowledge
onto corresponding knowledge about the speaker's career: he has as much

status as he can get in that particular career, it was difficult to get to that point in the career, it probably involved some temporary loss of status along the way, it will be difficult to maintain this position, and he will probably lose status before long. All this follows with nothing more than the conventional CAREER-AS-JOURNEY mapping, which we all share as part of our metaphorical systems, plus knowledge about climbing greasy poles.

The second example of Searle's I will consider is "Sally is a block of ice." Here there is a conventional metaphor that AFFECTION IS WARMTH, as in ordinary sentences like "she's a warm person," "he was cool to me," and so forth. "A block of ice" evokes the domain of temperature and, since it is predicated of a person, it also evokes knowledge of what a person can be. Jointly, both kinds of knowledge activate AFFECTION IS WARMTH. Since "a block of ice" is something very cold and not warmed quickly or easily, this knowledge is mapped onto Sally as being very unaffectionate and not able to become affectionate quickly or easily. Again, common knowledge and a conventional metaphor we all have is all that is needed.

Finally, Searle discusses "the hours crept by as we waited for the plane." Here we have a verb of motion predicated of a time expression; the former activates the knowledge about motion through space and the latter activates the time domain. Jointly, they activate the time-as-moving-object mapping. Again the meaning of the sentence follows only from everyday knowledge and the everyday system of metaphorical mappings.

Searle accounts for such cases by his Principle 4, which says that "we just do perceive a connection" which is the basis of the interpretation. This is vague and doesn't say what the perceived connection is or why we "just do" perceive it. When we spell out the details of all such "perceived connections," they turn out to be the system of conceptual metaphors I have been describing. But given that system, Searle's theory and his principles become unnecessary.

In addition, Searle's account of literal meaning makes most of the usual false assumptions that accompany that term. Searle assumes that all everyday, conventional language is literal and not metaphorical. He would thus rule out every example of conventional metaphor described not only in this chapter, but in the whole literature of the field.

The study of the metaphorical subsystem of our conceptual system is a central part of synchronic linguistics because much of our semantic system, that is, our system of concepts, is metaphorical, as we saw above. Because this huge system went unnoticed prior to 1980, authors like Searle, Sadock, and Morgan could claim, incorrectly as it turns out, that metaphor was outside of synchronic linguistics and in the domain of principles of language use.

The experiential basis of metaphor

The conceptual system underlying a language contains thousands of conceptual metaphors – conventional mappings from one domain to another, such as the Event Structure Metaphor. The novel metaphors of a language are, except for image metaphors, extensions of this large conventional system.

Perhaps the deepest question that any theory of metaphor must answer is this: why do we have the conventional metaphors that we have? Or alternatively: is there any reason why conceptual systems contain one set of metaphorical mappings rather than another? There do appear to be answers to these questions for many of the mappings found so far, though they are in the realm of plausible accounts, rather than in the realm of scientific results.

Take a simple case: the MORE IS UP metaphor, as seen in expressions like prices rose; his income went down; unemployment is up; exports are down; the number of homeless people is very high.

There are other languages in which MORE IS UP and LESS IS DOWN, but none in which the reverse is true, where MORE IS DOWN and LESS IS UP. Why not? Contemporary theory postulates that the MORE IS UP metaphor is *grounded in experience* – in the common experiences of pouring more fluid into a container and seeing the level go up, or adding more things to a pile and seeing the pile get higher. These are thoroughly pervasive experiences; we encounter them every day of our lives. They have structure – a correspondence between the conceptual domain of quantity and the conceptual domain of verticality: MORE corresponds in such experiences to UP and LESS corresponds to DOWN. These correspondences in real experience form the basis for the correspondences in the metaphorical cases, which go beyond real experience: in "prices rose" there is no correspondence in real experience between quantity and verticality, but understanding quantity in terms of verticality makes sense because of a regular correspondence in so many other cases.

Consider another case. What is the basis of the widespread KNOWING IS SEEING metaphor, as in expressions like I see what you're saying; his answer was clear; this paragraph is murky; he was so blinded by ambition that he never noticed his limitations? The experiential basis in this case is the fact that most of what we know comes through vision, and in the overwhelming majority of cases, if we see something, then we know it is true.

Consider still another case. Why, in the Event Structure Metaphor, is achieving a purpose understood as reaching a destination (in the location subsystem) and as acquiring a desired object (in the object subsystem)? The answer again seems to be correspondences in everyday experience. To achieve most of our everyday purposes, we either have to move to some destination or acquire some object. If you want a drink of water, you've got to go to the water fountain. If you want to be in the sunshine, you have to move to where the sunshine is. And if you want to write down a note, you have to get a pen or pencil. The correspondences between achieving purposes and either reaching destinations or acquiring objects is so utterly common in our everyday existence, that the resulting metaphor is completely natural.

But what about the experiential basis of A PURPOSEFUL LIFE IS A JOURNEY?

Recall that the mapping is in an inheritance hierarchy, where life goals are special cases of purposes, which are destinations in the event structure metaphor. Thus, A PURPOSEFUL LIFE IS A JOURNEY inherits the experiential basis of PURPOSES ARE DESTINATIONS. Thus, inheritance hierarchies provide *indirect experiential bases,* in that a metaphorical mapping lower in a hierarchy can inherit its experiential basis indirectly from a mapping higher in the hierarchy.

Experiential bases motivate metaphors, they do not predict them. Thus, not every language has a MORE IS UP metaphor, though all human beings experience a correspondence between MORE and UP. What this experiential basis does predict is that no language will have the opposite metaphor LESS IS UP. It also predicts that a speaker of a language without that metaphor will be able to learn it much more easily than its reverse.

Realizations of metaphor

Consider objects like thermometers and stock market graphs, where increases in temperature and prices are represented as being up and decreases as being down. These are objects created by humans to accord with the MORE-IS-UP metaphor. They exhibit a correlation between MORE and UP and are much easier to read and understand than if they contradicted the metaphor, if, say, increases were represented as down and decreases as up.

Such objects are ways in which metaphors impose a structure on real life, through the creation of new correspondences in experience. And once created in one generation, they serve as an experiential basis for that metaphor in the next generation.

There are a great many ways in which conventional metaphors can be made real. They can be realized in obvious imaginative products such as cartoons, literary works, dreams, visions, and myths, but they can be made real in less obvious ways as well, in physical symptoms, social institutions, social practices, laws, and even foreign policy and forms of discourse and history.

Let us consider some examples.

Cartoons. Conventional metaphors are made real in cartoons. A common example is the realization of the ANGER IS A HOT FLUID IN A CONTAINER metaphor, in which one can be "boiling mad" or "letting off steam." In cartoons, anger is commonly depicted by steam coming out of the character's ears. Social clumsiness is indicated by having a cartoon character "fall on his face."

Literary works. It is common for the plot of a novel to be a realization of the PURPOSEFUL LIFE IS A JOURNEY metaphor, where the course of a life takes the form of an actual journey. *Pilgrim's Progress* is a classic example.

Rituals. Consider the cultural ritual in which a newborn baby is carried upstairs to ensure his or her success. The metaphor realized in this ritual is

STATUS IS UP, as in: he clawed his way to the top; he climbed the ladder of success; you'll rise in the world.

Dream interpretation. Conceptual metaphors constitute the vocabulary of dream interpretation. The collection of our everyday conceptual metaphors makes dream interpretation possible. Consider one of the most celebrated of all examples, Joseph's interpretation of Pharaoh's dream from Genesis. In Pharaoh's dream, he is standing on the river bank when seven fat cows come out of the river, followed by seven lean cows that eat the seven fat ones and still remain lean. Pharaoh dreams again. This time he sees seven "full and good" ears of corn growing and then seven withered ears growing after them. The withered ears devour the good ears. Joseph interprets the two dreams as a single dream. The seven fat cows and full ears are good years and the seven lean cows and withered ears are famine years that follow the good years. The famine years devour what the good years produce. This interpretation makes sense to us because of a collection of conceptual metaphors in our conceptual system – metaphors that have been with us since biblical times. The first metaphor is TIMES ARE MOVING ENTITIES. A river is a common metaphor for the flow of time; the cows are individual entities (years) emerging from the flow of time and moving past the observer; the ears of corn are also entities that come into the scene. The second metaphor is ACHIEVING A PURPOSE IS EATING, where being fat indicates success, being lean indicates failure. This metaphor is combined with the most common of metonymies, A PART STANDS FOR THE WHOLE. Since cows and corn were typical of meat and grain eaten, each single cow stands for all the cows raised in a year and each ear of corn for all the corn grown in a year. The final metaphor is RESOURCES ARE FOOD, where using up resources is eating food. The devouring of the good years by the famine years is interpreted as indicating that all the surplus resources of the good years will be used up by the famine years. The interpretation of the whole dream is thus a composition of three conventional metaphors and one metonymy. The metaphoric and metonymic sources are combined to form the reality of the dream.

Myths. In the event structure metaphor, there is a submapping EXTERNAL EVENTS ARE LARGE MOVING OBJECTS that can exert a force on you and thereby affect whether you achieve your goals. In English the special cases of such objects are "things," fluids, and horses. Pamela Morgan (in unpublished work) has observed that in Greek mythology, Poseidon is the god of the sea, earthquakes, horses, and bulls. The list might seem arbitrary, but Morgan observes that these are all large moving objects that can exert a force on you. Poseidon, she surmises, should really be seen as the god of external events.

Physical symptoms. The unconscious mind makes use of our unconscious system of conventional metaphor, sometimes to express psychological states in terms of physical symptoms. For example, in the event structure metaphor, there is a submapping DIFFICULTIES ARE IMPEDIMENTS TO MOTION which has, as a special case, DIFFICULTIES ARE BURDENS. It is fairly common for someone encountering difficulties to walk with his shoulders stooped, as if "carrying a heavy weight" that is "burdening" him.

Social institutions. We have a TIME IS MONEY metaphor, shown by expressions like he's wasting time; I have to budget my time; this will save you time; I've invested a lot of time in that; he doesn't use his time profitably. This metaphor came into English use about the time of the industrial revolution, when people started to be paid for work by the amount of time they put in. Thus, the factory led to the institutional pairing of periods of time with amounts of money, which formed the experiential basis of this metaphor. Since then, the metaphor has been realized in many other ways. The budgeting of time has spread throughout American culture.

Social practices. There is a conceptual metaphor that SEEING IS TOUCHING, where the eyes are limbs and vision is achieved when the object seen is "touched." Examples are my eyes picked out every detail of the pattern; he ran his eyes over the walls; he couldn't take his eyes off of her; their eyes met; his eyes are glued to the TV. The metaphor is made real in the social practice of avoiding eye "contact" on the street, and in the social prohibition against "undressing someone with your eyes."

Laws. Law is a major area where metaphor is made real. For example, CORPORATIONS ARE PERSONS is a tenet of American law, which not only enables corporations to be "harmed" or assigned "responsibility" so they can be sued when liable, but also gives them certain First Amendment rights.

Foreign policy. A STATE IS A PERSON is one of the major metaphors underlying foreign policy concepts. Thus, there are "friendly" states, "hostile" states, and so forth. Health for a state is economic health and strength is military strength. A threat to economic "health" can be seen as a death threat, as when Iraq was seen to have a "stranglehold" on the "economic lifeline" of the United States. Strong states are seen as male and weak states as female, so that an attack by a strong state on a weak one can be seen as a "rape," as in the rape of Kuwait by Iraq. A "just war" is conceptualized as a fairy tale with villain, victim, and hero, where the villain attacks the victim and the hero rescues the victim. Thus, the United States and allies in the Gulf War were portrayed as having "rescued" Kuwait. As President Bush said in his address to Congress, "The issues couldn't have been clearer: Iraq was the villain and Kuwait, the victim."

Forms of discourse. Common metaphors are often made real in discourse forms. Consider three common academic discourse forms: the guided tour, the heroic battle, and the heroic quest. The guided tour is based on the metaphor that THOUGHT IS MOTION, where ideas are locations and one reasons "step-by-step," "reaches conclusions," or fails to reach a conclusion if engaged in "circular reasoning." Communication in this metaphor is giving someone a guided tour of some rational argument or of some "intellectual terrain." This essay is an example of such a guided tour, where I, the author, am the tour guide who is assumed to be thoroughly familiar with the terrain and the terrain surveyed is taken as objectively real. The discourse form of the heroic battle is based on the metaphor that ARGUMENT IS WAR. The author's theory is the hero, the opposing theory is the villain, and words are weapons. The battle is in the form of an argument defending the hero's position and demolishing that of the villain. The heroic quest discourse form is based on the metaphor that knowledge is a valuable but elusive object that can be "discovered" if one perseveres. The scientist is the hero on a quest for knowledge, and the discourse form is an account of his difficult journey of discovery. What is "discovered" is a real entity.

What makes all these cases realizations of metaphors is that in each case something real is structured by conventional metaphor, and thereby made comprehensible, or even natural. What is real differs in each case: an object like a thermometer or graph, an experience like a dream, an action like a ritual, a form of discourse, and so forth. These examples reveal that much of what is real in a society or in the experience of an individual is structured and made sense of via conventional metaphor.

Experiential bases and realizations of metaphors are two sides of the same coin: they are both correlations in real experience that have the same structure as the correlations in metaphors. The difference is that experiential bases precede, ground, and make sense of conventional metaphorical mappings, whereas realizations follow, and are made sense of, via the conventional metaphors. And as we noted above, one generation's realizations of a metaphor can become part of the next generation's experiential basis for that metaphor.

Summary of results

As we have seen, the contemporary theory of metaphor is revolutionary in many respects. To give you some idea of how revolutionary, here is a list of the basic results that differ from most previous accounts.

The nature of metaphor

Metaphor is the main mechanism through which we comprehend abstract concepts and perform abstract reasoning.

Much subject matter, from the most mundane to the most abstruse scientific theories, can only be comprehended via metaphor.

Metaphor is fundamentally conceptual, not linguistic, in nature.

Metaphorical language is a surface manifestation of conceptual metaphor.

Though much of our conceptual system is metaphorical, a significant part of it is nonmetaphorical. Metaphorical understanding is grounded in nonmetaphorical understanding.

Metaphor allows us to understand a relatively abstract or inherently unstructured subject matter in terms of a more concrete, or at least more highly structured subject matter.

The structure of metaphor

Metaphors are mappings across conceptual domains.

Such mappings are asymmetric and partial.

Each mapping is a fixed set of ontological correspondences between entities in a source domain and entities in a target domain.

When those fixed correspondences are activated, mappings can project source domain inference patterns onto target domain inference patterns.

Metaphorical mappings obey the Invariance Principle: The image-schema structure of the source domain is projected onto the target domain in a way that is consistent with inherent target domain structure.

Mappings are not arbitrary, but grounded in the body and in everyday experience and knowledge.

A conceptual system contains thousands of conventional metaphorical mappings which form a highly structured subsystem of the conceptual system.

There are two types of mappings: conceptual mappings and image mappings; both obey the Invariance Principle.

Some aspects of metaphor

The system of conventional conceptual metaphor is mostly unconscious, automatic, and used with no noticeable effort, just like our linguistic system and the rest of our conceptual system.

Our system of conventional metaphor is "alive" in the same sense that our system of grammatical and phonological rules is alive; namely, it is constantly in use, automatically, and below the level of consciousness.

Our metaphor system is central to our understanding of experience and to the way we act on that understanding.

Conventional mappings are static correspondences, and are not, in themselves, algorithmic in nature. However, this by no means rules out the possibility that such static correspondences might be used in language processing that involves sequential steps.

Metaphor is mostly based on correspondences in our experiences, rather than on similarity.

The metaphor system plays a major role in both the grammar and lexicon of a language.

Metaphorical mappings vary in universality; some seem to be universal, others are widespread, and some seem to be culture specific.

Poetic metaphor is, for the most part, an extension of our everyday, conventional system of metaphorical thought.

These are the conclusions that best fit the empirical studies of metaphor conducted over the past decade or so. Though many of them are inconsistent with traditional views, they are by no means all new, and some ideas – for example, that abstract concepts are comprehended in terms of concrete concepts – have a long history.

Concluding remarks

The evidence supporting the contemporary theory of metaphor is voluminous and grows larger each year as research in the field continues. The evidence, as we saw above, comes from five domains:

Generalizations over polysemy

Generalization over inference patterns

Generalizations over extensions to poetic cases

Generalizations over semantic change

Psycholinguistic experiments

I have discussed only a handful of examples of the first three of these, enough, I hope, to make the reader curious about the field.

Evidence is convincing, however, only if it can count as evidence. When does evidence fail to be evidence? Unfortunately, all too often. It is commonly the case that certain fields of inquiry are defined by assumptions that rule out the possibility of counterevidence. When a defining assumption of a field comes up against evidence, the evidence usually loses: the practitioners of the field must ignore the evidence if they want to keep the assumptions that define the field they are committed to.

Part of what makes the contemporary theory of metaphor so interesting is that the evidence for it contradicts the defining assumptions of so many academic disciplines. In my opinion, this should make one doubt the defining assumptions of all those disciplines. The reason is this: the defining assumptions of the contemporary theory of metaphor are minimal. There are only two.

1. The generalization commitment: To seek generalizations in all areas of language, including polysemy, patterns of inference, novel metaphor, and semantic change.

2. The cognitive commitment: To take experimental evidence seriously.

But these are nothing more than commitments to the scientific study of language and the mind. No initial commitment is made as to the form of an answer to the question of what is metaphor.

The defining assumptions of other fields do, however, often entail a commitment about the form of an answer to that question. It is useful, in an interdisciplinary volume of this sort, to spell out exactly what those defining assumptions are, since they will often explain why different authors reach such different conclusions about the nature of metaphor.

Literal meaning commitments

I started this chapter with a list of the false assumptions about literal meaning that are commonly made. These assumptions are "false" only relative to the kinds of evidence that support the contemporary theory of metaphor. If one ignores all such evidence, the assumptions can be maintained without contradiction.

Assumptions about literality are the locus of many of the contradictions between the contemporary theory of metaphor and various academic disciplines. Let us review those assumptions. In the discussion of literal meaning given above, I observed that it is taken as definitional that what is literal is not metaphorical. The "false assumptions and conclusions" that usually accompany the word "literal" are:

All everyday conventional language is literal, and none is metaphorical.

All subject matter can be comprehended literally, without metaphor.

Only literal language can be contingently true or false.

All definitions given in the lexicon of a language are literal, not metaphorical.

The concepts used in the grammar of a language are all literal; none is metaphorical.

We will begin with the philosophy of language. The generalization commitment and the cognitive commitment are *not* definitional to the philosophy of language. Most philosophers of language would feel no need to abide by them, for a very good reason. The philosophy of language is typically not seen as an empirical discipline, constrained by empirical results, such as those that arise from the application of the generalization and cognitive commitments. Instead, the philosophy of language is usually seen as an a priori discipline, which can be pursued using the tools of philosophical analysis alone, rather than the tools of empirical research. Therefore, all the evidence that has been brought forth for the contemporary theory of metaphor simply will not matter for most philosophers of language.

In addition, the philosophy of language comes with its own set of defining assumptions, which entail many of the false assumptions usually associated with the word "literal." Most practitioners of the philosophy of language usually make one or more of the following assumptions.

The correspondence theory of truth.

Meaning is defined in terms of reference and truth.

Natural language semantics is characterized by the mechanisms of mathematical logic, including model theory.

The very field of philosophy of language thus comes with defining assumptions that contradict the main conclusions of the contemporary theory of metaphor. Consequently, we can see why most philosophers of language have the range of views on metaphor that they have: they accept the traditional literal–figurative distinction. They may, like M. Johnson (1981), say that there is no metaphorical meaning, and that most metaphorical utterances are either trivially true or trivially false. Or, like Grice (1989, p. 34) and Searle (this volume), they will assume that metaphor is in the realm of pragmatics, that is, that a metaphorical meaning is no more than the literal meaning of some other sentence which can be arrived at by some pragmatic principle. This is required, since the only real meaning for them is literal meaning, and pragmatic principles are those principles that allow one to say one thing (with a literal meaning) and mean something else (with a different, but nonetheless literal, meaning).

Much of generative linguistics accepts one or more of these assumptions from the philosophy of language. The field of formal semantics accepts them all, and thus formal semantics, by its defining assumptions, is at odds with the contemporary theory of metaphor. Formal semantics simply does not see it as its job to account for the generalizations discussed in this chapter. From the perspective of formal semantics, the phenomena that the contemporary theory of metaphor is concerned with are either nonexistent or uninteresting, since they lie outside the purview of the discipline. Thus Jerrold Sadock in his chapter in this volume claims that metaphor lies outside of synchronic linguistics. Since he accepts mathematical logic as the correct approach to natural language semantics, Sadock must see metaphor as being outside of semantics proper. He must, therefore, also reject the enterprise of the contemporary theory of metaphor. And Morgan (this volume), also accepting those defining assumptions of the philosophy of language, agrees with Grice and Searle that metaphor is a matter of pragmatics.

Chomsky's (1981) theory of government and binding also accepts crucial assumptions from the philosophy of language that are inconsistent with the contemporary theory of metaphor. Government and binding, following my early theory of generative semantics, assumes that semantics is to be represented in terms of logical form. Government and binding, like generative semantics, thus rules out the very possibility that metaphor might be part of natural language semantics as it enters into grammar. Because of this defining assumption, I would not expect government and binding theorists to become concerned with the phenomena covered by the contemporary theory of metaphor.

It is interesting that much of continental philosophy and deconstructionism is also characterized by defining assumptions at odds with the contemporary theory of metaphor. Nietzsche (see Johnson, 1981) held that all language is metaphorical, a theory at odds with those results indicating that a significant amount of everyday language is not metaphorical (see subsection, "What is not metaphorical"). Much of continental philosophy, observing that conceptual systems change through time, assumes that conceptual systems are purely historically contingent, that there are no conceptual universals. Though conceptual systems do change through time, there do, however, appear to be universal, or at least very widespread, conceptual metaphors. The event structure metaphor is my present candidate for a metaphorical universal.

Continental philosophy also comes with a distinction between the study of the physical world, which can be scientific, and the study of human beings, which it says cannot be scientific. This is very much at odds with the conceptual theory of metaphor, which is very much a scientific enterprise.

Finally, the contemporary theory of metaphor is at odds with certain traditions in symbolic artificial intelligence and information processing psychology. Those fields assume that thought is a matter of algorithmic symbol manipulation, of the sort done by a traditional computer program. This defining assumption is inconsistent with the contemporary theory of metaphor in two respects.

First, the contemporary theory has an image-schematic basis. The Invariance Principle both applies to image metaphors and characterizes constraints on novel metaphor. Since symbol manipulation systems cannot handle image-schemas, they cannot deal with image metaphors or imageable idioms.

Second, those traditions must characterize metaphorical mapping as an algorithmic process, which typically takes literal meanings as input and gives a metaphorical reading as output. This runs counter to cases where there are multiple, overlapping metaphors in a single sentence, and which require the simultaneous activation of a number of metaphorical mappings.

The contemporary theory of metaphor is thus not only interesting for its own sake. It is especially interesting for the challenge it presents to other disciplines. If the results of the contemporary theory are accepted, the defining assumptions of whole disciplines are brought into question.

NOTE

This research was supported in part by grants from the Sloan Foundation and the National Science Foundation (IRI-8703202) to the University of California at Berkeley.

The following colleagues and students helped with this essay in a variety of ways, from useful comments to allowing me to cite their research: Ken Baldwin, Claudia Brugman, Jane Espenson, Sharon Fischler, Ray Gibbs, Adele Goldberg, Mark Johnson, Karin Myhre, Eve Sweetser, and Mark Turner.

APPENDIX: AN ANNOTATED BIBLIOGRAPHY

Most of the chapters in this edition also appeared in the first edition of 1979 and thus predate the contemporary theory of metaphor. It might therefore be a service to readers to provide a short annotated bibliography of fundamental books and papers on the contemporary theory written since the first edition of this volume appeared.

Gibbs, R. W., Jr. (1990). Psycholinguistic studies on the conceptual basis of idiomaticity. *Cognitive Linguistics*, 1, 417–462.
A survey of psycholinguistic results demonstrating the cognitive reality of conceptual metaphor and imageable idioms.

Johnson, M. (1981). *Philosophical Perspectives on Metaphor*. Minneapolis: University of Minnesota Press.
The best collection of papers by philosophers on metaphor. The author's introduction is the best short historical survey of the history of metaphor in philosophy.

(1987). *The Body in the Mind: the Bodily Basis of Meaning, Reason and Imagination*. Chicago: University of Chicago Press.
A discussion of philosophical issues arising from the discovery of the system of conceptual metaphor.

Kövecses, Z. (1990). *Emotion Concepts*. New York: Springer-Verlag.
A thorough and voluminously documented demonstration that emotion is conceptualized metaphorically.

Lakoff, G. (1987). *Women, Fire, and Dangerous Things: What Categories Reveal about the Mind*. Chicago: University of Chicago Press.
A survey of contemporary literature on categorization, including the role of metaphor in forming categories. Includes a general theory of meaning assimilating conceptual metaphor and other aspects of cognitive semantics.

(1989). Philosophical speculation and cognitive science. *Philosophical Psychology*, 2, 55–76.
A discussion of the differing assumptions behind generative semantics and generative grammar.

(1991). "Metaphor and War: The Metaphor System Used To Justify War in the Gulf." Distributed via electronic bulletin boards, January 1991. Reprinted in Brien Hallet (ed.), *Engulfed in War: Just War and the Persian Gulf*. Honolulu: Matsunaga Institute for Peace, 1991. Also in *Journal of Urban and Cultural Studies*, vol. 2, no. 1, 1991; in *Vietnam Generation Newsletter*, vol. 3, no. 2, November 1991; and in *The East Bay Express*, February 1991.
An analysis of the metaphorical system used in the public discourse and expert policy deliberations on the Gulf War, together with what the metaphors hid, and a critique of the war based on this analysis.

Lakoff, G., & Brugman, C. (1986). Argument forms in lexical semantics. In V. Nikiforidou, M. Van Clay, & D. Feder (eds.), *Proceedings of the Twelfth Annual Meeting of the Berkeley Linguistics Society*, 442–454.
A survey of the argument forms used in justifying metaphorical analysis and a comparison with corresponding argument forms in syntax and phonology.

Lakoff, G., & Johnson, M. (1980). *Metaphors We Live By*. Chicago: University of Chicago Press.
The first book outlining the contemporary theory of metaphor.

Lakoff, G., & Turner, M. (1989). *More Than Cool Reason: A Field Guide to Poetic Metaphor*. Chicago: University of Chicago Press.
A survey of the mechanisms of poetic metaphor, replete with examples.

Sweetser, E. (1990). *From Etymology to Pragmatics: The Mind-as-Body Metaphor in Semantic Structure and Semantic Change.* Cambridge: Cambridge University Press.
> The best work to date on the role of metaphor in semantic change, and the metaphorical basis of pragmatics.

Talmy, L. (1985). Force dynamics in language and thought. In *Papers from the Parasession on Causatives and Agentivity.* Chicago: Chicago Linguistic Society.
> The analysis that led to the study of the metaphorical basis of modality and causation.

Turner, M. (1987). *Death Is the Mother of Beauty: Mind, Metaphor, Criticism.* Chicago: University of Chicago Press.
> A study of the regularities behind all the kinship metaphors from Chaucer to Wallace Stevens, including the role of metaphor in allegory. Turner also noticed the prevalence of the CAUSATION IS PROGENERATION metaphor and the constraint that was the precursor to the Invariance Principle.

(1991). *Reading Minds: The Study of English in the Age of Cognitive Science.* Princeton: Princeton University Press.
> A reevaluation of the profession of English and the study of the English language in the light of recent studies on the nature of metaphor and other studies in the cognitive sciences.

Winter, S. L. (1989). Transcendental nonsense, metaphoric reasoning, and the cognitive stakes for law. *University of Pennsylvania Law Review, 137,* 1105–1237.
> The most comprehensive of Winter's many articles discussing the role of metaphor in law.

12

Process and products in making sense of tropes

RAYMOND W. GIBBS, JR.

Introduction

The study of tropes, or figures of thought and speech, has always been at the heart of scholarly interest in literature and rhetoric. Because figures twist the "proper" meanings of words – the Greek word for figure is *trope* meaning "turn, twist" – rhetoricians have closely analyzed the bewildering array of "turns and twists" used in poetry and literature and have provided a sometimes confusing list of labels for these poetic devices (metaphor, metonymy, irony, oxymoron, hyperbole, litotes, periphrasis, antithesis, and so on). Although the history of tropology, dating back to Plato's famous quarrel between philosophy and poetry, reveals tremendous skepticism about the cognitive value of tropes in philosophy and science, there has in recent years been a marked reaffirmation of the ubiquity of tropes in every intellectual discipline concerned with mind and meaning. The first edition of this collection brought to center stage many of the important ideas about figuration in linguistics, philosophy, psychology, science, and education. As befitting its title, the emphasis in that volume was on metaphor (and simile) in both its linguistic and conceptual guises. Very little discussion was devoted to tropes other than metaphor, which is understandable given the prominence of metaphor in intellectual thought starting with Aristotle over two thousand years ago.

Various scholars throughout history, however, beginning with Quintilian, Ramus, and Vico, have argued that a great deal of our conceptualization of experience, even the foundation of human consciousness, is based on figurative schemes of thought which include not only metaphor, but also metonymy, synecdoche, and irony. These tropes do not merely provide a way for us to talk about how we think, reason, and imagine, they are also *constitutive* of our experience. Work over the past fifty years demonstrates that the figurative schemes of metonymy, synecdoche, and irony play significant roles not only in everyday thought and language (Lakoff, 1987; this volume; Lakoff & Johnson, 1980; Johnson, 1987), but also in the development and practice of all intellectual disciplines in the arts and sciences (R. Brown, 1977, 1989; Burke, 1942, 1953; Derrida, 1978, 1982; Foucault, 1972; Hallyn, 1990; Pepper, 1942; Rorty, 1989; White, 1973, 1978).

My concern in this chapter is with how people make sense of tropes. There has been significant work in psycholinguistics and related disciplines on trope understanding. I will describe some of these ideas focusing specifically on the importance of conceptual and pragmatic knowledge in comprehension of a variety of related tropes. The research on tropes such as metonymy, irony, hyperbole, understatements, oxymora, and idioms is not nearly so extensive as that on metaphor. Nevertheless, there are good reasons and experimental evidence to suggest that these tropes do not require special cognitive processes to be understood, contrary to the widely held assumption in linguistics and philosophy that tropes violate, or "flout," norms of cooperative conversation. The ease with which many figurative utterances are comprehended has often been attributed to the constraining influence of context. But the context for linguistic understanding is specifically limited to the common ground – the knowledge, beliefs, and attitudes recognized as being shared by speakers and listeners (or authors and readers) in any discourse situation (Clark & Carlson, 1981). A major focus of this chapter is on the exact role that common ground plays in making sense of tropes. At the same time, our ability to conceptualize experience in figurative terms must also explain why nonliteral speech is normally understood so effortlessly. I shall argue that a major reason why people use different tropes so frequently in everyday speech and writing is that human cognition is fundamentally shaped by various processes of figuration (also see Lakoff, this volume). Speakers can't help but employ tropes in everyday conversation because they conceptualize much of their experience through the figurative schemes of metaphor, metonymy, irony, and so on. Listeners find tropes easy to understand precisely because much of their thinking is constrained by figurative processes.

The first section of this chapter briefly describes the traditional view of trope understanding. I attempt to explain why figurative language is often seen as violating conversational norms to be cooperative by looking at how scholars in different disciplines view the activity of linguistic understanding and the distinction between literal and figurative meaning.

Why are there conversational maxims?

The most influential ideas about trope understanding come from Grice's theory of conversational implicature and Searle's work on speech act theory. Grice (1975, 1978) noted that much of the information conveyed in conversation is implied rather than asserted. He argued that speakers and listeners expect each other to interpret their utterances as if they were acting in a rational and cooperative manner (the *cooperative principle*). To do this, speakers and listeners operate according to several maxims that include *quantity* (make your contribution as informative as needed), *quality* (do not say what you believe to be false), *relevance* (be relevant), and *manner* (avoid ambiguity). Listeners determine the conversational inferences (or "implicatures") of nonliteral utterances by first analyzing the literal meaning of the sentence. Second, the listener assesses the appropriateness and/or truthfulness of that literal meaning against the context of the utterance. Third, if the literal meaning is defective or inappropriate for the context, then and *only* then will listeners derive an alternative nonliteral meaning that makes the utterance consistent with the cooperative principle. Grice assumes that figurative language requires additional cognitive effort to be understood because such utterances violate one of the conversational maxims (usually quantity and/or quality). Searle (this volume) offers a similar rational analysis of figurative language interpretation. He proposes various principles that allow listeners to figure out just how sentence and speaker meanings differ in metaphor, irony, indirect speech acts, and so on. Searle believes that Grice's principles of cooperative conversation and the rules for performing speech acts are sufficient to provide the basic principles for figurative language understanding. In general, the Grice/Searle view follows the centuries-old belief that literal language is a veridical reflection of thought and the external world whereas figurative language distorts reality and only serves special rhetorical purposes.

The standard view that figurative language violates various communicative norms suggests three related claims about how tropes are understood (Gibbs, 1984; Glucksberg & Keysar, 1990). First, the analysis of a sentence's literal meaning is obligatory, and always derived before figurative meanings can be determined. The results of many psycholinguistic experiments have shown this claim to be false (e.g., Gibbs, 1982, 1984, 1989; Gibbs & Gerrig, 1989; Hoffman & Kemper, 1987). Listeners and readers can often understand the figurative interpretations of metaphor (e.g., "billboards are warts on the landscape"), metonymy ("the ham sandwich left without paying"), sarcasm ("you are a fine friend"), idioms ("John popped the question to Mary"), proverbs ("the early bird catches the worm"), and indirect speech acts ("would you mind lending me five dollars?") without having first to analyze and reject their literal meanings when these tropes are seen in realistic social contexts.

Another implication of the standard view is that understanding tropes requires that a defective literal meaning be found before searching for a nonliteral meaning. Figurative meaning can be ignored if the literal meaning of an utterance makes sense in context. But people apprehend the nonliteral meaning of simple comparison statements ("surgeons are butchers") even when their literal meanings fit perfectly with context (Glucksberg, Gildea, & Bookin, 1982; Shinjo & Myers, 1987). Even without a defective literal meaning to trigger a search for an alternative figurative meaning, metaphor, to take one example, can be automatically interpreted.

A final claim of the standard view is that additional inferential work must be done to derive figurative meanings that are contextually appropriate. However, metaphor, metonymy, irony, and indirect speech acts require the same kind of contextual information as do comparable literal expressions (Gibbs, 1986a; Gildea & Glucksberg, 1983; Keysar, 1989; Ortony, Schallert, Reynolds, & Antos, 1978).

Such experimental findings are damaging to the claim that people understand tropes as violations of conversational maxims. Similar psychological mechanisms appear to drive the understanding of both literal and figurative speech at least insofar as very *early* cognitive processes are concerned, though individuals may at a later time reflect on the *products* of trope understanding and make different judgments about these meanings or interpretations. There are many times when a particular trope makes us "stand up and take notice," where the meaning of some phrase reverberates in our minds, generating new interpretations, perhaps endlessly, over time. Readers may slowly ponder the potential meanings of a literary metaphor, such as Shakespeare's "The world is an unweeded garden," and this experience provides much of the basis for the assumption that tropes require "extra work" to be properly understood. Interpreting tropes often places us squarely in the web of "iterability" so that we never experience a final, definitive "click of comprehension." But the indeterminacy of figurative meaning doesn't demonstrate that tropes violate communicative norms to speak clearly and truthfully, nor does it mean that readers or listeners are unable to create *some* interpretation for a trope during the earliest moments of comprehension.

One reason many scholars believe figurative language violates communication maxims is that they confuse the *processes* and *products* of linguistic understanding. All language interpretation takes place in real time ranging from the first milliseconds of processing to long-term reflective analysis. This temporal continuum may be roughly divided into moments corresponding to linguistic comprehension, recognition, interpretation, and appreciation. Comprehension refers to the immediate moment-by-moment process of creating meanings for utterances. Recognition refers to the products of comprehension as types (i.e., determining whether an utterance conveys a particular type of meaning such as literal, metaphorical, ironic, and so forth). Interpretation refers to the products of comprehension as tokens (i.e., determining the specific content of the meaning type). Appreciation refers to some aesthetic judgment given to a product either as a type or token.

Philosophers, linguists, and literary theorists focus on trope understanding as a product and generally study recognition, interpretation, and appreciation. From an examination of the various products of trope recognition and interpretation, these scholars often try to infer something about figurative language comprehension. Psychologists or psycholinguists study comprehension processes with an eye toward explicating something about the products of trope interpretation and recognition. Many figurative-language theorists make the mistake of assuming that a theory constructed to explain one temporal moment of trope understanding can easily be generalized to account for *all* aspects of understanding. But one cannot conclude that the comprehension of figurative language is fundamentally different from literal language simply because speakers can, at times, consciously identify some utterances as literal and others as figurative. To say that people employ distinct cognitive mechanisms to understand a trope such as "Juliet is the sun" because we can identify the expression as metaphorical makes an unwarranted inference about a process of understanding from an examination of a product of understanding. Similarly, to say that some metaphors are more apt or aesthetically pleasing than others does not necessarily indicate that people understand "good" metaphors differently from "bad" ones. Psycholinguistic evidence has demonstrated that judgments of metaphor aptness entail a different kind of psychological act than is used in comprehension (Gerrig & Healy, 1983). This is not surprising given that comprehension and appreciation of metaphor are different mental activities, each reflecting different parts of the temporal continuum of linguistic understanding. One cannot simply infer something about the process of understanding (e.g., comprehension) from examining only the products of understanding (e.g., appreciation). In the same way, one cannot use evidence about the earliest temporal moments of trope understanding to say much about the later products of understanding. Thus, the psycholinguistic evidence that trope comprehension does not differ from understanding of literal language should *not* automatically be taken as evidence against the legitimacy of figurative meanings as special *products* of understanding. Each temporal moment of understanding requires its own theoretical explanation (Gibbs & Gerrig, 1989). The confusion between the processes and products of linguistic understanding offers one reason why many theorists mistakenly assume that tropes violate conversational norms of truthfulness and require special mental processes to be understood.

Another reason for the widespread belief that figurative language violates communication maxims arises from a questionable assumption about what constitutes literal meaning as distinct from figurative meaning. There has been tremendous debate about the role of literal meaning in the interpretation of tropes. One difficulty with this debate seems to be the lack of consensus as to the definition of literal meaning (Dascal, 1987, 1989; Gibbs, 1984, 1989; Lakoff, 1986; Rumelhart, this volume; Wilensky, 1988). At least five different meanings for literal have been identified (Lakoff, 1986, suggests the first four).

Conventional literality in which literal usage is contrasted with poetic usage.

Subject-matter literality in which certain expressions are the usual ones used to talk about a particular topic.

Nonmetaphorical literality, or directly meaningful language, in which one word (concept) is never understood in terms of a second word (or concept).

Truth-conditional literality in which language is used to refer to existing objects and can be judged as true or false.

Context-free literality in which the literal meaning of an expression is its meaning in a "null" context.

Both everyday talk and scholarly discourse suggest that some of these definitions of "literal" are closely equivalent. For example, ordinary conventional language is directly meaningful and therefore not figurative. Conventional language is also capable of referring to objective reality and of being objectively true or false. Furthermore, there is only one objectively correct way to understand a subject and the conventional language used to speak of a subject is capable of being true or false. Finally, truth conditional meaning refers to the meaning of an expression apart from any special discourse context.

These definitions of literal meaning contribute to the cluster of beliefs that researchers often assume without comment when they describe tropes as violating maxims of cooperative communication. But which, if any, of these views of literal meaning are used when listeners assess whether an utterance adheres to communicative norms? Each definition of literal meaning provides a different assessment of quality, quantity, relevance, and manner (Grice's maxims). Some notions of literality seem to have little to do with quality or quantity (e.g., conventional, subject-matter, and nonmetaphorical literality). Ordinary people's intuitions about the literal meanings of various tropes differ depending on their own assumptions about literal meaning. In one study, I have recently found that college students rated metonymic expressions (e.g., "the ham sandwich spilled beer all over himself") as being more literal under a context-free definition than either the nonmetaphorical or truth-conditional views. The opposite was true, however, for metaphorical comparisons (e.g., "a garbage truck is a hungry scavenger"). Similarly, people rated hyperboles ("Jane felt hotter than the sun") as being more literal under the nonmetaphorical definition than for the context-free view of literal meaning, but the opposite was true for literary metaphors ("the soul is a rope that binds heaven and earth"). Even without specific instructions about the definition of literal meaning, people appear to judge the literality of tropes based on a complex cluster of notions. These arguments and findings on literal meaning and its relationship to the maxims of truthfulness raise serious questions for the traditional view of trope understanding.

I have argued that scholars often assume that tropes violate maxims of cooperative communication because of some conceptual confusions about literal meaning and the time course of understanding. The following sections describe in more detail some of the evidence suggesting that people make sense of tropes without any tacit recognition of these phrases as violations of communicative norms. I specifically discuss the strong influences of conceptual and pragmatic knowledge on people's understanding of metonymy, irony, hyperbole, understatement, oxymoron, and idiomaticity.

Metonymy

There has been widespread debate among rhetoricians, linguists, and literary theorists regarding the differences between metaphor and metonymy. These tropes appear to be similar because each describes a connection between two things where one term is substituted for another. Some theorists suggest that metonymy is a type or subclass of metaphor (Genette, 1968; Levin, this volume; Searle, this volume). Other theorists argue that metaphor and metonymy are opposed because they are generated according to opposite principles (Bredin, 1984; Jakobson, 1971). Metaphor is based on similarity whereas metonymy expresses simple contiguous relations between objects, such as part-whole, cause-effect, and so on.

Regardless of the debate in literature and philosophy on the definitions of metaphor and metonymy, these two figurative types can be distinguished because the connections made between things are different in each case (Lakoff & Turner, 1989). In metaphor, there are two conceptual domains and one is understood in terms of the other. For instance, when a boxer is compared to a creampuff as in "the boxer was a creampuff," two separate conceptual domains are contrasted (athletes and food) and the fighter is viewed as similar to a pastry in being soft and easy to devour. Metonymy involves only one conceptual domain in that the mapping or connection between two things is done within the same domain. Traditional rhetoric defines metonymy as a figure of speech wherein the name of one entity is used to refer to another entity that is contiguous to it. This process of transferred reference is possible in virtue of what Nunberg (1979) calls *a referring function.* Thus, referring to a baseball player as a glove, as in "we need a new glove at second base," uses a salient characteristic of one domain (the glove part of the baseball player) to represent the entire domain (the player). When the two things being compared form a part-whole relationship (that is, when glove is part of the whole baseball player), the metonymic expression is often referred to as *synecdoche* (Lanham, 1969).

Like metaphor, metonymy has a conceptual basis that is easily seen in the similarity between various metonymic expressions. Consider first the following statements:

Washington has started negotiating with Moscow.

The White House isn't saying anything.

Wall Street is in a panic.

The Kremlin agreed to support the boycott.

Hollywood is putting out terrible movies.

Paris has dropped hemlines this year.

These examples do not occur one by one, but reflect the general cognitive principle of metonymy where people use one well-understood aspect of something to stand for the thing as a whole or for some other aspect of it (Lakoff & Johnson, 1980). All the above expressions relate to the general principle by which a place may stand for an institution located at that place. Thus, a place like Hollywood stands for a particularly salient institution located at that place, namely the motion picture industry.

I claim, following Lakoff and Johnson (1980), that there are various metonymic models in our conceptual system that underlie the use of many kinds of figurative and conventional expressions such as OBJECT USED FOR USER (e.g., "the sax has the flu today," "we need a better glove at third base"), CONTROLLER FOR CONTROLLED ("Nixon bombed Hanoi," "Ozawa gave a terrible concert last night"), and THE PLACE FOR THE EVENT ("Watergate changed our politics," "let's not let Iraq become another Vietnam"). Many of these models depend on conventional cultural associations, which reflect the general principle that *a thing may stand for what it is conventionally associated with* (Turner, 1987). This principle limits the use of metonymy to only certain relationships between entities. For example, we can use the name of any well-known creative artist to refer to the artistic creations of the artist as in "does he like Hemingway?" or "I saw a Jasper Johns yesterday." But not any product can be referred to by the name of the person who created the product. I could hardly say "Mary was tasty" meaning by *Mary* the cheesecake that Mary made, in spite of the analogy between Mary mixing and processing ingredients to produce her cake and Jasper Johns mixing and applying colors to produce his paintings. Any given instance of a referring function needs to be sanctioned by a body of beliefs encapsulated in an appropriate frame (Nunberg, 1979; Taylor, 1989). Thus, one widespread belief in our culture is that the distinctive value of a work of art is due uniquely to the genius of the individual who created it. But we do not normally believe that such a relationship always holds between a cake and the person who baked it.

Certain contexts, however, permit the use of referring functions that are not sanctioned outside those situations. For instance, the metonymic sentence "the ham sandwich is getting impatient for his check" makes little sense apart from some specific context as when one waiter informs another that his customer, who was served a ham sandwich, wants to receive the check (Nunberg, 1979). Metonymy serves in these instances as a kind of *contextual expression,* words or phrases whose meanings depend on the context in which they are embedded (Clark & Clark, 1979; Clark, 1983; Gerrig, 1986). Because potential contexts are unlimited, contextual expressions have an unlimited number of potential meanings. For example, listeners must create the meaning "uniformed police officers" for the word *uniforms* in the utterance "there are 20,000 uniforms in the city" (Gerrig, 1989). The word *uniform* is metonymic (or a synecdoche) because it exhibits a stands-for relationship where a salient part (the uniform) stands for a whole (the person wearing the uniform).

Psycholinguistic research has shown that readers can easily determine the appropriate referents for metonymic expressions in discourse (Gibbs, 1990a). Thus, readers can easily recognize that the word *tuxedo* in the statement "John fired the tuxedo because he kept dropping the tray" refers to a butler, despite the literal incongruity of this sentence. How do readers arrive at the correct interpretation of this seemingly anomalous utterance, one that violates Grice's maxim of quality. Most theories of sentence processing assume that all the possible senses for each word in an utterance are listed in the mental lexicon, and that listeners select among them given context to understand a word (Clark, 1983; Clark & Gerrig, 1983). But understanding contextual expressions involving metonymy requires that a process of *sense creation* must operate to supplement ordinary *sense selection.* For instance, the contextually appropriate meaning of *tuxedo* cannot be selected from a short list of potential meanings in the lexicon because these potential senses are unlimited. Listeners must instead create a new meaning for a word that already has a conventional interpretation. One proposal, called the error recovery model (Gerrig, 1989), assumes that sense creation is initiated only after the conventional meaning has been found to be in error. This model posits that listeners recognize the need for a figurative interpretation for utterances such as "the ham sandwich is getting impatient for his check" after it is seen as violating some communication maxim. It is, after all, untruthful to claim that inanimate objects, such as ham sandwiches, exhibit human traits, such as impatience. An alternative view of how metonymic expressions are understood, called the concurrent processing model (Gerrig, 1989), claims that sense creation and sense selection processes operate simultaneously, perhaps in competition with each other, in the determination of tropological meaning.

An experimental test of these hypotheses had participants read short stories that established preempting meanings for old words (Gerrig, 1989).

For example, people read stories ending with "the horse race is the most popular event." In a conventional context, this final phrase referred to a standard race between horses, whereas in the innovative situation the final phrase referred to a unique situation where snails competed in a race that was the length of King Louis' horse. Readers took roughly the same time to comprehend this statement in both contexts. The overlap in reading times suggests that error recovery cannot be operating. Instead, readers seem to be creating and selecting meanings for the phrase "the horse race" at the same time. These data are similar to those obtained for metaphor comprehension that show that contextual expectations drive the recovery of metaphorical meanings at the same time that their literal meanings are being rejected (Gerrig & Healy, 1983; Inhoff, Duffy, & Carroll, 1984; Ortony, Schallert, Reynolds, & Antos, 1978).

Data from experiments such as these provide initial support for the concurrent processing model for understanding metonymic expressions. Other evidence suggests that listeners make immediate use of common ground information – the beliefs, knowledge, and attitudes shared by both speakers and listeners – to figure out the meanings of contextual expressions. Consider the sentences "while I was taking his picture, Steve did a Napoleon for the camera" and "after Joe listened to the tape of the interview, he did a Nixon to a portion of it." These utterances contain eponymous verbs (i.e., verbs created from proper nouns) that are metonymic in that each action stands for some specific act conventionally associated with an individual. Traditional models of language comprehension in both linguistics and psychology have significant difficulty understanding contextual verb phrases such as "did a Napoleon for the camera" and "did a Nixon to a portion of (the tape)" (Clark, 1983). But experimental research has shown that people usually experience little problem interpreting these phrases, especially when they have specific knowledge of the person referred to by the eponymous verb phrase (e.g., the famous painting of Napoleon) (Clark & Gerrig, 1983). In other cases it is less clear which acts are most salient for an individual so we often have greater difficulty understanding such utterances (e.g., "I met a girl at the Coffee House who did an Elizabeth Taylor while I was talking to her"). The problem in these instances is that listeners do not recognize which piece of information, or in this case which salient act of Elizabeth Taylor's, constitutes part of the common ground between themselves and the speaker (Clark & Gerrig, 1983). This makes it more difficult to understand exactly what a speaker means by the eponymous phrase "did an Elizabeth Taylor."

The evidence therefore suggests that understanding contextual expressions involving metonymy requires quick access to common ground information to create novel interpretations for these nonliteral utterances. The difficulty sometimes associated with making sense of metonymic phrases is not in the extra time it takes to resolve the apparent violation of communication maxims, but in the effort needed to access particular information that supposedly constitutes part of the common ground between speakers and listeners in any discourse situation.

Irony

Irony is traditionally seen as referring to situations that postulate a double audience, one of which is "in the know" and aware of the actor's intention, whereas the other is naive enough to take the situation or utterance at its face value (Fowler, 1965). In literature, irony refers to the technique of using incongruity to suggest a distinction between reality and expectation, saying one thing and meaning another with the audience aware of both. Perhaps the most famous example of irony comes from Jonathan Swift who, in *A Modest Proposal* (1729), contended with apparent gravity that the answer to the social problems in Ireland lies in cannibalism:

I have been assured by a very knowing American of my acquaintance in London, that a young healthy child well nursed is at a year old a most delicious, nourishing, and wholesome food, whether stewed, roasted, baked, or boiled, and I make no doubt that it will serve in a fricassee, or a ragout. (Swift, *A Modest Proposal*)

Despite his ironic intentions, Swift was widely criticized for this unthinkable proposal. A more recent case of irony that was frequently misinterpreted came from the songwriter and performer Randy Newman who recorded a song in the late 1970s called "Short People." The song began by stating that "short people got no reason to live, short people got no reason, short people got no reason to live," and went on to detail the inadequacies of short people, including their small voices, beady little eyes, and the inconvenience of having to pick them up in order to say hello. Soon after its release, various groups organized to lobby against the song even though Newman repeatedly stated that it was not his intention to ridicule short people, but rather to comment on a subject of prejudice so absurd that it might expose the absurdity of all prejudice, whether against women, Jews, Blacks, homosexuals, or whomever. Newman claimed that he was simply being ironic (Newman himself, as he pointed out, was a short individual).

As both Swift and Newman found out, irony is a risky business. One can never be sure that readers or listeners will detect the true meaning behind one's use of irony or even whether people will recognize that one is speaking ironically in the first place.[1]

Yet the ability to conceptualize situations as being ironic must explain why people speak ironically as often as they do. If someone says "it's a lovely day" in the midst of a rainstorm, the speaker recognizes the incongruity of some expectations that it would be a nice day and the reality of rain. In the same way, we judge some event as ironic because of an awareness of the incongruity between expectation and reality even though other participants in the situation appear to be blind to what is really happening. O'Henry's classic short story "The Gift of the Magi" is a wonderful example of this. Two very poor newlyweds want to give each other a special gift for Christmas, but neither has any money. The only thing of value the wife owns is her beautiful long hair; the husband's only valuable possession is a beautiful watch. The husband sells his watch to buy an ornate comb for his wife's hair and the wife sells her hair to buy her husband a gold chain for his watch. This ironic twist is common to many situations in life. We conceptualize such situations as ironic and often comment on them in everyday discourse by speaking ironically.

How do listeners arrive at the meanings of ironic statements in conversation? One common view of irony states that people can readily detect ironic meaning by assuming the opposite of an utterance's literal meaning once the literal meaning is seen as being contextually inappropriate (Searle, this volume), or as violating the maxim of quality (Grice, 1975, 1978). Ironic statements are seen as deliberately intended by speakers, and unlike metaphor, do not invite further elaboration of their meanings once understood because only the overt words in some local discourse have been violated (Booth, 1974). This traditional view attempts to limit how irony works so that the undermining of overt or literal meaning will have a fixed and specifiable shape.

One immediate problem with the traditional view of irony is that it assumes a process of interpretation that rests on a single point, specifically the perspicuity and independence of literal meaning. But literal meaning is no more stable than the eventual interpretation it supposedly authorizes. For example, the difficulty some people experienced in understanding Newman's statement "short people got no reason to live" was not simply their inability to derive an ironic meaning from a literal one. Instead, people had problems trying to figure out *which* literal meaning the statement "short people got no reason to live" actually conveyed in the first place. If one assumes, as did Newman's critics, that the speaker was rendering a judgment in saying that "short people got no reason to live," the words will literally and immediately mean that short people do not deserve to live. But if one conceives of the speaker as a short person (as Newman is), the utterance will be recognized literally as a complaint. Under this literal reading, short people have nothing to live *for* because of the indignities they must suffer. In both cases, there is a literal meaning that is obvious and inescapable, but it is not the same one. It is a mistake, then, to say that the incongruity of an utterance's literal meaning, given some context, signals the mark of irony. Literal meaning is itself an interpretation given some contextual assumptions; it is a product of understanding and as such cannot provide the grounds for subsequent interpretations of irony (Fish, 1983).

Another problem with the traditional view is that whereas irony is properly understood by assuming the opposite of a sentence's literal meaning, in many cases the opposite of a sentence's literal meaning is unclear or doesn't come close to specifying a speaker's true ironic intent. For example, if you commit a grievous deed toward a good friend and he says to you "thanks," the traditional view suggests that taken literally the utterance is grossly inappropriate, violating the maxim of quality, and so listeners are forced to render the utterance appropriate by determining in what way the sentence and speaker meanings, as Searle (this volume) calls them, differ. The opposite of your friend's comment "thanks" would be something like "no thanks" or "it is not the case that I'm thanking you." These interpretations do not capture the true ironic intention of this utterance, "you have done something that I do not appreciate." The ironic meaning of "thanks" denies a felicity, not truth, condition because it is infelicitous to thank someone who deserves ingratitude. In other cases speakers do mean literally what they say but are still speaking ironically (Sperber & Wilson, 1981). For example, a driver can say to a passenger, "I love people who signal," when another car has just cut in front without signaling, and mean this sarcastically, which is an especially negative form of irony, though the statement is literally true. Once again, it is incorrect to assume that irony violates some communicative maxims.

These criticisms of the traditional view of irony have led psycholinguists to examine whether understanding irony really requires some tacit recognition that these utterances violate maxims of cooperative communication. Research has shown that readers take no longer to interpret ironic, or specifically sarcastic, remarks, such as "he's a fine friend," than they do to interpret the same sentences in literal contexts, or to read nonsarcastic equivalent sentences, such as "he's a bad friend" (Gibbs, 1986a). Similar findings have been reported for understanding sarcastic indirect requests (e.g., "why don't you take your time washing the dishes?" meaning "hurry up and wash the dishes") (Gibbs, 1986b). One must be careful not to draw conclusions based on null results, but the empirical findings are clearly contrary to any theory suggesting that irony should be *more* difficult to process than literal utterances with roughly equivalent meaning. Thus, people do not usually appear to go through some process of analyzing the literal meanings of ironic utterances before recognizing that such meanings violate communication norms.

Another view that better captures what goes on psychologically in understanding irony is the *echoic mention theory* (Jorgensen, Miller, & Sperber, 1984; Sperber & Wilson, 1981). This theory proposes that irony involves the distinction between use and mention, rather than the distinction between literal and nonliteral meaning. The sentence "please be quiet," for example, can be *used* to tell people to be quiet, but it is only *mentioned* in "the sign says 'Please be quiet.' " This distinction is useful because the truth value of the mentioned expression is irrelevant to the truth of the proposition it specifies. According to the echoic mention theory, there is no nonliteral proposition that hearers must substitute for the literal proposition. Rather, the listener is *reminded* echoically of some familiar proposition (whose truth value is irrelevant), and of the speaker's attitude toward it. Consider this example: a mother says to her son "you're a big help," when her son has not assisted her in doing some task. The irony here comes from the fact that the mother has echoed some previously mentioned statement or belief, or perhaps some unspoken agreement between herself and her son. The son might have earlier offered to help his mother or it might be his job to do so. When the mother says "you're a big help," she is, in a sense, quoting the earlier offer or verbalizing a mutually shared belief that the son is supposed to help her as part of his job.

Various research demonstrates that people judge ironic utterances with explicit echoic mentions as being more ironic than statements that do not have such mentions (Gibbs, 1986a; Jorgensen et al., 1984). People also process sarcasm based on an explicit echo faster than they do sarcastic expressions based on less explicit or nonexistent echos (Gibbs, 1986a). Kreuz and Glucksberg (1989) have extended the echoic mention theory to emphasize the reminding function of irony based on the shared attitudes and expectations held by conversational participants. Although all ironic utterances accomplish their communicative intent by reminding listeners of some antecedent event, not all such reminders are echoic, nor do they all refer to actual or implied utterances. For example, the utterance "another gorgeous day!" declared when it has been gray and raining for over two weeks need not echo anyone's utterance, thought, or opinion. It alludes to a generalized expectation or desire for good weather and, in doing so, expresses the speaker's disappointment in the weather. Swift's essay on eating small children also does not appear to involve previous mention.

The echoic reminder theory explains why positive statements, such as "a fine friend you are," can convey sarcasm so much better than negative statements, such as "you're a terrible friend" (Gibbs, 1986a; Kreuz & Glucksberg, 1989). Positive statements do not require explicit antecedents because these expressions implicitly allude to societal norms and expectations that are invariably positive (e.g., if you don't have anything nice to say, then don't say anything). But negative statements such as "you idiot!" said to a friend who has just solved some difficult problem, do not implicitly allude to these positive norms and require explicit antecedents to be easily understood (Kreuz & Glucksberg, 1989). Echoic mention may well be a special case of reminders that allude to prior occurrences or states of affairs.

An alternative view of irony suggests that verbal irony involves pretense rather than echoic meaning or reminding (Clark & Gerrig, 1984; Fowler, 1965). For example, a speaker who says, in the context of a rainstorm, "what lovely weather we're having," pretends to be an unseeing person,

perhaps a weather forecaster announcing the beautiful weather to an unknown audience. If pretense required only asserting the opposite of what
clearly is the case, then pretense theory would be a notational variant of the
echoic mention theory (Clark & Gerrig, 1984). But pretense goes beyond
this because the speaker is pretending to be someone else (an unseeing
person) and is also pretending to be talking to some person other than the
listener. When listeners recognize this pretense, they should understand
that the speaker is expressing a derogatory attitude toward the idea expressed, the imaginary speaker, and the imaginary listener. These imaginary speakers and listeners may be recognizable individuals (like some
specific weather forecaster) or people of recognizable type such as inaccurate weather forecasters in general. Both Swift's essay and Newman's song
can be treated as though the authors are pretending to be someone else,
speaking to an imaginary audience that might accept their ideas in all
seriousness.

   Pretense theory and reminder theory have much in common; both theories suggest that the communicative purpose of irony is to call attention to
some idea or attitude that both speaker and listener can derogate (Kreuz &
Glucksberg, 1989; Williams, 1984). Pretense theory, however, can also be
applied to other kinds of nonliteral language. When someone makes an
indirect speech act such as "can you pass the salt?" the speaker is only
pretending that some obstacle might prevent the addressee from complying
with the request (Gibbs, 1986c). Similarly, when someone says "it sure is
hot in here," the speaker only pretends the comment is on room temperature alone: he or she really wants some listener to open a window (Kreuz &
Glucksberg, 1989). The next section examines two other tropes that may
similarly be understood as pretense. My discussion in this section reinforces
the idea that understanding tropes does not require people to recognize
these figures as violating the maxims of truthfulness. Other pragmatic information, such as what speakers and listeners mutually believe about each
other and the situation at hand, permits the easy recovery of what speakers
mean when they use irony.

Hyperbole and understatements

In classical rhetoric, hyperbole and understatement are closely related to
irony in that each misrepresents the truth. In hyperbole speakers assert more
than is objectively warranted, as when Professor Smith says to Professor
Jones "I have ten thousand papers to grade before noon." Hyperbole should
be contrasted with simple overstatement, wherein a person unconsciously or
unintentionally expresses a proposition stronger than the evidence warrants.
The same proposition can be overstatement in one person's mouth and
hyperbole in another's. A person who states "all Americans can attain their
dreams of success" without realizing that circumstances of nature and society

prevent some people from achieving their full potential has simply over-stated the truth. However, a person who realizes the truth might intend his audience to understand the same proposition as hyperbole for rhetorical effect. Many hyperboles are apparent because they are patently absurd, such as the idiomatic expressions "it makes my blood boil" and "it is raining cats and dogs."

Understatement also distorts the truth: speakers say less than is objectively warranted as when someone comments about a very drunk person that "he seems to have had a bit too much to drink." *Litotes* are a particular kind of understatement in which the speaker uses a negative expression where a positive one would have been more forceful and direct. Litotes express an overt lack of commitment and so imply a desire to suppress or conceal one's true attitude. Paradoxically, litotes, like hyperbole, involve intensification, suggesting that the speaker's feelings are too deep for plain expression (e.g., "it's not bad," "he's no Hercules," "she's no beauty," "he's not exactly a pauper"). Because of their two-layer significance – superficial indifference and underlying commitment – litotes are often treated as a category of irony. In everyday speech, hyperbole and litotes represent antithetical postures and tend to go with contrasting attitudes: optimism and idealism in the case of hyperbole, pessimism and cynicism in the case of litotes. Both hyperbole and understatement are thus tradition-ally viewed as violations of Grice's maxims, with hyperbole violating the maxim of quality (say what you believe to be true), whereas understate-ment violates the maxim of quantity (contribute neither more nor less to the conversation than is required). In both cases, according to the Gricean framework, the speaker urges the addressee to seek an implicature beyond the straightforward literal interpretation of what is said.

Hyperbole and understatement violate truthfulness maxims, however, only if one assumes that a speaker's utterance must be identical to his or her beliefs. They do not violate or flout truthfulness maxims when one assumes that a speaker's utterance need only resemble his or her beliefs, sharing some logical and contextual implications with what the speaker believes (Wilson & Sperber, 1990). For example, when Jane says "my boyfriend is the strongest man in the world," she is conveying some implica-tions about her boyfriend, but not all of them need to be identical with the proposition stated. Only some implications need mirror what Jane truly believes. As with irony, when people use hyperbole and understatement, they pretend some state of affairs holds in the world to communicate ideas or attitudes regarding their stated propositions. When Jane goes on to say "My boyfriend is almost ten feet tall," she is adopting the pretense that her friend is close to ten feet tall to express the idea that he is tall. With both hyperbole and understatement, the speaker's meaning is always somewhat indeterminate because there is only a resemblance between what someone says and what the person really believes to be true. Thus we recognize by

Jane's statement that she believes her boyfriend to be quite tall, but we never know for sure exactly how tall he might really be. Similarly, when Bob says of his wife's special apple pie "it's not bad," we recognize that Bob thinks positively of his wife's pie, but we are somewhat unsure exactly how good he believes the pie to be.

The indeterminacy associated with understanding many tropes, such as irony, hyperbole, and understatement, shows how important it is to specify the time course of understanding in theories of figurative language comprehension. Listeners may comprehend a hyperbolic statement such as "I've got ten thousand papers to grade before noon" in the sense of immediately recognizing the speaker's belief that he or she has many papers to grade before noon. But on further processing or conscious reflection, the listener may, perhaps through his knowledge of the speaker, realize that the speaker probably has only four or five papers to grade, is slow in grading them, and feels enormous pressure conveyed through hyperbole. This elaboration of the speaker's intention and the true state of affairs requires a different theoretical description than needed to explain what goes on in the first few moments of trope comprehension.

There is no published experimental research in understanding hyperbole and understatement. My discussion of irony, hyperbole, and understatement suggests, however, that these tropes do not necessarily violate communication maxims. People's understanding of them may be readily explained by weakening the traditional maxims of cooperative communication in two ways. When making some statement, speakers want to attribute the belief in the proposition they express not to themselves necessarily, but to someone, perhaps by alluding to some cultural norm, and their statements need not be identical to their own beliefs, they need only resemble them (Wilson & Sperber, 1989). These alternative conceptions of the standard conversational maxims provide for a more accurate picture of the complexity of irony, hyperbole, and understatement, as well as better specifying the pragmatic information used when people make sense of these tropes in conversation.

Oxymoron

Oxymora are traditionally defined as figures of speech that combine two seemingly contradictory elements, as in Shakespeare's "O heavy lightness! serious vanity! / Misshapen chaos of well-seeming forms! / Feather of lead, bright smoke, cold fire, sick health!" (Shakespeare, *Romeo and Juliet*). Literally speaking, these statements seem nonsensical in that smoke isn't bright, fire isn't cold, and to be healthy isn't to be sick. We do have an ability to take contradictory, paradoxical stances toward people and events. This ability is more than just seeing in some person or situation alternative sides that cannot be grasped at the same time (in the way we see ambiguous figures). Rather, we seem able to conceptually grasp in a single instance two things that are apparently contradictory. Winston Churchill's quip that "America and England are two countries separated by a common language" makes sense to us through our cultural understanding of these two nations despite the contradiction of two entities divided by a common trait. Oxymora, such as "bright smoke," "lead feathers," and "sick health," do not simply represent figures of speech. They also reflect poetic schemes for conceptualizing human experience and the external world. Developments in the history of science have often been characterized as expressing oxymoronic thought. For instance, the transition from the cosmological views of Ptolemy and Copernicus to those of Kepler involved a shift from thinking in terms of antithesis to thinking in terms of the oxymoron that sees celestial motion as composed of both curves and straight lines (Hallyn, 1990). More generally, oxymora are frequently found in everyday speech, many of them barely noticed as such, for example "intense apathy," "internal exile," "man child," "loyal opposition," "plastic glasses," "guest host," and so on. The ubiquity of these figures suggests some underlying ability to conceive of ideas, objects, and events in oxymoronic terms.

How do people normally understand oxymora such as those seen in Shakespeare and in everyday speech? What makes some contradictory statements more meaningful to us than others? There appear to be two types of oxymora (Shen, 1987). Direct oxymora consist of two terms that are antonyms, or two terms whose only difference consists of a change in the plus or minus sign of their lowest, distinctive feature, all other features being identical (e.g., "a feminine man" and "living death"). Indirect oxymora consist of two terms that are not the direct antonyms of each other, but have one term that is the hyponym of the first term's antonym. Consider the example "the silence whistles" (taken from the Hebrew poet Nathan Altherman's *Summer Night*). The antonym of "silence" is lexically realized by the word "sound" whose semantic specification consists of the same features for "silence" except for the replacement of the "+" sign of the distinctive feature "silence" (namely "−sound") by the "−" sign. The second term of the oxymoron "the silence whistles" is not "sound," however, but its hyponym "whistle," which also shares the same feature list as does "sound" with an additional feature of something like +sharpness. Other indirect oxymora include "sacred garbage" in which the second term "garbage" is a hyponym of the category "defiled entities," the direct antonym of the first term "sacred." Shakespeare's "bright smoke" has a second term "smoke" that is the hyponym of "dim," which is the direct antonym of "bright." Finally, the oxymoron "sweet sorrow" has a second term "sorrow," conceived of as an example (that is, a hyponym) of the category "bitter entities," which is the antonym of the first term "sweet."

One empirical analysis of the oxymora found in modern Israeli poetry and in classical literary dictionaries indicated that only 16 percent of oxymora were of the direct type, whereas 84 percent were indirect (Shen, 1987). Why are indirect oxymora much more frequent than direct? Shen (1987) argued that indirect oxymora are more poetic than direct ones, and as such, should require the most complicated processing to be understood. This idea of equating complexity of processing with "poeticality" is commonly shared by many theories of tropes and poetic texts, but earlier work on the psycholinguistics of metaphor indicates that aptness (which is related to "poeticality") is independent of comprehension (Gerrig & Healy, 1983), and data from my laboratory show that readers take no longer to interpret indirect oxymora than direct ones. If anything, direct oxymora, such as "bittersweet" are more difficult to interpret than indirect ones, such as "sweet sadness."

Although indirect oxymora do not seem more difficult to process than direct expressions, indirect oxymora might still be viewed as more poetic. One might try to determine the poeticality of oxymora by the conceptual structure of the categories they designate. For instance, in the phrase "the silence whistles," the superordinate category "sound" has several subordinate members that are specific types of sounds such as "cries," "whispers," "shouts," and "whistles." These different members of the category "sound" give speakers a range of examples to choose from in forming new oxymora, specifically in selecting the actual hyponym for the second term of the phrase. The choice of hyponyms is constrained by the prototypical structure of the category. Members of a category differ in their degree of goodness, so hyponyms differ in their typicality with respect to their superordinate category. Some oxymora have hyponyms of their first terms' antonyms that are prototypical examples of the superordinate category. For example, in the oxymoron "the silence cries" the hyponym "cries" is a prototypical example of its superordinate category "sound." Shakespeare's "cold fire" has a second term that is a prototypical example of the category "hot" which is the first term's antonym. These unmarked cases of indirect oxymora are thought to be the least poetic because they require the least degree of processing given the easy availability of their hyponyms (Shen, 1987).

Medium cases of oxymora might require more complex processing because their hyponyms are medium examples of superordinate categories with some terms very good or typical examples of a category and other terms poor examples of a superordinate category. Consider again "the silence whistles" in which some instances of the category "sound," such as "cry" and "shout," are better examples than "whistles," whereas others, such as "sigh," are worse, and still others, such as "whistle," are intermediate or medium examples of the category. In "sacred garbage," the antonym of the adjective "sacred" is something like "defiled" or "impure" (in the religious sense) so that the second term "garbage" is a medium example of "defiled." "Sweet sorrow" has the hyponym "sorrow" that represents a medium example of the category "bitterness."

Finally, marked cases of oxymora include phrases in which the hyponym is a very bad exemplar of its superordinate category. For example, in the phrase "the silence sighs" the hyponym "sighs" is a very bad example of the category "sound." Marked cases of oxymora should be viewed as most poetic, requiring the greatest amount of processing to be interpreted. Shen's analysis of a corpus of eighty-five indirect oxymora showed that fifty-seven (65 percent) were medium cases, nineteen (22 percent) were unmarked examples, and eleven (22 percent) were marked cases. At the very least, medium cases of oxymora appear to be more typical in poetry and literature.

My own recent research suggests that people's understanding of oxymora is not directly related to their judgments of poeticality for these phrases. People find medium cases of indirect oxymora the most difficult to process among the three types identified by Shen (1987), but these medium phrases were also viewed as being the least poetic. The dissociation between comprehension and appreciation (or poeticality judgments) of oxymora is similar to that found in studies with metaphor (Gerrig & Healy, 1983). These findings provide further support for the inappropriateness of inferring anything about comprehension processes from data or introspections about the products of trope understanding (e.g., judgments of appreciation or poeticality). The data on oxymora suggest, nevertheless, that there is some link between people's conceptual knowledge and their understanding of these figurative phrases. Oxymora might even be characterized as forming ad hoc categories similar to the categories created by metaphorical comparison statements (Glucksberg & Keysar, this volume).

Idioms

Most taxonomies of tropes do not include idioms as separate figures; these phrases are traditionally conceived of as "dead" or frozen metaphors that speakers make sense of by learning arbitrary links between them and their figurative meanings. Readers and listeners do not generally recognize them as violating truthfulness norms because the arbitrary links between idioms and their figurative meanings are highly conventionalized (e.g., "spill the beans" is to reveal a secret, "button your lip" is to keep a secret, "lose your marbles" is to go crazy, and so on). But do people have greater insight into the figurative meaning of idioms other than to realize that they have conventional, nonliteral meanings? Even though idioms are not often seen as tropes, there has been substantial work on these figurative phrases that takes issue with the long-standing belief in the "dead" metaphor view of idiomaticity. This work has shown that the individual words in many idioms systematically contribute to their overall figurative interpretation, contrary to the noncompositional view of idioms (Fillmore, Kay, & O'Connor, 1988; Gibbs & Nayak, 1989; Lakoff, 1987; Langacker, 1986; Nunberg, 1978). For example, speakers know that "spill the beans" is analyzable since "beans" refers to an idea or secret and "spill" refers to revealing the secret. Similarly, in the phrase "pop the question," it is easy to discern that the noun "question" refers to a particular question ("Will you marry me?") when the verb "pop" is used to refer to the act of uttering it. People's intuitions about the analyzability of idioms play an important role in determining their syntactic productivity (Gibbs & Nayak, 1989), lexical flexibility (Gibbs, Nayak, Bolton, & Keppel, 1989), and ease of comprehension (Gibbs, Nayak, & Cutting, 1989). It appears that people ordinarily perform some sort of compositional analysis, though not necessarily a literal analysis, when comprehending idiom phrases to attach meanings to their specific parts (Gibbs, Nayak, & Cutting, 1989). These empirical studies suggest that the meanings of idioms can be partially motivated in that speakers recognize some relationship between the words in idioms and their overall figurative interpretation.

Although it is often assumed that idioms are "dead" metaphors, it may very well be that people make sense of idioms because they tacitly recognize the metaphorical mapping between two conceptual domains of information that partially explains why idioms mean what they do. For example, the idiom "John spilled the beans" maps our knowledge of someone tipping over a container of beans to a person revealing some secret. English speakers understand "spill the beans" to mean "reveal the secret" because there are underlying conceptual metaphors, such as THE MIND IS A CONTAINER and IDEAS ARE PHYSICAL ENTITIES, that structure their conceptions of minds, secrets, and disclosure (Lakoff & Johnson, 1980). The mapping of source domains such as containers and physical entities onto minds and ideas results in very specific entailments about the act of revealing a secret. Thus, the act of revealing a secret is usually seen as being caused by some internal pressure within the mind of the revealer, the action is thought to be unintentional and is judged as being performed in a forceful manner (Gibbs & O'Brien, 1990). One interesting possibility is that people draw these inferences each time they comprehend the idiom phrase "spill the beans." It is less likely, however, that people draw such inferences about causation, intentionality, and manner when they encounter literal paraphrases of idioms, such as "reveal the secret." Literal phrases are not motivated by the same set of conceptual metaphors as are specific idioms. Therefore, people do not view the meanings of "spill the beans" and "reveal the secret" as equivalent despite their apparent similarity.

One way to uncover speakers' tacit knowledge of the metaphorical basis for idioms is through a detailed examination of their mental images of idioms (Gibbs & O'Brien, 1990; Lakoff, 1987). Consider the idiom "spill the beans." Try to form a mental image for this phrase and then ask yourself the following questions. Where are the beans before they are spilled? How big is the container? Are the beans cooked or uncooked? Is the spilling accidental or intentional? Where are the beans once they've been spilled? Are the beans in a nice, neat pile? Where are the beans supposed to be? After the beans are spilled, are they easy to retrieve?

Gibbs and O'Brien (1990) examined people's mental images for groups of idioms with similar figurative meanings, idioms about revelation ("spill the beans," "let the cat out of the bag," "blow the lid off"), anger ("blow your stack," "hit the ceiling," "flip your lid"), insanity ("go off your rocker," "lose your marbles," "bounce off the walls"), secretiveness ("keep it under your hat," "button your lips," "keep in the dark"), and exerting control ("crack the whip," "lay down the law," "call the shots"). Participants were asked to describe their mental images for these idioms and to answer questions about the causes, intentionality, and manner of action in their mental images. We expected a high degree of consistency in participants' descriptions of their mental images for idioms with similar meanings because of the constraints conceptual metaphors (THE MIND IS A CONTAINER, IDEAS ARE PHYSICAL ENTITIES, and ANGER IS HEAT) impose on the link between idiomatic phrases and their nonliteral meanings. If people's tacit knowledge of idioms is not structured by different conceptual metaphors, there should be little consistency in participants' responses to questions about the causes and consequences of actions within their mental images of idioms with similar nonliteral interpretations.

The descriptions of mental images were remarkably consistent for different idioms with similar figurative meanings. Across the five groups of idioms we studied, 75 percent of participants described similar general images. These general schemas for people's images were not simply representative of the idioms' figurative meanings, but captured more specific aspects of the kinesthetic events. For example, the anger idioms such as "flip your lid" and "hit the ceiling" all refer to the concept of "getting angry," but participants specifically imagined for these phrases some force causing a container to release pressure in a violent manner. There is little in the surface forms of the different idioms to tightly constrain the images participants reported. After all, lids can be flipped and ceilings can be hit in a wide variety of ways, under many different circumstances. But our participants revealed little variation in the general events of their images for idioms with similar meanings.

Participants' responses to the questions about the causes and consequences of the similar actions described in their images were also highly consistent (over 88 percent similar responses when averaged across both the different probe questions and the five groups of idioms). Consider the most frequent responses to the probe questions for the anger idioms ("blow your stack," "flip your lid," "hit the ceiling"). When imagining anger idioms, people know that pressure (that is, stress or frustration) causes the action, that one has little control over the pressure once it builds, its violent release is unintentional (for example, the blowing of the stack), and that once release has taken place (once the ceiling has been hit, the lid flipped, the stack blown), it is difficult to reverse the action. Each of these responses is based on people's folk conceptions of heated fluid or vapor building up and escaping from containers (our participants most frequently envisioned the containers as the size of a person's head). Thus, the metaphorical mapping of a source domain (e.g., heated fluid in a container) into a target domain (e.g., the anger emotion) partially explains why people have consistent mental images, and specific knowledge about those images, for different idioms about anger. Other studies showed that knowing the figurative meaning (e.g., "getting angry") of an idiom does not by itself account for people's systematic knowledge of their images of idioms (e.g., "blow your stack" or "flip your lid"). Furthermore, people were much less consistent in their mental images for literal phrases (e.g., "blow your tire") than for idioms (e.g., "blow your stack") because they do not possess the same degree of conceptual knowledge about their images for literal phrases as they do for idiomatic expressions.

The results of these studies support the idea that the figurative meanings of idioms can be accounted for by various conceptual metaphors that exist independently as part of our conceptual system. These data provide evidence on the systematic relationship between idioms with similar figurative interpretations. Traditional theories of idiomaticity have no way of accounting for these findings because they assume that the meanings of idioms are mostly arbitrary. But are all idioms with similar meanings motivated by identical kinds of conceptual metaphors? For instance, the idioms "blow your stack" and "bite your head off" both express extreme degrees of anger. "Bite your head off" might make sense, however, because people can link the lexical items in this phrase to the conceptual metaphor ANGRY BEHAVIOR IS ANIMAL BEHAVIOR. An animal jumping down a victim's throat is similar to someone shouting angrily. On the other hand, people might understand the figurative meaning of "blow your stack" through the conceptual metaphor ANGER IS HEAT IN A PRESSURIZED CONTAINER where a person shouting angrily has the same explosive effect as does the top of a container blowing open under pressure.

Psycholinguistic research has shown that people's knowledge of the metaphorical links between different source and target domains provides the basis for the appropriate use and interpretation of idioms in particular discourse situations (Nayak & Gibbs, 1990). Participants in one study, for example, gave higher appropriateness ratings to "blew her stack" in a story that described a woman's anger as being like heat in a pressurized container whereas "bit his head off" was seen as more appropriate in a story that described a woman's anger in terms of a ferocious animal. Thus, readers' judgments about the appropriateness of an idiom in context are influenced by the coherence between the metaphorical information depicted in a discourse situation and the conceptual metaphor reflected in the lexical makeup of an idiom.

The empirical studies reviewed here paint a very different picture of idiomaticity than that assumed by traditional theories in linguistics, philosophy, and psychology. Many idioms are not simple "dead" metaphors that are noncompositional in meaning. Nor are the figurative meanings of many idioms arbitrarily stipulated and listed as simple, literal paraphrases in the mental lexicon. Instead, idioms are partially compositional and their figurative meanings are motivated by the conceptual knowledge people possess of the domains to which they refer. People partially conceptualize experiences such as anger, revelation, joy, fear, and so on via different metaphorical mappings between source and target domains. These mappings provide part of the link between the lexical makeup of idioms and their figurative meanings such that many idioms make sense in having the meanings they do.

Conclusions

My aim in discussing tropes other than metaphor is partly motivated by a desire to stem the inflation of metaphor to the status of the master trope. Figurative language researchers in the cognitive sciences have been especially guilty of ignoring tropes other than metaphor. This neglect stems partly from the belief that only metaphors have real cognitive value, whereas oxymora and figures involving irony, metonymy, and hyperbole are just rhetorical devices that neither serve conceptual purposes nor are motivated by figurative processes of thought. Despite the speculative nature of much of my discussion, I have laid the groundwork for the view that many tropes represent figurative schemes of thought by which people make sense of themselves and the world. The ubiquity of tropes throughout everyday speech testifies to the idea that much of our thinking is based on figurative processes that include not only metaphor, but a vast array of tropes.

The evidence presented here seems clearly contrary to the notion that tropes are understood as apparent violations of maxims of cooperative communication. I have suggested that researchers mistakenly assume that the products of linguistic understanding can tell us something about the processes by which utterances are understood and vice versa. Moreover, scholars often view trope understanding as being different in kind from literal language use because of various confusions over the perspicuity and independence of the notion of literal meaning. Understanding tropes does not require, however, that listeners replace a literal proposition with a nonliteral interpretation. Many tropes, particularly irony, hyperbole, and understatement, make sense because they are recognized as instances of pretense where speakers attribute their utterances to someone other than themselves. Other tropes, such as metonymy and idioms, make sense because of specific metaphors and metonymies that form part of the basis for thought. These arguments against the traditional, pragmatic view of trope understanding should not be regarded as a wholesale rejection of the Grice/Searle theoretical framework. It is clearly the case that making sense of tropes critically depends on recognizing what speakers and listeners mutually know, as well as on the specific recovery of what people intend to communicate when they speak figuratively.

NOTES

Preparation of this chapter was sponsored by Grant MH42980 from the National Institute of Mental Health and by a faculty Research Grant from the University of California, Santa Cruz.

1 Irony is not limited to verbal acts, but is also a characteristic of situations that are often referred to as *dramatic irony*. One way of distinguishing between verbal and dramatic irony is that one can intend to say something ironic, but one cannot intend to do something ironic. I cannot say that I will do three ironic acts today because when I say that some act is ironic, I am asserting that it is somehow unexpected or inconsistent from my point of view, and I cannot claim this with respect to my own intentions. But I can say of my past actions that it was ironic that I should have done such-and-such, or I could say of some hypothetical action that were I to do such-and-such, it would be ironic (Booth, 1974).

13

Metaphor, induction, and social policy: The convergence of macroscopic and microscopic views

ROBERT J. STERNBERG, ROGER TOURANGEAU, AND GEORGIA NIGRO

Metaphor can be studied in many different ways and at many different levels, any one of which may lead to valid insights into the nature of metaphoric generation, comprehension, and appreciation. The insights of any one approach to metaphor are perhaps most convincingly validated when they converge with the insights of a distinctly different approach, leading the student of metaphor to much the same conclusions without regard to the particular method from which the conclusions derived.

In his lucid and enlightening analysis of generative metaphor, Schön has reached conclusions strikingly similar in many ways to those we have reached in our analyses of metaphor and induction. As anyone might expect, where two independent research programs are involved, there are a number of theoretical issues that are addressed by one of the research programs but not by the other. However, in the central core of overlapping issues, there is clear convergence in the conclusions we have independently drawn. In this chapter we should like to point out and discuss the sources of convergence.

What follows is divided into three sections. In order to relate our world to Schön's, it is necessary in the first section to say something about the motivation, approach, theory, and methods that underlie the work in our laboratory on metaphor and induction. These underpinnings of our research differ in many respects from Schön's. Then, it is possible in the second section to draw parallels between our conclusions and those of Schön regarding metaphor, induction, and social policy. In the third section, we restate five basic questions about metaphor posed by Verbrugge and McCarrell (1977) and by Schön, and discuss how they are answered, or at least addressed, within our view of metaphor.

Metaphor and induction

This section is divided into three parts. In the first two, we describe two different lines of research that address the relationship between metaphor and induction in somewhat different ways. In the third part, we discuss how the theoretical points of view from the two lines of research can be integrated.

Theory of representation

We shall start by discussing a theory of representation in metaphor.[1] The discussion deals with four topics, namely, the motivation, approach, theory, and methods underlying this work.

The basic goals motivating the research are, first, to use a representation for information in semantic memory that is flexible enough to handle metaphors in a variety of domains; second, to propose a small set of rules that account for the differential aesthetic appeal and comprehensibility of metaphors; and third, to relate the representations – and the set of rules operating upon the representations – to their counterparts in a highly general theory of induction.

Our approach to these problems is in many respects an outgrowth of research on analogical reasoning done by Rumelhart and Abrahamson (1973).[2] These investigators began with the assumption that information can be represented by means of a multidimensional "semantic space" in which each dimension represents some graded characteristic of the set of concepts under consideration. Some limited support for this assumption had been obtained earlier by Henley (1969) in her study of the semantics of animal names. Henley had subjects rate the dissimilarities between all possible pairs of thirty animal names, and then used a multidimensional scaling program to derive a three-dimensional solution that seemed to represent these terms adequately. The three dimensions of the space (in order of appearance and therefore "strength" in the solution) were size, ferocity, and humanness. Animals like *giraffe* and *elephant* were near one extreme on the size dimension, whereas animals like *mouse* and *rabbit* were near the other extreme. The ferocity dimension contrasted animals like *tiger* and *gorilla* with those like *pig* and *cow,* and the humanness dimension contrasted animals like *monkey* and *gorilla* with those like *cow* and *mouse.*

According to Rumelhart and Abrahamson, each term of an analogy problem can be represented by a point in this three-dimensional space. For any analogy problem of the form *A:B::C:?,* there is a concept, *I,* that is the ideal solution to the analogy in the sense that the vector distance from *C* to

I is the same as that from *A* to *B*. The probability of choosing any answer option, X_i, as the best solution to the problem is a monotonic decreasing function of the distance between the locations in the space of *I* and X_i. Consider, for example, the analogy RAT:PIG:GOAT: _____ ; (A) CHIMPANZEE, (B) COW, (C) RABBIT, (D) SHEEP. There is no animal among these options, or in the semantic space, for that matter, that falls exactly where an ideal solution should. But the animal closest in the space to this hypothetical ideal animal is *cow,* followed by *sheep,* then *rabbit,* and then *chimpanzee.* So if subjects are asked to choose the best solution, the largest proportion of subjects should choose *cow,* then *sheep,* then *rabbit,* and then *chimpanzee.*

The theory of response choice was strengthened by assuming the applicability of Luce's (1959) choice axiom, and by assuming that the probability of choosing an alternative, X_i, as best is an exponentially decreasing function of the distance of that alternative from the ideal point. Thus, a quantitative choice rule is added to supplement the qualitative specification of rank order. With a little bit of mathematics, one can extend the quantitative predictions to all rank orderings, so that if subjects are asked not only to select the best option, but to rank order all the options as well, it is possible to predict the proportion of subjects assigning each rank ordering to each option.

Rumelhart and Abrahamson tested their theory in three ingenious experiments, of which only the first will be briefly summarized here. They asked thirty-five subjects to solve thirty animal-name analogies, rank ordering the options for goodness of fit. The authors then estimated a single parameter for the exponential function, and tested the ability of the mathematical model to account for the response-choice data. In fact, the model provided an excellent fit to the data, suggesting that subjects were indeed following a rank-ordering strategy similar to that proposed by the theory.

We have suspected that a common set of processes and strategies underlie performance on a variety of induction tasks (see, for example, chapter 13 of Sternberg, 1977b), and so it seemed possible that the same choice rule could be applied to other induction tasks as well. This possibility was investigated experimentally (see Sternberg & Gardner, 1978). Sternberg and Gardner administered thirty animal-name analogies, thirty animal-name series completions, and thirty animal-name classifications to thirty students from the Yale community. The analogies were those from Experiment 1 of Rumelhart and Abrahamson (1973). The series problems took the form exemplified by the problem, RABBIT:DEER: _____ ; (A) ANTELOPE, (B) BEAVER, (C) TIGER, (D) ZEBRA. Subjects were asked to rank order the options in terms of how well they completed a series from the first term to the second and from the second term to the third. The classification problems took the form exemplified by the problem MOUSE, CHIMPANZEE, CHIPMUNK, _____ ; (A) GORILLA, (B) RAT, (C) SQUIRREL, (D) ZEBRA. Subjects were asked to rank order the options in terms of how well they fit in with the three terms preceding the options.

It was hypothesized that in each of the three tasks, subjects would employ a different strategy that was nevertheless aimed at a common goal: the discovery of an ideal point. The strategies can be conceptualized geometrically in terms of the "construction of vectors." In the analogies task, subjects would construct a vector from the first term to the second, and then attempt to construct a vector from the third term to an ideal point such that the new vector was parallel to the first vector and equal to it in length and direction. In the series-completion task, subjects would construct a vector from the first term to the second, and then construct a vector from the second term to an ideal point such that the new vector was collinear with the first vector and equal to it in length and direction. In the classification task, subjects would construct a vector from the first term to the second, another vector from the first term to the third, and then use the centroid of the triangle formed by these vectors as an ideal point. Thus, although the proposed strategies required to arrive at an ideal point differed across the three types of tasks, it was hypothesized that subjects would indeed construct an ideal point in each task, and that the rule by which the subjects rank ordered responses (by relating them to the ideal point) would be the same in each task.

A single exponential parameter was estimated from the response-choice data for each task, and the values from the three estimations were remarkably similar. Moreover, the identical mathematical model provided an excellent fit to the data in each of the three tasks. Apparently, then, Rumelhart and Abrahamson's extension of Luce's choice axiom to the analogies task can itself be extended to other forms of induction tasks as well.

We have viewed metaphoric comprehension and appreciation as inductive in nature, because these global processes seem to involve, at bare minimum, induction of the relationship(s) between the tenor and vehicle of the metaphor. It therefore seems plausible that an approach similar to that employed in the animal-name induction study might be useful in investigating metaphor. Certain problems need to be dealt with, however. First, although the multidimensional scaling paradigm might work well enough in well-delineated semantic fields such as animal names, it seemed less likely to work well, or at least to yield comparable dimensions, across a variety of semantic domains. Second, it seemed necessary to us to generalize the notion of semantic space by introducing a concept of "orders" of spaces in order to accommodate our theory of metaphoric comprehension and appreciation. These orders represent the level of abstraction of the terms in the various spaces. It is to this theory that we now turn.

Imagine an array of "local subspaces" comprising sets of terms, such as U.S. historical figures, modern world leaders, mammals, birds, fish, airplanes, land vehicles, and ships. Each local subspace represents the terms within it as points with coordinates on each of several dimensions. Each of these local subspaces might also be viewed as of roughly the same order (level of abstraction), and as of a lower order than a higher-order hyperspace that contains the lower-order subspaces as points embedded within it. Thus, the points of the higher-order hyperspace map into the lower order subspaces, and can be labeled by the names of these subspaces. This hyperspace can, in turn, be viewed as one of multiple subspaces of some still higher-order hyperspace. However, possible hyperspaces of successively higher orders will not concern us here; we shall need to deal only with local subspaces of a lower order and one hyperspace of a higher order.[3]

We shall also need some rule for restricting the subspaces that map into a single hyperspace, and some way of establishing comparability across subspaces. Both of these goals can be accomplished by requiring all subspaces to have at least one corresponding dimension.[4] Thus, for example, the subspaces of modern world leaders, bird names, and ships must have at least one corresponding dimension if they are to be local subspaces of the same order and of a common hyperspace.

The conventional multidimensional scaling paradigm of requiring, say, dissimilarity ratings between all possible pairs of elements within each of these domains does not seem likely to fill the bill. Viewed in isolation, the domains simply do not seem to bear much resemblance to each other. One possible solution to this problem would be to have subjects rate dissimilarities between all possible pairs of objects both within and between domains, although this procedure quickly becomes impractical with large numbers of objects; moreover, the theoretical status of the cross-domain ratings would have to be thought out. We have followed another alternative, drawing upon the success of Osgood, Suci, and Tannenbaum (1957) and others in achieving uniform dimensions across domains, using the device of the *semantic differential*.

Subjects were asked to rate each of twenty terms within each domain on twenty-one scales, such as *warlike–peaceful, noble–ignoble,* and *strong–weak,* with a different group of sixteen subjects supplying ratings for each of the eight domains. We hoped in this way to obtain a corresponding set of dimensions for the eight domains (U.S. historical figures, modern world leaders, mammals, birds, fish, airplanes, land vehicles, ships). It seemed plausible to us that at least two such corresponding dimensions would obtain: prestige (similar to Osgood et al.'s "evaluative" dimension) and aggression (similar to Osgood et al.'s "potency" or "activity" dimensions). The adjective pairs for each domain were then factor-analyzed.[5]

Visual inspection of the results of the factor analyses supported our hypothesis: Two corresponding dimensions of prestige and aggression appeared for each domain, although the order in which the two dimensions appeared was variable across domains. In order to confirm our visual impression, we computed correlations between the loadings of the adjective pairs on dimensions we believed either to correspond, or not to correspond, across domains. Correlations for corresponding dimensions (prestige in each of two domains or aggression in each of two domains) were very high, and correlations for noncorresponding dimensions (prestige in one domain and aggression in the other) were very low, suggesting that the dimensions did indeed have the statistical properties our visual inspection had suggested they had.

A separate group of thirty subjects rated the eight domain names on each of the twenty-one adjective scales, and these results were also factor analyzed, giving us a three-factor hyperspace with each factor roughly representing a type of content (types of people, types of animals, types of vehicles). The results from this and the preceding factor analyses served as the representational basis for our further theoretical work.

Given our representational framework, what rules might identify metaphors that are either easily comprehensible or aesthetically pleasing? It seems that two basic considerations need to be taken into account in assessing the comprehensibility and aesthetic quality of a metaphor: the superimposed within-subspace distance between the tenor (first term) of the metaphor and the vehicle (second term), and the between-subspace distance.

Consider first the meaning of "superimposed within-subspace distance." Since at least two dimensions are corresponding (or at least, very similar) for each domain, one can imagine superimposing the dimensions of one local subspace onto the corresponding dimensions of another local subspace. Once this superimposition is accomplished, it is also possible to imagine computing the superimposed within-subspace distance between two points that are actually in different subspaces. One simply computes the distance between points as though they were in the same subspace. Thus, if the coordinates of some point in one subspace were (x, y), then the superimposed within-subspace distance to some point in another subspace would be 0 if that point also happened to occupy location (x, y), and would depart from 0 as the Euclidean distance of that point from (x, y) increased.

An example may help clarify the concept. The superimposed within-subspace distance from *wildcat* to *hawk is* very small, because the coordinates of *hawk* in the bird subspace are very close to those of *wildcat* in the mammal subspace. The superimposed within-subspace distance from *wildcat* to *robin* is quite large, however, because the coordinates of *wildcat* and *robin* are quite disparate. Similarly, the superimposed within-subspace distance from *wildcat* to *ICBM is* small, whereas the superimposed within-subspace distance from *wildcat* to *blimp* is large.

Consider next the meaning of "between-subspace" distance. In order for the concept to have meaning, it must be possible somehow to compute the distance between a pair of subspaces. This computation is possible, in our representational formulation, because the distance between two subspaces is equal to the distance between the corresponding points within the appropriate hyperspace. Thus, if the coordinates of some local subspace in the hyperspace are *(x, y)*, the distance from that subspace to another subspace increases as the Euclidean distance of that subspace from *(x, y)* increases.

Let us return to our earlier example to illustrate the concept of between-subspace distance. The between-subspace distance from *wildcat* to *hawk* is the same as that from *wildcat* to *robin*, since both *hawk* and *robin* are in the same local subspace. This distance is small, since mammal and bird names are viewed as relatively close to one another in the hyperspace. The between-subspace distances from *wildcat* to *ICBM* and *blimp* are also the same, since these latter two terms fall within the same local subspace; and this distance is relatively large, since mammal names and names of airplanes are viewed as relatively far from one another in the hyperspace.

Turning now to the theory of metaphor, we propose that *a metaphor is comprehensible to the extent that both the superimposed within-subspace distance and the between-subspace distance between tenor and vehicle are small. A metaphor is aesthetically pleasing to the extent that the superimposed within-subspace distance is small, but the between-subspace distance is large.* Thus, a smaller superimposed within-subspace distance between tenor and vehicle works in favor both of comprehensibility and aesthetic pleasingness, whereas a smaller between-subspace distance works in favor of comprehensibility, but against aesthetic pleasingness.

Consider some example metaphors derived from the terms discussed above:

(1) A wildcat is a hawk among mammals
(2) A wildcat is a robin among mammals
(3) A wildcat is an ICBM among mammals
(4) A wildcat is a blimp among mammals.

What empirical claims does the proposed theory make about each of these metaphors?

A first set of empirical claims addresses the relative comprehensibility of the various metaphors. According to the theory, (1) should be a highly comprehensible metaphor, because both the superimposed within-subspace distance and the between-subspace distance between tenor and vehicle are small. Metaphor (4), on the other hand, should be only poorly comprehensible, because both distances are large. Thus, whereas it is easy to discern relations between a wildcat and a hawk, it is difficult to discern relations between a wildcat and a blimp. Metaphors (2) and (3) should be intermediate in comprehensibility, because in each case, one distance is small but the other is large. *Wildcat* and *robin* occupy locations that are remote with respect to each other in their respective subspaces, but they are located in subspaces that are relatively close to one another (as measured by distance within the hyperspace). Conversely, *wildcat* and *ICBM* occupy locations in their respective subspaces that are quite close to one another, but they are located in subspaces that are relatively remote from one another. The qualitative assumptions of the theory do not distinguish between the comprehensibility of (2) and (3), although the experiments described below will enable us to assign quantitative weights to the use of superimposed within-subspace distance and between-subspace distance in judgments of metaphoric comprehensibility. Our strong expectation is that the former distance will carry a larger weight than the latter one – that latter superimposed within-subspace distance is more destructive to the comprehensibility of a metaphor than is larger between-subspace distance. If this expectation proves to be correct, then (3) will be judged as more comprehensible than (2). To summarize, the metaphors as ordered from most comprehensible to least comprehensible are (1), (3), (2), (4).

A second set of empirical claims addresses the relative aesthetic pleasingness (or quality) of the various metaphors. According to the theory, (3) should be the metaphor of highest quality, since although *wildcat* and *ICBM* are quite close to one another in terms of superimposed within-subspace distance, they are from distant local subspaces. Metaphor (2) should be lowest in quality, because the tenor and vehicle occupy discrepant positions in their respective subspaces, and are from proximal subspaces. Metaphors (1) and (4) should be intermediate in quality. Again, we expect superimposed within-subspace distance to carry more weight than between-subspace distance. Hence, we expect metaphor (1) to be perceived as higher in aesthetic quality than metaphor (4), since the greater superimposed within-subspace distance should be more destructive to the quality of the metaphor than the lesser between-subspace distance. To summarize, the metaphors as ordered from most to least aesthetically pleasing are (3), (1), (4), (2).

Although the theory that we are advancing may well not apply to all metaphors of all kinds, we do believe that it is fairly general and applicable to metaphors whose tenors and vehicles may not be from obvious semantic subspaces (like those for mammals or modern world leaders). Donne's famous metaphor (or conceit) linking lovers to stiff twin compasses, for example, is not readily comprehensible, according to our theory, because although the superimposed within-subspace distance between lovers and stiff twin compasses is small (at least within the context of "A Valediction: Forbidding Mourning"), the between-subspace distance is large. But it is precisely this pair of properties that renders the metaphor so aesthetically pleasing and, ultimately, so memorable. "The moon is a ghostly galleon" has also survived (perhaps too long!) because although one does not usually link heavenly bodies to ships at sea (large between-subspace distance), one can easily visualize an eerie orb sailing through the sky, impervious to the demands made upon ordinary sailing vessels.

At the opposite end of the spectrum, the theory can also explain why some statements are utter failures as metaphors. A literal statement or definition, such as "An ICBM is an intercontinental ballistic missile," fails as a metaphor because although *ICBM* and *intercontinental ballistic missile* occupy identical locations within their respective local subspaces (and hence the superimposed within-subspace distance is 0), the subspaces are identical (and hence the between-subspace distance is also 0), so that whereas satisfaction of one criterion for a good metaphor is maximized, satisfaction of the other criterion is minimized. An anomalous statement equating two seemingly unrelated concepts, such as "An ICBM is a haystack," fails as a metaphor because although *ICBM* and *haystack* come from subspaces that presumably are quite distant from one another, their locations in these subspaces are quite discrepant.

Our theory may require supplementation in order fully to account for either the comprehensibility or aesthetic quality of certain metaphors. For example, we are attracted to Ortony's notion (see Ortony, 1979, and this volume) that good metaphors tend to be those in which salient properties of the vehicle are linked to nonsalient properties of the tenor. In our representational framework, the relative salience of a property is a function of the relative order in which that property emerges as a dimension. In a standard principal component or factor solution, factors are ordered in terms of their relative strength in accounting for variation in the data. Stronger (more salient) dimensions appear earlier.

It would be possible to supplement our proposed theory (although we have not yet done so) with weights that take into account the possible interaction between the order in which a dimension appears and its role in the metaphor. Dimensions establishing the principal correspondence between tenor and vehicle (that is, the earliest corresponding dimensions) would be weighted as contributing to the goodness of the metaphor if they were both early dimensions of the vehicle and later dimensions of the tenor; dimensions would be weighted as contributing to the badness of the metaphor if they were both early dimensions of the tenor and later dimensions of the vehicle. An aesthetically pleasing metaphor, then, would be one in which the principal correspondence is between an earlier dimension of the vehicle and a later dimension of the tenor.

It should be pointed out that our theory is only one of a class of theories that may be derived from the general representational framework that we have proposed. One could imagine alternative theories in which either superimposed within-subspace distance or between-subspace distance are weighted zero, or in which predictions about which way these distances should go are either opposite or orthogonal to our own predictions. An appealing alternative to our hypothesis regarding the relation between between-subspace distance and aesthetic quality of a metaphor has been suggested by Michael Gardner. His suggestion is that the function is curvilinear rather than linear: The best metaphors are ones in which the between-subspace distance is moderate. If the distance is too small, the connection appears to be trivial, but if the distance is too large, the connection appears to be remote; or possibly, after a certain point, the dimensions cease to match up at all. One might imagine a rubber band stretched further and further, until it snaps: Beyond a certain distance, the metaphor simply cannot withstand the strain. To summarize, the representational framework is flexible enough to accommodate a variety of rules for operating upon that framework, but is not so flexible as to be vacuous: It does make empirical claims as to what kinds of distances should affect the comprehensibility and quality of a metaphor.

We are conducting two experiments designed to test some of the empirical claims and implications of the theory we have described (Tourangeau & Sternberg, 1981). Each of the experiments looks at the theory in a slightly different way.

In the first experiment, subjects are presented with sixty-four metaphors, such as "A wildcat is a hawk among mammals," and are asked to rate, among other things, the aesthetic quality or comprehensibility of each metaphor. The basic independent variables for predicting these two dependent variables (via multiple regression) are superimposed within-subspace distance and between-subspace distance. Other variables, such as the dimensional salience variable mentioned earlier, may also be considered if the initial two appear to need supplementation. Each subject also received two ability tests, one measuring skill in verbal analogical reasoning (e.g., PATIENT:CLIENT:: _____ ; (A) SURGEON:ACTOR, (B) HOSPITAL:PENITENTIARY, (C) DOCTOR:LAWYER, (D) TUBERCULOSIS:FELONY) and the other measuring skill in judging the quality of poetry (Rigg, 1937). Subjects are presented with two passages of poetry, one by a famous poet, the other (doggerel) by the author of the test, and are asked to select the better verse. We plan to use the tests to determine whether individual differences in measured verbal abilities are predictive of differences in parameters of the model (i.e., differential weights assigned by individual subjects to the superimposed within-subspace distance and the between-subspace distance). In the second experiment, subjects are divided into two groups, each of which receives one of two types of items. In both groups, subjects receive a metaphor in which a tenor is supplied, but the vehicle is missing. Subjects in one group are offered four alternative vehicle completions, all from the same local subspace. The subjects' task is to rank order these completions in terms of their aesthetic quality. Subjects in the other group are also offered four alternative vehicle completions; the completions are each from a different local subspace, but they are approximately matched in terms of their locations within their local subspaces. Thus, the alternatives in the items presented to the first group are at an approximately constant between-subspace distance from the tenor, but at a variable superimposed within-subspace distance; the alternatives in the items presented to the second group are at an approximately constant superimposed within-subspace distance from the tenor, but at a variable between-subspace distance. The theory makes clear qualitative predictions regarding the rank orders subjects should give for each type of item: Lower ranks (signifying better metaphors) should be assigned to completions that minimize superimposed within-subspace distance and maximize between-subspace distance. In these studies, it is possible to supplement the qualitative predictions with quantitative predictions as well. By extending the Rumelhart-Abrahamson adaptation of Luce's choice axiom to the present situation, we hope to predict the proportion of subjects who should assign each ranking to each option. If this application of the choice axiom is successful, then it will appear that the same decision rule that is used in a variety of induction tasks (analogies, series completions, and classifications) is used in the metaphor task as well. Indeed, metaphoric comprehension and evaluation might then be viewed as inductive processes in much the same way that analogical, serial, and classificational reasoning are. The induction can proceed either from tenor to vehicle or from vehicle to tenor. Thus, the second experiment might equally have been conducted (and further research will be conducted) in such a way that the tenor rather than the vehicle is missing. Such a study, in addition to testing the generalizability of the theory from both ends of the metaphor, would enable one to investigate Ortony's (1979) hypotheses regarding asymmetry in metaphor.

Theory of information processing

The theory of representation that we have described addresses itself to the form in which information is represented, and to rules that act upon that form of representation. It does not, however, specify an information-processing model for metaphoric comprehension and appreciation. In this part of the paper,[6] we discuss a theory of information processing in metaphor. This discussion, like the preceding one, deals with four topics; namely, the motivation, approach, theory, and methods underlying our work.

The basic goals motivating our research parallel those in the research on representation. These goals are, first, to construct a theory of information processing that is flexible enough to handle metaphors in a variety of domains; second, to propose a small set of processes that account for time to comprehend and evaluate metaphors, in conjunction with rules that explain why some metaphors are more easily comprehended, or more highly regarded, than others; and, third, to relate the information processes to their counterparts in a fairly general theory of induction.

Our approach to the problems listed above is in many respects an outgrowth of earlier research on analogical reasoning (Sternberg, 1977a, 1977b). Thus, the approach to information processing, like the one to representation, began with a theory of analogical reasoning, although the two theories of analogical reasoning (Rumelhart and Abrahamson's, and Sternberg's) deal with virtually nonoverlapping theoretical issues.

According to the "componential" theory of analogical reasoning, solution of analogies of the form $A:B::C:D_1 \ldots D_k$; is accomplished through the execution of up to six component processes. Consider, as an example, the analogy,

WASHINGTON:ONE::LINCOLN: _____ ; (A) TEN, (B) FIVE.

An individual solving this analogy must *encode* the terms of the problem, identifying the terms and retrieving from long-term memory the attributes and values that may be relevant for analogy solution. The individual must also *infer* the relation between the first two analogy terms, ascertaining what it is that *Washington* and *one* have in common (e.g., that Washington was the first president, or that Washington's is the portrait on a one-dollar bill). Next, the individual must *map* the relation from the first term to the third, recognizing what it is that links the domain (or first half) of the analogy, which is about Washington, and the *range* (or second half) of the analogy, which is about Lincoln. Then the individual must *apply* the inferred relation as mapped to the range of the analogy from the third analogy term to each answer option, determining which option bears the same relation to *Lincoln* that *one* does to *Washington*. Optionally, the individual may need to *justify* one of the options as preferred, but nonideal. The individual may find, for example, that neither option meets his or her criterion for an acceptable response, and therefore may need to check previous operations to determine whether there were any errors of omission or commission. An example of an error of omission would be one in which the individual inferred the ordinal position of Washington's presidency, but failed to infer that Washington's is the portrait on a one-dollar bill. An example of an error of commission would be one in which the individual believed that Lincoln's is the portrait on a two- rather than a five-dollar bill, and thus failed in application. Finally, the subject must *respond,* communicating his or her answer choice.

This theory was tested in a series of three experiments, using schematic-picture, verbal, and geometric analogies (see Sternberg, 1977b). Subjects were asked to solve analogies of varying difficulty and content under various experimental conditions that permitted isolation of the hypothesized component processes. The results of the experiments lend strong support to the theory, suggesting that response times to analogies of various types can be viewed as the sum of the times spent on each of the component processes specified by the componential theory of analogical reasoning.

It seemed plausible that this information-processing theory of analogical reasoning, like the Rumelhart–Abrahamson theory of representation and response choice, could be extended to other induction tasks as well. So in a series of nine experiments, the generalizability of the theory has been tested on analogies, series completions, and classifications with schematic-picture, verbal, and geometric content (Sternberg, 1978). A typical classification problem took the form:

(A) N.J., N.Y.   (B) N.C., S.C.
PA.

The subject's task was to determine whether the target item, here, *Pa.,* belonged more appropriately in category A or in category B. According to the componental theory of induction, the individual must encode the terms of the problem, infer the relation between *N.J.,* and *N.Y.,* infer the relation between *N.C.* and *S.C.,* map the differences that distinguish between the two categories, apply this relation to *Pa.* to determine in which category *Pa.* belongs, optionally, justify one of the categories as preferred, and then respond. A typical series completion problem took the form:

LOUIS XIII:LOUIS XIV:LOUIS XV
TRUMAN: (A) EISENHOWER, (B) ROBESPIERRE.

The subject's task was to determine which of the answer options should follow the last term, here, *Truman,* in the series. Subjects must recognize the relation of succession for the French kings, and then use this relation of succession for American presidents. According to the theory, the individual must encode the terms of the problem, infer the relation between *Louis XIII* and *Louis XIV,* infer the relation between *Louis XIV* and *Louis XV* (using only those attributes that are still deemed relevant after the first inference between *Louis XIII* and *Louis XIV*), map the relation from *Louis XV* to *Truman,* apply the inferred relation as mapped to the range of the problem from *Truman* to each answer option, optionally, justify one of the answer options as preferred, and finally, respond. To summarize, the same component processes seem to be involved in the solution of each of the three kinds of induction problems. Are these same processes involved in metaphoric understanding and appreciation? The information-processing theory about to be described suggests that they are.

We propose that the componental theory of induction can be extended to the comprehension and evaluation of metaphors (Sternberg & Nigro, 1978). What are the processes involved in comprehending and evaluating metaphors? Consider the metaphor, "Bees in a hive are a Roman mob (a) in the streets, (b) in the Coliseum." The individual faced with a choice between the two completions must encode the terms of the metaphor, infer the relation between *bees* and *hive,* map the relation between *bees* and a *Roman mob,* and apply the inferred relation from *a Roman mob* to *in the streets* and *in the Coliseum.*[7] Presumably, the individual will choose the latter as the preferred completion because a Coliseum encloses a multitude in a way somewhat analogous to the way a hive encloses a multitude. Neither completion seems ideal, however, so that the individual may spend some time justifying *in the Coliseum* as preferred but nonideal. Finally, the individual responds. Thus, the metaphor considered here is analogical in nature, and seems to require the same processes to comprehend it as does an analogy.

Not all metaphors are stated in analogical form. For example, the metaphor "My head is an apple without a core" is missing a term. The individual attempting to comprehend the metaphor must infer the relation between *apple* and *core,* map from *apple* to *head,* and then apply the previously inferred relation to *head,* completing the metaphor with the missing *brains* (or some such). In this metaphor, comprehension requires insertion rather than selection of a missing term. Consider four variants of the "bees and Romans" metaphor:

   (5) Bees in a hive are a Roman mob in the Coliseum
   (6) Bees in a hive are a Roman mob
   (7) Bees are a Roman mob in the Coliseum
   (8) Bees are a Roman mob.

In the first metaphor, all terms are supplied. In the second and third metaphors, one term is missing, and in the fourth metaphor, two terms are missing. What effects do the missing terms have upon the comprehensibility and aesthetic quality of the metaphor? We believe, with Miller (this volume), that when terms are deleted, the individual must insert the missing terms, attempting to place constraints upon the metaphor that render it interpretable. Deleting terms decreases the ease with which the metaphor is comprehended, because of the extra cognitive processing involved in the generation of missing terms. If the subject is unable to insert missing terms, or inserts inappropriate missing terms, comprehension may be thwarted altogether.

Deleting terms, however, is proposed to increase the aesthetic quality of the metaphor. Part of what makes a metaphor pleasing, we believe, is the insertion of the missing terms or constraints. Part of the beauty of Donne's metaphor linking lovers to stiff twin compasses, for example, seems to derive from the cognitive work required to insert the links between lovers and stiff twin compasses. In the language of the theory of representation stated earlier, this work is expended toward bridging the between-subspace distance.

Appreciation of a metaphor requires a certain amount of active participation on the part or the comprehender, which is reduced in the interpretation of literal statements (where the between-subspace distance is zero or close to it), and this active participation, we believe, cannot be separated from any beauty that may be "inherent" in the metaphor. As mentioned earlier, the perceived beauty of the metaphor may only increase with between-subspace distance up to a certain point, beyond which the metaphor may become utterly opaque. This point seems likely to differ for different individuals. The preferred distance between tenor and vehicle may be greater for highly verbal or trained individuals than for modestly verbal or trained individuals. Active participation contributes to the beauty of a metaphor only if the participation is in the bridging of between-subspace distance. Greater superimposed within-subspace distance can only destroy the beauty of a metaphor.

To summarize, the information-processing theory proposed here, like the representational theory proposed earlier, derives from a theory of analogical reasoning that was first extended to series completion and classification tasks, and then to metaphor. The proposed theory is flexible enough to accommodate a variety of types of metaphor, but not so flexible as to fail to make well-specified empirical claims. This theory, like the representational theory, is only in the earliest stage of testing, and is thus readily subject to change if the data demand it. It is to a description of two initial experimental tests of the theory that we now turn.

In a first experiment, designed to isolate the components of information processing (Sternberg & Nigro, 1978), subjects are presented with metaphors such as "Bees in a hive are a Roman mob _____ (a) in the streets, (b) in the Coliseum." Subjects are asked to select the preferred completion as quickly as they can while still making a carefully reasoned choice. The metaphors are always presented in trials consisting of two parts. The second part always consists of the full metaphor. The content presented in the first part differs as a function of the experimental condition.

Each subject receives half the metaphors in each of two conditions. In the first condition, the first part of the trial consists merely of presentation of a blank field. Subjects press a button when they are ready to see the full metaphor. After they press the button, the full metaphor appears immediately, and the subjects solve it as quickly as they can. In the second condition, the first part of the trial consists of presentation of the first half of the metaphor, for example, *bees in a hive*. Again, subjects press a button when they are ready to see the full metaphor, and the metaphor appears immediately after the button is pressed. The purpose of having the two conditions is to enable us to separate component processes that otherwise would be confounded. (See Sternberg, 1977b, for the rationale of componential task decomposition.) Subjects also receive tests of verbal reasoning, including a standard analogies test, which are used to assess the extent to which individual differences in component information processing in the metaphorical reasoning task are related to individual differences in verbal – and particularly verbal analogical – reasoning ability.

In a second experiment, designed to investigate the determinants of metaphoric comprehensibility and pleasingness, subjects are presented with metaphors taking the four forms described earlier for the "bees and Romans" metaphor. Although each metaphor is presented in each of the four forms, a given subject sees a particular metaphor in only one of the four forms. Each subject receives equal numbers of metaphors in each of the four forms. The subject's task is to rate either the aesthetic quality, or the comprehensibility, of each metaphor presented. A given subject supplies only one kind of rating. Unbeknownst to the subjects, they are being timed while making their ratings. Our expectations are that (a) aesthetic quality will decrease with increasing numbers of explicitly presented terms, (b) comprehensibility will increase with increasing numbers of explicitly presented terms, and (c) time to respond will decrease with increasing numbers of explicitly presented terms, despite the slightly increased reading load, because of the reduced amount of cognitive work required – that is, there is less need to insert missing terms.

Integration of theories of representation and information processing

The theories of representation and information processing that we have presented look at metaphoric comprehension and appreciation from distinct but complementary points of view. These points of view can be integrated. In *encoding,* the individual locates the tenor and vehicle of the metaphor in their respective local subspaces. In *inference,* the subject constrains those dimensions of the tenor that are likely to be relevant. *Mapping* is the heart of metaphoric comprehension and appreciation: The subject "computes" the superimposed within-subspace distance and the between-subspace distance between tenor and vehicle. In *application,* the subject constructs or selects a completion to the vehicle that satisfies the same constraints as those inferred for the tenor. If the subject is unable to find such a completion, then *justification* is used to construct or select the best possible, nonoptimal completion. Finally, the subject offers whatever kind of *response* is required.

The comprehensibility and quality of a metaphor can be influenced in all but the last (response) stage of metaphoric reasoning. If a term is particularly difficult to encode, then the comprehensibility and aesthetic quality of a metaphor may be reduced. Terms in remote local subspaces (i.e., in remote regions of the hyperspace), terms whose coordinates are unknown, or terms that are particularly ambiguous and thus may not have a unique set of coordinates, are all likely to be difficult to encode. Requiring insertion of a missing term during inference will generally decrease the comprehensibility of a metaphor while increasing its quality. If, however, explicit constraints are presented that are highly unusual or conceptually opaque, then comprehensibility may actually be reduced by supplying the subject with the difficult-to-process constraints. Mapping is without question the major source of variance in metaphoric comprehensibility and quality: A metaphor is highly comprehensible if both superimposed within-subspace distance and between-subspace distance are small, and highly pleasing if superimposed within-subspace distance is small but between-subspace distance is large. Requiring insertion of a missing term during application will generally reduce the comprehensibility of a metaphor while increasing its quality. Requiring selection of one of several metaphoric completions, none of which is very satisfactory, will increase the amount of justification required, and reduce the comprehensibility and quality of the metaphor. To summarize, we speculate that although comprehensibility and aesthetic quality are determined primarily by the outcome of the mapping process, each is complexly determined, as our analysis has shown.

Metaphor, induction, and social policy

In his analysis of generative metaphor, Schön attacks the problem of metaphor at a global level. Nevertheless, he points out that "with respect to the workings of the process itself, we need much better descriptions of the component activities [of] 'restructuring' and 'coordination.'" The analysis presented in the preceding section was an attempt to provide such a description – an attempt to analyze at a *microscopic level* the elements of metaphor that Schön has analyzed at a *macroscopic level*. There is no one correct level of analysis: Each level of analysis is capable of providing its own unique form of enlightenment. The present section is divided into five parts in each of which we take one of Schön's macroscopic constructs and explicate it in terms of the more microscopic constructs proposed in the present theories.

Generative metaphor

Schön conceives of the central construct in his theory, generative metaphor, as the "'carrying over' of frames or perspectives from one domain of experience to another." Not all metaphors are generative: Some merely capitalize upon already existing ways of seeing things. A generative metaphor, however, actually generates "new perceptions, explanations and inventions." The perception of the relation between tenor and vehicle creates in the perceiver a fresh way of viewing the nature of the tenor of the metaphor.

In our information-processing account of metaphor, the process most directly giving rise to what Schön calls "generative metaphor" is mapping, a term Schön himself uses. In structural terms, the perceiver sees a correspondence between a term located at a particular point in one local subspace and some other term located at the corresponding point in another local subspace. The metaphor is generative by virtue of the correspondence never having been perceived before: thus it results in a new perspective on the tenor of the metaphor.

Consider a few examples. A metaphor presented earlier, "A wildcat is an ICBM among mammals," might result in a new perception of a wildcat, one of a deadly hurling projectile whizzing in a long arc through the air, about to strike and destroy an unsuspecting victim. Schön cites another example of interest, "Man is a wolf." This metaphor may result in a new or enhanced perception of man as a fierce, untamed, destructive animal, ready to pounce in an instant upon his unsuspecting victims. The example is also of interest for the structural theory proposed earlier, because it calls attention to a new situation, one in which the tenor and vehicle of the metaphor seem, at least on the surface, to be at different levels of abstraction. In our implementation of the structural theory, *man* was at a higher level of abstraction, and thus in a higher-order space, than *wolf. Wolf* was an element in the local subspace of mammals, whereas *man* might have been considered as a higher-order space containing *modern world leaders* and *U.S. historical figures* as local subspaces. How does the structural theory handle metaphors constructed from terms of seemingly different levels of abstraction?

We believe that in comprehending this metaphor, the individual does not assign to every man (or woman) he or she has known the properties of a wolf. *Man* is not defined in terms of its full extensional meaning, any more than *wolf* is. Rather, the individual constructs two prototypes, one for *man* and one for *wolf,* that represent composites of the attributes associated with each term. Most of us today do not have highly differentiated notions about, or diverse acquaintances with, wolves, so that the prototype for *wolf* may be nothing more than an already assigned point for *wolf* in a single local subspace. (Among hunters, wolves might comprise a whole subspace of their own.) *Man,* on the other hand, is likely to be a highly differentiated concept, and the prototype may be viewed as the centroid of the points corresponding to the salient men we know or know of. The centroid need not be, and probably is not, an unweighted average of coordinates. We suspect it is a weighted average, with the weights influenced by context. In this case, *wolf* sets up a minimal context. Thus, the dimension of aggression noted earlier may well receive a higher weight than that of prestige. These prototypes are used as the basis for mapping. Note that the formation of the prototype is by what was earlier called the encoding process – that process by which the location of a point in space (in this case, the centroid corresponding to the prototype) is identified.

Problem setting versus problem solving

Schön believes that the major difficulties in social policy are in problem setting rather than in problem solving. The greater challenge is to frame the purposes to be achieved rather than to select optimal means of achieving them. He cites case-study examples in which the way the problem was framed was largely responsible for the way in which the problem was solved. Schön's examples reminded us of Graham Allison's (1969) classic paper, in which Allison compared different frames in which the Cuban missile crisis might have been viewed, each of which suggested a different conception of the enemy (primarily the Soviet Union) and of how to deal with it.

We think Schön is almost certainly correct in this regard. In his words, "Problems are not given. They are constructed by human beings in their attempts to make sense of complex and troubling situations." In terms of our proposed structural and process theories, problem-setting style can be determined by any of a number of predilections. Consider the forms individual differences in each of the component processes of metaphorical reasoning might take.

The policymaker has a number of options in encoding the available information. First, he or she may view certain dimensions as more salient than others. For example, some individuals seem to view the aggression dimension as particularly salient, adopting a "cold war" mentality wherever possible. Second, individuals may differ in their placements of points within a particular local subspace. For example, *Brezhnev* was scaled as the most aggressive of the modern world leaders included in our sample of leaders. However, *Brezhnev's* location in the subspace was computed as an average for the individuals supplying ratings. Some individuals might see him as less aggressive, resulting in a very different perception of him as the tenor of an implicit metaphor.

Policymakers may also differ in their inferences about the topics of their metaphors. For example, a pacifist might be viewed either as a lion or a mouse, depending upon whether the individual constructing the metaphor inserts as implicit terms "among senators" or "in the Senate" on the one hand, or "among soldiers" or "on the battlefield" on the other. Either metaphor might be acceptable, depending upon the constraining context the individual chose to insert.

Mapping can also influence the way in which problems are set. Presumably, everyone tries to match terms as closely as possible in their respective local subspaces; but there may be substantial individual differences in preferred distances between subspaces. As was noted earlier, it seems plausible that highly verbal or literate individuals might prefer larger between-subspace distances than do less verbal or literate individuals. Similarly, some individuals may have greater vision in reaching beyond the mundane metaphors that can be formed from very close local subspaces.

Policymakers may also differ in the constraints they apply to the vehicle of the metaphor. To continue with an earlier example, viewing a pacifist as a lion might mean very different things, depending upon whether the lion is viewed as being in its native jungle habitat or in the captivity of a cage at the zoo. A politician compared to a Spartan might be viewed either as a jingoist in the legislature, or as an austere individual in his personal life, depending upon whether the Spartan is viewed in the context of the battlefield or the home.

Finally, like everyone else, policymakers may differ in their tolerance of imperfection in metaphor, where imperfection is viewed in terms of the superimposed within-subspace distance between two points. Stated otherwise, policymakers may differ in their willingness to justify as valid, meta-phors of varying degrees of imperfection. Gerald Ford, for example, often compared himself to Harry Truman, a comparison that seems shaky at best. It would seem that an intermediate degree of willingness to justify metaphors as acceptable would be best. Very high willingness to justify metaphors might result in outright distortion of the facts, whereas very low willingness to justify metaphors might result in tunnel vision.

Frame awareness, frame conflict, and frame restructuring

Schön argues that there are "certain pervasive, tacit generative metaphors" that govern thinking about social policy problems, and that "we ought to become critically aware of these generative metaphors, to increase the rigor and precision of our analysis of social policy problems by examining the analogies and 'disanalogies' between the familiar descriptions . . . and the actual problematic situations that confront us." Once again, we are in agreement with Schön's position. We cannot evaluate the quality of our solutions to problems without knowing what the problem is that we have set out to solve. And this problem is one of our own construction. We have structured external events, although we may not know how. In terms of the structural and process theories described above, we are only dimly aware (if that) of the structure and content of our various orders of subspaces, and of the operations we perform on them. Surely, the research of Nisbett and Wilson (1977) on our awareness of internal processes suggests minimal access to these processes. We should like to believe that although the internal representations and processes are not accessible to conscious intro-spection, they are accessible to the kinds of experimental analyses that we have described.

Frame conflict, according to Schön, arises when "several different sto-ries about the same situation" are constructed; "each story is internally coherent and compelling in its own terms but different from and perhaps incompatible with all the others." Schön provides an example of frame conflict, showing how an urban slum can be viewed either as blighted and decayed or as healthy and natural. In terms of our own theories, frame conflict can arise because of different encodings of terms, different in-ferred constraints, different between-subspace mappings, different ap-plied constraints, or different tolerances in justification of nonzero super-imposed within-subspace distances.

Now, according to Schön, frame conflict is resolved by frame restructur-ing, in which "we respond to frame conflict by constructing a new problem-setting story, one in which we attempt to integrate conflicting frames by including features and relations drawn from earlier stories, yet without sacrificing internal coherence or the degree of simplicity required for ac-tion." In terms of the theories proposed earlier, there seem to be two major ways of resolving frame conflict. The first is to seek new encodings, inferences, mappings, applications, and justifications that resolve conflict by selective inattention to conflicting details. A "frame story" is created that integrates only those features of two previous stories that are consistent with each other. The second is to create new aspects of the stories that resolve inconsistencies. For example, a sly general initially compared to a fox turns out to be ruthless on the battlefield. He is then compared to a rabid fox. An insertion further describing the vehicle restructures the metaphor to render it minimally acceptable.

A domestic example of the development of a generative metaphor may help show the course of frame awareness, frame conflict, and frame restructuring. The example is one of policymaking "in the small." One of us (Sternberg) recently had to decide whether to buy a house. The major problem with the house seemed to be that its price was at the very limit of affordability; the house might therefore be difficult to maintain. This particular house happened to be located on a cul-de-sac named Wolf Tree Drive. The owners mentioned one day that a wolf tree is a tulip tree. That same day, Sternberg looked up "tulip tree" in a dictionary and found it to be a tree with pretty flowers resembling tulips. This definition resulted in the generation of a metaphor comparing the house to a tulip tree, a metaphor that was very pleasing. Sternberg then looked up "wolf tree," and found it to be "a forest tree whose size and position cause it to prevent the growth of many small and potentially more valuable trees around it by usurping their space, light, and nourishment." This definition also led to generation of a metaphor, and an unpleasant one at that: By buying the house, Sternberg and his wife were investing in a wolf tree that would restrict their ability to do a number of things in life that were important to them. Travel and family plans, for example, might have to be postponed because of the cost of the house. They became aware not only of the two frames, but of the obvious conflict between them. They resolved the conflict, eventually, with the discovery that the flowers of the tulip tree appear only very high on the tree and when the tree is fully mature. They thus concluded that after a few years had passed and their financial position had become more secure, their investment would flower! They had resolved the conflict by means of the first way of resolving frame conflict. They had ignored those aspects of the wolf tree that were inconsistent with the tulip tree. How else could they justify their decision to buy the house?

Life cycle of a generative metaphor

Schön proposes that a generative metaphor has a life cycle all its own.

In the earlier stages of the life cycle, one notices or feels that *A* and *B* are similar, without being able to say similar with respect to what. Later on, one may come to be able to describe relations of elements present in a restructured perception of both A and B which account for the pre-analytic detection of similarity between A and B, that is, one can formulate an *analogy* between A and B. Later still, one may construct a general model for which a redescribed A and a redescribed B can be identified as instances.

Note that Schön, too, sees the construction of a metaphor as tantamount to the formulation of an analogy. His account of the life cycle of a metaphor is consistent in several respects with our laboratory findings regarding the "life cycle," or information-processing model of analogy solution.

First, analytic solution of analogies via attribute-by-attribute comparison does appear to be accompanied by what has been variously called holistic processing or a preliminary scan (Sternberg, 1977a, 1977b). This processing is pre-analytic in the sense that the comparison does not rely on serial, "reasoned" attribute comparisons. Thus, dual processing of both a pre-analytic and an analytic nature appears to be common to the processing of both standard analogies and generative metaphors.

Second, it has been found that in analogy solution, subjects are not only unaware of what they have mapped from the domain (first half) to the range (second half) of the analogy, but are unaware of having mapped at all! In contrast, subjects are at least marginally aware of having encoded, inferred, applied, or justified, although they are often unaware of the particular attributes they have processed. The A to C mapping in analogy solution corresponds to the A to B similarity recognition in metaphor generation referred to by Schön. In analogy solution, as in metaphor generation, one can later state the similarity relations that may have been used. Consider, for example, the analogy WASHINGTON:ONE::LINCOLN:FIVE. Subjects will have no difficulty recognizing that Washington and Lincoln are similar in a number of ways. But they will not be aware of having generated these similarities during the course of analogy solution.

Third, a subject, after reflection, may well be able to describe the two terms as special cases, in the example analogy, of presidents whose faces appear on currency. In terms of the proposed structural theory of metaphor, the subject recognizes the dimensions of similarity that overlap between local subspaces and that form the basis for mapping. The individual may even recognize the hyperspace in which the local subspaces reside. But these recognitions follow rather than precede the detection of relations that makes possible understanding of an analogy or generation of a metaphor.

Surface metaphors versus deep metaphors

Schön distinguishes between surface and deep metaphors. The surface metaphor is that contained in the explicit language of a story about some object or phenomenon. But this language may not disclose what lies beneath the story.

The deep metaphor, in this sense, is the metaphor which accounts for centrally important features of the story – which makes it understandable that certain elements of the situation are included in the story while others are omitted, that certain assumptions are taken as true although there is evidence that would appear to disconfirm them; and, especially, that the normative conclusions are found to follow so obviously from the facts. Given a problem-setting story, we must construct the deep metaphor which is generative of it.

How do people ascertain the deep metaphor that underlies one or more surface metaphors? We suspect people do so by filling in terms of an implicit analogy.

Consider, as a first example, John Dean's description of the Nixon presidency and Dean's relation to it as told in Dean's congressional testimony. Dean conveys to President Nixon his fear of a cancer on the presidency. This surface metaphor, and the story surrounding it, seem intended to suggest a deep metaphor of John Dean as cancer surgeon. Dean's first function, in many ways the most difficult of all, is the recognition that a cancer exists. His second function is to excise the cancer, operating in a way that will remove the cancer while at the same time doing minimal damage to the patient's healthy organs. His final function is to restore the patient to an appearance of good health, stitching up any incisions that may have been made and making the patient presentable to the outside world. In this account, the blemishes signifying a cancerous state reappear because the root causes of the cancer – the internal dispositions of Nixon and the (other) men who surrounded him – were beyond the cancer surgeon's control. But an alternative reading is also possible, one of John Dean as cosmetic surgeon. As cosmetic surgeon, Dean first recognizes the appearance of external blemishes, and shows no concern for the internal malignant state that may have been responsible for these blemishes. Next, Dean performs cosmetic surgery, attempting to remove the blemishes while remaining oblivious to the internal states that may have generated them. Finally, Dean restores the patient to his preblemished appearance, substituting healthy-looking skin for the now-removed blemished skin. In this account, the blemishes quickly reappear because nothing was done to correct the internal state that generated them.

Consider as a second example the case of the White House "plumbers" operating during the Nixon administration. Again, there are two alternative readings of the actions of the so-called plumbers. In the White House-sponsored reading, the plumbers were plugging leaks in the flow of information along the pipeline that conveys state secrets from one security agency (for example, the FBI) to another (for example, the CIA). Leaks in the pipeline could be disastrous to national security, and thus needed to be corrected immediately and often without much regard as to the means used to correct them. In the alternative reading, the pipeline being treated was not one between security agencies, but between informants and the press. The information traveling along this pipeline was not state secrets, but secrets damaging to Nixon's prestige and possibly his longevity as president as well. Most importantly, the proper deep metaphor was not one of plumbers plugging leaks in pipelines, but one of demolition experts blowing up the pipelines that provide information to the press and thus protect our rights under the First Amendment.

In deciding between the appropriateness of two or more alternative deep metaphors, one has to decide between the appropriateness of two or more implicit analogies. Consider the case of John Dean. The two implicit analogies are:

(1) External actions of Dean:Internal state of Dean::External actions of cancer surgeon:Internal state of cancer surgeon;

(2) External actions of Dean:Internal state of Dean::External actions of cosmetic surgeon:Internal state of cosmetic surgeon.

The two analogies are identical in their A and B terms (domains). They differ only in their C and D terms (ranges). Thus, the major difficulty in choosing between analogies is in deciding upon the preferred mapping from domain to range of the analogy. There are other difficulties, however. First, the A term of the analogy may be incompletely or incorrectly given: Dean's account of his actions may be wholly inadequate, and must be checked against other sources of information. Second, the content of the B term is not a given, but must be inferred from the content of the A term. But it is difficult to infer internal states from external actions. Any of a number of inferences is usually possible, and the choice of inferences may well determine the mapping that is made. Third, neither analogy can be expected to be perfect, and so the individual will have to decide which is better, and whether the better analogy is close enough to a perfect analogy to justify it as being valid. To summarize, the construction of a deep metaphor is fraught with difficulties – difficulties that can be characterized in terms of the components of the information-processing theory of analogical reasoning described earlier.

We have attempted to take the major concepts in Schön's broadly based and conceptually rich theory of metaphor, and to show how they relate to concepts in both the theories of metaphor and of analogy (and induction) presented in the preceding section of this paper. We believe that the major difference between Schön's research and ours is one of approach rather than substance. His approach might be characterized as macroscopic, ours as microscopic. But the commensurability of the conclusions reached by the two different approaches is a powerful argument in favor of their validity. Converging operations have led to converging conclusions, suggesting that there is a common core of knowledge that transcends specific methodologies. With time, we can hope to see the substance of this core extended.

Conclusion

We shall conclude our discussion of metaphor, induction, and social policy by re-posing five major issues in the theory of metaphor posed by Verbrugge and McCarrell (1977) and by Schön, and by showing how the theories of representation and processing described in this paper deal with these issues.

One issue posed by Verbrugge and McCarrell is that of how semantic information is represented. We have proposed a spatial representation in which local subspaces can be mapped into points of higher-order hyperspaces, and vice versa. This representation is more flexible than conventional spatial representations because of its ability to characterize terms of different levels of abstraction. We have proposed that a common set of dimensions underlies many (although almost certainly not all) of the local subspaces, and our factor-analytic data were consistent with this notion.

A second issue posed by Verbrugge and McCarrell is that of what makes some metaphors more successful than others. We have proposed two rules that we believe govern successful, that is, aesthetically pleasing, metaphors. The first is that the superimposed within-subspace distance between tenor and vehicle be minimized; the second is that the between-subspace distance be maximized (at least within that range of distances for which the dimensions of the local subspaces remain correspondent). Comprehensibility, unlike aesthetic quality, is maximized by minimization of both superimposed within-subspace distance and between-subspace distance.

A third issue posed by these authors is that of how the tenor and vehicle of a metaphor interact. There seem to be three sources of interaction in the proposed theory. The first is an interaction between superimposed within-subspace distance and between-subspace distance: Aesthetically pleasing metaphors minimize the first while maximizing the second. The second source is in the constraints placed by the inference and application processes. It has been proposed that the explicit or implicit constraints set by the context of the metaphorical sentence result in tenor and vehicle being perceived in restricted ways that delimit their possible relations to each other. The third source of interaction was not discussed in this paper for lack of space, although it is discussed elsewhere in the context of research on reasoning by analogy (Sternberg, 1977a, 1977b; Sternberg & Rifkin, 1979). There exist alternative process models by which individuals can encode, infer, map, and apply attributes. At one extreme is a completely noninteractive model, in which the outcome of each operation is independent of the outcome of every other operation. At the other extreme is a completely interactive model, in which the outcome of each operation can influence the outcome of every other operation. It seems likely that metaphors are comprehended in a highly interactive way, with the results of operations directly affecting each other.

A fourth issue, this one posed by Schön, is that of how we decide whether people are using generative metaphors, and if they are, what these generative metaphors are. In two of the experiments we have described, subjects were asked to choose among alternative completions for metaphors. Preferences could thereby be discerned. But in both of these experiments, subjects were given at least part of the metaphor as stimulus material. We have not yet attempted to infer subjects' implicit metaphors when the subjects are given no experimentally controlled stimulus material at all.

A fifth issue, also posed by Schön, is that of discovering how people generate metaphors. The theories proposed here only begin to answer this fundamental question. We have proposed a structure and rules for operating upon this structure. In the mapping process, individuals will generate metaphors that minimize superimposed within-subspace distance and meet their preference for between-subspace distance. We have suggested that individuals may differ in this latter preference. Individuals may also differ in the ways in which they encode, infer, and apply attributes. Different encodings of an urban slum, to take Schön's example, result in very different generative metaphors. But we are certainly a long way from a full description of what leads people to generate certain metaphors, and in particular, those metaphors rather than others.

We have attempted to demonstrate in this paper a convergence between macroscopic and microscopic views of metaphor, induction, and social policy. The demonstration began with a description of the microscopic views we have adopted, continued with an integration of these views with the macroscopic views of Schön, and ended with a discussion of how the microscopic view deals with some fairly macroscopic questions about metaphoric generation, comprehension, and appreciation. The convergence of Schön's views with our own strengthens our conviction that an understanding of metaphor can be attained that is independent of the means used to attain that understanding.

NOTES

Some of the ideas we present evolved out of conversations of the first author with Amos Tversky who has investigated similar hypotheses regarding semantic domains and their relations to metaphorical goodness. We acknowledge his contribution with gratitude. We are also grateful to Andrew Ortony, to Sandra Scarr, and to the members of Robert Sternberg's research seminar at Yale for comments on an earlier draft of this chapter. Preparation of this chapter was supported by a contract from the Office of Naval Research to Robert Sternberg.

1 The research described in this section has been done as a collaboration between Roger Tourangeau and Robert Sternberg (see Tourangeau & Sternberg, 1978).

2 Our thinking about and approach to metaphor has been influenced by the notions of others as well, including those of interaction between tenor and vehicle (Black, 1962b) and of basic natural categories (Rosch, 1975b; Rosch, Mervis, Gray, Johnson, & Boyes-Braem, 1976).

3 Although the spatial representation described here has provided a useful theoretical basis and heuristic for our thinking about metaphor, we believe it likely that the theory could be mapped into other forms of representation as well, such as a feature representation (Tversky, 1977) or an attribute-value representation (Sternberg, 1977a, 1977b).

4 Dimensions may correspond in the sense that a common label applies to them. The dimensions are not viewed as equivalent, however: "Prestige" in the domain of modern world leaders may not mean the *same* thing as "prestige" in the domain of mammal names.

5 Factor analyses were performed via principal-factor solutions rotated to the varimax criterion.

6 The research described in this section has been done as a collaboration between Robert Sternberg and Georgia Nigro (see Sternberg & Nigro, 1978).

7 The metaphor may also be set up so that inference occurs in the vehicle and application in the tenor. The nature of the task determines the order of processing.

METAPHOR
AND
UNDERSTANDING

14

*Psychological processes in metaphor comprehension and memory

ALLAN PAIVIO AND MARY WALSH

For the student of language and thought, metaphor is a solar eclipse. It hides the object of study and at the same time reveals some of its most salient and interesting characteristics when viewed through the right telescope. The object is linguistic meaning. Metaphor obscures its literal and commonplace aspects while permitting a new and subtle understanding to emerge. Thus, metaphor highlights the capacity of language users to create and understand novel linguistic combinations that may be literal nonsense. An advertisement that urges you to "Put a tiger in your tank" is anomalous semantically but not in what it symbolizes for the driver who likes to take off with a roar. Most metaphors are not newly created by their users, but all were once novel and new ones arise constantly even in the most commonplace of conversations. Thus, semantic productivity must be regarded as a salient design feature of metaphorical language, just as syntactic productivity is of language in general, despite the repetitiousness of specific grammatical constructions in everyday speech. We know even less, however, about the psychology of semantic creativity than we do about syntactic creativity, and the former must be counted among the most challenging theoretical problems that confront those who are interested in a scientific understanding of language behavior.

The degree of semantic creativity in metaphorical language, and the problem it poses for language theory, have been emphasized by psychologists (e.g., Anderson & Ortony, 1975; Bransford & McCarrell, 1975; Honeck, Riechmann, & Hoffmann, 1975; Olson, 1970). Honeck et al. (1975), using proverbs to study the problem, found that conceptually related interpretations and stories were judged to be highly relevant to target proverbs and also served as effective prompts for the recall of the latter in a memory task. For example, "Your actions are bound to be accounted for eventually" was the relevant prompt for the proverb, "In due time, the fox is brought to the furrier." The authors emphasized that the interpretations did not share any major vocabulary, phrase structure, or propositional structure with the corresponding proverbs. Thus, they concluded that no existing theory adequately describes the semantic relationship between a proverb and its interpretations. Similar arguments were made by Anderson and Ortony (1975) in regard to the general problem of polysemy in language comprehension which, they argued, requires a theory that provides for the construction of a novel particularized representation that integrates the disparate elements of linguistic expressions in an infinitely productive way. Most contemporary and traditional approaches to linguistic semantics, and to semantic memory, lack the necessary flexibility and integrative power, or so it is claimed by those who adopt the constructivist approach. Be that as it may, the apparent creativity involved in the use of metaphor poses a major conceptual challenge for students of language, regardless of their theoretical preferences.

Although not pretending to solve the problem, we hope to show that some of the theoretical ideas and research findings arising from recent studies of memory and cognition have direct relevance for the student of metaphor, providing both clarification and testable hypotheses concerning metaphor comprehension. Our review takes account of the research progress in these areas since the earlier review in the first edition.

We discuss, in turn, the psychological issues associated with metaphorical behavior and traditional and recent psychological approaches to those issues, including an updated analysis based on a general theoretical approach to language and thought that has been applied to the problem of metaphor (Paivio, 1971, chap. 13; 1986, chap. 10; Walsh, 1988). In what follows, we sometimes use the term "metaphor" to refer to metaphorical or figurative expressions in general, including proverbs, but the paradigm case will be the similarity metaphor in which *topic* and *vehicle* are the key terms. Thus, in our introductory expression, "Metaphor is a solar eclipse," the topic is "metaphor" and the vehicle is "solar eclipse." Whatever it is that they have in common that permits a figurative interpretation is the *ground*.

Psychological problems related to metaphor

Metaphorical behavior includes both motivational and cognitive aspects. One motivational issue concerns the reasons for the creation of metaphorical expressions: why do they arise at all in communication? Ortony (1975) discussed the problem in terms of a general assumption and three hypotheses related to it. The general assumption is that metaphor fulfills the necessary communication function of conveying continuous experiential information, using a discrete symbol system. The three hypotheses pertain to the way in which metaphor fulfills this general function. One hypothesis is that a metaphor provides a compact way of representing the subset of cognitive and perceptual features that are salient to it. A metaphor allows large "chunks" of information to be converted or transferred from the vehicle to the topic. The second is the "inexpressibility" hypothesis, which states that a metaphor enables us to talk about experiences which cannot be literally described. The third is the hypothesis that, perhaps through imagery, metaphor provides a vivid and, therefore, memorable and emotion-arousing representation of perceived experience. These functions obviously implicate cognitive processes, but they are intended to explain what motivates the use of metaphor in communication.

The other side of the motivational issue has to do with the effect of incongruity and novelty on the hearer. C. Anderson (1964) discussed the effects of metaphorical novelty in terms of Berlyne's (1960) theory of arousal induction and reduction: the incongruity of metaphor induces arousal, which the person seeks to reduce by means of a "conceptual resolution" of the disparate elements. The motivational basis of metaphorical expression has been of particular interest to psychoanalysts as well as students of poetry (see Billow, 1977). Such views have received almost no direct research attention by psychologists interested in metaphor. Moreover, they have not clarified the cognitive problems associated with metaphors, and we shall not pursue them further in this chapter.

The comprehension of metaphor is basically a cognitive problem which centers around the following question: how does a novel conceptual entity arise from apparently disparate parts? It is central in regard to the production, as well as comprehension, of metaphor; for the creator of the metaphor must first grasp the significance of a metaphorical relation before it is uttered. The problem as stated entails the concepts of *similarity, relation,* and *integration,* as well as the idea of novelty. Similarity and relation are implied in definitions of metaphor. According to one definition, linguistic metaphor involves "the application of a word or expression that properly belongs to one context to express meaning in a different context because of some real or implied similarity in the referents involved" (C. Anderson, 1964, p. 53). The basis of similarity may lie in shared attributes of some kind, as in referring to a submissive person as a "sheep." Or it may involve relational similarity, as in the proportional metaphor in which four or more elements of a sentence are related proportionately (Billow, 1977, p. 82). Thus, the injunction to "Put a tiger in your tank" which a well-known gasoline company used some years ago could be analyzed as a proportionate metaphor which implies that a certain gasoline is to a car as power is to a tiger.

The centrality of the concepts of similarity and relation is particularly interesting because both are old and thorny conceptual problems in psychology. Similarity has always played a key role in the analysis of generalization, transfer of training, and forgetting, in tasks ranging from motor performance to paired associate learning of nonsense syllables (see, for example, Osgood, 1953). The basis of similarity, however, continues to be a theoretical puzzle. An operational definition seems straightforward in the case of formal similarity, which can be defined in terms of the number of identical elements shared by two stimuli, although the concept of identical elements itself was highly controversial in the early debates concerning transfer of training. The analysis of meaning similarity is even more difficult, particularly in regard to the nature of the common elements. It became necessary to invoke such concepts as "functional equivalence," "response similarity," and "mediated similarity," all of which also led to conceptual problems in their own right. These problems are further accentuated in the case of metaphor, which involves a particularly subtle form (or forms) of semantic similarity. They are only now being raised, and have not yet been solved in that context. Osgood (1953; 1963; 1980) was an early contributor to the theoretical interpretation of mediated similarity as well as metaphor. Tversky (1977) proposed an influential weighted feature-matching approach to similarity, which appears to solve some of the classical problems, generates novel predictions, and has testable implications for metaphor (see Ortony's discussion of the present chapter in this volume, and Glucksberg & Keysar's 1990 criticism of that approach).

The concept of relation has been historically prominent in perceptual psychology, particularly in the context of the "transposition problem" (Reese, 1968), where the debate turned on the degree to which an organism will respond to relations as compared to absolute stimulus properties. Gestalt psychologists championed the view that relational responding usually predominates. The gestalt view is particularly relevant to the assumption that the comprehension of metaphor involves a special kind of relational perception or response (cf. Lakoff & Johnson, 1980; Verbrugge & McCarrell, 1977).

The concept of relation is also implicated in another key term, integration, because relational perception is often interpreted as involving the perception of a new entity, which is distinct from the related elements considered separately. This conceptualization extends directly to metaphor, where, according to one writer, "The two (or more) ideas of the metaphor work together to produce a new concept for which there may be no other expression" (Billow, 1977, p. 82).

All these concepts – similarity, relation, and novel integration – are implicated in the various psychological approaches to metaphor, to which we now turn.

Psychological approaches to metaphor

All psychological theories of metaphor are *mediational approaches,* in the sense that they are concerned with processes that mediate the similarity, relational, and integrative reactions involved in the comprehension of metaphor. Contemporary cognitive psychologists would interpret such processes primarily in terms of structural and functional characteristics of long-term or *semantic memory*. Skinner's (1957) analysis is an apparent exception, since he rejects mediational and cognitive terminology. Nonetheless, close examination suggests that he, too, must assume mediational responses to explain metaphorical extension.

The Skinnerian interpretation is based on the idea of generalization of verbal responses to properties of stimuli that happen to be present along with the salient discriminative stimuli when the responses were originally reinforced. The following examples illustrate how some common figurative expressions may have arisen by such a mechanism (Winokur, 1976, pp. 54ff.). The verbal response "eye" would be reinforced in the presence of a stimulus cluster which includes, in addition to an eye, a "person," together with such properties as "recessed," "oval," "near the top," "part," "surrounded by flesh," and "contains fluid." Later, some of the parts occur as part of another whole, and the verbal response will also tend to occur. A needle, for example, would include the parts "recessed," "oval," "near the top," and "part," hence the metaphorical verbal response, "eye of needle." This approach implies quite a different interpretation of the novelty of metaphorical behavior than is the case in more traditional analyses. The response is not *created* by the speaker, it is simply *controlled* by stimuli through the mechanism of generalization.

The analysis apparently does not depend on any elaborate mediating process, unless one seeks explanations for generalization itself and inquires into the nature of the identity of the "parts" in two very dissimilar wholes. Other examples more obviously call for mediational constructs. For example, Skinner's analysis of "Juliet is the sun" is explicitly couched in terms of a common mediating reaction. Thus, "The metaphorical extension might have been mediated by, say, an emotional response which both the sun and Juliet evoked in [Romeo]" (1957, p. 97).

Contemporary memory theorists analyze comprehension of metaphor primarily as a semantic memory problem (for example, Kintsch, 1972). This is implicit in the idea that metaphor is a problem of meaning, which is based on long-term memory information associated with the terms of the metaphor. Comprehension accordingly involves the retrieval of such information. The nature and organizational structure of the information is crucial to the analysis of metaphor, because that structure will determine what attributes of the topic and vehicle will be likely to enter into, or mediate, the metaphorical relationship, given that there is access to those attributes by appropriate retrieval cues.

Different theories assume different mediating structures in the comprehension of metaphorical relations. Traditional verbal associative theory assumes that the relation is mediated by the structure of verbal associations. Imagery-based theories stress the structural similarities in perceptual memories. Other theories stress overlap in abstract semantic representations, which may be organized into networks or hierarchies. Each class of theory asserts or implies that the click of comprehension of a metaphor depends on some kind of structural match in regard to the information activated by the linguistic metaphor, or the construction of some new, relational entity from such information.

But comprehension also involves episodic memory (Tulving, 1972) for the metaphorical expression, and the linguistic and extralinguistic context in which it was uttered. The linguistic context includes the ongoing topic of conversation. The extralinguistic context includes the general communicational setting and the persons involved in the exchange. All these situational stimuli will determine precisely what semantic memory information is relevant to the interpretation of the metaphor. In brief, the metaphorical expression and the situation provide the *retrieval context* that guides the "search" through long-term memory. Since the linguistic aspects of the context are episodic events that fade rapidly, their influence will depend on their memorability, which in turn depends on such long-term memory characteristics as their concreteness or meaningfulness.

The preceding account provides a general framework for the analysis of metaphor in terms of mediation processes, long-term memory information, retrieval cues, and the like. We turn now to a more specific analysis of such processes in relation to metaphorical behavior. Four approaches are considered, one based on imagery, another on verbal associations, a third on abstract representations, and a fourth on a dual-coding approach that combines imagery and verbal processes in a systematic analysis.

Perceptual experience and imagery

Traditionally, metaphor has been analyzed in terms of perceptual imagery of a rather abstract nature. Susanne Langer, for example, wrote that "Metaphor is our most striking evidence of *abstractive seeing,* of the power of the human mind to use presentational symbols" (1942 reprint, p. 14). Conversely, the symbolic function of images is revealed in "their tendency to become metaphorical . . . [they are] our readiest instruments for abstracting concepts from the tumbling stream of impressions" (p. 117). These symbolic images are not only comprised of visual ingredients but are complex elements more appropriately described as "fantasies." They derive from experience, but the original perception of experience is "promptly and spontaneously abstracted, and used symbolically to represent a whole kind of actual happening" (p. 118). Further abstraction of this literal generality under appropriate circumstances results in a metaphorical fantasy, a figurative meaning.

Langer finds the origin of metaphorical thinking, not in language but in the nature of perception itself, in abstractive seeing. Her account is in striking agreement with Arnheim's (1969) analysis of visual perception as an abstractive process. Particularly relevant is an experiment by one of Arnheim's students, in which observers were asked to describe their impressions of two paintings of quite different style, shown side by side. One painting was then replaced by another and the effects of this new combination on the perception of the remaining picture were noted. These changes had strong effects, often leading to distortions in the perception of a picture. The experiments were actually "designed to illustrate the psychological mechanisms on which metaphors are based in literature. There, the pairing of two images throws into relief a common quality and thereby accomplishes a perceptual abstraction without relinquishing the context from which the singled out quality draws its life" (p. 62). The confrontation of the two images "presses for relation," which produces changes in the related items – changes in keeping with the structure of the context. Even single pictures can be vehicles for such perceptual abstractions, as Kennedy (1976) has demonstrated, particularly in regard to movement indicators in static pictures. Postural cues, lines of motion, and the like, are essential pictorial metaphors that elicit sensations, or images, of movement.

A number of other psychologists have also emphasized the perceptual basis of the metaphor without necessarily referring explicitly to imagery. Roger W. Brown (1958) suggested that metaphorical extensions involving the vocabulary of sensations, as when words like "warm," "cold," "heavy," and "dull" are applied to personality and social manners, may be based on "correlations of sense data in the non-linguistic world" (p. 154). Asch (1958) referred to functional similarities between the referents of metaphors and corresponding literal terms. Osgood (1953) related metaphor to the intersensory experience of "synesthesia," a form of imagery. Werner and Kaplan (1963) reported that subjects who were required to express relational statements in terms of lines or images often did so in an abstract, metaphorical way (see also Miller's chapter in this volume). Such interpretations do not in themselves *explain* how the perceptual processes and images achieve their abstract functions, or how they become linked to language, but they do emphasize the primacy of such processes in the origins of metaphor.

Direct empirical studies of the role of imagery in metaphor comprehension and memory began in the 1970s, with investigators manipulating three classes of variables. These included (1) variation in the imagery value of metaphor components or of accompanying stimuli, (2) use of imagery instructions, and (3) measures of individual differences in imagery use. Billow (1975) found that pictorial accompaniment facilitated comprehension of similarity metaphors in children. However, the effect was not large (about 10 percent above a prior presentation of the metaphors without any pictures) and the pictures also produced interference; 26.3 percent of the changes in interpretation when pictures were presented were from an initially correct to an incorrect interpretation. Billow concluded that "the results emphasized the linguistic nature of the metaphor task and the relatively minor input supplied by pictorial accompaniment" (p. 421). Note, however, that the results do not justify the conclusion that *imagery* played only a minor role in the task. The metaphors were originally "chosen for their relative concreteness. The compared objects were tangible and shared an attribute referring to tangible qualities or familiar actions or functions" (p. 416). Thus, the pictures presumably added little relevant imagery – and sometimes contributed irrelevant detail that led to enormous interpretations.

Recent studies concerned with the role of imagery in metaphor comprehension reveal a complex pattern as well. On the one hand, there is empirical evidence for a relationship between imagery and metaphor. For example, sentences constructed as similarity metaphors are rated as increasingly metaphorical as their predicates increase in rated imagery value (Marschark, Katz, & Paivio, 1983). The same relationship between sentence imageability and metaphoricity has been found in English proverbs (Walsh, 1988). Walsh used a measure of metaphoricity derived from Searle's (this volume) distinction between literal and metaphorical meanings, and found that high imagery proverbs were more likely to suggest metaphorical meanings than were low imagery proverbs. Some experimental studies have also shown that imageability is associated positively with comprehension and memory for metaphors (Paivio & Clark, 1986; Marschark & Hunt, 1985; Marschark et al., 1983; cf. Harris, 1979) and with higher levels of free recall of proverbs (Honeck, 1973).

On the other hand, the empirical picture is clouded by reported failures to find evidence that imagery has straightforward effects on specific measures of metaphor comprehension. Reichmann and Coste (1980) summarized results of studies in which subjects were asked to use either imagery or comprehension strategies to encode a list of proverbs; later, interpretations of the proverbs devised by the experimenters were presented along with unrelated distractors, and subjects were to indicate which interpretations were related to meanings of the proverbs presented earlier. Subjects who had used comprehension strategies did better than the imagery subjects in this task, which suggests that reliance on imagery to encode the meanings of proverbs results in memory representations that are not general enough to allow recognition of novel interpretations. However, it is not possible to rule out a functional role for imagery in proverb comprehension because, as Reichmann and Coste acknowledge, comprehension subjects may have used imagery in conjunction with other strategies to derive meanings for the proverbs. Such an assumption would help integrate Reichmann and Coste's findings with others described above (Walsh, 1988), which showed that high imagery proverbs were more likely to suggest metaphorical meanings than were low imagery proverbs.

Studies using other measures of comprehension also reveal mixed effects of imagery. Fainsilber and Kogan (1984) found that imageability was negatively related to the rated novelty of similarity metaphors, but positively related to the aptness of the comparisons in the metaphors. The authors concluded that, since overall quality of metaphors could be defined as a joint combination of novelty and aptness, then imageability is not related to *overall* metaphor quality. Katz (1989) found that participants in his metaphor construction task consistently preferred to use concrete, high imagery nouns to complete metaphor sentence frames. However, since individual differences in reported use of imagery for solving cognitive tasks did not predict choices in metaphor construction, he concluded that imagery was not the basis for this preference. Finally, Harris, Lahey, and Marsalek (1980) found that, although people rated metaphors as harder to image than literal paraphrases, they more frequently reported using imagery to encode the meanings of the metaphors.

The complex patterns of results in the above studies suggests that establishing the precise role of imagery in metaphor comprehension requires an analysis of metaphor in terms of more than a single cognitive component. Consistent with that suggestion, work by Bucci (Bucci & Freedman, 1978; Bucci, 1984) indicates that cognitive abilities that integrate imaginal processes with verbal ones may be related to metaphor production. The relevant findings are that individuals who tend to use metaphors relatively more often in spontaneous production also have high referential ability as measured by the speed with which they generate verbal labels for nonverbal experiences. We return to the idea that metaphor involves both imaginal and verbal processes later, in the context of a dual coding approach.

Verbal associative processes

Verbal interpretations of metaphor attribute the similarity relation between the key terms to common verbal associations. The common associations may vary in their remoteness, that is, their position in the hierarchy of associations to the key terms. Presumably, the more remote the common associates to the key terms, the longer it would take to "find" them and the more difficult the metaphor would seem. A similar analysis is applicable to associative priming effects that occur when associations to a target word are modified by the presence of a preceding context. Such priming effects, together with other processing mechanisms, could provide an associative account for the asymmetry puzzle in metaphor comprehension (e.g., Ortony, Vondruska, Foss, & Jones, 1985; Glucksberg & Keysar, 1990). The puzzle is that the elements that contribute to the perceived similarity between topics and vehicles in metaphor can often change if the order of the two terms is reversed in the metaphor (compare, for example, the interpretation of "His house is an old shoe" with "His old shoe is a house"). The challenge for associative models, and their new realizations in connectionist models of information processing (e.g., Hinton, 1981), is to account for the activation of the associations that are appropriate for metaphor interpretation so that a different association is activated when the order of the terms in a metaphor is reversed. In addition, it may be necessary for associative models to take account of the differences in associative patterns for metaphors ("His house is an old shoe") and literal sentences ("His Nike is an old shoe"; see Glucksberg & Keysar, 1990).

The associative model has often been applied to anecdotal data or literary examples, but direct research studies of metaphor from this viewpoint are relatively scarce. Koen (1965) obtained experimental evidence for the model in a situation in which subjects selected either a *metaphor* or a *literal* word to complete a sentence, such as "The sandpiper ran along the beach leaving a row of tiny STITCHES/MARKS in the sand." They were instructed to choose the word ("stitches" or "marks") most closely related to the group of ideas suggested by four cue words, which, according to associative data obtained from a separate group of subjects, were more often associated with either the metaphorical word or the literal word, or equally often with each. The results showed that the metaphor was greatly preferred over the literal word when cued by its frequent associates, but not otherwise. The finding is consistent with the verbal associative interpretation of metaphor processing, as are other findings that show both priming and interference effects on metaphor comprehension time, depending on the characteristics of prime words in a preceding context (Gildea & Glucksberg, 1983; Shinjo & Myers, 1987; see also Evans & Gamble, 1988, for evidence of associative effects on children's interpretations of metaphor). Such findings do not rule out imagery as an effective variable, in that cue words could arouse images that are consistent or inconsistent with critical words in metaphoric sentences, but verbal mediation is a plausible mechanism, and we accept it as a partial explanation, together with other processes, when we turn later to our own account.

Abstract representations

The third approach differs from the imagery and verbal associative interpretations in the assumption that the mediating process in metaphor comprehension is abstract, rather than modality specific. Osgood (1953, 1963) was probably the first psychologist to apply such a theory systematically to the analysis of language phenomena, including metaphor. His theoretical work began with the analysis of synesthesia. For Osgood, the basis of similarity, or transfer, in synesthesia and metaphor is in the common affective reactions that are aroused by different sensory stimuli and by words. "Evaluation," "potency," and "activity" are primary components of these affective reactions, according to factor-analytic studies. Osgood proposed that the highly generalized nature of the affective reaction system – the fact that it is independent of any particular sensory modality and yet participates with all of them – is at once the reason why Evaluation, Potency, and Activity appear as dominant factors *and* the psychological basis for metaphor and synesthesia. It is because such diverse sensory experiences as a *white* circle (rather than black), a *straight* line (rather than crooked), a *rising* melody (rather than a falling one), a *sweet* taste (rather than a sour one), a *caressing* touch (rather than an irritating scratch) – it is because all these diverse experiences can share a common affective meaning that one easily and lawfully translates from one sensory modality into another in synesthesia and metaphor. (1963, p. 312)

The common affective reactions are abstract in the sense that they are independent of "particular sensory modality," as well as in the sense that the representational affective reactions themselves are assumed to be abstractions of reactions originally made to things. Specifically, Osgood views the representational process as a simultaneous bundle of response-like components which differentiate among classes of meaning.

Research on the semantic differential has provided extensive indirect support for the relevance of Osgood's model. When individuals use scales such as "fast-slow," "hard-soft," and "weak-strong" to rate such diverse concepts as "mother" and "democracy," they must do so in a metaphorical way. Moreover, the emergence of stable factors indicates that individuals within a culture largely agree in their metaphorical interpretations of the relationship between the specific concepts that are rated and the bipolar terms in the rating scales. Such agreement is necessary if the model is to be relevant to the comprehension of metaphorical expressions, which must be amenable to common interpretations when they are used for communicative purposes within a linguistic community. Indeed, there is considerable cross-cultural generality in the metaphorical application of nonverbal visual form of the semantic differential to translation-equivalent words (Osgood, 1963, pp. 247–48). More recently, Osgood (1980) showed how the semantic differential model can be applied directly to the analysis of metaphor comprehension.

Others have recently suggested a variety of different abstract representational approaches to the analysis of metaphor. Malgady and Johnson (1976; see also Johnson & Malgady, 1980) proposed a model in which metaphor processing is described in terms of elementary units of meaning called "cognitive features." Features are inferred from association data, most particularly adjectival, descriptive associations to nouns (cf. Johnson, 1970). This aspect renders it operationally similar to the verbal associative approach, but features are theoretically viewed as units that are more elementary and abstract than words. In this general respect, the conceptual approach is similar to that of Osgood. Malgady and Johnson's experiment involved measures of similarity of constituents, as well as goodness and interpretability of metaphors involving noun pairs that were initially chosen to be high or low in rated similarity. The pair members were modified by adjectives that were associatively related to

(1) both nouns together (e.g., "soft hair is shiny silk"),

(2) each noun separately ("long hair is elegant silk"),

(3) the opposite (nonadjacent) noun in the pair ("elegant hair is long silk"), and

(4) neither noun ("distant hair is fatal silk").

A fifth condition involved two unmodified nouns ("hair is silk"). It was found that constituent similarity, goodness, and interpretability were all related to the pattern of modification. Metaphors in which the adjectives were associated with both nouns were generally highest in constituent similarity, goodness, and interpretability. The three variables were moderately intercorrelated when the individual nouns were initially high in similarity, but interpretability was essentially uncorrelated with nonconstituent similarity and metaphorical goodness when the nouns were low in similarity.

Malagady and Johnson interpreted their results in terms of the idea that, in metaphor interpretation, the constituents are encoded into a single feature representation. The degree of similarity of the constituent nouns, together with adjectival modifiers, will influence the integrity of the whole. Similar but "deviant" constituents, such as the noun pairs in this experiment, will be synthesized into a well-organized whole that is readily interpreted and viewed as a good metaphor. Dissimilar noun constituents usually result in a disintegrated representation that is difficult to interpret, and goodness will be judged only on the basis of phrase similarity.

The idea that the separate, feature-defined meanings of the constituents are assumed to form a single representation with a qualitatively distinct meaning is intriguing. The problem remains, however, of further specifying the psychological nature of the elementary features and the novel integrated representation that presumably results from their combination. Given their definition in terms of controlled associations, the features could be interpreted in verbal associative terms unless independent evidence suggests otherwise. In fact, there is reason to believe that descriptive associations are related to several different processes. A. N. Katz (1976) factor-analyzed a variety of measures obtained on concept instances, including descriptive associative norms available in Underwood and Richardson (1956). The associations consisted of sense-impression words, the frequency of which defined the relative dominance level of the instance with respect to a given sensory attribute. Thus "globe" has a higher dominance level than "pearl" with respect to the attribute "round," because "round" was a more frequent response to the former. It can be seen that associations define a subset of features in the Malagady and Johnson sense. Katz found that the dominance level correlated substantially with several different measures, including "image salience" (the degree to which the attribute is a salient aspect of the image aroused by the instance), the rank of the attribute in the verbal associative hierarchy, and the judged goodness of the instance as an example of a sense-impression category. In all, dominance level had loadings from three different factors and was unrelated to a fourth. Subsequent experiments showed that each of these factors independently predicted the ease of concept discovery. These results suggest that the elementary cognitive features and integrated representations involved in metaphor research might be similarly decomposable into different components, including verbal associative and imaginal mechanisms, and each might play a role in metaphor comprehension. In regard to imagery, it is interesting that Johnson (1977; Johnson & Malgady, 1980) also has stressed the perceptual basis of metaphor processing, without necessarily implying that the perceptual process "spills over" into conscious imagery.

The ultimate nature of the abstract representational process is similarly indefinite in other current theories of metaphor processing. We have already referred to the conceptual base hypothesis proposed by Honeck and his co-workers. They left the characteristics of the conceptual base relatively undefined except for the assertion that it is abstract and perhaps imagery-free. A number of psychologists have proposed similar views (for example, Brewer, 1975; Anderson & Ortony, 1975) in regard to the semantic processing of sentences. Verbrugge and McCarrell (1977) stressed the perceptual origins and relational nature of the common abstract representations that emerge in metaphor processing. The support for such representations emerged from a series of experiments in which the recall of metaphors was prompted by the topic, vehicle, or ground of the metaphor. Thus, for the metaphor "Billboards are warts on the landscape," the prompts were "billboards," "warts," or the (implicit) ground, "are ugly protrusions on the surface." The grounds from a different list served as irrelevant prompts. The results of one experiment showed that topic, vehicle, and relevant ground were all effective prompts, in that they produced recall levels that far exceeded levels obtained with the irrelevant prompts. The interesting result, of course, is the high recall with grounds as prompts, since they contained no words that appeared in the related sentences. Other experiments showed that the ground was a more effective prompt for the entire metaphor than for either topic or vehicle alone, and that the prompting effects should not be explained in terms of preexperimental verbal associations between grounds and metaphoric components.

Verbrugge and McCarrell concluded that metaphor processing involves the recognition of an abstract relation between the vehicle and topic domains, which is more than the sum of the attributes of each constituent. However, the precise nature of this abstract perceptual relation and how it arises from the separate parts remained unspecified, as did the abstract representational mechanisms postulated by Malgady and Johnson (1976), Honeck et al. (1975), and Reichmann and Coste (1980).

A dual-coding approach

The preceding views all have merit, but each suggested process is incomplete and insufficient in itself. Here, we discuss a dual-coding approach, which in principle combines the imagery and verbal associative views, in that both processes are assumed to be cooperatively involved in language (including metaphor) processing generally. The two processes represent the activity of independent but interconnected systems that are specialized for picking up, storing, organizing, retrieving, and manipulating stimulus information. The imagery system deals with information concerning concrete objects and events, the verbal system with linguistic information. Independence implies that the systems can be active separately or in parallel. Interconnections between the systems permit information to be transferred from one to the other or, more accurately, for one system to initiate activity in the other. Thus, words can evoke imagery, and concrete events can evoke verbal descriptions. The systems are assumed to differ qualitatively in the nature of the information they handle and generate. The imagery system presumably constructs synchronously organized, integrated informational structures, analogous to the continuous, structural layout of the perceptual world. Thus, imaginal representations (not necessarily experienced in the form of conscious imagery) are assumed to have just those properties that would account for the integrated representation that appears to emerge when a metaphor is understood. The verbal system organizes discrete linguistic units into higher-order sequential structures. Taken together, these assumptions imply that the two systems can contribute independently, yet cooperatively to such tasks as metaphor comprehension. They provide the cognitive mechanisms for conveying continuous experiential information, using a discrete symbol system – the communication function that Ortony (1975) considers so essential to metaphor. We now consider more specifically how these processes might contribute to metaphor comprehension and memory, supporting our suggestions with relevant experimental findings.

Dual coding enhances the probability of finding a common ground in long-term memory. The first point is that two independent, but interconnected sources of information in long-term memory increase the probability of finding a connection between topic and vehicle. The mechanism is simply additivity of independent systems. A relevant verbal-associative connection might be found in verbal memory, or some similarity might be found in the imagistic referents of the topic and vehicle, or both processes might contribute somehow to the construction of an integrated symbolic image, or a reasonable verbal interpretation, that could constitute the ground of the metaphor.

The additivity hypothesis has been supported in memory experiments and other tasks. Memory studies have shown that the availability of nonverbal images increases verbal recall. For example, pictures are recalled better than words, and concrete words that readily evoke images are recalled better than abstract, low-imagery words. A number of findings suggest that these differences can be explained partly in terms of dual coding (Paivio, 1986). The reasoning is that pictures of familiar objects are highly likely to be named implicitly during input, concrete words are quite likely to evoke images, and abstract words are most likely to be named and rehearsed. Dual coding similarly provides a partial explanation of the facilitating effect of instructions to use imagery mnemonics on verbal recall: such techniques ensure that an imaginal representation will be added to the verbal base. It is particularly relevant here that such techniques are most effective when they are used in associative learning tasks, which require the mental construction of a link connecting two unrelated terms, much as one is required to do in understanding a new metaphor.

There is evidence that subject-generated imaginal mediators are sometimes related metaphorically to the memorized items. Some dual coding experiments have required subjects to learn pairs of abstract nouns, using images. Such image-mediated learning is understandable only in terms of concretization, or instantiation, of the abstract information. Occasionally, this seemed to occur in the form of an image that symbolized both members of a pair. For example, one subject reported "boy scout" as an imaginal mediator for the pair "chance-deed." The image in this case is clearly metaphoric, symbolizing a complex idea that incorporates the meaning of both terms: a boy scout is someone who takes the "chance" (or opportunity) to do a good "deed." The example is relevant because the metaphorical connection was constructed by the subject in a manner analogous to the discovery of a common ground between the vehicle and topic of a novel metaphor. The discovery presumably involved dual coding in that the image had to be generated from verbal cues.

Another study illustrates more directly the discovery of a common mediator. Katz and Paivio (1975) asked subjects to learn pairs in which nonsense words were associated with instances of several concepts. The subject's task was to learn the concepts that were represented by the nonsense words. Although the specific instances did not differ in imagery value, the to-be-learned concepts themselves were either high or low in imagery value. Thus, "a four-footed animal" is relatively high in imagery, whereas "an optical instrument" is relatively low in imagery value. In addition, some individuals were instructed to use visual imagery to learn the pairs, whereas others were not. The results showed that the imagery value of the conceptual categories as well as imagery instructions, facilitated concept acquisition. Katz and Paivio interpreted this to mean that the addition of high-imagery conditions increased the probability that concept learning would be mediated by either imaginal or verbal representations, or both.

The study is relevant to metaphor interpretation, because such interpretation is analogous to concept discovery. The subject must discover what the vehicle and topic have in common in a semantic, conceptual sense. The experiment demonstrated that verbal conditions that encourage image arousal also facilitate concept discovery.

There is considerable evidence that imagery also contributes to the comprehensibility of sentences (Denis, 1984; Klee & Eysenck, 1973; O'Neill & Paivio, 1978; Paivio & Begg, 1971). The general assumption is that imagery provides a subjective referential context for sentence interpretation. It is reasonable that imagery would contribute similarly to the comprehension of metaphorical expressions, although, as noted earlier, the imagery context would be inappropriate if it draws attention to its literal aspects. Suggestive evidence emerged from a study in which subjects rated normal and anomalous sentences for comprehensibility (O'Neill & Paivio, 1978). In the anomalous case, selection restrictions were violated by interchanging nouns from different sentences. The pertinent result was that anomalous sentences were rated as less sensible than normal ones, but the manipulation had little effect on imagery ratings. Something similar might occur in the case of novel metaphorical expressions that initially seem somewhat anomalous – if they contain highly concrete terms, one might easily image those terms without arriving at an appropriate metaphorical understanding. On the other hand, if the situation draws attention to nonliteral possibilities, concrete terms might prompt figurative interpretations of anomalous sentences as well as of metaphors. Pollio and Burns (1977), for example, found that subjects could interpret anomalous sentences under instructions to do so, and that many of the interpretations were metaphorical in nature. The study did not indicate whether imagery played any special role in such figurative interpretations, but it does suggest ways of investigating the problem.

The discussion now turns to the qualitative differences that might result in different contributions by the two systems.

Integrated images make for efficient information storage. The organizational characteristics of the imagery system provide for a large storehouse of potentially relevant information. The assumption is that imagistic information in long-term memory is organized synchronously into large, integrated chunks. This idea goes back to the British associationists, who distinguished between simultaneous and successive associations. The former are especially characteristic of visual perception and imagery, although they can be multimodal as well. Think of the sun and you simultaneously think of the sky. Image your home and you have available, more or less at once, its components and contents – windows, doors, rooms, furniture, colors, and so on. Integration also implies redintegration, so that access to part of the structure tends to redintegrate the whole. This means that a large amount of information becomes quickly available when it is stored in the form of integrated images. Just as in perception, however, the simultaneously available image components may have to be processed (e.g., described) successively.

Relevant evidence again comes from laboratory studies of associative memory. Begg (1972) showed that high-imagery phrases, such as "white horse," tended to be remembered as holistic units, as though each phrase took up no more memory space than either word alone. Abstract phrases, such as "basic theory," on the other hand, seemed to take up twice as much memory space as the individual words, as though the words were concatenated onto each other. Begg's theoretical explanation was that the concrete phrases activate holistic long-term memory images, in which the components are unitized in a single representation, for example, an animal that is at once a horse and white.

To appreciate the implications of this analysis for metaphor, consider the vehicle in the expression "A metaphor is a solar eclipse." The term "solar eclipse" will tend to arouse a compound image that includes the blackened center, together with the glowing ring that surrounds it. Both components, obscurity and light, will then be simultaneously available to arouse further associations relevant to the metaphorical context. These may involve further imagery, or the component information may be described verbally, and the descriptions, in turn, evoke further verbal associations or imagery, and so on, in a continuous exchange until a reasonable interpretation is achieved – reasonable presumably being determined by the communicative context in ways that are yet to be fully understood.

Imagery ensures processing flexibility. The synchronous nature of imaginal representations also promotes efficient memory search, because such information can be processed in a way that is flexible and relatively free from sequential constraints. If you are asked how many windows there are in your house, you can arrive at the answer by imagining your house from different positions and counting the windows from the image. You could do so by working around the house in either direction, inside or out. By contrast, the processing of organized verbal information in long-term memory is sequentially constrained to a high degree. We can recite the alphabet forward more quickly than backward, and backward recitation of a poem would be painfully slow.

This imaginal-verbal difference in processing flexibility (freedom from sequential constraints) has been experimentally demonstrated by measuring the time required to process mental images and verbal strings in different ways (Paivio, 1986, pp. 198–200). The advantage in processing flexibility applies as well to the generation of novel images, as compared to sentences (Segal, 1976, described in Paivio, 1975b): things can be put together in various ways in a meaningful image, but words do not enjoy the same freedom in sentences.

The flexibility of image processing implies a special advantage in creative discovery and invention; specifically, it makes for speed and efficiency in the search for relevant information, as well as in the construction of novel combinations from component information. The implication for metaphor processing is that imagery can increase the efficiency of the search for relevant information, as well as the generation of a novel, integrated representation that would constitute the common ground for vehicle and topic. However, the term "relevant" is crucial in this context. A completely unconstrained search, or constructive process, could not guarantee metaphorical relevance. We assume that relevance is ensured by the retrieval cues provided by the topic and vehicle of the metaphor and the constraints associated with verbal processes.

Topic and vehicle as retrieval cues for relevant information. Relevance requires a guided search through long-term memory, which is initiated by appropriate retrieval cues. This function is served by the metaphorical expression itself, together with contextual information. We propose that the vehicle and topic are the key terms, and that the former is usually prepotent at the figurative processing stage, when its properties are to be "conveyed" to the topic. Moreover, the concreteness of the vehicle should be crucial, because a concrete term provides rapid access to information-rich images.

The idea originated with paired-associate learning tasks, in which the concreteness or image-evoking value of stimuli and responses have been systematically varied. Individuals are presented with pairs of nouns varying in concreteness or nouns paired with pictures. They are then presented with one member of each pair and are required to recall its associate. It turns out that recall accuracy depends particularly on the concreteness of the item that is presented as the retrieval cue: pictures or concrete nouns are good reminders for their associates, abstract nouns are not. This effect was metaphorically interpreted in terms of the "conceptual peg" hypothesis: concrete nouns and pictures are effective pegs for storage and retrieval of associated information (Paivio, 1963; Paivio & Yarmey, 1966).

In the case of metaphor comprehension, we extend the idea to the retrieval of relevant information from long-term memory. The vehicle serves as an efficient conceptual peg for metaphor comprehension to the extent that it promotes retrieval of images and verbal information that intersects with information aroused by the topic. Retrieval of integrated images will be particularly useful for reasons already discussed: they are information-rich and in addition they permit flexible processing.

The hypothesis has been supported by experimental findings and some informal observations. Verbrugge and McCarrell (1977) found that the vehicle was generally superior to the topic as a retrieval cue for an entire metaphor. This supports the special salience of the vehicle in episodic memory for the metaphorical expression, but it does not necessarily follow that the vehicle is also prepotent in retrieval of information from semantic memory or other aspects of the comprehension process. Moreover, Verbrugge and McCarrell's study was not designed to provide any evidence on the role of imagery in their task.

Tversky's (1977) demonstration that similarity relations are not symmetrical is also relevant to the present hypothesis. Specifically, he found systematic asymmetries in comparative tasks (*A* is like *B*) as well as production tasks (producing the most similar response to a given stimulus). The direction of the asymmetry was determined by the relative salience (that is, judged prominence, figural goodness, prototypicality) of the two stimuli, so that similarity was greater when the less salient stimulus was compared to the more salient one than vice versa. Thus, if *B* is more salient than *A*, *A* is more likely to be compared with and viewed as similar to *B* than *B* to *A* (see also Rosch, 1975a). The application to metaphor and simile is obvious: such expressions should be more acceptable when the more salient noun serves as the vehicle than when it serves as the topic. Moreover, Tversky suggested that the interpretation of similes and metaphors involves "scanning the feature space and selecting the features of the referent that are applicable to the subject" (1977, p. 349). The relevant point in the present context is not the feature model per se, but Tversky's emphasis on the priority of the vehicle (i.e., the referent) in the interpretation process. That aspect seems consonant with the present hypothesis, but Tversky's analysis is open to alternative interpretations (e.g., Harwood & Verbrugge, 1977; Ortony, this volume).

Some informal observations bear more directly on these features of the hypothesis. One of us (Paivio) asked a number of colleagues and graduate students to interpret the "meta-metaphor" that introduced this chapter, namely, the statement that "for the student of language and thought, metaphor is a solar eclipse." They then were asked to describe how they arrived at their interpretation. Most agreed at least partly with the intended interpretation: in a metaphor, as in an eclipse, something is obscured. In addition, several respondents gave interpretations completely in agreement with the intended one, saying, for example, that both a metaphor and an eclipse enlighten while they obscure, that they cover up the real thing so that you can see it better, or that they block out the central stuff so that you can see the subtle stuff around it better.

What would be expected in regard to their introspective reports concerning the manner of arriving at an interpretation? The hypothesis that the vehicle functions as a conceptual peg suggests that it should have been processed before the topic, and as an image. This seemed to be generally the case. One person spontaneously reported that the statement made no sense until he imagined an eclipsed sun. Another said that he first imaged a partial eclipse and then a full one. A third said that he certainly imaged "that thing with all the fuzzy stuff around it." And so on. There was one exception, who said that he first thought of what metaphor might be for the student of language, then what an eclipse means for the student of astronomy, and then what the two have in common. He *may* have imaged, he said, but it did not seem salient. It is interesting that this respondent was also the only one whose interpretation did not include the idea of something being obscured. He referred instead to "exotic events from which one can learn something." This certainly is an appropriate interpretation, although not the most common one for this group of respondents. His interpretation and his introspections are consistent with the conclusion that he used the topic rather than the vehicle as his conceptual peg, whereas the others apparently were drawn to cast the vehicle in that role. Both strategies are logically possible, but one was generally preferred.

Controlled studies have supported aspects of the informal observations and produced new information that leads to a more precise statement of the conceptual-peg hypothesis as applied to metaphor. Marschark, Katz, and Paivio (1983) had participants rate novel metaphors on various attributes. The pertinent results were that the imagery value of the topic and vehicle predicted metaphor goodness and interpretability even when a number of other variables were statistically controlled. Moreover, vehicle imagery was the better predictor. Related memory effects were reported by Marschark and Hunt (1985).

Other studies have confirmed the dominance of the vehicle in metaphor interpretation once the context has been provided by the topic. In a test of the conceptual-peg hypothesis, Paivio and Clark (1986) varied the imagery value of the two components independently. Subjects presented with written metaphors were asked to press a reaction-time key when they had interpreted a metaphor and then write a paraphrase indicating their understanding. This aspect of the experiment showed that interpretation time was facilitated only when both topic and vehicle were high in rated imagery and the metaphor had been previously rated as relatively easy to understand. A second aspect yielded more striking results. Some subjects were primed with either the topic noun or the vehicle noun before the entire metaphor was presented. Topic priming speeded up metaphor interpretation relative to an unprimed control condition, whereas vehicle priming retarded interpretation time. These results are consistent with those of Gerrig and Healy (1983) who similarly found interference effects when the vehicle came before the topic in a reading task.

The priming results prompt the following restatement of the conceptual-peg hypothesis. The vehicle dominates in metaphor comprehension in the sense that its meaning determines the interpretation of the topic, but the topic must be known before the relevant meanings of the vehicle can be considered. The topic constrains the associative reactions evoked by the vehicle, so the topic must be processed first; hence the benefit of topic priming. The negative effect of vehicle priming occurred because isolated presentation of the vehicle evoked associations, verbal or imaginal, that were irrelevant to a metaphorical interpretation of the metaphor. Paivio and Clark tested this in a second experiment. Subjects were required to interpret metaphors and then to indicate which component, the topic or vehicle, they had thought about first, and which one they had thought about most. The results supported the up-dated application of the conceptual-peg hypothesis to metaphor: subjects generally reported thinking about the topic first but spent relatively more time thinking about the vehicle. In brief, once the topic is known, the associative search process is dominated by the vehicle.

Verbal processes keep search and retrieval on track. The conceptual-peg results have implications for the special role of the verbal system in metaphor processing. We suggested that imagery contributes specifically to the speed of accessing long-term memory, and to the speed and flexibility of the search for information that would provide the basis of a relevant interpretation of a metaphor. We propose, finally, that relevance itself is largely determined by the verbal system. The sequential nature of verbal processes contributes to an orderly logical sequence in the flow of ideas (cf. Paivio, 1975b). In brief, the verbal system keeps the search process "on track" in regard to the goal of discovering a relevant relational idea. Thus, in our thematic metaphor, the image of a solar eclipse could lead to flights of fantasy bearing no relevance to the meaning of metaphor for a student of language, just as the Paivio and Clark (1986) results suggested. It is one's episodic memory for the verbal concepts themselves that keeps one from being blinded by the glare of the solar image and thereby stumbling aimlessly through one's memory storehouse.

Conclusion

We have reviewed theories and psychological research findings concerning metaphor comprehension and memory. The theoretical ideas still fall into the same basis categories that were described in the 1979 original of this chapter, but they have become better defined and the amount of relevant research has increased greatly. The basic problems of language comprehension and memory also are better understood perhaps partly because of the advances in the study of metaphor. There seems to be general consensus in any case that "ordinary language" and metaphor are continuous phenomena, involving common cognitive and linguistic processes. Research might prove otherwise but without it we shall never know. Until recently, much of the psychological research on metaphor was not directed at really fundamental problems in the area. The original suggested that such work might require the systematic development of a large pool of novel metaphors that vary in type, difficulty, concreteness, and whatever other dimensions may seem relevant. At least one pool of that kind is now available (Katz, Paivio, Marschark, & Clark, 1988). Other advances include systematic extensions of some of the traditional paradigms that have been developed in verbal memory and language research, and more factual information on precisely how people respond to a novel metaphorical expression. Finally, our own suggestions concerning the role of the vehicle and topic as retrieval cues have begun to be translated into systematic observational studies and experiments that have contributed to progress in this area.

NOTE

This chapter is a revision of the one by Allan Paivio that appeared in the first edition under the title "Psychological processes in the comprehension of metaphor." The authors' research cited in this chapter was supported by grants from the Natural Sciences and Engineering Research Council of Canada.

15

The interpretation of novel metaphors

BRUCE FRASER

Paivio concludes his chapter in the first edition of this collection with the lament that much of the psychological research on metaphor had not been directed at really fundamental problems in the area. In the last paragraph, he wrote:

> Such work might require the systematic development of a large pool of novel metaphors that vary in type, difficulty, concreteness, and whatever other dimensions may seem relevant. It may demand systematic extensions of some of the traditional paradigms that have been developed in verbal memory and language research. It would require detailed factual information about precisely how people respond to a novel metaphorical expression.

The present chapter describes a step toward redressing this lack of relevant research.

The particular issues I am addressing involve the last point raised by Paivio and Walsh, namely, the nature of the speaker's response to a novel metaphor. However, I want to go further than just determining the facts of what interpretation is provided by the native speaker to a novel metaphorical utterance and suggest that in order to evaluate such facts, we must examine the following general question: To what extent is the interpretation of a metaphorical expression (or at least the most probable interpretation) predictable on the basis of the linguistic properties of the utterance alone? There are several subquestions: If the metaphorical utterance is given out of context, do speakers agree on the most likely interpretation? Where speakers differ, are the differences explainable in terms of speaker characteristics, such as age, education, sex, cultural background, and the like? Where there is agreement, can we specify the properties which give rise to this agreement, and if so, are these properties part of the linguistic characterization of the sentence used, or more a component of the belief system of the language users?

Since the questions I am raising cannot be adequately answered through introspection, a portion of this chapter will deal with the details of an empirical attempt to arrive at some of the answers. First, however, I shall establish a framework by providing a partial account of metaphor: what it is, and how it is signaled.

What is a metaphor?

Although I shall talk as though all metaphors were the same, there is, in fact, a continuum. At one end there is what might be called the *live metaphor,* at the other end the *dead metaphor.* The latter is simply an idiom, which was once a live metaphor, but which is now to be treated as a conventionalized form in the language. The phrase "to kick the bucket," once used literally and then metaphorically to refer to the final struggles of animals lashed by their feet to a beam called a "bucket," has now lost any sense of its original source. On the other hand, there are expressions such as "John is married to his tennis game" or "Irrigate your mind a little" that require both a context and a certain creativity to interpret adequately. It is only these last that I shall be concerned with here.

Now, it may seem redundant and unnecessary to try to provide a definition of metaphor. After all, the topic has been discussed by many eminent writers (for example, Aristotle; Black, 1962b; Dubois et al., 1970; Koestler, 1964; Richards, 1936a), and one might expect to find an acceptable definition amongst such writings. Perhaps one can, but at the risk of replowing old ground, I want to address the question anew, looking at metaphor within the context of a more general theory of pragmatics. The main point that underlies this orientation is an obvious fact about metaphor, but one that is often overlooked in the linguistic literature, namely, that a metaphor involves the use of language. As such, metaphor is not to be accounted for within the grammar of a language – at least not in the sense of grammar proposed by Chomsky, which, although having undergone various modifications in the last fifteen years, is still intended to be a characterization of the language user's knowledge about the relationship between strings of sounds and their meanings, and not the knowledge about how such sentences might be used in context to communicate intentions. Black (1962b) presents this view when he writes:

The rules of our language determine that some expressions must count as metaphors; . . . but we must also recognize that the established rules of language leave wide latitude for individual variation, initiative, and creation. There are indefinitely many contexts (including nearly all the interesting ones) where the meaning of a metaphorical expression has to be reconstructed from the speaker's intentions (and other clues) because the broad rules of standard usage are too general to supply the information needed . . . to know what the user of a metaphor means, we need to know how seriously he treats the metaphorical focus . . . We must not expect the "rules of language" to be of much help in such inquiries. (There is accordingly a sense of "metaphor" that belongs to "pragmatics" rather than to "semantics" – and this sense may be the one most deserving of attention.) (pp. 29–30)

Black does not provide an account of what he means by "pragmatics," but since he contrasts it with "semantics" in the passage cited, I think we can take it as being consistent with the recent work that is aimed at developing a theory of pragmatics – a theory which attempts to explain how it is that a speaker can consistently exploit factors of the context of speaking, as well as the manner in which something is said, to convey to the hearer an utterance meaning that differs from the literal meaning of the linguistic expression he has used. The literal interpretation of the sentence, "Where are your shoes?" for example, is a request for information about the location of the hearer's shoes. Spoken by a mother to a child late for school, the utterance takes on (or we may assert that on many such occasions it takes on) the meaning of "Get going"; spoken by a nurse to an elderly patient, it may be intended to mean "I offer to get your shoes for you if you tell me where they are," and so forth.

The precise domain of such a theory, as well as its relationship to a theory of grammar, is a subject of current disagreement. This need not concern us here, though there are several concepts we shall need for the subsequent discussion.[1]

The first of these involves the choices a speaker may make in determining how to convey his intended meaning. There is one major distinction, that of speaking literally versus speaking nonliterally. To speak literally is to intend to convey the literal meaning of the sentence uttered; that is, to mean what you say. On the other hand, to speak nonliterally (figuratively) is to intend to convey *not* the literal meaning of the sentence uttered but, rather, some different meaning – one that is related in some conventional way to the literal meaning. A good example of the nonliteral use of language is found in irony. For example, I might be driving you in my car when someone from the right-hand lane cuts in front of us to make a left-hand turn, thereby causing me to slam on the brakes. My response might be to say, "I just love people who don't signal." (I might also say several other things, but they are not relevant here.) Clearly, the native speaker of English who has heard my utterance would recognize that I did not mean what I said, that I was speaking ironically, and that my intended meaning was something like, "I really hate people who don't signal." Note, however, that the sentence I used in being ironic is, in fact, a well-formed English sentence which has a clear literal interpretation. It just happens that I do not want to be taken as intending to convey this meaning at this particular moment. I shall argue later that metaphors involve only language used nonliterally.

It is, however, important to recognize that metaphor is not the only use of nonliteral language. I have already mentioned how irony ("I just love people who don't signal") requires that the speaker intend the expression nonliterally. Hyperbole, another rhetorical device, involves the conveying of a proposition that so distorts the obvious truth that the hearer recognizes the nonliteral intention on the speaker's part; for example, when one says, "Thousands showed up," when in fact hundreds were there. Synecdoche involves the substitution of one term for another within a predetermined hierarchy. Jacobson and Halle (1956) suggested that this replacement is of a syntagmatic sort, as opposed to metaphor, in which the replacement is paradigmatic. For synecdoche, one referring term replaces another that is either more general or more particular than the actual term itself. What binds the two terms together may be based on anatomical classification (for example, "all hands on deck"), or a perceptual relationship (for example, "Get that smell out of here," where "smell" is referring to the bag of garbage). Metonymy, on the other hand, involves a replacement of a term where the relationship of the first to the second is felt to be more functional: cause/effect, actor/action, container/contained, and the like. We find examples like the "lands belonging to the Crown," "The White House announced that . . . ," and "The Fords won all the prizes at le Mans this year." None of the expressions above can be taken literally, and each reflects a substitution of one term for another because of some preexisting relationship. An interesting analysis can be found in J. D. Sapir (1977).

A second distinction involves what it is that we convey to a hearer when we say something. Without going into any detail, I think we can adopt the position of Searle (1969) who argues that every sentence carries two sorts of information. It carries information that signals the intended propositional content, and it carries information that signals the intended speech act force. In a sentence such as "I promise that I will be there," the propositional content is clear and unambiguous: "I will be there." And the intended force of promising is also clear and unambiguous. In other sentences, the information signaling the force and propositional content may be collapsed, and in some cases, incomplete. For the purposes of this discussion, I shall be concerned only with the propositional content of the example sentences, and I shall usually treat them as simple propositions, rather than as compound propositions.

Let us return to the question posed at the beginning of this section: What is a metaphor? As a working definition, I define a metaphor as: "an instance of the nonliteral use of language in which the intended propositional content must be determined by the construction of an analogy."[2] I shall now elaborate on this definition.

First, that a metaphor does not exist without someone saying something seems clear. I think there would be general agreement that in seriously uttering "My brother is a spinster," or "The chairman plowed through the discussion," one is using a metaphor. However, to claim that the sentence "My brother is a spinster" is a metaphor seems just wrong. To say that the sentence "contains" a metaphor also seems unacceptable, because, at least in our view, a metaphor results from the speaker intending to use an expression nonliterally, and sentences surely do not have intentions. Of course, it might be fair to conclude that the use of the sentence would ordinarily involve the intention to speak metaphorically.

The requirement that a metaphor involve only the nonliteral use of language is perhaps more controversial. Sentences such as "John is a pig," "The chairman plowed through the discussion," and "Sheathe your impatience" are often suggested as incontestable examples of metaphor. Moreover, it is pointed out that they are all semantically anomalous and thus *cannot* be interpreted literally – they are literally meaningless. But just as there are many semantically anomalous expressions used metaphorically, so there are many which are semantically unexceptional; that is, there is an acceptable literal interpretation. Suppose, for example, that we are discussing my neighbors and I remark that "John is our priest," referring to John, who is, in fact, a plumber, but who provides us counsel. I have used a perfectly acceptable sentence, but one which I intend to be taken nonliterally in that context. Clearly I do not believe what I say, nor do I expect you to take me to believe it. The point here is not whether or not there are more metaphors which rest on semantically acceptable or unacceptable expressions; rather, the point is that, acceptable or not, the speaker *intends* the expression to be taken nonliterally. We return to this point in the following section, which deals with the signaling of a metaphor.

If the above claim restricting metaphors to the intended nonliteral use of language is correct, it should be clear that the truth or falsity of a sentence intended metaphorically is irrelevant. For semantically anomalous declarative sentences which cannot be interpreted literally, the issue of their being true or false cannot arise. In such cases, if the speaker is serious about the conversation and trying to communicate something, the hearer *must* take the expression as being nonliterally intended in order to understand it. For imperative sentences such as "Root out your faults, one by one," which are intended as orders of some sort, the issue of truth also cannot arise. The same is true for sentences which have an interrogative form but which are used metaphorically. Sentences such as "John is our priest," which are semantically well formed may or may not reflect a true or false claim. But this is beside the point if the speaker intends the expression to be taken nonliterally, thereby intending the hearer to infer some different interpretation of the utterance.

The final point in the definition which bears clarification is the requirement that the interpretation of a metaphor requires that the hearer establish an analogy. Indeed, a metaphor is often defined as a type of analogy, as an implicit comparison, whereas a simile is called an explicit comparison. Aristotle, for example, called a simile "a metaphor with a preface." I must point out, however, that whereas I am arguing that a metaphor is a proposition used nonliterally which requires the establishing of an analogy for its interpretation, a metaphor is *not* an analogy. An analogy must play a crucial role in the interpretation of a metaphor, but this is analogous to saying that some sort of polarity reversal must play a role in the interpretation of irony. From the latter, it does not follow that irony is a type of polarity reversal. The form of this analogy is discussed by Miller (this volume), and in Fraser (1977), where I discuss in some detail the nature of the required analogy and the process of metaphorical interpretation. There, I not only argue that all metaphors should be treated in a similar way, but I also propose some pragmatic rules of metaphor interpretation, sensitive to the grammatical form of the metaphorical utterance.

How is a metaphor signaled?

I have suggested in the preceding section that a metaphor involves a nonliteral use of language. At issue now is how a speaker signals this intention. There appear to be three basic approaches.

The most obvious, though seldom mentioned, way to signal a metaphor is to announce it. To say, for example, "Speaking metaphorically, Harry is married to his work," is to make explicit that you intend the utterance to be taken nonliterally and to receive metaphorical processing.[3] In addition, the use of terms such as "practically," "actually," or "virtually," as in "He virtually purred at the news," often serve to announce the intention to use a metaphor.

The second, and probably the most noted way to signal a metaphorical intent is to use a semantically anomalous sentence.[4] Examples such as, "Harry is a wastebasket," when talking about Harry, or "The crowd floated through the market," when discussing the crowd, represent such cases. As will be discussed later, not all semantically anomalous propositions are intended to be metaphorically interpreted.

The third way of signaling metaphorical intention is to use a sentence which is pragmatically anomalous. In such cases, the sentence is literally meaningful (in contrast to the case above), but the propositional content represents a possible state of affairs that is clearly false or irrelevant under the conditions of utterance.

Let us consider the following examples, not all intended metaphorically. First, "John is our priest," under the circumstance of talking about John, our unreligious next-door neighbor; second, "That remark reflects an outstanding sensitivity," said to someone who had just made a remark in front of the hostess about the tasteless dinner, and third, "He swallowed gallons of water," said of someone who nearly drowned. All of these sentences are clearly meaningful, but all are, in the stipulated context, clearly untrue, and all signal the need for a nonliteral interpretation. However, while the former seems to be a clear case of metaphor, the second is an example of irony, the third of hyperbole.

Unfortunately, I have no adequate analysis that will successfully identify which figurative use of language has been intended. Various linguists have informally suggested that irony is always accompanied by a characteristic nasal intonation, but there is no empirical evidence. Such an intonation may well sometimes accompany intended irony, but it is by no means a necessary condition for it. Rather, there appears to be but one clear method to differentiate ironic from metaphorical or hyperbolic intention: if the meaning of the proposition is, roughly speaking, directly opposite to the meaning one might expect from the speaker under the circumstances, then irony is intended; if the meaning does not fall into this category, then metaphor or hyperbole is a possibility. One can, of course, ask how the hearer is to know "what is expected" in a given utterance context. I have no adequate answer to this at present. That the example, "He swallowed gallons of water," is a case of hyperbole, rather than irony or metaphor, seems clear. But here again, we have no definite way of "proving" it.

To summarize, I have suggested that there are three ways of signaling a metaphorical intent. First, the speaker can simply announce his intention to have the utterance interpreted as a metaphor. Second, the speaker can use a semantically anomalous sentence; such cases appear unequivocally to be instances of the speaker signaling a metaphorical intent. Third, the speaker can use a meaningful sentence, but one whose content, given the context of utterance, is either obviously false or simply irrelevant. Here there are three possibilities: The speaker can be intending to signal irony, hyperbole, or metaphor. The first of these would seem to be signaled if the expected propositional content is directly opposed to that expressed. Hyperbole would seem to be signaled if the predication overstates or understates the abilities or actions of the propositional subject referent. And finally, as a default case, metaphor would seem to be signaled if neither of the first two is indicated.

All the examples considered so far have involved cases in which the propositional subject directly referred to the focus of the conversation. There are, however, at least two other rhetorical devices which rely on the nonliteral use of the proposition expressed, but for both of these, the propositional subject does not directly refer to the conversational focus. As we have indicated earlier, synecdoche involves a syntagmatic replacement of what would be the appropriate directly referring term by an indirectly referring one, where the two are related by some predetermined hierarchy; for example, "The sail appeared on the horizon," where "sail" is used to refer to the entire object, the ship. Metonymy, on the other hand, involves a replacement of the focus term by another term related in some functional way to the first. For example, "The White House announced . . ." uses the term "the White House" for the direct term, "the president." Although I have not discussed the rules that guide the interpretation of either metonymy or synecdoche, they would seem to bear close resemblance to those involved in metaphorical interpretation.

There may, of course, be problems with the account of how a metaphor is signaled that has been presented in this section. I may have overlooked a nonliteral use of language that will confound the recognition problem, or I may be oversimplifying the task of recognition by choosing examples too obvious. However, I think the basic outline of the program is sound, and I now wish to turn to the question initially posed concerning the interpretation of novel metaphors.

A pilot study

To pursue my response to Paivio's challenge to provide some real data on the interpretation of novel metaphorical expressions, I developed a set of test items which were clearly semantically anomalous, thereby signaling the need for a metaphorical interpretation. The principal questions I wished to investigate were those posed initially in this paper:

First, if a metaphorical utterance is given out of context, do speakers agree on the most likely interpretation? My hypothesis was that they would not, since context plays such a crucial role.

Second, where speakers do differ are their differences explainable in terms of speaker characteristics, such as age, education, sex, cultural background, and the like? My hypothesis was that they would be, particularly with respect to cultural orientation.

Third, where there is agreement, can the properties which give rise to this agreement be inferred, and to what extent are such properties part of the linguistic description of the utterance? My hypothesis was that we can specify the properties, but that they relate to connotative aspects (salient features) of the lexical items involved rather than any denotative lexical information.

There was, however, a second agenda, namely, to determine the extent to which metaphors and the similes which appear to be related structurally to them (for example, "John is a pig" and "John is like a pig") receive the same zero-context interpretation. Although various linguists have speculated informally on the translatability of metaphors to similes, and vice versa, no one, to my knowledge, has enquired empirically into the similarity of hearer interpretation.

To investigate some of these questions, at least at a preliminary level, we constructed four sets of twenty-eight sentences, each sentence having been judged clearly semantically anomalous by two or more native speakers. The groups consisted of declarative sentences having the following form:

Group A: "He's an *X*"

Group B: "She's an *X*"

Group C: "He's like an *X*"

Group D: "She's like an *X*."

Thus, groups A and B contained metaphorical expressions, differing only in the gender of the subject; groups C and D contained similes, again differing only in the subject gender. By using only pronominal subjects, I hoped to avoid specific images associated with a more specific noun phrase. The values of the *X* in the test were nouns chosen in as completely an unsystematic fashion as possible: A list of objects observed or mentioned during a day was compiled, and from it twenty-eight objects were selected which seemed "interesting," and which clearly would not receive a semantically acceptable interpretation in the test game. No attempt was made to control the conceptual categories from which values for the *X* were chosen.

The subjects for this first set of judgments consisted of ten men and thirty women, all native English-speaking college students in the greater Boston area. The age range was from nineteen to thirty-eight; the mean was twenty-six. No attempt was made to control for ethnic or cultural background.

Each subject was given a set of pages stapled together, consisting of a set of instructions followed by 30 separate examples: These included two practice examples (*X* = "dog," *X* = "snail") followed by seven from each of the four groups. The sheets of items were arranged in several random orders within each group of 28. Four different test sets of 28 items were compiled, thereby exhausting the (4×28) 112 test items.

Results

The basic question – whether a metaphor in zero context receives a consistent interpretation – was answered clearly in the negative, except for the two practice items ("He is a dog" and "She is like a snail" – dogs are nearly always ugly; snails are almost always slow). Several examples will illustrate this. Combining the metaphor and simile responses, for the *X* = "termite" cases, the following (edited) responses were obtained:

He: is a pest, is destructive, eats a lot, eats a little, is little, tears at your sense of self, bores into any conversation, is deceptive, picks things apart, is a parasite, is always worrying about you, is always in the way, is petty, is undermining, is insidious, is devious;

She: is nosey, is always eating, is tiny, eats you out of everything, is a pain in the ass, spends money quickly, is small, is bothersome, is a leech, is relentless, hides, is unwanted, keeps nagging, digs into others' business, is destructive, has a small brain, is dumb, is afraid of herself.

For X = "a peanut butter and jelly sandwich":

He: is always falling on his face, is delicious, is mediocre, is difficult to get rid of, is mushy minded, is sweet, has no backbone, is nice but dull, is easy going, is All American, is an acceptable substitute when no one else is around, is well put together, kids like him, is sometimes boring but basically good for you, is ubiquitous, is plain, is uninteresting;

She: is a good standby, is a slob, is mushy, is hard to get rid of, has got it, has no backbone, is a "common type," is plain, has mush for brains, is nice to have around, is not refreshing, is familiar.

For X = "a compass":

He/She: is stylish, is well-oriented, is rigid and set in direction, always does the right thing, is scientific, always knows where and how to go, follows you if he likes you, is very aware, has a good sense of direction, is indecisive, is decisive, has a girl in every place, is disorganized, is well organized.

For X = "a ripe banana":

He: is soft, is an OK person, is malleable, is mushyheaded, "too dirty to write down," is old and worn, is outmoded, is overripe, is soft, is all yellow, is nice, is friendly, is always ready, is harmless, is eccentric, is good now but rotten soon, is well hung, is phallic;

She: is oversexed, is raring to go, is crazy, stands out to be picked on, has appeal, is mushy, is too soft, is fully developed, is hot to trot, is voluptuous, is provocative, is soggy, is sensitive, is easy to hurt, is slender, takes care of herself, is waiting to be peeled, is too hot, is available.

Finally, for X = "an octopus":

He: is all arms, climbs, does a lot, is clumsy, is aggressive, is motor-oriented, is into everything, can't keep his hands off girls, is grabby (these last three a number of times);

She: does lots at once, is always hugging and touching, has fingers in many pies, is domineering, is manipulative, is great on first dates, is all over the place, touches everything, is grabby.

I think that without much fear of argument, I can conclude that for the zero-context interpretation of the similes and metaphors with pronominal subjects, but separated in terms of the sex of the referent of whom the expression is predicated, there is no one "most-probable" interpretation. Whether this would be true for nonpronominal subjects is an open question.

Four things, however, do stand out from the examples above, which I have taken to be representative. First, there is often a clear interpretation in terms of a positive or negative evaluation of the expression. Predicating "termite" of someone nearly always produced a negative interpretation. This might, of course, follow from the shared belief that termites are generally undesirable. For the case of X = "a caterpillar," however, where we might expect caterpillars to be pretty generally disliked, there were many more positive responses; for example, "He has potential," "She is very smooth," and "He is slow and cautious." Perhaps some general criteria of disdain can explain these differences.

Second, there is often (though not always) a significant distinction between the predication of the expression for "he" as opposed to "she" for both male and female judges. If a male is an octopus, he is nearly always aggressive, all hands, after a woman, oversexed, and only occasionally a busy person. A female who is an octopus, however, is much less aggressive, and grabby, and is more often seen as busy, liberated, ambitious, and the like.

Third, although none of the examples was (consciously) picked for any sexual connotation, nearly every test item evoked two or more interpretations which were sexually oriented. It is easy to see how this might arise with "a ripe banana," "an octopus," and "a geometric figure"; but one is far less likely to predict such a response with "a peanut butter and jelly sandwich" ("She's a good standby"), "a compass" ("He has a girl everyplace"), "a caterpillar" ("She's a good date, crawls all over you"), "a pack of chewing gum" ("She's cheap"). These sexual interpretations were by no means located solely with one or two individuals (though one person did seem to get carried away), nor were they made predominantly by the male as opposed to the female judges. One subject suggested that the reason for this might be that metaphors are so often used as a device to mask sexual information; I know of no empirical evidence which bears on this.

Fourth, and finally, though there is wide variation in the interpretations provided by the judges, they do not vary totally indiscriminately. Leaving aside those more idiomatic expressions (for example, "He's a dog," "She's a pig"), we can analyze the aspect of the X being evoked by the expression as relating what is believed to be (a) a physical characteristic; (b) a behavioral characteristic; or, (c) a functional characteristic of the object. Many of the interpretations fit into one of these three categories. Take, for example, the case X = "a woodchuck," where, in terms of the above framework, we find:

1. *Physical:* has buckteeth, is ugly, is fat, is hairy;
2. *Behavioral:* is industrious, is an introvert, is shy, eats continually, waddles, is always digging, is a careful eater, is plodding, is persistent;
3. *Functional:* (None, but a possibility would be "predicts spring").

However, we also have:

He: is timely, wears glasses, is always in your business, is a workhorse, needs braces, . . .

which do not appear to fit well into this classification, although there are associations which can be suggested. For nearly all of the test X's, the same sort of analysis resulted: Many of the interpretations could be easily related to one of the three aspects of the referent as was done above for "a woodchuck"; in all cases, however, there was a substantial residue which did not seem amenable to this classification. Whether this residue would increase with more subjects, or whether it was an artifact of the present research remains to be clarified.

To summarize, though there is often a definite orientation to the interpretation (positive/negative), often an obvious differentiation between the interpretation when predicated of a male versus a female, sometimes a definite sexual connotation, and sometimes some properties of the X that can be related to the interpretation, there is little evidence of the kind of consistency that would be needed to predict a zero-context interpretation.[5] This, of course, is exactly what one would hope, if the interpretation of a metaphor is to be based within the rules of language *use,* rather than within the rules of grammar. That is, to the extent to which a metaphorical interpretation is determined by the context in which it is uttered, the least consistent interpretations should be the zero-context ones.

I have much less to say on the other questions I raised. There was no evidence that the sex of the judge played any role in the resulting interpretation, though with a larger sample some effect might have become apparent. Since the other possibly important variables, such as education, and cultural and ethnic background were not controlled, I cannot comment on their roles.

The purpose of providing both metaphor and simile test items was, as indicated, to determine if there was any difference in their interpretation. Since the range of responses was so large, it was not possible to find any clear-cut trends. One, however, that did appear to be tenable is the following: The simile was more likely than the metaphor to evoke an interpretation involving the behavior of the X. For example, for "She's like a caterpillar," there were several responses of the sort, "She's in the process of development," whereas there were none for "She's a caterpillar." For "He's like a frog," there were several "He jumps around a lot," but there was only one such response for "He's a frog." Whether such a trend would show significance on conventional statistical tests remains to be seen.

In conclusion, I began this chapter by indicating that I wanted to respond to Paivio's challenge by investigating the interpretation of novel metaphors. I think that I have done so in a small but significant way. I have presented some precise, factual information about how native speakers interpret novel metaphors, and I have indicated that these interpretations suggest strongly that there is little consistency across speakers, thereby supporting the position that the interpretation of metaphor is based within a theory of language use, not of grammar. Paivio and Walsh say that "A metaphor is a solar eclipse." I suggest, rather, that "Metaphors are black holes in the universe of language": We know that they are there; many prominent people have examined them; they have had enormous amounts of energy poured into them; and, sadly, no one yet knows very much about them.

NOTES

I have benefited greatly from discussions with Jean Fraser, John Ross, and George Miller on the ideas presented here. All, however, have expressed reservations about them!

1 I believe that a theory of pragmatics and a theory of illocutionary acts are equivalent. This appears to be the position of J. J. Katz (1966), as well as that of Bach and Harnish (1979). Searle (1969, 1975) does not mention the term "pragmatics" but does make it clear that in his view, illocutionary acts cannot be separated from a theory of semantics. R. Lakoff (personal communication) sees pragmatics to encompass a much larger domain, perhaps that suggested by Hymes (1973) under the term "communicative competence."

2 In Fraser (1977) I argue that it is only the predicating expression of the propositional content that must be determined by use of an analogy, and that the referring expression (the propositional subject) is unequivocal. Miller (this volume) takes this position as well.

3 Interestingly, we do not find the expressions, "Speaking similely," or "Speaking in a simile," to be acceptable ways to indicate that a simile is intended, perhaps because the presence of "like," "as," or other predicates of similitude serves the purpose. Nor do we find "Speaking ironically," which cannot be for that reason, since there are no syntactic or semantic indicators of irony which can be indicated only by certain performance features, most notably intonation.

4 As various linguists have pointed out, there is a fine line to be drawn between where syntactic generalizations end, and semantic ones begin. Some, in fact, argue that such a distinction is both irrelevant and impossible. It is not necessary for me to take sides in this argument here, inasmuch as all I require is an agreement that certain propositions cannot be interpreted literally because of the propositional structure and the meanings of the individual lexical items.

5 One obvious way to investigate predictability would be to ask the judges to provide salient characteristics for each of the X's and then determine if these correspond to their responses.

16

*The role of similarity in similes and metaphors

ANDREW ORTONY

The chapter by Alan Paivio and Mary Walsh is like a tool kit; it provides the potential for undertaking a serious examination of our problem. The question that now has to be asked is whether it contains the right tools. I suspect that as with most tool kits, some of the tools are useful for the problem at hand and some are not. In this chapter, I shall concentrate on the tool that I believe to be the most important, namely, *similarity*. I shall also discuss briefly two other issues raised by Paivio and Walsh, namely, integration and relation.

Paivio and Walsh argue that the central question surrounding the comprehension (and the production) of metaphors concerns the way in which a novel conception arises from apparently disparate parts. This question, they claim, involves three important concepts, namely those of integration, relation, and similarity. Similarity is involved because the two terms in a metaphor share attributes. Relation is implicated, because a metaphor may take advantage of common relations, and also because of its involvement in integration. Integration is significant because of the emergence of something new, presumably a result of integrating certain aspects of the parts. As I have said, I think that the most important of these three concepts is that of similarity. For that reason, I shall devote most of my attention to the role of similarity in metaphors, and especially in similes. I think that integration deserves a more thorough treatment than I am able to give it, whereas relation probably gets more than it deserves.

Accepting the importance of the question Paivio and Walsh take to be the central one, I shall start by making a few observations about integration and relation. Paivio and Walsh do not have much to say about integration beyond the fact that it gives rise to a gestaltlike representation. They presumably believe that this representation finds its home primarily in the imagery system, rather than in the linguistic system. But they cannot claim that it lies exclusively there, because they believe that abstract concepts having little or no image-evoking value are primarily handled by the linguistic system. If this is true, then it follows that metaphors involving very abstract ideas will be processed primarily in the linguistic system, such ideas having few if any connections to the imagery system. However, it does not seem likely that the linguistic system, as Paivio and Walsh describe it, is able to achieve the integration of disparate elements into a coherent whole. The kinds of representational systems that seem most suited to this task are the abstract representational systems that have been proposed by various psychologists, often of substantially different persuasions in other respects (e.g., Anderson & Bower, 1973; Bransford & McCarrell, 1974; Kintsch, 1974; Norman & Rumelhart, 1975; Rumelhart & Ortony, 1977; Pylyshyn, 1973). Paivio and Walsh do not appear to be very enthusiastic about such proposals.

The second concept that Paivio and Walsh consider to be important in metaphors is that of relation. Relation, without doubt, plays a role in metaphors, as it does in language in general, but I am not convinced that the distinction between similarity metaphors and proportional metaphors, which Paivio and Walsh raise, is a very fruitful one, in spite of its illustrious origins. When metaphors involve common relations, as they do in proportional metaphors, their essential structure seems to be the same as that of similarity metaphors. Typically, similarity metaphors have two terms – the first term, often called the *topic;* and the second term, often called the *vehicle.* A similarity metaphor such as "The man is a sheep," gains its currency from the fact that there is something in common between the topic (man) and the vehicle (sheep). In a proportional metaphor the only difference is that the topic and the vehicle refer to relations rather than to objects.[1] Thus, relations are no more nor less important to the nature of metaphors than are objects. Both are important in that they constitute the kinds of things that tie language to reality, but neither of them are powerful tools for explaining specific linguistic phenomena. To rely on them as basic explanatory devices would be like relying on grass to explain the operation of a lawn mower. When the lawn mower breaks, one calls in a mechanically minded repairman, not a horticulturalist who specializes in grass.

As Paivio and Walsh observe, the underlying principle of a proportional metaphor is that of analogy. Metaphors express an analogy in an indirect manner by leaving out some of its components (see Miller, this volume). At the same time, as does a simile, a proportional metaphor expresses a similarity between constituents that are not really alike. In the case of proportional metaphors, these constituents are relations (see also Gentner & Jeziorski, this volume). Consider the following example from Billow (1975): "My head is an apple without any core." This asserts that the relationship between my head (or at least, someone's) and something or other, is the same as the relationship between an apple and its (removed) core. Clearly, part of what is involved in understanding this is the solution of an analogy of the form, "X is to $?$ as Y is to Z." What makes it a metaphor is not the fact that common relations are involved, but rather the fact that, literally interpreted, the assertion is false. It is false because the relations that are allegedly similar, are not in fact similar at all. I shall have more to say on this question in due course. Actually, such a proportional metaphor can easily be reduced to a "similarity" metaphor by creating a predicate out of the relation, to give: "My head is (like) a coreless apple." The purpose of this apparently fruitless (sic) manipulation is to suggest that the role played by relations in the comprehension and production of metaphors does not have any special significance. Whatever the processes are that enable people to understand metaphors, these processes result in a coherent interpretation of something that if taken literally is either false, true but uninformative, or meaningless relative to the context in which it occurs. Whether the implicit comparison involves relations or objects seems to be a relatively unimportant question; some analogies are literal analogies and some are not. In either case, they involve alleged similarities – similarities between relations between objects, rather than between objects themselves. So, as Paivio and Walsh imply, the question of relations has to be subsumed partly under that of integration, and partly under that of similarity, which I take to be the guts of the problem, and which I shall now discuss.

It is often claimed that metaphors are merely implicit comparisons to be contrasted with similes, which are explicit ones. I have very little faith in this view: first, because I do not think that it is true of all metaphors; and second, because even if it were, it would be totally unilluminating. The fact that metaphors are frequently used to make comparisons, if it is a fact, does not mean that metaphors *are* comparisons. A metaphor is a kind of *use* of language, whereas a comparison is a kind of psychological process, which although quite possibly an essential component of certain kinds of language use, is not the same thing as such a use.

In any event, it is probably not possible to map all metaphors into similes; and if it is not, then it becomes necessary to explain why some implicit comparisons are incapable of being made explicit. But a more serious problem with the claim is that even if it were true, or even if it is interpreted in a way that makes it plausible, it has no explanatory power unless it is assumed that the comparison, implicit in a metaphor and explicit in its corresponding simile, is a *literal* comparison, that is, a literal use of language. If this assumption were true, then the claim would suggest a reductionist program whereby metaphors could be reduced to literal language. But, if the assumption is false, as I shall argue it is, then the comparisons involved in both metaphors ("John is an ox") and in similes ("John is like an ox") still require explanations, because they cannot be construed as literal uses of language. In other words, the problems posed by the existence of metaphors are also posed by the existence of similes, so that the reduction of metaphors to similes will contribute nothing to their solution.

The fact that metaphors are not to be identified with comparisons, however, does not mean that the process of making comparisons is not of the utmost importance in the comprehension of metaphors (although see Glucksberg & Keysar, this volume, for a different point of view). I shall argue that the process of making comparisons is of fundamental importance in the comprehension of similes, and that the process can be construed in such a way as to make it perfectly appropriate for metaphors, even though, unlike similes, they lack the surface structural linguistic signals (e.g., the presence of the word "like") which invite an attempt to make a comparison. Given my unwillingness to equate metaphors with "literal" similes (which I take to be a contradiction in terms), I feel justified in concentrating my efforts on similes, hoping thereby to distill the more general notion of "nonliteral" as a prelude to understanding what is involved in the comprehension of metaphors. For convenience, I shall sometimes refer to the terms in a simile in the same way as to the terms in a metaphor, using "topic" for the first term and "vehicle" for the second.

Comparisons are more or less successful or appropriate to the degree to which the things being compared are, or can be found to be, similar. So, if understanding similes and metaphors involves making comparisons, and if making comparisons involves making similarity judgments, then we need to focus on the nature of these judgments. That is why I think Paivio and Walsh are right to treat similarity as a central concept. But the current situation in psychology concerning the analysis of similarity, particularly of meaning similarity, is not quite so gloomy as Paivio and Walsh suggest. A seminal paper by Tversky (1977) attests to this fact. Tversky describes how, in most approaches to similarity, the degree of similarity between two terms is represented by an inverse function of the distance between their representations in a multidimensional space (e.g., Carroll & Wish, 1974; Henley, 1969; Rumelhart & Abrahamson, 1973; and Shepard, 1974). As Paivio and Walsh suggest, these approaches have their shortcomings. One is that they are only appropriate for certain kinds of stimuli, namely, those for which a small number of dimensions can be found (e.g., colors and tones). But for our purposes, there is a particularly serious problem. Since the distance between two points (say, A and B) in an n-dimensional Euclidian space is the same whether measured from A to B or from B to A, it follows that such models of similarity entail something that is empirically false; namely, that people's similarity judgments are symmetrical.[2] As Tversky notes in passing, similes and metaphors are very good counterexamples, for if the terms in them are reversed they may become meaningless, or their meaning may change substantially. This tends to be less true for literal comparisons. So, for example, blackberries are probably like raspberries to the same degree that raspberries are like blackberries, and for the same reasons. By contrast, billboards are probably more like warts than warts are like billboards; and even if they are not, asserting that billboards are like warts would mean something quite different from asserting that warts are like billboards. If the similarity relation were independent of the relative position of the terms in it, then those positions should make only a stylistic, not a semantic, difference.

Finding geometric models of similarity unsatisfactory, Tversky offers an alternative account – an account based on feature matching. In this context, a feature is to be thought of as an attribute or predicate in a rather general sense, so that a feature of X is "something that is known about X." The basis of Tversky's model, put in words, is that the degree of similarity between two objects is a weighted function of their intersecting features minus a weighted function of the features distinctive to one and of the features distinctive to the other. Tversky presents a good deal of evidence for the goodness of fit between similarity ratings predicted by his model and those reported by subjects, both for visual and verbal materials. Toward the end of his paper he says:

> It appears that people interpret metaphors by scanning the feature space and selecting the features of the referent [vehicle] that are applicable to the subject [topic] . . . The nature of this process is left to be explained.
>   There is a close tie between the assessment of similarity and the interpretation of metaphors. In judgments of similarity one assumes a particular feature space, or a frame of reference, and assesses the quality of the match between the subject and the referent. In the interpretation of similes, one assumes a resemblance between the subject and the referent, and searches for an interpretation of the space that would maximize the quality of the match. (p. 349)

I think that, for the most part, Tversky is right, and that his account goes a long way toward civilizing what Paivio and Walsh see as an underdeveloped area. However, in my discussion I shall not use the term "feature." I am anxious to avoid giving the impression that I am referring to semantic features in the traditional sense, for I am not. I am really referring to parts of the knowledge representations of the entities being compared. For simplicity of exposition, I shall refer to these as "predicates" because these subcomponents can be attributed to or predicated of something – they can represent knowledge, a belief, or an attitude toward or about something, and that is just what I want.

In returning to the topic of similarity, I shall start by comparing an ordinary statement of comparison with a simile. Certainly, both have the surface structure of explicit comparisons, as can be seen from (1) and (2).

(1) Encyclopedias are like dictionaries.
(2) Encyclopedias are like gold mines.

But I am going to argue that whereas (1) is a literal comparison (encyclopedias really are like dictionaries), (2) is a nonliteral comparison (encyclopedias are not really like gold mines). I have two principal arguments in support of this conclusion, and because I think that it is an important conclusion to establish, and because many people find it counterintuitive and simply assert that it is false, I shall spell out the arguments in detail.

The first argument pertains to the intuitions of ordinary people, as opposed to those of the theoreticians, who are so prone to ignore them. If one asks someone whether encyclopedias are really like gold mines one never gets a straightforward positive answer. Very often one gets a straightforward negative answer, particularly if the question is posed in contrast to the question: "Are encyclopedias really like dictionaries?" This must mean that people do not believe that (2) is true; they are more likely to say that it is false. By contrast, they normally believe that (1) is true. So, there is a prima facie case for saying that (2) is false. Related to this fact is a linguistic fact, namely, that similes such as (2) are much more likely to be found in conjunction with hedges such as "sort of," "kind of," "in a way," and so on. Indeed, when people do not straightforwardly deny the truth of assertions like (2) their acceptance of them is invariably accompanied by some kind of hedge. So, I think that there is evidence that people generally will assent to the truth of an ordinary comparison without hesitation, whereas they are quite willing to deny the truth of a simile if they are encouraged to evaluate its truth in the same literal way they use for ordinary comparisons. Consequently, I am inclined to believe that ordinary comparisons are generally literally true (if they are appropriately intended as such), whereas similes are literally false.

My second argument is a kind of reductio ad absurdum. Suppose one argues the other side of the issue. Suppose, that is, that one vigorously maintains that similes are literally true. On what basis is that argument advanced? The answer is that it is based on the belief that to some degree, and in some respect or respects, everything is like everything else. So, if everything is like everything else, then certainly encyclopedias are like gold mines, and they are also like ice cream, infinity, and anything else you care to think of. But this argument has some curious consequences, the most serious of which seems to be this. If all similarity statements are true by virtue of the fact that everything is like everything else, then there is no possibility of a similarity statement ever being false. This means that similarity statements are necessarily true, which means that they are tautologies. Since tautologies convey no new information, similarity statements can convey no new information. Apart from this conclusion being absurd, it is plainly false, for to say that the structure of an atom is similar to the structure of the solar system, can indeed be to say something that conveys new information. In fact, it is a fairly standard way of teaching the rudiments of atomic physics. Furthermore, if similarity statements have the characteristic (one that is not shared by any other class of widely used statements) of being always true, another problem arises. One of the reasons that assertions are meaningful is that there always exists the possibility that they are false, just as with orders there exists the possibility that they will not be obeyed, and with promises, that they will not be kept. There is nothing contradictory about asserting that encyclopedias are not like gold mines, yet there would have to be if one were to accept the position described above. Thus, again, one has to conclude that to deny that some similarity statements can be false is an untenable position, and if they can be false, there seems to be no objection to saying that similes, if interpreted like ordinary comparisons, constitute good examples of false similarity statements.

I have several times used the phrase "similes, interpreted like ordinary comparisons," or phrases like it. The time has now come to explain what that is supposed to mean. When we are faced with a similarity statement that is literally true, it is always the case that some of the predicates that are important to one of the terms are also important to the other term. The interpretation of ordinary similarity statements can therefore be regarded as involving the determination of shared high-salient predicates in much the way that Tversky envisions it. The point about similes is that this procedure will produce *no* such shared predicates at all, unless those predicates are themselves interpreted metaphorically.[3] In his chapter in this volume, Searle makes much the same point. Now, if the ordinary procedure for interpreting similarity statements involves finding shared high-salient predicates, and if, as both Tversky's theory and my intuitions tell me, one of the features determining the degree of similarity is the quality of the match, or the number of shared high-salient predicates, then, since the terms in a simile have no such shared predicates, the procedure will fail to find anything important in common between the two terms. Thus, to say that they are alike, is either false, or metaphorical. So, from now on I am going to refer to ordinary similarity statements as being "literal comparisons" and I am going to refer to similes as being "nonliteral" comparisons. The question that now has to be answered is: "What are the processes involved in arriving at a coherent interpretation of a nonliteral comparison?"

According to Tversky, one "assumes a resemblance . . . and searches for an interpretation of the space that would maximize the quality of the match." But how does one know to do that, rather than to do what he says has to be done for literal comparisons, namely to assume the feature space and find the match? Tversky seems to be proposing two related but different operations, but the surface structures of the comparisons provide no clues as to which one is applicable. Perhaps the default process is the one that applies to literal comparisons; then, if no match is found, the space is reinterpreted to produce one. But suppose the process for interpreting literal comparisons were just the one that Tversky says applies in the case of metaphors, namely, finding predicates of the second term that are applicable to the first. Then, the same process might work for both literal comparisons and for nonliteral comparisons (similes). Of course, this process ought not to succeed if just any old predicates can be applied, since the predicate "is a thing" can be trivially applied to both a gold mine and an encyclopedia. We will have to restrict the predicates to be applied, at least initially, to salient ones. Paivio and Walsh's interesting suggestion that concrete vehicles are better than abstract ones, may thus relate to the fact – if it is a fact – that concrete terms have more salient predicates associated with them than do abstract terms, as well as to the fact that they are more accessible. Before proceeding, it is important to point out that the distinction between salient and nonsalient predicates is not a sharp one. In extreme cases, however, it is obvious. There are doubtless large individual differences resulting from the different conceptions and experiences that different people have of things. My use of the notion of salience here is based on an operational definition, a solution that may satisfy psychologists, but that probably leaves philosophers cold.

The concepts of gold mines and encyclopedias, like all concepts, have predicates associated with them which vary in their salience according to the context in which they are used (see Anderson & Ortony, 1975). Suppose that the comparison process takes the predicates of "gold mines" and tries to apply them to "encyclopedias," starting with the most salient. We get back to Tversky's notion of matching by having the criterion for a predicate applying to a concept as being the appearance of that predicate somewhere in the topic concept's internal structure. Now, there are either very few – or more likely, no – high-salient predicates of "gold mines" that are also high-salient predicates of "encyclopedias"; and for that reason I have suggested that (2) is not a literal comparison; but there are high-salient predicates of "gold mines" that are lower-salient predicates of "encyclopedias," and for that reason (2) is an interpretable comparison. This leads to the following account: in a comparison, "*A* is like *B*," if high-salient predicates of *B* are also high-salient predicates of *A*, then the comparison is a literal one and the two referents will be judged as being "really" similar. If a high-salient predicate of *B* is a less-salient predicate of *A* whereas there are high-salient predicates of *B* that cannot be applied to *A* at all, then we have a simile. If no high-salient predicate of *B* can be applied to *A* then the comparison is either uninterpretable, or nonsense (if there is a difference).

It should be noted that similes can easily be modified so as to come very close to being literal comparisons. If a modifier is introduced that is in fact an attribute with respect to which both terms are comparable, then by temporarily increasing the salience of that attribute for the *A* term, the comparison may result in a match of high-salient predicates. So we can think of modifiers as emphasizing (that is, increasing the salience of) predicates that correspond to them, and consequently they serve to identify the matching salient predicates, by specifying them and accentuating them. Thus, while (3) is a simile, (4) is much more like a literal comparison:

(3) His face was like a beet.

(4) His face was red like a beet.

The difference between the two is that in (4) the salience of a predicate (redness) of the referent's face has been increased, thus rendering a match of high-salient predicates, whereas in (3) the match is of high- to low-salient predicates. It seems, therefore, that whether a particular use of language on a particular occasion is literal or nonliteral, is a question of degree rather than a question of kind.

I shall now review some preliminary data that I have collected which relate to the role of shared salient predicates in literal and nonliteral comparisons. In a predicate elicitation task, subjects were asked to list the predicates of 40 terms; 10 terms were given to each of four groups of subjects. The 40 items were derived from 10 triplets of comparisons. Each triplet contained a simile such as (2) and two literal comparisons, one for each of the terms in the simile. Thus, if (2) were the simile, (1) would be one of the literal comparisons (for encyclopedias), and (5) would be the other (for gold mines).

(1) Encyclopedias are like dictionaries.

(2) Encyclopedias are like gold mines.

(5) Gold mines are like oil wells.

Subjects listed an average of just over six predicates for each of their 10 items. Having listed the predicates for a particular item, each subject ranked the predicates for importance and then indicated how many of them, in order of importance, were felt to be necessary to identify the item to someone who did not know what it was. This was taken as the operational definition of salience. Subjects rated an average of about three predicates per term as being salient. The predicated similarities were computed in accordance with Tversky's formula; the resulting values were always much lower for the similes than for the literal controls.

The point of interest for the moment, however, is the relative likelihood of shared predicates appearing for the literal and nonliteral comparisons. Referring now only to salient predicates, about 25 percent of those listed for terms in literal comparisons were listed for both the terms, compared with only about one percent for similes. If these values are weighted according to the frequency of mention, the difference becomes even more dramatic. These data show that the terms from the similes had virtually no common salient predicates, whereas those in the literal comparisons had many. The conclusion to be drawn is that if, in saying that two things are similar, one means that they have important things in common, then the data strongly suggest that similes, or at least the terms in them, are not in fact similar, whereas the terms in literal comparisons are. This, of course, is

Table 16.1

Billboards	Warts
are used for advertising	are found on the skin
are found by the roadside	are usually removed
are large	are ugly
etc.	are growths
	etc.

not to say that a similarity between the terms in a simile cannot be found, but in finding such resemblances, the interpretation of the simile would cease to be a literal interpretation.

It is instructive to look at a particular example to see the relationships between high- and low-salient predicates. Consider the simile expressed in (6), which was alluded to earlier:

(6) Billboards are like warts.

Table 16.1 lists the predicates that were most frequently mentioned as being salient for each term. These predicates are listed in order of likelihood of mention. The most frequent one was listed by over 90 percent of the subjects, and the less frequent ones, by about 40 percent. It would not be unreasonable to use the probability of inclusion as a salient predicate as a first-order approximation to the degree of salience. On this basis, one would have to say that 0.40 was a high value. That happens to be the value for "ugly" with respect to warts. Now "ugly" did not occur at all as a high-salient predicate of "billboards," but it was listed as a predicate with a probability of about 0.07. Thus it seems justifiable to say that being ugly is a high-salient predicate of warts, though a low-salient predicate of "billboards." Notice that there is no high-salient predicate shared by each of the terms, so that the comparison expressed by (6) is a nonliteral comparison, or simile, rather than a literal comparison. Billboards are not really like warts, they are only like warts metaphorically speaking.

I argued earlier that there was a big difference between asserting (6) and asserting (7):

(7) Warts are like billboards.

An interpretation of (7) would involve finding high-salient predicates of "billboards" that are low-salient predicates of warts. So, one might suppose that the point of uttering (7) would be to emphasize the fact that warts can be large and conspicuous, and so on, rather than that they are ugly, for these are high-salient predicates of billboards that might be applicable to warts. The lack of symmetry in nonliteral comparisons is thus due to the fact that the terms have nonoverlapping sets of salient predicates. Literal comparisons may also be asymmetrical due to the fact that some applicable predicates of one of the terms are not high-salient predicates of the other.

But, since there are always shared salient predicates of both, the lack of symmetry is less obvious and less radical (Ortony, Vondruska, Foss, & Jones, 1985). The difference between the meanings of (6) and (7) seems to me to be far greater than that between (8) and (9):

(8) Warts are like sores.
(9) Sores are like warts.

In this pair, the primary difference is due to the change in what is being talked about; the basis of the comparison is substantially the same in each case, even though it might not be identical. The same is true for the raspberries and blackberries case discussed earlier. In any event, one thing is certain; any treatment of similes and metaphors must account for the fact that they are radically asymmetrical. The account I have offered seems capable of doing that if nothing else.

My discussion of the role of similarity has so far been primarily concerned with establishing an empirical criterion to distinguish literal from nonliteral comparisons. This criterion has been cast in terms of the degree to which high-salient predicates of the second term are high- or low-salient predicates of the first. I have suggested a way in which the same process could underlie the comprehension of both literal and nonliteral comparisons. The process would be a "predicate application" process whereby known salient predicates of the vehicle would be applied – as it were, experimentally – to the topic. But if we unpack the notion of "application," what do we get? If the process involves trying to apply a predicate to the topic, what criteria are there for determining whether the application was successful or possible? As we saw earlier, one way is to see if the predicate being applied is already known to be a predicate of the topic. So, it may be that predicate matching has to be construed as an integral part of the predicate application process, a part that is sometimes successful and sometimes not. This then raises the question of what happens if the to-be-applied predicate is not already a predicate of the topic (for the reader or hearer). If a great deal is known about the topic, matching could play a major role, but if little is known, insufficient to give a coherent match, it will be to no avail. Furthermore, in such cases, the process of predicate *selection,* in which predicates that *can* be applied *are* applied, may be much less efficient than a process of predicate *rejection* in which all predicates of the vehicle are assumed to apply unless there is some fundamental incompatibility. What is here being suggested is this: when very little is known about the topic, predicates from the vehicle which are clearly incompatible with it are rejected; the manner in which, and extent to which, the other predicates do apply is hardly determined at all. This sometimes results in the metaphor being misunderstood and misleading (Spiro, Feltovich, Coulson, & Anderson, 1989). On the other hand, if a great deal is known about the topic, the predicates that apply are selected and the resulting interpretation is more specific and more restricted. This distinction has, I think, some important consequences with respect to the creation of the "novel conceptual entity" that Paivio and Walsh talk about, and I shall return to it shortly.

The position that I have adopted is still basically one that denies any fundamentally important difference in the processing of literal and non-literal comparisons. I am inclined to believe that this is true for literal and metaphorical uses of language in general. Of course, there are cases in which a hearer or reader may fail to come up with a coherent interpretation using the processes we have described. There are often occasions upon which one says to oneself: "I wonder what on earth that was supposed to mean." In such cases, I think that some relatively more deliberate problem-solving strategies are brought to bear, initiated by a kind of Gricean pragmatic analysis (see Grice, 1975), as described in the chapter by Searle. Such an analysis would require a person to relate the utterance meaning to the speaker meaning by resolving apparent violations of the implicit conventions governing linguistic interactions. Specifically, I assume that when the reader or hearer fails to (sensibly) interpret something which he or she has reason to believe was intended to be meaningful, there follows an attempt to render the violation of the conventions (probably those of being relevant and of being sincere) only apparent. The hearer would then assume that there is a detectable basis for comparison and would engage in processes that might help find it. But, of course this general account applies equally well to obscure literal uses of language. There may be a difference in the particular linguistic conventions that are violated, but a deliberate "figuring out of the intended meaning" is certainly not something that is necessarily restricted to nonliteral uses of language (Ortony, Schallert, Reynolds, & Antos, 1978).

A reasonable complaint that could be made at this juncture is that my discussion has centered around similes and has left their relevance for the topic of metaphor unspecified. So I shall now devote a few moments to talking about that relationship. Insofar as the comprehension of metaphor involves making comparisons, one might suppose that the processes required to comprehend metaphors would overlap with those required to comprehend similes. It has been argued, for example by Kintsch (1974), that the comprehension of metaphor in fact proceeds by the conversion of the metaphor into a simile. But even if one were to accept this suggestion (assuming that the conversion is always possible, which I doubt), the manner in which, and the reason for which, the conversion takes place still has to be explained. Consider (10), which is a metaphorical statement of the simile (2):

(10) Encyclopedias are gold mines.

When a hearer (or reader) encounters (10) in a particular context, there might come a point at which he realizes that if it is interpreted literally it is either false or nonsensical. And, unlike a simile, it does not have the surface characteristics of a comparison; so even though the processes for interpreting similes may be the same as those for interpreting literal comparisons, there is initially no reason to suppose that those processes are engaged. It first has to be thought of as though it were a comparison, a comparison which cannot be literally true since (10) is not. It may be that the comprehension processes for comparisons then come into play. One possibility is that in such "attributive" metaphors predicates are attributed to the topic in just the same way as in similes, inapplicable predicates of the vehicle getting left behind. In some cases this may well happen, but I doubt that it does in all. In other cases an additional mechanism is required, namely a mechanism that relates sentence meanings to speaker meanings, as described above. This is the approach taken by Searle in his chapter.

Finally, I want to introduce a distinction between "predicate promotion" metaphors and "predicate introduction" metaphors – a distinction that relates to the one between predicate selection and predicate rejection that I mentioned a little while ago. In a predicate promotion metaphor it is assumed that the hearer (and presumably the speaker) knows enough about the topic to recognize that what is implicitly being said of it is true. Such metaphors often involve generic terms. Consider (10) again: Most people know that encyclopedias are a source of knowledge, and that sources of knowledge are useful and desirable, and so forth. Predicates such as these are also applicable to "gold mines." When somebody understands the metaphor in this way, I want to argue that he already knows that the predicates in question are true of the A term, so that the information extractable from the metaphor is old information and it is recognized as such by the speaker and hearer. Consequently, all that the hearer does in comprehension is to promote the salience of the relevant predicates for the A term. But there is another possibility, namely, cases where the hearer knows very little about the topic, and in comprehending the metaphor, discovers something new about it; or at least makes inferences about something previously unknown. In these cases I want to say that from the hearer's point of view, the metaphor is a predicate introduction metaphor, namely, one in which the salience of an existing predicate (or set of predicates) cannot be increased, because they are not yet predicates of the A term at all; they are introduced as new predicates as a result of the comprehension process.

I have been arguing that in similes, high-salient predicates of the vehicle are low-salient predicates of the topic, and this distinguishes similes from literal comparisons, where the match is of high to high-salient predicates. But now we can see that something more is happening. Consider (11), for example:

(11) Attila the Hun had manners like a cesspool.

Suppose someone utters (11) and the hearer knows nothing more specific about Attila the Hun than that he was a renowned barbarian. Then, although no high-salient predicates of cesspools are low-salient predicates of Attila, or of his manners, (11) is interpretable, and most people will interpret it correctly. Less salient predicates that the speaker has for Attila may include things like "being extremely unpleasant," "having repulsive manners," and so on. These are not attributes of Attila the Hun at all from the hearer's point of view. Indeed, the purpose of the simile may be to introduce these ideas. So, perhaps we should say the following: A simile, by using high-salient predicates of the vehicle that are lower-salient predicates of the topic, if they are predicates at all, has the effect of emphasizing or promoting the salience of those predicates if they were low-salient, and of introducing them if they were not there at all. In predicate promotion metaphors, the predicates are already there, and they get promoted or emphasized. In predicate introduction metaphors, they are not already there and they get introduced. I think that it might be the case that predicate introduction metaphors are one of the cornerstones of insight. Their comprehension results in richer representations – representations that may be to some extent inappropriate because they exclude only what is flagrantly incompatible. Their richness is partially a consequence of this. The predicates that are transferred from the vehicle to the topic are more holistic, less discrete, and can include perceptual and emotive aspects. As I have argued elsewhere (see Ortony, 1975, 1976), this may bring them closer to perceptual representations than most language-initiated representations. I think that this may be why imagery is so important in metaphors, as Paivio and Walsh believe. This more coherent, holistic representation helps us to see things in different ways. And, as has often been argued, seeing things in different ways is a necessary prerequisite for scientific discovery. As Whitehead put it: "Fundamental progress has to do with the reinterpretation of basic ideas."

Although I have argued that similes and metaphors are usually processed in much the same way as is literal language, there remain important differences between the two, differences which concern their uses and functions in communication. And there is another difference too. All uses of language tend to stretch it; but in literal uses, language bounces back. Metaphors stretch language beyond its elastic limit.

NOTES

This chapter is a slightly revised version of the one that appeared in the first edition under the same title.

I am particularly indebted to David Rumelhart. Some of the ideas in this chapter are at least partially a result of hours of discussion with him. I also wish to acknowledge the help afforded me by a Spencer Fellowship awarded by the National Academy of Education. The work described herein was supported by a contract from the National Institute of Education.

1 By "objects" I do not wish to imply "physical objects," but rather those entities, real or imaginary, which can enter into relations. For the dangers of treating "objects" as "physical objects," see the chapter by Searle.

2 It should be noted, however, that there have been proposals to modify geometric models so as to avoid this difficulty (see, for example, Krumhansl, 1978).

3 This is a complicated question that is beyond the scope of this paper. It is important to realize, however, that it need not lead to infinite regress. One can argue for a recursive comprehension process. The stop rule would either be a detection of a match prior to reaching some processing threshold, or the failure to do so. In this case, the result might be an awareness of failure to comprehend.

17

Images and models, similes and metaphors

GEORGE A. MILLER

I shall try to defend a version of the traditional view that a metaphor is an abbreviated simile, and that the thought provoked is the kind required to appreciate similarities and analogies. In the nineteenth century that kind of thought was called "apperception."

"Apperception" is one mentalistic term that has not been rehabilitated by cognitive psychologists in recent years; perhaps it is time we got around to it. For Herbart (1898) "apperception" was a general term for those mental processes whereby an attended experience is brought into relation with an already acquired and familiar conceptual system. Today our psychological journals are full of terms like "encoding," "mapping," "categorizing," "inference," "assimilation and accommodation," "attribution," and so on; perhaps "apperception" would be a useful superordinate for all of them.

If I understand Herbart correctly, his general claim was that new things are learned by being related to things already known; he built his educational psychology on the belief that if teachers know what their pupils know, they can relate ideas they want to teach to ideas the pupil has already mastered. Although Herbart's term has passed from fashion, the educational philosophy of maximizing transfer of training seems as sensible now as it did a century ago. In my view, much of the scientific interest of an analysis of metaphor derives from what it might contribute to a theory of apperception appropriate to the psychological and educational concepts of the twentieth century.

In order to stay within manageable limits, I shall ignore the sort of root metaphors whose detailed development can motivate elaborate literary or scientific constructions; I shall concentrate on what might be called local metaphors, which can enrich a single phrase or sentence. And, since any metaphor can be written, I shall refer to the recipient of the metaphor as "the reader."[1]

Textual concepts

The need to understand how people relate new ideas to old is particularly acute in the psychology of reading. As a person reads and understands a passage, the new information he encounters has to be related – both to his store of general knowledge – to his "apperceptive mass," as it used to be called – and to his internal representation of the passage itself. As new information is added, of course, it becomes part of the old information to which further new information can be added, and so a "textual concept" grows as reading proceeds. Reading with comprehension is a test-tube example of apperception in action. I shall first sketch my view of the apperceptive processes involved in reading comprehension, then discuss the comprehension of expressions of similitude, and finally consider metaphor as posing a particular kind of apperceptive difficulty.

Remembering

What happens as we read a descriptive prose passage? If we attend closely and try to understand, we do more than move our eyes along the lines and mumble words to our inner ear. It changes us. When we finish reading, we have something that we did not have before we began. The psychological problem is how to characterize the change that occurs in a reader when he has carefully read a passage of straight, expository, descriptive prose.

Images. One approach is introspective. Indulge me, therefore, by participating in an experiment in self-observation. Below is a descriptive passage taken from Henry Thoreau's (1937) *Walden.* Read it attentively, but at the same time try to keep track of what is going on as you read:

Near the end of March, 1845, I borrowed an axe and went down to the woods by Walden Pond, nearest to where I intended to build my house, and began to cut down some tall, arrowy white pines, still in their youth, for timber . . . It was a pleasant hillside where I worked, covered with pine woods, through which I looked out on the pond, and a small open field in the woods where pines and hickories were springing up. The ice in the pond was not yet dissolved, though there were some open spaces, and it was all dark-colored and saturated with water.

My introspections on reading this passage persuade me that I built something in my imagination – a sort of mental picture to which I added details as I encountered successive phrases and sentences. Let me call what I was building an "image." Since I am well aware that what took shape in my mind was different from a photographic image, or a perceptual image, of the episode and landscape that Thoreau was describing, I need to qualify this label in order to mark the difference: I shall call it a "memory image" whenever I feel there is danger of confusing it with something more substantial or detailed.

My memory image grew piecemeal in roughly the following way. First I read that the time was late March; I formed no image at this point, but filed it away for possible use later. (This is not a satisfactory account: I shall return to "March, 1845" below.) Next, I saw an indistinct Thoreau borrow an axe from an even less distinct somebody and walk, axe in hand, to some woods near a pond. The following phrase turned the trees into white pines, and I saw Thoreau, his back toward me, swinging his axe on them. The next sentence introduced a hillside; suddenly the ground in my image tilted and the scene became firm. Then it was a simple matter to add the pond, the open field, the melting ice.

I make no substantive claims about my personal imagery, which I know to be predominantly visual; you may have smelled the piney woods or heard the axe biting into the trees. My point is that I felt I was doing something constructive as I read the passage; the result of this constructive mental activity was a memory image that summarized the information I had extracted from the passage. Although the memory image remained vague in many respects, it was nonetheless a particular image, just as the prose passage by Thoreau is a particular passage. Indeed, part of my memory image was an image of the passage itself, as well as the scene it described.

One way to characterize the change that occurs in reading, therefore, is to say that you construct an image as part of the process of understanding the passage, and that the image helps you to remember what you have read. It helps you to remember in the following sense. If, after putting down the book, you were asked to repeat what you have read, you would probably not be able to repeat it verbatim. Nevertheless, you could reactivate your memory image and describe it, thus generating a different prose passage, but one that (if your memory is good) would be roughly equivalent to the original passage that inspired the memory image. Many psychological experiments have shown that people forget some details and embellish others, so the process is not perfect. But the memory image provides some record of the passage and of information extracted from it – a record that is constructed as the passage is read, phrase by phrase.

The iconic character of memory image should not be exaggerated. The passage from Thoreau was deliberately selected; many others would have been far more difficult to visualize. Moreover, some people claim not to have such imagery; they search their mental furniture in vain for anything resembling a picture of the description they are reading. If we are to believe these people (and I do), there must be other ways to remember

what is read. Let me generalize what I mean by "memory image," therefore, to include all mental processes that can construct a particular record
of a particular passage and of the information extracted from it. For some
people, it is convenient to exploit the apparently enormous storage capacity of the perceptual system in order to construct this record, but that is not
the only way, and, for some passages, it is not even an easy way to construct
and preserve that record in all its individual particularity. For highly abstract passages, the memory image may be predominantly an image, visual
or auditory, of the text itself.

All of this is surely familiar to anyone who has thought about it, but I
have gone over it in order to make clear what I mean by a memory image,
and what the intuitive basis is for claims that understanding a passage like
this one is a constructive mental process.

I shall add only one point that is sometimes overlooked when memory
images are discussed: the vagueness of the image is critical to its utility. If
memory images had to be completely detailed, like photographs, they
could not preserve the incomplete information given by written descriptions. Thoreau did not describe every detail of the hillside above Walden
Pond; a reader who wants to remember accurately what Thoreau *did* describe had better not clutter the memory image with details that were not
provided. It may be impossible to construct an image that does not contain
some extraneous information that is merely suggested, not entailed, by the
text (Anderson & Ortony, 1975); a reader lacking any knowledge of the
New England countryside, for example, would not construct the same
image as a reader who knew it well. My point is simply that such additions
from general knowledge are potential sources of error, even when they
appear highly probable in the given context.

Models. This account of imagery formation will be persuasive to many
people, but let me now describe another way to characterize what went on
as I read the sample passage.

First, I cleared my mind of other matters. This initial attitude was one in
which, potentially, any state of affairs at all could be represented. When I
read the first sentence and encountered Thoreau borrowing an axe, I used
that information to narrow down the variety of possible states of affairs to
just those that included Thoreau borrowing an axe. When I read next that
he went down to the woods by Walden Pond, I narrowed the potential set
even further, now to those that included Thoreau with his axe walking to
the woods by Walden Pond. As I continued to pick up information from the
passage, I used it phrase by phrase to restrict the set of possible states of
affairs that I was considering. By the time I finished, I had narrowed down
this set considerably, but there were still indefinitely many alternatives
left – alternatives I had not gathered sufficient information to distinguish
among.

When I described my imagery, I described the process as *constructive*. The second account I have given is not constructive, but *selective*. As each item of information is understood and added to the image, it is used to select a smaller subset of possible states of affairs compatible with the image. Constructing something is not the same as selecting it. Moreover, the end product is different. The constructive process results in a memory image, a single representation of a scene whose particularities correspond closely to the particularities of the passage. The selective process, on the other hand, results in a collection of possible states of affairs that correspond to the written passage only with respect to their shared features, but which differ from one another in all other respects.

On first hearing the selective account, many people feel it violates common experience. It is hard enough to hold one memory image before the mind's eye. How could anyone deal with an indefinitely large collection of images simultaneously? I agree completely with this complaint. Indeed, I would insist on it because it shows so clearly that whatever the mental representations are that the reader is selecting among, they cannot be images. If we are to take the selective hypothesis seriously, we must be clear that the sets of possible states of affairs among which the reader is choosing are not images. The simplest way to remember that is to give these sets a different name. I shall call them "models" of the passage. Since there are many different kinds of models (Black, 1962a), however, I shall call them *semantic models* when there is any possibility of confusion.

A semantic model for a given text, then, is the set of all possible states of affairs in which all of the information in the memory image for that text is true. In order to be a member of this set, any particular state of affairs must be consistent with all of the information the reader has been given. All of the facts stated in the description are necessarily true in the model – they are true of every element in the set. Any facts that would contradict the facts stated in the description are necessarily false. And any facts that have neither been given nor contradicted are possibly true – they are true of some state of affairs contained in the model, but need not be true of all.

Semantic models are more abstract than memory images. A model is a set of things, but I have not yet characterized those things – all I have said is that they are not images. We could, without violating the spirit of the selective hypothesis, think of them as potential, but as yet unimagined, images. Or, in keeping with a more linguistic interpretation, we could think of the model as the passage plus the set of all possible continuations of the passage. As we read the passage, we construct a memory image that enables us to narrow the set of possible continuations.

Consider models from the author's point of view. Thoreau had something in mind when he wrote the passage we read. If he wrote it as a description of an actual scene – if his model contained just one representation of a unique state of affairs – it is not difficult to understand how he could have used the model to determine that every sentence he wrote was true of that scene. On the other hand, if he was writing from memory, he had probably forgotten many specific details, in which case the model selected by his image contained more than one representation compatible with what he remembered, but he could still use his model to insure that every sentence he wrote was true in the model.

That is how semantic models are usually thought of. It is assumed that the model is given in advance, and sentences expressing various facts can then be judged as necessarily or possibly true or false in that model. In short, *an author uses a semantic model to select true descriptive sentences.*

Now consider models from the reader's point of view. Initially, the reader has a very general model if he has any at all. The reader is given, not a model, but a text, a string of descriptive sentences. He must discover a model that is compatible with those sentences – a model that includes the author's model as a subset. The reader's basic assumption must be that the sentences he is given are true. Then his task becomes just the reverse of the author's: *a reader uses the true descriptive sentence to select a model* (Cushing, 1977).

Textual concepts. I have now presented two ways to characterize what goes on when a person reads a passage of descriptive prose. Since they seem different, you might be tempted to ask which is correct. I claim that both are correct.

A reader has both a memory image and a model. They serve related but different purposes. The memory image serves as a mental surrogate for the descriptive passage itself. It is a historical record, accurate just to the extent that it contains all, and only, the information in the passage. The model, on the other hand, keeps the mind open to future possibilities. Its importance might be illustrated as follows:[2] reinstate your image of Thoreau's scene and use it to decide whether there was any snow. The passage did not mention snow; if your memory image is accurate, it will not have any snow either. If all that you had were this image, you would have to answer no, because there is no snow in your memory image. Yet you know that the fact that Thoreau did not mention snow in what you read does not mean that there was none. If you answer yes, however, you may be going too far beyond the information given. For all you know, the next sentence may say, "There was no snow that winter." All you can say is, "It is possible that there was snow, but I don't know yet."

What does your ignorance imply? If you were looking at a real scene and someone asked whether there was any snow, you would have little difficulty answering. In order to know that you do not know, there must be some mental machinery that supplements your memory image. That additional machinery is the semantic model, which differs from a real scene in being a whole set of representations of alternative states of affairs, some with snow and some without. Bishop Berkeley once argued that there can be no abstract ideas, because ideas are images and images are particular; you cannot have an image that simultaneously contains snow and does not contain snow. In order to answer Berkeley's objection, we must supplement images with models. Models, by definition, contain alternative representations that are incompatible with one another.

Images, insofar as they preserve information provided by the preceding discourse, are creatures of the pragmatic theory of language. That is to say, different sentences can lead to the construction of the same image, and the same sentence in different contexts can lead to the construction of different images. How a person constructs an image that a given passage is intended to describe on some particular occasion of its use is a central problem for any pragmatic theory of language. Models, on the other hand, provide a mechanism for assigning truth-values, and to that extent they are creatures of the semantic theory of language. There is no conflict here. The image, like the text it enables us to remember, is a particular image, corresponding to a particular list of criteria for selecting an abstract model compatible with that list.[3]

In short, remembering a descriptive prose passage depends on two complementary and mutually supporting processes, one constructive and particular, the other selective and abstract. The constructive process preserves the particular criteria given by the passage for the selection of an abstract model consisting of all the potential states of affairs that could satisfy those criteria.

I shall call the combined image/model that emerges during the process of reading the reader's "concept" of the passage; and I shall call the constructive/selective processes that are involved his "synthesis" of that concept. If the extension of a concept is understood to be the set of things that are instances of that concept, then the reader's model corresponds to the extension of his concept of the passage; if the intension of a concept is what a person must know in order to determine its extension, then the reader's image corresponds to the intension of his concept of the passage. In this respect, a reader's concept of a particular text is similar to the sentential and lexical concepts that are used to synthesize it. Since not all concepts are equivalent, however, I shall refer to the reader's concept of a text he is reading as a "textual concept" whenever there may be danger of misunderstanding.

At this point, I could begin to talk about metaphor. I could claim that a metaphor poses an apperceptive problem. I shall get around to such a claim eventually, but my account is still deficient in a very important respect.

Understanding

The study of reading comprehension is more than a study of how a reader extracts information by decoding, parsing, and interpreting a text, or how he uses that information to construct an image of the passage that will enable him to select a model of its possible continuations. It must also be a study of problem solving (Thorndike, 1924), in which anything the reader knows about the world, or about the uses to which texts are put, can be exploited to help him solve the problem: What concept did the author have in mind when he selected these particular sentences? In order to understand a passage, readers must relate the textual concept they are synthesizing to their general store of knowledge and belief.

Grounds. A notion that has received much attention is that one understands a sentence if one knows the conditions under which it could be true. There are good reasons to think this notion is too narrow, but let us take it seriously for a moment. It presumes that you already know a great deal about whatever it is that the sentence is about; you are expected to search what you know for the truth conditions of the sentence. Psychologically, this means that in order to understand a sentence you must establish a particular kind of relation (a verifiability relation) between the concept that the sentence expresses and your general knowledge of the world. If you cannot establish that relation, you do not understand the sentence; if nobody can establish the relation, the sentence is (presumably) meaningless.

A broader relation than verifiability must be established between the text and general knowledge. What that relation is and how it is established are central problems for the psychology of apperception. I have no solution to offer, but, in order to hold a place for whatever solution the future may bring, let us say that you understand a sentence if you know the conditions under which a person would use it. Use conditions are sufficiently broader than truth conditions to cover most apperceptive relations. I shall speak of use conditions as the author's "grounds" for what he says, and shall assume that the appreciation of the grounds for a sentence is drawn largely from general knowledge and belief about situations or events similar to those described or imagined in the textual concept.

Under this formulation, you can understand sentences that defy verification if you can appreciate the author's grounds for using them. We cannot completely abandon the notion of truth, however, because readers cannot begin to search for the author's grounds unless they are willing to accept what is said as true of the concept the author has in mind. In passages intended to convey literal truth, of course, use conditions are not very different from truth conditions, but not all writing is intended to convey literal truth. We must, therefore, reconsider the reader's truth assumption.

The truth assumption. I have said that the semantic model selected for a text contains all possible developments of the text that do not contradict anything in the memory image. The apperceptive problem concealed in this formulation is "contradict." I can illustrate it by supposing that the first sentence of Thoreau's passage had read as follows:

Near the end of March, 1845, I borrowed an axe and drove my automobile to the woods by Walden Pond, nearest to where I intended to build my house. . . .

You would immediately see a contradiction, since there were no automobiles in 1845.

Where does the knowledge required to recognize this contradiction come from? Not from the memory image. I, at least, have no more trouble imagining automobiles in 1845 than I had revising Thoreau's passage. And not from the model selected for the passage, since (as described so far) the model is constrained only by the image. The source of the contradiction is elsewhere. Somewhere in my store of general knowledge, I have the information required to infer that automobiles did not exist in 1845. General knowledge must play a role in the process of understanding. It must provide some grounds for what the author has written.

What happens when we encounter a contradiction? Obviously, the comprehension system does not blow a fuse and quit. In this example, we recognize that Thoreau could not have written the passage. Someone who lived since the invention of the automobile must have written it. Either the genre is not what it seemed to be – it is parody, perhaps, or science fiction – or perhaps there has been a misprint – "1945" being accidentally printed as "1845." That is to say, we revise our concept of the passage in such a way as to preserve our assumption that our textual concept is true.

It is banal to insist that reading comprehension depends in some way on general knowledge not given in the text. But how general knowledge makes its contribution is often misunderstood. We might, for example, think of the model for a passage as being selected, not solely on the basis of information extracted from the text, but from all the information the individual has gained from his experience throughout life, up to and including however much of the text he has just read. In a sense, this view is correct, as is indicated in recall by the intrusion of other knowledge that was not explicitly stated or entailed in the original text. On the other hand, it cannot be completely true, since if the textual concept of the present passage is not kept distinct from other knowledge in some degree, the memory image cannot serve its purpose – when asked to recall a text, any fragment of previous experience might be described. We must assume, therefore, that the memory image for a text is isolated from general knowledge as a record of the current episode. A reader will normally assume that what he knows about the real world can apply to the world he is reading about (unless the text says otherwise), but if he confuses those two worlds, he will not be able to recall the text accurately.

Another reason the memory image cannot be assimilated directly into general knowledge is that truth in the model must be kept distinct from truth in the so-called real world, or in our general knowledge of that world. Literary critics have long argued about the sense in which fiction in general, and poetry in particular, can be said to be true or false. Some claim that truth and falsity are irrelevant to the acceptance of such works, but I believe that Empson (1967) is on the right track when he says, "The point is not that their truth or falsity is irrelevant, but that you are asked to imagine a state of mind in which they would appear true" (p. 12). In my terms, by accepting them as true, a reader can hope to converge on the model that the author had in mind, which may or may not coincide with what the reader knows or believes about the real world. If, as in the example just given, we find an assertion that contradicts what we know or believe about the world, we cannot abandon our working assumption that what we have read is true in the model we are selecting. We must hold on to the truth assumption at all costs. If we are not to abandon our effort to understand, we must select a model that makes the passage true – even though that selection may tax our ingenuity.

Fortunately, people can be enormously ingenious in such matters. The extreme test of a reader's truth assumption is provided by the form of humor that deliberately compounds absurdities. An example (source unknown) that amuses children:

> One bright day in the middle of the night
> Two dead boys got up to fight.
> Back to back they faced each other,
> Drew their swords and shot each other.
> A deaf policeman heard the noise
> And came and killed those two dead boys.

Accepting such nonsense goes beyond the willing suspension of disbelief – belief is not even involved. Yet it is possible to construct an image for this jingle (spectral boys, swords that shoot bullets), and the general scenario (trouble between boys attracts police) is sufficiently familiar to hold it together in spite of the flat contradictions in every line. The lengths to which a reader will go in order to maintain the assumption that what he reads is true – true in his model of the text, at least – should not be underestimated. So strongly does this assumption constrain the reader that an author can exploit it to create a wide variety of special effects, of which humor is but one.

The reader's assumption of truth is not limited to the special case of texts that are intended to communicate objective truth. Thinking ahead to metaphor, it should be obvious why a distinction between "true in fact" and "true in the model" is required. Metaphors are, on literal interpretation, incongruous, if not actually false – a robust sense of what is germane to the context and what is "true in fact" is necessary for the recognition of a metaphor, and hence general knowledge must be available to the reader. Not every statement that is literally incongruous or false is a metaphor, of course, but it must be true in the model. Whether to invent a fictitious state of affairs or to search for an alternative interpretation that could be true in the real world represents an important decision that a reader must make: Whether, for example, "rusty joints" is taken as a figurative description of an old man or conjures up a rusty machine can have important consequences for a reader's comprehension of the text. But whatever trick a reader uses to preserve the truth assumption, a distinction between "true in fact" and "true in the model" must be included in any general theory of textual comprehension.

Metaphor presents an apperceptive problem. A metaphor that is literally false of the real world can still be added to our image and used to constrain our model, but it creates a tension between our conception of the real world and our conception of the world that the author had in mind. In order to be able to make as much use as possible of what we know about similar situations in the real world, we try to synthesize a textual concept as near to our concept of reality as possible – we try to add the metaphorical information in such a way that its truth conflicts as little as possible with our conception of the real world. That is to say, we try to make the world that the author is asking us to imagine resemble the real world (as we know it) in as many respects as possible.

If an author says that x is y when we know in fact that x is not y, we must try to imagine a world in which x is y. This act of imagination is facilitated if, in the real world, x is like y in some respects, for then we can take their similarities as the author's grounds for saying that x is y. If he says, for example, "Man is a wolf," we can honor the truth assumption by attributing properties of wolves to men (in much the way we would deal with "Man is an animal"). If however, the author says, "Typhoons are wheat," we shall have difficulty simultaneously selecting a model in which this statement is true and preserving resemblances between that model and the real world. Resemblances between x and y enable us to minimize the tension between our textual concept and our concept of reality, thus maximizing our ability to use what we already know.

It is tempting to make a stronger claim, namely, that resemblances enable a reader to understand what the author meant and that this understood information, rather than the literal statement, is added to the textual concept. For example, if an author says, "Man is a wolf," a reader might understand this sentence to have meant "Man is like a wolf," and add this information to the textual concept. It is indeed true that an attempt to understand "Man is a wolf" causes a reader to explore those respects in which men and wolves are similar, but to add "Man is like a wolf" to the textual concept violates the truth assumption that is a reader's only basis for determining the author's state of mind. "Man is a wolf" is a much stronger claim, and if that is what the author said, readers must assume that that is what the author meant.

"Man is a wolf" is false in fact. If it must be regarded as true, it can only be regarded as true in the textual concept the reader is synthesizing In order to understand it, however, the reader must associate it with "Man is like a wolf" or, even weaker, "Man seems like a wolf (to the author)." The simile cannot be added to the textual concept, because that is not what the author said, but it does provide a basis on which a reader can understand why the author might have said "Man is a wolf." Thus, the reader synthesizes a concept of the author, as well as a concept of what the author wrote.

The important point, however, is that when an author says something literally false or contradictory, readers do not translate it into something true and then assume that that was what the author meant to say. Rather, they assume that what the author said is true in the state of affairs he is describing, then search their general knowledge for plausible grounds for saying that in the given context. Their search for those grounds, however, is guided by whatever resemblances and analogies they can find between the world of the text and the world of reality.

Comparison statements

Since Aristotle, students of metaphor have said that it is used to express resemblances or analogies. Although it has long been recognized that there are figures of speech that look like metaphors and do not express resemblances or analogies, so great is Aristotle's authority that many followers have either ignored them or argued that they are not really metaphors. But whether or not similitude is a defining property of metaphor, no one could disagree with the claim that many metaphors are apperceived in terms of resemblances. I must, therefore, say a few general words about expressions of similitude before turning to their role in metaphor.

Directionality

In the abstract, most people assume that similarity is symmetric – that if A is similar to B, then B must be similar to A, and that either way of saying it is equivalent to saying that A and B are similar. This assumption is not above question, even at an abstract level, but at the level of the linguistic expression of similarities it is surely false (Tversky, 1977).

To begin with as pure a case as possible, let me take mathematical equality as my starting point. Everyone knows that "$=$" denotes a symmetric relation, that if $x = y$, then $y = x$. From a psychological point of view, however, even this symbol of total similarity is used asymmetrically. For example, you will not have to search through many algebra texts to find expressions like the following:

(1) $y = ax + b$

where "*a*" and "*b*" are constants and "*x*" and "*y*" are unknowns. As every student knows, this equation can be used to derive other equations:

(2) $y - b = ax$

(3) $x = (y - b) / a$

All three equations, and indefinitely many others that could be invented, convey the same information and, in all three cases, the term on the left of the equals sign could be interchanged with the term on the right without changing the truth conditions for the equation. Nevertheless, (1) and (3) are special, for psychological reasons: (1) says that if you know what x is, you can multiply it by a and add b in order to find out what y is; (3) says that if you know what y is, you can subtract b and divide the remainder by a in order to find out what x is. The convenience of (1) and (3) comes from the fact that we usually know or assume the value of one variable and want to find the corresponding value of the other variable. The equations are perfectly symmetric, but the way we use them is not: (1) and (3) respect the way we use them.

A similar observation holds for analogies. Verbal analogies of the form, "Day is to light as night is to darkness," characteristically allow many permutations of terms: "Day is to night as light is to darkness," "Darkness is to light as night is to day," and so on. In the abstract, therefore, verbal analogies, like equations, seem to have no intrinsic directionality. As soon as we consider how authors use analogies, however, we find that the context imposes a direction, that it is no longer possible to rearrange freely the order of the terms. An author who says, "Money is to a university as fuel is to an engine," is telling the reader something about money in a university, namely, that it is like fuel in an engine. If you know what fuel does for an engine, you can transfer that knowledge to the relation between money and universities. "Fuel is to money as an engine is to a university" would tell the reader something very different.

In order to stay close to equality, consider definitions of words. Suppose you do not know what a pickle is and decide to look the word up in a dictionary. You will find a definition along the following lines:

(4) *pickle:* any article of food, especially cucumbers, that has been preserved in brine or vinegar.

Here again the asymmetry is respected: "pickle" is defined as a function of food, especially cucumbers. If you know what cucumbers are, you can find out what pickles are by soaking cucumbers in brine or vinegar. Something new is defined in terms of something it is assumed you already know. Of course, if you do not know what cucumbers are, you will have to pursue your research further until, if you are lucky, you encounter some defining terms that are familiar.

Moving one step further away from equality, consider lay definitions. Suppose a child asks you what a zebra is. You might respond:

(5) A zebra is like a horse, except that it has stripes.

You would assume that the child knows what a horse is and you would explain the unknown word in terms of the known word.

The word "like" in (5) marks it as a simile; if you delete it, as in:

(6) A zebra is a horse with stripes,

some scholars might say that you had used a metaphor. However, others would deny it was a metaphor on the grounds that "horse" is commonly used (by synecdoche?) to denote the genus *Equus,* in which case (6) is a perfectly satisfactory definition. My purpose, however, is not to quibble about the bounds of metaphor, but to point to a pervasive directionality in our expression of similarities, a directionality that is not restricted to metaphorical expressions (Rosch, 1975a). If we revise the phrasing of (6) to obtain:

(7) A horse is a zebra without any stripes,

the direction is reversed; knowledge of zebras is taken for granted and used to explain what a horse is.

If we find asymmetry in the expression of equalities, analogies, and definitions, we should not be surprised to find it also in the expression of weaker degrees of similarity. Consider an example:

(8) John's wife resembles his mother
(9) John's mother resembles his wife
(10) John's wife and mother resemble each other.

Leaving aside questions of John's oedipal problems, (8) is what you would say to someone who knew John's mother and was asking about his wife, (9) is what you would say to someone who knew John's wife and was asking about his mother, and (10) is what you would say to someone who knew John's wife and mother equally well.

Another example can be patterned on Thoreau's passage:

(11) I went to a place near to where I intended to build my house
(12) I intended to build my house near to a place where I went
(13) The place where I went and the place where I intended to build my house were near to each other.

It was natural for Thoreau to use the pattern in (11), because the preceding text had already established that he intended to build a house – it answers the question, "Where did you go?" by relating it to something already known. On the other hand, (12) seems to assume that the reader already knows of some place where Thoreau habitually went, and is being given new information about the intended location of his house. And (13) is neutral; the reader is assumed to be equally knowledgeable about both. Note especially that the directionality of (8) and (9), and of (11) and (12), are different – sufficiently different to imply different intentions on the part of the author.

The reason for this directionality is transparent, but let me make it explicit. New knowledge is assimilated apperceptively by being related to old knowledge (see Haviland & Clark, 1974). One of the easiest ways to impart new knowledge is to state its relation to something already known.

The old knowledge may be either general information that the author can assume everyone knows, or it can be knowledge imparted earlier in the same text.

I will borrow a pair of terms from medieval logic to characterize this directionality. I will call the concept that is being talked about the "referent," and the concept to which the referent is being related the "relatum."[4] In sentences of the form, *A is similar to B,* for example, *A* is the referent and *B* the relatum. The reader is expected to transfer features of the relatum *B* to the referent *A.*

The distinction between referent and relatum enables a reader to determine what should be added to the memory image he is constructing. It is always the referent, enriched by the relatum, that should be added to the image; the relatum is either already part of the image or is part of general knowledge. Consider, for example:

"I didn't know he'd been married before."

"John's first wife looked like his mother. She came from Chicago."

In these sentences, it is clear that the antecedent of the anaphoric pronoun "she" is John's first wife, not his mother. This follows because the wife is the referent and the referent is added to the memory image; the relatum indicates how, where, or why the referent is to be qualified.

In terms of the distinction between old and new information, it should be noted that there is a sense in which both the referent and the relatum of a simile are old information. The referent is what the sentence is about; if a reader is to connect the sentence to the concept, its referent must already have been introduced. The relatum is something the reader is assumed to know already, either from the passage or from general knowledge. The new information in a simile is the statement of a similarity between the referent and the relatum. A more precise terminology, therefore, might distinguish between old, current, and new information: the relatum is old information, the referent is the current topic, and the relation of similarity between them is new information.

Classification of comparison statements

Comparison statements are easily recognizable by their use of one or another copula of similitude: "like," "is like," "acts like," "looks like," "as," "is as *Adj* as," "resembles," "reminds me of," "is the same as," "is similar to," "the same way," and so on. Different copulas of similitude are not interchangeable; they impose different syntactic requirements on the constituents being compared, and often have different meanings, but those differences will not concern us here.

I shall distinguish three types of comparison statements: literal comparisons, similes, and analogies. In literal comparisons, the grounds are obvious. For example, "John's wife is like his mother" can be understood to

mean that a description of John's wife would include many of the same
features as would a description of John's mother. In similes, the grounds for
the comparison are not obvious. For example, "John's wife is like his
umbrella" might be understood to mean that she is very thin or that she
protects him, or in some other way. Analogies generally involve four terms,
since they are patterned after the arithmetic analogies of proportionality:
for example, 3:4::9:12, or, more generally, x:y::nx:ny. "The toes are to the
foot as the fingers are to the hand" is a comparison statement using the
copula of similitude "as," but the grounds for the comparison are not stated
explicitly.

In all three types, however, it is possible for a reader to assume that the
statement is true, and all three can be taken as the basis for metaphors.

Declarative sentences of the form, "A is like B," can be understood as
expressing true statements to the effect that the author has observed a
resemblance between A and B. That the grounds for the resemblance may
be obscure does not imply that such sentences are not true descriptions of
the author's state of mind. If "statement" seems too strong for the expression of subjective and possibly idiosyncratic impressions, one could still say
that the author was using the comparison statement to make a proposal
(Loewenberg, 1975b) or a claim (Fraser, this volume) to which another
person could reasonably assent or dissent. The reader, who is under the
requirement to regard whatever an author writes as true in the semantic
model he is selecting, should face no special problem with comparison
statements if the referent, which is already part of the reader's textual
concept, is simply qualified by the new information that (in the author's
view) it resembles the relatum.

The qualification will not be understood, however, unless the reader can
discover the grounds for the claimed resemblance, and that is the central
problem of interpretation. In the nonobvious comparison, "John's wife is
like his umbrella," it makes a difference whether the grounds of similarity
are that John's wife is very thin or that John uses his wife to protect himself
from unpleasant situations. In "A woman without a man is like a fish
without a bicycle," it helps to know that the author is a proponent of
women's liberation and to recognize the rejected allusion to a fish out of
water. Once an interpretation is assigned, however, a simile poses no further apperceptive difficulties.

One type of comparison statement that might seem to contradict this
claim includes such similes as, "My love is like a red, red rose." It is not a
real rose that the author had in mind, but a symbolic rose – a flower that,
in our culture, has become symbolic of love. Or, to take a more extreme
example, "John eats like a pig" is not an expression of an observed similarity between John's eating and a pig's eating. A person who had never seen a
pig could use it if he had learned that, in our culture, the pig is a symbol of
uncouth gluttony. In some cases, symbolism can be tested by translation.

To the extent that the relatum is a symbol rather than a sign (Sperber, 1975), there could be languages into which the simile could not be translated directly, but would have to be translated indirectly by using the expression for the corresponding symbol, rather than the corresponding referent.[5] The reader of a symbolic simile must respect the symbolism; but once the simile is interpreted symbolically, it can be accepted as true in the model that the reader is selecting.

The importance of this point becomes clearer if it is also accepted that all the varieties of comparison statements are related to metaphors. Metaphors characteristically pose apperceptive problems: either they assert something that strains the reader's truth assumption, or they seem to bear no apparent relation to the reader's textual concept. This apperceptive problem is reduced if there is a resemblance between the reader's concept of reality and what the author has written. Finding that resemblance can be viewed as a process of paraphrasing the metaphor as a comparison statement. The reconstructed comparison is not then added to the reader's textual concept – the reader must honor what the author wrote – but it does enable the reader to construct an image for the text (in which the metaphor must be true) that resembles his conception of reality (in which the corresponding comparison could be true) as closely as possible. Whereas a comparison statement expresses a resemblance, a metaphor merely calls attention to it.

The outline of the argument should now be clear. In order to find a compromise between the requirements of the truth assumption and the need to relate the textual concept as closely as possible to general knowledge and belief, the reader must search for resemblances between the textual concept and general knowledge. These resemblances, which are the grounds for the metaphor, can be formulated as comparison statements. Once found and interpreted, the comparison is not added directly to the textual concept, but is used as a basis for imagining a minimally divergent state of affairs in which the metaphorical claim is true.

Similes

A simile is a comparison statement involving two unlike things. Precisely how unlike they must be before the comparison qualifies as a simile is not well defined, but the indistinctness of the boundary will not pose any problems for the present discussion.

I assume that there are two aspects to understanding a simile: (1) recognizing that a simile has occurred, and (2) interpreting the grounds for the simile and the author's reasons for using it in the given context.

Recognition. Similes contain a copula of similitude. Presumably, they are processed in the same way any other comparison statement is processed, so the initial step of simile recognition is the recognition that a comparison statement has occurred. It is probably only after some processing has occurred and the grounds for the comparison are found to be nonobvious (Ortony, this volume) that a reader is able to say with assurance that the comparison is a simile.

Interpretation. Interpretation of a simile may require an inference as to the grounds the author had for the claim of similitude. The inference may be based on the antecedent text, on general knowledge, or both. Let me give a simile and context and try to characterize the comprehension of literal prose:

I told him that everything would be all right. Telling John not to worry is like telling the wind not to blow. It made things worse, because he started arguing with me.

As I read the passage, I construct a memory image of the author and a worried friend. I hear the author tell his friend John that everything will be all right, but John continues to worry. John is so worried that he starts arguing with the author.

Although the passage mentions the wind blowing, the wind is not added to my memory image for the content of the passage. (If it were, the wind would have been a possible antecedent for the anaphoric pronoun "it" that begins the third sentence.) The referent of the simile, "Telling John not to worry is like telling the wind not to blow," is "Telling John not to worry"; I add this referent to my image, which is used to select a model in which the referent, not the relatum, is the antecedent of "it." The fact that the wind was mentioned, however, may be added verbatim to my memory image of the passage itself.

More interesting, however, is how I know (1) that telling John everything would be all right is the same as telling John not to worry, and (2) that John continued to worry. On the face of it, the sentence, "Telling John not to worry is like telling the wind not to blow," is an interruption of the literal narrative (it could be called a simile that is used as a sentential metaphor: see rule M3 below). The reader is thereby warned that special processing is required to integrate this sentence into the narrative. In this case, however, the additional processing is relatively simple: (1) is explained by general knowledge that people worry because they think everything is not all right; (2) is explained by the transfer of features from the relatum to the referent. Before the referent of a simile is added to the image, certain features are transferred to it from its relatum. What is the most obviously transferable feature of the relatum, "telling the wind not to blow"? Futility. When futility is transferred to the referent, it is implicated that the admonition failed, that John continued to worry. (Note, incidentally, that the futility of talking to the wind is also drawn from general knowledge, not from lexical knowledge.)

My account of this simile is still not complete, however. Comparing John with the wind does more than indicate that he continued to worry on this occasion. It attributes to John the trait of being an inveterate worrier. If the wind did not blow, it would not be the wind; if John did not worry, he would not be John. This feature, too, can be transferred, in this case from the argument of the relatum to the argument of the referent.

It is an understatement to say that the mechanism of this transference is not well understood. I have spoken here as if all the conceptual features required to characterize the referent literally were preserved and some features of the relatum were simply added on, as if an old friend were dressed in new clothes. This way of speaking is surely too simple, even for this example, and other examples seem to work differently. Black (1962b) speaks of the interaction of the two terms as a "filtering" process – the relatum provides a filter through which the referent is viewed – which suggests that some of the literal features of the referent are subtracted, rather than that new features are added. "Honest work is like prayer," for example, would be subtractive, since all features of honest work other than those associable with prayer – respect, devotion, dedication, perhaps – seem to be filtered out. The complexity of this transfer process poses a central problem for psychological research, a problem that becomes even more pressing when we turn to the analysis of metaphors (Ortony, 1975).

What makes a simile striking, of course, is an author's sensitivity to previously unnoticed resemblances; it can link together two spheres of knowledge or experience in novel and revealing ways. In such cases, finding grounds for the comparison may be a nontrivial task. When Eliot writes, for example, "the evening is spread out against the sky like a patient etherized upon a table," it challenges us to search for the similarity in our own experience of evenings and etherized patients – and may affect the way we see an evening sky thereafter. Similes are less interesting than metaphors only in that the terms of the similitude are explicit and require less work from a reader. As far as interpretation is concerned, it is important to recognize that similes can pose all the apperceptive problems that metaphors can.

With these examples of similes in mind, I should like to formulate some generalizations about them. This task will be much easier, however, if I interrupt the argument at this point in order to introduce some notations for the concepts that are involved in comparison statements and metaphors.

Some conceptual notation

A simple notation for conceptual functions and arguments will serve our present purposes (Miller & Johnson-Laird, 1976; Miller, 1978). For example, the sentence, "The patient slept," has an intransitive verb, and the sentential concept it expresses can be represented as a function with a single argument: SLEEP (the patient), where small capitals indicate the *function* and lower case letters indicate the *argument*. In a fully developed semantic theory it would be necessary to indicate how this function is computed. I would claim that SLEEP is a function that maps animate arguments into truth values, but since in the situation we are considering, the reader is constrained to assume that the value of all such functions is "true," I shall not pursue these matters, important as they are.

The general form that such sentential concepts take can be represented as $F(x)$. It is conventional to say that functions taking a single argument express properties of the argument – in this case, sleeping is a property attributed to or predicated of the patient. The sentence, "He writes poetry," has a transitive verb and can be said to express a sentential concept with two arguments: WRITE (he, poetry), where the general form is $F(x, y)$. It is conventional to say that functions taking two or more arguments express relations between those arguments in this case, "he" and "poetry" are related by "writing."

This notation for concepts should be reasonably transparent, but two complications will be needed later. First, it is possible (by a formal operation known as abstraction; see note 6) to treat relations as properties. For example, it is sometimes convenient to represent the concept expressed by sentences like, "He writes poetry," as WRITE POETRY (he), where writing poetry is a property attributed to "he."

Second, arguments are sometimes omitted. For example, the verb "eat" can be used either transitively or intransitively. For reasons having nothing to do with metaphorical language, it is convenient to assume that the mental lexicon contains a single entry for "eat" as a transitive verb; conceptually, "eat" expresses a relation between an eater and the eaten. It is also recorded in this lexical entry, however, that the second argument of "eat" need not be specified. One way to do this is to use the existential quantifier "∃" to bind the argument without assigning it a value (Bresnan, 1978). Thus, "John is eating" expresses the sentential concept $(\exists y)$EAT(john, y), which can be paraphrased as "John is eating something." In this way, we can explain the fact that it is sensible to ask, "What is John eating?" whereas it would not be sensible to ask, "What is the patient sleeping?" The point, however, is that omitting arguments from a conceptual representation is required for other reasons than the reason to be proposed later, when comparison statements will be related to metaphors by omitting arguments.

If all features of a sentential concept $G(y)$ are also features of a sentential concept $F(x)$, then $F(x)$ entails $G(y)$; if $G(y)$ also entails $F(x)$, then the two concepts are identical. I will use SIM to represent the relation of similitude between concepts:

S1. SIM[$F(x)$, $G(y)$] will be the general form from comparison statements, and will be used to mean that the two concepts have some features in common, but that neither entails the other. SIM can be expressed by a variety of copulas of similitude, as already indicated. I shall always use $F(x)$ or $F(x, x')$ to indicate the referent of the simile and $G(y)$ or $G(y, y')$ to indicate the relatum. Although S1 is given for a comparison between properties of x and y, I shall take it as standing in for comparisons between relational concepts as well. The features that two concepts may share must be understood broadly; they are not constrained to semantic markers, truth conditions, or logical entailments of the sort that result from semantic decomposition of the particular words used to express the simile. The shared features constitute the grounds for the expressed similitude, and identifying them is the first step in interpreting the comparison.

In this notation, "The brain works the way a machine computes" would be taken as expressing the sentential concept:

(14) SIM [WORK (the brain), COMPUTE (a machine)]

where "the way" expresses SIM, which links two constituent sentential concepts, "the brain works" and "a machine computes," having some (but not all) features in common.

Parts of S1 can be omitted in a comparison statement (as long as an expression for SIM is preserved): "The brain is like a machine," for example, expresses the sentential concept:

(15) SIM (the brain, a machine)

where SIM relates two nominal concepts, not two sentential concepts. I claim, however, that the missing functions are understood conceptually, and, therefore, "The brain is like a machine" can be taken as expressing the underlying concept:

(16) $(\exists F) (\exists G)\{SIM[F(\text{the brain}), G(\text{a machine})]\}$

which can be paraphrased as "Some properties of the brain are like some properties of a machine," just as "John is eating" can be paraphrased as "John is eating something." This claim is summarized in a general rule for transforming a comparison of nominal concepts into comparison of sentential concepts:

S2. $SIM[x, y] \rightarrow (\exists F) (\exists G) \{SIM[F(x), G(y)]\}$

Note that the functions F and G, which are missing from the left side of rule S2, are introduced in the right side as variables bound by existential quantifiers. S2 is a reconstructive rule for comparison statements, but it illustrates the kind of rule that will be proposed below for reconstructing comparisons that underlie metaphors.

Both S1 and S2 are intended as psychological, not linguistic, structures. In particular, when F and G are implicit, the reader is not constrained to some particular linguistic expression that must replace them but is free to explore a range of conceptual possibilities. For example, in the symbolic simile "My love is like a rose," rule S2 entitles us only to the paraphrase "Some properties of my love are like some properties of a rose." The reader is then free to consider such alternative properties as "beautiful," "thorny," or (closer to what the author probably had in mind) "affects me."[6] To paraphrase "My love is like a rose" as "My love affects me as a rose affects me" is to go far beyond the kind of recoverable deletions sanctioned by synthetic theories.

Analogies

In its broadest definition, any expression of similarity or resemblance can be called an analogy; in that general sense, we say that similes express analogies. In a narrower sense, however, analogies are stated between four terms: $x:x'::y:y'$. This is the sense familiar to psychologists from verbal analogy tests, where a person is required to judge an analogy true or false, or to determine an appropriate value for the fourth term. Let us consider the relation of such analogies, narrowly defined, to the conceptual form of comparison statements characterized in S1.

Take a simple example: "Toe is to foot as finger is to hand." SIM is expressed by "as," and on that basis it is recognized as a comparison statement. The arguments linked by SIM, however, are neither sentential nor nominal concepts, but idioms peculiar to analogies. Let us represent them in the general form "$x:x'$." Then the example can be said to express the concept SIM [(toe:foot), (finger:hand)], where the missing constituents of S1 are the functions F and G. The missing function is symbolized by ":" and is the same for both arguments, so we can assume that F = G. In order to reconstruct the comparison statement, therefore, we need a variant of rule S2:

S3. SIM $[(x:x'\ y:y')] \rightarrow (\exists F)\{$SIM $[F(x,x'),F(y,y')]\}$.

When we apply S3 to the example, the result can be paraphrased as "There is some relation between toe and foot that is similar to the relation between finger and hand." F is left for the reader to choose: it could be, say, "is part of" or "there are five per" (or both). Then the paraphrase could be either "The toe is part of the foot as the finger is part of the hand" or "There are five toes per foot as there are five fingers per hand." Note that the same function must be used for both arguments of the simile: "The toe is part of the foot as there are five fingers per hand" is nonsense.

Reasoning by analogy usually proceeds as follows. It is noticed that SIM [F(x, x'), F(y, y')] and, assuming H(y',y') is already known, it is conjectured that H(x, x'). In the example just considered, a child might notice that the toe is a part of the foot in the same way a finger is a part of the hand, and assuming it is already known that there are five fingers per hand, the child might reason by analogy that there are five toes per foot. In less trivial examples, the analogy might lead to a tentative hypothesis to be tested empirically.

The productivity of reasoning by analogy is not limited to four-term analogies. A more literary example is "His thoughts flow like a river, deep and clear," where the root simile that his thoughts follow one another as a river flows is elaborated: his thoughts are profound as a river is deep; his thoughts are intelligible as a river is clear. The same arguments – "his thoughts" and "a river" – are compared in several respects.

Such parallels suggest that we should search for deeper relations between analogy and simile. We might follow J. D. Sapir's (1977) suggestion that analogy be regarded as a kind of thought process, and simile as one product of such thought. Given an analogy between four terms, $x:x'::y:y'$, eight valid analogies can be stated:[7]

(17) $x: x'::y: y'$ $x: y::x': y'$ $x': x::y': y$ $y: x::y': x'$
       $y: y'::x: x'$ $x': y'::x: y$ $y': y::x': x$ $y': x'::y: x$

Thus, analogies allow combinatorial play that might well be part of an author's thinking as he decides how to express some similitude in a particular context. Moreover, when x' and y' are superordinate terms for x and y, respectively, the analogy can take the form $x:F::y:G$. For example "Washington was an American" and "Napoleon was a Frenchman" can be represented as AMERICAN (washington) and FRENCHMAN (napoleon); the uninteresting comparison "Washington was an American as Napoleon was a Frenchman" expresses the concept SIM [AMERICAN (washington), FRENCHMAN (napoleon)]. If we play combinatorially with the underlying analogy, however, we will come across $F:G::x:y$, or "Americans are to Frenchmen as Washington was to Napoleon," which might be an idea that a chauvinistic American author would want to express.

Metaphors

Perhaps the simplest way to characterize a metaphor is as a comparison statement with parts left out. This is, of course, the traditional view of metaphor, as indicated in *Webster's New International Dictionary* (2nd ed.), where we are told, "A metaphor may be regarded as a compressed simile, the comparison implied in the former being explicit in the latter." Making the comparison explicit is the first riddle that a reader must solve.

This characterization is a version of what is generally called the comparison view of metaphor, to which Black (1962b) has objected on the grounds that "it suffers from a vagueness that borders on vacuity" (p. 37). Black is not alone in his criticism of the traditional dogma,[8] but if vagueness is a fault of this view, we should not abandon it before attempting to clarify it. I shall argue that the comparison view of metaphor can be made considerably less vague, and that the result of doing so leaves the process of interaction, which Black takes to be the crux of the problem, in much clearer relief.

Relation to comparison statements

In principle, three steps, recognition, reconstruction, and interpretation, must be taken in understanding metaphors, although in the simplest instances the processing may occur so rapidly that all three blend into a single mental act. I shall discuss recognition and reconstruction here, and postpone interpretation until later (p. 391).

I have claimed that metaphors produce a problem of apperception because the reader's textual concept departs from known facts about the real world. It would be natural to claim, therefore, that the recognition of this discrepancy is the recognition that a metaphor has occurred. On this view, a reader recognizes that something is false or unrelated to the preceding context, examines it, and decides to activate a mental subroutine for the interpretation of metaphors.

This characterization may be correct, but it is not the only possibility. One alternative is that readers process metaphors in the same way that they would process any literal expression. That is to say, perhaps no special attention is paid to the falsity or irrelevance of the metaphor, because readers are bound by the nature of their task to take whatever they read as true in the replica of the author's concept that they are synthesizing, and to assume that there is an internal coherence to the text. Readers do not balk when nonexistent people are described performing fictional acts; perhaps they accept metaphors the same way, as true in the textual concept. But just as readers understand what they read by relating it to what they know about the real world, so readers try to understand metaphors by relating them to something that could be true in the real world.

According to this alternative view, recognition that an expression is a metaphor would be post hoc, based on a review of the mental processes it initiated. If the text says, "He is a pain in the neck," perhaps it is processed mentally in much the same way as "He is a lawyer" might be: "he" is assigned to the class of things labeled "pain in the neck."

In order to understand this assignment, however, the reader must relate it to what he knows of the real world, where "people" and "pain" label disjunct categories. This relation can be established with the minimal discrepancy between the text and reality by searching for resemblances. If it were the case that in the real world the person in question affected people as a pain in the neck affects them, then the author's sentence, "He is a pain in the neck," could be understood in terms of the related comparison statement. But the reader must remember that the author did not say, "He affects me like a pain in the neck"; the author said, "He is a pain in the neck," and the reader must try to imagine a state of mind in which this assignment would be true.

If the author had said, "He is a lawyer," "he" would be assigned to the class of things labeled "lawyer" and this assignment would also be understood in terms of the reader's knowledge of the real world. In this case, however, understanding does not lead to disjunct categories that must be reconciled in terms of assumed similarities. The post hoc realization that the processing required to understand the metaphor was different from what would be required to understand a literal expression would provide a basis for recognizing that the expression was a metaphor and that, outside the textual context, it could not be literally true.

Since the recognition of metaphors may not be an antecedent psychological process, prior to the search for similarities to general knowledge, I shall turn instead to the reconstructive step. Once reconstruction is clear, I shall reconsider recognition (p. 390), and shall claim that recognizing a metaphor must be a more complex process than recognizing a comparison statement.

Reconstruction of the implied comparison is a critical step in understanding a metaphor (Kintsch, 1974). I assume that reconstruction is a psychological process equivalent to the formation of a concept having the structure of S1. The comparison statement cannot be taken as the meaning of the metaphor, because it will have different truth conditions, but it represents a possible situation in the real world that could provide a basis for the author's use of the metaphor.

All metaphors omit any expression of the relation of similarity, SIM. For example, comparisons of the form "x is like y" can be converted into metaphors by simply replacing "is like" with "is." Thus, even such literal comparisons as "His wife is like his mother" can be transformed into the much stronger claim, "His wife is his mother." In this case, understanding the metaphor requires the reinsertion of "is like," and the comparison so reconstructed provides a basis for understanding the sentence as a metaphor. Probably this reconstruction goes on in parallel with processing "His wife is his mother" as a literal expression, because the sentence must be regarded as true in the textual concept, but then context and general plausibility are used to decide which of the two interpretations probably provided the author's grounds for using the sentence on the given occasion.

When the terms of a comparison statement are clauses or sentences, however, the simple substitution of "is" for "is like" is not always possible. For example, "The crowd rushed through the door like a river bursting through a dam" will not admit the simple omission of "like." We can obtain a metaphor, however, by nominalizing the initial sentence: "The crowd rushing through the door was a river bursting through a dam." But sometimes nominalization does not suffice: "The rich must enjoy their leisure as the poor must perform their duties" is different from "The rich who must enjoy their leisure are the poor who must perform their duties," for example; more drastic steps are required to eliminate "like": "The rich must perform leisure" was Thorstein Veblen's solution. There may be comparisons that cannot be expressed as metaphors, but the point is not crucial to my argument. I should like to relate all metaphors to comparison statements, not promote all comparisons into metaphors.

Classification of metaphors

I shall begin with the simplest cases. Take "Man is like a wolf." If "is like" is replaced by "is," we obtain Plautus's metaphor, "Man is a wolf." This pattern is found when a nominal concept is used metaphorically. Conceptually, SIM[F(man)], G(wolf)] becomes BE(man, wolf) or WOLF(man).[9] (In English, a form of *be* is usually required to express concepts like WOLF (man), but this is not always the case. Sometimes $y(x)$ can be expressed simply as "y of x": "coat of paint," "family of mankind," "filing cabinet of memory," "river of time," "ship of state," "stream of consciousness," "tree of life" are all metaphors that can be understood in terms of comparison statements of the form "x is like a y.")

"Man is a wolf" is a clear violation of categories – men are not wolves – but readers, who are committed to the assumption that all sentences have to be true in the model they are selecting, must figure out what to do with it. They can understand the author's grounds for using the sentence by reconstructing the conceptual basis of the comparison, "Man is like a wolf," and they can then proceed to interpret that comparison statement. Note that, as in the case of comparison statements, it is the referent, man, that will appear in the image; no wolf will be added to the cast of characters in the reader's concept of the text. Note also that assigning man to the category of wolves endows him with wolflike properties drawn from either lexical knowledge of *wolf* or general knowledge, factual or symbolic, of wolves. And note finally that a careful reader will remember that the author said, "Man is a wolf," which cannot be synonymous with "Man is like a wolf," because the two have different truth-values.

If the riddle of a metaphor is to be solvable, the conceptual elements of the comparison that are left out cannot be chosen haphazardly. What the metaphor is about can be inferred if the argument x of the referent of S1 is preserved; if the implied comparison is to be recoverable, something from the relatum must also be preserved. In some metaphors, SIM, F, and G are omitted, but the argument x of the referent is retained and the relatum is represented by its argument y. The constraints can also be satisfied if the relatum is represented by its function G, instead of its argument y. This pattern is found when a predicative concept is used metaphorically: SIM, F, and y are omitted, but the function G is predicated of the argument x.

For example, "Root out your faults one by one" might be based on a concept that could be expressed by a comparison statement like "Eliminate your faults as you would root out weeds, one by one." Conceptually, the metaphor is ROOT OUT(your faults); when it is reconstructed as a comparison, it becomes SIM[ELIMINATE(your faults), ROOT OUT(weeds)]. As Empson (1967, p. 339) points out, the same idea can lead to a different metaphor: "Rid your soul of weeds," in which case the formula for the metaphor would be RID OF WEEDS(your soul), and the corresponding comparison would be SIM[RID OF FAULTS(your soul), RID OF WEEDS(your garden)]. In either case, however, the metaphor applies the function of the relatum to the argument of the referent of the corresponding comparison statement.

We have seen two patterns of omissions, both of which can be summarized in general rules.

Nominal metaphors. When a nominal concept y is expressed by a noun phrase that is used metaphorically, we have:

M1. BE$(x,y) \rightarrow (\exists\text{F})\ (\exists\text{G})\ \{\text{SIM}\ [\text{F}(x),\ \text{G}(y)]\}$

where "BE" is some form of the verb "to be." Since a noun phrase is used metaphorically in M1, I shall call these *nominal metaphors*.

A common metaphoric figure follows the format, x is the y of x': "This is the leg of a table," "The lion is the king of beasts," "Britain was the ruler of the waves," "George Washington was the father of his country," "André Weil is the Bobby Fischer of mathematics," and so on. Such proportional metaphors are most easily understood as incomplete analogies (J. D. Sapir, 1977): for example, lion:beasts::king:y'. An analogy that we have already considered can be used to illustrate how such metaphors are formed: toes:foot::fingers:hand becomes "The toes are the fingers of the foot," where the fourth term is omitted. Note, however, that the freedom of rearrangement indicated in (17) is not available here. If we take the derived analogy, toes:fingers::foot:hand, we obtain "The toes are the foot of the fingers," which is nonsense.

In order to see that "The toes are the fingers of the foot" can be formulated as an instance of M1, take the metaphor as "the toes are the fingers," or BE (toes, fingers). Then, by M1:

(18) BE(toes, fingers) $\rightarrow (\exists\text{F})\ (\exists\text{G})\ \{\text{SIM}\ [\text{F}(\text{toes}),\ \text{G}(\text{fingers}]\}$

which can be paraphrased as "Some property of the toes is like some property of the fingers." If we assume that the relation of the finger to the hand is H, we can define the function G by abstraction from H(y, hand):

(19) G $= \lambda y.\text{H}(y,\ \text{hand})$

Since H is also the relation of the toe to the foot, we can also use it by abstraction to define F:

(20) F $= \lambda x.\text{H}(x,\ \text{foot})$

Then the relation of (18) to the underlying analogy can be seen as follows:

(21) BE (toes, fingers) $\rightarrow$

    $(\exists\text{H})\ (\exists x)\ (\exists y)\ [\text{SIM}\ \{[\lambda x\ .\ \text{H}(x,\text{foot})]\ (\text{toes}),$

    $[\lambda y.\text{H}(y,\ \text{hand})]\ (\text{fingers})\}]$

    $= (\exists\text{H})\ \{\text{SIM}\ [\text{H}(\text{toe, foot}),\ \text{H}\ (\text{finger, hand})]\},$

which is the analogy toe:foot::finger:hand expressed according to rule S3.

Since proportional metaphors are based on analogic comparisons, they provide particularly clear examples of the relation between metaphor and the thought processes involved in analogic thinking. The point to be noted here, however, is that they conform to rule M1.

Predicative metaphors. When a predicative concept G is expressed by a predicate phrase (verb, verb phrase, or predicate adjective) that is used metaphorically, we have:

M2. $G(x) \rightarrow (\exists F) (\exists y) \{ \text{SIM} [F(x), G(y)] \}$

Since a predicate phrase is used metaphorically in M2, I shall call these "predicative metaphors."[10]

Rules M1 and M2, like S1, stand in for relational metaphors as well as for those involving properties (having a single argument). For example, an author's grounds for saying, "The rich perform leisure," can be reconstructed by substituting relations for properties in M2:

(22) PERFORM (the rich, leisure)

$\rightarrow (\exists F) (\exists y, y') \{ \text{SIM} [F \text{ (the rich, leisure)}, \text{PERFORM} (y, y')] \}$.

The first step in interpreting this comparison is to find appropriate values for the missing terms. As already suggested, "the poor" and "duties" can serve as y and y', and "enjoy" can serve as F. With these substitutions, the right side of (22) can be interpreted as:

(23) PERFORM (the rich, leisure) $\rightarrow$ SIM (ENJOY (the rich, leisure),

PERFORM (the poor, duties)].

There is a pun here (as there often is in metaphors: Reddy, 1973) between the performance of a duty and the performance of a play. The dramatic sense of "perform" would suggest "actors" and "their parts" as values for y and y'. It is left to the reader to decide which interpretation (if not both) provided the author's grounds for the metaphor in the particular context of use.

A possible objection to this approach is that it seems to demand that F and G in M1 or F and y in M2 be particular words already present in the English lexicon, and that the reconstruction is not correct unless we are able to infer the exact words that the author had in mind. Since metaphor is often used to repair a gap in the lexicon, any demand for particular words is highly questionable. Moreover, the author may or may not have had some particular words in mind; as he did not use them, we can never know. In that respect, there can be no uniquely correct comparison statement.

This is a forceful objection and should be respected whenever these reconstructive rules are used. All that these rules entitle us to is the claim that some properties or arguments will complete the conceptual structure of an underlying comparison: we can rewrite a metaphorical concept in the format of a concept expressible by a comparison statement as in (18) or (22). The search for suitable values to convert (18) to (21) or (22) to (23) is, strictly speaking, a matter of interpretation, not reconstruction. A variety of words may be appropriate, or there may be none at all. The claim is not that the author had particular words in mind, but that he had a general concept – resemblance, comparison, analogy – that we are trying to appreciate and make explicit. Such concepts have a structure, and S1 makes that structure explicit. Rules M1 and M2 merely indicate what conceptual elements are missing in the metaphoric expression of the concept. Thus, M1 and M2, like S1, should be viewed as psychological, not linguistic, rules.

Another possible objection is that these rules are too simple and mechanical to characterize adequately the complexity of the mental processes involved in the comprehension of metaphor. When metaphors are complex, however, most of the complexity occurs in the process of interpretation. If we are to respect the speed with which an intelligent reader is able to grasp a simple metaphor, the reconstruction had better be as simple and mechanical as possible. With complex metaphors, of course, much longer times will be required to explore alternative interpretations, which may require alternative reconstructions, with uncertain results even for literary experts. But it is interpretation, not reconstruction, that can be complicated.

Sentential metaphors. Still another objection would be that M1 and M2 do not apply to metaphors that use an otherwise unobjectionable sentence in an incongruous context, as when, for example, "John has lost his marbles" appears in a text that otherwise has nothing to do with marbles. However, these, too, can be encompassed in this framework if we introduce a third general rule:

M3. $G(y) \rightarrow (\exists F)(\exists x) \{ \text{SIM} [F(x), G(y)] \}$

In such cases, which I shall call "sentential metaphors," nothing of the referent is preserved in the metaphor; the entire sentential concept $F(x)$ must be inferred from the text or context. Grice's (1975) notion of "implicature" may be particularly relevant here.

We have, therefore, classified metaphors into three types according to the constituents of the underlying comparison statement that are omitted:

Nominal metaphors: $\text{BE}(x, y)$ when an x is not a y.

Predicative metaphors: $G(x)$ when an x is not G.

Sentential metaphors: $G(y)$ when y is not a discourse referent.

If S1 is accepted as a correct conceptual representation of the underlying comparison, then it is possible to claim that this classification is complete.

Of the five terms in S1 – SIM, F, x, G and y – two, SIM and F, are always omitted in a metaphor. The omission of SIM is necessary because the words expressing it are the characteristic marker of a simile; the omission of F is necessary because the purpose of a metaphor is to create a substitute for a literal F. We are left, therefore, with three terms, x, G, and y, of which two are always retained; if only one were retained, there would be no incongruity to mark the expression as a metaphor. When G is omitted and x and y retained, we obtain a nominal metaphor; when y is omitted and G and x retained, we obtain a predicative metaphor; when x is omitted and G and y

retained, we obtain a sentential metaphor. Since there are only three possible pairs of three things taken two at a time, rules M1, M2, and M3 together exhaust the possibilities, and the resulting classification can be said to be complete.

Test cases

It would be a simple matter to show that a wide variety of metaphors have the conceptual structure given in these rules. No number of such demonstrations, however, would really test their completeness. For that, we must search for potential exceptions to the rules.

One type of exception poses a problem for any theory that assumes metaphors are always expressions of resemblance or analogy. "Giddy brink," for example, is not based on a simile of the form "A dangerous brink is like a giddy feeling," as rule M2 might suggest. It is possible to claim that the copula is not similitude, but causality:

(24) GIDDY (brink) → CAUSE [DANGEROUS(brink), GIDDY (feeling)].

The structure of rule M2 would thus remain intact, although CAUSE rather than SIM would be the copulative relation in the source expression.[11]

Richards (1936a, p. 108) offers a more imaginative interpretation of "giddy brink," however, in which the observer's own giddiness is projected onto the brink that causes it. This analysis is roughly equivalent to saying that "I stood on the giddy brink" should be understood as "I stood giddily on the brink" plus projection. Richards's analysis has the advantage of fitting other examples, like "He drank a mournful cup of coffee," where CAUSE is as inappropriate as SIM, but where "He mournfully drank a cup of coffee" plus projection provides a reasonable interpretation. This projective conversion of adverbs into misplaced adjectives results in a trope that poses many of the same apperceptive problems as do metaphors, but that cannot be resolved by the reconstruction of an underlying simile. If the brink or the cup of coffee could be construed as part of a larger situation, it might be possible to classify such tropes as instances of synecdoche or metonymy.

Another type of expression that looks like a metaphor but does not seem to express a resemblance or analogy can occur when two arguments of a relation are reversed, as in "John bores poetry" or "Golf plays John." If rule M2 is imposed willy-nilly, the resulting similes do not capture the natural interpretations. Most people I have asked have said that these figures of speech (if they mean anything at all) mean that something about John (his dullness, his compulsiveness) is expressed by reversing the conventional agent–patient roles: John is not prepared to appreciate poetry, or John plays golf obsessively. The rules I have given, however, make no provision for reversing the order of arguments within a function, so if these expressions are metaphors, they are counterexamples to the present analysis. My own preference is to classify them as instances of personification and irony.

One possible difficulty is that it may not always be clear whether a metaphor is nominal or predicative, and thus a reader will not know whether to reconstruct it by rule M1 or M2. "A watchdog committee," for example, seems at first glance to be a predicative metaphor, and M2 leads to the not implausible paraphrase, "Some property of the committee is like a watchdog of something." But "watchdog" is a noun that is being pressed into service here as an adjective; if we treat it as a noun in a nominal metaphor, M1 leads to "Some property of the committee is like some property of a watchdog," which is a clear improvement. But the choice is not always obvious. Consider the following pair of metaphors:

(25) a. John is married to his work.
    b. John is married to a gem.

The attempt here is to find a case, like (25b), where the formula must apply to an argument inside the analysis required for (25a), that is, to a noun phrase inside a predicate phrase. Consider (25a) first. If we apply rule M2, we obtain:

(26) MARRIED TO (john, his work) → SIM [RELATED TO (john, his work), MARRIED TO (a person, a spouse)].

This reconstruction is based on the assumption that the underlying comparison is something like, "John is related to his work the same way a person is married to a spouse." If we follow the same analysis with (25b), however, the result is:

(27) MARRIED TO (john, a gem) → SIM [RELATED TO (john, a gem), MARRIED TO (a person, a spouse)].

The comparison reconstructed in this manner is "John is related to a gem the same way a person is married to their spouse." Since this is not how we would normally understand (25b), we seem to have found a counterexample.

In order to defend my analysis, therefore, I must argue that (25b) is not a counterexample. The first step is to argue that, to someone unfamiliar with this weary "gem" metaphor, the comparison constructed in (27) might be a perfectly plausible paraphrase. Indeed, (25b) seems more interesting when I see it in this fresh manner. In short, (27) is a possible, though not the conventional, reconstruction of (25b). The second step is to argue for an alternative way to obtain the more conventional result: as a nominal metaphor rather than a predicate metaphor. In order to make this point, it is convenient to paraphrase (25b) so that the conventional interpretation is unavoidable:

(28) [The person] John is married to [is] a gem.

This expansion emphasizes the conventional sense of (25b), and the result is a nominal metaphor that can be reconstructed according to M1:

(29) BE (the person john is married to, a gem) →
    SIM [F(the person john is married to), G(a gem)],

388 GEORGE A. MILLER

which says that some property F of the person John is married to is similar to some property G of gems. The final step in the defense is to argue that this second reconstruction is also available for (25a). As before, we re-phrase (25a),

(30) [The person] John is married to [is] his work,

which can be reconstructed to give the comparison, "The person John is married to is like his work." It is not clear how this simile should be interpreted, but it suggests to me that the person John is married to makes him work like an employee.

We see, therefore, that (25a) and (25b) both permit (at least) two reconstructions, which accords well with the notorious subtlety of metaphoric analysis. The difference between the two derivations is a difference in the scope of the metaphor; the apparent counterexample arises from the fact that the conventional scope of one is different from the conventional scope of the other. It might be proposed that some further rule should be formulated to govern the correct scope, but that would be unwise. It is much better, in my opinion, to take (25) as a demonstration of the possibility of different reconstructions, and to leave to context the task of selecting the more appropriate one on any given occasion.

Still another test is provided by mixed metaphors. Ortony, Reynolds, and Arter (1978) quote Ronald Reagan as saying, "The ship of state is sailing the wrong way down a one-way street." The underlying comparison is presumably:

(31) SIM [SAIL (ship of state), DRIVE WRONG WAY (someone)].

If rule M2 were respected, the result would be "The ship of state is driving the wrong way down a one-way street," but this is hardly an improvement. Either metaphor alone would be unexceptionable: "The country is driving the wrong way down a one-way street," or "The ship of state is sailing in the wrong direction." But these, too, are no better. As Ortony, Reynolds, and Arter remark, Reagan said exactly what he meant. Pedants should keep their hands off such effective communication. I must admit, therefore, that mixed metaphors can violate M2 and get away with it. But I cannot resist adding that the general validity of the rules is evidenced by the fact that we are aware they have been violated.

Not all compound metaphors are incongruous; some poets have excelled at nesting one inside another. Unraveling such constructions may require an algebra of metaphor that goes well beyond the rules offered here. We can catch a glimpse of the latent complexities by analyzing an example.

Consider these lines from Dryden: "A fiery soul, which, working out its way,/ Fretted the pygmy body to decay,/ And o'er informed the tenement of clay." An old sense of "inform" is "give form to" (the communicative sense presumably derives from the need to give form to your ideas before expressing them) and a closely related sense is "to be the formative principle of" or "animate." If we consider only the fragment, "A fiery soul . . . informed the tenement of clay," the comparison underlying it is something like "His passionate soul was related to his body as fire informs the clay," or, conceptually:

(32) SIM [RELATED TO (passionate soul, body), INFORM (fire, clay)].

A straightforward application of M2, however, would yield, "A passionate soul informed his body," which, given the close relation of "inform" and "animate," is hardly a metaphor at all. In order to force the relatum of (32) to the surface, Dryden elaborated the metaphor. First, he used another metaphor to link "fiery" and "soul":

(33) FIERY (soul) → SIM [PASSIONATE (soul), FIERY (furnace)].

Next, he draws on two more figures: "The body is (like) the tenement of the soul" and "The body is (like) clay." When the second is nominalized (following a general rule that relates, for example, "The boat is aluminum" to "the boat of aluminum"), and substituted into the first figure, the result is, "The body of clay is like the tenement of the soul," which is the simile corresponding to "tenement of clay":

(34) TENEMENT OF (clay) → SIM [BODY OF (clay), TENEMENT OF (soul)]

Now, when (33) and (34) are substituted for the arguments of the referent in (32), we can finally represent Dryden's line:

(35) INFORM (fiery soul, tenement of clay) →

   SIM [RELATED TO (fiery soul, tenement of clay), INFORM (fire, clay)]

A full paraphrase in terms of all the comparisons we have reconstructed might go something like this: "As fire informs the clay, so a soul as passionate as a fiery furnace was related to his body, which is like the tenement of his soul." Not only is this paraphrase stylistically awkward, it is harder to understand than Dryden's metaphors. As an interpretation, it would be a mockery.

Since "fiery soul" and "tenement of clay" were probably familiar metaphors even in Dryden's time, we can surmise that he did little more than juxtapose them in an interesting way. The conceptual analysis in (35) is no flow chart of the author's mental operations, nor does it exhaust all we would like to know about such constructions. It is intended simply to illustrate the intricate conceptual structure that can be hidden in a line of only moderate metaphorical complexity. I would speculate that, although we have no algebra for nested metaphors, we can pick them off one by one – compounding does not discredit the reconstructive rules in principle.

Adverbial metaphors provide still other test cases. As described, the rules hold for only noun and verb or adjective phrases. What are we to make of expressions like "Rapidly is wastefully," or "He shouted silently"?

Conceptually, a predicate adverb is an operator that maps a function into another function. "He ran" expresses the concept RUN(he); the concept expressed by "He ran rapidly" can be represented as [RAPIDLY(RUN)](he), where [RAPIDLY(RUN)] is the new function. Using this notation, expressions like "He shouted silently" can be seen as special cases of rule M2,

(36) [SILENTLY(SHOUT)] (he) →

(∃F) (∃y)[SIM{[SILENTLY (F)] (he), SHOUT(y)}],

which would be paraphrased as "He did something silently like someone shouting." Such examples can, therefore, be accommodated in the present account.

Examples like "Rapidly is wastefully," however, have the conceptual structure

(37) (∃F) (∃x) [BE {[RAPIDLY (F)] (x), [WASTEFULLY (F)] (x)}]

which would be paraphrased as "To do something rapidly is to do it wastefully"; the general idea is that "wastefully" can be substituted for "rapidly" in any F(x). As in "Haste makes waste," it is not clear that any resemblance or analogy is being expressed; the relation seems to be one of causation or identity. If these expressions are considered to be metaphors, they are counterexamples to the present theory. Like metaphors, they involve ellipsis, but, unlike metaphors, they do not involve comparison.

The merits of the reconstructive rules should not be overstated. Cases not involving similitude can possibly be counted as exceptions; so, perhaps, can cases that do not involve the metaphorical use of a noun phrase, predicate phrase, or sentence (in Dylan Thomas's "a grief ago," "ago" is not a predicate adjective). Although most of the metaphors that have been discussed in the extensive literature on this topic can be reconstructed as comparisons by a relatively mechanical application of the rules, no doubt a determined critic could find still other exceptions.

Recognition reconsidered

These various test cases provide a basis for reconsidering what cognitive processes might be involved in the recognition that some expression is a metaphor. According to the view presented here, recognition is equivalent to the reconstruction of SIM in the underlying conceptual representation. In this view, therefore, it would be plausible to argue that the appropriateness of SIM cannot be determined until a reader has understood the components well enough to evaluate possible relations between them.

Take BE(x, y) as an example. If a sentence expresses an entailment, as in "Trees are plants," we might assume that there is a reconstructive process of the form:

E1. BE (tree, plant) → (∃F) (∃G) {ENTAIL [F(tree), G(plant)]},

where the entailment is verified by determining that all properties of plants are also properties of trees. That is to say, if all properties of y must also be properties of x, the appropriate reconstruction is as an entailment. If the sentence expresses a contingent relation, as in "This tree is a landmark," we might imagine that there is a reconstructive process of the form:

A1. BE(tree, landmark) →

(∃F)(∃G) {ATTRIBUTE[F(tree), G(landmark)]},

where the contingency is understood as adding all the properties of land-marks to the properties of this tree. That is to say, if all properties of *y* could be properties of *x*, yet are not entailed, the appropriate reconstruc-tion is as an attribution. These formulations of E1 and A1 are designed to show their similarity to M1, and thus to suggest that part of the cognitive activity required to understand a sentence expressing a concept of the form BE*(x, y)* is the determination of which relation is appropriate. A general statement of the reconstructive process, therefore, would be:

G1. BE $(x, y) →$ (∃R) (∃F) (∃G) {R [F (x), G (y)]}.

In order to determine an appropriate value for R, a reader must first under-stand F*(x)* and G*(y)*. If the sentence is a metaphor, like "A tree is an umbrella," neither E1 nor A1 will he judged appropriate, but the reader may decide that R = SIM. Only at this point would it be possible to judge that the expression was a nominal metaphor.

A similar generalization of M2 is possible. For example, "Trees are woody" would follow:

E2. WOODY (tree) → (∃F)(∃*y*) {ENTAIL [F(tree), WOODY(*y*)]},

and "Trees are beautiful" would follow:

A2. BEAUTIFUL (tree) → (∃F) (∃*y*) {ATTRIBUTE [F(tree), BEAUTIFUL(*y*)]},

leading to the general rule:

G2. G(x) → (∃R) (∃F) (∃*y*) {R [F(x), G(y)]},

where once again the selection of R = SIM must await the processing of the related constituent expressions, and the recognition that the expression was a predicative metaphor would be post hoc.

Recognition of a sentential metaphor would also be post hoc, since the sentence itself would not require SIM, but after it had been understood, it would be recognized as unrelated to the antecedent text.

According to this view, therefore, a special recognition process is unnec-essary. It would not be necessary first to recognize that an expression is metaphorical and then to resort to some special subroutine for processing it. Metaphorical expressions would be processed just as literal expressions are, up to the point where SIM must be introduced.

Interpretation

In sentences like "John is eating," where one conceptual argument of the verb is omitted, a reader understands that John is eating something. It is not necessary to know precisely what John is eating in order to understand what has been claimed. Similarly, in sentences like "John is a wolf," where the properties of the two arguments are omitted, a reader understands that some properties of wolves are to be attributed to John. It is not necessary to know precisely what property of wolves is to be attributed to John in order

to understand what has been claimed. Just as "John is eating" cannot lead
to a unique determination of what John is eating, so "John is a wolf" cannot
lead to a unique determination of John's lupine properties.

It would be futile, therefore, to view the interpretive process as a search
for the uniquely correct interpretation of a simile or metaphor. Nevertheless, there is a set of alternative interpretations that are plausible. In the case
of "John is eating," the missing argument is understood to be something
edible: lunch, enchiladas, strawberry shortcake, or whatever. What is given
places constraints on what can be understood, but without determining it
uniquely. Similarly, in the case of "John is a wolf," the missing properties are
understood to be something attributable to both wolves and men: properties
descriptive of appearance, disposition, behavior, or whatever. For "John is
eating," the constraints are conventional, whereas for "John is a wolf" they
are not. In the case of similes and metaphors, therefore, it is necessary to
search the text and context for the author's grounds. This search process is
one of interpretation. Interpretation is not a search for a unique paraphrase
of the implicit comparison, but rather a search for grounds that will constrain
the basis of the comparison to a plausible set of alternatives.

Sometimes the grounds for a comparison statement are relatively obvious, but when they are obscure, interpretation becomes especially important. Examples of nonobvious comparisons are provided by oxymora –
figures like "a mournful optimist" or "a laborious idleness" – where
grounds for conjoining antonymous words must be found.

Are oxymora metaphors? If so, they provide a special challenge for
comparison views of metaphor (Beardsley, 1962). Since oxymora combine
opposites, they seem to express contrasts, not comparisons, and it can be
argued that, on the comparison view, they should not be analyzed in the
same way as metaphors.

Let us treat "a cruel kindness" by rule M2, as if it were a predicative
metaphor. Conceptually:

(38) CRUEL (kindness) → (∃F) (∃y) {SIM [F(kindness), CRUEL(y)]}.

As a comparison, "Some property of kindness is like something cruel."
This paraphrase does not seem absurd to me, especially if I think of it as
referring to some particular act of kindness, rather than to kindness generically. From the comparison, moreover, we can explain the direction of
transfer: "a cruel kindness" is not the same as "a kind cruelty"; an oxymoron does more than merely contrast two opposing ideas.

The puzzle that remains, however, is to understand the circumstances
under which a kindness could be cruel, and that puzzle is much the same
for the comparison statement as for the oxymoron. Was the kindness so
overwhelming that it created a cruel obligation for the beneficiary. The
problem posed by oxymora is not that they cannot be recast as comparisons, but that reconstructing the comparison does so little to help us understand what the author had in mind.

Although the need for interpretation in addition to reconstruction is obvious in the case of oxymora, interpretation is also necessary in the case of more conventional metaphors. In every case, given a reconstructed comparison, a reader must try to appreciate how and why the author felt the referent was similar to the relatum, and what the similarity contributes to the larger concept of the text in which it occurs. A reconstruction that may seem acceptable out of context can prove unacceptable when seen in a broader perspective, in which case it may be necessary to seek alternative reconstructions. Thus, reconstruction and interpretation are mutually interacting processes. Their separation in theory is no sharp dichotomy, but more a difference in emphasis.

Finding appropriate classes of referents and relata is, strictly speaking, part of the task of interpretation. In order to make the discussion definite, let us assume that the author has given us some predicative metaphor having the conceptual structure $G(x)$, where x is something that G is not normally predicated of $G(x)$ will, of course, be added to the image, but it will be understood (related to other knowledge) by finding a plausible basis for the use of such an expression, that is, by reconstructing a concept of the form $(\exists F)\,(\exists y)\,\{\text{SIM}\,[F(x),\,G(y)]\}$ and interpreting it. In this case, our initial degrees of freedom in interpretation will be the freedom to choose values for F and y. Two readers who choose different values for F and y will, of course, arrive at different interpretations of the metaphor, but even the same choices of F and y can lead to different interpretations. Choosing these values is only part of the interpretive task.

Consider first the selection of y, since this often seems the less critical choice. Usually it is sufficient to take as y whatever the most generic argument G is conventionally predicated of. If, for example, the metaphor concept is $\text{COMMIT}(x)$, then we search for something y such that $\text{COMMIT}(y)$ is highly predictable: "faux pas," "adultery," "suicide," "murder," or, more generally, a "crime." We will choose a generic argument, since the author is telling us that x is one of the generic class of things that COMMIT can be predicated of. In Auden's lines, "Thou shalt not sit/With statisticians nor commit/A social science," for example, the concept expressed by the metaphor is COMMIT (a social science) and thus social science is assigned to the class of things, namely crimes, that are most commonly committed; precisely which crime Auden had in mind (if any) we can never know.

If you were to ask what features to transfer from y to x, I would answer, "Whatever features are necessary in order to include x in the class of things that G is commonly predicated of." What effect this may have on the concept of x is a question that must be considered separately in every instance – in some cases it will be much more obvious than in others – but the reinterpretation of x as a kind of y is part, and sometimes the most important part, of interpreting the metaphor.

A more difficult step, however, is the choice of an F that stands in an appropriate relation to both x and G. We could, of course, proceed as before: ask what function is most commonly predicated of x. In the case of "commit a social science," this procedure is not much help, since there is nothing that stands out as the chief predicate applied to this argument: "study," "practice," "like," "subsidize," are all acceptable, but so are "forget," "ignore," "dislike," "criticize." The mystery: how do we know (and we do know) that the basis for Auden's metaphor is a comparison of the form, "Practicing a social science is like committing a crime," and not a comparison of the form, "Criticizing a social science is like committing a crime"?

Let us turn to G for help in finding an appropriate F. Reinhart (1976) suggests that the effect of F should be to delete certain semantic features of G – that G should be allowed to stand as the function applied to x, but that only those semantic features of G that are compatible with F are to be effective. "Commit" means to perform, or even more generically, to do, but with unpleasant connotations. If we delete all semantic features that serve to differentiate "commit" from "do," the comparison becomes "Doing a social science is like committing a crime," and the poet's message is "Thou shalt not do a social science." If, on the other hand, we delete all semantic features that differentiate "commit" from "criticize," the unpleasant connotations of "commit" will not be deleted, since "criticize" shares them, so the comparison would become "Doing something unpleasant to a social science is like committing a crime," and the poet's message would be "Thou shalt not do anything unpleasant to a social science," for example, criticize it or, if Auden were punning, commit it to prison.

This version of filtering theory works well enough, but still does not explain why we prefer a positive over a negative version of F. The answer to that question, I believe, must come from the context. The whole poem points to Auden's opinion of social science. Given that opinion, "do," "perform," "practice," and the like, yield the only consistent interpretation; with F = "criticize," the poem self-destructs. A person who understood "Thou shalt not commit a social science" to mean "Thou shalt not commit a social science to memory" would not recognize that a metaphor had occurred, and a person who understood it to mean "Thou shalt not commit a social science to prison" would presumably regard it as an instance of metonymy. A person who understands the poem can only understand the metaphor to mean "Thou shalt not practice a social science."

The moral is not merely that interpretation is complicated, but that it requires an internally coherent configuration of all four terms. The interpretation of the referent cannot be independent of the interpretation of the relatum. When Richards (1936a) speaks of the "interaction" of two ideas to produce a new, resultant idea, different from either in isolation, at least part of what he means is that the reconstruction must produce a result that is internally coherent and interpretable, and that such a result cannot be obtained without taking full account of both ideas, their interrelations, and their relation to the context.

Another example may illustrate more dramatically that interpretation must be consistent with the context in which the metaphor is used. In most contexts, "Sheathe thine impatience" would probably he reconstructed by M2 as follows:

(39) SHEATHE(impatience)→
    SIM[RESTRAIN(impatience), SHEATHE(SWORD)],

where y is taken to be "sword" because swords are the chief objects that we think of putting into sheaths. The choice of F is again somewhat moot; "conceal," "contain," or "hold back" would probably serve as well as "restrain." This reconstruction would be appropriate if the metaphor were spoken in a conventional social situation. In the context of a woman speaking to her lover, however, a second level of interpretation can be added on the basis of the simile that a penis is like a sword, in which case a variety of interpretations of F compatible with "sheathe" are possible. We can imagine contexts, therefore, that require totally different arguments for y and functions for F.

The importance of interpretation is clearest when repair is most dubious, when rule M2 produces an obviously inadequate simile. Consider, for example, Beckett's phrase, "waiting till my corpse is up to scratch." Leaving aside the pun on Old Scratch (an old jocular term for the devil), I take this to mean "waiting to die," but the inadequacy of that paraphrase is obvious. When I force "my corpse is up to scratch" into a comparison statement, the best I can do is: "A corpse that is ready for burial is like a body that is up to scratch." But what an odd relatum! The question, "Is Samuel's body up to scratch?" would not normally be understood as asking whether Samuel is dead – just the opposite.

Part of the power of Beckett's phrase comes from irony; if the irony is removed by rephrasing it as "waiting till my body is ready for burial," the impact is lost along with the metaphor. It is obvious that this attempt to provide a literal paraphrase of the metaphor falls far short of a translation; as Black says, "it fails to be a translation because it fails to give the insight that the metaphor did" (1962a, p. 46). The steps involved in reconstructing a comparison will often leave us far short of a satisfactory interpretation. Although we can tease out a pun, a simile, and an irony by relatively routine analysis, interpretation must go beyond that.

I am no expert at squeezing out everything a phrase will yield, but I can offer a candidate interpretation. Beckett does not say "waiting to die" because everyone is dying all the time. Death is merely the final stage in the progressive corpsification of the body. But this idea is carried one step further by irony: we are asked to see death as an achievement. If these notions are on the right track, it is obvious that interpretation must include more than the characterization of a transfer, either subtractive or additive, of conceptual features from the relatum to the referent.

The search for a theory of interpretation usually presupposes that it must begin with lexical concepts assignable to x, y, F, and G, including, perhaps, any general knowledge associated with these concepts and any affect that words expressing them may arouse. A discussion of the interpretation of metaphors leads very naturally, therefore, into a discussion of lexical knowledge. Since this is a vast topic on which I have written elsewhere at considerable length (Miller & Johnson-Laird, 1976), I shall try to discuss it here suggestively, not exhaustively.

Lexicalization

The organization of a person's memory for the meanings of words in his language has become a topic for much psychological speculation and research in recent years. One attraction of metaphor for cognitive psychologists is that it might contribute to a better understanding of lexical memory. The judgment that a word can literally denote some novel instances involves an appreciation of the similarity of that instance to instances previously encountered; SIM represents a basic psychological function. And, as Paivio and Walsh (this volume) point out, the meanings that are combined in a metaphor must be retrieved from the reader's memory for what the words conventionally mean and how they are normally used.

The interpretation of the comparison underlying a novel metaphor sometimes requires merely that a subsidiary meaning of a word be favored over its core meaning. For example, Reinhart (1976) comments that the interpretation of "green ideas" depends on selecting a subsidiary meaning of "green," unripe. (Should we take this to mean that "green ideas" is not a metaphor?) Note, however, that "green ideas" can be reconstructed by rule M2:

(40) GREEN (idea) → SIM [UNDEVELOPED (idea), GREEN (fruit)].

Reinhart makes the point that when we hear the literal warning, "Don't eat that apple; it's green," as we are about to eat an apple that is not green in color, we must do precisely the same thing we do for "green ideas": pass over the color sense of "green" in favor of the unripe sense. On the assumption that "green" has several alternative meanings, the problem of finding an appropriate sense in an apparently metaphorical use is not basically different from the problem of finding an appropriate sense in a literal use. The rapid disambiguation of polysemous words on the basis of context is one of the standard enigmas facing any theory of language comprehension.

These considerations add further plausibility to the suggestion that "green apple" is processed in the same manner as "green idea":

(41) GREEN (apple) → ENTAIL [UNDEVELOPED) (apple), GREEN (fruit)],

which follows rule E2; ENTAIL is appropriate because all properties of green fruit are also properties of undeveloped apples. This proposal levels any sharp boundary between the literal and figurative uses of words, which is consistent with easy passage of overused metaphors into subsidiary senses – of "green," in this example, from a metaphor based on the color of unripe fruit to a subsidiary sense, unripe, applicable to many other nouns.

Metaphor is frequently cited as a source of polysemy. For example, there was presumably a time in the history of English when "leg" was not used to refer to a part of a table. At that time, therefore, "leg of a table" might have been a metaphor based on a comparison of the form:

(42) LEG (table) → SIM [SUPPORT (table), LEG (animal)].

With repeated use, however, "leg" acquired another meaning as the name for a part of a table. (Stern, 1965, calls this type of meaning change "adequation.") We are still able to recognize the similarity that led to the original metaphor, but we understand "leg of a table" literally by rejecting the animal-part sense in favor of the furniture part sense in appropriate contexts.

The adequation of a metaphor is only one way subsidiary senses can creep into the lexicon. I have discussed elsewhere (Miller, 1978) semantic extensions that are common to many different words, and have proposed that such lexical regularities should be called construal rules. I shall not review this claim that people appreciate regular relations between a core sense and various extended senses of many words, since the status of such rules is still a matter for investigation. But, however the regularities are formulated, some extensions are easily understood on first hearing. Since a metaphoric interpretation of a word can be viewed as a semantic extension of that word's core meaning – a radical extension, in some cases – it would obviously be worthwhile to look for correspondences between construal rules and metaphorical interpretations. If metaphor often involves favoring an extended meaning over the core meaning of a word, students of metaphor should be interested in how such extended meanings arise.

The danger I see in regarding the metaphorical use of a word as merely an extension of that word's meaning is that it tempts us to oversimplify our view of metaphor. In novel metaphors, it is not the meanings of the words that change, but rather our beliefs and feelings about the things that the words refer to. I have claimed that the reader must imagine a world in which the metaphor, however incongruous it may seem, is true. Readers try to be conservative in imagining such different worlds, but the exercise cannot help but broaden their conception of what a world can be. If we think of metaphor as nothing more than pouring new meanings into old words, we shall be hard pressed to understand how metaphor can enrich the way we see the world, or why word meanings change so slowly.

Conclusion

A psychological theory of metaphor should be guided by two objectives. On the one hand, it should attempt to account for the comprehension of metaphorical language in the same terms used to account for the comprehension of nonmetaphorical language. On the other hand, it should attempt to discover what literal comprehension must be if metaphoric comprehension is to be explained in terms of it. Taken together, these objectives imply that we must extend our theories of literal comprehension until they are sufficiently powerful to account for metaphorical comprehension.

I have taken apperception as the central process in textual comprehension – the process of assimilating new information by relating it to things already known. A concept of the text is synthesized on the assumption that whatever the author has written is true in the conceptual world that he is describing, and that the reader is trying to replicate. What is true in the text, however, may be very different from what is true in the real world; the textual concept and the concept of reality must be kept distinct.

Metaphor poses an apperceptive problem, because metaphors are either false in the real world or apparently unrelated to the textual concept. Although readers must take what the metaphor says as true in the world that they are trying to synthesize from the text, they can only understand that world if they can find a basis in the real world that might have led the author to think of the metaphor. This search begins by attending to those features of the textual world that are similar to what is known of the real world, since those features can provide a basis for relating the textual world to what the reader already knows.

The grounds for a metaphor, therefore, can be formulated as relations of similitude that can be expressed as comparison statements. A set of rules for reconstructing those comparisons has been proposed, and an argument has been presented that the resulting classification of metaphors is complete. How the reconstructed comparisons are interpreted has been discussed, but many important problems of interpretation are left unsettled.

In this way, I have attempted to account for the comprehension of metaphorical language in terms of the comprehension of comparison statements. And I have tried to argue that the comprehension of literal language requires all of the apperceptive psychological machinery needed to account for the comprehension of comparison statements.

NOTES

Preparation of this manuscript was supported in part by a grant from the National Institute of Education to the Rockefeller University. The title is intended to acknowledge my intellectual debt to the work of Max Black. More personal acknowledgements are due to Bruce Fraser and Morris Halle for conversations that helped me to understand better what the problem of metaphor is, and to Andrew Ortony and John Ross for helpful comments on an earlier draft.

1 Metaphors occur in conversation as well as in written prose and poetry; these different settings undoubtedly impose different demands on both the source and addressee of a metaphoric expression. Inasmuch as I do not intend to explore such differences, however, I have chosen to focus on readers (to the exclusion of speakers and hearers, and the near exclusion of authors). I hope that this decision will not seriously compromise what I shall say about those aspects of metaphor I do intend to explore.

2 I am indebted to Steven Cushing for this way to illustrate the point.

3 The image has the logical status of a list of presuppositions, containing constants or bound variables, which restrict (or relativize) the domain of interpretation over which variables in the model can be quantified (Cushing, 1977).

4 Tversky (1977) calls the referent the "subject" and the relatum the "referent." If I understand Chomsky (1971) correctly, the referent is a conceptual instance of what he calls the (linguistic) "focus," and the relatum is a conceptual instance of what he calls the (linguistic) "presupposition" of a sentence.

5 If I understand Black (1962b) correctly, what I call a "symbol" is what he calls the "system of associated commonplaces." Bruce Fraser has suggested to me that the distinction between literal and symbolic should not be viewed as a dichotomy, but as a continuum, comparable to the continuum between creative and idiomatic expressions. The criterion of nontranslatability, if it can be used at all, would have to be used with caution. Asch (1958) has pointed out that the use of certain adjectives (e.g, "warm," "hard," "straight") to describe both properties of objects and property of persons is sufficiently universal to justify challenging the common assumption that their application to persons is a metaphorical extension of their meaning in objective contexts. If some symbol proved to be similarly universal, its translatability could not be used to argue that it was not a symbol.

6 Strictly speaking, the verb "affect" is a relation, not a property: "My love affects me" expresses the sentential concept AFFECT (my love, me). It is possible to treat a relation as a property, however, by exploiting the logical abstraction operator λ. Thus, the relation $F(x, x')$ can be used to define a new function, $\lambda x.F(x, x')$, which is a property that takes x as its argument. In the example: $\lambda x.\text{AFFECT}(x,$ me) defines a new function (that can be represented as AFFECT ME) which is a property that can take "my love" or "a rose" as its argument x. By using that abstraction operator it is possible to deal with comparisons in which the functions F and G have different numbers of arguments. For example, "Fog swirls like a cat rubs its back" compares a function of one argument, SWIRL(fog), with a function of two arguments, RUB(cat, its back). We can define a new function RUB ITS BACK $= \lambda x.\text{RUB} (x,$ its back), in which case the conceptual structure of the simile can be written SIM [SWIRL(fog), RUB ITS BACK (cat)], which conforms to S1.

7 There are also degenerate analogies: $x:x::x:x$, or $x:x::y:y$, or $x:y::x:y$, which are valid regardless of the values of x and y (Sternberg, 1977a).

8 The history of the comparison view is reviewed by Mooij (1976), who concludes that the case against it is not convincing. Most objections, he says, are to "a careless application of the comparison view rather than the comparison view itself" (p. 60).

9 More precisely, G(y) is attributed to F(x). Applying the abstraction operator to SIM [F(x), G(y)] enables us to define a new function λF(x).SIM [F(x), G(y)], which is a property that can take F(x) as its argument. If we represent this new function as SIM G (y), as in note 6, we obtain [SIM G(y)] [F(x)] as an alternative formulation of S1 for comparisons: SIMILAR TO G (y) is attributed to F(x). When SIM is omitted, we obtain [G(y)] [F(x)]. Since, in the example, both F and G are implicit, the paraphrase of [G (a wolf)] [F (man)] will be "some properties of a wolf are attributed to be properties of man." Note that in literal statements of categorization, like "Man is a primate," this same paraphrase is possible, but the simile would be odd because all properties of a primate are properties of man, and we do not use "some" when we know that "all" is appropriate.

10 If I understand Richards (1936b) correctly, the referent F(x) of the underlying comparison is what he calls the "tenor" and the relatum G(y) is what he calls the "vehicle" of the metaphor. And if I understand Black (1962b) correctly, the argument y (in M1) or the function G (in M2) is what he calls the "focus," and the argument x of the referent is what he calls the "frame" of the metaphor. J. D. Sapir (1977), calls the referent the "continuous term" (since it is commensurate or continuous with the topic of discourse) and calls the relatum the "discontinuous term" of the metaphor.

11 A similar and probably related situation exists in the morphology of compound words, where an even greater variety of relational predicates must be inferred. Thus, a bulldog is a dog that "resembles" a bull, but a honeybee is a bee that "makes" honey, an armchair is a chair that "has" arms, a garden party is a party that is "in" a garden, and so on. Levi (1974) has proposed a list of six "recoverably deletable predicates" (CAUSE, HAVE, MAKE, USE, BE, IN, but no predicate of similitude) that will account for many such constructions.

18

How metaphors work

SAM GLUCKSBERG AND BOAZ KEYSAR

In his contribution to this volume, Searle asks, "why do we use expressions metaphorically instead of saying exactly and literally what we mean?" We propose that this question seriously misstates the nature of the problem. We will argue that when people use metaphors, they *are* saying exactly what they mean. When, for example, someone says that "Sam is a pig," that is precisely what is meant; that the person designated by the name "Sam" is a member of a superordinate category referred to by the word "pig"(Glucksberg & Keysar, 1990). To understand how metaphors of this type work requires an understanding of at least two processes. First, what is the nature of the category formed by the assertion that *S* is *P*? Second, what governs the choice of the metaphor vehicle, *P,* as a name for that category? Answers to these pivotal questions will provide answers to other questions about how metaphors work, including the question posed by Searle, why do we use metaphors at all? What communicative functions do metaphors serve in discourse that are not served by more or less comparable literal expressions?

We will first examine in detail how metaphors are understood. We will begin with an analysis of the standard pragmatics view of how people understand utterances that are intended nonliterally. The pragmatics view rests on the assumption that literal meanings have unconditional priority in language use. We will show that this assumption is wrong. We will then examine the comparison and interaction views of metaphor and show how these are at best incomplete because metaphors are, as we will argue, not implicit comparisons but instead are assertions of categorization. We then explore some of the implications of this view for comparison and interaction views and for the question of how metaphors are produced. Finally, we consider why people use metaphors instead of literal language to communicate certain kinds of information in discourse settings.

The standard pragmatics view

Linguistic meaning and speaker meaning

Ordinary conversation is filled with utterances whose intended (and understood) meanings differ from the compositional meanings of their words and phrases. Phenomenologically, hearers simultaneously apprehend two kinds of meanings: linguistic meaning and speaker's meaning. Both meanings are often relevant and intended. The linguistic meaning of the expression "it's hot in here," for example, refers to the ambient temperature of a particular place at a particular time. This kind of meaning has been variously referred to as literal or sentence meaning (Searle, this volume). Whether or not a sentence meaning is appropriate in the context of utterance, the speaker's full meaning cannot be determined without additional information. The speaker could, of course, merely be asserting that the ambient temperature is higher than normal. If such an assertion were to be plausible in the context of the conversation, and the speaker meant no more than this assertion, then this would be an instance of a speaker saying exactly and literally what he or she means. In such cases, utterance meaning and sentence meaning coincide. If there seems to be insufficient reason for merely asserting that it's hot, then the sentence meaning would not be taken as the speaker's full intended meaning. As Searle puts it (this volume), "when sentence meaning is defective, look for a speaker meaning that differs from sentence meaning." The speaker could be conveying a request to open a window, complaining that the air conditioning system is malfunctioning, or asserting that a toaster oven is working properly.

Metaphors of the form S is P are instances of sentence meaning not coinciding with speaker meaning. In many metaphors, the assertion S is P is false. After all, if Sam is a human being, then he is not really a pig; Juliet is a woman and so cannot really be the sun. False assertions are "defective" because they violate the conversational maxim to be truthful (Grice, 1975), but metaphors need not be false to be defective. Metaphors that happen to be literally true can also be defective, as in John Donne's observation "no man is an island." Readers presumably already know that no human being is a landmass surrounded by a body of water, and so this assertion is defective because it violates the discourse maxim to be informative (Grice, 1975). According to the standard pragmatics view, the first step in understanding metaphors is to recognize that a sentence meaning is defective in the context of utterance. Central to this account of how we arrive at metaphorical meaning is the assumption that literal, sentence meanings have unconditional priority. Sentence meaning is always generated by hearers and is always generated before any other meanings are even considered. Deriving literal meanings is always the first step in determining intended speaker meanings, including metaphorical meanings. The second step is to assess whether sentence meaning is plausible in context. If it is plausible (i.e., not "defective"), then the hearer accepts sentence meaning as speaker meaning. Understanding utterances literally thus involves just two steps: process utterance for sentence meaning and assess its plausibility in context. When sentence meaning is not plausible in context, the hearer must decide which kind of alternative meaning the speaker might intend.

As an account of how people determine the meaning of metaphors, the standard view is incomplete. A theory of metaphor comprehension must include an account not only of what triggers a search for nonliteral meanings, but also of what triggers a search for metaphorical meanings in particular rather than any other nonliterally intended utterances, such as indirect requests, irony, and the like. The problem is complicated further by the fact that a single expression may be used to convey several meanings simultaneously, as when someone says "Sam is a pig" to convey not only a description of Sam's detestable character but also a request that Sam not be invited to dinner . . . ever.

Incomplete as it is, two important implications follow from the standard view of how people understand metaphors. First, because literal meanings have unconditional priority, it should be easier to interpret utterances literally than nonliterally. The available evidence argues strongly against this claim. Conventional idioms such as "kick the bucket," for example, can be understood quite easily. Indeed, the idiomatic meanings of such familiar expressions are often the only ones that come to mind, suggesting that literal meanings can be bypassed entirely (Gibbs, 1980; 1984). More to the point, novel metaphors can be understood as easily as comparable literal expressions when used in appropriate contexts (Ortony, Schallert, Reynolds, & Antos, 1978).

The second implication of the standard pragmatics view is that people require a triggering condition – a defective literal meaning – before searching for metaphorical meanings. When sentence meaning suffices, hearers should not seek alternative or additional metaphoric meanings. Here, too, the evidence argues against the standard pragmatics view. People go beyond the literal even when the literal is perfectly sufficient in context. They simply cannot ignore metaphorical meanings even when a literal meaning is all they need in the situation. Glucksberg, Gildea, and Bookin (1982) asked college students to determine the literal truth value of sentences such as "some desks are junkyards." This sentence is obviously literally false, no different in truth value from sentences such as "some desks are roads." The important difference between these two sentences is that the former has a readily apprehensible figurative interpretation whereas the latter does not.

The former sentence is clearly metaphorically true. The people in this experiment took longer to respond no to the literally false sentences that had figurative interpretations than to literally false sentences that had no such interpretation. Glucksberg et al. (1982) concluded that metaphorical meanings were computed involuntarily and thus interfered with decisions about literal truth values.

There are two potential problems with this conclusion. The first concerns the types of metaphors that were used. All were relatively conventional, and so may have required little work or effort. As Morgan (this volume) points out, conventional or "stored" metaphors pose no interesting comprehension problems. It is only the class of fresh metaphors "that is the central problem for a theory of metaphor." Would people be able to ignore fresh metaphors in the context of a literal-truth verification task? Consider a fresh (albeit inapt) metaphor such as "all marriages are iceboxes." This is a metaphor that requires figuring out. Just how are marriages like iceboxes? Do marriages store or preserve things? Do marriages inevitably entail interpersonal coldness of some sort? Unlike metaphors such as "some desks are junkyards," whose meanings are immediately accessible, the marriage metaphor poses an interpretive problem because there are no readily apparent properties of the vehicle *iceboxes* that are unambiguously relevant to and informative about the metaphor topic, *all marriages*.

As with literally intended language, context and the setting of the conversation can be used to disambiguate such metaphors. If the marriage metaphor were uttered in a conversation about emotional warmth, for example, it should be readily understood. Would it, however, still require the triggering condition of a defective literal meaning? Gildea and Glucksberg (1983) examined this issue in a version of the metaphor-interference experiment that used metaphors not understood immediately when encountered in isolation. These metaphors appeared in a sentence-verification task either in a neutral context or in a context that called to mind a potentially relevant property of the metaphor vehicle. The people in this experiment read sentences that appeared on a screen, one at a time, and decided "true" or "false" to each one. The relevant context for a fresh and ambiguous metaphor consisted merely of a sentence that appeared immediately prior to the metaphor, containing a single word that called to mind the relevant property of interest. For example, the sentence "some summers are warm" could appear as a test sentence immediately prior to the metaphor "all marriages are iceboxes." The concept of warmth presumably calls to mind (to use Searle's phrase) the domain of temperature, broadly speaking. This should make the marriage–icebox metaphor immediately interpretable. In contrast, the sentence "some summers are rainy" would not bring the temperature domain to mind, and so should have no effect on the interpretation of this metaphor. Gildea and Glucksberg found that fresh, ambiguous metaphors were understood immediately when preceded by relevant context sentences, but not when preceded by neutral sentences. This strongly suggests that even fresh metaphors do not require a defective literal trigger in order to be understood. Metaphor comprehension is not, in this sense, optional.

Before accepting this conclusion, there is a second potential problem that must be dealt with. In both studies (Glucksberg et al., 1982; Gildea & Glucksberg, 1983) the metaphor sentences were all literally false. These sentences were not literally "defective" because the experiment used many literally false sentences and subjects expected equal numbers of true and false sentences. As Dascal (1987) pointed out, however, any false sentence might trigger a search for alternative interpretations, whether or not such false sentences are expected in a given situation. For sentences without a metaphorical interpretation, the search for alternative meaning would quickly fail and permit a rapid "false" decision. For sentences with available and accessible metaphorical interpretations, the search would succeed and the alternative meaning would interfere with a "false" decision. If this is so, then the metaphor interference effect would be perfectly consistent with a "literal-first/metaphor optional" model.

One could as well suggest that the reason [for the metaphor interference effect] is the difficulty in determining what does the sentence *literally* mean, which is a necessary condition for assessing its truth value . . . one could imagine that, although the subjects have been told to pay attention only to the literal meaning, they automatically generate and infer *also* a metaphorical interpretation, precisely because of the difficulty of generating a literal reading in the first place. (Dascal, 1987, p. 277, emphasis in original)

To deal with this criticism, Keysar (1989) used sentences that were not only literally true but whose literal meanings were also sufficient in context. These sentences could also have figurative interpretations that were either consistent or inconsistent with their literal meanings. Consider this brief description of Bob Jones:

Bob Jones is an expert at such stunts as sawing a woman in half and pulling rabbits out of hats. He earns his living traveling around the world with an expensive entourage of equipment and assistants. Although Bob tries to budget carefully, it seems to him that money just disappears into thin air. With such huge audiences, why doesn't he ever break even?

Given such a context, subjects tried to decide, as quickly as they could, whether a following target sentence was true or false. In this example, the target sentence was *Bob Jones is a magician,* which is literally true, but metaphorically "false." With respect to Bob's financial affairs, he is not a "magician" at all! If people simply stay with the literal when it makes sense, then the "false" metaphorical meaning should not play a role at all, yet it does. It interferes with and so slows the "true" decision about the true literal meaning, that Bob Jones is a magician by profession. When Bob

Jones is described in a slightly modified context as making a profit despite huge expenses, then people very quickly agree that he's a magician by profession. The metaphorical meaning can thus either reinforce or interfere with the literal meaning, even when that literal meaning is not "defective" in Searle's sense.

We can conclude that understanding metaphorical meaning is not an optional process that requires the triggering impetus of a defective literal meaning. There seems to be no general priority of the literal, and there is nothing optional about understanding the meanings of such fresh metaphors as "marriages are iceboxes," given an appropriate context. With respect to these broad issues, metaphor comprehension seems no different in principle from understanding utterances literally (see also Rumelhart, this volume). This general conclusion, however, hardly constitutes a theory of metaphor comprehension and use. Given that the failure of a literal meaning is neither necessary nor sufficient to trigger a search for metaphorical meanings, what properties of utterances enable people to recognize that an utterance is intended metaphorically, and how are metaphorical meanings determined?

Metaphors as implicit comparisons

Traditionally, nominative metaphors of the form S is P are recognized not as class-inclusion statements, but rather as implicit similes. When a listener hears such a statement, he or she interprets it as S is like a P. Thus, the statement "my job is a jail" is interpreted as "my job is like a jail." Once this is done – that is, once the class-inclusion statement is recognized as false and transformed into a simile – then the statement is treated as any other comparison statement. Ortony (1979; this volume) draws a related distinction between a metaphor as an indirect comparison and a simile which is a direct nonliteral comparison.

Both Black and Morgan (this volume) argue that metaphors are not simply elliptical similes. Black is correct in noting (this volume) that a metaphor can imply a comparison, but it is not in itself merely a comparison: "To call 'poverty is a crime' a simile or comparison is either to say too little or too much." Moreover, though many metaphors can be paraphrased as similes, the simile form seems weaker. Similes can always be intensified by putting them in metaphor form, whereas the reverse does not hold. As Morgan points out (this volume), it makes perfect sense to say "John's not just *like* a tree, he *is* a tree." We may add that it does not make sense to say "John's not just a tree, he is like a tree." Why are metaphors perceived as stronger than similes?

One reason that the comparison form might seem weaker is that assertions of similitude, be they literal or metaphorical, can be derived from a prior assertion of category membership. Consider how comparison assertions are ordinarily understood. The first step in understanding any comparison statement is to select just those properties that are relevant in context (Tversky, 1977). When interpreting the statement "Harvard is like Yale," for example, people will typically exclude such noninformative properties as "have classrooms," "have a library," "employ an administrative staff," and so on. Indeed, there are countless properties that two entities might share, from having atomic nuclei and electrons to being able to be thought about by Martians should any Martians exist (Goodman, 1972a).

How are the relevant properties of a comparison selected? For the Harvard–Yale example, the dimensions of comparison can be derived from the most specific category that includes these two as instances. For most people familiar with American institutions of higher learning, Harvard and Yale are prime examples of the Ivy League, a group of private universities in the northeast United States. If a person views the comparison in this light, then only those properties that Ivy League institutions share among themselves and do not share with universities in general will be taken as the grounds for the comparison. If Harvard and Yale are seen as belonging to the group of institutions that includes Princeton and no others, then only the properties shared by these three institutions (and not shared with others) will be taken as relevant. One can even imagine a more exclusive grouping, Harvard and Yale alone, and this will yield yet another set of properties as relevant to the comparison, just as the comparison of Cambridge with Oxford concerns only those properties unique to those two institutions (which together comprise the category referred to familiarly as Oxbridge).

This example illustrates how categorization can play a central role in how we understand literal comparison statements. If one were asked, for example, how lemons and limes are alike, the most likely answer would be that they are both citrus fruits. Questions about similarities appear in many IQ tests, and in such tests the instructions for people administering the test are unambiguous. The answers to questions such as "how are an orange and a banana alike?" and "how are a fly and a tree alike?" are uniformly in the form of a category assertion: oranges and bananas are both fruits; flies and trees are both living things. Note that the answers that first come to mind in these instances are the most specific categories that can subsume both items. Properties or features of similarity are then derived from the imputed category.

Comparisons come in many forms. When a comparison specifies the properties of interest, as when someone says "doesn't Sam sound just like Donald Duck?" no implicit category is imputed to Sam and Donald other than the set of creatures that sound like Donald Duck. Similarly, when the grounds of a comparison are not stated but are nevertheless obvious, as in "Diet Coke is exactly like Diet Pepsi," no implicit category is imputed. When the grounds for a comparison are neither explicitly stated nor obvious, then people can resort to the strategy of identifying the most specific category that includes the two terms of the comparison. The properties that are most characteristic of that category are then taken as the grounds for the comparison.

People can thus select the relevant grounds for a comparison in at least two ways, either directly by identifying the relevant properties or indirectly by identifying the most specific category that the entities in a comparison can belong to. Properties are directly identified when they are explicitly mentioned in a comparison statement, or when they are implied by such qualifiers as "exactly like" or "essentially like." When direct identification of properties is problematic, people will first assign the terms of a comparison to a single category, and then take the characteristic properties of that category as the relevant grounds for the comparison.

This analysis poses an interesting puzzle for the comparison view of metaphor comprehension. If literal comparisons are dealt with as implicit categorizations, why should metaphoric categorizations be treated as implicit comparisons? Problematic literal comparisons, such as "how are flies like trees?" can be understood by first grouping the terms of the comparison and then deriving the grounds of comparison from the grouping, that is, "living things." Metaphoric comparisons should pose the same problem as literal comparisons, and the problem may be solved in the same way. Metaphoric comparisons might also be understood by assigning the terms of the metaphoric comparison to an appropriate category and deriving the grounds for comparisons from the characteristic properties of that category. If this is a viable strategy, converting a metaphor *S is P* into a simile *S is like P* will accomplish absolutely nothing, because *S is like P* will just be converted right back into the original metaphor form, *S is P*! If indeed such metaphors are understood by classifying *S* in the category referred to by *P*, the issue then becomes, what is the nature of the category referred to by the metaphor vehicle, *P*?

Metaphors are class-inclusion assertions

Taxonomic and attributive categories

Imagine having a conversation with one of us (SG) about various kinds of dogs as pets, and I tell you that "my dog is an animal." On the face of it, this is a true class-inclusion assertion. Dogs are a proper subset of the larger category, animals. Though this is a true statement, you will not take it as my intended meaning. You will not take it as the intended meaning because you already know this fact, and I know that you know this fact, and I am not going to say "my dog is an animal" to inform you of a fact that you know, that I know, and that you know I know, and I know that you know that I know, and so forth.

Converting "my dog is an animal" into a simile "my dog is like an animal" doesn't reveal the intended meaning, primarily because it makes no sense to say that a dog is like an animal when it already is an animal. So what can I mean when I say to you that my dog is an animal? The intended meaning might be the same as in the assertion "Arnold Schwarzenegger is an animal" or the implication in the John Belushi movie *Animal House*. In each of these uses, the term "animal" can have one of several meanings: animal as the alternative to vegetable in biological taxonomies, or animal as the name of a different superordinate category, such as the category of animate beings that behave in particularly animalistic ways. We will refer to the latter kinds of categories as attributive categories because they are used primarily to attribute specific properties to their metaphor topics. In this attributive "animal" category, sheep would not be animals, but drunken fraternity members, awesomely muscular and violent actors, and some breeds of dogs would be animals.

To say that one's dog is an animal, then, is to use the word "animal" in a new and interesting way, to refer to a category of things that does not (at least yet) have a name of its own.[1] Might the same strategy be at work in metaphors such as "my job is a jail"? Can we use the word "jail" to allude to a prototypical confining thing, the "literal" jail, while simultaneously referring to a category of such things for which we have no commonly accepted label or name?

Naming superordinate categories

One answer to this question may come from languages that generally do not have superordinate category names. All languages have names for basic level objects (Rosch, 1973), but some do not have names for superordinate categories. One such language is American Sign Language (ASL). In ASL, basic level objects have primary signs, strictly analogous to such single-word English names as *chair, table,* and *bed.* The superordinate level category of *furniture* had, until recently, no sign of its own in ASL. To refer to the category *furniture,* ASL signers use basic object signs that are prototypical of that category, as in:

House fire [+] lose all chair-table-bed etc., but one left, bed

which is interpretable as "I lost all my furniture in the house fire but one thing was left: the bed" (Newport & Bellugi, 1978, p. 62). The strategy of using the name of a prototypical category member to refer to a superordinate category that does not have a conventional name of its own appears in spoken languages as well. A particularly striking example was reported in a newspaper article about the war crimes trial of John Demjanjuk, who was accused of being "Ivan the Terrible," a sadistic guard at the Treblinka death camp in Poland during the Second World War. "[T]he name Demjanjuk has become a noun in Israel, a word to identify *an ordinary person capable of committing unspeakable acts*" (emphasis added). That the category name and the person's name are quite distinct is revealed in the following interchange between an American newspaper reporter and an Israeli spectator attending the trial:

Israeli: "If he is a Demjanjuk, then he should be condemned to death."
Reporter: "But he is Demjanjuk, his name is John Demjanjuk."
Israeli: "I know his name is Demjanjuk, but I don't know if he is a Demjanjuk."
    (Shinoff, *San Francisco Examiner*, 1987)

Other examples of this type abound. A number of Native American languages occasionally use prototypical category member names for the category name itself. In Hopi, for example, the name of the most common deciduous tree, "cottonwood," is also used as the name for the class of deciduous trees (Trager, 1936–39). The word for eagle is used by Shoshoni speakers to refer to large birds in general as well as to eagles themselves (Hage & Miller, 1976). Sometimes, to avoid confusion, more specific terms may be introduced, such as "cottonwood" for trees in general and "real cottonwood" for the cottonwood tree itself as in the Kiowa language in western Oklahoma (Trager, 1936–39).[2] But even in this case, the general principle is clear. The name of a prototypical category member can be used to name a category that has no name of its own.

Naming metaphorical attributive categories

Are these special cases, or do they represent a common communicative device? In languages such as English or Hebrew that do have superordinate category names, this strategy can be used to construct ordinary, everyday metaphors (Glucksberg & Keysar, 1990). To refer to someone as a *Demjanjuk* alludes to the original war criminal, and also makes metaphorical use of his name, Demjanjuk. A person who says "my job is a jail" is using precisely this strategy of employing a prototypical basic object name to refer to a superordinate category that has no conventional name of its own. What is the category that is exemplified by the basic level object "jail"?

The category referred to as "a jail" can be described by a list of distinguishing features, but it is difficult to enumerate these features exhaustively (see Figure 18.1). By naming the category "jail," "my job" inherits those properties of "jail" that can plausibly be attributed to "my job." The words "a jail" can refer either to a specific instance, *jail*, or to the class, *jail*. As a metaphor vehicle, "a jail" refers to a class of things, whereas when "a jail" is used literally it would refer to an actual jail or jails. The difference between these two uses of the word "jail" is analogous to that between "Demjanjuk" used to name a person and the same term used to refer to a

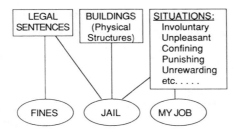

Figure 18.1. Cross-classification of *jails* and *jobs:* partial illustration (after Glucksberg & Keysar, 1990).

class of people with certain characteristics, namely, ordinary people capable of committing unspeakable acts. Similarly, a newspaper headline that states "Cambodia has become Vietnam's Vietnam" also uses a single referring expression, *Vietnam,* in two distinct ways, to allude to the entity itself (the country of Vietnam), and to refer to the category of situation that this entity has come to exemplify. Roger Brown captured this distinction when he argued in 1958 that metaphors involve categorization: "Metaphor differs from other superordinate-subordinate relations in that the superordinate is not given a name of its own. Instead, the name of one subordinate (i.e., the vehicle) is extended to the other" (p. 140; see also Elbers, 1988).

On this view, when someone says "my surgeon was a butcher," she means just that, not that her surgeon was like a butcher. In using this expression, the speaker alludes to a prototypical or ideal exemplar of the category of bungling and harmful workers, "butchers," and simultaneously uses that prototype's name to name the category. Thus, when new and novel metaphors are created, either new categories are created or new members are added to existing "metaphorical" categories, as in this particularly apt expression coined by Arthur Rosenthal in a *New York Times* editorial about the issue of economic aid to the Soviet Union: "The United States cannot patch up the Soviet economy because it is not a leaking tire, it is a blowout." Surely, Rosenthal did not intend the reader to understand this to mean that the Soviet economy is not a leaking tire (true), rather it is *like* a blowout (also true, but how inapt). When speakers or writers say that something *is* something, they do not mean merely that it is *like* something.

Categorization as a selection mechanism. When any two objects are compared, only a small subset of properties is usually involved, namely, those that are relevant to the context (Tversky, 1977). Comparison statements such as *olives are like cherries* involve selected properties of the predicate *cherries.* Both grow on trees, can be costly or cheap depending on the season, have pits, and so forth. Any one of these may be intended, as well as other properties that are shared by olives and cherries. The particular properties that are selected will depend on the context of the utterance. If the topic of conversation is about mixed drinks, then olives and cherries are alike in that both are used to garnish cocktails. The property selection can be induced by grouping, that is, by the way olives and cherries are classified (e.g., cocktail garnishes). The characteristic properties of this class become the ground for comparison.

For literal comparisons, as we have already seen, the properties to be shared are often based on an implicit categorization. Lemons and grapes are alike in that they are both fruits – recall that the similarity relation itself is most easily expressed in terms of joint category membership. The more specific the category, the greater the degree of similarity. Thus, lemons and limes are both citrus fruits and so are more similar to one another than are lemons and grapes, which must be categorized at a higher level in the hierarchy.

For metaphoric comparisons, we suggest that the categorization is made explicit by employing a predicate to name the class of things that it exemplifies. Thus, in the metaphor "cigarettes are time bombs," the term "time bombs" refers to a superordinate category that includes both cigarettes and actual time bombs as members. Of all the possible categories that these two can belong to, the one in focus is the category that "time bombs" typifies. This category selects all and only those properties that the metaphor attributes to cigarettes. Thus by placing cigarettes into this superordinate category, the concept "cigarettes" inherits the set of properties characteristic of the category. The same relationships hold for metaphorical comparisons or similes. Even though the simile "cigarettes are like time bombs" has the surface form of a comparison, it is understood as an implicit categorization. In addition to referring to the basic level category "time bomb," the second term of the comparison also names the superordinate category it typifies. Because of this dual function, the comparison can be expressed as a class-inclusion statement, "cigarettes are time bombs."

Class inclusion versus identity. The form *a* is *b* can be used to express identity relations as well as class-inclusion relations (see Brachman, 1983, on the ambiguity of the *isa* expression). Davidson (1978), for example, treats metaphors as expressions of identity statements. As such, they are usually false: "The most obvious semantic difference between simile and metaphor is that all similes are true and most metaphors are false . . . the earth is like a floor, but it is not a floor" (p. 39). Davidson even suggests that metaphors are comprehended as such: "What matters is not actual falsehood but that the sentence be taken to be false" (p. 40). If a metaphor expresses a false identity, it is only reasonable to resort to the simile form in order to recover the intended meaning.

However, if metaphor vehicles can have two referents simultaneously (e.g., time bombs can refer to the basic level actual bombs and to the superordinate, the class of deadly things), then the metaphor can be understood as class inclusion, not identity. How any particular *isa* statement is to be interpreted will depend upon our semantic knowledge and on rules of conversation and discourse. The statement "an ophthalmologist is an eye doctor" would usually be understood as an identity assertion that could be informative in context. In contrast, the statement "boys are boys" cannot be informative if it is an identity statement; it would be a truism (Gibbs & McCarrell, 1990; Glucksberg & Keysar, 1990). If interpreted as a class inclusion, then it can be informative. The first and second uses of *boys* have different referents. The first *boys* refers to individuals; the second *boys* refers to a class, people who behave in stereotypical boyish fashion. Similarly, in the assertion that Cambodia has become Vietnam's Vietnam the first and second uses of *Vietnam* have different referents. The first refers to the country itself, the second to a class of disastrous military and political interventions which the American-Vietnamese war has come to exemplify.

Reconsideration of comparison and interaction views

We are now in a position to specify why metaphors are not simply elliptical comparisons. When someone says "my job is a jail," the intention is for the hearer to understand that the job in question has all the properties of the attributive category that is called "jail." If instead one said "my job is *like* a jail," then one is likening that job to an actual "jail," not to the superordinate "jail." When the metaphorical form is chosen over the simile form, the very choice is communicative. If one chooses the simile, then the hearer presumably recognizes that choice and would therefore infer that the speaker was not attributing all the properties of the class "jail" to "my job," but only some of them.

Comparable speaker and hearer strategies are available for literally intended attributive expressions. In describing pearl onions to someone unfamiliar with them, I could say either that pearl onions are cocktail garnishes or that pearl onions are like olives. In the categorical description, I am being both more specific and more inclusive. Pearl onions, by being assigned to the category of cocktail garnishes, are grouped not only with olives but also with other garnishes such as lemon peel, maraschino cherries, and limes. In contrast, the comparison description leaves open the ways in which pearl onions and olives might be similar. How the comparison is understood will depend primarily on the implicit category inferred by the hearer.

Black's interaction view (1962b; this volume) captures some of the flavor of our category assertion view. Black argues that a metaphor vehicle (in his terms, the secondary subject) is not so much a single thing or entity but rather a system of relationships, an "implicative complex." Metaphor works by "projecting upon" the topic a set of "associated implications" that are selected by the hearer as relevant to the topic. This reciprocally induces a changed view of the metaphor vehicle. Viewing metaphor statements as categorical assertions provides a mechanism for the interactions described by Black. First, categorical assertions are more systematic, in Black's sense, than are simple similarity assertions. Attributive categories can "project" a complex of properties to metaphor topics that are simultaneously more specific and more inclusive than are simple similarity assertions (as in the onion–olive example, above). Second, when a new member is added to a category, this can not only change a category's extension (the set of entities included in the category), it can also change the category's intension. A category's intension, roughly speaking, is the conceptual basis for that category, and this includes criteria for deciding whether or not a candidate object is or is not a category member (Miller & Glucksberg, 1988). Before the advent of digital computers, the category *machines* did not include things that had memory. By adding computers to the category of machines, our concept of machines was changed. Machines could now have memories and perhaps could also be capable of thinking. On a smaller scale, by asserting that "Mary's marriage became a jail," the concept of involuntary, unpleasant, confining, punishing, unrewarding situations referred to by the metaphor vehicle "jail" is expanded to include such interpersonal relationships as marriage. Once this occurs, novel extensions of the metaphor can be created, as in "by marrying Jim, Alice sentenced herself to a long prison term."

Implications of the categorization view

The categorization approach to metaphor sheds new light on long-standing problems. In this section we address the following issues and problems of metaphor comprehension and use:

1. Literal comparisons are generally reversible, metaphoric comparisons are nonreversible. What accounts for this difference?
2. People can recognize a comparison as either literal or metaphorical. What cues do people use to make this discrimination?
3. Specifying the relevant attributed property in a metaphor typically makes the assertion less metaphorical, as in "cigarettes are time bombs" versus "cigarettes are as deadly as time bombs." Why do such specifications have this effect?
4. Metaphors vary in comprehensibility and in aptness. These two properties may vary independently. In some cases perfectly comprehensible metaphors can still be nonapt, as in "not even Einstein's ideas were all platinum." What determines the metaphor qualities of comprehensibility and aptness?

We deal with each of these issues in terms of the categorization view of metaphor.

Metaphors are not reversible

Class-inclusion statements, when one set is properly included in the other, are not reversible. The statement "trees are plants" is false or anomalous when it is reversed, "plants are trees." Because metaphors are class-inclusion statements, they behave in exactly the same way. Like literal class-inclusion statements, assertions such as "sermons are sleeping pills" are anomalous when reversed, "sleeping pills are sermons." There is, however, an important difference between literal class-inclusion statements and metaphors. Literal class-inclusion statements, such as "a tree is a plant," cannot be paraphrased as a comparison, "a tree is like a plant." In contrast, metaphors can be paraphrased as similes, for example, "my job is a jail" can be paraphrased as "my job is like a jail." The paraphrased metaphor, like its original, cannot be reversed: "a jail is like my job" simply makes no sense. We suggest that the principle governing the nonreversibility of metaphoric comparisons is that they are implicit class-inclusion assertions. They derive from the canonical metaphor form, *S* is *P*. As implicit class-inclusion statements, metaphoric comparisons simply obey the ordering constraint on such statements. They are not reversible.

The available data generally support this assertion (Ortony, Vondruska, Foss, & Jones, 1985). There are, however, two kinds of metaphors that appear to be reversible, though in both cases the reversibility is illusory. The first case is exemplified by such metaphors as "that surgeon is a butcher" and "that butcher is a surgeon." The only reason that such metaphors can be reversed is that the new vehicle happens to exemplify a category to which it can lend its name and in which the topic can be a member. But in such cases, the ground of the metaphor changes. In the surgeon–butcher example, characterizing a surgeon as a butcher is a negative attribution; the reverse is a positive attribution. It is purely coincidental that the concepts of *surgeon* and *butcher* happen to exemplify the categories to which they ordinarily belong, that is, precise and skillful craftsmen and bungling, atrocious workers, respectively.

The second kind of apparent reversibility is less well understood, though examples are easy to come by. Consider "A mighty fortress is our God." This can be considered a poetic inversion rather than a genuine reordering of "Our God is a mighty fortress." In each case, *our God* is identified with *a mighty fortress*. In neither case is a fortress intended as an object of worship. The semantics and pragmatics of the statement somehow combine to force only the single interpretation. The surface reversal is acceptable when the relative roles of topic and vehicle are unaffected by that reversal. The original topic remains an exemplar of the original vehicle category irrespective of surface ordering. Our God is assigned to the category of entities exemplified by the concept *mighty fortresses*, that is, things that provide protection against the ills of the world.

The general conclusion still holds. Reversing a metaphor reverses a class-inclusion statement. The same is true for metaphorical comparisons: a simile cannot be reversed just as a class-inclusion statement cannot be reversed. In the next section, we examine how this view of metaphors-as-categorizations provides the mechanism for distinguishing metaphoric comparisons from literal ones. Put simply, metaphoric comparisons involve items at different category levels and thus are implicit categorization statements. Recognizing a comparison as metaphorical involves the recognition that the comparison is intended as an implicit categorization.

Categorization as the source of metaphoricity in similes

Literal comparison statements typically involve objects at the same level of categorization, as in "harpsichords are like pianos." This statement cannot be paraphrased as "harpsichords are pianos." Similarly, when two objects differ in level of categorization, they cannot be literally likened to one another. One cannot sensibly say that "grand pianos are like pianos" or that "pianos are like musical instruments." Instead, the categorical relation must be expressed explicitly: "grand pianos are a type of piano"; "pianos are musical instruments." This is simply an extension of the observation made earlier, that a literal comparison statement cannot be paraphrased as a class-inclusion statement.

Metaphoric comparison statements do not obey these constraints. "Cigarettes are like time bombs," for example, can be paraphrased as the class-inclusion statement, "cigarettes are time bombs." In such class-inclusion statements, the predicate (metaphor vehicle) refers to a category that includes both the metaphor topic and the metaphor vehicle as exemplars, with the vehicle being a prototypical exemplar of that attributive category. In the metaphor, cigarettes are assigned to a category that is referred to as *time bombs,* with time bombs being a prototypical exemplar of the set of things that can abruptly cause serious damage at some unpredictable time in the future.

Metaphoric comparisons thus differ from literal comparisons in this central respect. They can be expressed as class-inclusion statements. They can be so expressed because, we suggest, that is what they are, implicit class-inclusion statements. This characteristic of metaphoric comparisons – that they are implicit class-inclusion statements – is a cue that people can use to identify metaphoricity.

The effect of hedges on metaphoricity. We have argued that a metaphoric comparison is actually an implicit class-inclusion assertion and that similes are identified as metaphorical because of this implicit categorization. It follows that the degree of metaphoricity of a statement should be a function of how strongly that statement suggests class inclusion. Therefore, hedges that affect the class-inclusion nature of a statement should affect its perceived metaphoricity.

The available data on this issue are sparse, but consistent. First, people can judge degree of metaphoricity reliably (Ortony, et al., 1985). Second, Ortony pointed out that judged metaphoricity of a comparison statement can be reduced by specifying a dimension of similarity, as in the statements "John's face was like a beet" versus the less metaphorical "John's face was red like a beet." Ortony interpreted this phenomenon in terms of salience imbalance. The original simile involves a match between a property that is not salient in the subject but salient in the predicate, redness. This constitutes a low-high property match, and because low-high matches typify metaphoric comparisons, the original simile is judged to be metaphorical. Specifying *redness* increases the salience of this property in the metaphor topic, *John,* and so converts the low-high match into a high-high match. "The result is a match of high-salient to high-salient attributes. Accordingly, judged metaphoricity should diminish from [the original simile to the now almost literal comparison]" (Ortony, 1979, p.170).

There are several problems with this interpretation. First, if specifying the color *red* makes the statement a high-high match, then it should make the statement reversible. Clearly, it does not. Second and more important, any such statements about *John* cannot involve a property-matching operation to begin with. A hearer's mental representation of John's face cannot have the property of *redness,* whether low- or high-salient, until the statement is perceived and understood. As Ortony himself pointed out, this is clearly a case of property *introduction,* not property matching as would be required by the salience imbalance model. Finally, the salience imbalance hypothesis cannot account for the systematic effect of hedges on perceived metaphoricity, as illustrated in the following statements:

    a. Cigarettes are literally time bombs.
    b. Cigarettes are time bombs.
    c. Cigarettes are virtual time bombs.
    d. Cigarettes are like time bombs.
    e. In certain respects, cigarettes are like time bombs.
    f. Cigarettes are deadly like time bombs.
    g. Cigarettes are as deadly as time bombs.

Statements *a* through *e* cannot vary in salience imbalance, yet they clearly vary in apparent metaphoricity, with *a* being most metaphorical, *e* least. Statements *f* and *g* are in fact literal: both cigarettes and time bombs can (and do), kill people.

What induces this gradation of metaphoricity? We would argue that the more a statement suggests a class-inclusion relation, the more metaphorical it will seem. Indeed, *a* to *c* have the surface form of class inclusion, and they seem more metaphorical than *d* to *g*, which are variants of a simile, with the surface form of a comparison. Black (this volume) captured this property of metaphors with his notion of "resonance" – the degree of implicative elaboration afforded by a metaphor. Strong metaphors provide a high degree of implicative elaboration; weak metaphors do not. Hedges, such as those illustrated above, reduce the degree of implicative elaboration, so should reduce resonance. In the extreme, a hedge that permits no implicative elaboration should transform a metaphor into a literal statement, and this is exactly what happens with such statements as *g,* above, "cigarettes are as deadly as time bombs."

Metaphor comprehensibility and aptness

Metaphors will be easily understood when the newly created classification is perceived as relevant and informative. Whether a classification is relevant and informative will depend on what a hearer already knows about any given metaphor topic, and whether the metaphor vehicle has salient properties that are diagnostic and relevant to that topic, as well as on the context of the utterance itself (Searle, this volume). Consider the statement "George Washington's dentists were butchers." Anyone who has been told the story of George Washington dying of a tooth infection caused by inept dental treatment should understand this metaphor with no difficulty whatsoever. The statement "George Washington's cobblers were butchers," in contrast, may be understood, but its relevance is obscure. With no prior knowledge of Washington's cobblers or their relative skills, we have no idea of precisely how they might have been butchers. They could even have been meat cutters in addition to being shoemakers. The statement about Washington's cobblers is ambiguous and thus difficult to interpret, although the proposition expressed by the sentence is apprehended. This is not different in principle from the comprehension problem posed by such statements as "dogs are animals," which is a true class-inclusion statement, but which also requires a communicative context for interpretation. Does the speaker want to inform the hearer that *dogs* belong to the category *animals* rather than *plants?* If so, why? Or, is the statement a comment on *dogs* that is intended to assert that dogs do not have humanlike traits and so should not be treated as we would treat people or children? Unless the relevance of a particular categorization is apparent, that categorization cannot be sensibly interpreted, whether it be conventional, as in ordinary taxonomic categorizations, or novel, as in newly created metaphors.

Beyond these general principles of discourse comprehension, the class-inclusion view of metaphors has specific implications for the role of the metaphor vehicle in metaphor comprehension: the vehicle's prototypicality is crucial for construing the category.

Vehicle prototypicality. Taxonomic categories have graded structure, with some members being more prototypical than others (Rosch, 1973). Apples, for example, are more typical of the category *fruits* than are blueberries. Functional categories created de novo also have graded structure (Barsalou, 1983). Yogurt, for example, is more prototypical of the category *foods to eat on a weight reduction diet* than are braised beet greens. Metaphoric categories, as a special case of newly created functional categories, should have graded structure as well. In the cigarette–time bomb metaphor, for example, *time bombs* would be a prototypical member of the category of things that can abruptly and unpredictably cause harm or injury some time in the future. Metaphor aptness may be a function of the prototypicality of a metaphor vehicle for a particular functional category. Consider the *time bomb* metaphor. Other things can also injure or kill at unpredictable times in the future, such as *strokes* and *airplane crashes.* Nevertheless, using either of these terms as the name for a category doesn't seem to work, as in "cigarettes are strokes" or "cigarettes are airplane crashes." One reason that these metaphors are not apt and also difficult to understand may be that neither *strokes* nor *airplane crashes* are prototypical members of the class of things that can suddenly cause harm.

Metaphor aptness may vary independently of metaphor comprehensibility and should be particularly sensitive to the typicality of the metaphor vehicle. In statements *a* through *d,* below, what is intended is easily understood, yet only the first seems apt:

    a. Not even Einstein's ideas were all gold.
    b. Not even Einstein's ideas were all platinum.
    c. Not even Einstein's ideas were all silver.
    d. Not even Einstein's ideas were all sapphires.

In each case, the meaning is clear: not all of Einstein's ideas were valuable. *Gold* is a prototypical member of the category of valuable, rare things; *platinum,* though more costly at times than *gold,* is not a typical member of that category, at least not in North American culture, and neither are *sapphires* or *silver.* The prototypicality of a metaphor vehicle may thus be one determinant of what Black (this volume) referred to as *emphasis* – the relative necessity of a particular metaphorical vehicle. Emphatic metaphors are, in general, more apt and usually more comprehensible than nonemphatic metaphors, as in the ideas–gold versus the ideas–platinum examples.

Many metaphor vehicles such as *butcher* and *gold* may be considered conventional vehicles for attributing properties to a topic of interest. Such conventional vehicles form part of the set described by Lakoff and Johnson as "metaphors we live by" (1980). These are metaphors that are conventional in a culture and that represent basic concepts such as love, time, communication, among many others. They are more systematic than the simple attributive metaphors we have discussed here, but they may follow the same principles. To say that a theory's foundation is crumbling implicitly acknowledges that the concept *theory* belongs to a category of *structures.* The particular *structure* category is specified by the exemplar–superordinate grouping of *theory* and *structure,* and it permits one to describe theories in terms of the appropriate parts of a structure. What parts of a metaphor vehicle category are appropriate?

Parts of objects vary in "goodness" (Tversky & Hemenway, 1984). Good parts are those that are functionally significant and often perceptually salient. The *wing* of an airplane is a good part, the *floor* of an airplane is not. This concept of part goodness is theoretically analogous to the concept of prototypicality or goodness of a category member, and so the goodness of a part may, for this purpose, be analogous to the prototypicality of a metaphor vehicle in simple nominative metaphors. This suggests that for the conceptual metaphor of *theories as structures,* some parts of *structures* should be more apt than others for describing *theories,* specifically, good parts. *Foundations, walls,* and *plumbing* may be "good" parts vis-à-vis the concept *structure* as it applies to *theories.* The parts *chimney, window,* and *corner* may be poor parts because their functional roles in the structure of a theory may not be important or salient.

In general, then, prototypical members of metaphorical categories should produce highly comprehensible and apt metaphors. Similarly, when a metaphor is systematic and has parts that may be functionally relevant to that metaphor, "good" parts should produce more comprehensible and more apt metaphors than less good parts. Examples discussed by Lakoff and Johnson (1980), including the *theory as structure* metaphor, are consistent with this hypothesis.

Why people use metaphors

Metaphors are generally used to describe something new by reference to something familiar (Black, 1962b), not just in conversation, but in such diverse areas as science (Gentner, 1982; this volume) and psychotherapy (Rothenberg, 1984). And, as Ortony (1975) argued, metaphors are not just nice, they are necessary. They are necessary for casting abstract concepts in terms of the apprehendable, as we do, for example, when we metaphorically extend spatial concepts and spatial terms to the realm of temporal concepts and temporal terms. All English words for temporal relations are derived from words that referred originally to spatial relations: *then* (from *thence*) and *when* (from *whence*) are two common examples of "dead" metaphors that were once transparently spatial terms (Traugott, 1985). This usage reflects our conception of time in terms of a unidimensional space, a timeline that extends ahead of us into the future and behind us into (or from) the past (Clark, 1973; Traugott, 1978).

Although the conceptual functions of metaphors are beyond the scope of this essay, the communicative and discourse functions are central. Any model of similarity presupposes the principle of relevance and diagnosticity: only those features of similarity that are relevant to a particular context will be involved in any particular comparison (Tversky, 1977). A model of classification must presuppose the same principles for the same reason that models of similarity do: both similarity and classification are, in isolation, unconstrained. Any two things are always alike in some way. Similarly, "there is always some category to which two terms belong" (Tourangeau & Sternberg, 1981, p. 28). For this reason, Tourangeau and Sternberg summarily reject both similarity and categorization models of metaphor comprehension. On either the similarity or categorization view, "there is not always some reasonable interpretation of a metaphor" (p. 28).

This is unarguable, just as there is not always some reasonable interpretation of a nonmetaphorical similarity statement or categorization statement. As we saw with the statement "dogs are animals," even true "literal" categorizations are uninterpretable without relevant contextual information. Principles of discourse are equally necessary for literal and nonliteral language comprehension, including principles of the kind proposed by Grice (1975) for conversations. For present purposes, we can assume that such principles operate in ways that make extraction of relevant properties possible, both for comparisons such as similes, and for categorizations as exemplified by nominative metaphors. The issue is not the comprehensibility of similes and metaphors per se, but why people would choose to use a metaphor – a class-inclusion statement – instead of a simile – a similarity statement.

Consider the problem of describing a particular actor named Xiao-Dong to a friend who has never seen him. The actor performs in the Chinese theater, typically playing roles that portray lurid characters, often of a supernatural nature, who do evil and macabre deeds, are often unctuous, sneaky, and generally eerie. If the speaker can assume that the hearer is familiar with American movies (can assume relevant mutual knowledge: Clark & Marshall, 1981) then he or she can use the metaphor, "Xiao-Dong is a Bela Lugosi." This provides not just one property of the Chinese actor, but a patterned complex of properties in one chunk: all those properties that Bela Lugosi, the quintessential player of Dracula and other vampirelike creatures, exemplifies. In Black's (this volume) terms, the metaphor provides a high degree of implicative elaboration. The simile form of this metaphor, "he is like a Bela Lugosi," does not quite capture the force of the metaphor, perhaps because the explicit "like" suggests that only some properties of the category "a Bela Lugosi" are to be applied to Xiao-Dong.

The clear implication that the properties of a metaphor-induced category are intended can thus be tempered by the simile form. Recall the striking example of Demjanjuk's name being used as a name for *an ordinary person capable of committing unspeakable acts* (Shinoff, 1987). To describe a person as *like Demjanjuk* is not nearly so forceful as identifying that person as *a Demjanjuk*. It may well be that people use metaphors instead of similes when such attributions are intended, and only use similes when they want to hedge or qualify the underlying metaphors.

A second possible function of metaphors, as compared with literal comparisons, is to alert a hearer that a specific relation is intended, not a more general assertion of similarity. The simile that likens an actor to Bela Lugosi can be transformed into a literal comparison by omitting the article, as in "he is like Bela Lugosi." Here, the comparison is with Bela Lugosi – with the individual. The two actors can be likened along a number of different dimensions, depending on how they are implicitly classified: gender, income level, height, acting style, and so forth. The literal comparison statement does not indicate which of these classifications is intended. Thus, the reader is not constrained to a specific interpretation. Each of these dimensions can contribute to the similarity between them. In contrast, the metaphorical comparison does suggest a specific grouping – Xiao-Dong is likened to *a* Bela Lugosi, or to the type of actor best exemplified by Bela Lugosi. As a result, Xiao-Dong takes on all the properties of this *type* of actor, not of the actor Bela Lugosi himself.

The crucial difference between similes and metaphors thus stems from the communicative function of metaphors. Metaphors are used to communicate a complex patterned set of properties in a shorthand that is understood by the members of a speech community who share relevant mutual knowledge. When I say that "my job is a jail," I communicate all those properties of the attributive category *jail* with that statement. I need not – indeed, I probably could not – list each of those properties exhaustively. In this way, the use of the metaphor is more efficent and precise than a partial listing of those properties that the attributive category name *jail* both denotes and connotes. If the attribution of all such properties is the communicative purpose, then the appropriate communicative form is the metaphor.

Conclusions

Aristotle (1952a) is the source of the comparison view of metaphor, as well as of the view that the topic and vehicle of a metaphor may belong to the same category. Contemporary theorists share this general view and treat comparison as the basic process underlying metaphor comprehension. George Miller (this volume), in perhaps the most well articulated development of this view, argues that metaphors are recognized as false and then treated as comparison statements: " 'man is a wolf' is false in fact. In order to understand it, the reader must associate it with 'Man is like a wolf' or, even weaker, 'Man seems like a wolf' (to the author)." Miller concludes that "the grounds for a metaphor . . . can be formulated as relations of similitude that can be expressed as comparison statements."

We have argued exactly the opposite case. Metaphors are not understood by transforming them into similes. Instead they are intended as class-inclusion statements and are understood as such. When metaphors are expressed as comparisons, that is, as similes, they are interpreted as implicit category statements, rather than the other way around. The grouping that is created by the metaphor induces the similarity relation, and so the grouping is prior.

This view of nominative metaphors, together with appropriate rules of discourse, provides a principled account of the following metaphor phenomena that have heretofore remained unexplained:

1. Metaphoric comparisons – two unlike things compared – can be expressed as class inclusion statements. Literal comparisons – two like things compared – cannot. This follows directly from the view of metaphoric comparisons as implicit class-inclusion statements.
2. Metaphoric comparisons are recognized as such because they involve a comparison between category levels in an assumed hierarchy. The categorization nature of the comparison is the cue to metaphoricity.
3. Metaphors, whether in canonical class-inclusion form or simile form, do not retain the same meaning when reversed. They are nonreversible because metaphors express class-inclusion relations that are in principle not symmetrical.
4. Hedges and specification of the grounds for similarity of a metaphor reduce perceived metaphoricity. These effects follow from the class-inclusion nature of metaphors. The canonical metaphor explicitly expresses an unqualified class-inclusion relation. Anything that qualifies the class-inclusion character or reduces its scope will reduce metaphoricity.
5. The simile, perhaps used as a qualifier or hedge, potentially poses a more difficult comprehension problem for a hearer. Hearers must recognize that the comparison is between levels of an assumed category and then treat the simile as an implicit categorization. This requirement may impose an additional cognitive burden on a hearer. If so, similes may be more difficult to understand than their corresponding metaphors because similes do not express the class-inclusion relation explicitly.

We have focused exclusively on nominative metaphor, but the account can be extended in principle to another important class of conversational metaphor, predicative metaphor. Predicative metaphors employ verbs in novel ways, as in "she hopped on her bike and flew home." In this case, the term *flew* can be construed to include the category of actions that are swift and direct. Flying can be considered a prototypical action in that category, and so the verb "to fly" can be used to refer to any action that belongs to that category. On this suggested analysis, action categories behave as do object categories and verbs can be used in the same way nouns can: to label categories that have no conventional names. A more detailed analysis of such metaphors must await further investigation of action categories.

Finally, a word of qualification. Our account of metaphors as categorizations that create new, relevant, and useful groupings simply recasts the problem of how people come to understand metaphors. It does not solve that problem, but does outline what an adequate psychological model might look like. Such a model of metaphor comprehension will have to include general principles of discourse comprehension, such as Grice's cooperative principle and the given-new convention, as well as the more specific principles of conversational interaction and inference discussed by Searle (this volume).

NOTES

We are grateful for the financial support provided by the National Science Foundation, grant No. BNS8819657, and by the Public Health Service, grant No. HD25826-01, and to Princeton University. Portions of this essay appeared in an earlier paper published in the *Psychological Review* (Glucksberg & Keysar, 1990).
1 One might argue that the word "animal" in the sense of being stereotypically animalistic has already become common in current American English. The *Random House Dictionary of the English Language* lists, as one sense of "animal," "an inhuman person; brutish or beast-like person, as in *She married an animal.*"
2 This usage is reminiscent of how English speakers treat metaphoric expressions. In "my job is a jail," the jail is not considered to be a "real" jail.

19

Metaphor and irony: Two levels of understanding

ELLEN WINNER AND HOWARD GARDNER

In defense of the literal–nonliteral distinction

Speakers often do not say what they mean. Both literal and nonliteral utterances require the listener to go beyond what is said to infer what is meant. Even the most literal of utterances is meant to convey unstated implications. To state (truthfully) that it is raining can mean not only that it is raining but also (depending on the context) (*a*) "Take your umbrella," (*b*) "The picnic is off," (*c*) "I told you so," and so forth. Despite the fact that these meanings are unstated, they are usually effortlessly apprehended, and conversataion typically proceeds thereafter in seamless fashion. A multitude of cues enables the listener to infer what is meant.

Since in both literal and nonliteral discourse speakers invariably mean more than they say, the distinction between literal and nonliteral usage cannot rest on whether the speaker says what is meant. Instead, the distinction rests on the reverse – whether the speaker means what is said (Searle, this volume). In literal discourse, speakers mean what they say *and more*. In nonliteral discourse, speakers do not mean what they say. Hence, what is said must be used but discounted in the interpretation process.[1]

In addition, the distinction between literal and nonliteral discourse in our view rests on the *relation* between what is said and what is meant. In literal utterances this relation is one of *consonance:* the implied meanings are consistent with the sentence meaning though they may range far afield from the actual statement, as in (*b*) and (*c*) above. In nonliteral utterances, the relation is one of *dissonance*. That the stated and implied meanings of nonliteral utterances diverge sharply follows from the claim that speakers of nonliteral utterances do not mean what they say.

Languages feature many ways of using words nonliterally (Gibbs, this volume). In all languages, however, the two major modes of nonliteral discourse are probably metaphor and irony. Both these forms of discourse pervade ordinary conversation (Booth, 1974; Lakoff & Johnson, 1980). In this chapter, we consider metaphor and irony together in order to determine the extent to which they work by common principles – as one might expect since both are instances of nonliteral language – and the extent to which they pose different comprehension challenges.

Two levels of understanding

As we show below, the ability to understand metaphor and irony is not an all or nothing affair. We distinguish two levels of understanding of nonliteral utterances. On one level, the listener must infer, or "pick up," the speaker's meaning. We refer to this level as that of *interpretation*. The interpretive level of understanding is the level typically studied in psychological research on the comprehension of nonliteral language (Ackerman, 1981; Demorest, Meyer, Phelps, Gardner, & Winner, 1984; Dent, 1984; Gibbs, 1984; Keil, 1986; Vosniadou, 1987; Winner, Rosenstiel, & Gardner, 1976). When listeners can demonstrate by some response (recognition, production, or some nonverbal measure) that they have gleaned the appropriate speaker meaning, they can be credited with having achieved adequate interpretation of the utterance.

On logical grounds, grasping the speaker's meaning is necessary, but not sufficient, for full understanding of nonliteral utterances. If interpreting the speaker's meaning is all there is to understanding nonliteral language, the listener hears right through the sentence meaning to the speaker meaning. Under these circumstances, nonliteral utterances function no differently from their literal equivalents.

For this reason we have come to believe that full comprehension of nonliteral utterances requires not only interpretation but also *metalinguistic awareness*. At this level, comprehension entails not only constructing the speaker's meaning, but also keeping in mind the literal sentence meaning and hearing the contrast between what is *said* and what is *meant* (Olson & Hildyard, 1983). Only with metalinguistic awareness does the listener recognize and appreciate the metaphoricity or irony of the nonliteral utterance. Only at this level do nonliteral utterances *feel* different (and hence function differently) from literal ones. Whether the two levels of comprehension always entail each other, or whether it is possible to attain one without the other, is an empirical question.

We do not mean that in a nonliteral utterance the speaker's meaning is *processed* differently from that of a literal utterance (Gibbs, 1984; this volume; Glucksberg, Gildea, & Bookin, 1982; Rumelhart, this volume). Rather, nonliteral utterances differ from literal utterances in their effect because the listener not only grasps the speaker's meaning but also *marks* the utterance as a special form of speech. (Gibbs, this volume, makes a similar distinction between the process and the product of comprehension, or between comprehension and recognition.) Full comprehension of nonliteral utterances entails not only inferring the speaker's meaning but also hearing the nonliteral utterances as different from just "plain talk" (Olson, 1988).

Four questions

In this chapter we will explore four questions about the abilities required for understanding metaphor and irony. First, what underlying abilities constrain and make possible metaphor comprehension at the interpretive level? Second, do these abilities differ from those that allow irony interpretation? Third, is the ability to recognize a distinction between what is said and what is meant a unitary ability that cuts across metaphor and irony? And finally, what is the relationship between metalinguistic awareness and interpretive understanding? Can metalinguistic awareness be a route to interpretive understanding or must it always follow interpretation?

There is more than one way to gain evidence to answer these questions. A particularly powerful method is to take a developmental approach. If metaphor and irony interpretation emerge on different developmental timetables, and if one can demonstrate that each form is related to a different set of cognitive competencies, one gains strong evidence that the two forms of understanding are constrained by different underlying abilities. If awareness at the metalinguistic level emerges at the same time for metaphor and irony, we gain evidence that metalinguistic awareness is a more general skill that operates independently of utterance type. And our final question is best asked using subjects who may not have acquired both levels of understanding (i.e., young children). Only in this way can we determine whether metalinguistic awareness can occur in the absence of an appropriate interpretation, or the reverse.

We will argue that metaphor interpretation is constrained *only* by the listener's domain knowledge. That is, there are no inherent limits on the kinds of similarities children can perceive. All that is necessary to interpret a metaphor is sufficient knowledge of the domains involved. In contrast, we will suggest that irony interpretation is made possible by the ability to infer other people's beliefs, and their beliefs about beliefs. That is, irony comprehension is constrained by one's "theory of mind" (Astington, Harris, & Olson, 1988; Wellman, 1990). Because children's theory of mind develops later than their domain knowledge the ability to understand irony is a later developing skill than the ability to understand metaphor.

With respect to the metalinguistic level, we will try to show that metaphor poses no less a challenge than irony, and children become aware of metaphor and irony as different from ordinary speech at about the same age – between six and seven. The relation between interpretation and metalinguistic awareness differs for metaphor and irony, however. In the case of difficult metaphors, one can be aware of the utterance as nonliteral yet not interpret it correctly; for irony, awareness of the utterance as ironic automatically *entails* a (roughly) correct interpretation of the speaker's meaning.

Metaphor and irony compared

Structure

At a general level, metaphor and irony have a common structure. Both are based on an opposition at the pragmatic level: what the speaker *says* is intentionally at odds with the way the speaker knows the world to be. However, it is in the *relationship* between what is said and what is believed and meant that metaphor and irony diverge in structure.

In metaphor, the relation between what is said and what is meant is one of similarity, whether this similarity is preexisting or created by the metaphor. In a metaphor, domains are juxtaposed and properties of the vehicle domain are attributed to the topic domain on the basis of some form of perceived resemblance. When we describe someone's mind as razor sharp, the razor's property of precision is attributed to the person's mind, and we interpret this to mean that the person has a precise, logical mind, whether interpretation involves mapping properties of the vehicle onto the topic (Ortony, this volume), or whether it involves conceiving of minds as belonging to the category of razor-sharp objects (Glucksberg & Keysar, this volume).

In irony, the relation between what is said and meant is one of opposition: the speaker conveys a negative attitude toward something by professing to have a positive attitude (Clark & Gerrig, 1984). When a waiter spills soup on a diner's suit, and the diner says, "oh, wonderful," he conveys not pleasure but displeasure. We shall exploit this structural difference between irony and metaphor to explain why metalinguistic awareness entails interpretation for irony but not for metaphor.

Communicative function

Metaphor and irony differ not only in structure but also in their communicative functions. Metaphor functions primarily to *describe,* and hence to clarify or explain. To show something in a new light (Gardner & Winner, 1986), it describes something new by referring to something old (Black, 1962a). For example, the by now often used mind–computer metaphor functions to describe and highlight certain properties of mind that may not have been previously noted. When metaphors are heard again and again, their novelty is lost, but novel metaphors always function to show the listener something in a new way. In addition, a metaphor is often the only way of communicating precisely and efficiently what one means. Hence, as Ortony (1975) has put it, metaphors are necessary and not just nice.

By contrast, the primary function of irony is not to describe something in the world, but to *show* something about the speaker. Irony functions to show the speaker's attitude toward something, and that attitude is almost always critical (Gibbs, this volume). The diner's comment, "oh wonderful," functions to express displeasure toward the waiter. Speakers can convey a negative attitude directly through literal discourse. The diner might have said, "oh, this is maddening!" A literal remark, however, is rarely if ever equivalent to an ironic one, because the choice of irony carries with it particular social effects. The ironist is perceived as being a certain kind of person – wittier, less confrontational, and more in control, than the utterer of a literal expression of displeasure (Dews, Kaplan, & Winner, 1992). The achievement of these side effects may be one of the primary determinants for a choice of irony over literal discourse.

Thus, metaphor functions to describe, to explain something in a particularly apt, memorable, and new way. In contrast, irony functions to show the speaker's evaluative attitude and, as a by-product, to show the kind of person the speaker is – one who can criticize indirectly, without emotional involvement. Although metaphor and irony may realize one another's communicative functions peripherally, their *primary* functions diverge in the above respects.

Comprehension demands

We have argued thus far that metaphor and irony differ in both structure and function. We now argue that because of these differences, metaphor and irony make different comprehension demands on the listener. To understand a metaphor's implied meaning, one must have enough knowledge about the topic and vehicle domains to discover a similarity between topic and vehicle (Keil, 1986). We refer to the possession of domain knowledge as having a "theory of matter" (Carey, 1985a). The recognition of some form of topic–vehicle similarity is *always* necessary for metaphor comprehension, whether one conceives of metaphors as implicit comparisons based on existent similarities (Miller, this volume; Ortony, 1979; Tversky, 1977), as topic–vehicle interactions (Black, 1962a; this volume), or as classinclusion assertions by which we construct similarities not previously recognized (Glucksberg & Keysar, 1990; this volume).

To understand the meaning of an ironic utterance requires, we suggest, a different set of competencies. What is necessary for irony is the ability to make inferences about the speaker's state of mind. In particular, listeners must be able to determine that ironic speakers do not *believe* what they say (and thus that they are not uttering unintentional falsehoods). Listeners must also be able to determine that ironic speakers do not want their listeners to believe their (literal) words (and thus that they are not uttering falsehoods to deceive). Mistaking irony for error or deception are the two pitfalls listeners face when confronted with irony. Thus, to understand irony's implied meaning, one is better off equipped with a theory of mind than a theory of matter.

As an illustration, consider a speaker who looks out the window, sees ominous clouds, and says, "nice day for our picnic." This is a false statement: it is *not* a nice day for a picnic. To avoid taking this falsehood as a mistake (the speaker did not *see* the clouds), one must infer what the speaker actually believes, that he saw the clouds and believes it to be a bad picnic day. To avoid taking irony as deception (the speaker is trying to *convince* someone that it is a fine day), one must infer what the speaker wishes the listener to believe – that it is *not* a fine day.

Because understanding irony requires the ability to reason about others' beliefs and intentions, we suggest that irony comprehension requires a theory of mind. In a very general sense all language understanding requires some ability to think about other minds. If communication is to proceed, one must infer the assumptions one shares with the speaker (Clark, 1983; Gibbs, this volume) and in the case of nonliteral language of any kind, one must recognize that the speaker intends to convey something other than what is said. But irony requires more than this. Because irony out of context is indistinguishable from error or deception the listener needs to make specific inferences about the speaker's beliefs and intentions.

Thus, understanding metaphor and irony rests on very different kinds of knowledge and skills. Knowledge of the construction/ontology of the world and the ability to map properties from one domain to another are the key skills for metaphor. The ability to make inferences about other people's beliefs, and about their intentions, is required for irony. Table 19.1 summarizes the distinctions we have set forth between metaphor and irony. We now turn to some of the evidence supporting these claims.

Interpreting metaphor

There is strong evidence that children can understand metaphors as early as they can be tested, providing only that they have sufficient knowledge of the domains on which the metaphors are based. Initial studies, however, have suggested that children could not understand metaphor – that is, could not grasp the speaker's implied meaning – until late childhood. For example, Piaget (1974) found that children as old as eleven could not explain proverbs, which led to the suggestion that the ability to understand metaphor may require the structures of formal operational thought (In-

Table 19.1. *Structural and functional distinction between metaphor and irony*

	Metaphor	Irony
Relation between sentence/speaker meaning	Similarity	Opposition
Communicative function	To *describe* or explain something about the world in a memorable, efficient, new way	To *show* the speaker's critical attitude and the kind of person the speaker is by virtue of choosing irony over literal criticism: witty, distanced, cool
Competencies required for interpretation	Ontological, domain knowledge; ability to map properties from one domain to another	Ability to make first- and second-order inferences about others' beliefs and intentions
Competencies required for metalinguistic awareness	Ability to recognize distinction between say/mean	Ability to recognize distinction between say/mean
Relation between interpretation and metalinguistic awareness	Interpretation can exist without metalinguistic awareness. Metalinguistic awareness can occur without adequate interpretation	Interpretation can exist without metalinguistic awareness, but metalinguistic awareness entails interpretative understanding

helder & Piaget, 1958; see also Elkind, 1969; Pollio & Pollio, 1974). Studies carried out in the 1960s and 1970s seemed to confirm metaphor comprehension as one of the last forms of language skills to emerge (Asch & Nerlove, 1960; Winner, Rosenstiel, & Gardner, 1976).

Three aspects of these early studies account for children's comprehension failure. First, the metaphors were sentences out of context. Tasks that require interpretations generated with no context reveal the kinds of similarities children *generate* on their own. But presentation of metaphors in context reveals the kinds of similarities children *recognize* (Ortony, Reynolds, & Arter, 1978; Winner, Wapner, Cicone, & Gardner, 1979). Naturally, therefore, the presentation of metaphors in context lowers the age at which comprehension is revealed (Ortony, et al., 1978; Vosniadou, 1987).

Second, comprehension was judged by the ability to generate verbal explanations of each sentence. The greater the reliance on such linguistic measures, the more likely is the measure to fail to reveal an adequate interpretation. The use of multiple choice or nonverbal matching measures has revealed comprehension in children at the very early stages of language acquisition (Dent, 1984; Gardner, 1974; Kogan, Connor, Gross, & Fava,

1980; Marks, Hammeal, & Bornstein, 1987; Vosniadou, Ortony, Reynolds, & Wilson, 1984; Winner, McCarthy, & Gardner, 1980; Winner, Wapner, Cicone, & Gardner, 1979).

The above two factors (context-free presentation and reliance on a linguistic comprehension measure) have to do with the *way* the tasks are presented. The third factor has to do with the *kinds* of metaphors presented. Metaphors can be based on one or both of two broad classes of similarity: (*a*) perceptual, surface similarity and (*b*) nonperceptual, deep similarity (cf. Vosniadou & Ortony, 1989, and Gentner, 1989, who make a similar distinction between similarities based on object attributes versus relational properties).[2]

Perceptual metaphors link objects that share noticeable, physical properties (e.g., "her cheeks were roses"). Here, the physical property of a rose's redness is mapped onto a person's cheeks. Nonperceptual metaphors are based on relational similarities that cannot be apprehended by our senses. Such metaphors are based on similarities between objects, situations, or events that are physically dissimilar but, often owing to parallel internal structures, function in a similar way. Thus, when we speak of the mind as a computer, we map the computer's property of being a (serial or parallel) processor of information onto the domain of minds. Psychological–physical metaphors, in which physical attributes are used to refer to psychological states, are an interesting and commonly used kind of nonperceptual metaphor. When we call a person hard or slimy or inflexible, we attribute to mental states and personality traits properties literally true only of physical objects.

The metaphors used in the early studies were based on nonperceptual forms of similarity. For example, Winner, Rosenstiel, and Gardner (1976) tested comprehension of psychological–physical metaphors such as "after many years of working at the jail, the prison guard had become a hard rock that could not be moved." Had the metaphors been perceptual ones, comprehension would have been found at a considerably earlier age. We base this claim on several studies comparing comprehension of perceptual and nonperceptual metaphors. For example, Gentner and Stuart (1983) asked children to paraphrase perceptual metaphors, called "attribute" metaphors in their study (e.g., cloud = marshmallow), relational metaphors (e.g., tree bark = skin), and metaphors based on both kinds of similarities (e.g., plant stems = drinking straws). *Despite* the lack of context and the linguistic response mode, five-year-olds performed as well as adults when asked to explain the similarity underlying the perceptual metaphors. These children offered fewer relational interpretations for the relational metaphors than did older children, however. Apparently they had more difficulty perceiving (or at least explaining) relational than perceptual similarities. Gentner (1989) has thus argued for a shift in focus from object attributes to relational properties of objects.

Other studies have also reported greater difficulty with nonperceptual than perceptual metaphors: six-year-olds were better able to choose endings for similes based on perceptual than nonperceptual grounds (Mendelsohn, Gardner, & Winner, 1981); and although kindergarten-age children distinguished perceptual metaphors from anomalies, they had considerably more difficulty with some forms of nonperceptual metaphors (Shantiris, 1983).

There are at least two reasons why children may seem to understand perceptual metaphors before nonperceptual ones (Winner, 1988). One possibility is that children's abilities to juxtapose domains and perceive similarities between these domains are not fully developed. Such lack of development limits the kinds of grounds they can perceive. The types of similarities that children cannot yet perceive should thus predict the types of metaphors that will be misinterpreted. On this account, children cannot understand what it means to call a person a hard rock because they do not have the ability to perceive the kinds of nonperceptual similarities between physical hardness and lack of emotional warmth.

Alternatively, metaphor comprehension may be constrained not by immature similarity perception skills but only by an incomplete knowledge of the domains involved. Metaphor comprehension requires a recognition that things in the world are classified into separate domains, that is, into the familiar categories of daily experience. Children must be able to make a preliminary delineation of the contents of these domains (e.g., inanimate matter, living matter, physical matter, mental matter), their physical appearance, internal structure, boundaries, and functioning. On this account, there are no inherent limits to the kinds of similarities children can construct. All that is necessary to map the appropriate vehicle properties onto the topic domain is sufficient *knowledge* about the domains involved. Failure to understand a nonperceptual metaphor would thus be due not to an inability to perceive nonperceptual similarity, but to insufficient knowledge about one or both of the domains on which the metaphor is based.

If children fail to understand because they lack the ability to perceive certain types of similarities, it is metaphoric ability per se that is incomplete. But if children fail only because they lack sufficient knowledge of topic and/or vehicle domains, it is domain knowledge and not metaphoric ability that is incomplete. To decide between these two alternatives, we must address what is known about children's abilities to perceive the kinds of similarities underlying nonperceptual metaphors.

There is compelling evidence in favor of the second hypothesis. Very young children can, in fact, perceive nonperceptual similarities. Evidence comes from lexical overextensions which are often based on nonperceptual similarities (Bowerman, 1977; Nelson, 1974), and from classification studies. For instance, one-year-olds prove sensitive to superordinate categories such as furniture, food, and animals even though the members of these categories are physically dissimilar (Ross, 1980). And infants appreciate the numerical equivalence of small arrays even when the physical arrays are dissimilar (Starkey, Gelman, & Spelke, 1983).

In addition, evidence from spontaneous speech suggests that children as young as three and four can understand nonperceptual metaphoric grounds. (Children below this age have not been tested.) Although the first metaphors that children produce tend to be primarily perceptual ones (Winner, 1979), nonperceptual grounds have also been noted. Gentner and Stuart (1983) report a three-year-old who described a new blanket as "full of gas" and a worn-out blanket as "out of gas." The four-year-old daughter of a friend of ours remarked on the similarity between a sympathetic physical pain (her mother had said her arm hurt when she watched her daughter get a shot) and a feeling of empathy for another person's sadness (the child had felt sad for her grandmother when the grandmother was sad). And another four-year-old, whose father had just died, seemed to gain insight into the irreversibility of death when a balloon she was holding soared forever out of reach, prompting her to sob for her father (Moore, 1986; see also Crisafi & Brown, 1983; Gentner, 1977; Holyoak, Junn, & Billman, 1984). There is thus no reason to conclude that a failure in metaphor comprehension is due to an inherent inability to perceive certain classes of similarities.

If preschoolers have the ability to perceive nonperceptual similarity, how can we explain the results of studies showing that perceptual metaphors are easier to understand than at least some kinds of nonperceptual metaphors? The most reasonable explanation is that difficulty in understanding nonperceptual metaphors has to do with lack of knowledge of the internal workings of things in the world. One does not need knowledge of the internal workings of things to understand most perceptual metaphors because these are based on surface similarities (shape, color, etc.). But to understand nonperceptual metaphors, one needs information about the domains that cannot be obtained through perception. For instance, to understand how plant stems can be like drinking straws, one must know that stems draw water up from the ground. One cannot know this from observation. Thus, comprehension of nonperceptual grounds is more difficult to demonstrate in young children than is comprehension of perceptual mappings only because the former often requires knowledge that must be acquired through experience, explanation, and exploration, rather than knowledge which is manifest to perception alone.

To test further the conclusion that problems in metaphor comprehension are the result only of limited domain knowledge, one would need to use nonperceptual metaphors based on domains highly familiar to young children (e.g., friends = magnets). And, indeed, when knowledge deficits do not intrude, children demonstrate no difficulty in understanding nonperceptual metaphors (Keil, 1986). For example, although five-year-olds could not understand nonperceptual metaphors ascribing physical properties to ideas (the idea bloomed/wilted/was planted), they had no difficulty with equally nonperceptual metaphors ascribing animate properties to cars (the car was thirsty/dead/lazy).

Further support for the "domain knowledge" explanation comes from evidence that the relative difficulty of types of metaphors is related to the order in which children acquire knowledge of different domains (Keil, 1986), or, in our terms, by the state of the child's theory of matter. For example, the distinction between animate and inanimate objects is mastered considerably earlier than that between abstract and physical objects (Carey, 1985a; Gelman & Spelke, 1981; Keil, 1979). It turns out that this order of domain distinctions predicts the developmental order in which different kinds of metaphors are correctly interpreted (Keil, 1986). Metaphors ascribing animate terms to cars were the earliest to be understood, whereas those ascribing physical object properties to ideas were grasped considerably later. We can thus understand why children have no difficulty making sense of metaphors such as "the car is dead," but have considerable difficulty with ones such as "the idea was planted." In the former, the distinction bridged is one that the child has mastered; in the latter, the distinction bridged is one not yet acquired.

The kinds of errors children make when interpreting metaphor also provide evidence for the kinds of competencies required for comprehension. When children misinterpret metaphors, they rarely take them as literally true statements (Winner et al., 1976). Nor do they take them as literal falsehoods (errors or lies). Rather, they typically derive a nonliteral meaning, that is, a meaning different from the sentence meaning. The meaning derived shows that children realize the speaker means something different from what was said. They use similarity in their interpretations, but fail to locate the intended similarity on which the metaphor is based. Thus, for example, six-year-olds typically interpret psychological–physical metaphors such as "the prison guard had become a hard rock" to mean he had strong muscles rather than that he was unfeeling. As we will see, when confronted with irony, young children make very different kinds of misinterpretations: they do not recognize that the speaker means to convey something other than what was said, and they take the utterance as some form of literal falsehood.

Thus, the problem for children in understanding metaphor is to zero in on precisely the kind of similarity linking the sentence and speaker meaning, and this means they must be able to perceive the similarity between the domains involved. Given what we know about infants' classification abilities, there is reason to believe that the ability to perceive similarities between domains does not develop but is present from the start.[3] What does develop, instead, is an increasingly articulated theory of matter – knowledge about more domains and more knowledge about particular domains that may be involved in a metaphor (their internal structures and their boundaries). As children's theories of matter grow, so also does the range of metaphors accessible to their understanding. Hence, there are no inherent limits on the child's potential to understand metaphor. The only limits are on the child's potential to understand *specific* metaphors.[4]

Interpreting irony

The comprehension demands posed by irony are very different from those posed by metaphor. There are empirical reasons for believing that irony understanding rests on the ability to attribute both first- and second-order beliefs and intentions to other minds (Perner & Wimmer, 1985; Wimmer & Perner, 1983). The term "first-order" belief refers to a belief about the world. Thus, recognizing that Sam believes it to be raining is to impute a first-order belief to Sam. A second-order belief refers to a belief about another person's belief state. Thus, recognizing that Sam believes Mary does not know it is raining is to attribute a second-order belief to Sam. Although children of three or four can attribute first-order beliefs that differ from their own beliefs (Hala, Chandler, & Fritz, 1991; Sullivan & Winner, 1991; Wellman, 1990; Wimmer & Perner, 1983), the ability to conceptualize second-order beliefs (that differ from their own) has not been demonstrated before the age of six (Perner & Wimmer, 1985).

The timing of the emergence of irony understanding, and the kinds of errors made by children in interpreting irony, lead us to claim that successful irony interpretation rests on the attribution of first- and second-order mental states. The ability to interpret irony correctly seems to emerge at about the same age as does second-order belief understanding. Confronted with an ironic utterance, in which the speaker says something positive to convey something negative, children under the age of six or seven typically miss the point (Ackerman, 1981).

For example, in one study (Demorest et al., 1984), we read children a story about a boy, Jay, who gets a very uneven haircut. On leaving the barbershop, he runs into a friend, Mike, who points at him and says, in mocking intonation, "your haircut looks terrific." We determined whether children knew that the haircut was in fact bad, that Mike believed it to be bad, and that Mike wanted Jay to feel that his haircut was bad. If children thought the haircut was bad but that Mike wrongly believed it to be good, they showed that they interpreted Mike's utterance as an error. If children thought the cut was bad, that Mike knew it was bad, and that Mike wanted Jay to feel it was good, they showed that they took Mike's utterance as a white lie. Only if children thought that Mike knew the haircut was bad and wanted Jay to know this could they be credited with taking the remark as ironic.

Surprisingly, children failed to take this remark as ironic until the age of eight or nine. Sometimes they took the utterance as literally true and

believed that the haircut was in fact good, ignoring the information provided that it was bad. Such literal interpretations were made by six-year-
olds. More commonly, they took the utterance as literal but false. They
believed that the haircut was in fact bad but either said that Mike mistakenly thought it was good, or (most commonly) that Mike knew it was bad
but pretended it was good. In other words, children under eight or nine
typically took the irony as a mistake or as a white lie. When they took the
utterance as a mistake, they heard the falsehood but missed the intentionality. When they took the utterance as a white lie, they heard the
falsehood and the intentionality of the falsehood, but missed the speaker's
communicative intent. Because the most common error was to take the
irony as a white lie, the stumbling block to comprehension appears to be
grasping the speaker's communicative intent – that is, that the speaker
does not want the listener to believe what is said.

When the task is simplified, children can distinguish irony from deception and error by six, but not before this age. For example, we reduced
memory demands (instead of listening to a story, children witnessed an
interaction between two people ending in an ironic remark) and simplified
the response measures (instead of responding to the above three questions,
children simply classified each remark as either a mistake, a lie, or teasing)
(Winner, Windmueller, Rosenblatt, Bosco, & Best, 1987). Even under
these conditions, children could not understand irony before age six.

The kinds of errors made in interpreting irony indicate that understanding irony rests on the ability to infer the speaker's actual beliefs (to avoid
taking the remark as a mistake) and the ability to infer the speaker's
intentions about the listener's beliefs (to avoid taking the remark as a lie).
The child who takes the irony as a white lie has not correctly inferred what
the ironic speaker wants the listener to believe. Thus, the child has failed to
attribute an *intention about a belief.* We refer to this as a "second-order
intention" attribution, given its structural similarity to "second-order belief" attributions – beliefs about beliefs (Perner & Wimmer, 1985).

Given that irony is logically distinguished from deception by what the
speaker wants the listener to believe, and given the parallels in the age of
emergence of irony comprehension and second-order belief attribution, we
suspected that the ability to understand irony (and distinguish it from
deception) is made possible by the ability to conceptualize a speaker's
second-order mental state. Thus, irony comprehension may be much more
highly constrained by the ability to reason about other minds than is the
comprehension of metaphor.

Some evidence for the suspicion that irony understanding rests on
second-order mental state attributions comes from a study in which we
examined children's ability to distinguish irony from a white lie (Winner &
Leekam, 1991). Understanding of irony was credited when the child perceived the ironic utterance as nasty in intent, and the white lie as nice.

Children were tested for their understanding of second-order intentions by determining whether they recognized that the ironist wanted the listener to know the truth but the white liar did not. Children had difficulty distinguishing irony from a white lie *unless* they also showed the ability to attribute second-order intentions. Almost *no* children distinguished irony from deception unless they also distinguished the speaker's second-order intentions. This pattern of results obtained even when the irony was presented in a mocking, sarcastic intonation. That is, children were unable to use the negatively tinged intonation to infer the speaker's attitude independently of their ability to infer the speaker's second-order intention.

Thus, irony comprehension is constrained by the child's developing "theory of mind." Why should this not also be true for metaphor? We suggest that irony is confusable with mistakes or lies because all three are based on the relation of opposition. Metaphor is not confusable with these other forms of falsehood because metaphor is based on another kind of relation, that of similarity. Children simply do not mistake metaphors for errors and lies. More typically, when children do not understand a metaphor, they infer an incorrect but nonetheless nonliteral meaning (Winner et al., 1976). Metaphors taken literally are usually so implausible that we rarely confuse them with other forms of literal falsehood. Children apparently experience the same implausibility constraint, for when they do offer literal interpretations for metaphors, they typically feel unsure of their interpretation and thus invent a magical, fairy-tale context to render more plausible their interpretation (Winner et al., 1976). Because metaphors taken literally are so implausible listeners need not reflect about whether the speaker really believes what is said, or whether the speaker wants the listener to really believe his actual words.

Thus far we have argued that, with respect to the level of interpretive understanding, metaphor comes easily to the child: mapping ability (or similarity perception) is there from the start, and metaphor comprehension is constrained only by domain knowledge. At the interpretive level, irony proves considerably more difficult: irony comprehension is constrained by the ability to represent, and reason about, other minds. More specifically, the ability to distinguish irony from deception (which children under six fail to do) rests on the ability to reason about second-order intentions, a skill that does not appear to emerge until the age of about six. Although metaphor and irony pose difficult comprehension demands at the interpretive level, however, there is reason to believe that these two forms of nonliteral language pose identical demands at the higher, metalinguistic level of understanding.

Metalinguistic awareness of metaphor and irony

According to Olson (1988), if we assume comprehension of metaphor to be present simply when the child understands the speaker's meaning, we miss the heart of metaphor. Crucial to understanding metaphor is the recognition of metaphor as a "marked" form of speech, in contrast to just "plain talk." Children need not know that what they are hearing is called a metaphor; all that is needed is that *at some level* they note the utterance as distinct from ordinary usage in that the speaker has said something that he did not mean. When children hear right through the sentence meaning to the speaker meaning, without noticing the tension between the two, they have not attained full understanding.

We take this argument to hold for all forms of nonliteral usage, and thus for irony as well. Interpretive understanding of irony allows the listener to recognize that the speaker is saying something critical. Thus, the listener would take an ironic remark such as "oh, wonderful" to mean something to the effect of "oh how maddening." However, at the interpretive level alone, the listener need not detect that the speaker had *said* something he did not mean. The listener can *in principle* achieve an adequate interpretation of irony by hearing directly through the positive words to the negative meaning without noticing the positive words. The remark can function as a literal one: the fact of irony need not be detected. Thus the effects carried by the choice of irony rather than literal discourse would go undetected: the remark could function as if it were a literal expression of displeasure.

When metalinguistic awareness of metaphor and irony is present, listeners not only infer what is meant, but are aware that what is said is not meant. This awareness enables the listener to hear a difference between metaphor and irony, on the one hand, and direct literal usage, on the other. (See Table 19.1.)

Almost all the research on nonliteral language comprehension has equated comprehension with accessing the speaker's meaning, and has thus ignored what Olson (1988) has called the "heart" of metaphor. We have investigated the development of the metalinguistic level of understanding to determine whether it emerges at the same time for metaphor and irony, and to determine the relation between metalinguistic awareness and interpretive understanding. Given the evidence that listeners can automatically access an utterance's nonliteral meaning without first accessing its literal meaning (Gibbs, this volume; Glucksberg & Keysar, this volume), we reasoned that children may well achieve an interpretive level of understanding without a hint of metalinguistic awareness of a speaker-meaning/sentence-meaning split. That is, children may hear right through a metaphoric or ironic utterance to the speaker's meaning: the sentence meaning might be transparent. Support for this would come from evidence that metalinguistic awareness emerges later than interpretive understanding. Given that both metaphor and irony are utterances in which speaker meaning diverges from sentence meaning, however, we reasoned that awareness of this split would occur no earlier for one form of utterance than for another: in both cases, one must have an awareness of sentence meaning as separate from speaker meaning.

Although metalinguistic awareness may emerge simultaneously for both kinds of utterances, there is reason to suspect that the relation between the two levels of understanding may differ. We have argued that for metaphors the major interpretive problem is in figuring out precisely how to map between two domains. Hence, it seems likely that listeners may be aware that the speaker says one thing but means something else without also being able to determine the metaphor's meaning. This pattern of results should occur in the case of "difficult" metaphors. But how could this occur with irony? It is difficult to conceive of a situation in which one knew a speaker was being ironic, yet could not interpret his meaning. The problem for irony is in recognizing the utterance as irony. But once recognized, at least a rough interpretation follows clearly. This asymmetry between metaphor and irony should occur because metaphor is based on similarity, irony on opposition. It is invariably easier to determine an opposite than to locate something similar to something else, because there is approximately one choice in the former case, but an infinite number in the latter case. (See Table 19.1.)

We investigated metalinguistic understanding of metaphor and irony, and its relation to the interpretive level, in children aged six and seven (Kaplan, Winner, & Rosenblatt, 1987). Children first heard a brief story about two characters, concluding with a literal utterance spoken by one character. They were told that this was an example of "one kind of story." They next heard a story with a nonliteral ending (either metaphor or irony, depending on whether the child had been assigned to the metaphor or irony condition). They were told that this was an example of "the way a boy named Max likes to talk."

Children then heard further stories, ending with either a literal or a nonliteral remark (either metaphor or irony). In a story used in the metaphor condition, an older sister is babysitting for her little brother. The brother has a prolonged temper tantrum. When her parents call to check in, she tells them of the ongoing tantrum. When they return, the brother is still angry. The sister says, "the storm is not over yet." In a story used in the irony condition, a girl takes out some library books and boasts that she never forgets to return books when they are due. Sure enough, she forgets. Her friend remarks (in sarcastic intonation), "you have such a good memory."

After each story we first assessed metalinguistic awareness (without equating such awareness with possession of the terms "metaphor" or "irony"). We asked children to decide in each case whether the final utterance "sounded like something Max would say." For the literal endings, the correct answer was no; for the nonliteral endings, the correct answer was yes. In other words, children were asked to classify the nonliteral remarks together and to discriminate them from the literal remarks. Those children who hear right through the sentence meaning to the speaker meaning should hear no difference between the literal and nonliteral remarks. Only if children are aware of the two levels of meaning can they succeed on this task. We then assessed the interpretive level of understanding. We read three paraphrases of each final utterance and asked children to choose the one that "meant the closest to what the character in the story meant." Interpretive understanding was always assessed after metalinguistic understanding to ensure that the information given by the paraphrases did not influence responses to the metalinguistic question.

With respect to metalinguistic understanding, the six-year-olds performed at chance for both the irony and the metaphor tasks. The seven-year-olds, however, showed a dramatic improvement. They discriminated literal remarks from both types of nonliteral remarks 73 percent of the time. The age at which metalinguistic understanding emerged was no earlier for metaphor than for irony. Thus, between the ages of six and seven, within the space of one year, what seems to emerge is a metalinguistic ability to step back and detect nonliterality.

It is intriguing to compare this emergence to the performance of children on first-order false belief tasks (Wimmer & Perner, 1983). Children can conceptualize false beliefs in others by four. Thus, the four-year-old can distinguish belief from *reality*. It is not until two or three years later, however, that children can distinguish belief (in the form of speaker meaning) from *sentence meaning* in nonliteral utterances. Why such a lag? We suggest that the concept of sentence meaning is less of an anchor than that of reality, that is, of facts known to be true by the child.

As we suspected, the relation between interpretive and metalinguistic understanding differed for the metaphoric and ironic utterances. For the metaphors, metalinguistic understanding sometimes occurred *without* an appropriate interpretation of the metaphor. That is, children recognized the metaphors as a special way of speaking but were unsure or wrong about what the speaker meant. Such late emergence of metaphor understanding at the interpretive level is undoubtedly due to the fact that the metaphors used were fairly difficult, nonperceptual ones. The important point here, however, is that the performance of the children demonstrates that metalinguistic awareness of metaphor does not immediately lead to interpretive understanding. In contrast, for irony, when children showed metalinguistic awareness, they also showed interpretive understanding. Thus, the relationship between interpretive understanding and metalinguistic awareness differs for metaphor and irony. As we suggested above, this is because metaphor is based on similarity, irony on opposition. If one recognizes that a metaphor is not literally intended, one still has the problem of determining in what way the vehicle is similar to the topic. Since there are an infinite number of similarities between objects, this task is a demanding one, and comprehension can go awry. But if one recognizes that an ironic remark is not literally intended, and that the relation between what is said and meant is one of opposition, the speaker's meaning is clear – it is the opposite of what was said.

Metaphor, irony, and theories of matter and mind

At the beginning of this chapter, we raised two questions about interpretive understanding of metaphor and irony, and two about metalinguistic awareness. What can we now conclude? First of all, metaphor understanding is constrained by domain knowledge and not by any inherent limits on the kinds of similarities children can perceive. Given sufficient knowledge of the objects/domains involved in the mapping, children can perceive any form of similarity at any age, even if these similarities are perceived on a global, nondimensional basis (Smith, 1989). Hence, metaphors can be understood as early as two or three, as long as the metaphor involves domains of which the child has knowledge. Second, irony understanding is constrained by the ability to infer others' beliefs (a first-order ability) and intentions to affect others' beliefs (a second-order ability). Because the relation between sentence and speaker meaning in irony is one of opposition within domain, the ironic comment is "domain relevant." The same comment that in one context is ironic can be, if the context is slightly altered, a mistake or a lie. Hence, the seductiveness of mistake and lie interpretations. The only way to avoid such interpretations is to infer what the speaker believes (to avoid a literally true or a mistaken interpretation) and to infer what the speaker wants the listener to believe (to avoid a deception interpretation). The ability to reason about second-order mental states does not develop until about six. Hence, irony interpretation is later to emerge than is metaphor interpretation.

Third, we have shown that metalinguistic awareness emerges at the same time for metaphor and irony – somewhere between the ages of six and seven. At this age, children become able to reflect about sentence meaning as distinct from speaker meaning. The concept of sentence meaning as separate from speaker meaning is an elusive one and thus it is not surprising that this ability does not develop until the age at which most children begin to read (Olson & Hildyard, 1983). And finally, the relation between metalinguistic awareness and interpretive understanding differs for metaphor and irony. In the case of metaphors, it is possible to recognize the utterance as nonliteral but not zero in on the appropriate speaker meaning. It is as if the listener said, "I know the speaker is being metaphoric, but I do not know what he is getting at." In the case of irony, once one recognizes that the speaker is being ironic, there is a click of comprehension and the speaker's meaning is grasped. It is difficult to imagine thinking, "I know the speaker is being ironic but I just don't know what he means." Rather, one is more likely to think, "Oh, *now* I understand. He was being ironic!"

We have suggested that, at the interpretive level, children call on their knowledge of domains to understand metaphor and on their theory of mind to understand irony. At the level of metalinguistic awareness, however, children must call on their theory of mind to understand both metaphor and irony. To recognize an utterance as nonliteral, the child must recognize that what the speaker says is not what he believes or means. As soon as one is consciously reflecting about the speaker's meaning, as separate from the surface, sentence meaning, then one is reflecting about the speaker's beliefs, the speaker's subjective mental state. Thus, *full* comprehension of both metaphor and irony requires the ability to represent and reflect about sentence meaning and mental states. The same requirement holds for any utterance in which speakers do not mean what they say, as, for example, in ambiguous utterances or in indirect requests. In this sense, metaphor and irony and all other forms of indirection are alike, and stand apart from veridical, direct literal uses of words.

NOTES

1 We disagree here with Glucksberg and Keysar (this volume), who claim that metaphors mean just what they say. We hold on to the distinction between say and mean. To reject this distinction is to obliterate the difference between literal and nonliteral utterances. Whereas nonliteral utterances may be processed identically to literal utterances, the conceptual distinction between them should be maintained.

2 To be sure, similarity is a philosophically problematic concept, since anything can be seen as similar to anything else *in one or more ways* (Goodman, 1972b). Moreover, determining what is and is not a perceptual similarity is not a simple matter. For instance, according to Gibson (1966), all similarities can be seen as in some way perceptual, even if some perceptual comparisons are more abstract than others (e.g., affordances versus shape). We define perceptual similarity as any similarity based on perceived physical properties of objects.

3 Smith (1989) has argued that children initially perceive only global similarities and later are able to recognize the dimensions along which two things are similar. We do not claim that children need be *aware* of the dimension on which the similarity is perceived. Hence, we see no conflict between this view and our position that the capacity to perceive all similarities is available from the start.

4 It has been shown that three-year-olds fail to distinguish metaphoric from literal similarity (Vosniadou & Ortony, 1983). This finding does not indicate, however, that metaphors are not interpretable by children this young. The three-year-olds in this study distinguished metaphor from anomaly, but not from literal similarity. Thus, this finding supports the position taken here, that on the interpretive level, metaphors can be understood as soon as the domains are known. However, metalinguistic awareness of the metaphor as different from "plain talk" (Olson, 1988) does not emerge until later.

METAPHOR
AND
SCIENCE

20

The shift from metaphor to analogy in Western science

DEDRE GENTNER AND MICHAEL JEZIORSKI

Analogy and metaphor are central to scientific thought. They figure in discovery, as in Rutherford's analogy of the solar system for the atom or Faraday's use of lines of magnetized iron filings to reason about electric fields (Nersessian, 1984; Tweney, 1983). They are also used in teaching: novices are told to think of electricity as analogous to water flowing through pipes (Gentner & Gentner, 1983) or of a chemical process as analogous to a ball rolling down a hill (Van Lehn & J. S. Brown, 1980). Yet for all its usefulness, analogical thinking is never formally taught to us. We seem to think of it as a natural human skill, and of its use in science as a straightforward extension of its use in commonsense reasoning. For example, William James believed that "men, taken historically, reason by analogy long before they have learned to reason by abstract characters" (James, 1890, vol. II, p. 363). All this points to an appealing intuition: that a faculty for analogical reasoning is an innate part of human cognition, and that the concept of a sound, inferentially useful analogy is universal.

In this essay we question this intuition. We analyze the way in which analogy and metaphor have been used at different points in the history of Western scientific thought, tracing their use backward from the present time. We begin by laying out the current framework for analogical reasoning, followed by two examples that conform to the modern aesthetic, those of Sadi Carnot (1796–1832) and Robert Boyle (1627–1691). We go on to consider a very different way of using analogy and metaphor in science, that practiced by the alchemists (about 300 B.C.–1600 A.D.). Based on these examples, we conclude that there are important differences in the kinds of similarities that were felt to warrant inferences about the world and in the kinds of predictions that were drawn from comparisons. In short, there appear to have been significant historical changes in what has counted as the scientific use of analogy and metaphor.

We will suggest that although an appreciation of similarity (including metaphorical similarity) is almost surely universal in human cognition, what to do with this sense of similarity is not. Opinions on how to tame the raw perception of likeness have varied. Many great thinkers have simply banned it. Berkeley pronounced that "a philosopher should abstain from metaphor" and Aristotle, although willing to permit metaphor as ornament, held that nonliteral language should not be used in argumentation. (He did concede, however, that the perception of similarities between disparate things could be a source of special insight.) At the opposite pole, the alchemists, as we will see, embraced metaphor and analogy with unbridled eagerness. Their excess was both quantitative and qualitative. They used vast numbers of metaphors and they imbued them with great power. They were, as Vickers (1984) puts it, owned by their analogies, rather than owning them. Finally, the modern view, as represented by Boyle and Carnot, values metaphorical similarity but observes firm constraints on its use in scientific reasoning. It can be summed up as follows: "And remember, do not neglect vague analogies. But if you wish them respectable, try to clarify them" (Polya, 1954, p. 15). Our focus is on the evolution in Western science from the alchemists' pluralistic use of all sorts of metaphorical similarities to the more austere modern focus on structural analogy. We begin by laying out what we take to be the current cognitive aesthetics for analogical reasoning.

A framework for analogy and similarity

Analogy can be viewed as a kind of highly selective similarity. In processing analogy, people implicitly focus on certain kinds of commonalities and ignore others. Imagine a bright student reading the analogy "a cell is like a factory." She is unlikely to decide that cells are buildings made of brick and steel. Instead she might guess that, like a factory, a cell takes in resources to keep itself operating and to generate its products. This focus on common relational abstractions is what makes analogy illuminating.

Structure-mapping and ideal analogical competence

Structure-mapping is a theory of human processing of analogy and similarity. It aims to capture both the descriptive constraints that characterize the interpretation of analogy and similarity (Gentner, 1982, 1983, 1989), and the processes humans engage in when understanding a similarity comparison (Markman & Gentner, in press). The central idea is that an analogy is a mapping of knowledge from one domain (the base) into another (the target) such that a system of relations that holds among the base objects also holds among the target objects. In interpreting an analogy, people seek to put the objects of the base in one-to-one correspondence with the objects of the target so as to obtain the maximal structural match. The corresponding objects in the base and target need not resemble each other; rather, object correspondences are determined by like roles in the matching relational structures. Thus, an analogy is a way of aligning and focusing on relational commonalities independently of the objects in which those relations are embedded. Central to the mapping process is the principle of *systematicity:* people prefer to map systems of predicates governed by higher-order relations with inferential import, rather than to map isolated predicates. The systematicity principle reflects a tacit preference for coherence and inferential power in interpreting analogy.

Consider, for example, Rutherford's analogy between the solar system and the hydrogen atom. A person hearing it for the first time (assuming some prior knowledge about the solar system) must find a set of relations common to the base and the target that can be consistently mapped and that is as deep (i.e., as systematic) as possible. Here, the deepest common relational system is the central-force causal system:

CAUSE {AND [ATTRACTS (sun, planet), MORE-MASSIVE (sun, planet)],
REVOLVES-AROUND (planet, sun)}

Isolated relations, such as HOTTER-THAN (sun, planet), that do not belong to this connected system, are disregarded. The descriptions of individual objects [e.g., YELLOW (sun)] are also disregarded. The object correspondences arrived at are those dictated by the system of relational matches: sun → nucleus, and planet → electron.

Although there are some differences in emphasis, there is a fair amount of convergence on the kinds of structural principles discussed above (Burstein, 1983; Hesse, 1966; Hofstadter, 1981; Holyoak & Thagard, 1989; Keane, 1985, 1988; Reed, 1987; Rumelhart & Norman, 1981; Winston, 1980, 1982). There is widespread agreement on the basic elements of one-to-one mappings of objects with carryover of predicates, and many researchers use some form of systematicity to constrain the interpretation of analogy (although there are exceptions; see Anderson, 1981). There is also empirical support for the psychological predictions of structure-mapping theory. Three findings are of particular relevance here. First, adults tend to include relations and omit attributes in their interpretations of analogy, and they judge analogies as more apt and more sound if they share systematic relational structure (Gentner, 1988; Gentner & Clement, 1988; Gentner & Landers, 1985; Gentner & Rattermann, 1991). Second, adults (and children) are more accurate in analogical transfer when there is a systematic relational structure in the base domain that can be used to guide the map-

Table 20.1. *Modern principles of analogical reasoning*

1. **Structural consistency.** Objects are placed in one-to-one correspondence and parallel connectivity in predicates is maintained.
2. **Relational focus.** Relational systems are preserved and object descriptions disregarded.
3. **Systematicity.** Among various relational interpretations, the one with the greatest depth – that is, the greatest degree of common higher-order relational structure – is preferred.
4. **No extraneous associations.** Only commonalities strengthen an analogy. Further relations and associations between the base and target – for example, thematic connections – do not contribute to the analogy.
5. **No mixed analogies.** The relational network to be mapped should be entirely contained within one base domain. When two bases are used, they should each convey a coherent system.
6. **Analogy is not causation.** That two phenomena are analogous does not imply that one causes the other.

ping (Gentner & Toupin, 1986; Markman & Gentner, in press; Ross, 1987). Third, adults asked to make new predictions from an analogy base their predictions on common relational structure. They are more likely to hypothesize a new fact in the target when the corresponding fact in the base is causally connected to a common structure (Clement & Gentner, 1991).

Analogical soundness. The foregoing discussion suggests a set of tacit constraints that modern scientists use in analogical reasoning. We believe there are six such principles, as given in Table 20.1. The first three principles, *structural consistency, relational focus,* and *systematicity,* have already been discussed. The fourth principle, *no extraneous relations,* expresses the point that analogy is about *commonalities.* Discovering other relationships between the base and target does not improve the analogy. For example, the fact that the sun and planets are made up of atoms does not strengthen the atom/solar system analogy.

The *no mixed analogies* principle reflects the sense that analogies constructed by mapping from several base domains into the same target are rarely sound. In the best case, such mixed comparisons tend to lack coherent higher-order structure, and in the worst case they contain contradictory mappings, as in these examples quoted in the *New Yorker:*

This college is sitting on a launching pad flexing its muscles.

The U.S. and the Middle East are on parallel but non-convergent paths.

In inferential reasoning we prefer that the relational system mapped into a target be drawn from a single base domain. There are exceptions in cases when different analogies are used to capture *separable* aspects or subsystems of the target (Burstein, 1983; Collins & Gentner, 1987). But such multiple analogies require firm rules of intersection to avoid inconsistent mappings (see Coulson, Feltovich, & Spiro, 1986, for a medical example). Unruly fusions violate the consensual rules of sound thinking.[1]

Finally, *analogy is not causation.* In our current cognitive practice, the presence of an analogy between two situations has no bearing on whether there is a causal relation between the two situations. Conversely, evidence of a causal relation between two analogous domains has no bearing on how similar or analogous they are. This point can be confusing, since *common* causal relations do contribute to the goodness of analogy. For example, given two possibly analogous situations A and B, the analogy between A and B is strengthened by adding like causal relations to both terms. Thus, analogy (2) is better than analogy (1).

	A	B
(1)	Ida pushed Sam.	Flipper pushed Shamu.
	Sam hit a tree.	Shamu hit a buoy.

	A′	B′
(2)	Ida pushed Sam.	Flipper pushed Shamu.
	CAUSED	CAUSED
	Sam hit a tree.	Shamu hit a buoy.

Adding common causal relations makes analogy (2) superior to (1) for three reasons: (*a*) adding common features increases the goodness of a match (Tversky, 1977); (*b*) more specifically, adding common features *that are connected to common systems* increases the goodness of a match more than does adding other commonalities, since interconnected elements support each other in the evaluation process; and (*c*) still more specifically, adding common *higher-order constraining relations* (such as the causal relation) increases the goodness of a match more than adding other connected commonalities, since the coherence and systematicity of the analogy is thereby increased (Clement & Gentner, 1991; Forbus & Gentner, 1989).

But although adding like causal relations *within* two situations strengthens an analogy, adding causal relations *between* them does not. Thus, analogy (3) between A and B is not better than analogy (1) between the same two event sets, even though analogy (3) has an additional causal relation between the analogs:

	A		B
(3)	Ida pushed Sam.	CAUSE	Flipper pushed Shamu.
	Sam hit a tree.		Shamu hit a buoy.

That is, the analogy does not improve if we are told that Sam's hitting a tree caused Shamu to hit the buoy. That A causes B may be an interesting connection, but it does not make A and B more similar or more analogous. In our current cognitive aesthetic, adding common causal relations to each of the domains increases the goodness of an analogy, but adding causal connections between the analogs does not.[2]

Analogy in reasoning. The constraints on analogical reasoning are closely related to the process of making new inferences. As mentioned above, analogical inferences are typically made by a process of *system completion* after some degree of match has been established. We have modeled this process in a computer simulation called SME (the structure-mapping engine) (Falkenhainer, Forbus, & Gentner, 1989; Forbus & Gentner, 1990; Forbus & Oblinger, 1990; Gentner, Falkenhainer, & Skorstad, 1988). The system first makes all possible local matches between like components and then attempts to link these into structurally consistent systems of matches. The largest and deepest global interpretation wins. Given such a common system, a new *candidate inference* is generated if a predicate belongs to the base system but its counterpart does not yet appear in the target system. That is, the partially matching system is completed in the target.

Candidate inferences are only conjectures. The six principles of analogical reasoning are concerned with whether the analogy is structurally sound, not with whether its inferences are factually correct. Verifying the factual status of the analogy is a separate process. Soundness principles simplify the task, however, because they specify what must be true in order for the analogy to hold. In a system of interconnected matches, even one significant disconfirmation can invalidate a whole analogy.

Metaphor and other similarity matches. Other kinds of similarity matches can be distinguished in this framework. Whereas *analogies* map relational structure independently of object descriptions, *mere-appearance matches* map aspects of object descriptions without regard for relational structure. *Literal similarity matches* map both relational structure and object descriptions. We view *metaphor* as a rather broad category, encompassing analogy and mere-appearance, as well as a variety of other kinds of matches. On this view, analogy is a special case of metaphor, one based on a purely relational match. The large-scale communication metaphor analyzed by Reddy (this volume), as well as other conceptual metaphors analyzed by Lakoff and Johnson (1980) and by Lakoff (this volume), are examples of systematic relational metaphors, that is, metaphors that could also qualify as analogies. There are also attributional metaphors – mere-appearance matches, based on shared object descriptions – for example, "her arms were pale swans," as well as metaphors based on mixtures of object and relational commonalities. Further, there are metaphors that cannot be analyzed in the simple terms we have used so far: for example, "the voice of your eyes is deeper than all roses" (e.e. cummings); or "On a star of faith pure as the drifting bread / As the food and flames of the snow" (Dylan Thomas). These metaphors are not bound by the one-to-one mapping constraint and can include mixtures of several bases, as well as thematic and metonymic relations (Gentner, 1982; Gentner, Falkenhainer, & Skorstad, 1988).

Historical uses of analogy

Despite the plurality of possible match types, the guidelines for use of analogy in scientific discovery and reasoning are quite selective. The strength of an analogy in licensing scientific prediction rests on the degree of systematic structural match between the two domains. We now ask whether western scientists have always adhered to these principles. We will consider evidence that the ascendancy of analogy over metaphor in scientific reasoning was not always the case. We begin with Carnot, a fairly recent example, and progress in reverse chronological order.

Sadi Carnot

The French scientist Sadi Carnot (1796–1832) was one of the pioneers of modern thermodynamics. He described the Carnot cycle for heat engines, still taught as an ideal energy conversion system, and laid the foundation for the later discovery of the equivalence of heat and work. In his treatise on heat, Carnot presented an analogy between heat and water that clarified his position and generated new questions. His use of analogy is prototypical of the rules of rigor described above and can stand as an example of the modern use of analogy. In 1824, Carnot published *Reflexions sur la puissance motrice du feu* (*Reflections on the Motive Power of Fire*). In this book, he describes the functioning of a hypothetical engine that can convert heat energy to work. This engine consists of a cylinder filled with gas and fitted with a frictionless piston that can move freely inside the cylinder. During a four-stage cycle, the gas inside is expanded by contact with a heat source (isothermal expansion) and allowed to continue dilating after the source is removed (adiabatic expansion). The gas is then compressed by transmission of heat to a colder body (isothermal compression), and the volume further decreases after removal of the cold body (adiabatic compression), restoring the original conditions of the system. During this period, the engine has absorbed a certain amount of heat and converted it to mechanical work through the movement of the piston. The operation of this ideal engine, known as the Carnot cycle, was an important theoretical contribution to the early development of thermodynamics.

In the *Reflexions*, Carnot utilized an analogy between water falling through a waterfall and caloric (heat) "falling" through a heat engine. The analogy between heat and fluid was not new. Indeed, the dominant theory of heat at the time was the caloric theory,[3] which defined heat as a weightless fluid that shared the properties of ordinary matter. Like other matter, caloric was considered a conserved quantity that could be neither created nor destroyed. Carnot's contribution was not the idea of viewing heat as a fluid but rather the thoroughness of his development of the heat/water analogy – the extent to which he applied explicit causal structures from the water domain to the heat domain:

1. According to established principles at the present time, we can compare with sufficient accuracy the motive power of heat to that of a waterfall. Each has a maximum that we cannot exceed, whatever may be, on the one hand, the machine which is acted upon by the water, and whatever, on the other hand, the substance acted upon by the heat.

2. The motive power of a waterfall depends on its height and on the quantity of the liquid; the motive power of heat depends also on the quantity of caloric used, and on what may be termed, on what in fact we will call, the *height of its fall*, that is to say, the difference of temperature of the bodies between the higher and lower reservoirs.

3. In the waterfall the motive power is exactly proportional to the difference of level between the higher and lower reservoirs. In the fall of caloric the motive power undoubtedly increases with the difference of temperature between the warm and the cold bodies; but we do not know whether it is proportional to this difference. We do not know, for example, whether the fall of caloric from 100 to 50 degrees furnishes more or less motive power than the fall of this same caloric from 50 to zero. It is a question which we propose to examine hereafter. (Carnot, 1977, p. 15; numbers and paragraph breaks are inserted for convenience; the original passage is continuous)

In section 1, Carnot introduces the analogy between the motive power of heat and the motive power of water and establishes and notes a simple yet important parallel: just as the amount of power produced by a given fall of water is limited, the power attainable from a given transfer of heat is limited. In section 2, Carnot establishes further correspondences and a shared higher-order principle. He compares the difference in temperature between two connected bodies to the height of the fall in a waterfall.[4] Carnot uses this correspondence in a proposed higher-order relation: he asserts that, in each case, the power produced by the system depends on both the amount of the substance (water or caloric) that "falls" and the distance of the "drop" between levels.

This qualitative combination – the fact that power depends on both the difference in level and the amount of "substance" involved – further sharpens the analogy. Figure 20.1 shows the common relational structure that holds for water and heat. Figure 20.2 sets forth the corresponding terms and assertions.

So far the enterprise has been one of *matching* structures between heat and water. In Section 3, a new candidate inference is *transferred* from water to heat, that is, the analogy is used to suggest a new hypothesis. Carnot notes a higher-order relation in the domain of water (the fact that the power produced by a given fall of water is directly proportional to the difference between levels). He asks whether the same relation exists for heat engines; that is, whether the power produced by a given "fall" of

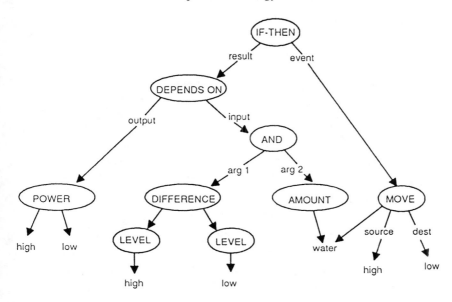

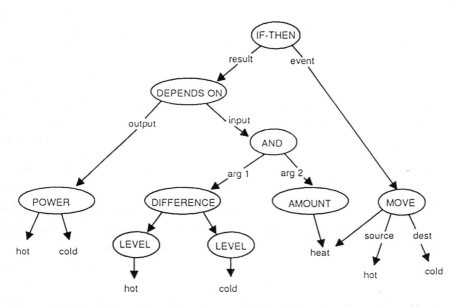

Figure 20.1. Carnot's analogy: the common relational structure for water and heat.

1. water: DIFFERENCE (level<h>, level<l>)
   heat : DIFFERENCE (temp<h>, temp<l>)

2. water: FLOW (h,l)
   heat : FLOW (h,l)

3. water: POWER (h,l)
   heat : POWER (h,l)

4. water: MAX POWER (h,l)
   heat : MAX POWER (h,l)

5. water: αQ(POWER (h,l), DIFFERENCE (level<h>, level<l>))
   heat : αQ(POWER (h,l), DIFFERENCE (temp<h>, temp<l>))

6. water: αQ(POWER (h,l), ami<h>)
   heat : αQ(POWER (h,l), ami<h>)

7. water: AND (αQ(POWER (h,l), DIFFERENCE (level<h>,level<l>)),
           αQ((POWER(h,l), ami<h>)

   heat : AND (αQ(POWER (h,l), DIFFERENCE (temp<h>, temp<l>)),
           αQ(POWER (h,l), ami<h>)

Figure 20.2. Terms and propositions derivable from Carnot's water/heat analogy. *Note:* αQ denotes qualitative proportionality (Forbus, 1984). A αQ B signifies that A is a monotonic function of B, but does not specify the nature of the function or whether other variables may also affect A.

caloric remains constant, regardless of the temperature at which that fall takes place.[5]

Carnot's development of his analogy is indistinguishable from the modern scientific use of analogy. It meets the six principles of rigorous analogical reasoning discussed earlier. Carnot paired the objects in the two domains in one-to-one correspondence. In so doing, he disregarded object-attribute matches. He was not concerned with whether corresponding components shared surface qualities, but with achieving a common systematic relational structure. Having explicated a higher-order relational system common to the two domains, Carnot was able to exploit that system to map across further hypotheses from the base to the target. Between-domain relations, such as "water can be hot," were avoided, as was any hint of a mixed analogy. In short, Carnot's use of analogy conforms to modern scientific practice.

Robert Boyle

We now move back another century and a half to the English scientist Robert Boyle (1627–1691). Boyle is considered among the founders of modern chemistry. He is best known for his work on the ideal gas law, but he also contributed to other domains, such as the theory of acids and alkalies. Probably his most influential work was the *Sceptical Chymist,* in which he criticized both the Greek division of matter into four elements and the later division into three principles. Appearing anonymously in 1661 and again in 1679 with additions, it "did more than any other work of the century to arouse a truly critical spirit of scientific logic in chemical thinking" (Stillman, 1960, p. 395). Boyle was a prolific writer, interested in philosophy and religion as well as the sciences. He was also a prolific analogizer. He often put forth several examples or analogies for each principle he wanted to prove.

A characteristic example of Boyle's use of examples and analogies occurs in his book *Of the great effects of even languid and unheeded local motion,* published in 1690. His purpose in this book was to demonstrate the importance of "local motion," the motions of many tiny particles. Boyle wanted to establish that the combined effects of the motion of many tiny particles – each invisible and insignificant in itself – can cause large-scale changes. He saw such effects as a unifying principle across domains such as light, sound, fire, and fluids. Although some of his points now seem to need no defense, such was not the case in his time. To marshal sufficient evidence for his conjecture, Boyle cited examples from one domain after another.

Boyle's examples appear to function in two ways. First, they serve as instances of local motion and its effects – that is, as instances of a principle that can be effectively applied to several domains. The more numerous and varied the instances, the more faith we can presumably have in the principle. Second, the examples serve as analogies that can be aligned with one another to yield common structural abstractions. By juxtaposing separate instances of local motion, Boyle led his reader to focus on the common causal system. The following excerpt illustrates his style of analogizing:

(Chap. IV) Observat. III. *Men undervalue the motions of bodies too small to be visible or sensible, notwithstanding their* Numerousness, *which inables them to act in Swarms.*

1. [Boyle grants that most men think of the particles of bodies as like grains of dust, which, although invisible, cannot penetrate the bodies they fall on. As a result, these grains cannot affect the bodies.]

But we may have other thoughts, if we well consider, that the Corpuscles we speak of, are, by their minuteness, assisted, and oftentimes by their figure inabled, to pierce into the innermost recesses of the body they invade, and distribute themselves to all, or at least to multitudes of the minute parts, whereof that body consists. For this being granted, though we suppose each single *effluvium* or particle to be very minute; yet, since we may suppose, even solid bodies to be made up of particles that are so too, and the number of invading particles to be not much inferior to that of the invaded ones, or at least to be exceedingly great, it not need seem incredible, that a multitude of little Corpuscles in motion (whose motion, may, for ought we know, be very swift) should be able to have a considerable operation upon particles either quiescent, or that have a motion too slow to be perceptible by sense. Which may perhaps be the better conceived by the help of this gross example:

2. *Example of the anthill*

If you turn an Ant-hill well stocked with Ants-eggs, upside down, you may sometimes see such a heap of eggs mingled with the loose earth, as a few of those Insects, if they were yoaked together, would not be able at once to draw after them; but if good numbers of them disperse themselves and range up and down, and each lay hold of her own egge, and hurry it away, 'tis somewhat surprizing to see (as I have with pleasure done) how quickly the heap of eggs will be displaced, when almost every little egge has one of those little Insects to deal with it.

3. *Example of wind in trees*

And in those cases, wherein the invading fluid does not quite disjoin and carry off any great number of the parts of the body it invades, its operation may be illustrated by that of the wind upon a tree in *Autumn:* for, it finds or makes it self multitudes of passages, for the most part crooked, not onely between the branches and twigs, but the leaves and fruits, and in its passing from the one side to the other of the tree, it does not onely variously bend the more flexible boughs and twigs, and perhaps make them grate upon one another, but it breaks off some of the stalks of the fruit, and makes them fall to the ground, and withall carries off divers of the leaves, that grew the least firmly on, and in its passage does by its differing act upon a multitude of leaves all at once, and variously alters their situation.

4. *Example of sugar and amber dissolving*

5. *Example of mercury compound dissolving*

6. *Example of flame invading metal*

But to give instances in Fluid bodies, (which I suppose you will think far the more difficult part of my task,) though you will easily grant, that the flame of Spirit of wine, that will burn all away, is but a visible aggregate of such *Effluvia* swiftly agitated, as without any sensible Heat would of themselves invisibly exhale away; yet, if you be pleased to hold the blade of a knife, or a thin plate of Copper, but for a very few minutes, in the flame of pure Spirit of wine, you will quickly be able to discern by the great Heat, that is, the various and vehement agitation of the minute Corpuscles of the metal, what a number of them must have been fiercely agitated by the pervasion of the igneous particles, if we suppose, (what is highly probable,) that they did materially penetrate into the innermost parts of the metal; and whether we suppose this or no, it will, by our experiment, appear, that so fluid and yielding a body, as the flame of Spirit of wine, is able, almost in a trice, to act very powerfully upon the hardest metalls.

7. *Example of animal spirits moving animals*

8. *Example of rope contracting from humidity*   (Boyle, 1690, pp. 27–35)

Boyle begins by noting that laymen may find it implausible that local motion could have large-scale effects. Laymen, he observes, consider such motion similar to the ineffectual motion of dust in air. By analogy with dust, if particles are very small, then although they can be moved easily, their movements are inconsequential. Having set forth the lay intuition – that local motion is ineffective – Boyle then defends the opposite position by differentiating the analogy further. The ineffectiveness of dust particles, he claims, is the result of their failure to penetrate other bodies and thereby to affect those bodies. He suggests that there are other kinds of particles involved in local motion that *are* small enough to diffuse through solid objects, and that it is this penetration that allows them to create large effects. (That is, he argues that dust is not small *enough*!) He then proceeds to present instances of this kind of local motion.

In paragraph 2, Boyle compares the ability of small particles to move large masses to that of ants to move their eggs. Although each ant is much smaller than the mass of eggs, the ability of each ant to "penetrate" the egg mass and move one egg causes the entire mass of eggs to be displaced. This example conforms well to the principles of analogizing (Table 20.1). There are clear one-to-one correspondences, based not on characteristics of individual objects but on relations between the objects, as shown in Figure 20.3. For example, Boyle does not suggest that the corpuscles involved in local motion are *like* ants – they are not living organisms, they do not have six legs, and so forth – nor does he suggest that particles of matter are white or soft or otherwise egglike. The only required matches are for the *relative sizes* of the ant, the egg mass, and the egg. The important commonality is a structural one: namely, that very large numbers can compensate for a very great size disadvantage, provided that penetration of the larger by the smaller can occur. Under these circumstances, many small bodies in motion can carry off a much larger body.

The remaining sections provide several additional analogous examples of the effects of local motion. For example, in paragraph 3, Boyle cites the example of wind passing through (penetrating) a tree, blowing off leaves and breaking branches. In paragraph 6, Boyle presents the effects of fire on a knife blade as an instance of local motion. He perceives fire as comprised of many small particles and explains the heating of metal in terms of the invasion of igneous particles into the metal, with the result that the corpuscles of metal themselves become "fiercely agitated" and the blade becomes hot. The remaining two paragraphs, which describe "animal spirits" and the contraction of rope, respectively, make analogous points. Boyle observes that although animal spirits may be minute enough to be invisible they are capable of propelling large animals such as elephants. He describes seeing hemp shrink in moist weather, and states that the "aqueous and other humid particles, swimming in the air, entering the pores of the hemp in great numbers, were able to make it shrink, though a weight of fifty, sixty or even more pounds of lead were tied at the end to hinder its contraction." Table 20.2 shows the correspondences across Boyle's set of examples.

Boyle's style of analogizing is very different from Carnot's. Rather than dwelling on one pair of examples, carefully explicating the critical common relational structure, he uses a rapid succession of analogies and examples

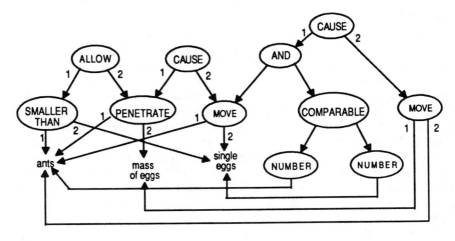

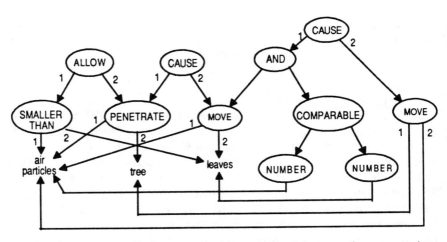

Figure 20.3. Boyle's analogy: the common relational structure for ants moving eggs and wind blowing leaves.

to demonstrate a central principle. The implicit message is that if all these phenomena occur, the model that summarizes them must be plausible. Each paragraph contains an instance of local motion, or contrasts situations in which the principles do or do not apply. By standards of modern knowledge, not all the comparisons are equally convincing. There is little surface similarity between these examples; they relate to one another by virtue of their common abstraction. They can be compared with one another to reveal an abstract model of local motion.

Table 20.2. *An overview of Boyle's series of analogies concerning local motion*

Abstract model	Layman's view (1)	(2)	(3)	(4)	(5)	(6)	(7)
					Analogs		
Small particles	Dust	Ants	Air particles	Aqueous particles	Igneous particles	Animal spirits	Aqueous corpuscles
Penetrate Large bodies	Large bodies	Mass of eggs	Tree	Mercury oxide	Metal	Animals	Rope
And move Fragments of bodies	Fragments of bodies	Single eggs	Leaves	Grains of oxide	Metal corpuscles	Animal (inner parts)	Rope (inner parts)

Despite these differences, Boyle's use of analogy falls roughly within the modern standards discussed in Table 20.1. In each of his analogies, the objects are placed in one-to-one correspondence. Object attributes are discarded, as in the wind analogy. Indeed, the sheer variety of the examples virtually guarantees that any specific object characteristics will cancel out. The analogies, as in the modern tradition, are about common relational systems. The complexity of the analogies is not great – they are no so deep as Carnot's, for example – but this is in part due to the state of knowledge of the subject matter. Boyle's point was to establish that the motion of many small particles can combine to produce powerful visible effects, and further, that the requirement for this to occur is that the smaller particles penetrate the larger matter. Boyle demonstrates that this system of commonalities holds throughout these examples. Finally, in spite of the large number of examples, there are no mixed analogies or between-analog relations; each example stands on its own as a separate instantiation of the relational structure.

Carnot and Boyle: A summary

At first glance, Boyle and Carnot seem to differ rather sharply in their use of analogy. Carnot uses one analogy, explaining it precisely and then going on to use the principles in further inferencing. Boyle, in contrast, offers a whole family of analogies, one after the other. It could be maintained that this sustained analysis marks Carnot as a more modern analogizer than Boyle.[6] Yet despite their stylistic differences, both Boyle and Carnot are essentially modern in their view of what constitutes a sound analogy.

The alchemists

We have moved back in time from Carnot (1796–1832) to Boyle (1627–1691). So far, the comparisons we have considered conform to the modern notion of a sound analogy. Now we move back still further, to the work of the alchemists, and analyze the forms of similarity they used in making their predictions. The alchemists were enthusiastic in their embrace of similarity, but as we shall see, their sense of how to use similarity differed markedly from the modern sense.[7]

Alchemy grew out of the fusion of Egyptian chemistry with Greek theory in about 300 B.C., continued in Persia after about 500 A.D., and entered the European sphere again after the first crusades at the end of the eleventh century A.D. It was a dominant force in western science, or prescience, until the seventeenth century A.D. Although there were many variants, there were some common themes.[8] Based on certain works of Plato and Aristotle, alchemical thought postulated a primordial source of all earthly matter. This First Matter was manifested in a small number of primary

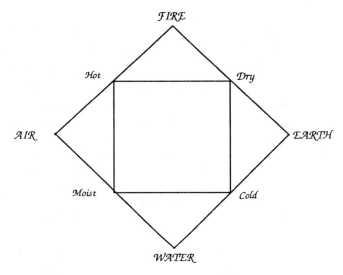

Figure 20.4. Schematic of the doctrine of four elements and four qualities.

elements – fire, air, water, and earth – each of which combined two of the primary qualities, hot, cold, wet, and dry. Fire was hot and dry, water was cold and wet, and so on (see Figure 20.4). A transmutation could occur if the proportions of the qualities changed: for example, fire (hot and dry) could be changed into earth (specifically, into ash) by losing heat to become cold and dry. The alchemists were particularly interested in transmutations of metals, especially the transmutation of base metals into gold, often with the help of a hypothesized catalyst known as the Philosopher's Stone (Redgrove, 1922). Besides bringing wealth, achieving such a transmutation would validate the theory.

The alchemists were peerless in their enthusiasm for analogy and metaphor. Their comparisons were numerous and striking. Metals were often held to consist of two components: mercury, which was fiery, active, and male, and sulphur, which was watery, passive, and female. Thus the combination of two metals could be viewed as a marriage (Taylor, 1949). This male-female division was extremely influential; with the addition of a third principle, it formed the *tria prima* of mercury, sulphur, and salt, which Paracelsus and other sixteenth-century alchemists held to underlie all matter. Metals were also compared to heavenly bodies or to mythological figures, as discussed below. Still other metaphors were taken from animals and plants. The eagle was used to convey volatility. Sal ammoniac, for example, was called *aquila coelestis* (heavenly eagle). In another metaphor, the raven, the swan, and the eagle stood for earth, water, and air (Crosland, 1978, p. 16).

A central comparison was a macrocosm–microcosm analogy (or meta-phor) by which man (the microcosm) was likened to the natural world. For example, it was said that copper, like a human being, has a spirit, a soul, and a body, with the spirit being the tincture (Crosland, 1978, p. 13). In a related vein, metals were compared with human states of health. Thus, gold corresponded to a man in perfect health and silver to "leprous gold" (Crosland, 1978, p. 15). In another analogy between the heavenly and the earthly planes, some alchemists counted twelve processes neces-sary to produce gold from base metal (calcination, solution, separation, conjunction, putrefaction, etc.), corresponding to the twelve signs of the zodiac. Others counted seven processes, corresponding to the seven days of creation and to the seven planets, each of which was held to generate its special metal in the earth (Cavendish, 1967, p.159). The importance of the microcosm–macrocosm metaphor stemmed partly from the fact that alchemy took as its domain the spiritual world as well as the physical world. A central belief was that the purification of base metals into gold was analogous to the spiritual purification of man (Redgrove, 1922). This analogy could be run in either direction, so that "some men pursued the renewal and glorification of matter, guiding themselves by this analogy, others the renewal and glorification of man, using the same analogy" (Taylor, 1949, p. 144).

The alchemists' willingness to heed similarities of all kinds derived in part from their belief that all things above and below are connected, and that similarity and metaphor are guides to those connections. This dogma was codified in the medieval *doctrine of signatures,* the sense that "It is through similitudes that the otherwise occult parenthood between things is manifested and every sublunar body bears the traces of that parenthood impressed on it as a signature" (Eco, 1990, p. 24). Vickers (1984) suggests that the alchemists invested analogy with extraordinary importance, even equating analogy with identity.

What were the rules that governed the alchemists' use of analogy and metaphor? We begin with a family of comparisons that used as the base domain the egg or the seed, and as the target domain either (or both) the principles of matter or the components of a human being.

The egg

The egg was used widely in alchemical analogies. Taken as a whole, the egg could symbolize the limitlessness of the universe, or infinity itself. The Philosopher's Stone was often called an egg (Cavendish, 1967; Stillman, 1960). The egg could also be divided into components. For example, Still-man (1960) notes that the shell, skin, white, and yolk of the egg were thought to be analogous to the four metals involved in transmutation: copper, tin, lead, and iron (although no pairings were specified between

Table 20.3. *Alchemical analogies of the Egg*

Domain	Dienheim's analogy		Further analogies		
	The Egg	Components of the Philosopher's Stone	Elements of matter	Male-female principles	Primary qualities
Number of elements	(3)	(?)	(3)	(2)	(4)
Correspondences					
	White	Soul	Sulphur	Male	Fire
	Yolk	Spirit	Mercury	Male-female	Air/Water
	Shell	Body	Salt (Arsenic)	Female	Earth

the components and the metals). Several additional correspondences are apparent in the following excerpt from the manuscript of St. Mark's in the tenth or eleventh century (copied in 1478, translated from Bertholet's [1887] *Collection des Anciens Alchemistes Grecs*).[9] The "egg" described is in fact the Philosopher's Stone:

Nomenclature of the Egg. This is the mystery of the art.
1. It has been said that the egg is composed of the four elements, because it is the image of the world and contains in itself the four elements. It is called also the "stone which causes the moon to turn," "stone which is not a stone," "stone of the eagle" and "brain of alabaster."
2. The shell of the egg is an element like earth, cold and dry; it has been called copper, iron, tin, lead. The white of the egg is the water divine, the yellow of the egg is couperose [sulfate], the oily portion is fire.
3. The egg has been called the seed and its shell the skin; its white and its yellow the flesh, its oily part, the soul, its aqueous, the breath of the air. (Stillman, 1960, pp. 170–171; notation in brackets added)

This brief excerpt illustrates the style of analogizing displayed by many alchemists. First, the egg is compared to several different analogs. The use of multiple analogs would not in itself differentiate this passage from the work of Boyle. However, what is distinctive here is that the number of components involved in the correspondence varies from analog to analog, as shown in Figure 20.5. (See also Table 20.3.) The first paragraph maps the "egg" first onto the four elements and then onto a series of single entities (e.g., "the stone which is not a stone," the "brain of alabaster"). In paragraphs 2 and 3, the components of the egg are successively compared to the four elements of ancient Greek philosophy (earth, water, air, and fire),[10] the layers of a seed, and the aspects of a human being. These multiple analogies are quite different from those of Boyle; the alchemist

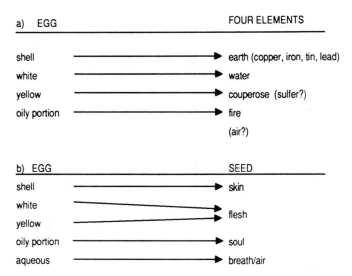

Figure 20.5. Object correspondences in the egg analogy.

does not attempt to delineate a common structure that holds across the several systems. (It would probably not be possible to do so.)

But a more striking difference arises when we consider the issue of one-to-one mappings. Figure 20.5 shows the object correspondences used in the above set of analogies. It is apparent that achieving one-to-one correspondence is not of primary concern. For example, as Figure 20.5a shows, the object correspondences for the analogy between the egg and the four elements of matter are such that the element of air must either be omitted or else placed in correspondence with a previously used element of the egg, yielding a mapping of four objects onto five. As Figure 20.5b shows, the mapping from the egg to the four divisions of the seed (or aspects of a human being) is also not one-to-one, since both the white and the yellow parts of the egg correspond to the flesh. Thus Figure 20.5b shows a $5 \rightarrow 4$ mapping, whereas Figure 20.5a shows a $4 \rightarrow 5$ mapping. When an analogy yields two or more competing mappings, the modern practice is to choose between them or to note that there are alternative interpretations. In contrast, the alchemists resolved the tension by combining both interpretations into a fused whole. This failure to preserve a one-to-one correspondence differentiates this reasoning sharply from that of modern scientists.

The alchemists invested metaphor with great importance. The belief that metaphors reveal essential categories, as discussed by Glucksberg and Keysar (1990), was taken to extreme lengths. For example, an attractive aspect of the egg was that it was recognized as something vital, as symbolic of a beginning. Any system that could be related to the egg was imbued with a similar significance. When some alchemists shifted from the Greek theory of four elements to the theory that three "principles" – usually defined as sulphur, mercury, and salt (or arsenic) – composed all matter, it was still possible to use the egg analogy:

As an egg is composed of three things, the shell, the white, and the yolk, so is our Philosophical Egg composed of a body, soul, and spirit. Yet in truth it is but one thing [one mercurial genus], a trinity in unity and unity in trinity – Sulphur, Mercury, and Arsenic. (Dienheim, quoted in Hamilton-Jones, 1960, p. 79; brackets are his)

Here the alchemist suggests a series of parallel analogies among the egg, the Philosopher's Stone, man, and matter, and gives the object correspondences among the (now three) parts of the egg, the three aspects of man, and the three principles of matter. Other alchemists extended the analogy, mapping the three parts of the egg onto the male-female principles and the four primary qualities, as shown in Table 20.3 (Cavendish, 1967, p. 169).

Analogies with symbols

Another striking aspect of alchemical analogizing was a willingness to use similarities between symbols and their referents. Vickers (1984) suggests that the alchemists were influenced by the occult tradition in which the word or symbol does not merely stand for its referent, but is *identical in essence* to it. This in turn led to a belief in the causal powers of words and other symbols. For example, Kriegsmann (1665) offered an analysis of the properties of the three principles – sulphur, mercury and salt – in terms of their symbology (Crosland, 1978, p. 233). Given the suppositions that a straight line denoted earth, a triangle fire, a semicircle air, and a circle water, he attempted to analyze the symbols for sulphur, mercury, and salt into the four basic elementary symbols. Even as late as 1727, Boerhaave analyzed copper by the following chain of thought. First, he noted that a circle indicates perfection, whereas a cross denotes something sharp and corrosive. It follows that gold is symbolized as a circle, and since copper is symbolized by a circle plus a cross, it can be seen to be "intimately Gold" but combined with some crude, sharp, and corrosive material. That this system was believed to be predictive, not merely conveniently iconic, can be seen in this passage by Boerhaave concerning iron (symbolized by a circle plus an outward arrow):

that this too is intimately Gold; but that it has with it a great deal of the sharp and corrosive; though with but half the degree of Acrimony as the former, as you see that it has but half the sign that expresses that quality. . . . Indeed it is almost the universal opinion of the adepts that the *Aurum vivum* or *Philosophorum* does lye concealed in Iron; and that here therefore we must seek for metalline Medicines, and not in Gold itself. (Crosland, 1978, p. 233)

That metaphors between symbols and material objects were held to be informative is a marked difference from the present aesthetic. It is related to the doctrine of signatures, the sense that similarity virtually guarantees significant connections. As Eco (1990, p. 24) puts it in his description of Renaissance hermeticism, .

> The basic principle is not only that the similar can be known through the similar but also that from similarity to similarity everything can be connected with everything else.

Paracelsus

Paracelsus (Theophrastus Bombastus von Hohenheim, 1493–1541) was a leading alchemist of the sixteenth century and a vigorous proponent of the value of empirical observation as opposed to received dogma. Despite this rather modern spirit, his use of the analogy remains distinctly different from modern usage. Here, he describes how gold and silver can be made:

> Some one may ask, what, then, is the short and easy way whereby Sol and Luna may be made? The answer is this: After you have made heaven, or the sphere of Saturn, with its life to run over the earth, place on it all the planets so that the portion of Luna may be the smallest. Let all run until heaven or Saturn has entirely disappeared. Then all those planets will remain dead with their old corruptible bodies, having meanwhile obtained another new, perfect and incorruptible body. That body is the spirit of heaven. From it these planets again receive a body and life and live as before. Take this body from the life and earth. Keep it. It is Sol and Luna. Here you have the Art, clear and entire. If you do not understand it it is well. It is better that it should be kept concealed and not made public. (quoted in Jaffe, 1967, p. 23)

Here Sol and Luna (the sun and moon, respectively) signify gold and silver, and other metals in the recipe are represented by the other planets, according to a widely used system of alchemical analogies (see below). Paracelsus does not detail the object correspondences between the two domains, nor does he explain how an action in one domain parallels an action in the other. The mappings and the theoretical basis for the procedure are left unstated. Indeed, it is not always clear which actual metals are being referred to. For example, to what do "earth" and "all those planets" refer? Does "heaven, or the sphere of Saturn" refer to tin? If so, is the final "spirit of heaven" derived from the process also tin? This last seems implausible, since the goal is to produce gold and/or silver; yet if the final "spirit of heaven" is gold or silver, then what about the initial "heaven"? Here, and also in the passages below, the alchemists go beyond similarity and into a wider set of what Gibbs (this volume) calls "tropes," including many instances of metonymy.

This passage, though it exemplifies the different rules of analogizing

Table 20.4. *The alchemical system of correspondences among planets, metals, and colors*

Planets	Metals	Colors
Sun	Gold	Gold, yellow
Moon	Silver	White
Mercury	Quicksilver	Gray, neutral
Venus	Copper	Green
Mars	Iron	Red
Jupiter	Tin	Blue
Saturn	Lead	Black

Based on Cavendish 1967, p. 26.

among the alchemists, also raises questions concerning the reasons for these differences. Paracelsus makes it clear that clarity is not his intention. The secretive nature of the enterprise, the fact that it was felt necessary to hide results from the common public and from competitors, could have led to the ambiguity of the writing. Is it possible that this ambiguity shielded a set of informative analogies? To answer this question, we must look more closely at the system of comparisons that supported this reasoning.

The system of correspondences

Since the goal of many alchemists was to transform base metals into higher metals (gold or silver), metals held an important place in alchemical analogy and metaphor. As illustrated above, metals figured in analogies with the principles of matter and with the aspects of human beings, and the transmutation of base metals into gold was felt to be analogous to the spiritual purification of man. A further set of correspondences existed between metals, planets, and colors, as shown in Table 20.4.[11] (This table and much of the surrounding explication are based on Cavendish's discussion [Cavendish, 1967, p. 26].)

The first thing that strikes us about this system is the importance of surface similarity – that is, common color – in determining the correspondences. The Sun, the metal gold, and the color gold are linked by a common color, as are the Moon, the metal silver, and the color white. But an equally striking aspect of this system is that this commonality is not uniformly maintained. The basis for the comparison shifts from one part of the system to another. For example, unlike the two triads just mentioned, the Jupiter/tin/blue triad is not entirely based on common color. Instead, blue (the color of the sky) is matched to Jupiter because Jupiter was lord of the sky. And although the match between Jupiter and tin may be a color match, based on the planet's silvery appearance, it may also have been based on an ancient belief that the sky was made of tin. Thus the set of similarities that figure in the correspondences changes from one row or column to another.

The set of relations that linked the rows of this table was remarkably rich and diverse, as illustrated in this discussion by Cavendish (1967, p. 27):

> Lead, the darkest and heaviest of the metals, was naturally assigned to Saturn, the dimmest and slowest-moving planet, which trudges heavily through its slow path round the sun. In the old cosmology Saturn is the farthest planet from the sun, the ruler of life, and is the lord of death. The analogy between death and night was drawn very early. Black is the colour of night and the colour invariably associated with death in Western countries.

The chain of connections between Saturn and black is a case in point. Saturn is the lord of death, death is similar to night, the color of a night sky is black, and blackness symbolizes death. Thus a chain is made between the planet Saturn and the color black. This rich metonymic chain is quite different from the simple "color of X and Y is Z" relation that holds for Sun/gold/yellow and Moon/silver/white. The heterogeneity of matches that could apply within a single tabular system contrasts sharply with the modern aesthetic. The preference for structural consistency and systematicity in modern analogy would dictate that identical relations should hold across the system: that is, we would expect to find

Moon:white :: Sun:yellow :: Jupiter:blue :: Saturn:black

In the alchemical system there is no such requirement: no two rows need have the same set of relational links.[12]

This example illustrates a further point of difference: the alchemists' system of correspondences violates the "no extraneous relations principle" in that cross connections of all kinds enter into the analogies. For instance, black, lead and Saturn are all linked through the chain described above; but the match between lead and Saturn was improved by the fact that both are slow and heavy. Saturn moves slowly in its orbit and was therefore thought of as massive (heavy); lead was known to be a dense (heavy) metal, which would presumably move slowly. This complex web of similarities was felt to improve the system, though it could not be applied uniformly.

As another instance of the prolific and heterogeneous nature of this relational system, consider the match between Mars and red. Cavendish (1967, p. 27) notes that it is based on several chains of associations: Mars looks red; Mars was the god of war, war is associated with bloodshed, and blood is red; faces are painted red in war; and Mars is held to rule violent energy and activity and red is the color symbolizing energy. These multiple metonymic paths strengthened the analogical connection between Mars and red.

This discussion of the alchemists' system of correspondences illustrates some marked differences in the rules of the game. The alchemists were not moved by the modern "no extraneous relations" rule. They accepted mixed metaphors and fused interpretations of a single metaphor. In the current aesthetic, once a parallel set of relations is established, adding local relations that hold only for a few cases does not improve the analogy. But for the alchemists, more was always better. A rich set of interrelationships, however idiosyncratic, was felt to strengthen the similarity bond.

Comparison between the alchemists and modern scientists

The alchemists embraced similarity in all its forms in reasoning about the natural world. Yet the examples we have considered show marked deviation from the current style of analogical reasoning as summarized in Table 20.1. Are there then historical differences in analogical reasoning? Before drawing this conclusion we must consider two other factors that may have contributed to the differences. First, the vagueness of alchemical analogy might have stemmed simply from a desire for secrecy, as discussed above. In order to prevent laymen from understanding the mysteries of alchemy, its practitioners disguised their recipes with symbolism and ambiguity. But although this is undoubtedly part of the story, it would be an oversimplification to try to explain all the differences in this way.[13] As discussed below, the alchemists' penchant for chaotic metaphor goes well beyond what a desire for secrecy will account for.

A second and deeper difference between the alchemists and modern scientists is the fact that the alchemists had more complex goals. They were concerned not only with understanding the material world, but with achieving spiritual transcendence. The alchemist invested the analogy between the spiritual and material planes with dual-causal powers and might strive to purify his spirit in order to transmute metals, or strive to transmute metals in order to purify his spirit. Modern science separates personal virtue from excellence in research. This separation has its disadvantages, but it does streamline the research enterprise.

Another possible difference in goals is that the alchemists were probably relatively more interested in the acquisition of power (as opposed to the acquisition of pure knowledge) than are modern scientists. But although the alchemists had a complex (and perhaps mutually incompatible) set of goals, we should not lose sight of the fact that a primary goal was to understand the material universe. The most convincing evidence that the desire to understand was at least part of their agenda is the fact that alchemy produced a large number of factual discoveries: useful compounds, tinctures, alloys, and so forth. We can also see a quest for knowledge in some alchemical writings. The alchemist Roger Bacon (1214–1292, not to be confused with Francis Bacon, quoted below) wrote in 1267:

I have laboured from my youth in the sciences and languages, and for the further-
ance of study, getting together much that is useful. I sought the friendship of all wise
men among the Latins, and caused youth to be instructed in languages and geometric figures, in numbers and tables and instruments, and many needful matters.
(quoted in Crosland, 1978, p. 119)

It is impossible not to recognize in this passage some commonalities with
scientists of any period. However complex the alchemists' goals, it is inescapable that among those goals was a desire for knowledge.

With the foregoing cautions, we now consider whether the disparities
in analogizing suggest a genuine difference in reasoning style. Some of
the differences – notably failure to show relational focus and to seek
systematicity – could reasonably be attributed to simple lack of domain
knowledge. Lacking deep domain theories, the alchemists perforce had to
rely more on surface similarity than later scientists. Indeed, there is considerable evidence from studies of the development of metaphor and analogy
(Billow, 1975; Chen & Daehler, 1989; Gentner, 1988; Gentner & Rattermann, 1991) and from novice–expert studies in learning physics (Chi,
Feltovich & Glaser, 1981) to suggest that young children and novices judge
similarity by common object descriptions, while older children and experts
use common relational structure. Many researchers have argued that the relational shift in development may be explainable largely by accretion of domain knowledge (Gentner, 1988; Gentner & Rattermann, 1991; Goswami,
1991; Goswami & A. Brown, 1989; Vosniadou, 1989), and the same arguments may apply here. Similarly, the alchemists' reliance on surface qualities
and their failure to show relational focus do not necessarily indicate a different style of thinking; they could be attributable to lack of knowledge.

Domain knowledge differences, however, will not account for all the
differences between the alchemists and modern analogists. The fact that
the alchemists felt no need for one-to-one correspondences, their fondness
for between-domain relations and mixed metaphors, and their propensity
to ascribe causal powers to analogy and similarity all seem to point to a true
difference in their sense of the implicit rules of analogizing. One hint that
this may be true comes from contemporary comments.

Transition: The discovery of analogy

Toward the end of the alchemists' reign, roughly between 1570 and 1640,
there occurred a fascinating period of explicit discussion of the proper use
of analogy and similarity. (For an extended discussion, see Vickers, 1984,
pp. 95–163.) For example, Francis Bacon in 1605 attacked the Paracelsans'
penchant for analogy:

The ancient opinion that man was Microcosmus, an abstract or model of the world,
hath been fantastically strained by Paracelsus and the alchemists, as if there were to

be found in man's body certain correspondences and parallels, which should have respect to all varieties of things, as stars, planets, minerals, which are extant in the great world. (quoted in Vickers, 1984, p. 134)

Some of this criticism rested on rejecting the seemingly absurd conclusions of the alchemists' analogies, such as the notion that man was made of vegetative or mineral matter. Van Helmont, for example, complained of the vast differences between the objects placed in correspondence, for example, stars mapping onto plants and herbs. (It is interesting that this argument would not be valid in the modern aesthetic.) Another complaint centered on the alchemists' tendency to "heap analogy onto analogy, spiraling off into the void" as Vickers (1984, p. 135) puts it. For example, Andreas Libavius attacked the alchemist Croll for his use of a cabalistic language of signs:

The Cabala is a falsehood and a deceit. For it presents things, not as they are, but as they are compared with other things in an indeterminately external fashion. Thus we are not able to know what constitutes a thing. (quoted in Vickers, 1984, p. 135)

Some critics recommended abandoning similarity altogether. Daniel Sennert (1619) wrote:

Therefore the soul that loves truth is not satisfied with similitudes only, but desires solid demonstrations; and volves things from their own, not from principles of another. . . . There is nothing so like, but in some part it is unlike. (quoted in Vickers, 1984, p. 142)

J. B. Van Helmont (1648) was even firmer, writing, "I have hated Metaphorical Speeches in serious matters," and also, "surely I do not apply figures or moving forces in Mathematicall demonstration unto nature: I shun proportionable resemblance [analogy]" (quoted in Vickers, 1984, p. 144).

Others responded to this crisis of confidence by trying to define the nature of true analogizing. Johannes Kepler was particularly articulate in attempting to explicate the kind of analogy that is warranted in scientific argumentation. Like Van Helmont, he was critical of the alchemical style of analogizing. He wrote in 1619 of Ptolemy's analogy between planetary motions and musical keys:

I have shown that Ptolemy luxuriates in using comparisons in a poetical or rhetorical way, since the things that he compares are not real things in the heavens. (quoted in Vickers, 1984, p. 153)

Kepler argued that analogies should be based on physical, measurable quantities, and not on the symbols that represent them. He rejected metaphors from the symbolic to the real world (such as Boerhaave's mappings of qualities from chemical symbols to the elements themselves, as discussed earlier).

Yet Kepler did not advocate avoiding the use of similarity. On the contrary, he was an ardent analogizer. For example, in 1604 he used an analogy with optics to explain the five conic sections (circle, ellipse, parabola, hyperbola, and straight line), an explanatory framework that is still useful. He notes that he speaks "contrary to normal use" but continues:

But for us the terms in Geometry should serve the analogy (for I especially love analogies, my most faithful masters, acquainted with all the secrets of nature) and one should make great use of them in geometry, where – despite the incongruous terminology – they bring the solutions of an infinity of cases lying between the extreme and the mean, and where they clearly present to our eyes the whole essence of the question. (quoted in Vickers, 1984, p. 150)

But Kepler's enthusiasm for analogy was tempered by a desire for independent confirmation of the analogical inferences. Later in the passage, giving examples of how to construct the conic sections, he notes "Analogy has shown, and Geometry confirms." In distinction to the alchemists, for whom similitude was sufficient evidence of a deep connection, Kepler regarded analogy as a source of hypotheses.

In a 1608 letter to a colleague, he wrote with great explicitness about the heuristic nature of analogy and of the need for analogies to preserve interrelationships and causal structure:

I too play with symbols, and have planned a little work, Geometric Cabala, which is about the Ideas of natural things in geometry; but I play in such a way that I do not forget that I am playing. For nothing is proved by symbols . . . unless by sure reasons it can be demonstrated that they are not merely symbolic but are *descriptions of the ways in which the two things are connected and of the causes of this connexion.* (quoted in Vickers, 1984, p. 155; italics added)

Kepler's symbols and principles – that analogies should in general hold between real domains, rather than between symbols and domains, that analogy is a source of hypotheses rather than a guarantor of truth, and that an analogy is useful in virtue of its ability to capture common causal relations – are remarkably modern. Further, this new sense of analogizing is apparent in practice as well as in theory. Both Kepler and his contemporary Galileo made frequent use of analogy, but in a style quite different from the alchemists. For example, Galileo (1629) used the analogy between dropping a ball from a tower on the earth and dropping a ball from the mast of a ship to argue that the earth moves despite the evidence of our senses. (See Gentner, 1982, for further details.) Kepler dealt with the notion of action at a distance with an analogy between light and a force he hypothesized to emanate from the sun. (See Vickers, 1984, for further details.) Like light, this motive force might travel unseen through space yet produce an effect at its destination, and like light, its strength would diminish with distance from the source. In each case, Kepler and Galileo examined the disanalogies as to whether they undermined the analogy, that is, as to whether they affected the common causal system sanctioned by the analogy.

There is a sharp contrast between this playful but stern view of analogy and the profligate metaphor of the alchemists. Kepler (1571–1630) and Galileo (1564–1642), each working within about fifty years of Paracelsus (1493–1541), used analogies as rigorously and systematically as Boyle or Carnot, or indeed as Feynman or Oppenheimer. The striking contrast in analogical style over this brief period, coupled with the intense discussion of the proper use of similarity that occurred during this time, leads us to speculate that a shift in the rules of reasoning by similarity occurred somewhere between 1570 and 1640. Vickers (1984) identifies this period as a transition period in the relation between analogy and identity. We could put it that analogy was (re)discovered in Western science[14] in about 1600.

Conclusions

Despite the seeming inevitability of our current constraints on similarity-based reasoning, they do not appear to be universal. The alchemists relied heavily on similarity and metaphor in their investigations of the nature of matter; but their use of similarity differed sharply from that of modern scientists. In particular, the alchemists lacked a sense that *analogy* in the modern sense had any advantage over surface similarity or over metonymic, richly interconnected but unclarified forms of similarity and metaphor.

A fascinating aspect of this historical change is the period, roughly 1570–1640, during which similarity itself became a focus of discussion among scientists. This period coincides with the waning of alchemical methods[15] and the rise of a more modern spirit. The shift from metaphor to analogy is one aspect of the general change in the style of scientific thought that occurred during this period. There is no way to tell whether the discussion of analogy was the cause or the result (or both) of the general shift in scientific reasoning. Nevertheless, the energy and explicitness with which Kepler, Van Helmont and others discussed the nature of proper analogizing commands attention. Among other things, it offers an opportunity to study the psychological intuitions of scientists 350 years past. The convergence between Kepler's account of analogy and our own current account is as remarkable as the divergence of both approaches with that of Paracelsus.

Cultural differences in the cognitive aesthetics of similarity and analogy

The marked difference in the style of analogizing between the alchemists and later scientists suggests that the uses of analogy and similarity are in part culturally defined. How far might such cultural differences extend? The strongest form of this conjecture would be that some human cultures have lacked the use of true analogy entirely, and that there is a cultural evolution toward such use. We hasten to stress that our evidence is much weaker than this. We do not suggest that the alchemists (or their compatriots) lacked the ability to use analogy; on the contrary, the prevalence of allegories and proverbs suggests that analogy was alive and well in western culture during the middle ages. Where the alchemists differed from modern scientists, we suggest, was in lacking an appreciation of analogy's special value in the pursuit of scientific knowledge.

There are modern instances of cultures that possess the various forms of similarity, including analogy, but use them in a different distribution from current western culture. Homeopathy and contagion (that is, similarity and contiguity/association) are the two pillars of folk magic across cultures (e.g., Rozin & Fallon, 1987). For example, in West Africa, a belief in *juju* – a kind of sympathetic magic that relies heavily on similarity and metonymy – exists side by side with the frequent highly relational use of proverbs in everyday human interactions. Thus our point is not that some cultures have lacked the ability to reason analogically, but that cultures have differed in their tacit theories of when and how to use analogy and other kinds of similarities.

Different kinds of similarities coexist in our own current cognitive practice as well. Although analogy is preferred in science (see note 16), literary metaphors are allowed to be rich, complex, and inconsistent, and to have many-to-one mappings and metonymies (Shen, 1987). (Recall the example from Dylan Thomas cited earlier, or this one from him: "All the moon long I heard, blessed among stables, the nightjars / Flying with the ricks, and the horses / Flashing into the dark.") To see whether people use different criteria for scientific and literary comparisons, we asked subjects to rate scientific and literary comparisons for their *clarity* ("how easy is it to tell what matches with what") and their *richness* ("how evocative is the comparison; how much is conveyed by the comparison"). We also asked them to rate either the scientific explanatory value or the literary expressiveness of the comparisons (Gentner, 1982). In judgments of scientific merit, clarity was considered crucial and richness was unimportant. In judgments of literary merit, both clarity and richness contributed, and neither was essential. These findings suggest a broader tolerance for nonclarified similarity in literary contexts than in scientific contexts.

This should not be taken to imply that unclarified metaphor has no role in scientific contexts in our culture. There is general agreement that unruly metaphors play a role in the discovery process, and that some degree of tolerance for loose analogy is important for creativity, as in Polya's (1954) advice (quoted earlier) to keep vague analogies but try to clarify them.

This speculation fits with recent research that has emphasized the plurality of similarity types and the context-sensitivity of similarity processes. For example, Medin, Goldstone, and Gentner (1993) have suggested that similarity is (implicitly) defined with respect to a large set of variables, and

Gentner, Rattermann, and Forbus (in press) and Ross (1984, 1987) have emphasized that different kinds of similarities participate differentially in different psychological subprocesses. For example, in similarity-based transfer, access to memory appears particularly sensitive to the degree of surface similarity, whereas evaluation of soundness is particularly sensitive to the degree and depth of common relational structure (Gentner, Rattermann, & Forbus, in press). To model a similarity comparison one must specify not merely the two comparands but also the sets from which they are chosen, the contextual goals, the task (e.g., memory access or inference or evaluation), and several other "respects." The present conjecture goes one step further in adding cultural factors to the list of variables that influence similarity.

Does child development parallel historical development?

In Western science we see a historical shift toward the belief that analogy rather than generalized metaphor provides a basis for scientific inquiry. We might ask whether such an evolution also occurs in children. (For related comparisons see Brewer, 1989; Carey, 1985a.) There are many differences between a child growing up in a culture that already possesses the analogical method and a scientist living in a time when the consensual rules for similarity were themselves evolving. But there may be some parallels. For example, Vygotsky (1962) observed that when preschool children are asked to sort varied objects into piles that go together, they tend to utilize thematic and metonymic connections, rather than consistent categories. They shift from one local similarity to another (e.g., the apple goes with the tomato because both are red, the knife goes with the apple because it can cut the apple, the spoon goes with the knife because they co-occur).

A second parallel is that in the development of metaphor and analogy, children show an early focus on surface object commonalities, followed by a developmental shift toward attention to relational commonalities (Gentner, 1988; Gentner & Toupin, 1986). For example, asked "how is a cloud like a sponge?" a preschool child says "both are round and fluffy," whereas older children and adults say "both hold water and later give it back." A similar shift occurs in perceptual similarity tasks, from object similarity to relational similarity and then to higher-order relational similarity (Gentner, Rattermann, Markman, & Kotovsky, in press; Halford, 1987, 1992). Smith (1989) has noted a developmental shift from the use of a vague sort of global magnitude (wherein, for example, *large* and *dark* are interchangeable positive magnitudes) to the use of dimensional orderings (wherein *small/medium/big* is structurally aligned with *light/medium/dark*). It is possible that children recapitulate some of the alchemists' journey in learning how to reason with similarity.

There are other possible parallels. Based on Rozin and Fallon's (1987) findings, we might ask whether young children in our culture are more swayed by homeopathy and contagion than are adults. Further afield, it is possible that children recapitulate the alchemists' journey from seeking *power* to seeking *knowledge*. Young children, even when instructed to find out how a device works, often approach the task in the spirit of gaining control rather than in the spirit of gaining knowledge (Klahr, 1990, personal communication).

But the issue of parallels between cultural evolution and children's development for similarity and analogy raises more questions than it answers. Most current accounts of the causes of the relational shift in similarity have emphasized accretion of domain knowledge, rather than changes in cognitive processing (e.g., A. Brown, 1989; Gentner, 1988; Gentner & Rattermann, 1991; Goswami, 1991; Goswami & A. Brown, 1989; Vosniadou, 1989). But if we take the parallel with alchemists seriously, it suggests that we might also look for changes in children's metacognitive rules about how and when to use similarity. Do children show a shift in their causal uses of similarity from valuing thickly interconnected metaphoric tropes to valuing rigorous analogy? If so, is there a transition period of explicit thought about the nature of explanatory analogy? And finally, if this kind of evolution occurs, what are its causes? Gentner and Rattermann (1991) have suggested that learning relational language is important in bringing about the relational shift in similarity. Other kinds of cultural experiences, including literacy and schooling (Bruner, Goodnow, & Austin, 1956), may be important as well.

Similarity is a central organizing force in mental life. This research implies that although the apprehension of similarity in its various forms may be universal among humans, conventions for how and when to use it are not. There is variation both across and within cultures in the ways humans use similarity to categorize and reason about the world. This survey suggests an evolution in Western science from metaphor to analogy: from profligate use of rich but unruly comparisons to the present preference for structural analogy in scientific reasoning. Finally, this research raises the fascinating question of how our current cognitive aesthetics are learned by children.

NOTES

This chapter is a substantially revised version of a paper by D. Gentner and M. Jeziorsky (1989), "Historical shifts in the use of analogy in science," in B. Gholson, A. Houts, R. A. Neimeyer, and W. R. Shadish (eds.), *The psychology of science and metascience* (New York: Cambridge University Press). Preparation of this chapter was supported by the Office of Naval Research under Grant No. N00014-85-K-0559, NR667-551, and by the National Science Foundation under Contract No. BNS 9096259. We thank Cathy Clement, Brian Falkenhainer, Ken Forbus, Robert Goldstone, Doug Medin, and Mary Jo Rattermann for discussions of these issues, and Andrew Ortony and Lance Rips for comments on prior drafts. We also thank Eva Hinton, Gina Bolinger, and Mike Park for editorial assistance.

1 The *no mixed analogies* rule does not apply to the case of multiple parallel analogies that all embody the *same* relational structure. Such parallel analogies can often illuminate a common abstraction (Elio & Anderson, 1981; Gick & Holyoak, 1983; Schumacher & Gentner, 1987).

2 As with the other principles, the "analogy is not causation" principle is violated occasionally. There are still believers in homeopathy and sympathetic magic, who implicitly subscribe to the belief that likeness implies causal connection. Closer to home, in a survey of the analogies used to explain cognition in the history of psychology, Gentner and Grudin (1985) found that certain analogies between the physical brain and the mind (such as "associations among images are analogous to white matter connecting regions of gray matter" [Starr, 1984]) seemed to take on extra authority because of the known causal connection between brain and mind.

3 The caloric theory was widely accepted until Joule and other experimenters demonstrated the interconvertibility of heat and work in the 1840s (Wilson, 1981). Carnot's reliance on the caloric theory did not invalidate his basic conclusions regarding the cycle, although some later statements in *Reflexions* are incorrect when viewed from the perspective of the mechanical theory of heat (Fox, 1971).

4 Although Carnot refers to a waterfall, his discussion may have been based not merely on waterfalls, but on some kind of water engine, such as a water wheel or a column-of-water engine (Cardwell, 1965).

5 According to Fox (1971), Carnot's answer to this question was affected by his reliance on the questionable data of other scientists.

6 It is possible that at least part of the difference in analogical style between Carnot and Boyle stems from differences in their respective intellectual traditions. As Hesse (1966) points out in her ground-breaking work on analogy in science, the English tradition is far more tolerant of mechanical analogies than the French tradition. Hesse notes that the French academic tradition views analogy as vague and unsatisfactory, at best a crutch to use until a formal model can be devised. In contrast, the English tradition values mechanical analogies as sources of insight, especially with respect to preserving causation. This point is brought home in Nersessian's (1984) analysis of the use of analogy by Faraday and Maxwell and in Tweney's (1983) discussion of Faraday. Thus it is possible that some of the differences in style between Boyle and Carnot may stem from differences in cultural tradition.

7 The alchemists' comparisons are usually referred to as "analogies" but, for reasons that will become clear, they might better be described as "metaphors." We will use both terms.

8 This discussion is culled from several sources, principally Asimov (1965, pp. 15–33), Cavendish (1967, pp. 143–180), Crosland (1978, pp. 3–107), Holmyard (1957), Stillman (1960), and Vickers (1984).

9 Although this passage was copied in 1478, its exact date of origin is difficult to pinpoint. Other manuscripts from this collection are believed to have existed since before the fourth century in one form or another (Stillman, 1960).

10 However, this is an unusual (perhaps a transitional) account of the elements. The elements listed are earth (or metal), water, couperose (or sulfate), and fire, with air not explicitly mentioned.

11 There were several minor variants of this system of correspondences (e.g., Crosland, 1978, p. 80).

12 An alternative way of describing the alchemical aesthetic would be to say that the relations involved are extremely nonspecific: for example, "associated with by some path." Under that description, the alchemists would not be guilty of shifting relations between parallel analogs. However, this degree of nonspecificity of relations would still constitute a marked difference from modern scientific usage.

13 For one thing, it is not clear that the alchemists' analogies are so much less accessible than modern analogies. To the extent that alchemical correspondences were based on surface similarity, they could often be readily guessed. In contrast, in modern scientific analogy the object correspondences are often impossible to grasp without a knowledge of the domain theory, since they are based purely on like roles in the matching relational system.

14 It might be better to say "rediscovered," since the Greeks, including Plato and Aristotle, used analogy in the modern way.

15 Alchemy continued into the eighteenth century and beyond, but with greatly decreased influence.

16 This is apart from variation in the degree to which individuals in our culture conform to our ideal of rationality, as opposed to relying on superstitions based on metaphor and metonymy.

21

*Metaphor and theory change: What is "metaphor" a metaphor for?

RICHARD BOYD

Introduction

In the now classic essay "Metaphor" (Black, 1962b), Max Black considers and rejects various formulations of the "substitution view" of metaphor, according to which every metaphorical statement is equivalent to a (perhaps more awkward, or less decorative) literal statement. Black devotes most of his critical attention to a special case of the substitution view, the "comparison view," according to which a metaphor consists in the presentation of an underlying analogy or similarity. It is clear from Black's discussion that he understands the comparison view as entailing that every metaphorical statement be equivalent to one in which some quite definite respect of similarity or analogy is presented, and that successful communication via metaphor involves the hearer understanding the same respect(s) of similarity or analogy as the speaker.

Black argues that, except perhaps in cases of *catachresis* – the use of metaphor to remedy gaps in vocabulary – the comparison view is inadequate. As an alternative, Black proposed the adoption of an "interaction view" of metaphor. According to this view, metaphors work by applying to the principal (literal) subject of the metaphor a system of "associated implications" characteristic of the metaphorical secondary subject. These implications are typically provided by the received "commonplaces" about the secondary subject. Although Black's position has many facets, it is clear that, at a minimum, it differs from the comparison view in denying that the success of a metaphor rests on its success in conveying to the listener or reader some quite definite respects of similarity or analogy between the principal and secondary subjects: metaphors are, on Black's view, more open-ended (this is not his terminology) than the comparison view would suggest.

In certain passages, Black appears to suggest even stronger points of divergence between his view and the comparison account. In addition to denying that successful metaphors must convey to the reader or hearer some quite definite respect of similarity or analogy, Black also denies that any analysis of an interaction metaphor in terms of explicit analogies or similarities, however elaborate, can capture the cognitive content which it is capable of conveying (Black, 1962b, p. 46). Black sees these features of metaphor as indicative of an important difference between metaphorical uses of language and those uses which have the features of explicitness characteristic of scientific usage.

We need the metaphors in just those cases where there can be no question as yet of the precision of scientific statements. Metaphorical statement is not a substitute for formal comparison or any other kind of literal statement but has its own distinctive capacities and achievements. (p. 37)

In particular, in this view, one should expect that when metaphorical language is employed in a scientific context, its function should either lie in the pretheoretical (prescientific?) stages of the development of a discipline, or in the case of more mature sciences, it should lie in the realm of heuristics, pedagogy, or informal exegesis, rather than in the realm of the actual articulation or development of theories.

In formulating my own views about the role of metaphor in theory change, I have found it valuable to compare and contrast my understanding of scientific metaphors with Black's account of metaphors in general. Roughly speaking, what I should like to argue here is this: There exists an important class of metaphors which play a role in the development and articulation of theories in relatively mature sciences. Their function is a sort of *catachresis* – that is, they are used to introduce theoretical terminology where none previously existed. Nevertheless, they possess several (though not all) of the characteristics which Black attributes to interaction metaphors; in particular, their success does not depend on their conveying quite specific respects of similarity or analogy. Indeed, their users are typically unable to precisely specify the relevant respects of similarity or analogy, and the utility of these metaphors in theory change crucially depends upon this open-endedness.

On the other hand, I shall argue, this particular sort of open-endedness or inexplicitness does not distinguish these metaphors from more typical cases of scientific terminology, nor need it be the case that these metaphors forever resist complete explication of the relevant respects of similarity and analogy; such explication is often an eventual consequence of successful scientific research. There are, I shall argue, cases in which complete explication is impossible, but far from being indications of the imprecision of metaphorical language in science, such cases reflect the necessity of obtaining a *precise* fit between scientific language and a messy and complex world. The impression that metaphors must lack the precision characteristic of scientific statements reflects, I shall argue, an extremely plausible but mistaken understanding of precision in science.

More precisely, what I shall argue is that the use of metaphor is one of many devices available to the scientific community to accomplish the task of *accommodation of language to the causal structure of the world*. By this I mean the task of introducing terminology, and modifying usage of existing terminology, so that linguistic categories are available which describe the causally and explanatorily significant features of the world. Roughly speaking, this is the task of arranging our language so that our linguistic categories "cut the world at its joints"; the "joint" metaphor is misleading only in that it obscures the fact that the relevant notion of "joint" may be context, or discipline, relative. An important special case of this task of accommodation (not under that description) has recently been investigated in some detail by Kripke (1972) and Putnam (1975a, 1975b), who have emphasized the ostensive character of some of the mechanisms by which the reference of certain natural-kind terms is fixed. Although their accounts of the "causal theory of reference" differ in important details, each of them emphasizes that it is by virtue of the ostensive character of these reference-fixing mechanisms that it is possible for natural-kind terms to refer to kinds which are determined by explanatory or "real" essences, rather than by definitional or "nominal" essences: that is, their account explains how it is possible for natural-kind terms to play a role in what I am calling *accommodation*. The accounts which Putnam and Kripke offer are particularly well suited to cases in which the reference of a term is specified by display of one or more examples of a substance whose real essence is its internal constitution. What I shall argue here is that the employment of metaphor serves as a nondefinitional mode of reference fixing which is especially well suited to the introduction of terms referring to kinds whose real essences consist of complex relational properties, rather than features of internal constitution.

If I am right, this conclusion provides the basis for a clearer understanding of the (itself metaphorical) notion that reference fixing in the case of theoretical terms in science involves *ostension*. I shall suggest that the notion of ostension, and indeed the notion of reference itself, are fundamentally epistemological notions, and that the issue of reference for a general term is the issue of its role in making possible socially coordinated *epistemic access* to a particular sort of thing or natural phenomenon. In terms of the notion of epistemic access, one can formulate an account of linguistic precision in science which allows an adequate treatment of ostensively defined terms in general and metaphor in particular.

I shall also argue that an understanding of certain uses of metaphor in science can teach us something about the nature of the "real essences" which define the natural kinds to which scientific terms refer. The cases of natural kinds defined by real essences on which Putnam and Kripke chiefly rely as examples are cases in which the real definition of the kind in question is (at least on a suitable idealization) provided by a set of necessary and sufficient conditions – conditions whose conceptual representation might become our concept of the relevant kind if our scientific investigations are sufficiently successful. Thus the examples of a posteriori real definitions of natural kinds on which the literature has largely been built suggest that the classical empiricist picture according to which a kind is properly defined by a set of necessary and sufficient conditions united by the mind is basically correct as an idealization. The error of empiricist philosophers, it would seem, was their failure to recognize that such conceptual unities are properly subject to an external and nonconventional requirement of accommodation to appropriate causal structures.

I shall argue that an emphasis on such cases draws our attention away from an important fact about the scientific task of accommodating our language and concepts to the causal structure of the world and that attention to the role of metaphors in science can help us to see how this is so. In particular, I shall argue that for a class of scientifically important kinds – *homeostatic property cluster kinds* – the conception of kind definitions as conceptually unified necessary and sufficient conditions fails even as an idealization. The definitions of such kinds, I shall argue, differ in three important ways from the definitions envisioned by empiricists. In the first place, the properties (relations, etc.) that constitute the definition of a homeostatic property cluster kind are united *causally rather than conceptually*. Such a kind is defined by a family of properties that are causally united in nature: there are causal mechanisms ("homeostatic" mechanisms to use the metaphor I prefer) that tend to bring about their co-occurrence. This fact, rather than any idealized conceptual representation of those properties, is what constitutes their unity as elements in a kind-definition.

Second, the properties that define a homeostatic property cluster kind do not, even as an idealization, specify necessary and sufficient conditions for kind membership. Imperfect homeostasis, I shall argue, dictates that we take homeostatic property cluster kinds to have irremediable indeterminacy in extension – indeterminacy which could not be remedied by any more "precise" definition without abandoning the scientifically crucial task of accommodation of kind definitions to actual causal structures.

Finally, the empiricist picture of kinds as defined by conceptually united sets of necessary and sufficient conditions is mistaken in yet another way when applied to homeostatic property cluster kinds. Sets are individuated extensionally so that the members of a set cannot change from time to time or place to place. Homeostatic property cluster definitions, by contrast, are individuated nonextensionally. Mechanisms of property homeostasis are often themselves not static and as they vary over time or from place to place the properties that make up the definition of a single kind may themselves vary. Numerically the same definition may embody different properties at different times (or places) although defining numerically the same kind!

Homeostatic property cluster kinds are relevant to our understanding of metaphors in science in at least four ways. In the first place, the role of theory-constitutive metaphors in science reflects in a perhaps surprising way the epistemological necessity (and hence the methodological necessity) for the accommodation of conceptual structures to the causal structure of the world. Scientific kinds and categories must be defined in ways which reflect a deference to the world even at the cost of conceptual complexity. The fact that scientific investigation sometimes requires reference to kinds whose definitions are necessarily causally rather than conceptually unified indicates the depth of that necessity.

Moreover, the existence of kinds with the sort of definitional complexity that homeostatic property cluster kinds exhibit helps to explain why theory-constitutive metaphors are so stable a feature of the study of complex systems; indeed such metaphors may be especially important for the investigation of homeostatic property cluster phenomena.

An understanding of homeostatic property cluster kinds also, I shall argue, enhances our understanding of technical matters that bear on our understanding of the semantics of theory-constitutive metaphors. In the first place, an understanding of the semantics of scientific metaphors requires a critique of empiricist conceptions of linguistic precision and recognition of the special features of homeostatic property cluster definitions greatly enhances that critique. More important, as I suggested earlier, an understanding of the semantics of theory-constitutive metaphors requires that we understand reference of linguistic expressions in epistemic terms – in terms of relations of socially coordinated *epistemic access* between language users and features of the world. I shall argue that both epistemic access and the more basic phenomenon of knowledge in terms of which it is defined are themselves homeostatic property cluster phenomena. Thus an understanding of such phenomena is central to the task of understanding the epistemic and semantic function of scientific terms generally and theory-constitutive metaphors in particular.

Examples of metaphor in science

There is, no doubt, a considerable variety of sorts of metaphors that play a role in science, and in theory change. Certain metaphors, which might be plausibly termed exegetical or pedagogical metaphors, play a role in the teaching or explication of theories which already admit of entirely adequate nonmetaphorical (or, at any rate, less metaphorical) formulations. I have in mind, for example, talk about "worm-holes" in general relativity, the description of the spatial localization of bound electrons in terms of an "electron cloud," or the description of atoms as "miniature solar systems."

The fact that these metaphors, and others like them, do not convey theoretical insights not otherwise expressible does not indicate that they play no important role in theory change. Kuhn's work has made it clear that the establishment of a fundamentally new theoretical perspective is a matter of persuasion, recruitment, and indoctrination. It cannot be irrelevant to those enterprises that there is a body of exegetically, or pedagogically, effective metaphors.

Nevertheless, it seems to me that the cases of scientific metaphor which are most interesting from the point of view of the philosophy of science (and the philosophy of language generally) are those in which metaphorical expressions constitute, at least for a time, an irreplaceable part of the linguistic machinery of a scientific theory: cases in which there are metaphors which scientists use in expressing theoretical claims for which no adequate literal paraphrase is known. Such metaphors are *constitutive* of the theories they express, rather than merely exegetical. It might seem doubtful that such theory-constitutive metaphors exist; after all, it is at least plausible that metaphorical language is fundamentally pretheoretical, and lacks the explicitness and precision characteristic of scientific theories. Still, if one looks at theory construction in the relatively young sciences like cognitive psychology, one finds theory-constitutive metaphors in abundance. The examples that I know best are metaphors in cognitive psychology that are drawn from the terminology of computer science, information theory, and related disciplines. The following examples are but a small subset of the actual cases:

1. the claim that thought is a kind of "information processing," and that the brain is a sort of "computer";
2. the suggestion that certain motoric or cognitive processes are "pre-programmed";
3. disputes over the issue of the existence of an internal "brain-language" in which "computations" are carried out;
4. the suggestion that certain information is "encoded" or "indexed" in "memory store" by "labeling," whereas other information is "stored" in "images";
5. disputes about the extent to which developmental "stages" are produced by the maturation of new "preprogrammed" "subroutines," as opposed to the acquisition of learned "heuristic routines," or the development of greater "memory storage capacities" or better "information retrieval procedures";
6. the view that learning is an adaptive response of a "self-organizing machine";
7. the view that consciousness is a "feedback" phenomenon.

I do not want to maintain that *all* of these examples are of fundamental importance to theoretical psychology. Nevertheless, the prevalence of computer metaphors shows an important feature of contemporary theoretical psychology: a concern with exploring analogies, or similarities, between men and computational devices has been the most important single factor influencing postbehaviorist cognitive psychology. Even among cognitive psychologists who despair of actual machine simulation of human cognition, computer metaphors have an indispensable role in the formulation and articulation of theoretical positions. These metaphors have provided much of the basic theoretical vocabulary of contemporary psychology (Neisser, 1966; G. A. Miller, 1974).

Moreover, it is clear that these computer metaphors are theory-constitutive: psychologists do not, generally speaking, now know how to offer literal paraphrases which express the same theoretical claims. This is made clearly evident by the current discussion among psychologists and philosophers about the doctrine called "functionalism" (Block & Fodor, 1972; Block 1977; Boyd, 1980; Fodor, 1965, 1968; Lewis, 1971; Putnam, 1967, 1975b, 1975f; Shoemaker, 1975b). It is widely agreed that some version or other of the doctrine that mental and psychological states are functional states of organisms represents the cognitive content of the metaphorical statement that the brain is a sort of computer. But even among psychologists and philosophers who are convinced that functionalism is true, there is profound disagreement about important issues regarding its interpretation. Thus, this metaphor, and other computer metaphors employed in psychological theorizing, share with more typical interaction metaphors, at least for a time, the property that their cognitive content cannot be made explicit.

In important respects, however, these theory-constitutive metaphors are highly atypical. In the first place, they undergo a sort of public articulation and development that is uncharacteristic of literary metaphors. Typically, a literary metaphor has its "home," so to speak, in a specific work of a specific author; when the same metaphor is employed by other authors, a reference to the original employment is often implicit. When the same metaphor is employed often, by a variety of authors, and in a variety of minor variations, it becomes either trite or hackneyed, or it becomes "frozen" into a figure of speech or a new literal expression (see Black on "orange"). Literary interaction metaphors seem to lose their insightfulness through overuse: the invitation to explore the various analogies and similarities between the primary literal subject and the metaphorical secondary subject becomes pointless or trite if repeated too often. Theory-constitutive scientific metaphors, on the other hand, become, when they are successful, the property of the entire scientific community, and variations on them are explored by hundreds of scientific authors without their interactive quality being lost. They are really conceits rather than metaphors – and conceits which extend not through one literary work, but through the work of a generation or more of scientists.

There is another closely related respect in which theory-constitutive metaphors are atypical. As Black points out, the task of offering explicit and literal paraphrases of literary metaphor is the appropriate task of literary critics and other commentators, but represents an enterprise relatively distinct from the production of the literary works in which the metaphors occur: the task of explication of metaphor is typically separate from the task of production and is often pursued by a quite different group of practitioners. In the case of scientific metaphors, on the other hand, especially in the case of theory-constitutive metaphors, this division of tasks and division of labor does not obtain. It is part of the task of scientific theory construction involving metaphors (or any other sort of theoretical terminology) to offer the best possible explication of the terminology employed. Although this task is sometimes also the preoccupation of professional philosophers (as in the case of functionalism), it is certainly the routine responsibility of working scientists. The sciences in general, and psychology in particular, are self-reflective disciplines, and the explication of theoretical concepts – metaphorical or not – is an essential part of the task of scientific inquiry.

Finally, whatever the merits of the claim that the cognitive content of literary metaphors can never be captured by literal paraphrase, there seems to be no reason to doubt that such explication is possible in the case of some theory-constitutive metaphors, nor is there any reason to doubt that complete explications are often the eventual result of the attempts at explication which are central to scientific inquiry. (For some reservations about explication of theory-constitutive metaphors for cases involving homeostatic property cluster kinds see the section in this chapter entitled "Homeostasis, reference, and precision.")

Literary interaction metaphors, it would seem, display what might be termed *conceptual open-endedness:* they work by inviting the reader (or hearer) to consider the principal subject of the metaphor in the light of associated implications – typically – of the commonplace conception of the secondary subject. Even in those cases in which the metaphor depends upon esoteric information about the secondary subject, the information is of the sort the sufficiently sophisticated reader might be expected to possess (sophisticated commonplaces, so to speak); indeed, the whole point of most literary metaphors would be lost if this sort of knowledge on the part of readers could not be presupposed. The function of literary metaphor is not typically to send the informed reader out on a research project.

Exactly the opposite is the case with theory-constitutive metaphors. They display what might be called *inductive open-endedness.* Although the intelligibility of theory-constitutive metaphors rests on the reader's being able to apply to her current understanding of the primary subject some of the associated implications appropriate to her current conception of the secondary subject, the function of the metaphor is much broader. The reader is invited to explore the similarities and analogies between features of the primary and secondary subjects, including features not yet discovered, or not yet fully understood. This programmatic research-orienting feature of theory-constitutive metaphors explains, I believe, the ways in which such metaphors both resemble and differ from ordinary interaction metaphors. Theory-constitutive metaphors are introduced when there is (or seems to be) good reason to believe that there are theoretically important respects of similarity or analogy between the literal subjects of the metaphors and their secondary subjects. The function of such metaphors is to put us on the track of these respects of similarity or analogy; indeed, the metaphorical terms in such metaphors may best be understood as referring to features of the world delineated in terms of those – perhaps as yet undiscovered – similarities and analogies. Thus, it is hardly surprising that, at least for a time, it is not known exactly what the relevant respects of similarity or analogy are; many have yet to be discovered or understood. Similarly, it is unsurprising that theory-constitutive metaphors can retain their interactive quality even though they are employed, in a number of variations, by a number of authors, and over a long time. Repeated employment of such metaphors does not consist (as it would in the case of more typical interaction metaphors) of merely repetitive and trite invitations to once again explore the same understanding of the principal subject in the light of the same body of associated implications about the secondary subject. Instead, the use of theory-constitutive metaphors encourages the discovery of new features of the primary and secondary subjects, and new understanding of theoretically relevant respects of similarity, or analogy, between them.

Precisely because theory-constitutive metaphors are invitations to future research, and because that research is aimed at uncovering the theoretically important similarities between the primary and secondary subjects of the metaphors, the explication of these similarities and analogies is the routine business of scientific researchers, rather than of some specialized body of commentators. Indeed, the explication of such metaphors is essentially an automatic consequence of success in the research programs that they invite. For this reason, and because we cannot know a priori that such investigations will not ultimately be completely successful with respect to the issues raised by any particular metaphor, we have no reason to deny that complete explication of theory-constitutive metaphors is sometimes possible. They do, however, share with literary metaphors the important property that their utility does not depend on the (even tacit) availability of such an explication. Indeed, the utility of theory-constitutive metaphors seems to lie largely in the fact that they provide a way to introduce terminology for features of the world whose existence seems probable, but many of whose fundamental properties have yet to be discovered. Theory-constitutive metaphors, in other words, represent one strategy for the accommodation of language to as yet undiscovered causal features of the world.

Accommodation and reference fixing

The possibility that linguistic usage in science might be accommodated to as yet unknown "joints" in the causal structure of the world is at least as old as the seventeenth century. In Book III (and, to a lesser extent in Books II and IV) of the *Essay Concerning Human Understanding* (Locke 1690/ 1959), Locke explores the consequences of the proposal that substance terms should be taken to refer to the "real essences" of substances in the sense suggested by Boyle's corpuscular theory of matter: that is, that terms like "gold" or "water" should be understood to refer to specific kinds of corpuscular structure. Locke's rejection of this proposal in favor of the view that general terms must refer to kinds specified by "nominal essences," that is, by criteria of membership fixed by definitional convention, has formed the basis for all subsequent empiricist discussions of meaning and reference.

It is important to remember that empiricist accounts of meaning and reference, from Locke to the present, have rested on what are essentially "verificationist" principles. It is insisted that the kinds referred to by general terms must be delineated by "nominal essences" precisely because attempts to delineate kinds by "real essences" or "secret powers" (Hume's phrase) would make knowledgeable use of language impossible. Thus, for example, Locke rejects the possibility of classifying substances on the basis of their atomic structure on the grounds that the limitations of the senses precludes our ever discovering atomic structures. He also concludes that, in general, our inability to discern the hidden inner constitution of things makes knowledge of general laws impossible (although, like all empiricists, he restrains such skepticism where it suits his own philosophical purposes).

More recent empiricists have departed from both Hume and Locke in holding that verificationism *is* compatible with the view that knowledge of general laws is possible. Nevertheless, contemporary versions of Locke's account of general terms – doctrines to the effect that the reference or cognitive content of general terms must be fixed by "operational definitions," "criterial attributes," "law-clusters," "reduction sentences," and the like – still have a verificationist foundation. We are to understand the kinds referred to by general terms to be specified by definitional conventions because – so the argument goes – knowledge of unobservable underlying "powers" or "inner constitutions" is impossible.

In recent years there has been a movement in the philosophy of science away from the instrumentalism implicit in this sort of position and toward the "scientific realist" position that knowledge of "unobservables" and of causal powers is indeed possible (Boyd, 1973, 1983, 1985a, Putnam, 1975a, 1975b, 1975c, Smart, 1963). To a large extent, this realist tendency has resulted from analyses of the actual findings and methods of the empirical sciences. More recently, it has also been associated with the development of distinctly non-Humean positions in epistemology: causal theories of perception, causal theories of knowledge generally, the increased realization that Locke and Hume were correct in insisting that inductive generalization is unfounded unless our categories correspond to causal powers or natural necessity, and the recognition that knowledge of general laws in science is – typically, at least – impossible without some knowledge of unobservable entities or powers (Boyd, 1973, 1983, 1985a, 1985b, 1990a; Goldman, 1967, 1976; Harré & Madden, 1975; Shoemaker, 1975a).

One of the most interesting aspects of this realist tendency has been the recently renewed interest in alternatives to the standard empiricist accounts of language. It has long been recognized that considerations of circularity preclude *all* general terms possessing reference-fixing descriptive definitions. Logical positivists, for example, typically assumed that general terms for qualities of sense-data (e.g., "orange" as a description of the qualitative character of sensation) and their reference (or extension) are fixed ostensively, that is, by association with examples of the relevant sensory qualities, rather than by verbal definition. A number of philosophers, most notably Kripke and Putnam, have recently defended and developed the view – which has occasionally tempted certain of the more realist logical empiricists like Feigl – that the reference of natural-kind terms (like "water" and "gold"), and of theoretical terms in science, might be fixed "causally" or ostensively rather than by definitional convention. Such a view accords with the realistic position that knowledge of "unobservable" causal powers and constituents of matter is possible, and with Quinean dicta to the effect that there are no analytic definitions, no truths by convention. These dicta, in turn, have been confirmed by the experience of philosophers of science, who have found it extraordinarily difficult to find rationally defensible grounds for deciding which measurement procedures are operational definitions or which laws are in law-clusters or which statements are reduction sentences: that is, by the experience of philosophers who have found it impossible in practice to distinguish scientific truths-by-convention from high level empirical truths.

Putnam's account of ostensive reference for theoretical terms (Putnam, 1975a, 1975b) is perhaps the most widely discussed (although, as he points out, it represents a preliminary discussion). The examples of ostensive reference fixing on which he concentrates are those in which terms are introduced that refer to substances like water, or to fundamental physical magnitudes like electrical charge. In these cases, on his view, we may think of the reference of terms like "water" or "electrical charge" as being fixed by "dubbing" or naming ceremonies (the latter terminology is Putnam's, the former, Kripke's) involving the association of the term in question with a sample or exemplary causal effect of its referent, or with a description of stereotypical samples or causal effects. One might, for example, imagine a ceremony in which someone says "Let's call 'water' whatever substance is present in this bucket over here" or "Let's call 'electrical charge' whatever fundamental physical magnitude is responsible for the deflection of the needles on meters of this sort." Of course, no general terms are actually introduced precisely by such ceremonies, but as an idealization such an account does indicate how unambiguous (or nearly unambiguous) reference could be achieved without explicit definition in terms of necessary-and-sufficient conditions, criterial attributes, or operational procedures. If the stuff in the bucket is nearly pure water, then we may take the dubbing to have fixed the reference of "water" as the chemical substance water, even though no one at the time of the dubbing may know what property is really essential to water (i.e., no one might know that water is H_2O and that ice and steam are, therefore, species of water). Similarly, if electrical charge is the only one fundamental magnitude which is the principal determinant of the position of needles in the meters in question, then we might think of the reference of "electrical charge" as having been fixed as electrical charge – even if no one knew how to detect electrical charge generally, or what its most fundamental properties are, or how, in other circumstances, to distinguish the effects of charge from the effects of other fundamental magnitudes. This sort of ostensive reference fixing, then, can be understood as a procedure aimed at accommodation of linguistic usage to as yet undiscovered causal structures: we introduce terminology for substances and fundamental magnitudes by appealing to situations in which we believe they are exemplified, prior to our discovery of their fundamental or essential features (that is, prior to the discovery of those properties which would have to be mentioned in an extensionally correct explicit definition).

The success of the particular style of ostensive reference fixing by citation of samples or exemplary effects also depends on the particular sorts of kinds at which the ostension "aims." It is possible to employ samples in fixing the reference of substance terms precisely because relatively pure samples of substances are possible – because it is possible to have situations in which only one kind of the sort in question is significantly present. However, in cases where terms are to be introduced ostensively to refer to kinds whose essential properties include causal relations to, and co-occurrence with, other kinds of the same sort, one must typically think of their reference as being fixed by practices with a much more complicated structure than the dubbings considered by Putnam. The avoidance of quite fundamental ambiguity requires that one think of the mechanisms of reference fixing as involving features which serve to disambiguate the references of each introduced term between two or more kinds of the same sort, all of which are manifested in the exemplary samples, or situations. There must, therefore, be differences between the ways in which the different terms are introduced corresponding to the differences in essential properties between the kinds referred to. The rationale for ostensive introduction of general terms is to permit reference to kinds whose essential properties may not yet be known – and thus to accommodate linguistic categories to as yet only partially understood causal features of the world. It is thus typically impossible that the differences between the essential properties of such co-occurring kinds should be marked, either in actual reference fixing or in idealized models of dubbing, by entirely accurate and complete descriptions of their respective essential properties.

If I am right, one of the important roles of theory-constitutive metaphors is to accomplish nondefinitional reference fixing of this sort. If the fundamental properties of the metaphorical secondary subjects of a body of related metaphors are sufficiently well understood, then these metaphors can be employed – together perhaps with exemplary circumstances of application – to fix nonliteral referents for the metaphorical expressions they contain. If the differences in essential properties of the secondary subjects are sufficiently great, analogy or similarity with them may suffice to disambiguate the (new) reference of the terms thus introduced. Subsequent metaphors which develop the same metaphorical theme may be used to report discoveries or theoretical speculations regarding the kinds to which the new reference of the metaphorical terms so introduced has been fixed. In such cases, as in the case of ostensive introduction of terms for substances, linguistic terminology is accommodated to the structure of natural phenomena whose fundamental features are not yet fully understood.

The case of computer metaphors in cognitive psychology, I believe, illustrates this sort of ostensive introduction of theoretical terminology. Mental and psychological states and processes are, almost certainly, among the sorts of kinds whose essential properties are relational – they are functional states or processes. Furthermore, it seems reasonable to hold about many psychological states and processes that their causal relations to *other psychological states and processes* are among their essential properties. (These claims make up what is least controversial about the doctrine called "functionalism.") Theoretical terms in psychology, then, are among those for which reference fixing must typically involve disambiguation between several quite different but co-occurring kinds of the same sort. Computational states and processes of the sort which are the secondary metaphorical subjects of computer metaphors in psychology are also functional states and processes: typically their essential properties are their causal relations to other computational states or processes or to the inputs and outputs of the machines which realize or manifest them. What I am suggesting is that – when computer metaphors in cognitive psychology are successful – the metaphorically employed computer terms come to have new referents in the context of psychological theory construction. They refer to functionally defined psychological states or processes which bear to each other functional relations analogous to those which the literal referents of these terms bear to one another. If the metaphors are apt, and if they are drawn in sufficient detail, the differences in functional (relational) properties of the literal referents of the computer terms will serve – by analogy – to disambiguate the referents of these terms in their theory-constitutive metaphorical applications.

The example of computer metaphors has several features that illustrate the programmatic character of theory-constitutive metaphors and, indeed, of nondefinitionally introduced theoretical terminology generally. In the first place, when we inquire about the referents of theory-constitutive metaphorical expressions, it is necessary to inquire about the aptness or insightfulness of the metaphors in which they are employed. The introduction of theory-constitutive metaphors, like the introduction of any theoretical terminology, represents an estimate that natural phenomena of the right sorts exist (see Putnam, 1975a, pp. 224–5). Computer metaphors are introduced into psychological theory on the basis of an informed "guess" that there are important similarities or analogies between their primary and secondary subjects. The aim of the introduction of such terminology is to *initiate investigation* of the primary subjects in the light of an informed estimate of their properties. In cases where a theoretical metaphor proves not to represent a real insight, we need no more inquire about the new referents of its metaphorical terms than we do with respect to the referent of the term "vital force": in such cases the "guess" does not work out, and the relevant terms do not refer at all. If there are no features of human cognition closely analogous to the fundamental features of machine computation, then, for example, there is nothing which is the referent of "information processing" in its use as a term of psychological theory.

It is also possible to see an important relation between the programmatic inductive open-endedness of theory-constitutive metaphors and their role as reference-fixing devices. Computer metaphors are introduced in order to make possible investigation of the similarities and analogies between human cognition and machine computation. These metaphors are (at least for a while) open-ended precisely because the research program they help to initiate is incomplete: we still do not know in exactly what respects human cognition resembles machine computation. What metaphorical uses of computer terminology permit is that we introduce at a relatively early stage theoretical terms to refer to various plausibly postulated computerlike aspects of human cognition, which then become the objects of further investigation. Two features of this sort of use of metaphors are worth remarking on here. First, it is by no means necessary – in order that fundamental ambiguities among the new referents of the metaphorical terms be avoided – that the fundamental or essential properties of their literal (nonmetaphorical) referents be fully understood. The relation between "indexing" of memory items and subsequent "information retrieval" may not be fully understood by computer specialists, for example, but this does not prevent the notions of "indexing" and "retrieval" from playing a role in successful psychological metaphor. Indeed, this sort of case illustrates the important point that successful theory-constitutive metaphors can have programmatic importance for the development of research about their metaphorical secondary subjects, as well as for research about their primary subjects and the new referents of their metaphorical terms. There is no doubt that analogies between human cognition and computer functioning have provided useful heuristics for computer scientists as well as for psychologists.

The second point is that subsequent developments in the research program initiated by the employment of theory-constitutive metaphors may well lead to further articulation of the metaphor in question, to the introduction of new theoretical terminology (metaphorical or not) and to a consequent refinement of usage and further reduction in ambiguity of such terminology. Thus, for example, the notion of "feedback," in its information-processing and computer usage, seems to cover a variety of sorts of phenomena, ranging from simple feedback circuits in analogue devices to "system monitoring" functions in complex computational devices. If there is some insight in the claim that consciousness is a sort of feedback, then one might expect that, as both applied computation theory and psychology progress, new terminology will be introduced (perhaps, but not necessarily, by employment of further computer metaphors), which will permit the drawing of finer distinctions among those cognitive processes that are analogous to the machine processes now grouped under the term "feedback."

These programmatic features of theory-constitutive metaphors – the fact that they introduce the terminology for future theory construction, refer to as yet only partially understood natural phenomena, and are capable of further refinement and disambiguation as a consequence of new discoveries – explain the fact that repeated employment and articulation of these metaphors may result in an increase in their cognitive utility rather than in a decline to the level of cliché.

What is significant is that these programmatic features of theory-constitutive metaphorical expressions are, in fact, typical of theoretical terms in science (in fact, they are true of general terms, generally). Normally, we introduce terminology to refer to presumed kinds of natural phenomena long before our study of them has progressed to the point where we can specify for them the sort of defining conditions that the positivist's account of language would require and, indeed, where no such conditions may exist at all (see the discussion of homeostatic property cluster kinds below). The introduction of theoretical terms does require, however, some tentative or preliminary indication of the properties of the presumed kinds in question. Any such terminology must possess a sort of programmatic open-endedness, inasmuch as its introduction fixes a presumed topic for future research. Thus the introduction of theoretical terminology generally requires just the features that theory-constitutive metaphors provide. One way of providing a tentative and preliminary account of the properties of presumed kinds – and of disambiguating terms referring to presumed kinds of the same general sort – is by open-ended analogy to kinds whose properties are in some respects better understood. One way of expressing such analogies is by metaphorical use of terms referring to those better understood kinds. Theory-constitutive metaphors, then, simply represent one strategy among many for the preliminary stages of theory construction.

Given the initial plausibility of the view that metaphorical uses of language are insufficiently precise to be scientific, it is surprising that the use of metaphors in science is so unsurprising. The fact of their utility in science is philosophically important, not because they represent an especially unusual phenomenon, but, instead, because they provide an especially apt illustration of ubiquitous but important features of scientific language generally.

Metaphor and linguistic precision: Challenges for a theory of reference

Black argues, and common sense concurs, that metaphorical language lacks the precision of scientific language. Against this eminently plausible position, I have proposed that there exist theory-constitutive metaphors in abundance, and that a nondefinitional "causal" or "ostensive" account of reference of the sort advanced by Kripke and Putnam can be employed to defend the view that the metaphorical terms occurring in theory-constitutive metaphors actually refer to natural kinds, properties, magnitudes, and so on – hereafter referred to simply as "kinds" – which constitute the nonliteral scientific subject matter of such metaphors. I suggested that, in fact, the use of theory-constitutive metaphors represents a nondefinitional reference-fixing strategy especially apt for avoiding certain sorts of ambiguity.

Is this the whole story? Is the intriguing issue of metaphor and theory construction, in reality, reducible to a footnote to an already extant theory of scientific language? Is it a mistake to believe that important theoretical questions are raised by the issue of metaphor in scientific theory construction?

That the answer to these questions is no is suggested not only by common sense, but also by the following consideration: nothing in the application of the causal theory of reference to theory-constitutive metaphors directly addresses Black's claim that metaphorical language lacks scientific precision. Supposing it is established that there are theory-constitutive metaphors, and that their metaphorical terms are to be understood referentially, the question still remains why their apparent imprecision does not render them unsuitable for scientific theory construction. No alternative to the common-sense understanding of linguistic imprecision has been offered. Furthermore, this deficiency – which the issue of theory-constitutive metaphors forces us to examine – reflects, not a defect in my presentation, but rather a serious limitation in the existing accounts of the causal theory of reference and, as I shall argue toward the end of this essay, in our understanding of the nature of the definitions of some scientifically important kinds.

There are, broadly speaking, two rival accounts of the ways in which reference is fixed for natural-kind terms and the other sorts of general terms that occur in scientific and everyday discourse. According to the empiricist account, for all but a special class of primitive terms, all general terms are to be understood as governed by stipulatory definitional conventions. Certain sentences (operational definitions, law-clusters, meaning conventions) involving such terms are true by stipulation, are known a priori, and fix the meaning (and the extension or reference) of the terms they define. According to the rival causal or ostensive accounts, for many general terms, reference is fixed by an appropriate sort of causal interaction between users of the term and instances of the kind to which it refers.

The empiricist account readily supplies criteria of linguistic precision. Two uses of the same term (or of two lexicographically different terms for that matter) are coreferential or co-extensive only when they are governed by the same definitional conventions. Vagueness arises from inexplicitness or intersubjective variation in definitional conventions, and ambiguity from the association of a single term with two or more nonequivalent definitional conventions. Both sources of linguistic imprecision have the same remedy: each general term should be associated with a single, quite explicit, and definite conventional definition which is accepted by the relevant linguistic community *prior to* the employment of the term in question. Linguistic precision can be identified with the existence of explicit, detailed, and intersubjectively accepted conventional definitions.

The empiricist account of general terms has other important consequences as well. It entails that there are certain (definitional) statements which are immune from revision or refutation by experimental evidence. It entails that these definitional truths can be established by convention prior to the conduct of experimental investigations. Futhermore, it entails that necessary truths are almost always a priori definitional truths, and (as Kuhn, 1970a, brilliantly observed, especially pages 101–2) it entails that major changes in scientific theories are almost always to be diagnosed as changes in subject matter or conceptual framework, rather than as new discoveries. Finally, although the empiricist account of general terms may be construed as a theory of *reference,* in important respects it represents a nonrealist, nonreferential account of general terms. The extensions of the "natural" kinds, or values of the magnitudes which are the referents of general terms are – according to the empiricist conception – largely fixed by arbitrary and empirically unrevisable definitional conventions. General terms are not understood as referring to independently existing kinds or magnitudes. Indeed, an antirealist and verificationist perspective has provided the defense of the empiricist account of language since its proposal by Locke (see Locke, 1690/1959, especially Book III). Characteristically, the empiricist account of language treats even precisely defined nonobservational ("theoretical") general terms as playing a merely heuristic, or conceptual (but nonreferential), role in scientific theory construction.

With the decline of logical empiricism, especially within the philosophy of science, each of these consequences of the empiricist account of language has come to seem unacceptable to a number of philosophers. It is the unacceptability of these consequences that has led philosophers like Kripke and Putnam (and, much earlier, Feigl – see Feigl, 1956) to advance causal or ostensive theories of reference. The reasoning goes something like this: The empiricist account of language has unacceptable philosophical consequences; on the other hand, if the reference of some general terms is fixed nondefinitionally, in a way somewhat analogous to ostension, baptism, or the employment of stereotypical "definitions," then one can accommodate the variety of antiempiricist findings of recent philosophy of science and philosophy of language. Thus, a nondefinitional account of reference fixing is probably correct for a wide variety of general terms.

There is nothing wrong with this sort of reasoning. Indeed, the proposal that reference-fixing mechanisms are typically nondefinitional promises to be one of the most important achievements of recent analytical philosophy. What has not happened, however, is the articulation of a genuine causal *theory* of reference as an alternative to the received empiricist theory. It is proposed that reference is somehow a nondefinitional causal relation, but no general theory of nondefinitional reference in the literature integrates all of the proposed nondefinitional reference-fixing strategies into a single unifying theory of reference. In particular, existing proposals lack an adequate account of ambiguity and coreferentiality, and, thus provide no account either of the nature of linguistic precision, or of the methodological or linguistic practices which are apt for achieving it. The causal account of reference arises from an attempt to defend the position that general terms (especially "theoretical" terms in scientific theories) should typically be understood referentially, that general terms can refer even though they do not possess unrevisable conventional definitions, and (what is important) that tokens of a term employed in different contexts, at different historical times, within different paradigms, or in different "possible worlds" may be coreferential, even though they are not associated with equivalent conventional definitions. The independent philosophical justification for these doctrines warrants the acceptance of a causal account of reference, but it remains true that no available account offers a satisfactory treatment of the crucial issues of coreferentiality, ambiguity, and linguistic precision. In particular, one must reject the "obvious" criterion for coreferentiality of ostensively introduced terms: that two tokens of a term are coreferential only when they are each connected (by a historical causal chain of speakers' intentions to corefer) to the same dubbing or introducing ceremony. There are almost never actual events which can be identified with idealized introducing ceremonies, and, furthermore, painful human linguistic experience makes it abundantly clear that good intentions are not sufficient to avoid unintended ambiguity or shifts in reference.

Arguably, the absence of an adequate account of coreferentiality does not seriously undermine the cogency of the considerations which favor a causal account of reference. The causal account does avoid unacceptable consequences of the empiricist theory of language, and the judgments about reference and about coreferentiality which the causal account protects – even if they are not assimilated into a general theory of reference – are quite well justified by independent philosophical, linguistic, and historical considerations. On the other hand, if we are concerned about the role of theory-constitutive metaphors in science, the situation is reversed. Both common sense and the best available treatments of metaphor suggest that metaphorical language must be imprecise, nonreferential, and essentially heuristic, just as the empiricist theory of language would suggest. In the previous section, I showed that it is *possible* to maintain that the metaphorical terms in theory-constitutive metaphors refer, even though they lack explicit definitions, by adopting a nondefinitional account of the way in which they refer. I have not, however, shown that such metaphorical terms *must* be understood referentially and, in particular, I have not replied to the plausible rebuttal that – precisely because their imprecision precludes their sustaining a definite reference over time, and from one occasion of use to another – metaphorical terms in science should be understood *nonreferentially,* and scientific metaphors should be seen as playing a largely heuristic role in theory construction. Existing causal theories of reference do not provide the machinery for a reply to this challenge.

The considerations that have persuaded many recent philosophers of science to abandon the empiricist (and especially the verificationist) position that theoretical terms play a heuristic or conceptual but nonreferential role in scientific theories are quite general and, if sound, should apply to almost all cases of theoretical language in successful scientific theory construction (see, for example, Boyd, 1973, 1983, 1990a, 1991; Byerly & Lazara, 1973; Feigl, 1956; Fodor, 1968; MacCorquodale & Meehl, 1948; Putnam, 1975a, 1975b; Smart, 1963). If considerations of linguistic precision should dictate a nonreferential and heuristic treatment of theory-constitutive metaphors, serious questions would be raised at least about the generality of the currently accepted antiempiricist account of scientific theory construction. If the considerations that support a referential treatment of theoretical terms, and that support the rejection of Kuhn's paradigm relativism regarding the meaning and reference of such terms, are sound then they should be applicable as well to metaphorical terms in science, and it should be possible to extend them to a general theory of reference which adequately treats the issue of coreferentiality and precision. I shall address the following questions which reflect the challenge we have just examined:

1. Given that it is *possible* to employ a nondefinitional account of reference fixing as an alternative to both the verificationist accounts of empiricists, and the related relativist accounts of Kuhn (1970a) and Hanson (1958), why is such a position preferable to a nonreferential treatment according to which the role of theoretical terms is purely heuristic or conceptual?

2. How do the considerations that constitute the answer to 1 apply to the especially difficult case in which the theoretical terms in question are metaphorical terms occurring in theory-constitutive metaphors?

3. Given that ambiguity and linguistic imprecision are real possibilities in the use of scientific language, what account of ambiguity, coreferentiality, and linguistic precision can the defenders of nondefinitional reference fixing offer as an alternative to the received empiricist account?

4. How does this alternative account treat the especially difficult issue of imprecison in theory-constitutive metaphors?

In order to answer these questions, it will be necessary to digress in order to develop, at least in outline, a general theory of nondefinitional reference and a nondefinitional alternative to the received empiricist account of coreferentiality, ambiguity, and linguistic precision. This digression will, I believe, prove fruitful. Scientific metaphors raise truly fundamental issues about language and linguistic competence, and the theory of reference required to understand them has several quite startling consequences, which are important both to an understanding of metaphorical language, and to an understanding of language in general. We shall discover, for example, that there is, in an important sense, no such thing as *linguistic* precision; there are rational strategies for avoiding referential ambiguity, but they are not a reflection of rules of linguistic usage (as the empiricist theory suggests). Rather, they reflect essentially nonlinguistic principles of rational inquiry. We shall also discover that a nonreferential but heuristic treatment of metaphorical language in science is ruled out (as are similar paradigm-relativistic treatments of theoretical terminology of the sort advocated by Kuhn) by quite general epistemological considerations.

Epistemic access: The basis of a theory of reference

Let us then begin our digression into the philosophy of language by addressing the general question: what is reference? What relation between the use of terminology and features of the world is at issue when the question of reference is raised? What sorts of phenomena is a theory of reference supposed to explain? One way to approach the issue of the nature of reference is to examine some of the doctrines about reference which have produced so much recent excitement in philosophy. It is clear that we sometimes refer by pointing, or by employing definite descriptions. If what Putnam and Kripke say is basically correct, then we can also refer to things by employing terminology which bears the right sort of historical relation to antecedent introduction ceremonies, or by employing stereotypical descriptions which look very much like definite descriptions, but are not. In his provocative papers, Field (1973, 1974) suggests that there is a relation of *partial denotation* between certain words and features of the world which is importantly like reference. Putnam (1975e) argues that a *principle of benefit of doubt* is appropriate when assessing the reference of terms in the work of previous scientists, and that a *division of linguistic labor* involving deference to scientists and other experts is essential to reference (Putnam, 1975a).

If these doctrines are even approximately correct (and I believe that they are) then the phenomenon of reference has some quite striking properties: it can be manifested by pointing, by explicitly defining, by dubbing, or by stereotyping; it is essentially connected to the knowledge-gathering efforts of experts and specialists; and it admits of partial manifestation. It is reasonable to ask what sort of relation between language use and the world it is, that has such varied manifestations. Indeed, it is reasonable to ask what the justification is for the presumption that there is a *single* phenomenon of reference with all these different manifestations.

So far as I have been able to ascertain, this question has almost never been explicitly addressed in the literature on reference. The one place in which I have found it treated is Putnam (1975a), where it is suggested that reference and truth should be "so construed that, at least in the 'paradigm case', at least for important classes of sentences, at least if things go as they should, sentences will tend to be accepted in the long run if and only if they are true." This standard for theories of reference and truth is seen as consonant with the "scientific realism" in epistemology defended in Boyd (1973). This principle is, as Putnam remarks, especially suited to explaining the principle of benefit of the doubt and other doctrines which link the notion of reference to issues regarding the opinions and investigations of experts.

The account of reference offered here (which was developed independently of the position of Putnam, 1975a) has Putnam's position as a special case, and may be viewed both as an explanation and a justification for Putnam's position, and as an extension of it which can provide a theoretical basis for a wider variety of recent discoveries about reference. I shall not attempt here to provide an analytic definition of reference, or to establish necessary and sufficient conditions for a word's referring to a particular thing or kind. On Quinean grounds, I doubt that such analytic definitions or specifications of necessary and sufficient conditions are ever to be found in the case of philosophically important concepts and, in any event, I shall argue that for reference no such necessary and sufficient conditions – analytic or otherwise – exist. Furthermore (following Field), I believe that it is a misleading idealization to portray the referential relation between language and the world as being constituted by relations of determinate reference between words and their unique referents. What I shall do is to try to describe the essential features of reference in such a way as to illuminate as much as possible the issues raised by discussions of reference in the recent philosophical literature. I shall be especially concerned to learn from, and to explicate, the grain of truth in each of the following doctrines:

1. Operationalism;

2. The law-cluster account of "meaning" and reference for theoretical terms;

3. Putnam's (1975a) claim that there is a "division of linguistic labor" involved in reference fixing;

4. The suggestion of Quine and Ullian (1970) that language "extends the senses";

5. Gibson's (1966) claim that perception is detection of "ambient information";

6. Putnam's principle of benefit of the doubt;

7. Putnam's suggestion that those who introduced general terms like "water" intended to name an explanatory real essence if there was one;

8. Field's claim that there is a relation of "partial denotation" which may obtain between a general term and more than one kind of natural phenomenon at a time when the distinction between those kinds has not yet been drawn;

9. Causal theories of knowledge and perception (Goldman, 1967, 1976) and the suggestion that they are closely related to causal theories of reference (especially the view that the general reliability of belief-producing mechanisms or methods is a crucial feature of knowledge);

10. The suggestion (Feigl, 1956; Byerly & Lazara, 1973) of a causal theory of detection and measurement for physical magnitudes analogous to causal theories of perception;

11. The view that a realist account of scientific theories (i.e., one which treats theoretical terms as referring to real kinds) is essential to a satisfactory account of the epistemology and method of science. Here we are especially concerned with the view that "theoretical" considerations are essential to the reliable assessment of evidence in science, that the reliability of such theoretical considerations rests on the approximate truth of the body of "collateral theories" upon which they depend, and that rational scientific practice, when successful, eventuates in the adoption of successively more accurate approximations to the truth. (For a defense of this

realist and cumulative account of method with respect to issues of measurement, see Cronbach & Meehl, 1956; for a similar treatment of ontological issues in science, see MacCorquodale & Meehl, 1948; for a realist treatment of principles of experimental design and assessment of experimental evidence, see Boyd, 1973, 1983, 1985a, 1985b.)

12. The suggestion of Goldstein (1978) that the metaphor of "ostension" in nondefinitional accounts of reference fixing for theoretical terms is to be understood in terms of the role of those terms in "pointing out" or indicating directions for future research programs.

It seems to me that the grains of truth in these doctrines can best be explained by an account of the essence of reference which generalizes the doctrine of Quine and Ullian that language extends the senses, the doctrine of Gibson that the senses are detectors of ambient information, and the doctrine of Feigl that "verifying evidence is to be viewed as causally related to the evidence's 'theoretical' entities" (Feigl, 1956, p. 17). In the light of these considerations, I propose to defend the following:

1. The notion of reference is fundamentally an epistemological notion. *Semantic Theory – insofar as it is a branch of Philosophy – is a branch of epistemology.*

2. The central task of a theory of reference is to explain the role of language in the acquisition, assessment, improvement, and communication of knowledge, especially the role of language in making possible social cooperation and rational deliberation within these activities. *What is to be explained is our (collective) capacity to successfully detect and discover facts about the world.*

3. The causal theory of reference is true not, primarily, because reference involves causal connections to dubbing or introducing ceremonies, but rather because the referential connection between a term and its referent is typically sustained by a variety of epistemically relevant causal connections both between users of the term and examples of its referent (measurement, perception, detection, experimental manipulation, etc.) and between different users (reporting, deliberating, justifying, disputing, etc.). *A causal theory of reference is true precisely because reference is an epistemological notion and causal theory of knowledge is true.*

4. In deciding issues in the theory of reference it is, therefore, appropriate to make use of the best available epistemological theories. *The true theory of reference will be a special case of the true theory of knowledge: the true theory of reference for theoretical terms in science will be a special case of the true theory of the epistemology of science.*

It also seems to me essential that one adopt a *dynamic* and *dialectical* conception of reference, in contrast to conceptions of reference which present a *synchronic, piecemeal,* and *nondialectical* idealization of the relation between individual words and features of the world. I intend to criticize conceptions of reference according to which the referential relation between a natural language and the world is entirely constituted by those relations of reference which obtain between particular words, and quite definite kinds.

One consequence of such accounts is to treat as nonreferential those connections between words and features of the world which (like Field's partial denotation) do not link words to unique referents. Equally important is the consequence that diachronic changes in linguistic usage, which alter relations of definite reference, are not themselves constitutive of the phenomenon of reference; they must be diagnosed as "changes of reference" in a sense which necessarily contrasts with "report of new discovery." One of the consequences of this sort of picture of reference is the plausibility of the empiricist doctrine that the definiteness and constancy of reference must be guaranteed by explicit and purely conventional definitions for all nonprimitive general terms. The remaining three claims are in opposition to this static conception of reference.

5. The accommodation of our language and conceptual categories to the causal structure of the world ("cutting the world at its joints") is essential in order that knowledge be possible. Since – in the absence of perfect causal knowledge – such accommodation cannot be accomplished by explicit and conventional definitions, nondefinitional procedures for accommodating language to the world are essential to knowledge. Since knowledge gathering is the essential core of reference, *the processes of linguistic accommodation are essential components of reference.*

6. Ostensive reference fixing, and other nondefinitional reference-fixing mechanisms – in the absence of perfect knowledge – will often establish referential connections between a word and more than one thing or kind. Routinely, terms with this sort of "imprecision" play a vital role in the socially coordinated discovery and communication of knowledge; indeed, the employment of terms of this sort appears to be essential to scientific inquiry (and rational inquiry generally). Thus, if reference is the relation between language and the world which explains the role of language in the acquisition and communication of knowledge, *nondeterminate referential connections between words and features of the world are essential components of reference.*

7. It is also routine that the acquisition of new knowledge, and the exploration of new areas of inquiry, require that linguistic usage be modified so as to mark newly discovered causal features of the world. This sort of dialectical modification of langauge use (which has what Field, 1973, calls "denotational refinement" as a special case) is essential to the process of accommodation of language to (newly discovered features of) the causal structure of the world, and is thus an essential component of reference. *Reference has an essential dynamic and dialectical aspect. Changes in language use – when they reflect the dialectics of accommodation – do not represent changes of reference in any philosophically puzzling sense of that*

term. Instead, such dialectical changes of reference are characteristic of refer-
ential continuity and represent perfectly ordinary vehicles for the reporting of
new discoveries.

In order to defend this epistemological account of reference, I propose to analyze the notion of reference in terms of the notion of *epistemic access.* I hold that, for any particular general term, the question of reference is to be understood as the question: to which kind (or kinds), or property (or properties), or magnitude (or magnitudes), . . . and so on, does our use of this term afford us epistemic access? When we conduct rational inquiry intended to discover facts about the referent of this term, about what kind(s) do we in fact gather information? A better picture of the relevant notion of epistemic access or information gathering can be obtained by first considering very simple cases of language use which illustrate Quine and Ullian's claim that language extends the senses. Consider, for example, the case of cries issued by sparrows to warn others of approaching predators. Such crying "extends the senses" in a perfectly straightforward sense. Sparrows, hearing such cries, are able to detect indirectly the presence of predators outside their line of sight through the efforts of others. The detection of predators takes on a social character: sparrows have, in such cases, socially coordinated epistemic access to certain kinds of predators. Even though it may be inappropriate to talk of "reference" in such cases, a "warning cry" is a warning cry rather than a mating call precisely because sparrows (a) can detect predators by sight with fair reliability, (b) typically issue warning cries only when they do so, and (c) typically respond to hearing warning cries in much the same way that they respond to seeing a predator.

The sort of epistemic access afforded by certain words in human languages (like "red" or "cold," for example) is quite analogous. Central to our employment of the term "red" are the facts that most speakers of English can detect the presence or absence of the color red, use the term "red" to report the presence of that color, and (under normal circumstances) take others' reports of "red" as indicative of the presence of the color red.

To these simple cases of language extending the senses, we may add cases in which the relevant "detection" skills are cognitive rather than merely perceptual (consider the case of the general term "refrigerator"), and where "discovery" rather than "detection" may be the more appropriate term (but not, I insist, "construction"). More relevant to the issue of reference for theoretical terms in science are cases in which epistemic access, the discovery of facts about the referents of terms, requires scientific investigation and serious theory construction. In such cases, the role of general terms in the social coordination of knowledge acquisition is substantially more complex. It remains true in these cases that one may be afforded a passive extension, if not of one's senses, then of one's research. I am, for

example, able to know that DNA carries the genetic code in mammals, by
relying on the testimony of experts whose research demonstrated this fact
about the referent of "DNA." Inasmuch as this is the only way I can obtain
such information about the substance which is the referent of "DNA,"
however, the sort of epistemic access which I have to its referent is not
central to determining the reference of "DNA."

What is important is the epistemic access which the term "DNA" affords
to DNA in virtue of the role that term plays in the organization of research.
Here there are at least three distinguishable ways in which use of the term
"DNA" makes it possible for the relevant scientific community to make of
itself an instrument for the detection (or discovery, if you prefer) of information about DNA:

1. Its use permits scientists to report to each other the results of studies
   of DNA.
2. Its use permits the public articulation, justification, criticism, debate,
   and refinement (in the light of justification, criticism, debate, *and*
   experimentation) of theories concerning DNA, thus making the interpretation of data and the evaluation of proposed theories – as well as
   the reporting of results – into a social enterprise.
3. Finally, the use of the term "DNA" makes possible verbal reasoning
   concerning DNA with respect to questions of data interpretation,
   theory evaluation, experimental design, and so forth. That is, the use
   of language makes possible not merely the formulation of theories and
   publicity and cooperation in their assessment; it makes it possible for
   reasoning (whether individual or public) to be *verbal* reasoning: to
   take place in words.

In discussing simpler cases of epistemic access, it was necessary to appeal
to the general and typical reliability of the human senses, or the commonplace cognitive ability to, for example, recognize refrigerators. In the context of theoretical terminology, the analogous factors are somewhat more
complex. In the first place, of course, the epistemic reliability which is
involved is (typically) that of the community of scientific experts, rather
than that of particular individuals, especially laymen. Furthermore, the
scope of the relevant notion of epistemic reliability must be formulated
with some circumspection. Scientific terms must be understood as providing the sort of epistemic access appropriate to the level of epistemic success
typical of scientific discoveries. Historical evidence suggests that the theories which are accepted by the scientific community are rarely entirely
correct in every respect, even when they reflect the discovery of fundamentally important truths. What is typical of successful scientific investigations
is successive improvements in partial but significant knowledge: scientific
progress typically arises from the replacement of revealing (though only
approximately accurate) theories with more revealing (and more nearly
accurate) theories. Similarly, it is true that the history of science reveals a

number of plausible but fundamentally mistaken "false starts" which are only corrected over time (for example, Darwin's belief in inheritance of acquired characteristics, or the theory of vital forces). Thus the sort of success which is characteristic of epistemic access in the case of a theoretical term in science involves the capacity of the scientific community, typically and over time, to acquire increasingly accurate knowledge about the referent of that term.

The mark of reference, then, is epistemic access, and the mark of epistemic access is the relevant sort of socially coordinated epistemic success. Roughly, a general term, T, affords epistemic access to a kind (species, magnitude, and so on), k, to the extent that the sorts of considerations which are (in the relevant historical context) rationally taken as evidence for statements involving T are, typically, indicative in an appropriate way of features of k. The following mutually supporting epistemic relations between a term, T, and a kind, k, are characteristic (but by no means definitive) of the sorts of relations which constitute epistemic access:

1. Certain of the circumstances or procedures which are understood to be apt for the perception, detection, or measurement of T are, in fact, typically apt for the perception, detection, or measurement of k.[1]

2. Some of the circumstances which are taken to be indicative of certain features or properties of manifestations of T are, in fact, typically indicative of those features or properties of manifestations of k.

3. Certain significant effects attributed to the referent of T by experts (or generally, in the case of nontheoretical terms) are in fact typically produced by k.

4. Some of the most central laws involving the term T are approximately true if they are understood to be about k.

5. There is some generally accepted, putative, definite description of the referent of T which is in fact true of k and of no other kind.

6. The sorts of considerations which rationally lead to modifications of, or additions to, existing theories involving the term T are, typically and over time, indicative of respects in which those theories can be modified so as to provide more nearly accurate descriptions, when the term T is understood as referring to k, so that the tendency over time is for rationally conducted inquiry to result in theories involving T which are increasingly accurate when understood to be about k.

It is, of course, possible for a term, T, to afford epistemic access to several quite different kinds. The term "demon" probably afforded epistemic access to a great variety of kinds of natural phenomena for centuries. What I am suggesting is that it is correct to talk of the referent of a general term precisely in those cases in which the term affords substantial epistemic access to a single kind or, at any rate, to a family of closely related ones. The mark of reference is continued epistemic success with respect to information gathering about a particular kind. In the case of general terms employed in the theoretical sciences, such continued success is typically reflected in theoretical advances and in new discoveries, but it is important to realize that the same phenomenon of continued epistemic success is reflected in a more mundane fashion in the case of everyday general terms. Even in the absence of profound discoveries or theoretical advances regarding refrigerators, the color blue, or candlesticks, it remains true that we daily succeed in conveying to each other new and reliable information regarding refrigerators, blue things, and candlesticks, by employing the terms "refrigerator," "blue," and "candlestick."

I want to defend the view that reference is constituted by just this sort of epistemic access, in part, by showing how such a view can make sense of our seemingly incompatible philosophical intuitions regarding reference. But it should be said at the outset that the analysis of reference in terms of epistemic access has considerable independent plausibility. It is hard to see how language could serve the vital social functions it does if epistemic access were not a central feature of its use, and – given the limits of human knowledge – it is hard to see how the relevant sort of epistemic access could be other than that which involves gradual improvement of knowledge. Furthermore, a referential treatment of theoretical terms – and a treatment which explains how reference is possible prior to definitive knowledge – is apparently essential to any adequate treatment of the role of theoretical considerations in the assessment of scientific evidence (Boyd, 1973, 1983, 1985a, 1985b, 1990a). Thus, considerations of both everyday and scientific epistemology favor an account of reference in terms of epistemic access. It remains to show that such an account also makes sense of the received body of philosophical truisms about reference.

In the first place, an account of reference in terms of epistemic access avoids the necessity for idealized reference to dubbing ceremonies and for an implausible emphasis on the role of speakers' referential intentions. The kind to which a general term refers is determined by the role that term plays in socially coordinated inquiry, rather than by any particular features of its introduction, or the intentions of the speakers who first introduced it. It is true, of course, that the history of a term's use, and the intentions of those who use it, will play a role in determining the kind(s) to which it affords epistemic access, but we are able to offer an account of reference which does not make introducing events or speakers' intentions definitive in this regard.

Similarly, we can see how an epistemic-access account of reference accommodates the insights of the two most important logical empiricist accounts of the meaning of theoretical terms: operationalism and the "law-cluster" account. Operationalism insists that the reference (or the cognitive content – many early defenders of operationalism rejected a referential treatment of theoretical terms) is determined by conventionally fixed procedures of detection or measurement. It is mistaken in holding that detection and measurement procedures are definitive in reference fixing, and even more mistaken in holding that the reliability of measurement or detection procedures is a matter of linguistic convention. Nevertheless, if an epistemic-access account of reference is correct, there is an important grain of truth in operationalism. In typical cases, substantial epistemic access to a natural kind or physical magnitude rests on the possession of relatively reliable detection or measurement procedures. Furthermore, the sort of continued theoretical understanding characteristic of reference for theoretical terms will typically result in the acquisition of even more sophisticated and accurate techniques of detection or measurement. This sort of centrality of detection or measurement to referential epistemic access represents the important grain of truth in operationalism.

In the case of the law-cluster account, there are several grains of truth which can be accommodated to the epistemic-access account. In the first place, of course, if continued epistemic success is characteristic of reference, then the intuition is vindicated that there is something absurd in the suggestion that all of our most fundamental beliefs about a "theoretical entity" might be fundamentally mistaken. Substantial and sustained epistemic access guarantees that we cannot be entirely mistaken all the time. Furthermore, inasmuch as scientific investigations tend to be influenced by those theoretical beliefs that the scientific community considers most fundamental, continued epistemic success provides strong indication that those beliefs are, in some respects at any rate, correct. None of these considerations, of course, supports the view that fundamental laws are true by linguistic convention, or that it is always true when reference occurs that most of them are even approximately correct.

The central importance of law-clusters in reference is also explained by a central feature of scientific methodology. Scientific methodology is heavily theory-determined: for example, one tests a proposed theory by trying to identify those alternative theories which are – in the light of the best available theoretical knowledge – most likely to be true, and by designing experiments or observational studies with the aim of choosing between a proposed theory and its *plausible* rivals (this is a point which Putnam has often emphasized). There is every reason to believe that this procedure for theory assessment is crucial to the success of scientific practice (Boyd, 1973, 1983, 1985a). Because the plausibility judgments involved in the practice of this methodological principle depend on applications of the best available theories, the most fundamental laws which the scientific community accepts about a given kind will play a methodologically crucial role in the discovery of new knowledge. Indeed, the approximate truth of such collateral theoretical beliefs is part of the explanation for future epistemic success. We have thus identified another important grain of truth in the law-cluster view: The approximate truth of many of the most important laws in a given subject area is not only a probable consequence of the sustained epistemic-access characteristic of reference, in many cases, it provides the explanation for the success of scientific method in producing the epistemic successes which constitute that epistemic access. Here again, of course, the doctrine that law-clusters are true by stipulation need not be invoked; indeed, that doctrine is contrary to the methodological picture of sustained experimental *and* theoretical criticism and subsequent modification of existing theories.

It is also apparent that the epistemic-access account of reference offers an explanation for many of the less empiricistic doctrines regarding reference and knowledge, which appear on the list with which I began this section. Indeed, the epistemic-access account straightforwardly incorporates causal theories of perception, detection, and knowledge; Quine and Ullian's doctrine that language extends the senses; realist accounts of scientific methodology; and Goldstein's suggestion that ostension involves indication of research directions.

The epistemic-access account also provides an important elaboration of Putnam's talk of a division of linguistic labor. Experts play a crucial role in reference for theoretical terms (and relatively esoteric terms generally) precisely because it is they who provide nonpassive epistemic access to the referents of those terms. In this regard, it is worth remarking that what occurs is not really a division of *linguistic* labor at all. Instead, what is involved is the social division of mental (or, better yet, cognitive) labor: some of us are auto mechanics and know what "accelerator pump" means, others of us are nurserymen and know what "beech" means, whereas still others are physicists who know what "black hole" means. This division of labor is not primarily a linguistic phenomenon, nor is it primarily an epistemological phenomenon: instead, as Putnam insists, it represents facts about social organization of labor at a certain stage of historical development. The division of cognitive labor is related to the issue of reference only because it is reflected in the ways people have of gathering information about features of the world, and because the notion of reference is essentially an epistemic notion.

Consider now the three remaining intuitions about reference on the list with which I began this section: Putnam's plea for "benefit of the doubt" in assessing reference, his claim that the earliest users of general terms like "water" intended to refer to the secret inner constitution of the substance in question, and Field's defense of a notion of partial denotation. If I am right, all three represent commentaries on the dialectical aspects of reference: the accommodation of language to the causal structure of the world.

What I am calling "accommodation" is a response to an epistemological problem, whose discovery represents the principal epistemological achievement of early empiricism: inductive generalization is reliable (or, at any rate, is nonaccidentally reliable) only if the categories in terms of which generalizations are formulated correspond in the right way to the causal powers of things in the material world (Locke, 1690/1959, Book IV, Chap. iii, Sections 14, 25, 29; Hume, 1739/1973, pp. 90–1). If all A's I have so far examined have produced the effect B under circumstances C, and I conclude on that basis that A's always produce effect B under circumstances C, I am going to be right (barring pure luck) only if the categories A, B, and C correspond in the right way to the kinds of causal powers that operated to produce the effects that I observed in the sampled cases. I can go wrong, for example, if all the observed A's actually belong to a smaller kind D, and in fact, only D's have the causal power to produce B under circumstances C; I can go wrong if the category C is too broad to capture the causal contribution which the observed instances of C made to the observed effect, or if the category B is so narrow that it excludes some of the very effects which are sometimes produced by the very mechanisms which were involved in the sample situations. As Locke and Hume (somewhat inconsistently) recognized, it follows that knowledge of general laws is impossible unless we are able to succeed at the "metaphysical" task of "cutting nature at its joints."

It was the fond hope of twentieth-century logical empiricists that a non-"metaphysical" nonrealist account of the meaning of scientific theories would prove to be compatible with an acceptable account of the possibility of their rational confirmation by experiment and observation. The failure of positivist philosophy of science indicates that this was a vain (if well motivated) hope. The emergence of realist conceptions of scientific epistemology reflects the recognition that Locke was right after all: it is impossible to understand scientists as being in the business of achieving non-accidental success at inductive generalization without understanding them to be in the business of learning about (typically "unobservable") causal powers and underlying mechanisms of structures (Boyd, 1973, 1983, 1985a).

It follows, then, that the business of inductive generalizations must be the business of "cutting the world at its joints" – the business of describing and classifying natural phenomena in ways which in fact correspond to underlying causal powers or mechanisms. In other words, the accommodation of language to the world is essential for linguistically mediated epistemic access. It is for this reason that I insist that the dialectical process of accommodation – the introduction of linguistic terminology, or the modification of current usage so that general terms come to afford epistemic access to causally important features of the world – is an essential component of reference. The sorts of epistemic success that are characteristic of reference are only possible in cases where general terms afford epistemic access to kinds which are "natural" in the sense of corresponding to important causal features of the world.

We are, thus, in a preliminary way, able to offer an explication of Putnam's doctrine that the earliest users of terms like "water" intended to name the underlying real essence, if any, which explained the observable properties of their samples of water. Taken literally, this claim is patently false. What is true, however, is that the earliest users of "water" were embarked on an enterprise – the socially coordinated and linguistically mediated discovery and transmission of information about natural substances – whose rational conduct eventually required the deployment of a general expression which holds of just the inner constitution of the substance which predominated in the samples they called "water." Although they were not in a position to intend, to know, or even to imagine it, the rational conduct of the enterprise upon which they were embarked was to require the employment of terminology coextensive with our term "H_2O."

In a somewhat similar way, we can explicate Putnam's principle of the benefit of the doubt. Suppose that earlier practitioners of some science have achieved a certain measure of success: Suppose, for example, that they have come to be able to make relatively accurate predictions about a significant range of observable phenomena. In the light of the best available accounts of scientific epistemology, we may say that it is overwhelmingly likely (as a partial explanation for their success) that the linguistic terminology of their field afforded them epistemic access to (at least many of) those kinds of natural phenomena that are crucial in the causal determination of the phenomena that they have been able to predict successfully.

Their terminology must have, with some success, "cut the world at its joints." Suppose that we are now in possession of an even more sophisticated theory of the same subject area – an even more sophisticated account of those "joints." If we now ask the question: "to which natural kinds did the terminology of those earlier scientists afford them epistemic access?" we shall (quite properly) answer the question in the light of the best available current theory about what natural kinds causally determine the phenomena at issue. In many typical cases, the most plausible answer will be that their terms were – in all or most cases – coreferential with the same terms as we currently use them. Such an answer – when it is justified – will constitute part of a causal explanation of the epistemic success of earlier researchers – an explanation informed both by historical data and by the best available account of the structure of the world they were studying. Such an account of Putnam's dictum accords perfectly with the claim that what a theory of reference should explain is the role of language in the acquisition, improvement, and communication of knowledge.

We are now in a position to see the wisdom of Field's talk about partial denotation. Consider how accommodation of linguistic usage to the causal structure of the world works in cases where existing practice reflects real errors in classification of natural phenomena. There seem to be two relatively distinct types of error-collecting procedures, which correspond to two different sorts of errors.

In type one cases, we have classified together (say, as A's) certain things which have no important similarity, or we have failed to classify together things which are, in fact, fundamentally similar. In cases of this sort, we typically revise our classifications and say that the things in the first instance really weren't A's after all, and that the things in the second instance really were A's after all.

In type two cases, the situation is more complicated. We have classified things as A's and have met with success in certain sorts of causal generalization or theory construction. We later discover that for certain other theoretical or practical purposes, the things we have classified as A's do not form so natural a kind. Instead, we are led to employ a classification which partly overlaps those cases which we have earlier classified as A's. It may later turn out that one or the other of these two classifications seems the more fundamental, in the sense that it plays a role in the more significant general laws, but it remains true that each of the categories is appropriate for the formulation of interesting generalizations or laws. (I have formulated the description of these two types of errors as though the terms in question referred to natural kinds of things. Obviously, similar cases obtain for properties, kinds of properties, magnitudes, and so on.)

If all cases of classificatory error were of the first type, then the two proposals of Putnam which we have been discussing would be entirely plausible. In such cases, it is plausible to say that we are correct in saying that the erroneous misclassifications represented saying of a non-A that it is A and saying of an A that it is not an A. Precisely because there is no other natural kind close to A which includes the deviant cases, it is plausible to say that the referent of A has remained the same, and that we simply learned more about it. There would be only one kind which might plausibly be thought of as the referent of "A," even before the anomalies were discovered, and it would be reasonable both to claim (in the metaphorical sense) that it had been the "intended" referent all along, and therefore to apply the principle of benefit of the doubt and to say that earlier speakers' use of "A" had been coreferential with our more sophisticated use. Cases of type one are cases in which no new kind has been discovered; rather they are cases in which the boundary of a previously known kind is fixed with greater accuracy.

Unfortunately, cases of type two are not so clear-cut. Consider the term "fish." At one time, whales and porpoises were classified under the term "fish." Later it was discovered that whales and porpoises are mammals and are quite distinctly unlike other marine vertebrates in many important respects. We now say that whales and porpoises are "not fish" or that they are "not true fish." It remains true, however, that porpoises and bonefish do have many interesting nonphylogenetic features in common. For purposes of many sorts of investigations (of fishing industries, or animal locomotion, for example) it may be perfectly rational to classify whales and porpoises together with the boney and cartilaginous fish.

Suppose that the response to the anatomical, behavioral, physiological, and evolutionary findings that make it rational to distinguish fish from marine mammals had instead been that people had begun to say that there were two importantly different sorts of fish: furry fish and scaled fish (with subsequent modifications of terminology to distinguish "true scaled fish" from, for example, sharks and rays), and that the general term "fish" had continued to be universally applied to bonefish, sharks, rays, porpoises, and whales alike. Suppose, that is, that the important biological discoveries about aquatic animals that we have discussed had not resulted in a change in the animals which people termed "fish," and that the term "fish" had retained its prescientific usage, rather than being employed as a relatively technical term approximately coextensive with "osteichthyes." Under the circumstances we are imagining, people would not have said, for example, "Whales really aren't fish after all," but they would have marked, with different terminology, the same distinctions between kinds of aquatic animals which we now make. Provided that our imaginary linguistic community gets its biological theories right in other respects, it is unreasonable to say that they are mistaken in saying, "Whales are fish." If it is also unreasonable to say that we are wrong in saying, "Whales are not fish," then we have constructed a situation in which Putnam's principle of benefit of the doubt is inapplicable, even though the linguistic communities in question have made no scientific errors. After all, the two communities have the same linguistic history prior to the relevant biological discoveries, and each could – with equal justification – apply the principle of benefit of the doubt to enshrine its own *current* usage as exemplary of the earlier reference of the term "fish."

Two facts are made obvious by examples of this sort. In the first place, the schemes of classification, or modes of measurement, that are inductively appropriate for the acquisition of general knowledge in one field of inquiry may be quite different from those that are appropriate to another. We can and must "cut nature at its joints," but the boundaries between joints are themselves context-specific. Ways of classifying animals which are appropriate for evolutionary biology may be inappropriate for commerce, or for ethological studies. To use Goodman's terminology, "projectability" is a context-of-inquiry relative property of predicates.

Second, when it first becomes evident that it is necessary to draw a distinction between kinds where none has been drawn before, it is often the case that nothing in previous linguistic usage or intellectual practice dictates which of the newly marked kinds, if any, should be referred to by whatever the relevant previously used general term is, and which should be referred to by newly introduced terminology. It is, for example, undetermined whether the old terminology should be co-opted for the more technical, or the less technical, of the subsequent distinctions. In the case of "fish" the term has come to be used in a relatively technical way, whereas in the case of the term "jade," the term has retained its old commercial usage, and new technical terms ("jadite" and "nephrite") were introduced to mark the relevant technical distinction. (This example is from Putnam, 1975a.) As we have seen, neither of these choices was dictated by constraints of rational usage: All that rationality required was that the relevant distinction be marked in the language.

This phenomenon illustrates, I believe, what Field calls partial denotation. It often happens that a term affords epistemic access to two (or more) relatively similar – but clearly distinguishable – kinds during the period before the relevant distinctions have been drawn. Prior to the discoveries that give rise to the drawing of those distinctions, substantial information is gathered about the kinds in question – and formulated with the aid of the general term in question – so that the epistemic access afforded by that term is often crucial to the discoveries in question. After the relevant discoveries have been made, relevant changes in linguistic usage are made, but linguistic and scientific rationality do not dictate a unique new referent for the term in question. These refinements of usage represent the paradigm case of the accommodation of language to the causal structure of the world.

It is clear that the epistemic-access account of reference fully explicates Field's notion of partial denotation. Field is right to think of partial denotation as very closely related to typical cases of reference, because partial denotation involves not only epistemic access but also – in the sorts of cases we are discussing – the sorts of epistemic successes characteristic of reference. Indeed, the eventual resolution of partial denotation in favor of ordinary reference is typically achieved in the light of those successes. It is precisely this sort of "denotational refinement" (Field's term) that one would expect to be commonplace when theory-constitutive metaphorical terms are introduced at early stages of theory construction. As I suggested earlier, the term "feedback" in psychology is a likely candidate.

Field is right in another way. If we think of reference as being the relation between expressions of language and features of the world by virtue of which communication and linguistically mediated discovery are possible, then partial denotation – and indeed epistemic access in general – must be counted as part of that relation between language and the world, and so must the process of linguistic accommodation. There are two reasons why these dialectical elements must be understood as part of the phenomenon of reference itself. First, what is central in reference is epistemic access and epistemic success, and both of these can be achieved to a considerable extent in cases of partial denotation. Second, the accommodation of linguistic categories to the causal structure of the world is essential to the very possibility of the epistemic success characteristic of reference. To think of the phenomenon of reference as excluding these dialectical elements, and as somehow consisting solely of cases in which a term affords epistemic access to only one kind, would be a denial of the basically epistemic character of reference, and might, as well, lead to the absurd conclusion that in early prescientific communities many extremely useful terms have no referential interpretation at all.

There is an even more important consequence of understanding the accommodation of language to the world to be a routine feature of the process of reference, and a routine response to the acquisition of new knowledge. According to the empiricist conception of general terms, there are two quite distinct sorts of changes in the ways we use language. On the one hand, we may use general terms in a way which preserves their current referents, in order to revise, modify, amend, or contradict things we have previously said. On the other hand, we may change our usage in such a way that one or more general terms change their referents (that is, we can "adopt" new criterial attributes, law-clusters, operational definitions, or reduction sentences for such terms). Only the former sort of change, according to an empiricist understanding of reference, represents an appropriate vehicle for the assertion of new discoveries or the refutation of former beliefs. Changes in linguistic practice of the second sort – which involve changes in the referents of the relevant terms – amount, on the empiricist view, to a decision to speak a language which is, with respect to the terms in question, a new language altogether. According to such a view, sentences containing those terms which are uttered before the change in reference are in no straightforward way comparable with sentences containing the same terminology after the linguistic shift: they have a quite different subject matter and their acceptance represents simply the adoption of a new linguistic convention (this is the essence of Kuhn's treatment of the term "mass" during the change from Newtonian mechanics to special relativity; Kuhn 1970a, pp. 101–2).

Against this empiricist relativism, it is possible to insist, as an epistemic-access account of reference does, that law-clusters, operational definitions, and reduction sentences are not definitive of the referent of a general term, are not established by defining conventions, and can be modified or disconfirmed without changing the entity to which a term affords epistemic access (and, thus, without changing its referent if it refers). Nevertheless, cases like those which provide counterexamples to Putnam's principle of benefit of the doubt *are* cases in which it seems impossible to maintain that the relevant term referred to just the same kind before and after the important change in language use.

What are we to say about these cases? Are they cases in which what has occurred is a change in linguistic convention (or "world view," or "conceptual scheme") *and not a discovery?* Or, alternatively, are we – having recognized that Putnam's principle of benefit of the doubt fails in these cases – forced to treat pre-Linnaean uses of "fish" and pre-Einsteinian uses of "mass" nonreferentially on the grounds that there is no unique kind or magnitude (respectively) to which such earlier uses afforded epistemic access? Are we to say that "fish" and "mass" did not refer at all? Or, similarly, are we to say that psychologists' uses of the term "feedback" do not refer because there may be several feedbacklike psychological processes?

According to the view that I am defending here (whether one chooses to say that these terms partially denoted in their earlier usage, or, alternatively, that they referred, but lacked unique referents), the important fact is that they provided substantial and sustained epistemic access to a sufficiently small number of kinds that their use resulted in sustained increases in knowledge (and eventually in the discovery that crucial distinctions had to be drawn between those kinds to which they did afford epistemic access). This sort of linguistically mediated epistemic success – *which necessarily includes modification of linguistic usage to accommodate language to newly discovered causal features of the world* – is the very core of reference. It is just a fact that circumstances arise relatively frequently in which a term affords epistemic access to two or more natural phenomena which are importantly different but which are similar enough in certain respects. Consequently, a considerable amount of theoretically and practically useful knowledge about them can be gathered before the relevant distinctions come to light. The epistemic access provided by such terms plays a crucial role in the acquisition of this information, and in the discovery of the relevant differences; furthermore, such sustained epistemic access is characteristic of reference. Thus, both the relation which such terms bear to the world originally, *and* the modification of usage which accommodates the relevant parts of language more precisely to the causal structure of the world in the light of subsequent discoveries, are central features of the phenomenon of reference.

Two conclusions now follow: in the first place, if we are interested in the "microstructure" of reference – the relations between individual words and the world which go together to constitute the referential relation between language as a whole and the world – then the notions of epistemic access and accommodation are more important than the notion of an individual word's possessing a distinct referent. The situation in which a term affords substantial epistemic access to more than one partial denotation, until more precise accommodation is achieved in the light of later discoveries, is so commonplace that we may think of it as one of the typical ways in which language is connected to the world.

In the second place, we can now see how to answer questions about the distinction between discovery, on the one hand, and the adoption of new linguistic conventions on the other, in cases of accommodation involving partially denoting terms. Contrary to the empiricist account, alterations in the reference (or the partial denotation) of general terms is a perfectly ordinary way of expressing the discovery of new natural kinds. Situations like that of "fish," "jade," and "mass," in which a partially denoting term comes to have a more definite referent as language is accommodated to newly discovered features of the world, are absolutely commonplace. Far from representing the adoption of a new and incomparable language with respect to the terms in question, such developments are marks of referential *success:* these partially denoting terms have facilitated the discovery of new and relevant features of the world.

Having developed an epistemic-access theory of reference, we are now in a position to address the questions regarding coreferentiality, ambiguity, and linguistic precision, which were posed at the beginning of this section and to return to the issue of theory-constitutive metaphors.

Consider first the question of why one should prefer to understand the reference of theoretical terms as continuous during scientific revolutions rather than as changing in ways which make comparison between successive theories impossible. This amounts to the question of why one should apply Putnam's principle of benefit of the doubt. We have just seen in some detail how Putnam's principle, amended in the light of Field's notion of partial denotation, is a consequence of an epistemic-access account of reference. Two points in favor of the continuity account are especially relevant because of their relation to the corresponding question about metaphors. First, according to the epistemic-access account, there are no particular features of the use of a theoretical term (like, for example, a law-cluster, or a particular set of measurement procedures, or a set of reduction sentences) which are conventionally definitive of its referent. Thus, we are not obliged to conclude that the referent of a theoretical term has changed whenever there has been a radical change in the relevant theory, provided that there is some reason to treat the change in theory as a response to additional evidence.

Second, in cases of scientific revolutions, the fact that the subsequent theory resembles the previous one in some important respects provides part of the evidence in support of the latter theory, and this evidential consideration makes sense only on the view that what is involved is the replacement of one approximately accurate and well-confirmed theory by another even better theory *with basically the same subject matter.*

This last point can be put in another way: certainly, in the case of the development of the theory of relativity, the earlier Newtonian theory served a valuable heuristic role in the development of the later theory. Newtonian mechanics provided a valuable guide to the construction of a new theory to account for new and surprising data. What the present account of scientific epistemology dictates is the conclusion that the overwhelmingly likely explanation of the heuristic value of a theory in such a situation is that its terms refer (or partially denote); that it is in important respects true; and that for that reason it can serve as a guide to the formulation of an even more nearly true theory *with relevantly the same subject matter,* that is, one in which most terms preserve their earlier referents

(Boyd 1973, 1989, 1991). The typically positivist move of distinguishing between a theory's being approximately true, and its merely providing a heuristically valuable way of looking at data, fails: in all but contrived and scientifically atypical situations, the only plausible explanation for a theory's heuristic value is that its terms refer, and that it is in some important respects approximately true.

Theory-constitutive metaphors, epistemic access, and referential precision

We can now ask the corresponding question about theory-constitutive metaphors: given that it is possible to employ a nondefinitional account of reference to defend the view that theory-constitutive metaphorical expressions should be understood as referring, why is this view preferable to the view that theory-constitutive metaphorical expressions are nonreferential and are merely heuristically useful?

First, the fact that we are typically unable to provide an explication of theory-constitutive metaphors – that we are typically unable to *define* the relevant respects of similarity or analogy between the primary and secondary subjects of these metaphors – does not, in the light of an epistemic-access account of reference, provide any reason to doubt that the relevant metaphorical expressions refer. The existence of explicit definitions is not characteristic of referring expressions, and is not even a typical accompaniment to sustained epistemic access.

Second, the option of treating theory-constitutive metaphorical expressions as serving a merely heuristic role, rather than treating them referentially, is ruled out by general epistemological considerations from the philosophy of science. If the articulation and refinement of a body of metaphors all involving the same metaphorical theme proves to be genuinely fruitful in scientific theory construction, then the only epistemologically plausible explanation is that most of the relevant metaphorical expressions refer, and that the metaphorical statements in question – when interpreted in the light of the nonstandard referents of their metaphorical terms – express important truths.

Finally, Field's notion of partial denotation, which the epistemic-access account explains, makes it possible to treat metaphorical expressions referentially without ignoring the strong intuition that it is unlikely that such expressions always refer to a single definite kind. The view that the metaphorical terms in successful theory-constitutive metaphors should be understood referentially, but perhaps as affording epistemic access to more than one kind, amounts to an understanding that the epistemic-access account of reference dictates for theoretical terms generally.

At the beginning of the last section, I raised the question of what the standard of coreferentiality was if the empiricist standard of preservation of law-cluster, operational definition, or reduction sentences were not cor-

rect. The epistemic-access account provides an answer: reference is continuous if the term in question continues to provide epistemic access to the
same kind, or if appropriate episodes of denotational refinement take
place. Similarly, several roughly simultaneous uses of the same term are
coreferential if they are embodied in patterns of usage which afford
epistemic access to the same kind(s).

It must be understood that the issue of epistemic access (and thus of
reference) for a particular term is a perfectly ordinary scientific question.
One is inquiring about the complex causal relationships between features
of the world and the practices of the relevant linguistic community;
whether, how, and/or to what extent they, in turn, give rise to the relevant
sort of epistemic relations between the term in question and one or more
kinds.

In typical cases, one might expect the outcome of such an inquiry to be
an independent specification of the kinds to which the term in question
affords epistemic access. In the case of theory-constitutive metaphorical
expressions, this outcome is precluded (at least until later research makes
the explication of the metaphor possible) inasmuch as an independent
specification of the relevant kinds would amount to the sort of analysis or
explication of which theory-constitutive metaphors typically do not admit.
Nevertheless, when we inquire whether a single metaphorical expression
occurring in a variety of different theory-constitutive metaphors which
develop the same theme, has the same referent (or the same partial
denotata) in each of those metaphors, we can have evidence for a positive
answer, even though an independent specification of its referent may be
impossible. For precisely the epistemological reasons which justify a realist
conception of scientific theories, we know that the only plausible explanation for genuinely substantial heuristic value in such an extended series of
metaphors is that there is a relatively small number of kinds to which their
constituent terms afford epistemic access. Thus, whenever an extended
series of related scientific metaphors has genuine scientific value, the overwhelmingly plausible explanation lies in the assumption that each of their
constituent metaphorical expressions affords epistemic access to at most a
small number of kinds – that is, that reference is constant from one employment of such a metaphorical expression to the other.

Thus, if an epistemic-access account of reference is sound, we have every
good reason to hold, in the case of genuinely fruitful theory-constitutive
metaphors, that all or most of their constituent metaphorical terms refer
and that each of them has the same referent (or approximately the same set
of partial denotata) in each of its applications within the relevant theoretical context.

Let us turn now to the question of exactness, or linguistic precision, as it
arises in the case of theory-constitutive metaphors. Black holds that metaphors lack the "precision of scientific statements," and that they must

therefore play a role in language different from the role played by the theoretical statements of science. It is evident that it is the open-endedness and inexplicability of interaction metaphors which leads Black to this conclusion. If, as I have argued here, such open-endedness and inexplicitness is typical of theoretical statements and of theoretical terms whose reference is not definitionally fixed, the question arises: what is the right account of linguistic precision in science?

According to the empiricist understanding of scientific terms and scientific method, there are two quite distinct kinds of precision in scientific practice. On the one hand, there is precision in the use of scientific language. Since Locke, the empiricist view has been that this sort of precision is achieved to the extent to which general terms are associated with fixed, conventional, and explicit definitions of their extensions or referents. On the other hand, there is what might be called methodological precision: precision in reasoning, careful experimental design, diligent reporting of data, proper control of experimental variables, precision in measurement, and so forth. The first sort of precision is wholly a matter of the proper following of linguistic rules, whereas the second is a matter of care in treating epistemological issues. Black's insistence that metaphors lack scientific precision must, I believe, stem from a recognition that the use of metaphorical terminology fails to meet the first of these empiricist tests of precision.

Against this view of precision in science, I want to maintain that there is only one sort of scientific precision – methodological, or epistemological precision – and that precision in the use of scientific language is merely one feature, and one consequence, of this methodological precision. There is no purely *linguistic* precision, no mere following of *linguistic* rules, which accounts for precision in the use of theoretical terms.

We may, at the outset, see why the empiricist account of linguistic precision is fundamentally mistaken. The aim of this account is to set standards of linguistic precision which guarantee that each general term will refer to exactly one quite definite kind. The referent (or the extension) of a general term is supposed to be precisely fixed once and for all by conventionally adopted defining criteria. Given human ignorance, it would inevitably be the case (as Locke and Hume recognized) that almost none of the terms introduced according to such pure conventions would correspond to "natural kinds," almost none would "cut nature at its joints." As both Locke and Hume recognized, such terms would in fact prove to be almost useless for the acquisition of any general knowledge whatsoever, and would thus be scientifically useless: indeed, it is hard to see what viable social arrangements could sustain the practice of abiding by such self-defeating conventions.

If the empiricist criterion of precision is a failure, we may still ask what sorts of linguistic difficulties it was designed to avoid. It seems that there are two sorts of linguistic imprecision against which empiricist standards of linguistic precision were directed, although the distinction between them does not seem to have been carefully drawn, even by Locke who may well be the most careful of the empiricists in discussing misuses of language.

On the one hand, there is the difficulty which would arise from idiosyncratic uses of a general term – from circumstances in which someone uses a general term with a different referent or extension from the referent or extension which it has in the idiolects of the typical speakers of his language, or from circumstances in which there was a corresponding sort of mismatch between the uses of a term in two communities which share the same language. On the other hand, there is the sort of difficulty which would arise if the linguistic community as a whole used a general term in an ambiguous or vague way – in a way which left it without any definite referent or extension. Empiricism proposes the same solution – definitional linguistic conventions – to both of these problems.

From the point of view defended here, the first of these problems takes on a somewhat different cast. Because, on the epistemic-access view, reference is a social rather than a private phenomenon, fewer circumstances fit the first of these cases than Locke, say, might have thought. For example, many cases in which an individual has atypical evidential standards for the application of a general term, but in which he also relies on indirect evidence provided by the testimony of others, would be diagnosed as cases in which his use of the term afforded him epistemic access primarily to the same kind to which others referred, but in which his own beliefs about the kind in question were seriously mistaken.

Similarly (and even more obviously), cases in which two communities employed different evidential standards in applications of the same term – standards which were in fact apt for the detection of two different kinds, but in which this fact went unnoticed, so that members of each community relied on reports from members of the other – would often be diagnosed as cases of partial denotation, rather than cases in which definite but different referents could be assigned to the term in the vocabulary of each community. Nevertheless, difficulties of the first sort no doubt do occur, and it is reasonable to inquire what remedy exists for them if an epistemic-access account of reference is correct. Here, it is interesting to note, the remedy involves principles of rational inquiry, which are not distinctly linguistic principles: assess evidence in the light of the best available *generally* accepted theory unless compelling evidence dictates its rejection. Rely on the advice of recognized experts. When your standards of evidence contrast sharply with those of others, seek to identify the source of the conflict, and so on. These are independently justifiable methodological principles, but the consistent application of principles of this sort provides the only rational procedure for uncovering or preventing the difficulties we have been discussing.

The second sort of difficulty arises when the use of a general term affords epistemic access to two or more quite distinct kinds, or (worse yet) to no particular kinds at all. What is to be avoided, then, are situations in which a general term partially denotes rather than refers, or situations in which it affords such diffuse epistemic access that even partial denotation is not achieved. The empiricist solution to this problem is to erect contrived categories as the referents of general terms at the cost of abandoning the project of "cutting nature at its joints." The alternative solution is provided by the ongoing project of continuous accommodation of language to the world in the light of new discoveries about causal powers. Here, the examples of the terms "demon," "fish," "jade," and "mass" are revealing. In each of these instances, a case of quasi-reference or worse was resolved by either a subsequent refinement of usage, or by the abandonment of a term altogether. In each case, the improvement in linguistic usage resulted from new discoveries about the world, rather than from attention to linguistic rules or conventions. In general, this sort of accommodation is achieved by careful and critical research about the structure of causal relations, and in particular by the pursuit of questions like: how reliable are the detection and measurement procedures which we now use? When we take several different procedures to be reliable tests for the same kind, or reliable measures for the same magnitude, are we right in believing that they are all indicative of the same kind or magnitude? How similar are the things we now classify together, and in what respects? How different? What new and undiscovered natural kinds, magnitudes, and so on, must be postulated to account for new data? It is in the *methodologically* precise and diligent pursuit of these scientific questions, rather than in any distinctly *linguistic* practices, that the solution to the problem of diffuse epistemic access lies.

Indeed, all of these questions, as well as the remedies for idiosyncratic usage, are a reflection of a single methodological principle: always inquire, in the light of the best available knowledge, in what ways your current beliefs about the world might plausibly be incomplete, inadequate, or false, and design observations or experiments with the aim of detecting and remedying such possible defects. All of the principles which serve to prevent diffuse epistemic access are special cases of this principle, and there is no application of it which is irrelevant to the dialectical task of accommodation. I conclude, therefore, that there are no distinct principles of *linguistic* precision in science, but rather that linguistic precision is one of the consequences of methodological precision of a quite general sort.

Turning now to the issue of metaphor in science, we can see what realist standards of precision should govern their use. One should employ a metaphor in science only when there is good evidence that an important similarity or analogy exists between its primary and secondary subjects. One should seek to discover more about the relevant similarities or analogies, always considering the possibility that there are no important similarities or analogies, or alternatively, that there are quite distinct similarities for which distinct terminology should be introduced. One should try to discover what the "essential" features of the similarities or analogies are, and one should try to assimilate one's account of them to other theoretical work in the same subject area (that is, one should *attempt* to explicate the metaphor). Such principles of methodological precision are, of course, not importantly different from those that properly govern the use of any sort of theoretical terminology in science, and it is for that reason that we may conclude that the "imprecision" of metaphors does not preclude their employment as constituents of scientific theories.

A final remark about the inexplicitness of theory-constitutive metaphors: theory-constitutive metaphorical terms – when they refer – refer implicitly, in the sense that they do not correspond to explicit definitions of their referents, but instead indicate a research direction toward them. The same thing is apparently true of theoretical terms in science generally.

Now, some thinkers have taken such phenomena as support for an *idealist* conception of scientific understanding, which treats implicit features of scientific knowledge as personal and constructive, rather than as objective and intersubjective. It is beyond the scope of this essay to explore this view in any detail. But it is interesting to reflect that the implicit character of scientific metaphors does not demand any such idealist interpretation. They refer by virtue of *social* and intersubjective (as opposed to personal) mechanisms, which connect scientific research with independently existing ("objective") features of the world.[2] Furthermore, when we understand a theory-constitutive metaphor, there is no reason to believe that we somehow *tacitly* understand the similarities and analogies to which its constituent terms afford epistemic access, just as there is no reason to believe that Newton tacitly understood the Einsteinian account of the referents of his theoretical terminology. These considerations are, of course, not conclusive with respect to an idealist and subjective conception of science; but, taken together with the independent evidence for a realist conception of scientific theories, the fact that an idealist explanation is not required in so obvious an area as that of metaphor in science should give a thoughtful idealist pause.

Metaphors, property homeostasis, and deference to nature

We have seen that there are theory-constitutive metaphors, that a naturalistic epistemic-access account of reference can explain their role in the accommodation of scientific language to the causal structure of the world, and that the same conception of reference can explain why the risk of referential ambiguity associated with such metaphors does not compromise their precision in any scientifically interesting sense of precision. If the role of theory-constitutive metaphors is thus rendered nonmysterious, questions about their role in scientific investigation still remain.

In the first place, there is the question of why metaphors prove so valuable in providing theory-constitutive conceptual frameworks in science. I have already suggested that the introduction of metaphorical terminology reduces the risk (or perhaps the extent) of ambiguity when terms are introduced to refer to functionally or relationally characterized phenomena. Is that it, or are there other ways in which metaphors are especially suited for the introduction of terminology in certain sciences?

There is, moreover, the question of the future of any given theory-constitutive metaphor. I have argued that there is no a priori reason to suppose that a theory-constitutive metaphor will forever escape complete explication, but should we expect that such an explication will typically be the fate of a theory-constitutive metaphor if things go well scientifically. Or should we routinely expect that theory-constitutive metaphors will eventually be abandoned or "frozen"? Suppose, for example, that a metaphorical term is introduced for a chemical compound whose (a posteriori) definition is discovered to be provided by the formula F. Should we not expect that after this discovery it will be referred to by F rather than by the original metaphorical term, or at any rate that the metaphorical term will become a dead metaphor once the essence of the compound has been discovered and research can be guided by that knowledge? Should this not be the fate of all theory-constitutive metaphors if things go well?

No doubt these questions have quite complex answers, but I think that we can make some headway with them if we examine certain cases of natural kinds and natural kind terms with respect to which our practice of deferring to nature in defining kinds goes somewhat further than the examples of natural definitions like "Water = H_2O" suggest.

The sorts of essential definitions of substances reflected in the currently accepted natural definitions of chemical kinds by molecular formulas (e.g., "water = H_2O") appear to specify necessary and sufficient conditions for membership in the kind in question. Recent *non*naturalistic property-cluster or criterial attribute theories in the "ordinary language" tradition suggest the possibility of definitions which do not provide necessary and sufficient conditions. Instead, some terms are said to be defined by a collection of properties such that the possession of an adequate number of these properties is sufficient for falling within the extension of the term. It is supposed to be a conceptual (and thus an a priori) matter what properties belong in the cluster and which combinations of them are sufficient for falling under the terms. It is usually insisted, however, that the kinds corresponding to such terms are "open textured" so that there is some indeterminacy in extension legitimately associated with property-cluster or criterial attribute definitions. The "imprecision" or "vagueness" of such definitions is seen as a perfectly appropriate feature of ordinary linguistic usage, in contrast to the artificial precision suggested by rigidly formalistic positivist conceptions of proper language use.

I doubt that there are any terms whose definitions actually fit the ordinary language model, because I doubt that there are any significant "conceptual truths" at all. I believe, however, that terms with somewhat similar definitions are commonplace in the special sciences which study complex phenomena. Here is what I think often happens (I formulate the account for monadic property terms; the account is intended to apply in the obvious way to the cases of terms for polyadic relations, magnitudes, etc.):

1. There is a family, F, of properties that are contingently clustered in nature in the sense that they co-occur in an important number of cases.

2. Their co-occurrence is, at least typically, the result of what may be metaphorically (sometimes literally) described as a sort of *homeostasis*. Either the presence of some of the properties in F tends (under appropriate conditions) to favor the presence of the others, or there are underlying mechanisms or processes which tend to maintain the presence of the properties in F, or both.

3. The homeostatic clustering of the properties in F is causally important: there are (theoretically or practically) important effects which are produced by a conjoint occurrence of (many of) the properties in F together with (some or all of) the underlying mechanisms in question.

4. There is a kind term, t, which is applied to things in which the homeostatic clustering of most of the properties in F occurs.

5. t has an analytic definition; rather all or part of the homeostatic cluster F together with some or all of the mechanisms that underlie it provide the natural definition of t. The question of just which properties and mechanisms belong in the definition of t is an a posteriori question – often a difficult theoretical one.

6. Imperfect homeostatis is nomologically possible or actual: some thing may display some but not all of the properties in F; some but not all of the relevant underlying homeostatic mechanisms may be present.

7. In such cases, the relative importance of the various properties in F and of the various mechanisms in determining whether the thing falls under t – if it can be determined at all – is a theoretical rather than a conceptual issue.

8. Moreover, there will be many cases of extensional vagueness that are not resolvable even given all the relevant facts and all the true theories. There will be things which display some but not all of the properties in F (and/or in which some but not all of the relevant homeostatic mechanisms operate) such that no rational considerations dictate whether or not they are to be classed under t, assuming that a dichotomous choice is to be made.

9. The causal importance of the homeostatic property cluster F together with the relevant underlying homeostatic mechanisms is such that the kind or property denoted by t is a natural kind reference important for scientific explanation or for the formulation of successful inductive inferences.

10. No refinement of usage which replaces t by a significantly less exten-

sionally vague term will preserve the naturalness of the kind referred to. Any such refinement would either require that we treat as important distinctions that are irrelevant to causal explanation or to induction, or that we ignore similarities that are important in just these ways.

11. The homeostatic property cluster which serves to define *t* is not individuated extensionally. Instead, the property cluster is individuated like a (type or token) historical object or process: certain changes over time (or in space) in the property cluster or in the underlying homeostatic mechanisms preserve the identity of the defining cluster. As a consequence, the properties which determine the conditions for falling under *t* may vary over time (or space), *whereas* t *continues to have the same definition*. This historicity in the way the property cluster definition is individuated is itself dictated by methodological considerations in the disciplines in which *t* is employed: the recognition of the relevant continuities in the historical development of the property cluster is crucial to the inductive and explanatory tasks of those disciplines. Thus the historicity of the individuation conditions for the property cluster is essential for the naturalness of the kind to which *t* refers. I do not envision that this sort of variability in definition will obtain for all of the kinds and kind terms satisfying 1 through 10 and I propose to employ the term "homeostatic property cluster" even in those cases in which 11 fails.

The paradigm cases of natural kinds – biological species – are examples of homeostatic cluster kinds. The appropriateness of any particular biological species for induction and explanation in biology depends on the imperfectly shared and homeostatically related morphological, physiological, and behavioral features that characterize its members. The definitional role of mechanisms of homeostasis is reflected in the role of interbreeding in the modern species concept; for sexually reproducing species, the exchange of genetic material between populations is thought by some evolutionary biologists to be essential to the homeostatic unity of the other properties characteristic of the species and it is thus reflected in the species definition that they propose (see Mayr, 1970). The *necessary* indeterminacy in extension of species terms is a consequence of evolutionary theory, as Darwin observed: speciation depends on the existence of populations that are intermediate between the parent species and the emerging one. Any "refinement" of classification that artificially eliminated the resulting indeterminacy in classification would obscure the central fact about speciation on which the cogency of evolutionary theory depends.

Similarly, the property cluster and homeostatic mechanisms that define a species must be individuated nonextensionally as a processlike historical entity. It is universally recognized that selection for characters that enhance reproductive isolation from related species is a significant factor in phyletic evolution, and it is one that necessarily alters over time the species' defining property cluster and homeostatic mechanisms (Mayr, 1970).

It follows that a consistently developed naturalistic conception of the accommodation of scientific language to the causal structure of the world *predicts* indeterminacy for those natural kind or property terms that refer to complex homeostatic phenomena; such indeterminacy is a necessary consequence of "cutting the world at its joints." Similarly, consistently developed naturalism predicts the existence of nonextensionally individuated definitional clusters for at least some natural kinds, and thus it treats as legitimate vehicles for the growth of approximate knowledge linguistic practices that would, from a more traditional empiricist perspective, look like diachronic inconsistencies in the standards for the application of such natural kind terms.

Homeostatic property cluster definitions represent a special kind of deference to the world: instead of being possible *conceptual phenomena* whose content is dictated by the causal structure of the world, they are themselves naturalistically and (perhaps) historically individuated causal phenomena *in the world*. They provide the most striking examples of the phenomenon of accommodation of scientific language to causal structures. They also provide us with a number of insights into the ways in which theory-constitutive metaphors may contribute to that accommodation.

In the first place, consider the question of why metaphors are so often valuable devices for the introduction of theoretical language. Recall that when a term, t, is employed metaphorically as a theoretical term scientists are invited to explore the similarities between the phenomenon referred to by t in its metaphorical uses and the phenomenon to which t literally refers. The cluster of properties that scientists associate with (real) t's is to guide their thinking about metaphorical t's. If the choice of metaphor is apt this strategy of investigation could be valuable for the study of any sort of phenomenon but, I suggest, it may prove especially valuable in the case in which the phenomenon referred to by t in its theory-constitutive metaphorical use is a homeostatic property cluster phenomenon whose essence is given by a property cluster rather than by a set of necessary and sufficient conditions. The metaphor may prove more valuable still if the literal referent of t is also a homeostatic property cluster kind whose essential structure is in that respect like that of its metaphorical referent.

I speculate that the latter sort of situation obtains in the case of many famous scientific metaphors like the sustained metaphors of economic competition which have underwritten much of evolutionary theory, the various (human) social metaphors invoked in descriptions of the behavior and ecology of nonhuman animals, and military metaphors in the description of bodily responses to disease.

Consider also the question of whether or not we should expect that theory-constitutive metaphors will in the course of successful science typically become fully explicated or otherwise "frozen." At least insofar as we think of explication of a theory-constitutive metaphor as involving the specification of the natural definition of the phenomenon to which it refers, the case of homeostatic property cluster phenomena suggests a negative answer. Where a theory-constitutive metaphor (or any other expression) refers to such a phenomenon, there is no reason in general to believe that such an explication is even possible. The properties that constitute the homeostatic property cluster may not even be finite in number and they may vary significantly from time to time or place to place, so that a finite characterization of them (much less a cognitively tractable characterization) need not be possible. It is a striking fact that, contrary to what empiricist accounts of scientific language and scientific concepts would suggest, we can refer to and study successfully phenomena that could not possibly have the sorts of definitions empiricists envisioned as essential for scientific investigation.

Homeostasis, reference, and precision

An understanding of homeostatic property cluster definitions can also enhance our understanding of the semantics of theory-constitutive metaphors and other linguistic expressions as well. In offering an epistemic-access account of reference I identified a number of mutually reinforcing factors which, I argued, contributed toward the establishment of a referential connection between a term and a feature of the world. I did not propose to offer a definition of reference in terms of necessary and sufficient conditions for a term to refer to a phenomenon and I suggested that no such conditions exist. I am now in a position to make that claim more precisely. I propose that reference itself is a homeostatic property cluster phenomenon and that the mutually reinforcing factors I identified are some elements of the defining cluster.

I propose, moreover, that reference is a homeostatic property cluster phenomenon precisely because reference is an epistemic phenomenon and knowledge is a homeostatic property cluster phenomenon. All plausible theories of knowledge have it that cases of knowledge differ from other cases of true belief in being appropriately justified, or appropriately reliably produced or regulated, or both. One challenge in epistemology is to specify the degrees and combinations of justification and/or reliability that suffice for knowledge. I suggest that knowledge is in fact defined by a homeostatic cluster of justificatory and reliability producing factors and that this fact explains both the "vagueness" of the notion of knowledge and the failure of efforts to provide (even as an idealization) necessary and sufficient conditions for a true belief to be an instance of knowledge. I develop this theme, without the terminology of homeostatic property cluster phenomena, in Boyd (1983) and I sketch a defense of the related claim that rationality is a homeostatic property cluster phenomenon in Boyd (1990a). I believe that almost all the phenomena of special interest to philosophers are homeostatic property cluster phenomena; for a treatment of moral categories along these lines see Boyd (1988).

An understanding of homeostatic property cluster phenomena also helps to clarify the issue of linguistic precision with respect to scientific terms generally and with respect to theory-constitutive metaphors in particular. We have already seen that with respect to the sort of imprecision that manifests itself as ambiguity in the use of theoretical language the appropriate remedy lies not in seeking a distinctly *linguistic* precision of the sort suggested by empiricists, that is, the adoption of conventional definitions in terms of necessary and sufficient conditions. Instead what is required is the sort of *methodological* precision capable of identifying cases of partial denotation.

Empiricists were concerned as well with a different sort of linguistic imprecision – that displayed by "vague" terminology lacking a determinate extension. Part of the motivation for the empiricist conception of conventional meaning was to provide a remedy for this sort of vagueness. Of course the considerations rehearsed in our earlier discussion of linguistic precision suggest that – where vagueness is a problem to be avoided – the remedy is methodological precision leading to the theoretical resolution of indeterminateness. But, what the homeostatic property cluster conception of some natural kinds indicates is that vagueness in extension is by no means always indicative of any imprecision at all. For some kinds, "vagueness" in the application of the associated terminology is precisely indicative of *precision* in the accommodation of language to the causal structure of the world. If, as I have suggested, many theory-constitutive metaphors refer to homeostatic property cluster phenomena, then we have an additional reason for rejecting the empiricist conception of precision for those cases.

I do not mean to suggest that for such metaphors all the vagueness in their application in practice will correspond to real vagueness in the associated phenomenon. Nor do I suggest that when a literal homeostatic property cluster term is metaphorically used to refer to a homeostatic property cluster phenomenon there will be a neat match between the respects of vagueness of its two referents. I do suggest, however, that the vagueness of scientifically useful theory-constitutive metaphors may serve to remind us of both the actual vagueness of some natural phenomena and the deep limitations of the empiricist conception of linguistic precision.

NOTES

The present chapter is for Herbert Feigl and James J. Gibson. In it I have focused on the question: how can we explain the role of metaphor in the articulation of new scientific theories? I have not addressed the question: what role does metaphorical thinking play in theory invention? I find the second question no less important, but I do not have anything interesting to say about it.

Especially in developing my views on epistemic-access and reference I have benefited from advice and criticism from a number of colleagues. I want especially to thank William Alston, Alex Goldstein, Hilary Kornblith, Barbara Koslowski, Richard Miller, Sydney Shoemaker, Robert Stalnaker, and Nicholas Sturgeon.

The present essay is a revision of the original version which appeared in the 1979 edition of this collection. Apart from minor revisions, the only new material is the material on homeostatic property cluster definitions described in the Introduction and developed in the sections entitled "Metaphors, property homeostasis, and deference to nature" and "Homeostasis, reference, and precision." This material is also developed in Boyd (1988, 1989, 1991).

I have not made any attempt to survey in the present version the extensive literature on naturalistic conceptions of knowledge and of reference that has appeared since the first version was published, nor have I surveyed the equally extensive literature on the relation between naturalistic conceptions of reference and issues in the philosophy of mind and the philosophy of psychology. The reader interested in recent developments might start with Burge (1986), Devitt (1981), Dretske (1981), Fodor (1981), Goldman (1986), and Stalnaker (1984).

Since Professor Kuhn has not rewritten his comments in light of the new material in the present version I want to say something about the relation of the new material to my disagreement with him over the relative merits of realist and social constructivist interpretations of scientific knowledge. I take the development of the homeostatic property cluster theory of (some) natural kind definitions to be important to the articulation of a naturalistic conception of scientific knowledge and of the semantics of scientific language on which the defense of realism ultimately depends. In that sense *only* I believe that it contributes to the defense of realism against social constructivism. The acknowledgment and articulation of a version of the homeostatic property cluster account of certain kind definitions is plainly compatible with social constructivism. After all, social constructivists are no more Humeans about causal structures than are realists, and they can certainly portray scientists as defining some terms in terms of causally determined property correlations in the world(s) they study. Nothing in the present essay is designed to show that constructivist accounts of how such accommodations to causal structure are secured in scientific research must be inferior to realist versions. I discuss the relative merits of realist and constructivist accounts of such accommodation in Boyd (1990a, 1990b, 1991) and especially in Boyd (1992).

1 Here, and in other entries on this list, I have abused the use–mention distinction. The reader will have no difficulty in providing (somewhat tedious) but correct reformulations of these points.

2 It is important to understand in just what respect natural kinds are "objective" or "independently existing." According to the account offered here, natural kinds are discipline- or interest-relative. That is, the "naturalness" of a natural kind consists in the fact that its members have relevantly similar causal powers (or causal histories, etc.). Relevance of similarity is assessed with respect to the sorts of everyday reports, inductive generalizations, or theory constructions that are required for the particular practical or theoretical projects that the relevant

linguistic community undertakes. Thus "jade" denotes a commercial and "gemological" natural kind, even though for purposes of geology, jadite and nephrite are quite distinct kinds. Indeed, the notion of a natural kind can be fully explicated in terms of the notion of linguistic accommodation in the setting of particular practical or theoretical projects.

This project relativity of natural kinds represents the *only* grain of truth in Locke's claim that, although nature makes things similar, men rank them into kinds (Locke, Book III, Chap. iv, Sections 35–8). In no other respect are kinds un-"objective." The causal structures to which our language is accommodated exist quite independently of our conceptual schemes or theory construction. We do not decide by convention where the boundaries of natural kinds lie. Neither do we, in any important sense, "construct" the world when we adopt linguistic or theoretical frameworks. Instead *we* accommodate *our* language to the structure of a theory-independent world (contrast Kuhn, 1970a; Putnam, 1977; for further discussion see Boyd, 1990b, 1991, 1992).

22

Metaphor in science

THOMAS S. KUHN

If I had been preparing the main paper on the role of metaphor in science, my point of departure would have been precisely the works chosen by Boyd: Max Black's well-known paper on metaphor (Black, 1962b), together with recent essays by Kripke and Putnam on the causal theory of reference (Kripke, 1972; Putnam, 1975a, 1975b). My reasons for those choices would, furthermore, have been very nearly the same as his, for we share numerous concerns and convictions. But, as I moved away from the starting point that body of literature provides, I would quite early have turned in a direction different from Boyd's, following a path that would have brought me quickly to a central metaphorlike process in science, one which he passes by. That path I shall have to sketch, if sense is to be made of my reactions to Boyd's proposals, and my remarks will therefore take the form of an excessively condensed epitome of parts of a position of my own, comments on Boyd's paper emerging along the way. That format seems all the more essential inasmuch as detailed analysis of individual points presented by Boyd is not likely to make sense to an audience largely ignorant of the causal theory of reference.

Boyd begins by accepting Black's "interaction" view of metaphor. However metaphor functions, it neither presupposes nor supplies a list of the respects in which the subjects juxtaposed by metaphor are similar. On the contrary, as both Black and Boyd suggest, it is sometimes (perhaps always) revealing to view metaphor as creating or calling forth the similarities upon which its function depends. With that position I very much agree and, lacking time, I shall supply no arguments for it. In addition, and presently more significant, I agree entirely with Boyd's assertion that the open-endedness or inexplicitness of metaphor has an important (and I think precise) parallel in the process by which scientific terms are introduced and thereafter deployed. However scientists apply terms like "mass," "electricity," "heat," "mixture," or "compound" to nature, it is not ordinarily by acquiring a list of criteria necessary and sufficient to determine the referents of the corresponding terms.

With respect to reference, however, I would go one step further than Boyd. In his chapter, the claims for a parallel to metaphor are usually restricted to the theoretical terms of science. I suppose that they often hold equally for what used to be called observation terms, for example "distance," "time," "sulphur," "bird," or "fish." The fact that the last of these terms figures large in Boyd's examples suggests that he is unlikely to disagree. He knows as well as I that recent developments in philosophy of science have deprived the theoretical/observational distinction of anything resembling its traditional cash value. Perhaps it can be preserved as a distinction between antecedently available terms and new ones introduced at particular times in response to new scientific discoveries or inventions. But, if so, the parallel to metaphor will hold for both. Boyd makes less than he might of the ambiguity of the word "introduced." Something with the properties of metaphor is often called upon when a new term is *introduced into* the vocabulary of science. But it is also called upon when such terms – by now established in the common parlance of the profession – are *introduced to* a new scientific generation by a generation that has already learned their use. Just as reference must be established for each new element in the vocabulary of science, so accepted patterns of reference must be reestablished for each new cohort of recruits to the sciences. The techniques involved in both modes of introduction are much the same, and they therefore apply on both sides of the divide between what used to be called "observational" and "theoretical" terms.

To establish and explore the parallels between metaphor and reference fixing, Boyd resorts both to the Wittgensteinian notion of natural families or kinds and to the causal theory of reference. I would do the same, but in a significantly different way. It is at this point that our paths begin to diverge. To see how they do so, look first at the causal theory of reference itself. As Boyd notes, that theory originated and still functions best in application to proper names like "Sir Walter Scott." Traditional empiricism suggested that proper names refer by virtue of an associated definite description chosen to provide a sort of definition of the name: for example, "Scott is the author of *Waverley.*" Difficulties immediately arose, because the choice of the defining description seemed arbitrary. Why should being the author of the novel *Waverley* be a criterion governing the applicability of the name "Walter Scott" rather than a historical fact about the individual to whom the name, by whatever techniques, does refer? Why should having written *Waverley* be a necessary characteristic of Sir Walter Scott but having written *Ivanhoe* a contingent one? Attempts to remove these difficulties by using more elaborate definite descriptions, or by restricting the characteristics on which definite descriptions may call, have uniformly failed. The causal theory of reference cuts the Gordian knot by denying that proper names have definitions or are associated with definite descriptions at all.

Instead, a name like "Walter Scott" is a tag or label. That it attaches to one individual rather than to another or to no one at all is a product of history. At some particular point in time a particular infant was baptized or dubbed with the name "Walter Scott," which he bore thereafter through whatever events he happened to experience or bring about (for example, writing *Waverley*). To find the referent of a name like "Sir Walter Scott" or "Professor Max Black," we ask someone who knows the individual about whom we inquire to point him out to us. Or else we use some contingent fact about him, like his authorship of *Waverley* or of the paper on metaphor, to locate the career line of the individual who happened to write that work. If, for some reason, we doubt that we have correctly identified the person to whom the name applies, we simply trace his life history or lifeline backward in time to see whether it includes the appropriate act of baptism or dubbing.

Like Boyd, I take this analysis of reference to be a great advance, and I also share the intuition of its authors that a similar analysis should apply to the naming of natural kinds; Wittgenstein's games, birds (or sparrows), metals (or copper), heat, and electricity. There is something right about Putnam's claim that the referent of "electric charge" is fixed by pointing to the needle of a galvanometer and saying that "electric charge" is the name of the physical magnitude responsible for its deflection. But, despite the amount that Putnam and Kripke have written on the subject, it is by no means clear just what is right about their intuition. My pointing to an individual, Sir Walter Scott, can tell you how to use the corresponding name correctly. But pointing to a galvanometer needle while supplying the name of the cause of its deflection attaches the name only to the cause of that particular deflection (or perhaps to an unspecified subset of galvanometer deflections). It supplies no information at all about the many other sorts of events to which the name "electric charge" also unambiguously refers. When one makes the transition from proper names to the names of natural kinds, one loses access to the career line or lifeline which, in the case of proper names, enables one to check the correctness of different applications of the same term. The individuals which constitute natural families do have lifelines, but the natural family itself does not.

It is in dealing with difficulties like this one that Boyd makes what I take to be an unfortunate move. To get around them he introduces the notion of "epistemic access," explicitly abandoning in the process all use of "dubbing" or "baptism" and implicitly, so far as I can see, giving up recourse to ostension as well. Using the concept of epistemic access, Boyd has a number of cogent things to say both about what justifies the use of a particular scientific language and about the relation of a later scientific language to the earlier one from which it has evolved. To some of his points in this area I shall be returning. But despite these virtues, something essential is lost, I think, in the transition from "dubbing" to "epistemic access." However imperfectly developed, "dubbing" was introduced in an attempt to understand how, in the absence of definitions, the referents of individual terms could be established at all. When dubbing is abandoned or shoved aside, the link it provided between language and the world disappears as well. If I understand Boyd's chapter correctly – something I do not take for granted – the problems to which it is directed change abruptly when the notion of epistemic access is introduced. Thereafter, Boyd seems simply to assume that the adherents of a given theory somehow or other know to what their terms refer. How they can do so ceases to concern him. Rather than extending the causal theory of reference, he seems to have given it up.

Let me therefore attempt a different approach. Though ostension is basic in establishing referents both for proper names and for natural kind terms, the two differ not only in complexity but also in nature. In the case of proper names, a single act of ostension suffices to fix reference. Those of you who have seen Richard Boyd once will, if your memories are good, be able to recognize him for some years. But, if I were to exhibit to you the deflected needle of a galvanometer, telling you that the cause of the deflection was called "electric charge," you would need more than good memory to apply the term correctly in a thunderstorm or to the cause of the heating of your electric blanket. Where natural-kind terms are at issue, a number of acts of ostension are required.

For terms like "electric charge," the role of multiple ostensions is difficult to make out, for laws and theories also enter into the establishment of reference. But my point does emerge clearly in the case of terms that are ordinarily applied by direct inspection. Wittgenstein's example, games, will do as well as another. A person who has watched chess, bridge, darts, tennis, and football, and who has also been told that each of them is a game, will have no trouble in recognizing that both backgammon and soccer are games as well. To establish reference in more puzzling cases – prize fights or fencing matches, for example – exposure is required also to members of neighboring families. Wars and gang rumbles, for example, share prominent characteristics with many games (in particular, they have sides and, potentially, a winner), but the term "game" does not apply to them. Elsewhere I have suggested that exposure to swans and geese plays an essential role in learning to recognize ducks (Kuhn, 1974). Galvanometer needles may be deflected by gravity or a bar magnet as well as by electric charge. In all these areas, establishing the referent of a natural-kind term requires exposure not only to varied members of that kind but also to members of others – to individuals, that is, to which the term might otherwise have been mistakenly applied. Only through a multiplicity of such exposures can the student acquire what other authors in this book (for example, Cohen and Ortony) refer to as the *feature space* and the knowledge of *salience* required to link language to the world.

If that much seems plausible (I cannot, in a presentation so brief, hope to make it more), then the parallel to metaphor at which I have been aiming may be apparent as well. Exposed to tennis and football as paradigms for the term "game," the language learner is invited to examine the two (and soon, others as well) in an effort to discover the characteristics with respect to which they are alike, the features that render them similar, and which are therefore relevant to the determination of reference. As in the case of Black's interactive metaphors, the juxtaposition of examples calls forth the similarities upon which the function of metaphor or the determination of reference depend. As with metaphor, also, the end product of the interaction between examples is nothing like a definition, a list of characteristics shared by games and only games, or of the features common to both men and wolves and to them alone. No lists of that sort exists (not all games have either sides or a winner), but no loss of functional precision results. Both natural-kind terms and metaphors do just what they should without satisfying the criteria that a traditional empiricist would have required to declare them meaningful.

My talk of natural-kind terms has not yet, of course, quite brought me to metaphor. Juxtaposing a tennis match with a chess game may be part of what is required to establish the referents of "game," but the two are not, in any usual sense, metaphorically related. More to the point, until the referents of "game" and of other terms which might be juxtaposed with it in metaphor have been established, metaphor itself cannot begin. The person who has not yet learned to apply the terms "game" and "war" correctly can only be misled by the metaphor, "War is a game," or "Professional football is war." Nevertheless, I take metaphor to be essentially a higher-level version of the process by which ostension enters into the establishment of reference for natural-kind terms. The actual juxtaposition of a series of exemplary games highlights features which permit the term "game" to be applied to nature. The metaphorical juxtaposition of the terms "game" and "war" highlights other features, ones whose salience had to be reached in order that actual games and wars could constitute separate natural families. If Boyd is right that nature has "joints" which natural-kind terms aim to locate, then metaphor reminds us that another language might have located different joints, cut up the world in another way.

Those last two sentences raise problems about the very notion of joints in nature, and I shall return to them briefly in my concluding remarks about Boyd's view of theory change. But one last point needs first to be made about metaphor in science. Because I take it to be both less obvious and more fundamental than metaphor, I have so far emphasized the metaphorlike process which plays an important role in finding the referents of scientific terms. But, as Boyd quite rightly insists, genuine metaphors (or, more properly analogies) are also fundamental to science, providing on occasions "an irreplacable part of the linguistic machinery of a scientific theory," playing a role that is *"constitutive* of the theories they express, rather than merely exegetical." Those words are Boyd's, and the examples which accompany them are good ones. I particularly admire his discussion of the role of the metaphors which relate cognitive psychology to computer science, information theory, and related disciplines. In this area, I can add nothing useful to what he has said.

Before changing the subject, however, I would suggest that what Boyd does say about these "constitutive" metaphors may well have a bearing wider than he sees. He discusses not only "constitutive" but also what he calls "exegetical or pedagogical" metaphors, for example those which describe atoms as "miniature solar systems." These, he suggests, are useful in teaching or explaining theories, but their use is only heuristic, for they can be replaced by nonmetaphorical techniques. "One can say," he points out, *"exactly* in what respects Bohr thought atoms were like solar systems without employing any metaphorical devices, and this was true when Bohr's theory was proposed."

Once again, I agree with Boyd but would nevertheless draw attention to the way in which metaphors like that relating atoms and solar systems are replaced. Bohr and his contemporaries supplied a model in which electrons and nucleus were represented by tiny bits of charged matter interacting under the laws of mechanics and electromagnetic theory. That model replaced the solar system metaphor but not, by doing so, a metaphorlike process. Bohr's atom model was intended to be taken only more-or-less literally; electrons and nuclei were not thought to be exactly like small billiard or Ping-Pong balls; only some of the laws of mechanics and electromagnetic theory were thought to apply to them; finding out which ones did apply and where the similarities to billiard balls lay was a central task in the development of the quantum theory. Furthermore, even when that process of exploring potential similarities had gone as far as it could (it has never been completed), the model remained essential to the theory. Without its aid, one cannot even today write down the Schrödinger equation for a complex atom or molecule, for it is to the model, not directly to nature, that the various terms in that equation refer. Though not prepared here and now to argue the point, I would hazard the guess that the same interactive, similarity-creating process which Black has isolated in the functioning of metaphor is vital also to the function of models in science. Models are not, however, merely pedagogic or heuristic. They have been too much neglected in recent philosophy of science.

I come now to the large part of Boyd's chapter that deals with theory choice, and I shall have to devote disproportionately little time to my discussion of it. That may, however, be less of a drawback than it seems, for attention to theory choice will add nothing to our central topic, metaphor. In any case, with respect to the problem of theory change, there is a great deal about which Boyd and I agree. And in the remaining area, where we clearly differ, I have great difficulty articulating just what we disagree about. Both of us are unregenerate realists. Our differences have to do with the commitments that adherence to a realist's position implies. But neither of us has yet developed an account of those commitments. Boyd's are embodied in metaphors which seem to me misleading. When it comes to replacing them, however, I simply waffle. Under these circumstances, I shall attempt only a rough sketch of the areas in which our views coincide and in which they appear to diverge. For the sake of brevity in that attempt, furthermore, I shall henceforth drop the distinction on which I have previously insisted between metaphor itself and metaphorlike processes. In these concluding remarks, "metaphor" refers to all those processes in which the juxtaposition either of terms or of concrete examples calls forth a network of similarities which help to determine the way in which language attaches to the world.

Presupposing what has already been said, let me summarize those portions of my own position with which I believe Boyd largely agrees. Metaphor plays an essential role in establishing links between scientific language and the world. Those links are not, however, given once and for all. Theory change, in particular, is accompanied by a change in some of the relevant metaphors and in the corresponding parts of the network of similarities through which terms attach to nature. The earth was like Mars (and was thus a planet) after Copernicus, but the two were in different natural families before. Salt-in-water belonged to the family of chemical compounds before Dalton, to that of physical mixtures afterwards. And so on. I believe, too, though Boyd may not, that changes like these in the similarity network sometimes occur also in response to new discoveries, without any change in what would ordinarily be referred to as a scientific theory. Finally, these alterations in the way scientific terms attach to nature are not – logical empiricism to the contrary – purely formal or purely linguistic. On the contrary, they come about in response to pressures generated by observation or experiment, and they result in more effective ways of dealing with some aspects of some natural phenomena. They are thus substantive or cognitive.

These aspects of Boyd's and my agreement should occasion no surprise. Another one may, though it ought not. Boyd repeatedly emphasizes that the causal theory of reference or the concept of epistemic access makes it possible to compare successive scientific theories with each other. The opposing view, that scientific theories are incomparable, has repeatedly been attributed to me, and Boyd himself may believe I hold it. But the book on which this interpretation is imposed includes many explicit exam-

ples of comparisons between successive theories. I have never doubted
either that they were possible or that they were essential at times of theory
choice. Instead, I have tried to make two rather different points. First,
comparisons of successive theories with each other and with the world are
never sufficient to dictate theory choice. During the period when actual
choices are made, two people fully committed to the values and methods of
science, and sharing also what both concede to be data, may nevertheless
legitimately differ in their choice of theory. Second, successive theories are
incommensurable (which is not the same as incomparable) in the sense that
the referents of some of the terms which occur in both are a function of the
theory within which those terms appear. There is no neutral language into
which both of the theories as well as the relevant data may be translated for
purposes of comparison.

With all of this I believe, perhaps mistakenly, that Boyd agrees. If so,
then our agreement extends one step further still. Both of us see in the
causal theory of reference a significant technique for tracing the continuities between successive theories and, simultaneously, for revealing the
nature of the differences between them. Let me provide an excessively
cryptic and simplistic example of what I, at least, have in mind. The techniques of *dubbing* and of *tracing lifelines* permit astronomical individuals –
say, the earth and moon, Mars and Venus – to be traced through episodes
of theory change, in this case the one due to Copernicus. The lifelines of
these four individuals were continuous during the passage from heliocentric
to geocentric theory, but the four were differently distributed among natural families as a result of that change. The moon belonged to the family of
planets before Copernicus, not afterwards; the earth to the family of planets afterwards, but not before. Eliminating the moon and adding the earth
to the list of individuals that could be juxtaposed as paradigms for the term
"planet" changed the list of features salient to determining the referents of
that term. Removing the moon to a contrasting family increased the effect.
That sort of redistribution of individuals among natural families or kinds,
with its consequent alteration of the features salient to reference, is, I now
feel, a central (perhaps the central) feature of the episodes I have previously labeled scientific revolutions.

Finally, I shall turn very briefly to the area in which Boyd's metaphors
suggest that our paths diverge. One of those metaphors, reiterated throughout his chapter, is that scientific terms "cut [or can cut] nature at its joints."
That metaphor and Field's notion of quasi-reference figure large in Boyd's
discussion of the development of scientific terminology over time. Older
languages succeeded, he believes, in cutting the world at, or close to, some
of its joints. But they also often committed what he calls "real errors in
classification of natural phenomena," many of which have since been corrected by "more sophisticated accounts of those joints." The older language may, for example, "have classified together certain things which

have no important similarity, or [may] have failed to classify together, things which are, in fact, *fundamentally* similar" (italics added). This way of talking is, however, only a rephrased version of the classical empiricists' position that successive scientific theories provide successively closer approximations to nature. Boyd's whole chapter presupposes that nature has one and only one set of joints to which the evolving terminology of science comes closer and closer with time. At least, I can see no other way to make sense of what he says in the absence of some theory-independent way of distinguishing *fundamental* or *important* similarities from those that are *superficial* or *unimportant*.[1]

To describe the successive-approximation view of theory change as a presupposition does not, of course, make it wrong, but it does point to the need for arguments missing from Boyd's paper. One form such arguments might take is the empirical examination of a succession of scientific theories. No pair of theories will do, for the more recent could, by definition, be declared the better approximation. But, given a succession of three or more theories directed to more-or-less the same aspects of nature, it should be possible, if Boyd is right, to display some process of bracketing and zeroing in on nature's real joints. The arguments which would be required are both complex and subtle. I am content to leave open the question to which they are directed. But my strong impression is that they will not succeed. Conceived as a set of instruments for solving technical puzzles in selected areas, science clearly gains in precision and scope with the passage of time. As an instrument, science undoubtedly does progress. But Boyd's claims are not about the instrumental effectiveness of science but rather about its ontology, about what really exists in nature, about the world's real joints. And in this area I see no historical evidence for a process of zeroing in. As I have suggested elsewhere, the ontology of relativistic physics is, in significant respects, more like that of Aristotelian than that of Newtonian physics. That example must here stand for many.

Boyd's metaphor of nature's joints relates closely to another, the last I shall attempt to discuss. Again and again, he speaks of the process of theory change as one which involves "the accommodation of language to the world." As before, the thrust of his metaphor is ontological; the world to which Boyd refers is the one real world, still unknown but toward which science proceeds by successive approximation. Reasons for being uneasy with that point of view have already been described, but this way of expressing the viewpoint enables me to phrase my reservations in a different way. What is the world, I ask, if it does not include most of the sorts of things to which the *actual* language spoken at a given time refers? Was the earth really a planet in the world of pre-Copernican astronomers who spoke a language in which the features salient to the referent of the term "planet" excluded its attachment to the earth? Does it obviously make better sense to speak of accommodating language to the world than of accommodating the world to language? Or is the way of talking which creates that distinction itself illusory? Is what we refer to as "the world" perhaps a product of a mutual accommodation between experience and language?

I shall close with a metaphor of my own. Boyd's world with its joints seems to me, like Kant's "things in themselves," in principle unknowable. The view toward which I grope would also be Kantian but without "things in themselves" and with categories of the mind which could change with time as the accommodation of language and experience proceeded. A view of that sort need not, I think, make the world less real.

NOTE

1   In revising the manuscript to which this paragraph and those following are addressed, Boyd has pointed out that both natural kinds and nature's joints may be context- or discipline- or interest-relative. But, as note 2 to his paper will indicate, that concession does not presently bring our positions closer together. It may do so in the future, however, for the same root note undermines the position it defends. Boyd concedes (mistakenly, I think) that a kind is "un-'objective'" to the extent that it is context- or discipline-dependent. But that construal of "objective" requires that context-independent bounds be specified for context-dependence. If any two objects could, in principle, be rendered similar by choice of an appropriate context, then objectivity, in Boyd's sense, would not exist. The problem is the same as the one suggested by the sentence to which this footnote is attached.

23

Metaphorical imprecision and the "top-down" research strategy

ZENON W. PYLYSHYN

In discussing Boyd's interesting and provocative thesis concerning the role of metaphor in the development of scientific understanding, I shall focus on several issues which strike me as particularly relevant to the new discipline of cognitive science (which takes a computational approach to the study of cognition). In doing so, I shall occasionally adopt a translation of some of his terminology into terminology more familiar to me, thus perhaps exhibiting some metaphorical usage of my own.

The four main points that I shall address are the following. First, I suggest that important as it is, the accommodation of linguistic usage is only one part of the sort of accommodation of conceptual schemata that occurs in ontogenetic development, and which in my opinion, remains as deep a mystery as it was in Socrates' time. Second, as I wonder why I find some of Boyd's own metaphors enlightening without at the same time compelling me to accept some of his conclusions, I suggest that in cases where views differ, "aiming at" will not substitute for detailed argument. Third, since I find Boyd's discussion of imprecision to be particularly interesting, I try to relate this notion to my own bias concerning the utility of certain kinds of imprecision (referential, not logical) in the development of cognitive theory. And finally, recognizing that Boyd and I do not share the same view concerning particular examples of metaphors in cognitive psychology, I speculate on what gives some scientific descriptions the right to bear the ascription "literal" – and suggest that computation is a literal rather than metaphorical view of cognition.

Conceptual accommodation and linguistic usage

Boyd's presentation can be viewed as related to a question of long standing in psychology as well as in the philosophy of science. It is that adaptive equilibrium between two essential but antagonistic processes by which our mental world comes to terms with our experiences. Piaget calls these processes "assimilation" and "accommodation." "Assimilation" refers to the process by which the environment is made cognitively accessible by incorporating some of its effects into relatively stable intellectual systems called "schemata." Accommodation, on the other hand, refers to the slower but no less systematic and persistent manner in which the schemata themselves change in response to the demands of the environment.

One way of presenting the difficult and far-reaching problem posed by this opposition – which some might even call the basic paradox of adaptation and learning – is in terms of the question: How is it possible to acquire new knowledge? If one's intellectual apparatus consists of a set of concepts or conceptual schemata which are the medium of thought, then one can only learn (or apprehend) what can be expressed in terms of these concepts. On the other hand, if it were possible to observe and to acquire new "knowledge" without benefit of these concepts, then such "knowledge" would not itself be conceptual or be expressed in the medium of thought, and therefore it would not be cognitively structured, integrated with other knowledge, or even comprehended. Hence, it would be intellectually inaccessible.

This paradox, in one form or another, has been with us at least since the time Socrates offered his "learning as recollecting" solution in the *Meno*. Almost every major cognitive theoretician – from Hume to Newell and Simon (1976) – has had a crack at it. Recently Fodor (1975) has made a strong case against the whole class of empiricist accounts of concept acquisition, thus giving the Socratic position new life.

The paradox arises because we need terms or categories or concepts in order to structure our experience and to serve as a vehicle for tokens of thought. But then we immediately run into the problem of explaining how it is possible to think about new things, and especially how new ways of carving up our experiences are possible. The universal solution in contemporary experimental psychology (as well as much of artificial intelligence) has been to consider new concepts as being characterized in terms of old ones (plus logical connectives), that is, a definitional view of concept acquisition. But this view, as many have argued (e.g., Fodor, 1975; Fodor, Fodor & Garrett, 1975; Kintsch, 1974), and as Boyd concurs, is fundamentally incapable of dealing with the problem. For one thing, since definitions are logically eliminable, this approach does not actually add new concepts but merely alters the accessibility to combinations of already available ones. For another, it simply appears to be an inconvenient fact of life that, with very few exceptions, there are no criterial definitions available for natural concepts.

In some psychological circles a recent response to this difficulty (and other closely related ones) has been to abandon, or at least to augment, conceptual schemata by introducing a number of *metaphorical* devices – such as internal analogues, images, prototypes, and the like. Now, one might wonder why I have been referring to concepts as literal things and then in the last sentence why I have switched to talking about analogues and images as metaphorical. At this point, I simply wish to present an example of an evaluative use of the term "metaphor" from my point of view (a sort of ostensive reference to metaphor) so that I can pick up this theme again later. For the present, I shall simply offer the claim that none of these expedients addresses the assimilation–accommodation paradox but merely postpones it in one way or another.

Before turning to Boyd's proposal, I should point out that in my view, Boyd only addresses a part of the problem – and not even what I take to be the most crucial part – because he confines himself almost exclusively to discussing the use of linguistic terms (verbal labels) rather than to the general case of the acquisition of internal concepts. This may partly reflect his concern in this essay with linguistic issues (metaphor in particular). But it may also be that he accepts the philosophical position to which many of the people Boyd cites subscribe which denies the existence of such abstract private terms.

For these people, thoughts are thought in English or some other natural language, not in a language-free "mentalese" – though many of these people reluctantly and uneasily leave open the possibility that images or some other sorts of entities may also play an as yet undetermined role (e.g., both Boyd and Fodor imply this possibility). I shall not take time to argue for the plausibility (or, indeed, the necessity) of such an abstract private conceptual system (but see Pylyshyn, 1978a; and Fodor, 1975). I do want to briefly suggest, however, that although some of Boyd's discussion may be relevant to concepts as well as to linguistic terms, much of it is not, so that the assimilation–accommodation problem is not resolved. The only aspect of this problem that is directly addressed is that of linguistic accommodation and, more specifically, that of accommodating linguistic usage.

In comparing the problem of linguistic usage with that of conceptual assimilation and accommodation, one might note several striking differences. Consider, for example, the process whereby the use of terms in the public natural language accommodates to various constraints. According to the view advocated by Boyd (which, as I understand it, is essentially that of Putnam, 1975a), we begin by applying a term to paradigm situations where we believe its referent is exemplified, and continue to refine and adjust the scope of the term as we discover new essential features of situations in which it seems appropriate to use that term.

Thus, when we use the term "water" to refer to the stuff in the bucket we are really "aiming at" a deeper essence (which we cannot yet define) and so are prepared to accommodate our use of the term when we discover that ice and steam contain the same essential substance (at least from certain perspectives relevant, say, to scientific theories and perhaps also to other contexts as well). In other words, a prerequisite for such accommodation is that our use of the term is not fixed by stable perceptual or biological conditions but depends on various kinds of common-sense considerations (such as who is likely to know best, where one can find out the relevant facts, how similar this is to other situations, what a plausible guess might be, and so on). Any change in usage, therefore, involves understanding, plausible reasoning, and decision.

Such, however, is not the case for terms in the private language for concepts – especially those for which there are no corresponding lexical items in the public vocabulary. Let us accept for the moment the need for a distinct internal vocabulary of symbols, which are amodal and refer to such things as equivalence classes of perceptual patterns and also serve as objects of such things as beliefs, desires, and fears. Whatever such terms are, it would seem that unlike public linguistic terms, there is no room here for reasoning about them and choosing the scope of their referents. While I may decide to call both *this* and *that* by the same name (for example, water and ice) I cannot in the same sense *decide* on the basis of evidence that *this* and *that* are really cognitively equivalent (that is indiscernible) and therefore fall under the same concept.

The reason for this difference between concepts and words is that the former are by hypothesis the elements over which our perception, comprehension, memories, beliefs, and reasoning take place. They are the *atomic* symbols which distinguish the content of our mental representation. Although we do have representations of words as lexical items, as phonetic shapes, as graphical shapes, and so forth, as well as independent representations of what words refer to (the latter being a prerequisite to learning the association of words with things, as well as prerequisite for some sense of reasoning in nonverbal organisms), we do not have such dual representations of concepts – at pain of infinite regress. To use a computer metaphor, concepts are terms of the wired-in machine language. That is why concepts, unlike words, cannot have the kind of ambiguity associated with homonyms or homographs.

Yet this dual representation or meta-access to concepts is what we would need in order to rationally alter the referents of concepts in response to changing beliefs. In other words, this suggests that we do not reason, or have beliefs, about *concepts* but only about what they refer to. A fortiori, we cannot change what the referents of concepts are in the same manner as we can change the way we publicly express such beliefs or the way we *use* linguistic terms. The difference is that in the case of *words* there is a component of reason and choice which mediates between cognitive content and outward expression. I can choose what words I use, whereas I cannot in the same sense choose the concepts in terms of which I represent the world.

All this, of course, is not to suggest that the concepts in terms of which our knowledge is structured are fixed, or that they cannot change in response to new knowledge. Indeed, it is the fact that they do change which raises the assimilation–accommodation problem in the first place. However, it suggests that the mechanisms by which concepts change their referents (or by which percepts and thoughts change their content) may not be the same as those by which the use of linguistic terms changes. Thus Boyd's paper is a contribution to understanding how *language usage* accommodates: The assimilation–accommodation puzzle of greatest concern to cognitive psychologists remains.

Reference and the metaphor of epistemic access

According to Boyd, reference fixing is a process of linguistic accommodation, whose goal is to provide continuing *epistemic access* to an intended essential aspect of some situation. Because language "extends the senses" by giving us indirect knowledge (such as shared social knowledge and reports of findings) by focusing our joint efforts (say to investigate certain phenomena) and enabling us to discuss referents of terms, Boyd takes this sort of reaching out for knowledge – or epistemic access – to be "the mark of reference." Though one might quarrel with the exclusive attention given to the communicative use of language, there is no doubt that providing access to knowledge is one of the fundamental values of language. By focusing on this aspect of language, Boyd does weave an interesting account of how language use evolves adaptively under certain pressures.

For example, the establishment of a reference for general terms (i.e., terms other than proper names) begins with an ostensive example or "dubbing" and the use of the term then gradually evolves under subtle pressure from its use by others (particularly experts) and by the demands of nature. Consequently (at least in science), the term eventually accommodates to the "causal structure of the world." Thus, general terms can truly be said to *refer,* even though what they refer to cannot be explicitly defined, because it is something like the functional essence of the exemplar, that is, it is that aspect which enters into causal relations, which has yet to be explicated in any detail, and to which linguistic usage will eventually accommodate.

This is an interesting and, in many ways, illuminating account of linguistic usage and its relation to the reasoned search for knowledge. It has a number of useful consequences quite apart from sharpening some technical issues in the philosophy of language. One is that the disturbingly variable and uncertain relation that (superficially) appears to exist between terms and what we think of as their referents is given an account in terms of a real underlying, currently "inarticulable," referent, together with pragmatic, social, and common sense reasoning principles, which tend to produce a convergence of usage onto these real underlying referents. This realist position has natural implications for viewing theory change in science (to which I shall return later).

Another consequence is that by denying a number of prevalent distinctions – such as that between modification of linguistic usage and genuine empirical discoveries, or that between linguistic and methodological precision – Boyd is able to illuminate an underlying unity among a variety of phenomena by relating them to the dialectical process of acquisition of knowledge or epistemic access. And finally, this view of the relationship between terms and their referents leads Boyd to locate a natural place for metaphor in science. Metaphor is seen as simply providing an alternative to ostension for initiating the reference fixing process by which linguistic usage eventually accommodates to the "causal structure of the world." By this account, metaphors are not qualitatively different from other general terms in science. They are all seen as having real underlying referents and serving as stages in the ongoing process of providing epistemic access.

Though this is an elegant story, there are nonetheless a number of things about it which are, at least, discomforting. For instance, I am somewhat uneasy about the recursive flavor of the discussion of metaphor, wherein the account itself is distinctly metaphorical. If I were to accept Boyd's conclusion, I would naturally appreciate the essential contribution which his theory of constitutive metaphors makes to his presentation. On the other hand, if I should find the metaphors (say, the metaphor of "aiming at") to be unilluminating, then I suppose I should not accept the claims about the value of metaphor in such arguments. This gives me a certain dizzy feeling, because I do find Boyd's metaphors illuminating, and yet at the same time, I feel that his long paper has been somewhat like the proverbial Chinese feast and that in a short time I shall be hungry again.

My problem is that while I enjoyed the insights and agree with much of what Boyd has to say, I do not see how this type of argument, which appeals to notions as seemingly diffuse as that of epistemic access, can be made to carry much explanatory weight. One must distinguish between the general programmatic enterprise of trying to illuminate a new phenomenon and the much more demanding goal of establishing the validity of an explanatory theoretical principle. For example, some quite specific strong claims that Boyd makes demand much more than the sort of "aiming at" treatment afforded by metaphorical discussion (however appealing that might be): They demand an argument.

Consider, for example, the claim that there is continuity of reference during scientific revolutions, rather than a change of reference, as many people have claimed (for example, that classical terms like "mass," "length," "time," and so on continued to have the same referents with the advent of special relativity or quantum mechanics). Now there is surely a sense in which the acquisition of knowledge about *something* continues undisturbed through revolutionary theory change. Furthermore, this something is doubtlessly somehow epistemically related to the use of the crucial terms. Thus, if reference is to be identified with epistemic access, I suppose one would be entitled to say that reference is maintained. But that seems like a distinctly unenlightening conclusion, inasmuch as it is more a stipulation of linguistic policy (i.e., on how to use the word "reference") than a fact about theory change. Of course, if we knew what it was that the terms were intended to designate, then we could say whether the referents had changed, but in the epistemic-access view this is not possible.

I do not see how the epistemic-access story allows one to draw the continuity conclusion. We can either attend to the common features of terms before and after the theory change, and conclude that they had always referred to the same essence, or else we can attend to their differences and conclude that the use of the same name was incidental. For example, the continued use of the same terms could be viewed as a consequence of trying to make the new referent intelligible in terms of old concepts, or it may be a retrospective rationalization of the earlier enterprise. At least, such alternatives are not a priori implausible – especially since the exegesis of earlier scientific and technical work is notorious in its tendency to rewrite history so as to give the appearance of unrelenting progress (cf. Smith, 1970).

According to such an alternative approach, metaphor might even be invoked to help build a bridge between two world views – not, as Boyd says, to introduce terminology for putative new features of the world, but to help make the two views mutually intelligible by emphasizing, or even inducing, a similarity between them. I am not seriously proposing this as a view of theory change but merely pointing out that so long as we confine our discussion of these issues to such general metaphorical levels as are involved when we invoke epistemic access, the arguments have little force over other plausible ways of talking.

What all this suggests to me is that while metaphors may be interesting and insightful in certain contexts and relative to certain goals, there are other contexts in which they are quite powerless to settle an issue. I think this is related to the notion of imprecision in science and to the way it can be exploited for progress. Because Boyd and I are in agreement that this is an important notion, I propose to devote the next section to it.

Precision and the "top-down" strategy

In arguing for the importance of the computational approach to cognitive psychology recently (Pylyshyn, 1978a), one of my points was related to the precision issue. Because I want to refer to this point later in the discussion, I shall begin by quoting what I wrote then.

... just as there are two sources of understanding – the empirical and the rational – so there are two corresponding loci of rigor. One can be rigorous by operationally defining one's constructs and sticking close to the experimental data. One can also be rigorous by ensuring that one's theoretical ideas are complete, consistent, and logically sound. One can then try to capture one's intuitions and bring everyday knowledge to bear on the development of theoretical ideas with some confidence that they are neither incoherent nor contradictory, and further-more with some way of exploring what they entail. The point is that there are better and worse places for introducing rigor into an evolving discipline.

What I was arguing for was the benefit, at certain stages in development of the theory, of what is sometimes referred to as a "top-down strategy." There are various ways of understanding and pursuing a top-down research strategy. Functional analysis as typically practiced is one sort of top-down approach. It attempts to account for the behavior of a system as a "black box," in terms of the interaction of smaller black boxes, which carry out subfunctions, and each of which is also explained in a similar way. Typically the regress ends when the function carried out by a black box is sufficiently simple, and its function can be subsumed under physical principles (for example, they are instantiated in a machine). This strategy is not only typical of functional analysis, but it is also fundamental to synthesis or design of systems. In computer science it is called "structured program-ming" and is the standard method of designing computer programs. Fur-thermore, some version of this sort of top-down approach is ubiquitous in scientific progress.

As Simon (1969) remarks,

We knew a great deal about the gross physical and chemical behavior of matter before we had a knowledge of molecules, a great deal about molecular chemistry before we had an atomic theory, and a great deal about atoms before we had any theory of elementary particles . . . This skyhook-skyscraper construction of science from the roof down to the yet unconstructed foundations was possible because the behavior of the system at each level depended on only a very approximate, simpli-fied, abstracted characterization of the system beneath. This is lucky, else the safety of bridges and airplanes might depend on the correctness of the "Eightfold Way" of looking at elementary particles. (p. 17)

It is useful to recognize several different dimensions which correspond to the top-down "direction." The functional analysis case and the examples cited by Simon emphasize the *systematic reduction* aspect. It is not that one gains precision in descending the explanatory reduction hierarchy. What one gains is a deeper, more general, and therefore a more *complete,* expla-nation. In artificial intelligence (a discipline generally viewed as committed to a top-down analysis of intelligent action), the primary goal is to discover methods which are sufficient for some particular problem domain, and to postpone concern over a number of other important questions, such as its detailed similarity to human mechanisms. As a methodology for theory construction in cognitive psychology, it contrasts with the more traditional bottom-up approach, which has typically been to infer isolated mechanisms to account for experimental results, while postponing the question of how these mechanisms might be employed, or how they might arise as part of a more general method.

Another traditional approach has been to operationally define properties or parameters that can be used to predict experimental results, while postponing the explanation of how these properties come about, or what more general role they might have in cognition. The difference between top-down and bottom-up approaches in this case is again not a question of precision so much as a question of the priority of various criteria and of what sort of incompleteness is considered most tolerable. The top-down approach of cognitive science and artificial intelligence tolerates incompleteness in specifiability of detailed correspondence with experiments in favor of accounting for the possibility of certain performance skills.

The latter way of putting it shows the top-down dimension to be rather closely related to the strategy, which Boyd discusses, involving the use of metaphor, and which he contrasts with the empiricist position. Use of metaphor is intended to "provide a way to introduce terminology for features of the world whose existence seems probable, but many of whose fundamental properties have yet to be discovered." This initiates a direction of research beginning with diffuse epistemic access and hopefully converging onto important causal entities. This convergent focusing strategy is a top-down approach, which like the other examples cited above, postpones certain crucial commitments (such as entailed by operational definitions) with the intention of avoiding the most costly potential dead ends.

There is a general principle behind this strategy which is recognized in artificial intelligence and variously referred to as the "principle of least commitment" or the "principle of procrastination" or the "wait and see strategy" (see, for example, Marr, 1976). This is a computational strategy applied to methods of visual processing, problem solving, and language analysis, which says, roughly, that one should proceed in such a way as to avoid, whenever possible, doing something (e.g., making an inductive guess) which subsequent discoveries may force one to undo. This, it seems to me, is the heart of most of the top-down strategies and contrasts with the empiricist method which, in Boyd's words, "erects contrived categories as the referents of general terms at the cost of abandoning the project of 'cutting nature at its joints'." Inasmuch as cutting nature at its joints is, however, a prerequisite to formulating general causal laws, the "contrived categories" frequently have to be changed, or else very complex systems have to be erected ad hoc as discoveries are made.

Despite the general top-down theme that is shared by the various examples cited above, there are significant differences among them. These differences, I believe, account for why I personally find some particular cases of top-down strategies to be more fruitful than others, and why I find certain types of imprecision to be more promising steps towards scientific progress than others. What I am trying to propose here is some way to distinguish between metaphors that I find revealing and those that I find stultifying.

Earlier, I referred to concepts and schemata as literal entities, whereas internal analogues, images, and the like, I took to be metaphors. Because I suspect that some people may feel that the converse is the case, it may be worthwhile to see whether there is anything systematic underlying such intuitions. I believe that there is more to this difference than mere idiosyncratic intuition or a commitment to a different theoretical system. I think what is at stake is a qualitative difference in the *type* of imprecision these terms entail – and here I believe that part of Boyd's discussion provides a useful basis for the comparison.

In addition to the obvious differences among various undefined terms and metaphors – for example, that some capture deeper underlying causal structures – is a difference in (1) the degree and the manner in which their referents are constrained, and (2) the extent to which they invite certain kinds of further explication. I shall try to elaborate briefly on these two aspects, which I believe differentiate different types of theoretical imprecision.

Systematic constraints

Many terms which appear in cognitive science – such as "schemata," "proposition," "representation," "control structure," "goal," and the like – are usually not given an explicit definition, and certainly not an operational definition in the empiricist sense. They are typically introduced by ostension in a context in which their essential properties are usually pretty clear to those familiar with the field. They are, in addition, usually rather tightly constrained in their possible referents by virtue of the fact that they must partake in an elaborate system. (This is related to the point I was driving at in my passage quoted above).

For example, suppose I have a theory of perception that claims that a certain class of scene is perceived in terms of entities which I shall call "visemes," of which there are eleven distinct types. Furthermore, the physical structure of objects is such that only certain specified arrangements of these visemes can occur in an image. Even if I am unable to give an operational definition of a viseme, or of its different types, the system as a whole is rather severely constrained, for it must be able to account for the appropriate set of equivalence classes of percepts. For example, these elements together with the system of rules or procedures must be capable of producing the correct perceptual distinctions and the correct description of the scene. Furthermore, they must form a *coherent system,* which remains fixed as the perceptual cases it is asked to deal with are changed. Such a set of units is not arbitrary – in fact, the demands are so severe that working examples such as this one are very rare.[1] A similar (though not so dramatic) story can be told about schemata, concepts, propositions, and so on, as these are used in cognitive science. Because their exemplars typically occur in large theoretical systems, the requirement that the system be coherent imposes tight constraints on their potential properties.

Such is generally not the case with other types of general terms (e.g., "analogue," "image," "prototype," and so forth). Though these are no less precise, their exemplars do not (at least not yet) play a part in large, intricate systems, whose coherence provides strong intrinsic constraints on their properties.

Openness to explication

The difference among metaphors or general terms with respect to the kinds of further explication they invite seems to me to be an even more important differentiating property. If one believes, as I do, that the appropriate kind of explanation of cognitive phenomena is one which proceeds along the functional-analysis and systematic-reduction lines sketched earlier, then any practice which tends to discourage this process would be viewed as counterproductive. For instance, any metaphor which leaves one feeling that a phenomenon has been "explained," even though only a superficial level of functional reduction or process explanation has been offered, is, to my mind (and presumably also by Boyd's criteria), unproductive. This would, for instance, be the case with certain of Boyd's examples, such as "demon," or with the Freudian metaphors of energy and flow.

Closer to home, I believe that it is also the case with a large number of metaphors in cognitive psychology. It is, in my view, particularly serious in those cases where the metaphor makes prediction possible without affording explanation. For example, there is a view that mental comparison (of, say, sizes or colors) is performed by an "internal psychophysics," wherein images of the objects in question are compared in the "mind's eye." Because empirical generalizations concerning psychophysical comparison of external stimuli are available (for example, the time it takes to make a comparison is linearly related to the similarity of the objects compared), these can then be used to make predictions and are therefore taken as accounts of the mental comparison cases. Although the detailed explanations of this and other cases involving mental comparisons and mental manipulation are considerably more complex than this illustration, they nevertheless invariably come to rest on the same set of metaphors involving the "mind's eye," or the metaphor of "mental access" as a species of internalized perception.

Despite the fact that every time I raise this point I am accused of attacking a straw man, and although the latest appeals to imagery as an explanatory notion have been more carefully hedged, I have seen no reason to revise the view I held in 1973 (Pylyshyn, 1973) that the apparent cognitive satisfaction of these accounts rests on a comfortable metaphor. That the accounts involve metaphor is, as Boyd has emphasized in his chapter, not a sign of ultimate deficiency. But that the accounts come to *rest* on it because of its subjective comfort is to my mind a more serious problem.

I might add that the metaphor here is not unproductive of research – any more than the Freudian, or for that matter, the demonic, ones (taking a liberal view of "research"). On the contrary, the very intuitiveness of the metaphor inspires a bumper crop of experimental research. What it does tend to inhibit, however, is the process of functional reduction. Consider the following example, which has occupied me personally for several years (see, e.g., Pylyshyn, 1978b). The story goes that in order to judge whether two differently oriented figures are identical in shape one "mentally rotates" a mental image of one of them until it is in the same orientation as the other and then tests them for congruence – presumably by superimposition or template matching. This account nicely "explains" why the comparison time is a linear function of the relative orientation of the two figures (it takes more time to rotate through a larger angle) and a lot of other experimental findings as well. Now, the term "rotate" is clearly a metaphor here since there is no spatially extended rigid object to rotate. However, there is little pressure to explicate the metaphor by further functional reduction. There seems to be no need to explain *how* rotation occurs as a cognitive process, because it is obvious how rotation occurs in the subsidiary subject of the metaphor (that is, in the case of real rotation of physical objects).

Elsewhere (Pylyshyn, 1978c) I argue that this is not a matter of methodological sloppiness or mere heuristics. The difference between those who accept the sort of cognitive metaphors illustrated above and those who, like myself, do not, lies deeper – in differing views concerning what, in principle, would constitute an ideal complete explanation. It may be that no theory-building enterprise can, or should, avoid metaphors any more than it should avoid general terms with which – as Boyd has argued – they share a great deal in common. But some resting places are more sound than others, and I believe that there are principled reasons for preferring some types of imprecision to others (in particular, for preferring imprecision that occurs in a framework that clearly marks it as an explanatory I.O.U.). But a detailed argument for that claim is a topic for another occasion.

Literal descriptions as world views

The last point I shall take up was prompted by the fact that it appears that Boyd and I have differing views concerning what constitute instances of the use of metaphor in science. I want to challenge the examples Boyd has chosen to illustrate the use of metaphor in cognitive psychology – since many of these examples do not seem to me to be metaphors at all. But to do this, we need to have some idea of what it would mean for a theoretical system to be a *literal* account. And this, in view of the very generality of the process of reference fixing which Boyd introduces, seems to be an even more difficult notion to explicate than is metaphor. Metaphor, as a type of reference-fixing process affording epistemic access to relational complexes, is apparently to be found whenever general relational notions are introduced (even possibly when relational terms are introduced by ostension, inasmuch as that can be viewed as an instance of the metaphor implied in the comparison statement "*X* shall refer to all things that are essentially like *this*." But where are the *literal* uses of general terms in science?

Clearly, there are uses of language – other than simple statements using proper names and definite descriptions – that deserve to be called "literal." Indeed one of the defining characteristics of Boyd's theory-constitutive metaphors is that they "express theoretical claims for which no literal paraphrase is known." Later Boyd adds that "complete explications are often the eventual result of the attempts at explication that are central to scientific inquiry."

But one may well ask what distinguishes a metaphor from its complete explication – or, for that matter, from any literal description. Surely not the syntax of the description – for instance, the presence of comparative construction or the violation of selectional restrictions. Neither is the difference likely to rest on implied imprecise comparisons or on the vagueness of descriptions, since surely we can be literal in our intention though vague in the way we formulate our description. Are explicit criteria for distinguishing literal from metaphoric description possible, or must that distinction itself be (as Boyd's title implies) metaphorical?

As an illustration of how this distinction might be problematic, consider the following example of Boyd's of a metaphor which is not theory constitutive (but merely exegetic) because a literal paraphrase is available. According to Boyd the metaphor that atoms are "miniature solar systems" is theoretically eliminable, because "one can say *exactly* in what respects Bohr thought atoms were like solar systems without employing any metaphorical devices." Though I agree with this conclusion it seems to me that we need some way to justify this claim. One could surely argue that any of the ways of explicating the solar-system metaphor itself involves other, perhaps more familiar, metaphors. For instance, it is not clear that reference to electrons as *objects* travelling in elliptical *orbits* in a three-dimensional *space* does not itself involve a metaphorical extension of our notions of object, orbit, and space to include subatomic domains, which are prima facie very different from the objects, orbits, and space with which we are familiar in macrophysics. Indeed, even the leap from the mechanics of middle-sized objects to astronomy was vigorously resisted in

Galileo's time, for there is a sense in which a metaphorlike extension of reference was called for.

If this is the case, then there does remain a problem of distinguishing literal from nonliteral descriptions. Without some clearer explication of the metaphor of "metaphor" we are not in a good position to discuss, say, why certain approaches of cognitive science appear metaphorical to Boyd whereas I see them as literal.

My own tentative feeling is that the difference between literal and meta-phorical description lies primarily in such pragmatic considerations as (1) the stability, referential specificity, and general acceptance of terms; and (2) the perception, shared by those who use the terms, that the resulting description characterizes the world *as it really is,* rather than being a conve-nient way of talking about it, or a way of capturing superficial resem-blances. The first of these is in line with Boyd's notion of epistemic access becoming less diffuse and more focused on true causal entities as the scien-tific enterprise progresses. The second consideration – the perception-as-reality of the description – is, however, no less important. It represents what might be thought of as a perceptual phenomenon rather than a re-search strategy, and reflects the tacit acceptance of a certain view regarding what an ultimate explanation of certain puzzles will have to be like.

The case of space, to which I have already alluded, provides a revealing example of the latter phenomenon. Our current scientific conception of space is a projection of geometry onto the observations of mechanics. But plane geometry was well known and widely used by the ancient Egyptians in surveying and building. Later it was developed into an exquisite formal system by the Greeks. Yet, for the Egyptians, it was a way of calculating, like a system of ciphers, whereas, for the Greeks, it was a demonstration of the perfect Platonic order. It was not until two millennia later that Galileo began the transformation which eventually resulted in the view that is so commonplace and mundane today that virtually no vestige remains of the Aristotelian ideas of natural motions and natural places. Everyone imag-ines space as that perfectly empty infinite isotropic three-dimensional recep-tacle, quite independent of the earth or any object, and capable of locating such mathematical entities as points and infinite straight lines. Such a strange idea was literally unthinkable before the seventeenth century. In fact not even Galileo totally accepted it. For him a straight line was still bound to the earth's surface. It was not until Newton that the task of "geometrization of the world" (to use Butterfield's, 1965, phrase) was completed.

The transformation that led to the reification of geometry – to accepting the axioms of Euclid as a literal description of physical space – profoundly affected the course of science. Both Hanson (1958) and Polanyi (1966) have argued that the importance of accepting a system as a literal account of reality is that it enables scientists to see that certain further observations are possible and others are not. It goes beyond merely asserting that certain things happen in certain ways and becomes a way of seeing. It is thus quite distinct from metaphor, which by contrast remains a rather self-conscious imposition of an unrelated extrinsic system believed to reflect important aspects of similarity to the primary phenomena. Whereas metaphor *induces* a (partial) equivalence between two known phenomena, a literal account describes the phenomenon in the authentic terms in which it is "seen."

The reason I have gone into this digression concerning the reification of geometry is that for me the notion of computation stands in the same relation to cognition as geometry does to mechanics: It is not a metaphor but part of a literal description of cognitive activity. This is not to say that there are not also metaphorical uses of computer concepts. Indeed most contemporary writing about cognition (especially by philosophers) does make extensive use of the computer as a metaphor for the brain, and of software as a metaphor for mind.

But is seems to me that *computation,* and all that it entails regarding rule-governed transformations on intentionally interpreted symbolic expressions, applies just as literally to mental activity as it does to the activity of digital computers. Such a term is in no sense a literal description of the operation of electronic computers that has been metaphorically transported to the primary subject of mind. The relation between computation and artifacts is just as abstract as the relation between computation and mental activity (the same can be said of the term "information"). Both require that we give terms an interpretation in these domains, precisely the way Euclidean axioms are given a realistic interpretation in classical space, and the axioms of non-Euclidean geometry are given a realistic interpretation in the space of special relativity. I see no significant differences here which would lead me to characterize computation, but not geometry, as metaphor.

Of course, accepting computations as a literal account imposes a special burden on those who take that road (and currently they are not all that numerous). We can no longer get away with certain kinds of permanent imprecision. Being committed to the view that we are literally describing mental activity we take on the responsibility of giving an explanation by functional reduction – an explanation which does not itself terminate with an appeal to metaphor, empirical generalizations, stipulated properties of different media (e.g., analogue media), similarity spaces, and the like, *except* as these are clearly marked to be explanatory debts to be repaid at a later time and in a particular manner (that is, as further explicated computations). Thus, imprecision is permitted – as it must be if science is to develop – but within a clearly circumscribed top-down research strategy, and with the character of the ultimate explanatory terms specified by the particular realist view of the enterprise.

Naturally a great deal more needs to be said concerning this position – and I have already said some of it elsewhere (Pylyshyn, 1978c). For the present purposes, my point is that although Boyd's account of the utility of metaphor in science is insightful, it might be of additional value to distinguish among various kinds of imprecision associated with metaphor, and to try to characterize what constitutes literal usage along the lines I have sketched – especially for those cases which are not in the empiricist mold of linguistic rigor and consequently might appear to the outsider to be cases of theory-constitutive metaphor.

NOTE

1   This example is a slightly disguised reference to the work of Waltz (1975) who designed an elegant system for perceiving scenes consisting of polyhedral objects and shadows. The "visemes" in this case were edges which were classified into eleven labeled categories. Grammarlike constraints on co-occurrence of different label combinations at various types of vertices, further constraining when two vertices share a common edge, made "parsing" the image straightforward.

METAPHOR
AND
EDUCATION

24

The instructive metaphor: Metaphoric aids to students' understanding of science

RICHARD E. MAYER

The goal of science is to describe and explain how things in the universe work. It follows that a goal of science education is to help students understand these descriptions and explanations. In this chapter, I explore the language of science and of science education – including the respective roles of precise quantitative description and metaphoric qualitative explanation – and I focus on the *instructive metaphor hypothesis,* the idea that metaphoric language can play a productive role in fostering students' understanding of scientific descriptions and explanations. The chapter deals with three subjects: the language of science, the language of science education, and metaphoric aids to science learning.[1]

The language of science

This section considers the role of descriptive and explanative language, and of literal and constructive language in science.

Descriptive and explanative language

Historians of science (Bronowski, 1978; Cohen, 1960; Kearney, 1971; Westfall, 1977) have viewed description and explanation as two successive stages in the historical development of scientific knowledge. For example, Westfall (1977, p. 1) distinguished between the *Pythagorean tradition* based on the idea that "the cosmos was constructed according to the principles of mathematical order" so that the goal of science is to provide "an exact mathematical description," and *mechanistic philosophy* based on the idea that "natural phenomena are caused by invisible mechanisms entirely similar to the mechanisms in everyday life" so that the goal of science is the elucidation of cause-and-effect systems.

Description refers to the specification of relations among observable variables that may be stated as verbal rules or quantitative laws. For example, a commonly used science textbook sometimes states some relations in words, such as "materials take up more space when heated" (Pasachoff, Pasachoff, & Cooney, 1986, p. 142) and at other times in equations, such as "current = voltage/resistance" (Pasachoff, Pasachoff, & Cooney, 1986, p. 390). Description may also take the form of a list of the order of events in a process, such as the stages in the nitrogen cycle. Bronowski (1978) refers to description as the "idea of order."

Explanation refers to the mechanisms that underlie and connect descriptive rules. For example, a textbook may describe the mechanism underlying the expansion rule in terms of the movement of particles (Pasachoff, Pasachoff, & Cooney, 1986, p. 142): "When a steel rod is heated, its particles move around and bump into each other more. Because the particles knock each other further apart, the space between the particles grows. So the rod expands." Similarly, to explain Ohm's law, a science textbook asks the student to compare electricity to water flowing in pipes (Pasachoff, Pasachoff, & Cooney, 1986, p. 390):

To understand this idea, compare the pictures of pipes. [Pictures show water coming out of a narrow pipe and water coming out of a wide pipe.] The only difference in the pipes is their diameters. The pump pushes water equally in both cases. But more water passes through the pipe with the large opening. The larger pipe offers less resistance to the flow of water than the smaller pipe. In a similar way, more current flows through a conductor with less resistance than through a conductor with more resistance.

In explanation, we seek to explain cause-and-effect relations, leading Bronowski (1978) to refer to explanation as the "idea of causes."

Literal and constructive language

How should we express descriptions and explanations in science and in science education? In his introductory chapter to this volume, Ortony distinguishes between two approaches to scientific language – the literal and the constructivist. Literalism is based on the idea that scientific communication involves the direct transmission of information from one person to another – it is based on a teaching-as-transmission (learning-as-reception) metaphor. According to the literal approach, the words and pictures we use to describe a scientific principle must portray that principle as unambiguously and clearly as possible. For example, a literal statement describing the relations between volume and heat is: "objects expand when heated." As Ortony puts it:

Science is supposed to be characterized by precision and the absence of ambiguity, and the language of science is assumed to be correspondingly precise and unambiguous – in short, literal.

Constructivism is based on the idea that human understanding is the result of mental construction by the learner – it is based on the learning-as-construction metaphor. According to the constructivist approach, the language of science serves to help people construct an understanding of scientific descriptions. For example, to help understand the relation between heat and volume, students may need to construct the concept of particles in a box. In characterizing the constructivist approach, Ortony writes:

Knowledge of reality, whether occasioned by perception, language, or memory, necessitates going beyond the information given. It arises through the interaction of that information with the context in which it is presented and with the knower's preexisting knowledge.

The literal and constructive views entail different approaches to science and scientific language. On one side is the argument for literal, precise, and unambiguous language in science. When we describe a phenomenon, the description should not be embellished. To avoid embellishment and vagueness, formal mathematical notation can be used to express relations among variables. For example, a literal description of Ohm's law is "current = voltage/resistance" and a literal description of Charles' law is "at constant pressure, an increase in temperature causes an increase in the volume of a gas" (Eby & Horton, 1986, p. 450).

On the other side is the argument for metaphoric language in science. To understand how a system works, we need to view that system as a machine. We need to represent the mechanism that underlies the causal relations expressed in the description. For example, to understand Ohm's law it useful to think in terms of an underlying mechanism such as the flow of electrons, and to envision concrete referents for abstract concepts such as current, voltage, and resistance. To understand Charles' law it is useful to think in terms of vibrating particles and to envision concrete referents for abstract concepts such as volume, mass, density, and pressure.

Given the established history of science, one might justifiably ask about the relative contributions of literal and constructive language. My field of interest, the psychology of learning, has a history that bears on this question. During the first half of this century (and before), the language of the psychology of learning consisted largely of literal description – the goal was to establish a list of behavioral laws that expressed precise, mathematical relations among observable variables. For example, the classic work of Ebbinghaus (1885) in the late 1800s focused on finding the quantitative relation between variables such as amount of practice and amount learned (expressed as the learning curve) or the time since learning and the amount remembered (expressed as the forgetting curve). Yet, underlying Ebbinghaus' precise descriptions lurked an associationist model of learning that contained an explanatory metaphor – the mechanism by which learning occurs is the strengthening and weakening of connections among elements.

The rise of behaviorism in the first half of this century formally restricted psychology's task to providing precise descriptions of the relations among observable variables (Bower & Hilgard, 1981; Skinner, 1938) – the epitome of the literal view of scientific language. During the behaviorist period, the literal view reached its summit in 1943 with the publication of *Principles of Behavior* by Clark Hull, a book that sought to mathematize the laws of learning. Based largely on animal-learning research, Hull provided formulas specifying the relations among variables such as response strength, habit strength, drive level, and inhibitory strength. In creating his precise mathematical formulas, however, Hull also seemed to provide a theory of the internal intervening mechanisms in learning. Today, Hull's attempt to build mathematical laws of learning is largely viewed as a failure:

Despite Hull's love for the quantitative aspects of his theory, the consensus judgment of subsequent generations of psychologists, even of those sympathetic to Hull, was that the specific quantitative details were the most arbitrary, least important, least interesting, and least enduring of Hull's theorizing. (Bower & Hilgard, 1981, p. 106)

Hull's theoretical constructs, however, are now seen as a major contribution: "It is doubtless wiser to consider Hull's theory at the informal, verbal level . . . the concepts and interrelated ideas being of more enduring significance" (Bower & Hilgard, 1981, p. 106). Even when the main goal of a science was precise description, the enduring value of the work turned out to be the underlying mechanisms used to explain the learning process. Accounts that leave open the possibility of metaphoric language seem to be more enduring.

During the second half of this century, as psychology moved from behaviorism to cognitive psychology, the call for precise descriptions was most strongly heard from a chorus of mathematical psychologists (for example, Estes, 1976; Estes & Straughan, 1954). Bower & Hilgard (1981, p. 212) note that "the type of program for which Hull argued appeared in significant form after 1950 under the banner of mathematical learning theory." Yet, as with Hull's work, the main contribution of mathematical learning theory may have rested not so much in its mathematical language as in the learning mechanisms that were modeled. For example, Estes' mathematical models of probability learning were originally based on the view of learning as conditioning of responses whereas his later models were based on the idea that learners store event frequencies that are used in conjunction with decision rules (Bower & Hilgard, 1981). In short, mathematical precision alone was unable to provide an accepted account of learning; underlying explanatory constructs seem to be needed at the heart of any useful mathematical model. Constructs such as learning-as-hypothesis-testing or learning-as-response-strengthening may be useful because they serve as metaphors of the mechanisms that underlie learning.

Most recently, literalism has been the hallmark of that segment of the cognitive science revolution concerned with computer simulation and artificial intelligence (Gardner, 1985; Johnson-Laird, 1988). Cognitive scientists place great value on a particular type of precise language – computer programs – and cognitive science doctrine holds that descriptions of cognitive processing should be computational – that is, stated in the language of a computer program. The underlying metaphor is that of the mind as a computing machine: "Cognitive science . . . tries to elucidate the workings of the mind by treating them as computations" (Johnson-Laird, 1988, p. 9).

One of the best known computer simulations of cognition is presented in Newell and Simon's (1972) classic *Human Problem Solving.* In terms of literalism, its major achievement was to specify means-end analysis as a precise computer-implemented algorithm – a contribution that has been greatly diminished by subsequent research showing that means-end analysis is not the method of choice for expert problem solvers (Larkin, Mc-Dermott, Simon, & Simon, 1980). In terms of constructivism, Newell and Simon's major achievement was the development of mechanisms such as subgoal construction, subgoal stacking, condition testing, and so forth, all under the overarching metaphor of cognition-as-computation – a contribution that seems to have stood the test of time.

What can one conclude from this brief survey of the history of research on the psychology of learning? The literal view, that the goal of science is to provide precise descriptions, has been a dominating force in each phase of this enterprise. It can be argued, however, that precise language by itself has not contributed substantially to scientific progress in the psychology of learning. In retrospect, even when precise descriptions were stipulated to be the most acceptable language of science, the enduring contributions also came from the underlying metaphors and models.

In taking a constructivist view, one could argue that progress has occurred mainly in the way that we now view learning and its underlying explanatory mechanisms. Kuhn (1970a) has asserted that scientific progress occurs when one model or metaphor comes to replace a less useful one and Schön (this volume) shows how the metaphors we use for framing problems affect the kinds of solutions we generate. For example, Sternberg (1990, p. 3), in his *Metaphors of Mind,* has systematically shown how, for the field of human intelligence, "each metaphor generates a series of questions . . . which the theories and research seek to address." Similarly, the constructs at center stage in this chapter are learning-as-knowledge-acquisition (which suggests a metaphor supporting the argument for literal descriptions in science) versus learning-as-knowledge-construction (which suggests a metaphor supporting the argument for metaphoric explanations in science).

This discussion of scientific language suggests that description without explanation is incomplete, and that literal precision without models or metaphors of the underlying mechanisms is sterile. To be useful, the language of science must provide not only precise descriptive information but also cues for how to understand and interpret the information. The appropriate use of metaphoric aids to learner understanding of scientific information is the subject of the next section.

The language of science education

In this section, I examine the processes by which students come to understand scientific descriptions and explanations. In particular, I address the question: when the goal is to promote meaningful science learning, what is the role of scientific descriptions expressed in precise quantitative terms and of scientific explanations expressed in qualitative (including, metaphoric) terms?

Quantitative and qualitative knowledge

One of the simplest and most precise ways to communicate scientific information to students is in quantitative form, as in a formula. Converging evidence from a variety of sources, however, points to the crucial role of qualitative, conceptual knowledge as a key to science learning.

Research on students' misconceptions of scientific principles shows, for example, that students often enter the physics classroom with a well-established set of incorrect concepts built up from their everyday experience (McCloskey, 1983; McCloskey, Caramazza, & Green, 1980). Students' intuitions can include the idea that "motion implies force" – that is, force is required to keep an object in motion. These students will predict that a ball dropped from an airplane traveling in one direction at a constant velocity will fall straight down (or will fall behind the plane). Although students in school physics courses are taught all the appropriate formulas involving force and motion, this formal training does not eliminate their misconceptions (Clement, 1982). In contrast, instruction aimed at building a qualitative understanding of the relations among force, velocity, and motion within the context of a video game does improve students' conceptions and, later, their understanding of quantitative laws (White, 1984). The power of students' qualitative intuitions about the concepts underlying the physical sciences suggests that instruction should be aimed at the conceptual level before emphasizing the more formal, quantitative language of science.

Research on mental models demonstrates that the metaphor students use for understanding a scientific formula influences how they go about solving problems. For example, Gentner and Gentner (1983) found that students who used a "flowing waters" metaphor for understanding Ohm's law performed differently on solving Ohm's-law problems than students who used a "teeming crowd" metaphor. Similarly, research on qualitative reasoning about physical systems (Bobrow, 1985) shows that successful physics reasoning is based on the reasoner's model of the physical system – a model that does not involve quantitative language. White and Frederiksen (1987) propose that students' progress in learning about a physical system can be viewed as a series of progressively more useful mental models – that is, as the development of qualitative models rather than the development of expertise in using quantitative formulas.

Research on expertise shows that experts tend to reason qualitatively about the model underlying a problem before focusing on quantitative computations (Chi, Feltovich, & Glaser, 1981; Larkin et al., 1980). For example, Chi and her colleagues (Chi, Bassok, Lewis, Reimann, & Glaser, 1989) found that good physics students produced more "self-explanations" than poor physics students as they examined a worked-out physics problem involving computations with various formulas. The self-explanations were aimed at connecting the quantitative language of the worked-out example to the student's qualitative knowledge of the underlying concepts and principles. In another study, Chi, Feltovich, and Glaser (1981) found that novices tended to categorize physics problems based on their surface characteristics such as whether an inclined plane was involved whereas experts categorized problems based on the underlying principle such as conservation of energy. Interestingly, Larkin (1983) found that when novices are given a physics problem they describe the problem in terms of its surface features such as pulleys and ropes and carts, whereas experts describe the problem in terms of underlying physics mechanisms such as forces and velocities. In summarizing research on expertise in scientific problem solving, White and Frederiksen (1987, p. 281) noted that experts "rely initially on qualitative reasoning and, if the problem requires it, employ quantitative models after they analyzed the problem in conceptual, qualitative terms."

Research on students' solutions to arithmetic story problems provides evidence that successful students build a "situation model" of the problem – that is, a nonquantitative representation of the relations in the problem – before using the numerical quantities in the problem to compute an answer (Greeno, 1989; Kintsch & Greeno, 1985; Lewis, 1989; Paige & Simon, 1966). Supporting this conclusion is some recent evidence from our laboratory. An analysis of students' eye movements as they solved story problems revealed that successful students tended to begin by looking mostly at the words in the problem and later at the numbers (Hegarty, Mayer, & Green,

1992). In a converging study, Lewis (1989) found that training students in how to generate a situational understanding of the problem – before focusing on numbers – greatly improved their performance on solving story problems.

A consistent theme running through these various research literatures is that in successful scientific problem solving qualitative reasoning precedes quantitative reasoning. It follows that if we want students to understand quantitative descriptions such as formulas they must first construct qualitative models of the underlying explanatory mechanisms. Accordingly, a primary goal of science education is to help students to build qualitative models that will aid their understanding of scientific descriptions and explanations.

Models for understanding

Based on a long series of research studies, I have proposed that instructional models can be used to help students build mental models for to-be-learned scientific material (Mayer, 1989a). Instructional models offer a type of instructional representation – materials presented by the instructor that invite the learner to construct a model of the to-be-learned situation. For example, to help students understand Ohm's law, an instructor might invite the student to envision a water-flow system in which the water pipes correspond to metal wires, water pumps correspond to batteries, and narrow pipes correspond to resistors; within the water-flow system, the rate of water flow corresponds to electrical current, the narrowness of the pipe corresponds to resistance, and water pressure corresponds to voltage (Gentner & Gentner, 1983). The water-flow model provides an example in support of White and Frederiksen's (1987, p. 282) assertion that "scientific theories need not at all times be algebraic and quantitative."

Mental models refer to the model of the system actually constructed by the learner. White and Frederiksen (1987) have shown that the development of mental models can progress through a series of stages, from zero-order qualitative models to first-order qualitative models to quantitative models. For example, a student who possesses a zero-order model of an electrical circuit can reason about gross aspects such as what happens to a light when the switch is opened or closed. A student who possesses a first-order model can engage in more sophisticated qualitative reasoning such as judging whether the light will get brighter or dimmer when the resistance is increased. Finally, a student who possesses a quantitative model will be able to determine exactly how bright the light will be when the switch is closed, or how much dimmer the light will get when resistance is increased by a certain amount.

This view of the progression of mental models from qualitative to quantitative suggests important implications for instruction:

In instruction, one should start by helping students to acquire a progression of increasingly sophisticated, zero order, qualitative models . . . that help them to understand how changes in one part of the [system] can cause changes in other parts. . . . Once these fundamental aspects of [system] behavior have been mastered in qualitative terms, we argue that one should introduce students . . . to first order qualitative models. . . . Finally, only after students can reason . . . in qualitative terms, should quantitative reasoning be introduced. Further, the form of quantitative . . . analysis taught should be a logical extension of the qualitative reasoning that students have already mastered. (White & Frederiksen, 1987, pp. 283–284)

White and Frederiksen (1987, p. 284) note that the qualitative-to-quantitative, explanation-to-description sequence "represents a radical departure from how physics theories are typically taught."

As an example, consider the formal statement that "matter expands when heated." As an instructional model, students can be asked to envision matter as a collection of colliding particles that respond to heat:

As heat is added to a material . . . the particles move faster. As the particles move faster, they collide with each other more violently. These violent collisions push the particles further apart. As the particles move further apart in a material, the material's volume increases. Thus, the material is said to expand. (Heimler & Price, 1984, p. 400)

In support of this instructor's model, the student might conduct an experiment in which a cup of coffee is heated in a microwave oven. At first blush, the coffee does not appear to have expanded. To test the idea in more detail, however, the student could focus on the hypothesis that material expands only slightly when heated. To detect the slight expansion, the student might use a type of thermometer arrangement: a full cup with a plastic top and a straw through the middle of the top. When the cup is placed in the microwave oven the coffee level in the straw is at the top of the cup but after 20 seconds in the microwave the coffee level has progressed up the straw. In this case, the student envisions and constructs a thermometer. As other experimental tests, the student might determine what happens to the space between railroad tracks on hot and cold days, or might take a steel ball that barely passes through a ring, heat the ball, and then see if it can pass through the ring. Each of these instructional episodes serves to help the student build a mental model of the relation between heat and volume.

Physics textbooks tend to emphasize precise quantitative statements of physical laws – such as Charles' law for the relation between temperature, volume, and pressure for gases – as well as hands-on activities – such as constructing a thermometer out of a beaker, stopper, tube, and burner. Yet only a few sentences are devoted to the qualitative model – such as colliding particles – required for interpreting the results of hands-on experimentation or quantitative calculations. In summary, I propose that hands-on experience is empty without an underlying mental model that predicts and explains the results; quantitative computations using a formula are meaningless unless the variables and relations in the formula correspond to a mental model possessed by the student. My own view of science education is that students attain scientific understanding mainly when they are able to construct mental models of the to-be-learned system.

This approach is consistent with Black's (this volume) "interaction view" of metaphor in which "every metaphor may be said to mediate an analogy or structural correspondence" and may be used "as an instrument for drawing implications." Similarly, the instructional program proposed in this section is consistent with Petrie and Oshlag's (this volume) conclusion that:

Metaphors in education have traditionally been viewed as occasionally heuristically useful but essentially ornamental, and sometimes as downright pernicious. We have argued that metaphors are essential for learning . . . they are epistemically necessary in that they seem to provide a basic way of passing from the well known to the unknown.

Metaphoric aids to science learning

In this section, I explore the hypothesis that metaphors can be used to help students understand scientific descriptions and explanations of how things work. For example, in a lesson on radar, students may be told to think of radar as an echo:

The phenomenon of acoustic echoes is familiar; sound waves reflected from a building or cliff are received back at an observer after a lapse of a short interval. If the initial sound is a short sharp one such as a hand-clap and if the speed at which sound waves travel is known, the interval between the initial clap and its echo is a measure of the distance of the reflecting object or surface. Radar uses exactly the same principle except that waves involved are radio waves, not sound waves. (Clarke, 1977, p. 176)

In this passage, sound waves are used to represent radio waves.

The practical problem facing educators and the theoretical problem facing researchers is that all metaphors are not equally instructive. Some metaphors may have no effect on student learning whereas some may be so misleading as to give rise to misconceptions (Spiro, Feltovich, Coulson, & Anderson, 1989); alternatively, others may have strong positive effects on what is learned (Mayer, 1989a). I define *instructive metaphor* as metaphoric information[2] in a passage that improves problem-solving transfer; for example, metaphoric information for the radar passage could include words and pictures depicting radar as a bouncing ball. I define *problem-solving transfer* as the ability to use information in a lesson to solve problems that were not presented in the lesson; for example, to evaluate problem-solving transfer from the radar passage students could be asked to devise ways to increase the area under surveillance. Unfortunately, little is known concerning the characteristics of instructive metaphors (Sticht, this volume).

Table 24.1. *A framework for metaphoric aids to learning*

Cognitive process	Description	Example	Outcome
none	none	Video-camera metaphor	no improvement (retention of nonuseful information)
selecting (or selective encoding)	encode key events	Echo metaphor: clap hands sound hits object hear echo measure time convert to distance	retention of key information
organizing (or selective combination)	build internal connections among events in metaphor	clap hands ↓ sound hits object ↓ hear echo ↓ measure time ↓ convert to distance	near transfer
integrating (or selective comparison)	building external connections between events in metaphor and events in target domain	clap hands ↔ transmit radio waves hear echo ↔ reception of radio waves	far transfer

The theory that has driven our research over the past two decades can be called *analogical transfer theory:* instructive metaphors create an analogy between a to-be-learned system (target domain) and a familiar system (metaphoric domain). This approach has been successfully applied to the analysis of transfer from one problem to another (Gick & Holyoak, 1980, 1983; Vosniadou & Ortony, 1989). The creation of an analogy requires one-to-one correspondence between events in the target and metaphoric systems (Gentner, 1983). For example, in the analogy between how radar works and how echoes work, there are one-to-one correspondences between clapping (or shouting) and transmitting a radio wave from an antenna, between hearing the echo and receiving a reflected radio wave back at the source, and between the time from shouting to hearing an echo and the time from transmission to reception of the radio wave.

Framework for metaphoric aids to learning

How do instructive metaphors affect student learning? Table 24.1 lists four possible effects of metaphoric language on the cognitive processing of the learner. First, the metaphor may have no positive effect on learning processes. For example, in the radar passage, we could create a metaphor between radar and a video-camera system by inserting the sentence: "think of radar as a TV screen connected to a video camera." This metaphor would not, however, allow the creation of an analogy because the events in the video-camera system do not correspond to events in the radar system. Analogical transfer theory predicts that a metaphor that fails to create a familiar analogy would have no positive effect on retention or transfer.

Second, the metaphor may direct the learner's attention toward key information. This is a cognitive process that Mayer (1984, 1989a) calls *selecting* and that Sternberg (1985, 1988) calls *selective encoding*. In the radar passage, the learner must selectively encode the five major events in the process of radar detection: transmission of a radio wave, reflection of the wave off a remote object, reception of the reflected wave back at the source, measurement of the time between transmission and reception, conversion of time to a measure of distance. The echo metaphor creates an analogy that emphasizes these events. When learners engage in an appropriate selecting process, their scores on tests of retention of key information should be improved.

Third, the metaphor may encourage the learner to connect the events into a coherent structure. Mayer (1984, 1989a) refers to this process as *selecting,* whereas Sternberg (1985, 1988) uses the term *selective combination* to refer to this process. For example, in the radar passage, the echo metaphor suggests how the key events should be ordered into a causal chain: transmission enables reflection, which enables reception, which enables measurement of time, and this in turn enables conversion to distance. Learners who engage in these cognitive processes should show improvement in retention of key information and in near transfer involving text-based inferences.

Fourth, in addition to guiding attention and building internal connections, the metaphor may also encourage the learner to build external connections between the metaphoric domain and the target domain – a process Mayer (1984, 1989a) calls *integrating* and Sternberg (1985, 1988) calls *selective comparison.* For example, in the radar passage, the events in the radar system can be mapped onto the events in the echo metaphor: transmitting corresponds to shouting, and so on. Learners who have engaged in selecting, organizing, and integrating should show improvement in retention of key information, near transfer, and far transfer.

In summary analogical transfer theory predicts that instructive metaphors (i.e., metaphors that create familiar analogies) foster the learning processes of selecting, organizing, and integrating. These processes lead to learning outcomes that support improved selection retention of key information and improved problem-solving transfer. In short, improvement in conceptual recall and problem-solving transfer occurs when three cognitive conditions are met: selecting, organizing, and integrating. During the last decade or so, my colleagues and I have been testing various aspects of these predictions. I turn now to a brief discussion of this research as it applies to three exemplary metaphors: radar as a bouncing pulse, density as particles in a box, and the computer as an instruction follower.

Radar as a bouncing pulse

Clues concerning the nature of metaphoric aids to learning emerged when we asked students to read, recall, and answer questions about a passage on radar (Mayer, 1983). First we noticed that concrete metaphors are more salient than other aspects of text for most students. On recall tests, students remembered 26 percent of the part of the text that described concrete metaphors such as an echo or dropping a pebble into a pond versus 12 percent of the text material that described the technical operation of radar devices (Mayer, 1983). Apparently, when metaphors are familiar and concrete they can attract the reader's attention, meeting the first criterion for meaningful learning (that is, selecting).

Unfortunately, however, students often fail to create an effective analogy between radar and bouncing pulses (or dropping pebbles) thus failing to meet the second and third criteria for meaningful learning (organizing and integrating). For example, our results showed that students did not perform well on tests of problem-solving transfer after reading the radar passage. To ensure that students build the needed internal and external connections, I developed a five-step introduction to the passage that emphasized the metaphor of radar as a bouncing pulse (Mayer, 1983):

1. Transmission: a pulse travels from an antenna.
2. Reflection: the pulse bounces off a remote object.
3. Reception: the pulse returns to the receiver.
4. Measurement: the difference between the time out and the time back tells the total time traveled.
5. The time can be converted to a measure of distance, since the pulse travels at a constant speed.

The introduction also contained simple diagrams showing an arrow moving from a source, striking an object, and returning to the source.

Our hypothesis was that the bouncing-pulse metaphor presented in the introduction would help the learner to build internal connections by organizing the system into five cause-and-effect events; similarly, the metaphor would help the learner build external connections between the five events in the metaphor and the five events in the operation of a radar system. For example, the principle underlying radar was expressed in the passage as: "thus, radar involves simply measuring the time between transmission of the waves and their subsequent return or echo and the converting that to a distance measure." These connections are summarized in Figure 24.1.

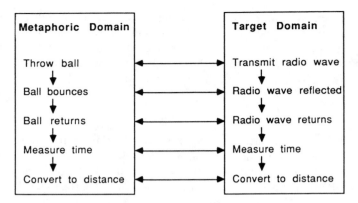

Figure 24.1. Radar as a bouncing pulse.

The results showed that the bouncing-pulse metaphor affected student learning. Students who received this information in their radar lesson recalled 50 percent more of the principles in the passage and generated approximately twice as many answers to the problem-solving transfer questions as students who did not receive the bouncing-pulse metaphor (Mayer, 1983). Thus, the results are consistent with the predictions of analogical transfer theory.

Density as particles in a box

As another example in our search for metaphoric aids to learning, consider the following excerpt from a passage on the concept of density (Mayer, Dyck, & Cook, 1984, p. 1104):

The formal definition of density is the mass per unit volume of a substance. Mathematically density is defined as a ratio of:

$$D = M/V$$

where D is density, M is mass, and V is volume. . . . An important fact about density is that most substances expand when heated. Therefore, when a certain weight of a substance is hot, it occupies a larger unit volume than it does when it is cool. This means that the density of the substance will decrease as it is warmed.

Students typically focus on recalling the formula in mathematical and numerical form, but not on the words about the formula (as shown above). When students lack a concrete metaphor for understanding density, they pay attention to the numbers and formulas in the passage.

To help direct students' attention toward the conceptual information – such as the words in the above excerpt – we inserted an introduction that

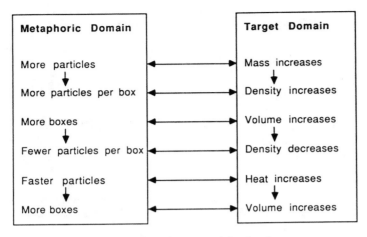

Figure 24.2. Density as particles in a box.

described volume as a cube and mass as particles (Mayer, Dyck, & Cook, 1984):

> Volume tells us how much space an object takes up. Finding the volume of an object is like finding how many individual cubes there are in a specific object. In the case below, volume is $3 \times 4 \times 2 = 24$ cubes. [A $3 \times 2 \times 4$ inch box is shown.] We could theoretically even take a cube out. [A 1×1 box is shown.] Mass is the number of particles within an object. Obviously, some substances have more particles than others. For example, BOX A mass is 3 particles [box with 3 black dots inside is shown], BOX B mass is 6 particles [box with 6 black dots inside is shown]. BOX B has two times as many particles and thus twice the gravitational pull.

As you can see, the student could build the analogy between density and particles in a cube. Figure 24.2 shows the analogical relation between particles in a box and the relations among variables in the density formula.

Does the density-as-particles-in-a-box metaphor affect student learning? Students who read a density passage that began with the metaphoric information recalled approximately twice as much of the conceptual information in the passage and generated approximately 50 percent more correct solutions to problem-solving transfer questions than students who read the passage without metaphoric information. Again, the metaphoric information seems to have helped learners to build a useful analogy.

The computer as an instruction follower

A heavily traveled path in my search for metaphorical aids to learning has involved the development of instructional materials for computer pro-

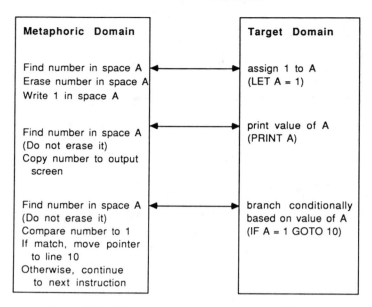

Figure 24.3. The computer as an instruction follower.

gramming. For example, consider a manual to teach students about elementary BASIC programming statements, such as INPUT, LET, PRINT, READ, DATA, IF, GOTO, FOR, NEXT. A typical manual (e.g., Bayman & Mayer, 1988, p. 298) describes the correct syntax for a statement and gives an example, such as:

A value is assigned to a variable by using the LET statement. For practical reasons, all the variable names used throughout this minicourse will be letters of the alphabet. Now assume that you type in:
LET A = 1
and press the RETURN key. The value 1 will be stored in variable A.

A metaphoric aid to understanding the concept of a variable is the concept of an erasable memory space, as in the following example (Bayman & Mayer, 1988, p. 298):

The steps the computer carries out are:
  1. Find the number stored in memory space A.
  2. Erase the number stored in memory space A.
  3. Write the number 1 in memory space A.
  4. Wait for the next statement to be entered from the keyboard.

Figure 24.3 summarizes the analogy between assigning values to variables and writing numbers in memory spaces, as well as several other connections.
    Does learning about programming statements within the context of a

familiar metaphor affect student learning? To answer this question, we compared the retention and transfer performances of students who read a programming manual that described each statement in standard form or one in standard form with metaphoric information added (Bayman & Mayer, 1988; Mayer, 1975, 1976; Mayer & Bromage, 1980). For example, variable assignment with LET statements was described in terms of erasing and writing numbers in a labeled memory space; flow of control using IF, GOTO, FOR, and NEXT statements was described in terms of moving a pointer arrow along a list of instructions; entering data using READ and DATA statements was described in terms of processing tickets at a ticket window; and so on. The metaphors were presented in verbal and in pictorial form. Over the course of eight experiments, students who received instructive metaphors during learning subsequently solved more than twice as many transfer problems and recalled approximately one-third more conceptual information than students who had not received metaphoric information in their manuals (Mayer, 1989a).

In summary, we see that in three quite different domains (the principles of radar, the concept of density, and elementary computer programming) the results are basically the same. The use of instructive metaphors facilitates meaningful learning and problem-solving transfer.

Conclusion

In the first two sections of this chapter, I examined the role of qualitative models in science and science education. In reviewing the language of science, I suggested that mathematical precision and metaphoric models both have a place in science, and that scientific language should both describe and explain. In discussing the language of science education, I reviewed evidence that learner understanding evolves from the qualitative to the quantitative, and that instruction should begin with instructional models that invite students to build progressively more sophisticated mental models of the to-be-learned system.

In the final section of this chapter, I provided several examples of metaphors that instruct – radar as bouncing pulse, density as particles in a box, and the computer as instruction follower. In each case, the metaphor was intended to help the learner build an analogy between a cause-and-effect system in the text (target domain) and in a familiar context (metaphoric domain). As predicted, each metaphor resulted in improved retention of conceptual information and improved problem-solving transfer. The next step in this program of research is to examine the boundary conditions for instructive metaphors: what are the distinguishing characteristics of instructive and noninstructive metaphors?

In conclusion, not all metaphors in a science textbook have the same effect on the knowledge construction processes of the learner: some may have a deleterious effect, others may have no effect at all, and yet others can enhance the selecting, organizing, and integrating processes. As empirical work on the instructional effects of metaphors continues, we can expect to gain a better understanding of how metaphoric language affects the learning processes and learning outcomes of science students. The respective roles of words and illustrations in helping students construct mental models is also an issue that requires additional study (Mayer, 1989b; Mayer & Gallini, 1990).

NOTES

1 For purposes of this chapter, I use a broad definition of metaphor as a description in which one object or event substitutes for another. This definition is broad because it allows a metaphor to involve more than a figure of speech, and because I emphasize the distinction between metaphors that systematically create analogies and those that do not. A more traditional definition is provided by Flexner and Hauck (1987): a metaphor is "a figure of speech in which a term or phrase is applied to something to which it is not literally applicable in order to suggest a resemblance" as exemplified by "A mighty fortress is our God." A simile is "a figure of speech in which two unlike things are compared" as exemplified by "she is like a rose." An analogy is "a similarity between like features of two things on which a comparison may be based" as exemplified by "the analogy between the heart and the pump."

2 Unlike the traditional definition of metaphors as being based solely on words, metaphoric information can contain words and pictures.

25

*Metaphor and learning

HUGH G. PETRIE AND REBECCA S. OSHLAG

Metaphor in education

There seem to be two main views of the role of metaphor in education. On the one hand, there is the idea that metaphors are primarily of aesthetic value, with perhaps some secondary utility as heuristic aids. This view concentrates on metaphors along with other linguistic forms, such as analogies, similes, and synecdoche, as figures of speech in literature, especially poetry. The poet's insight is often expressed through metaphor. Occasionally, proponents of the aesthetic value of metaphor also admit that it has some heuristic value in educational contexts outside of literature. For example, some of metaphor's relatives, like analogies and models are often used as teaching aids (see for example, Mayer, this volume; Petrie, 1976). The solar system model of the atom is familiar to high school physics students. But even in such a positive view of the pedagogical value of metaphors, it is usually claimed that although possibly useful and often ornamental, the metaphors and models are not essential to a cognitive understanding of what is being taught and learned. This is at least part of the position held by those whom Black (this volume) called the appreciators of metaphor.

On the other hand, metaphors occasionally receive a bad press in education. Metaphors are used when one is too lazy to do the hard, analytic work of determining precisely what one wants to say. Consequently, metaphors encourage sloppy thought. In addition, metaphors can be tremendously misleading. There are a number of different ways in which metaphors can be understood and so the possibility of mistake abounds. If metaphors are eliminated, there will be fewer mistakes. Finally, metaphors and their close cousins, slogans, are often used to cloud educational issues and reduce complex matters to simple-minded banalities. In short, as has been noted in other connections, metaphors have all the advantage over explicit language as does theft over honest toil (for example, R. M. Miller, 1976). Such views are often held by those whom Black (this volume) called the depreciators of metaphor.

Notice that both appreciators and depreciators of metaphors in education tend to agree that the *cognitive* significance of metaphor is severely limited. The main home of metaphor is in poetic insight and any more general cognitive function is ideally better served by explicit analytic language. At best, metaphors may be nice, but they are scarcely necessary for comprehension, communication, or coming to know (but cf. Ortony, 1975).

That view was challenged by Petrie in his chapter in the first edition of this volume where he argued that metaphors had a number of important cognitive roles, in particular, a possibly unique educational role in helping in the acquisition of new knowledge. One thing seems quite clear: in the intervening years, a number of cognitive roles for metaphors have been widely discussed and investigated (see, for example, Williams, 1988, for a summary of work on the cognitive roles of metaphor; Stepich & Newby, 1988, for an analysis of the function of analogies as learning aids within an information processing paradigm; and various chapters in Vosniadou & Ortony, 1989). The cognitive importance of metaphor, especially in instructional settings, has been clearly acknowledged since the first edition of this work. Furthermore, the importance of metaphor for the acquisition of new knowledge is being more and more widely accepted. In this sense, the purpose of the first chapter has already been to some extent fulfilled.

At the same time, despite the explosion of interest in the cognitive functions of metaphor, there remain sharp conflicts over the exact nature and use of metaphor in education. In this revision, therefore, we hope to use some of the work that has appeared since the first edition to augment the core ideas expressed by Petrie some 10 years ago. We are convinced that the major emphases of the earlier chapter are still essentially correct, but we also believe that these emphases can now be more perspicaciously and usefully expressed. Consequently, what follows represents in some cases a significant rewriting of the original chapter. We have tried to keep the basic format and the major conclusions so that the commentary that follows still has point, but we have tried at the same time to incorporate new work and clarify obscure points.

The work on metaphor's cognitive significance since 1979 has proceeded primarily on two fronts. On the one hand, it has been argued that metaphor enables one to transfer learning and understanding from what is well known to what is less well known in a vivid and memorable way, thus enhancing learning. This claim is essentially a psychological one, asserting a connection between vividness, or more precisely, imageability, and learning (e.g., Davidson, 1976; Ortony, 1975; Paivio, 1971; Reynolds & Schwartz, 1983). It is an extremely important result that metaphorical teaching strategies often lead to better and more memorable learning than do explicit strategies.

The memorableness of metaphors can also lead, however, to several undesirable consequences. Not only are metaphors sometimes misleading and misused, we have also learned that on occasion they are taken as literal truth, thereby interfering with the later development of more adequate knowledge. Rand Spiro and his associates (Spiro, Coulson, Feltovich, & Anderson, 1988; Spiro, Feltovich, Coulson, & Anderson, 1989; Spiro, Vispoel, Schmitz, Samarapungavan, & Boerger, 1987), for example, have shown that certain very common and useful analogies and metaphors used in the instruction of physicians come to interfere with later learning and a more adequate understanding of the concepts. Despite these dangers Spiro's suggested solutions do not include eliminating the metaphors, but rather utilizing multiple, cross-cutting metaphors and knowledge sources. Thus, even if we grant the possible misuse and misleadingness of metaphor, especially in advanced learning, and even if we were to assume the goal of making what is learned more explicit, it still appears that metaphors and analogies play a central, even indispensable role in the pedagogical process of acquiring that subject. We call this use of metaphor the pedagogical use.

S. I. Miller (1987), however, in criticizing Petrie's original chapter implicitly distinguished between what we call pedagogical metaphors (or analogies) and theory-constitutive metaphors (see Boyd, this volume; Gentner & Jeziorski, this volume). The former may be useful for the teacher in introducing certain difficult concepts. Theory-constitutive metaphors, however, are integral parts of the very structure of a theory at any given time in its development. All theories contain such metaphors, and their usefulness consists of both their ability to help us learn the theory and their inductive fruitfulness in guiding further research in the theory. They are, for Miller, always to be conceived of as way stations toward a more explicit and literal rendering of the theory.

S. I. Miller's (1987) concern was that educational theorists not ignore the problems of the theory-constitutive metaphors embedded within typical "educational" theories, such as operant conditioning and functionalism. He pointed out, correctly, that it is not always clear how metaphors such as, for instance, "shaping" behavior can be of any practical pedagogical use. It is also important to realize that one can, in principle, look at any theoretical approach and question its metaphors. In short, we can, and sometimes should, examine the theory-constitutive metaphors of educational psychology, physics, or even metaphor comprehension itself.

In a similar vein Reyna (1986) described pedagogic metaphors as a type of functional metaphor used to introduce novel concepts by relating them to familiar concepts. These can be contrasted with technical metaphors which are used to describe abstract concepts in terms of more explicit concepts. This distinction appears very close to the characterization of pedagogic and theory-constitutive metaphor described above. Reyna went further, however, in introducing the distinction between mundane and elite metaphors with the former more easily comprehended than the latter.

For our purposes we wish to lump together as educational metaphors all the various categories of metaphors which are useful for increasing understanding by students. Thus mundane, pedagogic metaphors as well as elite theory-constitutive metaphors can be seen as educational metaphors if they are used by teachers and students to enhance learning. There may even be a category that we would call "residual metaphors" which can function as educational metaphors on certain occasions of their use. These are typically concepts and phrases that may be viewed as literal by people fully familiar with a field, but that would be seen as metaphorical from the point of view of a student just learning a field. The "frames of reference" example in Petrie's original chapter, and repeated here later in abbreviated form, can be seen as an example of a residual metaphor that can have an educational use.

Within the category of educational metaphorical use we wish to focus here on Petrie's original claim that the very possibility of learning something radically new can only be understood by presupposing the operation of something very much like metaphor (see Rumelhart & Norman, 1981, and Vosniadou & Brewer, 1987, for examples of researchers who have been seriously investigating the claim that radically new knowledge requires the operation of metaphor). This is not just the heuristic claim that metaphors are often useful in learning, but the epistemic claim that metaphor, or something very much like it, is what renders possible and intelligible the acquisition of new knowledge.

Plato first posed the problem of the acquisition of radically new knowledge in his famous paradox of the *Meno:*

You argue that a man cannot enquire either about that which he knows or about that which he does not know; for if he knows, he has no need to enquire; and if not, he cannot; for he does not know the very subject about which he is to enquire. (Plato, *Meno* 80E; Jowett translation)

How *is* it possible to learn something radically new? – a question also raised by Pylyshyn (this volume).

There is an educational formulation of the issue raised in the *Meno* paradox. If we assume that we can simply pour knowledge into the heads of students, then we are faced with the problem of how those students can ever recognize what they receive as knowledge, rather than as something to be rote-memorized. If, however, we insist, as current conventional wisdom as well as constructivist psychology (Anderson, 1977; Rumelhart & Ortony, 1977; Schank & Abelson, 1977) would have it, that learning must

Figure 25.1

always start with what the student presently knows, then we are faced with the problem of how the student can come to know anything radically new. It is our thesis that metaphor is one of the central ways of leaping the epistemological chasm between old knowledge and radically new knowledge (see also Petrie, 1976, 1981).

The belief that there is such an epistemological chasm depends on certain presuppositions for which we shall not here argue. Although still somewhat controversial 15 years ago, these presuppositions are now widely accepted. First, experience is never directly of the world as it is, but is always in part constituted by our modes of representation and understanding, by our schemas, scripts, or mental models. For example, we experience the chairs on which we sit as dense and impenetrable, although they are, physicists tell us, composed of clouds of very tiny particles. Second, most learning consists of processing that which impinges on us in terms of a context of rules or representations. These representations form our modes of understanding. Much learning is thus coming to be able to process our experience in terms of existing contexts and schemas and the relations among them. We learn about the Civil War by seeing it is a war within a nation. Third, however, on some occasions we learn by actually changing our representations. The result of *changed* representations is what we call radically new knowledge. For example, the phenomenon of experiencing something in different ways if approached with a different schema is graphically illustrated by the so-called ambiguous figures. Figure 25.1 can be seen as either a duck or a rabbit. Piaget (1972) noted the distinction between these two kinds of learning by distinguishing between assimilation and accommodation. During assimilation, we learn by changing experience to fit our concepts. During accommodation, we learn by changing our concepts to fit our experience.

The problem posed by the *Meno* paradox occurs with accommodation. If understanding and learning involve being able to put that which is learned into a schema, as noted in the first assumption above, then how can we ever rationally come to *change* our schemas? It seems we would either have to presuppose that we already possess, at least implicitly, the schema which renders intelligible the radically new thing we are attempting to learn, or else we would have to admit that the learning of something radically new is arbitrary and subjective. Both alternatives, unfortunately, have considerable precedent in education. What we shall suggest here is a third alternative – that metaphor can provide a *rational* bridge from the known to the radically unknown, from a given context of understanding to a changed context of understanding. The central question for us is "how is radically new knowledge possible?" With the presuppositions noted above, that question becomes "how is rational change of schemas possible?" Finally, these "how?" questions are to be taken in the epistemic and not the psychological sense. In other words, the question is "how is one to make intelligible the acquisition of new knowledge?" not "what are the processes involved?"

Our concern with metaphor is derivative from this central educational concern. We believe an examination of metaphor will show that it does, on occasion, play this crucial epistemic role of rendering the acquisition of radically new knowledge intelligible. We have now learned that there are many devices other than metaphor that serve as a bridge from the known to the unknown (see, for example, Gentner & Jeziorski, this volume; Reigeluth, 1980; Rumelhart & Norman, 1981; Vosniadou & Brewer, 1987). Analogies, models, and exemplary problem solutions also sometimes perform this function and, we believe, in very similar ways to metaphor. The feature that all these have in common is that they invite the use of a familiar rule-governed device for dealing with the material to be learned in ways that require the bending or even breaking of the familiar rules. Metaphor is one crucial way this happens; analogies, models, and exemplars are others. Our purpose is to argue that metaphor, as traditionally understood and as an exemplar of these other types of figurative devices, often plays a central role in the acquisition of radically new knowledge.

Metaphor

There are two issues in the voluminous literature on metaphor that are of particular interest for our purposes. The first is the distinction between comparative and interactive metaphors. On the comparative view of metaphor, what a metaphor does is to say implicitly that two apparently dissimilar things have something in common after all. Thus, in speaking of the "flow" of electricity, despite the obvious dissimilarities between electricity and liquids, it is held that there is a fundamental similarity – they both move in a fluid kind of way. On this view, a metaphor is an implicit comparison, whereas a simile or an analogy is an explicit comparison (Green, 1971); metaphors transfer meaning and understanding by comparison. It should be noted that the notion of a comparative metaphor would not serve to make intelligible the acquisition of radically new knowledge. The problem is that radically new knowledge results from a *change* in modes of representation of knowledge, whereas a comparative metaphor occurs within the existing representations which serve to render the comparison sensible. The comparative level of metaphor might allow for extensions of already existing knowledge, but it would not provide a new form of understanding.

There are problems, however, with attempting to construe all metaphors as implicit comparisons. Consider the example (Haynes, 1975), "Virginity is the enamel of the soul." Is the implicit comparison to be between the positive features of clarity, strength, and protectiveness, or the negative features of rigidity, brittleness, and enclosure? Nothing in the metaphor tells us and only nonlinguistic contextual knowledge of speaker or hearer seems useful. For reasons such as this, many writers have claimed that there is also an interactive level of metaphor. Black says, "It would be more illuminating in some of these cases to say that metaphor creates the similarity than to say that it formulates some similarity antecedently existing" (Black, 1962b, p.37). The interactive level of metaphor is peculiarly appropriate for our purposes, because if it *creates* similarities, then it could provide the bridge between a student's earlier conceptual and representational schemes and the later scheme of the totally unfamiliar subject to be learned by the student. Interactive metaphor would allow truly new forms of knowledge and understanding to be acquired by the student without presupposing the student already knows, in some sense, that which is being learned.

The discussion so far points to the fact that a metaphor, comparative or interactive, depends on the cognitive scheme presupposed for its understanding. One and the same metaphor can be comparative *and* interactive, depending on the point of view taken. An educational metaphor like "The atom is a miniature solar system" is probably a comparative metaphor from the point of view of the teacher. The teacher already knows both about the solar system and about atoms and is relying on the similarity between them that already exists in our collective understanding. But from the point of view of the student just beginning physics, the metaphor, assuming it is successful, will be interactive. It will (help) create the similarity *for the student*. It provides a way of understanding how the student's existing modes of representation and understanding can be changed through interaction with the new material, even granting that experience is dependent on a particular mode or scheme of understanding.

In the original chapter, Petrie discussed the issue of whether a metaphor can be identified by some set of linguistic features independent of its use on particular occasions. The purpose of the discussion was to address the apparent fact that metaphors are, if interpreted literally, clearly false. The question then became, how do students interpret their teachers when they are uttering falsehoods? In retrospect, this issue is almost certainly a red herring. The common situation in the classroom is that students typically take the teacher to be serious and sincere and when teachers do introduce metaphors, their reports indicate a carefully planned, strategic use of metaphors as part of teaching the new material (e.g., Biermann, 1988a; Marshall, 1984; D. B. Miller, 1988; Whitman, 1975; Zegers, 1983). Given the care and thought that typically go into teachers' use of metaphor, it is unlikely that students will be surprised by pedagogical metaphors. Good teachers know from long experience that certain topics and fields are difficult for students to understand. What happens is that good teachers carefully signal the introduction of something new and the necessity for the students to suspend the normal conversational implications regarding literal truth and falsity. Thus, students will typically try to make sense of the metaphorical utterance, making use of clues that the teacher is serious and attempting to say something important and useful.

Recent work by Glucksberg and Keysar (1990; this volume) throws important new light on the "problem" of the literal falsity of metaphorical assertions. They argue persuasively for the view that, in the final analysis, metaphorical statements are not implicit similes, a view we have at least partially endorsed in arguing for Black's (1962b) interactive view of some metaphorical utterances. Instead, they suggest that typical nominative metaphors are class-inclusion assertions in which the topic of the metaphor is assigned to an abstract category referred to by the vehicle of the metaphor. The vehicle thus functions as both the name of the category and as a prototypical example of it. Their example, "My job is a jail," thus receives the interpretation that my job, the topic, is assigned to the class of entities that confine one against one's will, are unpleasant, are difficult to escape from, and so on. The vehicle, jail, is a prototypical exemplar of this new category and serves in this instance as a name for the category.

Glucksberg and Keysar (1990) gave numerous examples of such uses in the language, including a fascinating comment by an Israeli during the war crimes trial of John Demjanjuk who was accused of being "Ivan the Terrible," a sadistic guard at the Treblinka death camp in Poland. Apparently the name Demjanjuk had become a noun in Israel to identify an ordinary person capable of committing unspeakable acts. Thus, it was quite sensible during the trial for an Israeli to say of John Demjanjuk, the defendant, "I know his name is Demjanjuk, but I don't know if he is a Demjanjuk."

This dual role for the vehicle of a metaphor as both prototypical example and name of a newly created class sheds considerable light on how metaphors can actually create the similarity to be noted. As has often been noted, everything is similar to everything else in some respect or other. Some similarities are typically worth drawing attention to and eventually become enshrined as "literal" truth or falsity in terms of typical conceptual schemes. At any point in time, then, the schemas of most people contain certain connections of inclusion, similarity, and relationship, and not oth-ers. Good metaphors suggest new connections by picking out an exemplary and well-known example of a certain category, and, by grouping it with a member of another category which is typically *not* related to the meta-phor's category, the relevant similarity is created. The particular grouping of existing categories causes the appropriate selection of properties which are to be related by the metaphor in its role as prototypical example of the new class. If such a predication of a prototypical example to the topic continues to make sense, the metaphor may pass into literal truth and become a "dead" metaphor. If it is a bad metaphor, the similarity will not be seen as worth making, or at least not making in that way, and the metaphor will not even be understood or will not catch hold. In either case, the metaphor is anomalous in the sense that a well-known prototypical example of a certain category is connected to parts of our conceptual schemes with which it is not usually associated.

We shall have more to say about how students utilize metaphors to change their cognitive structures. For now we simply want to emphasize that it is the *anomalous* character of an interactive metaphor, anomalous in terms of a student's *current* set of rules for understanding, that distin-guishes the way in which metaphors transfer chunks of experience from the way in which literal language or comparative metaphors do. Literal lan-guage requires only assimilation to existing frameworks of understanding. Comparative metaphor requires simple extensions of the framework in the light of a more comprehensive framework. Accommodation of anomaly requires changes in the framework of understanding. While these changes in cognitive structures almost certainly fall along a continuum, it is the general requirement of a fairly radical change in cognitive framework that provides the distinction between the ways interactive metaphor and literal language are to be understood. It is this change in framework that secures the importance of metaphor in considering how radically new knowledge is acquired.

Metaphor and the growth of science

The brief description that we have presented of how an interactive metaphor can create an anomaly for a student so as to lead toward changes in cognitive structure bears a striking analogy to Kuhn's description of the workings of science during scientific revolutions (Kuhn, 1970b). During the periods of normal science, puzzles and problems are solved by the use of the accepted paradigm of the moment. Occasionally, such problems or disturbances resist current paradigm efforts to solve them, and they become anomalies. The scientist then searches for a new metaphor or model that can remove the anomaly. The main difference between the scientist on the frontiers of knowl-edge and the student is that in the student's case the metaphor provided by the teacher, if it is a good one, is likely to be more immediately helpful than are the variants tried out by the scientist. Except for a kind of trust in the teacher, however, the student does not really know any more about where he or she will end up than does the scientist. This seems to us to go directly against the educational dogma that one should always lay out in advance for the student exactly what the goals of the learning experience are taken to be. In cases where the goals are to change significantly the student's current cognitive structure, it will not be possible to lay out learning outcomes the student can initially understand. Only metaphorically and ex post facto can the student be brought to understand the goals expressed in the terms and categories of the to-be-learned subject matter.

One of the crucial senses of "paradigm" for Kuhn (1974) is what he called an exemplar. An exemplar is a concrete problem with its solution, which together constitute one of the scientific community's standard examples. Acquiring these exemplars is a critical part of the scientist's training, and they serve the absolutely central function of allowing the student to "apply theory to practice," although, as we shall show, this is a misleading way of making the point. The exemplar is what enables the student to deploy the symbolic generalizations of the theory being learned in particular problem situations. This role is extremely important, because on Kuhn's view, we do not always link up theory and observation statements by means of correspondence rules, nor is there any direct access to the world independent of our theoretical language. In short, having denied a direct perceptual link to the world "as it is," and having accepted the fact that observation is theory-laden, another account of the link between our beliefs and nature must be provided. Kuhn's suggestion is that, in an important sense, exemplars serve this function.

How do exemplars work? Kuhn (1974) gave an extended example of a young boy learning to recognize ducks, swans, and geese by repeated ostensive definition and correction of mistakes. His account went no further than the simple observation that this is indeed how such learning often happens. Kuhn claimed that what the boy learned is not "rules" of application, but rather a primitive perception of similarity and difference. This perception precedes any linguistic formulation of the similarity relations. Can these nonlinguistic similarity relations be spelled out in more detail? If so, perhaps a third alternative, besides direct access and correspondence rules between theory and observation, can be given some plausibility as a way of accounting for the link between observation and nature or between theoretical language and observational language about nature.

What we wish to suggest is that understanding an interactive metaphor includes, as an essential part, activities similar to those involved in acquiring an exemplar. For when a metaphor has effected a change of cognitive structure (where the "rules" of the cognitive structure need not be explicitly formulated or formulatable), the student has a new way of dealing with, describing, and thinking about nature, just as the science student, in acquiring an exemplar, has a new way of deploying symbolic generalizations in nature. Furthermore, if Glucksberg and Keysar (1990) are right in suggesting that metaphors are class-inclusion assertions, with the vehicle of a metaphor being a prototypical example of the new category to be learned, the similarity to the Kuhnian (1974) description of learning new perceptual categories is even more striking. What happens in both cases is that our cognitive structures or schemas are expanded and linked up in different ways through the use of an exemplar of the category being learned. "The atom is a solar system" thus becomes the attribution of the atom to those categories of systems in which there are central bodies around which revolve other bodies with certain forces and relations obtaining, of which the solar system is a prototypical exemplar.

The key to understanding the learning of new categories such as ducks and geese on the one hand, and comprehending metaphors on the other, is that both processes are bound up with *activities* on the part of the student. It is not simply a case of hearing words, understanding them literally, and applying them directly. In both instances it is a case of *acting* in the ecology. For the science student, this is brought out by Kuhn's (1974) insistence that in acquiring exemplars the student requires diagrams, demonstrations, and laboratory exercises and experiments. Even the young boy learning about ducks, swans, and geese is doing something. He is classifying and being corrected. Of course, language is involved, not as a kind of labeling, but as a prod to *activities* of sorting, classifying, and perceiving similarities and differences. In the case of the metaphors, the activities are again those of classification, building new relationships, testing hypotheses suggested by the new class-inclusion relationship, and the like. We believe our subsequent discussion of interactive metaphor in a pedagogical situation, especially as viewed from the student's perspective, will be directly relevant to Kuhn's claims that exemplars provide the way of understanding how language relates to the world.

Thus the educational functions we are proposing for metaphor are that it does, indeed, make learning more memorable, and that it does, indeed, help move one from the more familiar to the less familiar. But we are also claiming that metaphor is what enables one to pass from the more familiar to the unfamiliar in the sense that it provides a key mechanism for changing our modes of representing the world in thought and language. It provides this mechanism not through a direct labeling, or through explicit rules of application, but rather because in order to understand an interactive metaphor, one must focus one's *activities* on nodes of relative stability in the world. Language bumps into the world at those places where our activity runs up against similar boundaries in diverse situations.

Metaphors and pedagogical content knowledge

Perhaps one of the most influential developments in education since the first edition of this book has been the widespread acceptance of the notion of pedagogical content knowledge (Shulman, 1986; 1987). This is a kind of knowledge that expands on ordinary content knowledge in the direction of those aspects that are particularly germane for teaching the particular content. Shulman has identified two major subcategories of pedagogical content knowledge – first, the most useful forms of metaphors or representations of a subject and, second, the features that render any given topic more or less easy to teach or understand. An example of a powerful metaphor in Newtonian mechanics would be conceiving of the action of objects on each other as if they were a system of billiard balls. With respect to the issue of typical difficulties teachers ought to know about, an example might be the fact that even many college students believe, incorrectly, that if one gave a puck a push on an infinite, frictionless air hockey table, eventually the force imparted to the puck would "wear out" and the puck would stop moving. That is, students tend naturally to hold an impetus theory of motion rather than a Newtonian one. Clearly, both these kinds of knowledge would be very useful for a teacher to know in attempting to teach mechanics.

For our purposes, there are at least two important consequences of the increasing significance of the notion of pedagogical content knowledge. First, it encompasses an explicit acknowledgment of the centrality of metaphor in teaching. We shall return to this feature in a moment. Second, it challenges the traditional conception of learning how to teach. That conception implicitly assumes that one first learns the content of a subject and then one learns general theories of pedagogy. General pedagogical and psychological learning theories are then applied to the content, and, perhaps to the specific students, in order to devise instructional strategies for the content and context in question. Furthermore, it is assumed by many that, on the whole, learning how to teach is more or less content-free. That is, the difference between a physics teacher and an English teacher is believed to lie almost wholly in their respective content knowledge. How to teach it is largely the same for the two and consists of knowing things like how to motivate students, how to structure a lecture, how to manage a class, how to use small group discussions, how to construct grading schemes, and so on.

The concept of pedagogical content knowledge, without denying the usefulness of general pedagogy, invites us to look beyond such principles and focus on the different ways in which content knowledge may be held by both teacher and student. Some of those ways may be more pedagogically useful than others. Some ways of representing that knowledge may make it easier to acquire than others. Some ways of representing a given knowledge domain may be useful for one group of students in one context, but it may be necessary for the expert teacher to have a variety of ways of representing and *re*-presenting content knowledge so that different kinds of students in different contexts can learn.

Reminding us that there are extremely important pedagogical features specifically connected to the content being taught or learned reinforces the importance of the use of metaphor in education that we have been urging. Indeed, as noted above, Shulman (1986; 1987), has characterized knowledge of the metaphors of a field as one of the key features of pedagogical content knowledge. We would urge that Shulman's metaphors need to include all of what we have called educational metaphors – the theory-constitutive metaphors of the field, the pedagogic metaphors (sometimes they will be the same as the theory-constitutive metaphors) which help introduce students to the field, and even the residual metaphors, those parts of a field which may be viewed as literal truth for people already knowledgeable in the area, but which may involve radically new knowledge for someone just being introduced to the field.

If, therefore, one thinks of the typical student and the typical teacher as each having some sort of conceptual representation or schemas of, say, physics in their minds at any given time, two features stand out. First, as noted earlier, the use of a metaphor, pedagogical, theory-constitutive, or residual, by the teacher may be comparative in that the teacher already knows enough physics to comprehend both the old and new knowledge domains. For the student, on the other hand, the very same metaphor may be interactive, creating the similarity under consideration. Second, the student may well be acquiring one of the constitutive or residual metaphors of the field for the first time.

In the following section we repeat the example from Petrie's original chapter, although in a shortened form. Originally Petrie offered the example as a clear case of the use of a metaphor in a teaching situation. In retrospect, the case does not seem so clear, although as an example of how a given concept that might be viewed as literal truth by those familiar with the field and as a metaphor by students just learning the field, it still seems to us to have merit. We will follow the frames of reference discussion with an example from more recent work which clearly does illustrate how metaphor seems to be the only way in which to overcome student misconceptions.

Educational metaphors: Some examples

One of the interesting features that seems to characterize most people's unreflective concept of motion is that there is no difficulty in deciding whether something is in motion or not. One simply looks and sees. Yet, an essential feature of motion is that it is properly describable only relative to a coordinate system. Where the observer happens to be located when trying to decide whether something is in motion is essential to understanding motion (for simplicity's sake we assume a stationary observer). After noting several examples of motion, one secondary-school science text (Fisk & Blecha, 1966, pp. 217–18) suggested that the reader look at a nearby object, for example, a chair, and decide whether or not it is moving. The authors assumed the answer would be no, and then they pointed out that the chair is on the earth's surface, and the earth is moving, so is not the chair moving after all? The authors were attempting to introduce into the student's conceptual scheme an anomaly analogous to Kuhn's (1974) description of anomalies in the growth of science. Does the chair move or does it not?

Fisk and Blecha had to assume two things about the student; first, that his or her standard unreflective judgment would be that the chair is not moving, and second, that the student knows the earth moves. Without these two assumptions, the attempt to introduce an anomaly into the student's view of the world will fail, for the student will simply reject one of the things he or she is being invited to consider, probably the claim that the earth moves. What this illustrates is that an anomaly will *be* an anomaly only from the standpoint of a conceptual scheme. If the student does not know about the earth's movement, no anomaly will occur. This point illustrates the feature that in order for metaphors to work, at least one of the categories being used metaphorically must be part of the student's conceptual scheme.

Next, Fisk and Blecha (1966) tried to make the anomaly explicit by suggesting that it may seem strange to say a book is both moving and not moving. Here they were relying on the idea that everyone probably finds contradictions anomalous. The theory-constitutive, or, possibly residual metaphor to be used to solve the anomaly is then introduced. The book's moving and not moving seems strange only because the book is being observed from two different *frames of reference*. We take it that the metaphorical term here is "frame of reference."

The authors next define "frame of reference" as "a place or position from which an object's motion may be observed and described" (Fisk & Blecha, 1966, p. 218). It might be objected that "frame of reference" is not a metaphor at all. For the student, however, it may have no literal referent whatsoever. Does it mean that the student is to put up a picture frame and block out part of his or her experience? That would be one "literal" meaning. The point is crucial for pedagogy. A technical term may have a literal meaning for those who understand the subject but be completely metaphorical for the student just learning the subject.

It will be objected that the term was *given* a literal definition and so still fails to be metaphorical. The plausibility of this objection rests on the presupposition that the students have already grasped the notion of *different points of view* – which is, after all, the core of the frame of reference idea. If they have, then "a place or position from which an object's motion may be observed and described" makes sense as referring to different places at the same time with putative observers at those places at the same time. But if the student has not yet grasped the notion of different points of view, then "a place or position from which an object's motion may be observed" may literally mean to the student his or her own place or position. Thus, unless one presupposes that most of the work of grasping the metaphor has already occurred, the "literal" definition may not do the trick at all.

This point can be brought out another way. In order to demonstrate their grasp of the term, the students will have to be able to do things with it. They will have to be able to solve problems, answer questions, in short, to engage in activities guided by the concept of frame of reference. In the current case, those activities are largely confined to thought experiments (as they necessarily must be in most written materials). The student is asked to imagine the chair on the earth's surface, the thought experiment taking on the logical role of activities that help one to triangulate on motion. The metaphor "frame of reference," however that is initially understood by the student, provides the other leg of the triangulation. If thought experiments do not provide sufficient activity for the student to converge on the idea of relative motion, they could be supplemented by actual activities of the same type.

However, the first attempts at convergence may result in fairly gross approximations, and corrections may be needed. Fisk and Blecha (1966) referred back to the chair example and, using frame of reference language, explicitly suggested that the student look at the chair from a position in space near the moon, and as they put it, somewhat hopefully, "You would probably say that the chair is moving because the earth is moving" (p. 218). With the chair–earth example, they are implicitly correcting a possible mistake which they anticipate some students may initially have made.

In addition to the metaphor of frames of reference, the text uses an interesting diagram (Figure 25.2) and a different example to supplement in a perceptual way the new conceptualization suggested by the metaphor. Through the sequence of pictures, Fisk and Blecha (1966) tried to show how important "point of view" is. They took it for granted the student would, if in a spaceship, say the book fell to the floor. By presenting a schematic series of pictures of the spaceship ascending, another anomaly is created, for the floor is also rising. The pictures also illustrate the alternative conceptualization which can solve the problem. The pictures quite plainly *demand* that one take up a point of view outside the spaceship, and it is that "other point of view" that is the point of the lesson. Again the activity is left to thought experiments. *Both* "book falling" and "floor rising" seem appropriate from the point of view from which the pictures are seen. For the students to check out their ideas on such a fairly subtle point provides opportunity for correction and successive triangulations.

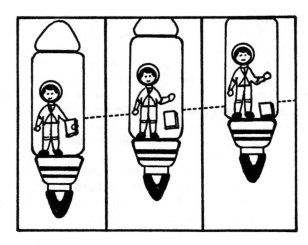

Figure 25.2

The overall point of this example is that, if successful, it has changed the student's conceptual framework in a fairly fundamental way through the use of the term "frame of reference." The notion was given a literal definition in terms of place of observation, but the appropriateness of that definition depended on the *nonlinguistic* ability to take up alternative points of view (another metaphor?), so that place of observation did not simply mean to the student "where I happen to be at the time."

Another, even more dramatic example of an educational metaphor is provided by Joshua and Dupin (1987). They studied the evolution of change-resistant student conceptions and the methods used to overcome these "epistemological obstacles" or "interpretive grids" through which students observe phenomena and then draw conclusions different from those the teachers intended to establish. Of interest were the conceptions of simple direct current held by French students about 12 and 14 years old, in grades comparable to six and eight in the United States.

Four main preinstructional conceptions were identified by Joshua and Dupin (1987) during clinical interviews. The "contact" conception, a simplistic view, emphasized the mechanical contact between the battery and the bulb and was held by relatively few students. Similarly, the "single wire" conception which assumes that electricity travels through just one wire to the light did not enjoy a wide following. The "clashing currents" conception which suggests that two currents leave the battery and supply the bulb but do not return to the battery was held by a majority of the students. Finally, the "current wearing out" view which holds that the current goes one way around the circuit but wears out in its travels through the bulb was maintained by a number of students, particularly the older ones.

Joshua and Dupin (1987) observed the development of these conceptions during a series of activities presented by regular classroom teachers. In the first of two class discussions, students presented their explanations and discussed the various interpretations. No students in either grade put forth the contact conception, perhaps because the teachers' cues and the responses of the other students indicated that more elaborate explanations were sought. The single-wire conception was eliminated based on classroom discussion. The current-wearing-out view was rarely presented, although a "circulatory" conception that did not mention wearing out was voiced. The circulatory view and the clashing current position, held by the majority of the students, remained as competitors at the end of the lesson.

During the second session Joshua and Dupin (1987) observed that students discussed the competing views in small groups but did not typically change positions until a particularly animated class discussion. In the younger group, there was considerable clarification and systematization of views and little change of opinion. Changes did occur in both directions in the older group, but most students simply deepened their initial conception. The circulatory conception was modified and eventually expressed as the current-wearing-out view. This notion had the majority of adherents at the end of the discussion.

Once both the clashing current and current wearing out conceptions were seen as accounting for the phenomenological data equally well, experimentation was used to gain additional information. Joshua and Dupin (1987) reported that the children were not very good at identifying experiments, but they did agree that they needed to know the direction and quantity of current in each wire to decide between the theories. The teachers proposed a method, and the students were required to anticipate the results of the experiment based on their models, carry out the experiment, and draw conclusions. The results of the first experiment failed to support the clashing-current view and were accepted, with some disappointment, by the proponents of that view.

Joshua and Dupin (1987) noted that the teachers had to insist on conducting a second experiment to test the current-wearing-out theory. The supporters of that theory could not accept the possibility of a circulatory model without losses and did not see the purpose of the experiment. When the results demonstrated the same amount of current before and after crossing the light bulb, the younger students were surprised and then unanimously rejected the results, suggesting flaws in either the equipment or its reading. The older students were also surprised by the results but were not so critical of the findings. Most did not reject the experiment, but they also did not accept a result that did not seem logical, that is, the conservation of the electrical fluid in its material form and exhaustion in its energy form. At that point existing student conceptions were simply inadequate to deal with the anomaly presented by the experiment.

To overcome this "epistemological obstacle," Joshua and Dupin (1987) had the teachers employ a "modeling analogy," an analogy operating as a thought experiment. They presented a diagram of a train without a locomotive that operates on a closed-track loop. Workers in a station (the battery) permanently push on train cars going past them, maintaining the movement by tiring their muscles. In their discussion the teachers tried to establish connections between the analogy and the "without loss" conception. The older students gradually began to grasp the analogy whereas the younger children grasped only the connection between the battery and the workers with the remaining connections, such as current-and-train and wires-and-tracks, introduced by the teachers. Joshua and Dupin found that the doubts and criticisms of students in both classes decreased immediately once it was accepted that the battery wears out but the current is the same along the circuit.

Students then became interested in testing the limits of the analogy. They wanted to know what would happen if the tracks were cut. Joshua and Dupin (1987) reported that the students hypothesized, based on the analogy and contrary to their normal experience, that the bulb would stay on temporarily like a train-car derailment. Clearly they were trying out the new metaphor (model) and correcting its implications with thought experiments and actual activities.

Joshua and Dupin (1987) concluded that the students' incorrect conceptions (from the point of view of physics) were, nevertheless, clearly used as a rational basis for their reasoning and evaluative behavior. Implicitly illustrating Shulman's (1986; 1987) notions of what should be included in teachers' pedagogical content knowledge, Joshua and Dupin argued that for instruction to be effective it must take into account and counteract the natural conceptions that students have, conceptions that have a great capacity for logical, if incorrect, adaptation to experience. In short, students do try to account for new experience using their existing schemas, and only if faced with an anomaly and a new way of conceiving of the anomaly, something very much like a metaphor, can they acquire radically new knowledge.

What we believe these examples illustrate is the kind of convergence of thought and activity that can lead through a succession of iterations from a given way of conceiving a situation to a radically different way of conceiving it. In most cases of learning, bringing to bear thought and action in their ordinary literal guises is all that is necessary to resolve the problematic situation. The kind of learning that goes on in such cases is what we have called ordinary learning. It is primarily the utilization of existing cognitive structures to deal with our experience. In other cases involving the use of a metaphor that may be comparative from the point of view of the student, the process is only slightly more complicated. The larger cognitive structure in terms of which the implicit comparison makes sense is already possessed by the student and is straightforwardly brought to bear and the similarities noted. This may be what was going on, for example, as the French students rejected the single-wire conception during the class discussions. In cases like the frame of reference example and the final use of the train analogy in the electricity case, however, neither ordinary learning nor a simple extension of cognitive frameworks allows the student to deal with the problematic situation. In such cases, a change of cognitive structure, or as we have called it, the acquisition of radically new knowledge, is necessary.

The continuum briefly sketched above, from ordinary learning to understanding comparative metaphors to the structural changes consequent on construing an interactive metaphor (probably with a number of other steps between), is very important. The continuum illustrates that one need not be consciously aware of anything so esoteric as metaphors or the need for radical change in one's cognitive structure. In this sense, the process of construing a metaphor is, as Searle (this volume) says, a natural extension of ordinary thought and activity. Educationally, we can start with what we know, and by an iteration of triangulations of thought and activity on our experience, end up with radically new knowledge.

Let us now try to analyze this process of acquiring radically new knowledge by means of triangulation on the world. We call the first component of the process the "anomaly step." This consists subjectively of the student's perception of the situation as problematic enough to require a minimal amount of cognitive activity. Objectively, the activity will need to be of a sufficient magnitude to require a change in cognitive structure, although as we have noted, the student need not be aware of this. During the students' initial encounter with the electricity example, they were totally unaware that the result would require a radical restructuring of their schemata.

Assuming, then, that attempts at assimilating the problematic situation to ordinary cognitive structures have failed, or would not work, and there really is an anomaly in the technical sense of a problem requiring a change of cognitive structure, the second step, which we shall call "providing a metaphor" begins. In the typical educational situation the most important source of an alternative classification for the student is the metaphor provided by the textbook or teacher. Yet because the schema suggested by the metaphor has not yet been applied by the student to the material to be learned, the learning process will necessarily be interactive for the student. The metaphor is a guide in that it essentially says, "Look at and deal with this new situation as if it were like one you already know about." Thus, the second step in the process of understanding a metaphor is conceiving of possible variant classifications as if they were like what is already known, so as to create new class-inclusion relations in Glucksberg and Keysar's (1990; this volume) sense.

The third step in the process is actually acting in the world and observing the results. An interactive metaphor is not going to succeed unless activity takes place. The activity is guided by the metaphor. On the first trial, one can conceive of the activity taking place as if the metaphor were literally true. Recall the "train derailment" hypothesis in Joshua and Dupin (1987). One behaves in the new area as one would have behaved in the area in which the metaphor is literally true. The point of the metaphorically suggested activity is to see if it will remove the anomaly. Does the teacher respond positively to the students' papers, questions, and examination answers? Do experiments turn out as predicted? Do thought experiments make sense? If not, do the responses indicate that the activity was close?

Notice that each of the steps thus far mentioned – recognizing an anomaly, conceiving the problematic situation as if the metaphor were literally true of it, and acting on the situation in those terms – provides a triangulation on the problematic situation. The anomaly step focuses on the situation in terms of the existing framework and characterizes the situation in existing framework terms. The metaphor suggests a new characterization of the situation, and activity in the situation provides a third perspective. Of course, some of the steps may be combined, as when a good metaphor creates the anomaly because it is literally false and simultaneously creates a new characterization that can guide subsequent activity.

The fourth step in construing an educational metaphor is the correction of the activity. Typically, the first activity carried out in terms of the metaphor's suggested conceptualization will not be quite right; yet, from the point of view of the anomaly, it will show promise. Much of the problem in the electricity case in Joshua and Dupin (1987) was removed once the students could see how something could wear out, the workers' muscles, while something else could remain the same, the train cars traveling around the track. At the same time more had to be done, especially with the younger students.

The teacher, typically, will provide such a correction, and a new activity – close to, but slightly different from, the original – will be attempted. The corrected activity provides a triangulation of the problematic situation and can be compared to the original metaphorical conception, beginning to show in what sense the ultimately correct conceptualization will differ from and in what sense it will be the same as the initial metaphorically suggested conceptualization. The corrected activity also shows the extent to which the anomaly is being removed by the corrected activity and its evolving conceptualization. It is essentially the iterative process of triangulation of conceptualization and activity, powered by the perception of remaining anomaly, that enables the students gradually to change conceptual schemes to accommodate totally new experiences. And it is the reaching of a final equilibrium of conceptualization and activity that is the test of the success of the metaphor, not whether we can explain its meaning (R. M. Miller, 1976).

The same steps are present when one considers metaphor from the external point of view of the teacher, but they look somewhat different. The teacher must pay special attention to both the initial intelligibility to the student of the metaphor and the appropriateness of activity for triangulation on the new material. The teacher must also consider the ecology in which corrections leading ultimately to a reflective equilibrium in the student take place. For in triangulating on the new material, the student will stop when conception and activity have combined to remove the anomaly. Recall that among the students studied by Joshua and Dupin (1987) those who held the current-wearing-out conception were quite unwilling to have their theory tested. They thought they had removed all the problems through disproving the alternative clashing-current conception. There are equilibria that do not match the collective understanding the teacher is trying to impart, and those are the ones that must be avoided. They tend to be the typical mistakes made by students in any given subject and were referred to above in describing Shulman's (1986; 1987) discussion of pedagogical content knowledge. Probably the best way, in general, to avoid these mistakes is to provide an ecology rich in opportunities to apply the student's newly established equilibrium of conceptualization and activity. For if the student's triangulation is just a bit off, it is more likely to become apparent to the teacher dealing with a variety of cases. This is what the teachers in Joshua and Dupin's study essentially did and it is also the strategy advocated by Spiro, Coulson, Feltovich, and Anderson (1988) in dealing with the misconceptions and oversimplifications of the medical students they studied.

The power of metaphor as one of the ways of intentionally bringing about conceptual change should now be apparent. The teacher presumably has a grasp of both the student's current ways of structuring his or her experience and the conceptual structure as it is found in the material to be taught. The teacher can, therefore, choose instructional metaphors that will serve to remove incipient anomalies for the student, as well as suggest initial conceptual guides to removing the anomalies. Furthermore, activities for the student can be chosen with a view to guiding the successive triangulations of thought and action toward the material to be learned. Students can learn something radically new without metaphors, but only if their variant conceptualizations serve the same function as metaphors – providing new ways to look at old material.

Returning for a moment to Kuhn (1974), the importance of his exemplars or concrete problem solutions is now apparent. For these are the *activities* that provide one of the crucial legs in the triangulation of conceptualization and activity on the subject area. Such problem solutions are indeed how the science student learns to deploy the disciplinary matrix in dealing with the world. The four-step process we have outlined of anomaly, metaphor, activity, and correction can be seen as explicating Kuhn's ostensive definition as an activity in which the student must *construct* the experience to which the definition is to apply. At the same time, if the process of learning a new paradigm is at all like what we have described as the process of a student coming to change conceptual frameworks through the operation of interactive metaphor, then the process of paradigm shift is both intelligible and intelligent. It is intelligible as an iteration of triangulations of thought and action on the world. It is intelligent in that it proceeds *from* the rules of reasonableness currently held by the scientist/student at any point in the historical process.

How are metaphors used in education?

Teachers' anecdotal data support Petrie's original and our continued contention that teachers can use metaphors to bring about structural changes in the cognitive apparatus of students. They also suggest that metaphors can be employed to promote changes in the affective characteristics of students who are learning unfamiliar subject matter which they perceive as irrelevant. Moreover, they indicate that *student* production of metaphors can result in important changes in students' cognitive structures and affective responses. What follows are, first, illustrations of how the components of anomaly, provision of metaphor, acting in the world, and correction of activity are carried out in the real world to effect cognitive change in students. Although the steps frequently overlap in the classroom, and divisions between one step and another are, to some extent, arbitrary. Next is an account of how teachers use metaphors to make unfamiliar material more interesting and relevant to students. Last are indications of how teachers assist students to produce metaphors and descriptions of the kinds of changes in knowledge and meaning that are brought about through metaphor production.

Cognitive change

The use of metaphors and analogies has been reported in the teaching of major subject areas such as biology, business, chemistry, geometry, literature, physics, political theory, psychology, and statistics. Teachers use metaphors to teach concepts that students ordinarily find difficult to learn through factual presentations because the concepts are unfamiliar or complex (Biermann, 1988b; D. B. Miller, 1988; Zegers, 1983). The concepts may be derived from concrete experiences that the students have not had or they may describe abstract realms where direct sensory experience is not possible. For some students, abstract, nonvisual knowledge may be a radically new *type* of knowledge to learn, a type of knowledge they may be unprepared to learn (DiGiovanna, 1987; Garde, 1987; Licata, 1988). Although an occasional analogy may be described as appropriate for middle school students (Allen & Burlbaw, 1987), metaphors are most often used in high schools and colleges. Students at these levels are frequently expected to rather rapidly learn unfamiliar, abstract, and complex concepts, and teachers are more likely to find that conventional methods – examples, arguments, and the drawing of inferences – are insufficient.

Teachers become highly proficient at producing and providing metaphors. DiGiovanna (1987), for example, presented suggestions for other teachers in selecting and using analogies. Like DiGiovanna, teachers are careful to draw vehicles from domains of knowledge that the students have already acquired, especially from important and familiar aspects of students' lives such as school, sports, social relationships, food, and money (Best, 1984; Licata, 1988; Marshall, 1984; Poskozim, Wazorick, Tiempetpaisal, & Poskozim, 1986). Best stated that she had identified domains of knowledge from which to draw analogies for various types of concepts related to political theory. Furthermore, she reported routinely viewing aspects of everyday activity as vehicles for her subject matter. "The technique can be learned. The more that I use it, the easier it gets. Now I see metaphors for my subject matter everywhere I look" (p. 168).

Teachers provide metaphors within contexts that support comprehension. They ensure that students are familiar with the vehicle or direct attention to aspects of the vehicle that students are to use to structure new information (Allen & Burlbaw, 1987; Whitman, 1975). Teachers assist students to visualize metaphors and analogies by describing the vehicle in some detail and directing students to imagine the topic as that situation (Biermann, 1988a; Garde, 1987; Last, 1983). Additionally, teachers present analogies through diagrams, demonstrations with concrete objects, or student participation in actively representing the metaphor (Ball, 1987; Bonneau, 1987; Kangas, 1988; Kolb & Kolb, 1987/88). The provision of a metaphor can be an extended and dramatic affair. D. B. Miller (1988) taught the concept of the interrelationship between genes and experience in the development of organic structure and behavior using the model of a cooking demonstration. The demonstration involved flour (the genetic base), different cooking methods (experimental factors), and different food items (the developmental outcomes).

Teachers typically direct student activity and further guide student thinking. They encourage their students to discuss the metaphor (Cavese, 1976; DiGiovanna, 1987; Garde, 1986), develop examples and solve problems based on the metaphor (Laque, 1978), apply the metaphor in new situations (Polyson & Blick, 1985), or attempt to extend the metaphor past the point where it begins to break down (Marshall, 1984). Teachers may require students to examine limitations of analogies to encourage exploration of the new concept (Licata, 1988), ensure that students will not later be misled by the analogy (Biermann, 1988a), or provide the teacher with feedback on whether the analogy and the related concept have been understood (Webb, 1985).

Correction of activity can occur throughout instruction. Teachers determine whether a given metaphor is being understood based on students' questions, arguments, applications, and various affective responses (Best, 1984; DiGiovanna, 1987; Polyson & Blick, 1985). The extended explanations and demonstrations provide ongoing opportunities for students to compare their construals of the metaphor to that of the teacher and correct accordingly. Students who attend to the remarks of classmates may also compare their own characterizations to those of their peers, and, depending on the responses of others, either maintain their own construals or bring theirs in line with those of the others.

Teachers' use of conferences and professional journals to communicate their successful employment of metaphors points to the development of an area of pedagogical content knowledge. Since 1980, for example, *The Journal of Chemical Education* has featured a collection of applications and analogies designed to assist students understand difficult concepts. The reports also suggest that teachers often perceive the use of metaphors as advisable, if not necessary, when presenting certain new concepts. With the exception of Joshua and Dupin (1987), noted above, empirical research on classroom use of metaphor has generally been directed toward demonstrating the effectiveness of metaphor-based or analogy-based instruction relative to conventional instruction (e.g., Burns & Okey, 1985; Evans, 1988), determining the effectiveness of various types of analogical learning aids (e.g., Bean, Searles, Singer, & Cowen, 1990), or testing competing theories of how and why metaphors are effective (e.g., Evans & Evans, 1989; Simons, 1984). (See Zeitoun, 1984, for a model for teaching scientific analogies that attempts to incorporate research on learning and instruction.) These studies indicate that metaphors aid in the acquisition of knowledge and that lessons employing metaphors or analogies are more effective than conventional methods. Empirical research is needed to identify situations in which metaphors are clearly necessary and how metaphors make possible the acquisition of new knowledge in classroom settings.

Metaphors as Motivators

Teachers have indicated that the learning of unfamiliar and abstract concepts is further complicated by affective characteristics of students. Students who are unaccustomed to learning abstract material may dislike dealing with it (Best, 1984), or students may simply not be interested in learning material they perceive as far from their own lives or as difficult (Polyson & Blick, 1985). Some students may have had experience in learning complex and abstract concepts in their own fields of study, but they may find such concepts in other domains uninteresting or irrelevant (Biermann, 1988b; DiGiovanna, 1987). Yet such teachers and others (Hirsch, 1973; Marshall, 1984) have noted that students become interested in learning difficult concepts that are presented through metaphor or analogy.

Haynes (1978) argued that the educational power of metaphors comes from their capacity to bridge the gap between the teachers' rational knowledge and the lack of knowledge of the student by drawing from the shared experiences of the students and teacher. The metaphors or common examples serve the cognitive function of shared rules, but, because they draw from the experiential base of the students, they also include aspects of knowledge that are vivid, emotive, and experiential. This often tacit knowledge assists students to understand new knowledge in their own terms and gives metaphor a dimension of meaningfulness.

The meaning that the vehicle has for the students may not necessarily have been considered during production, but it can have a positive impact on learning. To assist her students read a manometer, a U-shaped instrument for measuring difference between gas pressure and atmospheric pressure, Garde (1986) compared the mercury levels in the two sides of the tube with children on a seesaw. The lower mercury level was associated with the heavier child on the seesaw, the child who made the seesaw go down. Garde reported the effectiveness of the analogy in assisting students to learn to read the manometer, but she also observed that the reference to the seesaw elicited memories of more carefree days and the discussion of the weight of children held the high school students' attention because of their concern with body weight.

Metaphors also permit teachers to provide or transmit meaning for unfamiliar or abstract concepts. Marshall (1984), for example, reported the use of an anthropomorphism that involved telling students they would meet many new "friends" during the year to help them learn. Students initially found it artificial and somewhat embarrassing to refer to unit factors in chemistry as friends, but later in the year, when Marshall would become engrossed in presenting a new concept, it was the students who asked if what was being taught was a new friend, something helpful and nice to have around. Haynes (1978) stated that she transmits her values associated with philosophy by telling her students the study of philosophy is like an orange – requiring effort to remove the tough, bitter covering but sweet and nourishing once one is inside. Hirsch (1973) used behavioral and social phenomena strategically as vehicles for analogies to present physics concepts to liberal arts students who regarded science as boring.

Metaphors also enable teachers and students to share meaning. A metaphor used by Polyson and Blick (1985) to present concepts in experimental psychology to students who typically found such concepts boring and difficult operated by construing basketball as a psychology experiment. A basketball game was presented as a means of testing a hypothesis concerning which team is better in the various mental and psychomotor skills required by the game. The teachers used this analogy during the season when the intercollegiate basketball team at their university had a very successful year and was of great interest to both faculty and students. Although this metaphor clearly established the similarity of structure between the experimental method and rational aspects of basketball games, it would seem to have drawn from emotive aspects of knowledge such as those related to the uncertain outcomes and comparisons of performance that most likely were encompassed in the meaning of basketball games for students and teachers that year and, presumably, to an extent, in the meaning of the experimental method for the two psychologists.

Polyson and Blick's (1985) construal of a basketball game as a psychology experiment is an anomaly in that unlike the typical nominative metaphor the topic, basketball game, is the known situation and the vehicle, psychology experiment, is the unknown situation. Although the students knew nothing more about basketball games immediately after the provision of the metaphor than they did before it was presented, the statement probably did signal the students that they were going to learn about something in which they were interested.

This unusual metaphor can also be analyzed in terms of Glucksberg and Keysar's (1990; this volume) presentation of a metaphor as a class-inclusion statement. *Psychology experiment,* as the vehicle, is the prototype of a category that encompasses certain scientific testing of human performances, a concept that was probably as unfamiliar to the students as was psychology experiment. But whatever psychology experiment was to the students, it was no longer irrelevant because it had become a means of learning about something that they wanted to know about (Polyson & Blick, 1985). The metaphor established the similarity between basketball games and psychology experiments and from that point, the teacher's explanations could be directed toward clarifying just what the similarities were.

The metaphor enabled the development of a new schema for basketball games. During the year, students acquired substantially new knowledge about basketball games, and by the end of the year, they could view them in a very different way. Their concept included much of what they had already known about the games, but it now included the rational structure of psychology experiments as well. Basketball games perceived as psychology experiments would include knowledge related to rules, procedures, the players, and so on. Certain vivid and emotive properties of basketball games such as the high rate of physical energy, mass expression of emotion, and the gymnasium would have been selected out, but aspects of basketball games as highly interesting events involving competition and important but uncertain outcomes would have remained as properties of the topic.

The grouping of the topic and vehicle created similarity between them. This is because the similarity of grouped objects is both causal and derivative (Glucksberg & Keysar, 1990). The ground of the new category was provided by both the topic and vehicle specifying the category in which they had joint membership. As the prototype of the category to which the topic and vehicle belonged, psychology experiments exemplified basketball games and had those properties of basketball games that comprised the ground. Both category members included knowledge related to outcomes and comparing performance. In addition, basketball games had an experimental base from which to draw. This base most likely would have included a high level of such aspects of affect as interest, importance, and excitement. These aspects would have been correlated in the real world with outcomes and performances and would have thereby constituted part of the ground of the category established by the metaphor.

Although for a number of teachers (e.g., Ball, 1987; Garde, 1986) metaphors are useful simply because they enable the presentation of rational structures of concepts, teaching metaphors do have a dimension of meaningfulness or what Carroll and Thomas (1982) called "emotional tone" for teachers to draw on. Under Black's (this volume) view, teachers' metaphors are resonant with implications that are highly familiar and meaningful to students. The reports of teachers such as Best (1984), DiGiovanna (1987), and Marshall (1984) suggest that it may be necessary for teachers to make use of this aspect of metaphor when students perceive new concepts as irrelevant.

Student production of metaphors

Although metaphor *comprehension* may make it possible for students to acquire radically new knowledge, metaphor *production* requires some knowledge of the topic. Even though analogies can be produced based on nothing more than the recognition of some similarity in salient properties between a known system and a relatively unfamiliar system (Vosniadou, 1989), the production of metaphors and analogies is more typically used as an instructional device when students know enough about a situation to at least tentatively identify salient elements, conceptualize their relationships, and then search for a similar, familiar situation (e.g., Licata, 1988). Thus, production is used in the mastery rather than the initial acquisition of new concepts. Production of analogies has been employed to assist students to analyze literary works (McGonigal, 1988) and to apply social studies concepts (Wragg & Allen, 1983). Metaphor production can also be used in the acquisition of procedural knowledge. Skills in technical and expository writing have been taught through metaphor production (Catron, 1982; Wess, 1982) as have reading comprehension skills (Kuse & Kuse, 1986).

At this point, our concern is with the production and explication of metaphors for the purpose of communicating conceptual knowledge. Catron (1982) taught advanced science students to produce metaphors in writing for lay readers. His students could already write knowledgeably about scientific subject matter. Their task was to view reality from outside the concepts and theory-constitutive metaphors of their own fields and select concepts from everyday life onto which to map their knowledge.

Sunstein and P. M. Anderson (1989; see also P. M. Anderson & Sunstein, 1987) taught college freshmen to use metaphors to write about unfamiliar science topics. In representing a connection between their personal experiences and a scientific model these students learned writing skills and acquired scientific knowledge. In spite of the differences in the two sets of students and the complexity of their production tasks, the components of anomaly, provision of metaphor, activity, and correction were evident in the instruction described by their teachers.

Each of the components was presented in all four assignments described by Catron (1982). His students did not initially perceive themselves as lacking skills in transmitting their subject matter, and Catron generated disturbances to enable students to perceive the discrepancy between their use of jargon and the strategies needed to convey information to nonscientists. For example, in the first assignment, he required students to describe an unfamiliar object to a general reader, leading them to view artifacts as lay readers. Catron provided examples of metaphors and other figures of speech, often from scientific and technical writings, to demonstrate the technique of their creation or to illustrate their effectiveness. The discussion and writing exercises that ensued permitted students to act on the information and to have activity corrected.

Sunstein and P. M. Anderson's (1989) students perceived an anomaly of substantial magnitude in that they did not regard themselves as competent in writing or knowledgeable about science topics. During prewriting activities students read and analyzed essays by noted science writers and completed worksheets designed to assist them to investigate a topic and compare it to something else. These activities provided the students with examples of the use of metaphor and enabled them to produce a simile or analogy.

Students' early drafts consisted of extended analogies or similes. After students successively revised their work and identified an audience, Sunstein and P. M. Anderson (1989) encouraged them to think metaphorically about their subject matter. They were led to brainstorm, redraft, and shift from communicating new information to representing experience metaphorically. Writers drew more and more directly from their own experiences as they reconceptualized the topic as the vehicle. One student employed a "verb pass" which involved using verbs from the vehicle to describe the topic. Another presented facts following the order produced by the metaphor (P. M. Anderson & Sunstein, 1987). Metacognitive evaluations by students indicated greater scientific understanding and awareness of the production process.

Similarly, Wess (1982) taught students to use analogies to generate ideas for writing, to discover resemblances, and to see the world in a different way. Although Wess analyzed student writing and retrospective data in terms of a process of inquiry framework of preparation, incubation, illumination, and verification, the four components are evident. The anomaly was represented by Wess' presentation of the assignment. Provision of metaphor was accomplished by the presentation of one of his own analogical essays and a description of the creation process. Students' retrospective essays indicated an awareness of a disturbance followed by considerable activity directed toward determining a topic, an audience, and their roles as writers. Students reported that they regarded the assignment as very difficult and that they initially reviewed class examples, reflected, discussed possible topics with others, and engaged in brainstorming. Topics were identified during these activities or simply came to mind later during diverse and unrelated activities. Once a topic was identified and writing began, correction took place throughout the writing process. Although students wrote about subjects that were relatively familiar, many reported that they gained a great deal of new knowledge about the topic, and some reported affective changes as well. Student comments also indicated a sense of rightness about the analogies that they eventually explicated. Teacher verification provided external correction.

Production studies demonstrate that students can be taught to produce and explicate metaphors. They also indicate the importance of providing examples of metaphors and their use and of teaching the process of production, either through relatively structured activities or a portrayal of the process. The assignment creates the anomaly, and the examples and the information on the process suggest to the students a schema that incorporates information on what will correct the situation as well as the cognitive and behavioral acts that will result in a solution. This schema guides student production and is corrected through that activity.

These studies also demonstrate that production enables the acquisition of knowledge, even for students who are already knowledgeable about the topic. It also makes possible the integration of new knowledge with previous knowledge and thereby aids in thinking about the topic as a member of the same class as the vehicle. Production of metaphor supports both cognitive and affective changes. Sunstein and P. M. Anderson's (1989) data, in particular, indicate the importance of metaphor as a form of language in inducing these changes. The language form required their students to imagine the topic as if it were the vehicle and apparently led the students to draw directly from their experience. In short, students can learn to produce metaphors and thereby form new connections, view things in a different way, and generate explanations.

Conclusion

We have tried to sketch the educational centrality of metaphor for bridging the gap between old and new knowledge. Educational metaphors need to be viewed from two perspectives – that of the student and that of the teacher. From the latter standpoint, the metaphor may look like a concealed analogy, but what the teacher must never forget is that from the student's point of view, in those cases in which the metaphor really is to effect a cognitive change, it will *not* be merely an analogy.

Metaphors in education have traditionally been viewed as occasionally heuristically useful but essentially ornamental, and sometimes as downright pernicious. We have argued that metaphors are essential for learning in a number of ways. They may provide the most memorable ways of learning as well as critical affective aids to learning, and thus be our most efficient and effective tools. But further, they are epistemically necessary in that they seem to provide a basic way of passing from the well known to the unknown. Such a formulation is somewhat misleading, however. The crucial use of metaphor is in moving from one conceptual scheme with its associated way of knowing to *another* conceptual scheme with *its* associated way of knowing. Finally, and of suggestive importance for current philosophy of science, it seems that the activity phase of understanding metaphors has much in common with the use of exemplars – concrete problem solutions – in providing an alternative to immediate observation as one of the crucial legs for triangulating our theories and observations on the world.

One new feature in the recent literature is of particular interest to a discussion of the educational implications of metaphor. Metaphors appear to be construable as class-inclusion statements where the vehicle serves as both a prototypical exemplar of the category being predicated and as a name for that category. This feature shows how metaphors can be used to create an anomaly for the student, how they can provide a new view of the situation, and how they can be judged better or worse without having to speak of "metaphorical truth"; rather, one judges them as more or less successful in suggesting a fruitful new way of organizing our schemas.

Our positive account of how educational metaphors work contains four steps. First, an anomaly is "created" for the student, often through the fact that good teachers know where students tend to have problems with the material to be learned and also know the best pedagogical metaphors and the core theory-constitutive metaphors in the subject in question. Consequently, teachers often introduce new material with metaphors *assuming* that standard factual presentations would create an anomaly for the students. The metaphor provides one leg of a triangulation by suggesting a way of looking at new, unknown material as if it were old, known material. In addition to the new view, opportunity to be active with the new material is critical. This activity may be either directly experiential or may take the form of thought experiments. In either case the activity, the acquisition of nonlinguistic similarity relationships, is essential in providing the other leg for triangulating on the material to be learned. Corrections of initial triangulations and iterations of the whole process provide a mechanism whereby eventually the student's understanding of the material to be learned and his or her manner of acting on the material provide a triangulation that is significantly different from where the student began, and significantly like the triangulation enshrined in the disciplinary, collective understanding of the material, justifying our claim that the student has learned something radically new. The metaphor has been successful, not when we can say what it means, but when the triangulation allows the student to make judgments similar to those of experts in similar specific cases.

Empirical work on the use of educational metaphors in the past decade tends to confirm the centrality of metaphors in acquiring new knowledge as well as being consonant with the four-step analysis we have provided. This work has also suggested an increased importance for the affective characteristics of metaphor and has begun to examine the role of student-produced metaphors in knowledge acquisition by the students. Thus, understanding the process involved in construing metaphor is what makes intelligible the ability to learn something new while admitting we must always start with what and how we already know.

NOTE

This chapter is a revision of the one by Hugh Petrie that appeared in the first edition under the same title.

26

Learning without metaphor

THOMAS F. GREEN

In his chapter in the first edition of this collection, Petrie wishes to establish the claim that metaphor is "epistemologically necessary" for "learning something that is radically new." I believe that his attempt is unsuccessful. Seeing *that* it fails, however, is neither as difficult nor as interesting as seeing *why*. To discover the sources of his failure, we may begin with the following, rather complex, conditional. If one holds to a very narrow and limited conception of the reach of reason and inference in ordinary life, and if one is captured by the paradox of the *Meno* into believing that there is a particular mystery in understanding how anyone can learn something radically new, and if, finally, one discovers that metaphor is often pedagogically helpful in leading a student to bridge the gap between the known and the unknown, then one is likely to conclude that metaphor is "epistemologically necessary" to learning something radically new.

It seems to me that this sequence of thinking sets forth pretty well the path that Petrie follows. I wish to propose a counterpath, one that might reveal the reasons why Petrie believes that metaphor is epistemologically necessary and why we may believe that it is not. That path begins with a reconsideration of how large and inclusive is the role of reason in ordinary life. But more of that in a moment. We must first consider what it is that Petrie means by "learning something radically new."

Petrie, I understand, is referring to learning that has two important features. First, it is learning something that is not strictly implied by anything that we already know; and secondly, it is learning something that has the result of reorganizing what we do already know. So this is not any mere accretion of information that he has in mind. It is not, for example, like arriving at the doctor's office and learning that he is out. There may be mystery in that kind of learning; but if there is, it is not the mystery that he has in mind. Neither does he have in mind the sort of surprise that comes upon us from time to time when we discover a theorem in logic that, despite its everlasting presence, was once concealed to our consciousness and is now revealed. That is still a learning of something that is implied by what we know already. Nor, I believe, does Petrie have in mind that rare case of somebody learning something that is not entailed by *anything* that *anybody* knows. These are cases that might better be described as "discovery," "invention," "creation," or even "inspiration," but surely not as "learning." We would not say that Newton "learned" Newtonian mechanics in the same sense that students learn it now.

Petrie has in mind the experience of students who need to learn something that is not implied by anything that *they* may know, even though it is, no doubt, well understood by their teachers. Such learning is surely the most important kind that we try to bring about by teaching. If we cannot make that kind of learning understandable, then surely we cannot make the most lofty aims of pedagogy intelligible.

Petrie suggests that this kind of learning is quite common. I suspect that it is not. Consider carefully what it would mean to learn something that is not entailed by *anything* that one already knows. That, it seems to me, is a fairly rare occurrence in teaching, although when it does occur, it is terribly important. But add to that the second condition, namely, that learning something radically new is that kind of learning that has the consequence of reorganizing what we already know. This too, is an experience that we all can recognize. But, in my own memory at least, the most drastically reorganizing ideas or concepts have been those that are derivable from what I had known already. Indeed, that is where part of the power of such learning enters. It turns out, as students sometimes say, that "I knew it all along." When we put together these two features of learning something radically new – logical independence and the capacity to reorganize what is already known – then we have, it seems to me, an experience that is quite extraordinary. It rarely happens in the day-to-day affairs of teaching. But it is immensely important when it does occur. It seems to me that the paradigm case of learning something radically new in Petrie's sense would occur in the case of religious teaching. I do not see how one can come to possess religious knowledge as more than an agreeable possibility except through the use of metaphor. Yet this quite unusual occurrence is clearly not what Petrie has in mind, even though it could quite clearly be described as "learning something radically new."

But let us begin to construct the counterpath. My point is not that metaphor is never useful in leading a student to learn something radically new. My point is rather that all we need to understand how such learning occurs in the normal course of teaching, *and perhaps even to bring it about,* is contained in the standard logical categories of truth, argument, and inference. Reason has a much larger role in ordinary life and in everyday teaching than Petrie is willing to acknowledge. Consider the simple observation that even jokes, for the most part, are arguments. The very possibility of their existence rests upon the human capacity to reason. Comedians even use the language of arguments in discussing the comedic art. First, they say, you must establish the premise. Sometimes, having established the premise, and having waited for the hearer to draw his conclusion, the joke is then produced by introducing an entirely different conclusion, a conclusion no less valid, but for all that, unexpected. A man goes to the doctor and says, "Doctor, I am dead." The remark immediately suggests both diagnosis and treatment. The doctor replies, "You will agree, won't you, that dead men do not bleed?" "Of course." The doctor then pierces the patient's finger and draws blood. Whereupon the patient says, "I was wrong, doctor, dead men do bleed." The argument of the joke is so explicit that it can be formalized with ease. Its presence needs no comment.

But jokes do not always depend upon this possibility of drawing multiple inferences from a set of established premises. Sometimes the turn comes from the sudden exposure of a missing or ambiguous premise. A man enters a country inn to take a room for the night. He registers at the desk and turns to go upstairs, but the way is blocked by a pipsqueak of a dog barking furiously. The visitor turns to the innkeeper. "Does your dog bite?" "Certainly not!" And so the visitor turns to ascend the stairs and is promptly bitten. (Notice the anomaly. The dog bites; the dog does not bite.) "You told me your dog doesn't bite!" "Ah? yes! But that's not my dog." (Note the disappearance of the anomaly.) Here the joke has the structure of an enthymeme. The joke is delivered by revealing the missing premise.

I suppose that there are exceptions to this general rule that jokes are always arguments. But I would venture to guess that the exceptions are fewer than we might think. Even sight gags contain a kind of argument. There is a difference between seeing a person of slovenly demeanor and mean disposition slip on a banana peel and seeing a person dressed as a banker do the same. Different premises are established by dress and manner and thus different inferences are drawn by the person watching. Can anyone honestly suppose that Laurel and Hardy, those masters of the sight gag, paid no attention to their dress and to the character presented by their actions? I doubt it. Serious attention to such matters is essential in establishing the premises of the sight gag. Even one-liners have their argument. When a sociologist kisses his beloved does he multiply her face into a crowd? When philosophers make love do they advance a proposition? The inferences are multiple, and yet they are clearly present. The success of the joke depends upon which inferences are drawn from an established set of premises. I repeat: A joke is an argument.

What happens if the inferences of the joke are not negotiated? We have a perfectly familiar way of describing the result. We say, "I don't get it!" Recall, if you can, the sense of dismay and helplessness that we all experience on hearing that announcement. It is a kind of signal to make the argument of the joke explicit, yet we know, even before starting, that making it explicit is precisely what is sufficient to destroy the joke. If you don't "get it," then you cannot make the argument of the joke explicit. If you do "get it," then the argument of the joke does not need to be made explicit. And finally, if you do make the argument explicit, then there is no longer any joke "to get."

These observations about the arguments of jokes parallel almost exactly Petrie's remarks when he presents his strongest claims for the epistemological necessity of metaphor in learning something radically new. In his carefully developed example of how students might learn the concept of relative motion, he says, "Unless one presupposes that most of the work of grasping the metaphor has already occurred, the 'literal' definition may not do the trick at all." Unless the student has, in large measure, already "got it," the verbal definition will not help. And in another place, when discussing what is involved in learning to take up alternative points of view, he writes, "Indeed the students may say something like, 'Ah, it depends on how you look at it,' but the verbal formula is unlikely to be *what* it is that they have learned in learning to take up alternative points of view."

Notice the close parallel of these remarks of Petrie's to my own observations about the claim that a joke is an argument. My claim, recall, is that what Petrie says about the role of metaphor in learning something radically new can be said quite satisfactorily with sole reference to the categories of argument and inference. Part of the reason that the presence of arguments in jokes so often escapes our attention is that we all clearly recognize that *telling* a joke is by no means the same as giving an argument. *Telling* a joke is something like a speech act. Giving the argument of the joke is not. Giving the argument of the joke is so distant a thing from *telling* the joke that, in fact, we all recognize it is the quickest way to destroy the joke. Nonetheless, if we wish to *remember* a joke that we have heard and have "got," then the best way to do it is to remember the argument of the joke, that is, the premises and the conclusion. Likewise, when we learn what it means to think of relative motion, then *what* we have learned is not any verbal formula or definition. The definition is merely the summary of what we have already learned, but now put in a form that is orderly and systematic so that we can remember, and better use, what we have learned.

Now, there is something about this last point that seems to me correct, profound, and surprising. Petrie, early in his paper, reminds us of a view that we are all familiar with. It is the view that the function of metaphor in education is to make memorable, in a compact expression, what we have learned through literal, but more extended, language. This is the view that metaphor is a mnemonic or heuristic device. And surely, that is sometimes true. But now comes Petrie. And, if I understand him correctly, he says precisely the opposite. It is through the metaphor that we learn – in several stages – and the literal rendering of what we have learned, rather than metaphor, is the mnemonic device, the summary.

If I have represented him faithfully, then I believe that this insight of Petrie's is true and profoundly important for pedagogy. If I have not represented him faithfully, then I apologize, but still declare that he has taught something radically new to me about the practice of teaching. What I have learned, I may now express. What, as a teacher, I have often thought was to be learned by the students, I now see was only the mnemonic device; and what I thought sometimes was merely a mnemonic device, I now see was what really advanced learning. That confusion is like supposing that in telling the *argument* of a joke, I was telling the *joke*.

Yet, there is something about my comments on the argument of a joke that does not quite fit with Petrie's topic. What is that lack of fit? Petrie finds it necessary to use a rather extended and enlarged sense of the term "metaphor." He says that his meaning will include such things as models, similes, physical objects of certain sorts, and even theories. I mean to make no such enlargement of the concepts of arguments and inference. Jokes are arguments in a quite literal and standard sense of "arguments." If my meaning seems to involve an extended meaning of "argument" that is simply due to the profound difference between telling the joke and telling the argument of the joke. These indeed, are not the same. But there is this further peculiarity about jokes. In telling them, we rely heavily upon our capacity to establish the premises. That is possible only within a context of discourse in which references and allusions have a high probability of eliciting the same inferences in the minds of many hearers. Thus, the telling of jokes depends upon a shared experience and a generally predictable pattern of reasoning about the shared experience. There must, in short, be nothing conceptually new in the argument of a joke. Thus, it may seem, these observations about the arguments of jokes do not shed light on what it means to learn something radically new. Jokes do not take us beyond what we already know and what we are already disposed to conclude from what we know. They must rely heavily upon our shared common experience, and they go only most cautiously beyond those limits. Thus, to continue exploring my counterthesis, we need a fresh start from a different direction.

Let us consider the steps that Petrie actually describes. He says there are four. Metaphor figures in all four, but is predominant in only one. The four steps are: *anomaly, metaphor, action,* and *correction.* Let us begin with Petrie's account of this first step and see where the argument will lead. In only one place, as far as I can see, does he give us an example of what he means by an anomaly. And in that case – the example from the physics text – he is quite clear that the anomaly appears, *for the student,* not because the student's conception of the world is anomalous, but precisely because it is not. Because we can rely upon the student's conception of the world to produce a rather standard set of inferences, and to include a rather standard and widely accepted set of premises, therefore, it is possible for us to introduce a contradiction in the mind of the student. *And this contradiction* is, according to Petrie, what constitutes the anomaly. It is clearly not the metaphor that creates the anomaly. Nor is the anomaly created by the fact that the student's conceptualization of the world is anomalous. On the contrary, the introduction of the anomaly is accomplished by constructing an argument that rests upon a set of inferences that we believe students, in general, will make. It rests, therefore, upon our conviction that the students' conceptualizations of the world are not anomalous.

The point is that Petrie's account of anomalies is confusing. I am trying to take the step of action and correction by seeing what sorts of inferences we are, and are not, permitted to make on the basis of what he says. Let us see, then, what he actually describes as a case of learning something radically new. The curious fact is that his own illustration fits the counterthesis that I have been exploring more precisely than it fits his own.

Petrie describes the introduction of an anomaly. But what he describes, in fact, is a process by which we introduce an argument – or a pair of arguments – whose conclusion Petrie describes as a contradiction. In doing this, the teacher – the textbook writer – like the teller of jokes, takes care to see that the premises of the argument are premises established in the minds of the students. This is a chair, and it is at rest. This is a chair; it is on the surface of the earth; the earth is moving; therefore, the chair is moving. *Conclusion:* The chair is moving and the chair is at rest. Petrie says of this step that it "fairly clearly fits the idea of introducing an anomaly into the student's conceptual scheme."

On this point, I think that Petrie makes a mistake. We have not *introduced* an anomaly at all. Assuming that the students' beliefs are quite usual, and not anomalous in *that* sense, we seek to expose those premises that they are already disposed to accept and to draw those inferences that they are already disposed to make. Petrie describes the result as the introduction of a contradiction, saying, "Everyone probably finds a contradiction anomalous." I suggest that it is a pedagogical mistake to speak thus of *introducing* the contradiction. Rather we uncover it, we elicit it, and in speaking thus, we are already taking the view of the student. And that is what Petrie wants us to do. Only later, by his view, do we introduce something into the mind of the student.

But it is a mistake of another sort to suggest that in this step we elicit a contradiction. What is produced, in this case, is not a contradiction but a paradox. The difference may seem small, but it is enormously important, especially for our understanding of pedagogy. A contradiction is usually understood as a pair of propositions which, *as a minimum,* cannot both be true. The pedagogical purpose of exposing a contradiction might then be to lead the student to reject one or the other side of the contradiction. There is a place for such a thing in teaching. But that is not the purpose here at all.

A paradox, in contrast to a contradiction, is produced by the juxtaposition of a pair of propositions that *appear* to be contradictory, but which are, in fact, both true. Clearly, what is wanted in Petrie's example is not the description of the anomaly as a contradiction, but its description as a paradox. What we want is to lead the student to see a way of holding to the truth of *both* propositions about the chair – that it is in motion, and that it is at rest – without thinking they are in opposition. The teacher who follows Petrie's account on this point will make a substantial mistake in pedagogy.

The tension that the student experiences, and that Petrie speaks of, is not then created by a metaphor. Rather it is created by an argument, or series of arguments, that establish a paradox in the mind of the student on the basis of premises that he already accepts. What is needed to remove that tension is the introduction of some premise that will permit the student to hold on to both sides of the paradox as true. Introducing that premise is what Petrie describes as "solving the anomaly." If we want students to learn something radically new, then what we must do, according to Petrie's illustration, is to cast about for the paradox from which the new concept, formulated as a premise, will provide an escape. First, we expose to the student a paradox implicit in what he already believes Then we show the student how to escape from it by introducing a fresh premise into the argument in the mind of the student. This last step may require metaphor as a kind of practical necessity or it may not. But it will certainly require something like Petrie's steps of test and correction. *What* the student must test are the inferences permitted by the escape from the paradox. *What* he must correct are mistaken inferences. Being able to make the correct inferences permitted by the escape from the paradox is precisely what we mean by having learned something radically new. When that happens, the student has learned, as Petrie puts it, "to make the same moves as the professor."

Introducing the premise needed to escape the paradox is the step that, I believe, Petrie wants to say *requires* metaphor. I can certainly understand and appreciate his inclination to that view. No doubt, such a step does require imagination on the part of the student. We may even say that it requires invention or discovery. Here we are with another person, "caught" as it were, in a paradox quite of his own making. Now we are asking him to find a way out, and unless there is something for us to do, we are quite helpless in offering any assistance. The problem is not that the task is ill-defined. On the contrary, it is quite well-defined by the paradox itself. One wants to find some way of maintaining both that the chair is in motion and that it is at rest, without these claims being in apparent contradiction. How are we to help anyone who is faced with such a difficult task to find the right way? How are we to help anyone to "get it"? About the best that we can do is to present a symbol, a model, a verbal formula of some kind, which the "drowning victim" can grab hold of and with which he can begin to reason – throw out a suggestion that he can grab to start the steps of testing and correction. Indeed, it seems that what is needed is an interactive metaphor, one that *creates* likenesses, comparisons, and aids in creating the inferences that are to be tested in the search for rescue.

But how can Petrie settle on the metaphor as the necessary step? I think it goes something like this. One of the conditions of the problem that Petrie sets is that the premise needed to escape the paradox must be something new. If it is not, then we do not have a case of learning something radically new. It follows that whatever we do to bring about the rescue must be something so new *to the student,* so much a fresh addition to his understanding of the world, that it will have some of the features of a metaphor. Even though the idea of relative motion is old hat to us, it is not to the student who is captured by the paradox. It turns out then that *anything* that works will have some of the features of metaphor, whether it is a symbol, or a statement, or a physical model, or whatever. If it works, then it must be new to the student, not derivable from what the student knows already, and it must create the needed similarities to permit the reasoning to begin that constitutes the steps of testing and correction.

It turns out then that the *necessity* of metaphor flows from the terms of the problem that Petrie sets. It is simply analytic that *anything* that works *must* have the properties of an interactive metaphor, because the properties of interactive metaphor are simply defined as those that work in the effort to effect rescue from the paradox. Now Petrie knows very well that there are, in fact, many things other than metaphor, in the normal sense of "metaphor," that will work, and so he finds it necessary to his view that the concept of "metaphor" be extended to include them. I suspect that whatever device of rescue we may find successful, Petrie will expand his list to include it. It turns out that anything that works to effect rescue from the paradox will be included as metaphor. This, I believe, is how he develops the view that metaphor is epistemologically necessary for learning something radically new.

But of course, there are other ways of introducing to the student the premise needed to escape the paradox. We can, for example, cast about for *other* experiences on which to base *other* premises in the mind of the student, from which the testing and correction of inferences can begin. *And this is precisely what the textbook writers in Petrie's example do.* They ask the students, "Have you ever been in a car, a bus, or a train and felt that the vehicle was moving when it was not moving? If so, what happened to cause the feeling of movement?" This is a move that is precisely of the same order as the moves made in the lesson to establish the premises of the arguments producing the paradox. Petrie describes this step in the text as a "fairly difficult extension of the concept." But that is his account. My own is that this step is an effort to find the premise already established in the mind of the student, from which reasoning may begin to test a possible escape from the paradox. It still requires imagination on the part of the student, and perhaps even a kind of invention. But I see no reason to say that there is here any metaphor involved.

Petrie's presentation is full of excellent advice to anyone who will take his teaching seriously. It is full of good advice to writers and students also. Indeed, on the conduct of teaching, Petrie's presentation contains more wisdom than I have seen in any similar work for many years. I believe, however, that we may accept that advice, and even cherish it, without accepting any of the account of metaphor in learning that goes with it.

For example, Petrie says that he has *shown* that "an anomaly will *be* an anomaly only from the standpoint of a conceptual scheme." Now, I think that what he says here is true in a quite limited sense, but that he has not *shown* it to be true in any sense. The claim that the chair is in motion and that it is at rest is a paradox in *any* conceptual scheme, though it is true that it is not *paradoxical* except to some people. What Petrie wants us to grasp is that we who are teachers know the way out, and that what we must do to be effective teachers is to make sure that we present the paradox, or develop it in teaching, so that it will indeed have the force of paradox to the students, and even so that once again it may strike *us* as paradoxical. That requires that we forget, for the moment, that we as teachers know the way out. But this need, though extremely important to point out, is also quite understandable from the perspective of the conventional categories of argument and inference. It is also understandable from the requirements of telling jokes. The premises must be established in the minds of the hearers. We cannot expect "in jokes" to be successful when told to an "out group." But that is only because the premises of the argument of the joke cannot be established in such a group. It is good advice to both humorists and teachers to keep that fact in mind.

There is, of course, in both teaching and learning, such a thing as the exercise of imagination. I have already suggested that in introducing to the student the premise that he needs to escape the paradox, something even like discovery and invention is called for. This element is an essential requirement that must be acknowledged in any theory of pedagogy.

I have students, for example, who are so "literal-minded" and "empirically biased" by their studies that they seem unable to entertain imaginary circumstances that would reveal important truths to them, because they see such imaginary circumstances only as patently contrary to well-known fact. Sometimes, I find that metaphor, even the effort to revive dead metaphors, is helpful in overcoming this difficulty. Whenever I encounter it, it always strikes me as something particularly odd. It seems a strange kind of incapacity to entertain counterfactual conditionals. Suppose we lived in a world where there was no work at all. What would it be like? How would we, as humans, be different creatures if there were no death and no birth in the world? What would be missing from the world if we were missing the capacity for memory? Yet, it usually happens that students who have difficulty entertaining such questions read science fiction and have no similar problem in grasping what their friends may mean when they say, "If today were Saturday, I would be swimming."

The "thought experiment" that Petrie describes is a similar exercise. "How would the chair appear, if I were on the moon?" He points out that the thought experiment, that is, the capacity to entertain a counterfactual conditional, may not work. I agree. If it does not work, then one must find another way to establish the premise needed to generate the paradox. But what really is the difference between, "If I were on the moon, then . . . " and "If today were Saturday, then . . . "? Why is the imagination free always to consider the one, but not the other?

I suspect that it is due to something peculiar in the classroom setting, something there that tends to inhibit the "epistemic conditions" of learning something radically new. After all, the role of the teacher is a peculiarly authoritative one. Both student and teacher share the belief that the teacher knows the way out of the paradox, even though the students do not. And furthermore, what is wanted is to "get" the way out. So the tendency of the teacher is to forget the necessity of exploiting the premises needed and already implicitly present in the mind of the student. And the student is likely to be impatient, knowing that after all, it is not the premises that are important. It is "the way out" that counts.

Perhaps in this way of viewing the matter, we have a description of what often happens with both bad students and bad teachers. They omit the step that requires the exercise of imagination and forge on to what is to be understood literally as true. What both leave out of the process is thinking. Truth passes from the professor's notes to the student's notes without going through the head of either. Perhaps that is why, as we all know, students from time to time are able to identify the teacher that they admire and why they are so often just those teachers who, as the students say, "make them think."

Petrie has described what is needed to "make them think." I accept his advice. What he has not described is any epistemological necessity for metaphor. Rather he has been able to help us see how metaphor might be useful sometimes in that essential step of learning that I have described as "exercising imagination," or entertaining the counterfactual conditional, or "getting" the premise needed to escape the paradox.

In short, I believe that what Petrie has taught us about learning something radically new is quite understandable through traditional concepts of argument and inference. Learning something radically new is quite understandable – as understandable as it can be – without the introduction of metaphor at all. Metaphors are nice; sometimes they are needed; oftentimes they are useful; but epistemologically necessary they are not. If there is any setting in which metaphors come closest to being absolutely indispensable, it would be, I believe, in those settings where they are used by religious teachers. But that is another topic entirely.

Still, there may be something missing in this quite traditional and conventional account that I have given. I still do not know how they "get it." But here Petrie and I are on equal ground. If either of us needs an account of "getting it," then both of us do. He does not explain how anyone "gets the metaphor." But neither can I explain how anyone "gets the joke," or "gets the parable," or "gets" the premise needed to escape the clutches of paradox. Perhaps, after all, it turns out on this point that the best we can do is to say there are those who have eyes to see and ears to hear, who are gifted, inspired, talented, or inventive. And, of course, all this is true. There are such people. Petrie is one of them. But the fact that we may have to rest at this point, and the fact that some do not "get it" is no excuse for sloppy, slovenly, or unskillful teaching, anymore than it is an excuse for telling jokes badly. Petrie has described such skillful teaching, even though, it seems to me, he has not described the role of metaphor in learning something radically new. Perhaps, on the other hand, my conclusion should be more modest. It does not seem to me, that Petrie, by his metaphors, has described the role of metaphor in learning any better than I have without them.

27

*Educational uses of metaphor

THOMAS G. STICHT

As educators, the goal of our inquiries into the nature of cognitive processes is to achieve an understanding of these processes that can be put to use in improving students' learning through improved educational practice. In Petrie and Oshlag's presentation the inquiry focuses on the improvement of educational practice by the more effective use of metaphor. Petrie and Oshlag discuss three topics: (1) the nature of metaphor (as "speech act" rather than "linguistic entity"); (2) the manner in which the metaphor "works" (by creating a cognitive anomaly in the listener); and (3) a prescription for the teacher's use of metaphor (first create an anomaly; next offer opportunity for the student to actively discuss or otherwise become active with the new ideas addressed by the metaphor; and then provide corrective feedback, with several iterations if necessary, to get the student to understand the relationships between the knowledge domains addressed in the metaphor).

In this chapter, I shall follow Petrie and Oshlag's lead and comment on the nature and mechanism of action of metaphorical speech acts. I will make my comments within the context of a discussion of metaphor as a tool for communication and thought. Evidence will be presented to suggest that children and marginally literate adults who lack skills in analytical thinking can be taught aspects of these skills in relatively brief training periods, and that such training can improve their ability to produce and comprehend metaphors. This discussion extends Petrie and Oshlag's consideration of the educational use of metaphor to include the development of students' abilities to produce and comprehend metaphors as tools of communication and thought.

Metaphors as tools for communication

To understand the nature of metaphor as a speech act, we need to understand how metaphors serve as linguistic tools for overcoming certain cognitive limitations – limitations that we all have by virtue of the way we are built. As with other tools, metaphors provide a way of extending our capacities, in this case, for communication. Just as the tool function of the hammer is to extend the strength of the arm and the hardness of the fist, and just as the tool function of the telescope is to extend the range of the eye, so the tool function of the metaphor is to extend the capacity of active memory *using the medium of speech.*

The fact that speech is a fleeting, temporally linear means of communicating, coupled with the fact that, as human beings, we are limited in how much information we can maintain and process at any one time in active memory, means that as speakers we can always benefit from tools for efficiently bringing information into active memory, encoding it for communication, and recoding it, as listeners, in some memorable fashion. Metaphors appear to serve as one of a variety of special linguistic devices facilitating these activities. Other such devices for overcoming the ephemeral nature of speech include rhyme and rhythm, both of which apparently aid in the learning of speech, as in the memorizing of poetry. Ortony's (1975) discussion of metaphor elaborates on the role of metaphor as a tool for overcoming active memory limitations in the use of spoken language. Ortony discusses three different theses to explain how metaphor may facilitate learning: the *compactness thesis,* in which it is asserted that metaphors work by transferring chunks of experience from well-known to less well-known contexts; the *vividness thesis,* which maintains that metaphors permit and impress a more memorable learning due to the greater imagery or concreteness or vividness of the "full-blooded experience" conjured up by the metaphorical vehicle; and the *inexpressibility thesis,* in which it is noted that certain aspects of natural experience are never encoded in language and that metaphors carry with them the extra meanings never encoded in language.

Both the compactness and inexpressibility theses are compatible with the view that metaphor has its origins in the oral language and that it serves as a tool for cognitive economy by helping to transfer information in large chunks. More recent research underscores the importance of the "functional context" in learning and communicating (Lave, 1988; Sticht, Armstrong, Hickey, & Caylor, 1987). From this point of view, the compactness and inexpressibility theses suggest that metaphors work by efficiently providing a meaningful, functional context for acquiring new knowledge by means of old knowledge. Furthermore, the mnemonic function of metaphor as expressed in Ortony's vividness thesis also points to the value of metaphor as a tool for producing durable learning from unenduring speech.

The importance of metaphor as a tool for active memory may be demonstrated by the use of a key metaphor for bringing coherence to discourse. Here is an example from *Moby-Dick* (cited by Upton, 1973):

Queequeg and I were mildly employed weaving what is called a sword-mat, for an additional lashing to our boat. . . . As I kept passing and repassing the filling or woof of marline between the long yarns of the warp, using my own hand for the shuttle, and as Queequeg, standing sideways, ever and anon slid his heavy oaken sword between the threads, and idly looking off upon the water, carelessly and unthinkingly drove home every yarn: I say so strange a dreaminess did there then reign all over the ship and all over the sea, only broken by the intermitting dull sound of the sword, that it seemed as if this were the Loom of Time, and I myself were a shuttle mechanically weaving and weaving away at the Fates. There lay the fixed threads of the warp subject to but one single, ever returning, unchanging vibration, and that vibration merely enough to admit of the crosswise interblending of other threads with my own. This warp seemed necessity; and there, thought I, with my own hand I ply my own shuttle and weave my own destiny into these unalterable threads. Meantime, Queequeg's impulsive, indifferent sword sometimes hitting the woof slantingly, or crookedly, or strongly, or weakly, as the case may be; and by this difference in the concluding blow producing a corresponding contrast in the final aspect of the completed fabric; this savage's sword, thought I, which thus finally shapes and fashions both warp and woof; this easy, indifferent sword must be chance – aye, chance, free will, and necessity – no wise incompatible – all interweavingly working together. The straight warp of necessity, not to be swerved from its ultimate course – its every alternating vibration, indeed, only tending to that: free will still free to play her shuttle between given threads; and chance, though restrained in its play within the right lines of necessity, and sideways in its motions directed by free will, though thus prescribed to by both, chance by turns rules either, and has the last featuring blow at events.

In this example, two vivid chunks, or domains of knowledge, one dealing with weaving, the other with human destiny, are brought into juxtaposition in active memory and are discussed in an extended manner. In this case, the metaphor initiates an interactive mode of thought between the two domains that is distinctly different from the linear processing that precedes and follows the metaphor. This has the effect of producing a certain saliency in the discourse which makes it "stick together" or cohere. In this regard, the metaphor serves a similar function to various discourse structures which are currently being shown to affect comprehension and learning (for instance, Irwin, 1986).

The educational implications of metaphor as a tool for efficient communication are mentioned, in passing, by Petrie and Oshlag, but they do not elaborate on them. Instead, they focus on the use of metaphor as a tool of thought for creating new knowledge, and they concentrate on the teacher's use of metaphor, which induces considerable cognitive anomaly or puzzlement on the part of students.

However, when teachers use metaphors as efficient tools of communication it is *not desirable* to produce excessive puzzlement in students. Rather, the effective use of metaphor for producing a functional context for communication and learning requires the teachers to know that students possess the knowledge addressed in the metaphor. It also requires the teacher to have a technique for determining that this knowledge is recalled and structured according to the metaphor. Indeed, determining that students understand what is being said is a crucial problem in all teaching. But it is a particularly important consideration for metaphor, because the metaphor is itself frequently used as a way of trying to explain something else. This problem is compounded in schools with students from widely varying cultural backgrounds. It also takes on different dimensions with students of different ages. Young children are not so well equipped to comprehend the wide variety of metaphors that depend on the extra meaning addressed in Ortony's inexpressibility thesis (Winner, Rosenstiel, & Gardner, 1976).

Perhaps an example from a classic metaphor will help convey the importance of the teacher's understanding of students' knowledge for choosing metaphors that are efficient communication tools. Consider the well-known example, "The Lord is my shepherd." In this case, we can imagine that the psalmist who is trying to convey his feelings about the Lord faces crowds who are familiar with the ways of shepherds. They know that shepherds take care of sheep, they protect them, take them to good pastures, and so forth. The psalmist wonders how he can convey something about the Lord to his audience. So he thinks, "Well, the Lord takes care of me as a shepherd takes care of sheep." Without hesitation then, the psalmist tells the audience: "The Lord is *my* shepherd" and so on. In this case, he intends the audience to recognize that the Lord is someone who will take care of them, protect them, love them, and so forth. It is generally assumed that the context of the statement and the situation will guide the audience to the intended interpretation of the statement in an efficient manner. Additionally, it may be at least tacitly understood by the psalmist that the use of metaphor is likely to cause the audience to make inferences beyond those statements that can be literally expressed, as in Ortony's inexpressibility thesis, and hence a degree of affect may accompany the interpretation which would be lost if the psalmist simply listed the important features of the Lord.

The use of metaphor in written text is a particularly hazardous venture for both the teacher and the reader. Typically, the teacher as writer has only the most global notions of who the potential readers might be. Thus, when transferred to the written language, particularly in the mass production of textbooks, metaphors, like other more or less "context-bound" figures of speech, run the risk of leading to misunderstanding, because a large number of readers may not share the required experiences for receiving the large chunks of information to be transferred by the metaphors. Typically, the author is not available, and so readers cannot resolve ambiguities through question-and-answer techniques. This may well lead to many activities to reduce the feeling of anomaly, as Petrie and Oshlag suggest, but these activities reflect a lack of understanding, which might not occur if a metaphor which fitted the reader's experience were used. To the extent that the writer can better understand who the reader is, and what experiences the reader has had that are relevant to the material to be presented, the more skillfully the writer should be able to use metaphor to facilitate learning.

From the point of view of the student, the metaphor is something to be comprehended. To comprehend the metaphor, the student must first infer that the teacher means the student to shift from a mode of cognition in which ideas are being fitted to an existing knowledge structure, to a metaphorical mode in which the construction of a third knowledge structure consisting of the relations educed between the two domains referenced by the metaphor is accomplished.

Petrie and Oshlag identify, correctly I believe, one of the cues for inferring the need for metaphorical thinking: a cognitive anomaly created by a statement that does not fit well into the knowledge structure being developed in response to the language preceding the metaphor. The inference that metaphorical thinking is called for by the cognitive anomaly requires that the student rely on his or her understanding of the conventions of language use, which as Petrie and Oshlag also note, includes the notion that people try to make sensible utterances. If the student has no reason to think that the teacher is mistaken or confused, then the inference that sense should be made of what was said by applying metaphorical thinking may be appropriate.

In metaphorical thinking, the student must strive to find some basis for similarity between the two domains in the metaphor, the juxtaposition of which created the cognitive anomaly. Analysis of a traditional Aristotelian "proportional" metaphor (Upton, 1973, p. 76), in which two seemingly disparate domains are shown to be related to one another by virtue of some similarities in structure, function, or some derived relation, illustrates this type of thinking.

In this example, imagine an educator who states that "the teacher is the fertilizer of budding minds."[1] To comprehend the metaphor, it is necessary for the student to understand something about teachers, where they work, with whom, what they do; and it is necessary to understand something about fertilizers, where they work, with what, what they do. The domain of knowledge about teachers (Knowledge Domain I) and the domain of knowledge about fertilizers (Knowledge Domain II) must be searched to discover some basis for establishing a relation, or set of relations, between teachers and fertilizers, as required in the metaphor. This search leads to the discovery of the analogical relationship that the teacher is to children's minds ($A:B$) what fertilizer is to plants ($C:D$), that is, a stimulant to growth.

What the student now constructs in his or her mind is a knowledge structure that is not signaled at all in the language of the speaker, that is, "A teacher stimulates the growth of children's minds." This structure is a third structure consisting of relationship(s) understood to hold between the two given domains. Whether it is the precise knowledge structure the teacher had in mind cannot be certain to the student without additional information. However, if the teacher has carefully considered what it is the student is to learn about a topic, in this case teaching, and what domains of knowledge the student possesses that can be used to reason analogically, then communication should be fairly efficient, and the student's learning should be facilitated both through the mnemonic powers of metaphor and through engagement in the analytical thought processes involved in metaphorical thinking.

Metaphors as tools for thought

In the preceding section, metaphor was discussed as a tool for communication. It was noted that the metaphor is a linguistic device particularly well suited to overcoming problems involved in using an ephemeral medium like speech. Ortony's (1975) compactness thesis deals with metaphor as a means of efficiently transmitting large chunks of information, so that active memory processing is made more efficient, whereas his vividness thesis points to the role of metaphor as a tool for making information more memorable through the mnemonic powers of vivid images. Both the chunking and the mnemonic functions are illustrated by the passage of *Moby-Dick* which "coheres" a segment of prose into a vivid, recallable chunk.

When metaphor is considered as a tool for communication, attention is focused on its use for the exchange of information among speakers and listeners. The consideration of metaphor as a tool for thought, on the other hand, is concerned with the discovery of relationships between seemingly disparate domains and an exploration of the extent to which they can be related. For instance, the metaphor "the brain is a computer," discussed by others in this volume, is based on some similarities in structure and function that are easily identified between the domains of knowledge about brains and computers. The attempt to exhaustively enumerate the similarities and differences between these domains may lead, however, to the discovery of relationships or differences not thought of at the time the metaphor was formed. Here, Ortony's (1975) inexpressibility thesis seems relevant, because the continued consideration of a metaphor may lead to the recognition and explicit formulation of similarities and differences latent in a metaphor.

To understand the function of metaphor as a tool for thought, we have to distinguish between the tool functions of metaphors when they are used in an intuitive manner, and those tool functions involved in the use of metaphor as a "metacognitive" tool for creative problem solving (as discussed by Schön in this volume), for rhetorical purposes, for literary effect, or for the types of educational purposes with which Petrie and Oshlag are concerned.

It seems to me that the function of metaphor as a tool for thought, when used intuitively, is to extend our capacities for perceiving relationships in the perceptual domain to the conceiving of relationships in the conceptual domain. Let me explain this notion a bit.

In the domain of visual perception, the fact that we perceive both the onset and the offset of a light suggests that we react to stimulus change, that is, relative stimulus values, rather than to the stimulus energy per se. Similar examples hold in other sensory modalities. Perceptually, then, we are built to perceive relationally.

At the level of conception, examples, such as metaphor, simile, analogy, suggest that we are likely to be able to conceive only on a relative basis. That is, we can only know something in relation to our knowledge of something else (Sticht & Hickey, 1991, p. 82). Metaphor, as condensed simile, permits us to think about one thing or event being like (and in that regard related to) something else. From the speaker's point of view, the metaphor permits the use of language to express conceived relations in a less than exhaustively analyzed fashion, as Ortony's inexpressibility thesis suggests. In the act of placing conceptions into language, there is a clarification and stabilization of similarities which may have earlier been only vague conceptions. In the same way as a stereoscope brings a third dimension to what would otherwise have been a flat picture, the juxtaposition of two seemingly disparate domains of knowledge may produce a stable third domain made up of conceptual relationships between the first two. In both cases, the whole is greater than the sum of its parts – the parts are essentially incomplete descriptions.

From the listener's point of view, a metaphor provides both a cue to what kind of thinking should be done (a search for similarities of some sort), and two domains of knowledge, or relative conceptual positions, from which to conduct the mental search.

Although metaphors contain the ingredients for producing new knowledge domains from old ones, as Petrie and Oshlag indicate, there is no guarantee that students will be able to perform this task without considerable interaction with the teacher. Indeed, there is evidence that many adults may lack skill in forming categories into which objects or events may be sorted on the basis of some similarity. For instance, Figure 27.1 presents a task, having commonalities with metaphor production and comprehension, on which adults having low literacy skills perform poorly. In this task, the person studies Parts *A* and *B* to understand that the matrix of Part *B* is constructed from information in Part *A*. The person's task is then to study Part *C* and construct a matrix as Part *D*. Notice that this task, like the proportional metaphor discussed above, is an analogy problem of the sort *A*:*B*::*C*:*D*. The student's task is to discover by studying the *A*:*B* terms that

A

Types of Bars

Crowbars are used for moving timbers and rocks. They are available in 4 and 5 foot lengths with a diameter of 1 or 1-¼ inches. Pinch bars are from 12 to 36 inches long and are used for prying out spikes and nails. Pinch bar diameters range from ½ to 1 inch depending on their length. Wrecking bars have diameters of ½ to 1-⅛ inches and are available in lengths from 12 to 60 inches. They are used for the same things as crowbars. Pry bars are used for prying out gears and bushings. They are 16 inches long and have a diameter of 1-1/16 inches.

B

Type	Use	Length	Diameter
Crowbar	Moving timbers and rocks	4–5 feet	1 or 1-¼ inches
Pinch bar	Prying out spikes and nails	12–36 inches	½ to 1 inch
Wrecking bar	Moving timbers and rocks	12–60 inches	½ to 1-⅛ inch
Pry bar	Prying out gears and bushings	16 inches	1-1/16 inches

C

When You Are Lost – EAT PLANTS

If you are lost and out of food there are many types of plants that you can eat. Marsh marigolds are best during early spring. They are found in swamps and in streams. The leaves and stems are the only parts that you should eat. The leaves, stems, and flowers of the rock rose are all good to eat. You can find them along streams and lakes in early spring. Fireweed is also good to eat. It is usually found in burned-over areas during spring and summer. You can eat the leaves and flowers of the fireweed but not the stem. The roots of the mountain willow are also good to eat. Mountain willow is found in high mountains in early summer.

D

Figure 27.1. Analogical reasoning task similar to that involved in metaphorical thinking.

Table 27.1 *Types of errors made by literacy students from three levels of reading skill on the analogies task*

	Reading levels		
Errors	Less than 5 ($n = 10$)	5–8 ($n = 10$)	9 and greater ($n = 10$)
Format			
Did not use matrix	2	0	0
Column headings copied from sample	5	0	0
Missing headings	1	1	0
No headings	2	3	1
Table cells			
Copied sample cell information	5	0	0
Cell information missing:			
Types of plants	9	2	2
Locations of plants	8	3	3
Edible parts	9	4	2
Time of year	9	4	3
Information combined in cells	5	2	2

the column headings of Part *B* are superordinate category names for the elements contained in the column. In solving the *C:D* problem, the person must study *C*, tentatively identifying features of the things being referred to in the paragraph. The person must develop a hypothesis about a superordinate category label, check some more of the elements, confirm the hypothesized category label or generate a new one; and then, given appropriate category labels, sort elements in the paragraph into the appropriate columns of the matrix.

That this is a difficult task, highly related to literacy level, is indicated by data for adult men in a remedial literacy program who attempted the task. Men reading at the fourth grade level, or below, got less than 20 percent correct, those reading at the sixth grade level got nearly 50 percent correct, whereas men reading at the tenth grade level or higher got nearly 100 percent correct.

Table 27.1 presents an analysis of the types of errors made by men at these three different reading ability levels on the matrix task. Clearly, the problem of developing appropriate headings for matrix columns is highly related to the making of errors in sorting elements into cells, as evidenced by the data for men reading below the fifth grade level. The data for the better readers, however, those scoring at the ninth grade or higher, clearly indicate that even though proper column headings may be inferred from study of the passage, this does not necessarily guarantee that elements will be identified and sorted into cells correctly.

The results of six weeks of literacy training, in which students reading below the fifth grade level practiced producing classification matrices based on reading text passages, and then inferring superordinate categories, resulted in a 40 percent increase in the number of people getting 90 percent correct or better on the task of Figure 27.1. This training was very similar to that used by Silverman, Winner, and Gardner (1976) to teach sensitivity to style in art, and comprehension and production of metaphoric language, to preadolescents. It consisted essentially of group discussion in which students and teachers talked about picking out things in a text that in some respects are similar. Thus, various attributes that things can differ on, or resemble each other on, were discussed, and the need to develop semantic category labels was stressed.

The method of Silverman, Winner, and Gardner for teaching children to produce metaphors and the method for teaching literacy students to represent information in matrices, incorporated most of Petrie and Oshlag's prescription of the teacher's use of metaphor. In each case, a "cognitive anomaly" is established by posing a challenging task requiring problem solving. Opportunity is given for the students to become active with the problem, to try solutions, to learn about related matters, such as categorization skills and semantic categories, and to receive corrective feedback from the teacher or peers. Thus, Petrie and Oshlag's method for improving the educational utility of metaphor is not uniquely reserved for the use of metaphor. Though this weakens its value as a specific instructional methodology, it is of value to recognize that this generally used instructional method, which is a basic form of inquiry, may be fruitfully applied using metaphor. Empirical evidence regarding the value of this type of application is yet to be adduced.

The fact that preadolescents and marginally literate adults can so readily be taught certain of the analytical skills used in producing representation formats such as matrices and metaphors, suggests that what is being learned is not some fundamentally new, difficult mode of thinking. Rather, it appears that what is happening is that students are learning meta-cognitive skills of categorization applied to situations where the propensity for such activities is low. Cole and Scribner (1974) point out that one function of schooling is apparently to increase the range of situations in which people use the fundamental cognitive processes involved in classification; schooled persons seek relationships in a greater variety of situations by appealing to a broader range of ways in which things, events, and processes could be related.

As an intuitive tool for thought, metaphor embodies the principles of semantic growth identified by Slobin (1971): "New forms first express old functions, and new functions are first expressed by old forms" (p. 317). These principles appear to fit neatly into Piaget's processes of assimilation and accommodation, identified by Petrie and Oshlag as mechanisms underlying the function of metaphor in producing new knowledge from old. By Slobin's principles, children first acquire a conceptualization that they intend to express. Then they acquire the linguistic means of expressing it, the form. Soon they acquire a new function or conceptualization. Not yet having the form necessary to express this new function, children may use a simile or metaphor, as an old form of expression. The use of such figures of speech is reinforced because of their effectiveness in overcoming active-memory limitations.

When the use of metaphor is made explicit as a metacognitive tool for thought, then it is more likely to serve the process of accommodation when it is used intuitively to assimilate new functions by use of old forms. The training of analysis skills underlying the specifications of relations between semantic categories, as in the literacy and metaphor-training programs discussed, may facilitate the development of metacognitive skill in the use of metaphor to stimulate knowledge *invention* not simply knowledge *retention,* which is a major function for metaphor when communicating in the ephemeral medium of speech.

Metaphor as a tool for knowledge invention seems to underlie Black's concept of the "interactive" metaphor, as discussed by Petrie and Oshlag. It also seems to be the aim of Petrie and Oshlag's prescription for the teacher's use of metaphor. This assumes the analytical skills that I have discussed.

In Petrie and Oshlag's scheme, metaphor is used as a metacognitive tool by the teacher to produce a cognitive anomaly and to provide the potential for resolving the anomaly by use of the domains expressed in the metaphor. For the student, Petrie and Oshlag's paradigm calls for going beyond some superficial similarities between the domains to an extended consideration of the full ramifications of the metaphor. Often, considerable surprise may be experienced as the implications of a metaphor are understood, and an "accommodation" of thought may occur. Such surprise is not a unique feature of metaphor, however; it also occurs in the most "literal" languages, mathematics and formal logic, when a long argument reveals a surprising, though perfectly predictable, conclusion.

The metacognitive knowledge of how to manipulate ideas explicitly in metaphor so as to transform either one's own or another's knowledge into new knowledge makes metaphor a major tool for extending our capacities for analytical thought, at the same time changing us as tool users. Though the types of changes produced by the use of metaphor as a tool for thought may not yet be fully understood, it can be argued by analogy that just as the repeated use of a hammer may strengthen the arm, the repeated use of metaphors may strengthen the powers of analysis and synthesis. Also, much as the telescope may produce knowledge that changes our basic assumptions about ourselves and the nature of our universe, the use of metaphors may, as Petrie and Oshlag have argued, bring about basic changes in how we understand ourselves and the world around us.

NOTES

This chapter is a revised version of the one that appeared in the first edition under the same title. The ideas and opinions expressed herein are those of the author. Helpful comments on an earlier version of this chapter were received from Carl Frederiksen, Marcia Whiteman, and Joe Dominic.

1 I am indebted to Virginia Koehler for this insightful metaphor. It is recognized that the analysis of the metaphor given in the text is oversimplified and incomplete, for example, terms such as "budding mind" and "growth of children's minds" are themselves metaphorical. Although the appearance of metaphors within metaphors complicates metaphorical thinking, no new processes of thought seem to be implicated.

References

Abraham, W. (1975). *A linguistic approach to metaphor.* Lisse, Holland: Peter de Ridder Press.

Ackerman, B. (1981). Young children's understanding of a speaker's intentional use of a false utterance. *Developmental Psychology, 17,* 472–480.

Allen, M., & Burlbaw, L. (1987). Making meaning with a metaphor. *Social Education, 51,* 142–143.

Allison, G. T. (1969). Conceptual models and the Cuban missile crisis. *American Political Science Review, 63,* 689–717.

Anderson, C. C. (1964). The psychology of the metaphor. *Journal of Genetic Psychology, 105,* 53–73.

Anderson, J. R. (ed.). (1981). *Cognitive skills and their acquisition.* Hillsdale, NJ: Erlbaum.

Anderson, J. R., & Bower, G. H. (1973). *Human associative memory.* Washington, D.C.: Winston and Sons.

Anderson, P. M., & Sunstein, B. S. (1987). *Teaching the use of metaphor in science writing.* Paper presented at the 38th annual meeting of the conference on College Composition and Communication, Atlanta, GA. (ERIC Document Reproduction Service No. ED 281 204.)

Anderson, R. C. (1977). The notion of schemata and the educational enterprise: General discussion of the conference. In R. C. Anderson & R. J. Spiro (eds.), *Schooling and the acquisition of knowledge.* Hillsdale, NJ: Erlbaum.

Anderson, R. C., & Ortony, A. (1975). On putting apples into bottles: A problem of polysemy. *Cognitive Psychology, 7,* 167–180.

Aristotle. (1952a). *Rhetoric.* Translated by W. R. Roberts. In W. D. Ross (ed.), *The works of Aristotle* (vol. 11): *Rhetorica, de rhetorica ad Alexandrum, poetica.* Oxford: Clarendon Press.

(1952b). *Poetics*. Translated by I. Bywater. In W. D. Ross (ed.), *The works of Aristotle* (vol. 11): *Rhetorica, de rhetorica ad Alexandrum, poetica*. Oxford: Clarendon Press.

Arnheim, R. (1969). *Visual thinking*. Berkeley: University of California Press.

Asch, S. E. (1958). The metaphor: A psychological inquiry. In R. Tagiuri & L. Petrullo (eds.), *Person perception and interpersonal behavior*. Stanford, CA: Stanford University Press.

Asch, S. E., & Nerlove, H. (1960). The development of double function terms in children: An exploratory investigation. In B. Kaplan & S. Wapner (eds.), *Perspectives in psychological theory: Essays in honor of Heinz Werner*. New York: International Universities Press.

Asimov, I. (1965). *A short history of chemistry*. New York: Anchor.

Astington, J., Harris, P., & Olson, D. (eds.). (1988). *Developing theories of mind*. Cambridge University Press.

Auster, P. (ed.). (1984). *The Random House book of twentieth century French poetry*. New York: Random House.

Austin, J. L. (1961). Truth. In J. L. Austin, *Philosophical papers*. Oxford: Clarendon Press.

Bach, K., & Harnish, R. M. (1979). *Linguistic communication and speech acts*. Cambridge, MA: MIT Press.

Bain, A. (1888). *English composition and rhetoric*. New York: Appleton.

Ball, D. W. (1987). Another auto analogy: Rate-determining steps. *Journal of Chemical Education, 64*, 486–487.

Barsalou, L. (1983). Ad hoc categories. *Memory & Cognition, 11*, 211–227.

Bartlett, F. C. (1932). *Remembering*. Cambridge University Press.

Bayman, P., & Mayer, R. E. (1988). Using conceptual models to teach BASIC computer programming. *Journal of Educational Psychology, 80*, 291–298.

Bean, T. W., Searles, D., Singer, H., & Cowen, S. (1990). Learning concepts from biology text through pictorial analogies and an analogical study guide. *Journal of Educational Research, 83*, 233–237.

Beardsley, M. C. (1958). *Aesthetics: Problems in the philosophy of criticism*. New York: Harcourt Brace and Co.

(1962). The metaphorical twist. *Philosophy and Phenomenological Research, 22*, 293–307.

(1967). Metaphor. In P. Edwards (ed.), *Encyclopedia of philosophy* (vol. 5). New York: Macmillan.

Begg, I. (1972). Recall of meaningful phrases. *Journal of Verbal Learning and Verbal Behavior, 11*, 431–439.

Bellush, J., & Hausknecht, M. (eds.). (1967). *Urban renewal: People, politics and planning*. Garden City, NY: Doubleday Anchor.

Berger, P. L., & Luckmann, T. (1966). *Social construction of reality: A treatise in the sociology of knowledge*. Garden City, NY: Doubleday.

Berlyne, D. E. (1960). *Conflict, arousal and curiosity*. New York: McGraw-Hill.

Bertholet, M. (1887). *Collection des anciens alchimistes grecs*. Paris.

Best, J. A. (1984). Teaching political theory: Meaning through metaphor. *Improving College and University Teaching, 32*, 165–168.

Biermann, C. A. (1988a). Hot potatoes – high energy electrons: An analogy. *The American Biology Teacher, 50*, 451–452.

(1988b). The protein a cell built (and the house that Jack built). *The American Biology Teacher, 50,* 162–163.

Billow, R. M. (1975). A cognitive developmental study of metaphor comprehension. *Developmental Psychology, 11,* 415–423.

(1977). Metaphor. A review of the psychological literature. *Psychological Bulletin, 84,* 81–92.

Binkley, T. (1974). On the truth and probity of metaphor. *Journal of Aesthetics and Art Criticism, 33,* 171–180.

Black, M. (1962a). *Models and metaphors.* Ithaca, NY: Cornell University Press.

(1962b). Metaphor. In M. Black, *Models and metaphors.* Ithaca, NY: Cornell University Press.

(1962c). Models and archetypes. In M. Black, *Models and metaphors.* Ithaca, NY: Cornell University Press.

(1962d). Linguistic relativity: The views of Benjamin Lee Whorf. In M. Black, *Models and metaphors.* Ithaca, NY: Cornell University Press.

Block, N. (1977). Troubles with functionalism. In C. W. Savage (ed.), *Minnesota studies in the philosophy of science* (vol. 9). Minneapolis: University of Minnesota Press.

Block, N., & Fodor, J. A. (1972). What psychological states are not. *Philosophical Review, 81,* 159–181.

Blumer, H. (1969). *Symbolic interactionism; perspective and method.* Englewood Cliffs, NJ: Prentice-Hall.

Bobrow, D. G. (ed.). (1985). *Qualitative reasoning about physical systems.* Cambridge, MA: MIT Press.

Bonneau, M. C. (1987). Enthalpy and "Hot Wheels" – An analogy. *Journal of Chemical Education, 64,* 486–487.

Booth, W. (1974). *A rhetoric of irony.* Chicago: University of Chicago Press.

Bower, G. H., & Hilgard, E. R. (1981). *Theories of learning* (5th ed.). Englewood Cliffs, NJ: Prentice-Hall.

Bowerman, M. (1977). The acquisition of word meaning: An investigation of some current topics. In P. Johnson-Laird and P. Wason (eds.), *Thinking: Readings in cognitive science.* Cambridge University Press.

Boyd, R. (1973). Realism, underdetermination and a causal theory of evidence. *Nous, 8,* 1–12.

(1980). Materialism without reductionism: what physicalism does not entail. In N. Block (ed.), *Readings in philosophy of psychology* (vol. 1). Cambridge. MA: Harvard University Press.

(1982). Scientific realism and naturalistic epistemology. In P. D. Asquith & R. N. Giere (eds.), *PSA 1980* (vol. 2). E. Lansing, MI: Philosophy of Science Association.

(1983). On the current status of the issue of scientific realism. *Erkenntnis, 19,* 45–90.

(1985a). Lex Orendi est Lex Credendi. In P. M. Churchland & C. A. Hooker (eds.), *Images of science: Scientific realism versus constructive empiricism.* Chicago: University of Chicago Press.

(1985b). Observations, explanatory power, and simplicity. In P. Achinstein & O. Hannaway (eds.), *Observation, experiment, and hypothesis in modern physical science.* Cambridge, MA: MIT Press.

(1985c). The logician's dilemma. *Erkenntnis, 22,* 197–252.

(1988). How to be a moral realist. In G. S. McCord (ed.), *Moral realism.* Ithaca, NY: Cornell University Press.

(1989). What realism implies and what it does not. *Dialectica, 43,* 5–29.

(1990a). Realism, approximate truth and philosophical method. In W. Savage (ed.), *Minnesota studies in the philosophy of science* (vol. 14). Minneapolis: University of Minnesota Press.

(1990b). Realism, conventionality, and 'Realism About.' In G. Boolos (ed.), *Meaning and method.* Cambridge University Press.

(1991). Realism, anti-foundationalism and the enthusiasm for natural kinds. *Philosophical Studies, 61,* 127–148.

(1992). Realism, constructivism and philosophical method. In J. Earman (ed.), *Inference, explanation and other philosophical frustrations.* Los Angeles: University of California Press.

(in press). *Realism and scientific epistemology.* Cambridge University Press.

Boyle, R. (1690). *Of the great effecs of even languid and unheeded local motion.* London: S. Smith.

Boyle, R. R. (1954). The nature of metaphor. *Modern Schoolman, 31,* 257–280.

Brachman, J. R. (1983). What IS-A is and isn't: An analysis of taxonomic links in semantic networks. *Computer, 16,* 30–36.

Bransford, J. D., & McCarrell, N. W. (1974). A sketch of a cognitive approach to comprehension. In W. B. Weimer & D. S. Palmero (eds.), *Cognition and the symbolic processes.* Hillsdale, NJ: Erlbaum.

Breal, M. (1899). *Essai de sémantique.* Paris: Hachette.

Bredin, H. (1984). Metonymy. *Poetics Today, 5,* 45–48.

Bresnan, J. (1978). A realistic theory of transformation grammar. In M. Halle, J. Bresnan, & G. A. Miller (eds.), *Linguistic theory and psychological reality.* Cambridge, MA: MIT Press.

Brewer, W. F. (1975). Memory for ideas: Synonym substitution. *Memory & Cognition, 3,* 458–464.

(1989). The activation and acquisition of knowledge. In S. Vosniadou & A. Ortony (eds.), *Similarity and analogical reasoning.* Cambridge University Press.

Bronowski, J. (1978). *The common sense of science.* Cambridge, MA: Harvard University Press.

Brooks, C., & Warren, R. P. (1938). *Understanding poetry.* New York: Holt, Rinehart and Winston.

Brown, A. L. (1989). Analogical learning and transfer: What develops? In S. Vosniadou & A. Ortony (eds.), *Similarity and analogical reasoning.* Cambridge University Press.

Brown, R. (1958). *Words and things.* New York: Free Press.

Brown R. (1977). *A poetic for sociology: Toward a language of discussion for the human sciences.* Chicago: University of Chicago Press.

(1989). *Social science as civic discourse.* Chicago: University of Chicago Press.

Brown, R. H. (1976). Social theory as metaphor. *Theory and Society, 3,* 169–198.

Brown, S. J. (1927). *The world of imagery.* London: Kegan Paul, Trench, Trubner.

Bruner, J. S., Goodnow, J. J., & Austin, G. A. (1956). *A study of thinking.* New York: Wiley.

Bucci, W. (1984). Linking words and things: Basic processes and individual variation. *Cognition, 17,* 137–154.

Bucci, W., & Freedman, W. (1978). Language and hand: the dimension of referential competence. *Journal of Personality, 46,* 594–622.

Burge, T. (1986). Individualism and psychology. *Philosophical Review, 95,* 3–45.

Burke, K. (1942). *A grammar of motives.* Berkeley: University of California Press.
  (1953). *The philosophy of literary form: Studies in symbolic action.* Berkeley: University of California Press.

Burns, J. C., & Okey, J. R. (1985). *Effects of teacher use of analogies on achievement of high school biology students with varying levels of cognitive ability and prior knowledge.* Paper presented at the 58th annual meeting of the National Association for Research in Science Teaching, French Lick Springs, IN. (ERIC Document Reproduction Service No. ED 254 431.)

Burstein, M. H. (1983). *Concept formation by incremental analogical reasoning and debugging.* Paper presented at the international machine learning workshop. Monticello, IL.

Butterfield, H. (1965). *The origins of modern science* (rev. ed.). New York: Free Press.

Byerly, H. C., & Lazara, V. A. (1973). Realist foundations of measurement. *Philosophy of Science, 40,* 1–27.

Campbell, D. T. (1963). Social attitudes and other acquired behavioral dispositions. In S. Koch (ed.), *Psychology: A study of a science* (vol. 6). New York: McGraw-Hill.

Cardwell, D. S. L. (1965). Power technologies and the advance of science, 1700–1825. *Technology and Culture, 6,* 188–207.

Carey, S. (1985a). *Conceptual change in childhood.* Cambridge, MA: MIT/Bradford Press.
  (1985b). Are children fundamentally different kinds of thinkers and learners than adults? In S. F. Chipman, J. W. Segal, & R. Glaser (eds.), *Thinking and learning skills: Current research and open questions* (vol. 2). Hillsdale, NJ: Erlbaum.

Carnot, S. (1977). *Reflections on the motive power of fire.* Translated by R. H. Thurston. Gloucester, MA: Peter Smith. (Original work published 1824.)

Carroll, J. D., & Wish, M. (1974). Multidimensional perceptual models and measurement methods. In E. C. Carterette & M. P. Friedman (eds.), *Handbook of perception.* New York: Academic Press.

Carroll, J. M., & Thomas, J. C. (1982). Metaphor and cognitive representation of computing systems. *IEEE Transactions on Systems, Man and Cybernetics, 12,* 107–116.

Cassirer, E. (1946). *Language and myth.* New York: Dover.

Catron, D. M. (1982). *The creation of metaphor: A case for figurative language in technical writing classes.* Paper presented at the 33rd annual meeting of the Conference on College Composition and Communication. San Francisco, CA. (ERIC Document Reproduction Service No. ED 217 470.)

Cavell, S. (1976). *Must we mean what we say?* Cambridge University Press.

Cavendish, R. (1967). *The black arts.* New York: Capricorn Books.

Cavese, J. A. (1976). An analogue for the cell. *The American Biology Teacher, 38,* 108–109.

Chen, Z., & Daehler, M. W. (1989). Positive and negative transfer in analogical problem solving by 6-year-old children. *Cognitive Development, 4*, 327–344.

Cherry, C. (1966). *On human communication* (2d. ed.). Cambridge, MA: MIT Press.

Chi, M. T. H., Bassok, M., Lewis, M. W., Reimann, P., & Glaser, R. (1989). Self-explanations: How students study and use examples in learning to solve problems. *Cognitive Science, 13*, 145–182.

Chi, M. T. H., Feltovich, P. J., & Glaser, R. (1981). Categorization and representation of physics problems by experts and novices. *Cognitive Science, 5*, 121–151.

Chomsky, N. (1964). The logical basis of linguistic theory. In H. G. Lunt (ed.), *Proceedings of the ninth international congress of linguistics.* The Hague: Mouton.

(1965). *Aspects of the theory of syntax.* Cambridge, MA: MIT Press.

(1971). Deep structure, surface structure, and semantic interpretation. In D. D Steinberg & L. A. Jakobovits (eds.), *Semantics: An interdisciplinary reader in philosophy, linguistics, and psychology.* Cambridge University Press.

(1981). *Lectures on government and binding.* Dordrecht, Holland: Foris.

Chomsky, N., & Halle, M. (1968). *The sound pattern of English.* New York: Harper & Row.

Clark, E., & Clark, H. H. (1979). When nouns surface as verbs. *Language, 55*, 767–811.

Clark, H. H. (1973). Space, time, semantics and the child. In T. E. Moore (ed.), *Cognitive development and the acquisition of language.* New York: Academic Press.

(1983). Making sense of nonce sense. In G. B. Flores d'Arcais & R. Jarvella (eds.), *The process of understanding language.* New York: Wiley.

Clark, H. H., & Carlson, T. (1981). Context for comprehension. In J. Long & A. Baddeley (eds.), *Attention and performance* (vol. 9). Hillsdale, NJ: Erlbaum.

Clark, H. H., & Gerrig, R. (1983). Understanding old words with new meanings. *Journal of Verbal Learning and Verbal Behavior, 22*, 591–608.

(1984). On the pretense theory of irony. *Journal of Experimental Psychology: General, 113*, 121–126.

Clark, H. H., & Lucy, P. (1975). Understanding what is meant from what is said: A study in conversationally conveyed requests. *Journal of Verbal Learning and Verbal Behavior, 14*, 56–72.

Clark, H. H., & Marshall, C. (1981). Definite reference and mutual knowledge. In A. Joshi, B. Webber, & J. Sag (eds.), *Elements of discourse understanding.* Cambridge University Press.

Clarke, D. (1977). *The encyclopedia of how it works: From abacus to zoom lens.* New York: A and W Publishers.

Clement, C. A., & Gentner, D. (1991). Systematicity as a selection constraint in analogical mapping. *Cognitive Science, 5*, 121–151.

Clement, J. (1982). Students' preconceptions in introductory mechanics. *American Journal of Physics, 50*, 66–71.

Cohen, I. B. (1960). *The birth of a new physics.* Garden City, NJ: Doubleday Anchor.

Cohen, L. J. (1970). *The implications of induction.* London: Methuen.

(1971). Some remarks on Grice's views about the logical particles of natural language. In Y. Bar-Hillel (ed.), *Pragmatics of natural language.* New York: Humanities Press.

(1977a). Can the conversationalist hypothesis be defended? *Philosophical Studies, 31,* 81–90.

(1977b). *The probable and the provable.* Oxford: Clarendon Press.

(1985). A problem about ambiguity in truth-theoretical semantics. *Analysis, 45,* 129–134.

Cohen, L. J., & Margalit, A. (1972). The role of inductive reasoning in the interpretation of metaphor. In D. Davidson & G. Harman (eds.), *Semantics of natural language.* Dordrecht, Holland: D. Reidel.

Cohen, T. (1976). Notes on metaphor. *Journal of Aesthetics and Art Criticism, 34,* 249–259.

Cole, M., & Scribner, S. (1974). *Culture and thought.* New York: Wiley.

Collins, A. M., & Gentner, D. (1987). How people construct mental models. In D. Holland & N. Quinn (eds.), *Cultural models in language and thought.* Cambridge University Press.

Coulson, R. L., Feltovich, P. J., & Spiro, R. J. (1986). *Foundations of a misunderstanding of the ultrastructural basis of myocardial failure: A compounding of oversimplifications.* Prepublication manuscript.

Crisafi, M., & Brown, A. L. (1983). *Flexible use of an inferential reasoning rule by very young children.* Paper presented at the biennial meeting of the Society for Research in Child Development, Detroit.

Cronbach, L. J., & Meehl, P. E. (1956). Construct validity in psychological tests. In H. Feigl & M. Scriven (eds.), *Minnesota studies in the philosophy of science* (vol. 1). Minneapolis: University of Minnesota Press.

Crosland, M. P. (1978). *Historical studies in the language of chemistry.* New York: Dover. (First published 1962 by Heinemann Educational Books, Ltd., London.)

Cushing, S. (1977). *Discourse, logical form, and contextual model selection: The unity of semantics and pragmatics in presupposition and anaphora.* Discussion paper. Higher Order Software, Cambridge, MA.

Dascal, M. (1987). Defending literal meaning. *Cognitive Science, 11,* 259–281.

(1989). On the roles of context and literal meaning in understanding. *Cognitive Science, 13,* 253–257.

Davidson, D. (1978). What metaphors mean. *Critical Inquiry, 5,* 31–47.

Davidson, R. E. (1976). The role of metaphor and analogy in learning. In J. R. Levin & V. L. Allen (eds.), *Cognitive learning in children.* New York: Academic Press.

Demorest, A., Meyer, E., Phelps, E., Gardner, H., & Winner, E. (1984). Words speak louder than actions: Understanding deliberately false remarks. *Child Development, 55,* 1527–1534.

Denis, M. (1984). Imagery and prose: A critical review of research on adults and children. *Text, 4,* 381–401.

Dent, C. (1984). The developmental importance of motion information in perceiving and describing metaphoric similarity. *Child Development, 55,* 1607–1603.

Derrida, J. (1978). The retrait of metaphor. *Enclitic, 2,* 5–33.

(1982). White mythology. Metaphor in the text of philosophy. In J. Derrida (ed.), *Margins of philosophy.* Chicago: University of Chicago Press.

Devitt, M. (1981). *Designation.* New York: Columbia University Press.

Dewey, J. (1938). *Logic: The theory of inquiry.* New York: Holt.

Dews, S., Kaplan, J., & Winner, E. (1992). *Why not say it directly? The social functions of ironic discourse.* Unpublished manuscript.

DiGiovanna, A. (1987). Making it meaningful and memorable. *The American Biology Teacher, 49,* 417–420.

Dretske, F. (1981). *Knowledge and the flow of information.* Cambridge, MA: MIT Press.

Dubois, J., Edeline, F., Klinkenberg, J. M., Minguet, P., Pire, F., & Trinon, H. (1970). *Rhétorique general.* Paris: Larousse.

Ebbinghaus, H. (1964). *Memory.* New York: Dover. (Originally published in German in 1885.)

Eberle, R. (1970). Models, metaphors and formal interpretations. In C. M. Turbayne (ed.), *The myth of metaphor* (rev. ed.). Columbia: University of South Carolina Press.

Eby, D., & Horton, R. B. (1986). *Physical science.* New York: Macmillan.

Eco, U. (1990). *The limits of interpretation.* Bloomington: University of Indiana Press.

Elbers, L. (1988). New names from old words: related aspects of children's metaphors and word compounds. *Journal of Chicago Language, 15,* 591–617.

Elio, R., & Anderson, J. R. (1981). The effects of category generalizations and instance similarity on schema abstraction. *Journal of Experimental Psychology: Human Learning and Memory, 7,* 397–417.

Elkind, D. (1969). Piagetian and psychometric conceptions of intelligence. *Harvard Educational Review, 39,* 319–337.

Empson, W. (1951). *The structure of complex words.* New York: New Directions. (Reprinted by the University of Michigan Press, 1967.)

Estes, W. K. (1976). The cognitive side of probability learning. *Psychological Review, 83,* 37–64.

Estes, W. K., & Straughan, J. H. (1954). Analysis of a verbal conditioning situation in terms of statistical learning theory. *Journal of Experimental Psychology, 47,* 225–234.

Evans, G. E. (1988). Metaphors as learning aids in university lectures. *Journal of Experimental Education, 56,* 91–99.

Evans, M. A., & Gamble, D. L. (1988). Attribute saliency and metaphor interpretation in school-age children. *Journal of Child Language, 15,* 435–449.

Evans, R. D., and Evans, G. E. (1989). Cognitive mechanisms in learning from metaphors. *Journal of Experimental Education, 58,* 5–19.

Fainsilber, L., & Kogan, W. (1984). Does imagery contribute to metaphoric quality. *Journal of Psycholinguistic Research, 13,* 383–391.

Falkenhainer, B., Forbus, K. D., & Gentner, D. (1989). The Structure-Mapping Engine: Algorithm and examples. *Artificial Intelligence, 41,* 1–63.

Feigl, H. (1956). Some major issues and developments in the philosophy of science of logical empiricism. In H. Feigl & M. Scriven (eds.), *Minnesota studies in the philosophy of science* (vol. 1). Minneapolis: University of Minnesota Press.

Field, H. (1973). Theory change and the indeterminacy of reference. *Journal of Philosophy, 70,* 462–481.

(1974). Quine and the correspondence theory. *Philosophical Review, 83,* 200–228.

Fillmore, C., Kay, P., & O'Connor, M. (1988). Regularity and idiomaticity in grammatical constructions. The case of *let alone. Language, 64,* 501–538.

Fish, S. (1983). Short people got no reason to live: Reading irony. *Daedalus, 112,* 175–191.

Fisk, F. G., & Blecha, M. K. (1966). *The physical sciences*. River Forest, IL: Doubleday.

Flavell, J., & Ross, L. (eds.), *Social cognitive development*. Cambridge University Press.

Flexner, S. B., & Hauck, L. (eds.), (1987). *The Random House dictionary of the English language* (2d ed.). New York: Random House.

Fodor, J. A. (1965). Explanations in psychology. In M. Black (ed.), *Philosophy in America*. Ithaca, NY: Cornell University Press.

   (1968). *Psychological explanation*. New York: Random House.

   (1975). *The language of thought*. New York: Crowell.

   (1981). *Representations*. Cambridge, MA: MIT Press.

Fodor, J. A., Fodor, J. D., & Garrett, M. F. (1975). The psychological unreality of semantic representations. *Linguistic Inquiry, 6*, 515–531.

Forbus, K. D. (1984). Qualitative process theory. *Artificial Intelligence, 24*, 85–168.

Forbus, K. D., & Gentner, D. (1989). Structural evaluation of analogies: What counts? In *Proceedings of the eleventh annual conference of the Cognitive Science Society*. Hillsdale, NJ: Erlbaum.

Forbus, K. D., & Oblinger, D. (1990). Making SME greedy and pragmatic. In *Proceedings of the twelfth annual conference of the Cognitive Science Society*. Hillsdale, NJ: Erlbaum.

Foucault, M. (1972). *The archaeology of knowledge and the discourse on language*. New York: Pantheon.

Fowler, H. (1965). *A dictionary of modern English usage* (2d ed.). Oxford: Oxford University Press.

Fox, R. (1971). *The caloric theory of gases: From Lavoisier to Regnault*. Oxford: Clarendon Press.

Fraser, B. (1977). *An account of metaphor*. Unpublished manuscript, Boston University.

Frederiksen, C. (1977). Structure and process in discourse production and comprehension. In M. Just & P. Carpenter (eds.), *Cognitive processes in comprehension*. Hillsdale, NJ: Erlbaum.

Gans, H. (1962). *The urban villagers*. New York: Free Press.

Garde, I. B. (1986). An easy approach for reading manometers to determine gas pressure: The analogy of the child's seesaw. *Journal of Chemical Education, 63*, 796–797.

   (1987). An analogy for soluble and insoluble mixtures: Sand and magnetic iron filings. *Journal of Chemical Education, 64*, 154–155.

Gardner, H. (1974). Metaphors and modalities: How children project polar adjectives onto diverse domains. *Child Development, 45*, 84–91.

   (1985). *The mind's new science: A history of the cognitive revolution*. New York: Basic Books.

Gardner, H., & Winner, E. (1986). Attitudes and attributes: Children's understanding of metaphor and sarcasm. In M. Perlmutter (ed.), *Perspectives on intellectual development. The Minnesota symposia on child psychology* (vol. 19). Hillsdale, NJ: Erlbaum.

Gazdar, G. (1976). *Formal pragmatics for natural language implicature, presupposition and logical form*. Doctoral dissertation, University of Reading, Reading, England.

Geertz, C. (ed.). (1974). *Myth, symbol and culture.* New York: Norton.

Gelman, R., & Spelke, E. (1981). *The development of thoughts about animate and inanimate objects: Implications for research on social cognition.* Cambridge University Press.

Genette, G. (1968). La rhétorique des figures [The rhetoric of figures of speech]. Introduction to P. Fointainne's *Les figures du discours.* Paris: Flammarion.

Gentner, D. (1977). Children's performance on a spatial analogies tasks. *Child Development, 48,* 1034–1039.

(1982). Are scientific analogies metaphors? In D. Miall (ed.), *Metaphor: Problems and perspectives.* Brighton, England: Harvester Press.

(1983). Structure-mapping: A theoretical framework for analogy. *Cognitive Science, 7,* 155–170.

(1988). Metaphor as structure mapping: The relational shift. *Child Development, 59,* 47–59.

(1989). The mechanisms of analogical learning. In S. Vosniadou & A. Ortony (eds.), *Similarity and analogical reasoning.* Cambridge University Press.

Gentner, D., & Clement, C. (1988). Evidence for relational selectivity in the interpretation of analogy and metaphor. In G. H. Bower (ed.), *The psychology of learning and motivation* (vol. 22). New York: Academic Press.

Gentner, D., Falkenhainer, B., & Skorstad, J. (1988). Viewing metaphor as analogy. In D. H. Helman (ed.), *Analogical reasoning: Perspectives of artificial intelligence, cognitive science, and philosophy.* Dordrecht, Holland: Kluwer.

Gentner, D., & Gentner, D. G. (1983). Flowing waters or teeming crowds: Mental models of electricity. In D. G. Gentner & A. L. Stevens (eds.), *Mental models.* Hillsdale, NJ: Erlbaum.

Gentner, D., & Grudin, J. (1985). The evolution of mental metaphors in psychology: A ninety-year retrospective. *American Psychologist, 40,* 181–192.

Gentner, D., & Jeziorski, M. (1989). Historical shifts in the use of analogy in science. In B. Gholson, A. Houts, R. A. Neimeyer, & W. R. Shadish (eds.), *The psychology of science and metascience.* Cambridge University Press.

Gentner, D., & Landers, R. (1985). Analogical reminding: A good match is hard to find. In *Proceedings of the international conference on systems, man and cybernetics.* Tucson, AZ.

Gentner, D., & Rattermann, M. J. (1991). Language and the career of similarity. In S. A. Gelman & J. P. Byrnes (eds.), *Perspectives on thought and language: Interrelations in development.* Cambridge University Press.

Gentner, D., Ratterman, M. J., & Forbus, K. D. (in press). The roles of similarity in transfer: Separating retrievability from inferential soundness. *Cognitive Psychology.*

Gentner, D., Rattermann, M. J., Markman, A. B., & Kotovsky, L. (in press). The development of relational similarity. In G. Halford & T. Simon (eds.), *Developing cognitive competence: New approaches to process modeling.* Hillsdale, NJ: Erlbaum.

Gentner, D., & Stuart, P. (1983). *Metaphor as structure-mapping: What develops?* (Tech. Rep. 5479). Cambridge, MA: Beranek & Newman.

Gentner, D., & Toupin, C. (1986). Systematicity and surface similarity in the development of analogy. *Cognitive Science, 10,* 277–300.

Gerrig, R. (1986). Process models and pragmatics. In N. Sharkey (ed.), *Advances in cognitive science 1*. Chichester, England: Ellis Horwood.

(1989). The time course of sense creation. *Memory & Cognition, 17*, 194–207.

Gerrig, R. J., & Healy, A. F. (1983). Dual processes in metaphor understanding. Comprehension and appreciation. *Journal of Experimental Psychology: Learning, Memory, and Cognition, 4*, 667–675.

Gibbs, R. W. (1980). Spilling the beans on understanding and memory for idioms in context. *Memory & Cognition, 8*, 149–156.

(1982). A critical examination of the contribution of literal meaning to understanding nonliteral discourse. *Text, 2*, 9–27.

(1984). Literal meaning and psychological theory. *Cognitive Science, 8*, 274–304.

(1986a). On the psycholinguistics of sarcasm. *Journal of Experimental Psychology: General, 115*, 3–15.

(1986b). Comprehension and memory for nonliteral utterances: The problem of sarcastic indirect requests. *Acta Psychologica, 62*, 41–57.

(1986c). What makes some indirect speech acts conventional? *Journal of Memory and Language, 25*, 181–196.

(1989). Understanding and literal meaning. *Cognitive Science, 13*, 243–251.

(1990a). Comprehending figurative referential descriptions. *Journal of Experimental Psychology: Learning, Memory, and Cognition, 16*, 56–66.

(1990b). Psycholinguistic studies on the conceptual basis of idiomaticity. *Cognitive Linguistics, 1*, 417–462.

Gibbs, R., & Gerrig, R. (1989). How context makes metaphor comprehension seem special. *Metaphor and Symbolic Activity, 3*, 145–158.

Gibbs, R., & McCarrell, N. S. (1990). Why boys will be boys and girls will be girls: Understanding colloquial tautologies. *Journal of Psycholinguistic Research, 19*, 125–145.

Gibbs, R., & Nayak, N. (1989). Psycholinguistic studies on the syntactic behavior of idioms. *Cognitive Psychology, 21*, 100–138.

Gibbs, R., Nayak, N., Bolton, J., & Keppel, M. (1989). Speakers' assumptions about the lexical flexibility of idioms. *Memory & Cognition, 17*, 58–68.

Gibbs, R., Nayak, N., & Cutting, C. (1989). How to kick the bucket and not decompose: Analyzability and idiom processing. *Journal of Memory and Language, 28*, 576–593.

Gibbs, R., & O'Brien, J. (1990). Idioms and mental imagery: The metaphorical motivation for idiomatic meaning. *Cognition, 36*, 35–68.

Gibson, J. J. (1966). *The senses considered as perceptual systems*. Boston: Houghton Mifflin.

Gick, M. L., & Holyoak, K. J. (1980). Analogical problem solving. *Cognitive Psychology, 12*, 306–355.

(1983). Schema induction and analogical transfer. *Cognitive Psychology, 15*, 1–38.

Gildea, P., & Glucksberg, S. (1983). On understanding metaphor: The role of context. *Journal of Verbal Learning and Verbal Behavior, 22*, 577–590.

Gleicher, P., & Fried, M. (1967). Some sources of residential satisfaction in an urban slum. In J. Bellush & M. Hausknecht (eds.), *Urban renewal: People, politics and planning*. Garden City, NY: Doubleday Anchor.

Glucksberg, S., Gildea, P., & Bookin, H. (1982). On understanding nonliteral speech: Can people ignore metaphors. *Journal of Verbal Learning and Verbal Behavior, 21,* 85–98.

Glucksberg, S., & Keysar, B. (1990). Understanding metaphorical comparisons: Beyond similarity. *Psychological Review, 97,* 3–18.

Goldman, A. (1967). A causal theory of knowing. *Journal of Philosophy, 64,* 357–372.

(1976). Discrimination and perceptual knowledge. *Journal of Philosophy, 73,* 771–791.

(1986). *Epistemology and cognition.* Cambridge, MA: Harvard University Press.

Goldstein, A. (1978). *Meaning, reference and theory change.* Doctoral dissertation, University of Michigan.

Goodman, N. (1968). *Languages of art.* Indianapolis: Bobbs-Merrill.

(1972a). *Problems and projects.* New York: Bobbs-Merrill.

(1972b). Seven strictures on similarity. In N. Goodman, *Problems and projects.* New York: Bobbs-Merrill.

Goswami, U. (1989). Relational complexity and the development of analogical reasoning. *Cognitive Development, 4,* 251–268.

(1991). Analogical reasoning: What develops? A review of research and theory. *Child Development, 62,* 1–22.

Goswami, U., & Brown, A. L. (1989). Melting chocolate and melting snowmen: Analogical reasoning and causal relations. *Cognition, 35,* 69–95.

Green, T. (1971). *The activities of teaching.* New York: McGraw-Hill.

Greeno, J. G. (1989). Situation models, mental models, and generative knowledge. In D. Klahr & K. Kotovsky (eds.), *Complex information processing: The impact of Herbert A. Simon.* Hillsdale, NJ: Erlbaum.

Greimas, A. J. (1970). *Du sens. Essais sémiotiques.* Paris: Editions du Seuil.

Grice, H. P. (1975). Logic and conversation. In P. Cole & J. Morgan (eds.), *Syntax and semantics* (vol. 3): *Speech acts.* New York: Academic Press.

(1978). Further notes on logic and conversation. In P. Cole (ed.), *Syntax and semantics* (vol. 9): *Pragmatics.* New York: Academic Press.

(1989). *Studies in the way of words.* Cambridge, MA: Harvard University Press.

Hage, P., & Miller, W. R. (1976). 'Eagle'='bird': A note on the structure and evolution of Shoshoni ethno-ornithological nomenclature. *American Ethnologist, 3,* 481–488.

Hala, S., Chandler, M., & Fritz, A. (1991). Fledgling theories of mind: Deception as a marker of 3-year-olds' understanding of false belief. *Child Development, 62,* 83–97.

Halford, G. S. (1987). A structure-mapping approach to cognitive development. *International Journal of Psychology, 22,* 609–642.

(1992). Analogical reasoning and conceptual complexity in cognitive development. *Human Development, 35,* 192–217.

Hallyn, F. (1990). *The poetic structure of the world: Copernicus and Kepler.* New York: Zone Books.

Hamilton-Jones, J. W. (ed.) (1960). *Bacstrom's alchemical anthology.* London: John M. Watkins.

Hanson, N. R. (1958). *Patterns of discovery.* Cambridge University Press.

Harré, R., & Madden, E. (1975). *Causal powers.* Totowa, NJ: Rowman and Littlefield.

Harris, R. J. (1979). Memory for metaphors. *Journal of Psycholinguistic Research, 8,* 249–265.

Harris, R. J., Lahey, M. A., & Marsalek, F. (1980). Metaphors and images. Rating, reporting and remembering. In R. P. Honeck & R. R. Hoffman (eds.), *Cognition and figurative language.* Hillsdale, NJ: Erlbaum.

Harwood, D. L., & Verbrugge, R. R. (1977). *Metaphor and the asymmetry of similarity.* Paper presented at the annual meeting of the American Psychological Association, San Francisco.

Haviland, S. E., & Clark, H. H. (1974). What's new? Acquiring new information as a process in comprehension. *Journal of Verbal Learning and Verbal Behavior, 13,* 512–521.

Haynes, F. (1975). Metaphor as interactive. *Educational Theory, 25,* 272–277.
  (1978). Metaphoric understanding. *Journal of Aesthetic Education, 12,* 99–115.

Hebb, D. O. (1949). *The organization of behavior.* New York: Wiley.

Hegarty, M., Mayer, R. E., & Green, C. E. (1992). Comprehension of arithmetic word problems: Evidence from students' eye movements. *Journal of Educational Psychology, 84,* 76–84.

Heimler, C. Y., & Price, J. S. (1984). *Focus on physical science.* Columbus, OH: Merrill.

Hempel, C. G. (1965). *Aspects of scientific explanation and other essays in the philosophy of science.* New York: Free Press.

Henle, P. (ed.). (1965). *Language, thought, and culture.* Ann Arbor, MI: University of Michigan Press.

Henley, N. M. (1969). A psychological study of the semantics of animal terms. *Journal of Verbal Learning and Verbal Behavior, 8,* 176–184.

Herbart, J. H. (1898). *Letters and lectures on education.* Translated by H. M. Felkin & E. Felkin. London: Sonneschein.

Hesse, M. B. (1966). *Models and analogies in science.* Notre Dame, IN: University of Notre Dame Press.

Hinton, G. E. (1981). Implementing semantic networks in parallel hardware. In G. E. Hinton & J. A. Anderson (eds.), *Parallel models of associative memory.* Hillsdale, NJ: Erlbaum.

Hirsch, G. O. (1973). *Social examples in teaching physical concepts.* Paper presented at the 21st national convention of the National Science Teachers Association, Detroit, MI. (ERIC Document Reproduction Service No. ED 093 598.)

Hoffman, R., & Kemper, S. (1987). What could reaction-times tell us about metaphor comprehension? *Metaphor and Symbolic Activity, 1,* 149–186.

Hofstadter, D. (1981). Metamagical themas: Roles and analogies in human and machine thought. *Scientific American, 245,* 18–30.

Holmyard, E. J. (1957). *Alchemy.* Harmondsworth, England: Penguin Books. (Reprinted by Dover Publications, Mineola, NY, 1990.)

Holyoak, K. J., Junn, E., & Billman, D. (1984). Development of analogical problem solving skill. *Child Development, 55,* 2042–2055.

Holyoak, K. J., & Thagard, P. (1989). Analogical mapping by constraint satisfaction. *Cognitive Science, 13,* 295–355.

Honeck, R. P. (1973). Interpretive versus structural effects in semantic memory. *Journal of Verbal Learning and Verbal Behavior, 12,* 448–455.

Honeck, R. P., Riechmann, P., & Hoffman, R. R. (1975). Semantic memory for metaphor: The conceptual base hypothesis. *Memory & Cognition, 3,* 409–415.

Horn, L. R. (1976). *On the semantic properties of logical operators in English.* Bloomington: Indiana Linguistics Club.

Hull, C. L. (1943). *Principles of behavior.* New Haven, CT: Yale University Press.

Hume, D. (1973). *A treatise of human nature.* Edited by L. Selby-Bigge. London: Oxford University Press. (Originally published 1739.)

Hymes, D. (1973). *Towards linguistic competence.* Working paper in sociolinguistics, 16. Austin: University of Texas, Department of Anthropology.

Inhelder, B., & Piaget, J. (1958). *The growth of logical thinking from childhood to adolescence.* New York: Basic Books.

Inhoff, A., Duffy, P., & Carroll, P. (1984). Contextual effects on metaphor comprehension in reading. *Memory & Cognition, 12,* 558–567.

Irwin, J. (ed.), (1986). *Understanding and teaching cohesion comprehension.* Newark, DE: International Reading Association.

Jaffe, B. (1967). *Crucibles: The story of chemistry.* (rev. ed). New York: Dover.

Jakobson, R. (1971). Two aspects of language and two types of aphasic disturbances. In R. Jakobson (ed.), *Selected writings* (vol. 2). The Hague: Mouton.

Jakobson, R., & Halle, M. (1956). *Fundamentals of language.* The Hague: Mouton.

James, W. (1890). *The principles of psychology.* New York: Dover.

Johnson, M. (1981). *Philosophical perspectives on metaphor.* Minneapolis: University of Minnesota Press.

(1987). *The body in the mind: The bodily basis of meaning, reason and imagination.* Chicago: University of Chicago Press.

Johnson, M. G. (1970). A cognitive feature model of compound free associations. *Psychological Review, 77,* 282–293.

(1977). *The abstraction of meaning from complex pictures.* Paper presented at the annual meeting of the Psychonomic Society, Washington, D.C.

Johnson, M. G., & Malgady, R. G. (1980). Toward a perceptual theory of metaphoric comprehension. In R. P. Honeck & R. R. Hoffman (eds.), *Cognition and figurative language.* Hillsdale, NJ: Erlbaum.

Johnson-Laird, P. N. (1988). *The computer and the mind: An introduction to cognitive science.* Cambridge, MA: Harvard University Press.

Johsua, S., & Dupin, J. J. (1987). Taking into account student conceptions in instructional strategy: An example in physics. *Cognition and Instruction, 42,* 117–135.

Jorgensen, J., Miller, G., & Sperber, D. (1984). Test of the mention theory of irony. *Journal of Experimental Psychology: General, 113,* 112–120.

Kangas, P. (1988). A chess analogy: Teaching the role of animals in ecosystems. *The American Biology Teacher, 50,* 160–162.

Kant, E. (1963). *Critique of pure reason.* Translated by N. K. Smith. London: Macmillan. (Originally published 1787.)

Kaplan, J., Winner, E., & Rosenblatt, E. (1987). *Children's abilities to discriminate and understand irony and metaphor.* Unpublished data.

Karttunen, L., & Peters, S. (1975). Conventional implicature in Montague grammar. In *Proceedings of the first annual meeting of the Berkeley Linguistics Society.* Berkeley: University of California.

Katz, A. N. (1976). *Verbal concept identification: Disentangling the dominance effect.* Doctoral dissertation, University of Western Ontario.

(1989). On choosing the vehicles of metaphors: referential concreteness, semantic distances, and individual differences. *Journal of Memory and Language, 28,* 486–499.

Katz, A. N., & Paivio, A. (1975). Imagery variables in concept identification. *Journal of Verbal Learning and Verbal Behavior, 14,* 284–293.

Katz, A. N., Paivio, A., Marschark, M., & Clark, J. M. (1988). Norms for 204 literary and 260 nonliterary metaphors on 10 psychological dimensions. *Metaphor and Symbolic Activity, 3,* 191–214.

Katz, J. J. (1966). *The philosophy of language.* New York: Harper & Row.

(1977). *Propositional structure: A study of the contribution of semantic meaning to speech acts.* New York: Crowell.

Katz, J. J., & Fodor, J. A. (1963). The structure of semantic theory. *Language 39,* 170–210.

Keane, M. (1985). On drawing analogies when solving problems: A theory and test of solution generation in an analogical problem-solving task. *British Journal of Psychology, 76,* 449–458.

(1988). *Analogical problem solving.* New York: Halsted Press.

Kearney, H. (1971). *Science and change.* New York: McGraw-Hill.

Keil, F. (1979). *Semantic and conceptual development: An ontological perspective.* Cambridge, MA: Harvard University Press.

(1986). Conceptual domains and the acquisition of metaphor. *Cognitive Development, 1,* 73–96.

Kennedy, J. M. (1976). *Pictorial metaphor: A theory of movement indicators in static pictures.* Paper presented at the Information through Pictures Symposium, Swarthmore College, Swarthmore, PA.

Keysar, B. (1989). On the functional equivalence of literal and metaphorical interpretations in discourse. *Journal of Memory and Language, 28,* 375–385.

Khatchadourian, H. (1968). Metaphor. *British Journal of Aesthetics, 8,* 227–243.

Kintsch, W. (1972). Notes on the structure of semantic memory. In E. Tulving & W. Donaldson (eds.), *Organization of memory.* New York: Academic Press.

(1974). *The representation of meaning in memory.* Hillsdale, NJ: Erlbaum.

Kintsch, W., & Greeno, J. G. (1985). Understanding and solving word problems. *Psychological Review, 92,* 109–129.

Klee, H., & Eysenck, M. W. (1973). Comprehension of abstract and concrete sentences. *Journal of Verbal Learning and Verbal Behavior, 12,* 522–529.

Koen, F. (1965). An intra-verbal explication of the nature of metaphor. *Journal of Verbal Learning and Verbal Behavior, 4,* 129–133.

Koestler, A. (1964). *The act of creation.* New York: Macmillan.

Kogan, N., Connor, K., Gross, A., & Fava, D. (1980). Understanding visual metaphor: Developmental and individual differences. *Monographs of the Society for Research in Child Development, 45.*

Kolb, K. E., & Kolb, D. K. (1987/88). Classroom analogy for addition polymerization. *Journal of College Science Teaching, 17,* 230–231.

Kövecses, Z. (1990). *Emotion concepts*. New York: Springer-Verlag.

Kreuz, R., & Glucksberg, S. (1989). How to be sarcastic: The echoic reminder theory of verbal irony. *Journal of Experimental Psychology: General, 118,* 374–386.

Kriegsmann, W. (1665). *Taaut, oder ausslegung der chemischen zeichen*. Frankfurt.

Kripke, S. A. (1972). Naming and necessity. In D. Davidson & G. Harman (eds.), *The semantics of natural language*. Dordrecht, Holland: D. Reidel.

Krumhansl, C. L. (1978). Concerning the applicability of geometric models to similarity data: The interrelationship between similarity and spatial density. *Psychological Review, 85,* 445–463.

Kuhn, T. S. (1970a). *The structure of scientific revolutions* (2d. ed.). Chicago: University of Chicago Press.

(1970b). Reflections on my critics. In I. Lakatos & A. Musgrave (eds.), *Criticism and the growth of knowledge*. Cambridge University Press.

(1974). Second thoughts on paradigms. In F. Suppe (ed.), *The structure of scientific theories*. Urbana: University of Illinois Press.

Kuse, L. S., & Kuse, H. R. (1986). Using analogies to study social studies texts. *Social Education, 50,* 24–25.

Lakoff, G. (1971). On generative semantics. In D. D. Steinberg & L. A. Jakobovits (eds.), *Semantics: An interdisciplinary reader in philosophy, linguistics and psychology*. Cambridge University Press.

(1986). The meaning of literal. *Metaphor and Symbolic Activity, 1,* 291–296.

(1987). *Women, fire and dangerous things: What categories reveal about the mind*. Chicago: University of Chicago Press.

(1989). Philosophical speculation and cognitive science. *Philosophical Psychology, 2,* 55–76.

Lakoff, G., & Brugman, C. (1986). Argument forms in lexical semantics. In K. Nikiforidou, N. Van Clay, & D. Feder (eds.), *Proceedings of the twelfth annual meeting of the Berkeley Linguistics Society*.

Lakoff, G., & Johnson, M. (1980). *Metaphors we live by*. Chicago: University of Chicago Press.

Lakoff, G., & Turner, M. (1989). *More than cool reason: A field guide to poetic metaphor*. Chicago: University of Chicago Press.

Langacker, R. (1986). *Foundations of cognitive grammar* (vol. 1). Stanford, CA: Stanford University Press.

Langer, S. K. (1942). *Philosophy in a new key*. Cambridge, MA: Harvard University Press. (Reprinted by Mentor Books, New York, 1948.)

Lanham, R. (1969). *A handlist of rhetorical terms*. Berkeley: University of California Press.

Laque, C. F. (1978). *Mathematical designs for teaching and learning composition*. Paper presented at the 29th annual meeting of the conference on College Composition and Communication, Denver, CO. (ERIC Document Reproduction Service No. ED 159 719.)

Larkin, J. H. (1983). The role of problem representation in physics. In D. G. Gentner & A. L. Stevens (eds.), *Mental models*. Hillsdale, NJ: Erlbaum.

Larkin, J. H., McDermott, J., Simon, D. P., & Simon, H. A. (1980). Expert and novice performance in solving physics problems. *Science, 208,* 1335–1342.

Last, A. M. (1983). A bloody nose, the hairdresser's salon, flies in an elevator, and dancing couples: The use of analogies in teaching introductory chemistry. *Journal of Chemical Education, 60,* 748–750.

Lave, J. (1988). *Cognition in practice: Mind, mathematics, and culture.* Cambridge University Press.

Levi, J. N. (1974). On the alleged idiosyncrasy of nonpredicate NP's. In *Papers from the tenth regional meeting, Chicago Linguistic Society.* Chicago: University of Chicago.

Lévi-Strauss, C. (1963). *Structural anthropology.* Translated by C. Jacobson & B. G. Schoepf. New York: Basic Books.

Levin, S. R. (1977). *The semantics of metaphor.* Baltimore, MD: Johns Hopkins University Press.

(1988). *Metaphoric worlds.* New Haven, CT: Yale University Press.

Lewis, A. B. (1989). Training students to represent arithmetic word problems. *Journal of Educational Psychology, 81,* 521–531.

Lewis, D. (1971). An argument for the identity theory. In D. M. Rosenthal (ed.), *Materialism and the mind-body problem.* Englewood Cliffs, NJ: Prentice-Hall.

Licata, K. P. (1988). Chemistry is like a . . . *The Science Teacher, 55,* 41–43.

Locke, J. (1959). *An essay concerning human understanding.* Edited by A. C. Fraser. London: Dover. (Originally published 1690.)

Loewenberg, I. (1973). Truth and consequences of metaphors. *Philosophy and Rhetoric, 6,* 30–46.

(1975a). Denying the undeniable: Metaphors are *not* comparisons. *Mid-American linguistics conference papers.*

(1975b). Identifying metaphors. *Foundations of Language, 12,* 315–338.

Luce, R. D. (1959). *Individual choice behavior.* New York: Wiley.

MacCorquodale, K., & Meehl, P. E. (1948). On a distinction between hypothetical constructs and intervening variables. *Psychological Review, 55,* 95–107.

Malgady, R. G., & Johnson, M. G. (1976). Modifiers in metaphors: Effects of constituent phrase similarity on the interpretation of figurative sentences. *Journal of Psycholinguistic Research, 5,* 43–52.

Markman, A. B., & Gentner, D. (in press). Evidence for structural alignment during similarity judgments. *Cognitive Psychology.*

Marks, L., Hammeal, R., & Bornstein, M. (1987). Perceiving similarity and comprehending metaphor. In *Monographs of the Society for Research in Child Development, 52.*

Marr, D. (1976). Early processing of visual information. *Proceedings of the Royal Society of London,* Sev. B 275, 483–534.

Marschark, M., & Hunt, R. (1985). On memory for metaphor. *Memory & Cognition, 13,* 413–424.

Marschark, M., Katz, A. N., & Paivio, A. (1983). Dimensions of metaphor. *Journal of Psycholinguistic Research, 12,* 17–40.

Marschark, M., & Paivio, A. (1977). Integrative processing of concrete and abstract sentences. *Journal of Verbal Learning and Verbal Behavior, 16,* 217–232.

Marshall, J. K. (1984). Classroom potpourri. *Journal of Chemical Education, 61,* 425–427.

Matthews, R. J. (1971). Concerning a "linguistic theory" of metaphor. *Foundations of Language, 7,* 413–425.

Mayer, R. E. (1975). Different problem-solving competencies established with and without meaningful models. *Journal of Educational Psychology, 67*, 725–734.

(1976). Some conditions of meaningful learning for computer programming. Advance organizers and subject control of frame order. *Journal of Educational Psychology, 68*, 143–150.

(1983). Can you repeat that? Qualitative effects of repetition and advance organizers on learning from scientific prose. *Journal of Educational Psychology, 75*, 40–49.

(1984). Aids to text comprehension. *Educational Psychologist, 19*, 30–42.

(1989a). Models for understanding. *Review of Educational Research, 59*, 43–64.

(1989b). Systematic thinking fostered by illustrations in science text. *Journal of Educational Psychology, 81*, 240–246.

Mayer, R. E., & Bromage, B. K. (1980). Different recall protocols for technical texts due to advance organizers. *Journal of Educational Psychology, 72*, 209–225.

Mayer, R. E., Dyck, J. L., & Cook, L. K. (1984). Techniques that help readers build mental models from scientific text: Definitions pretraining and signaling. *Journal of Educational Psychology, 76*, 1089–1105.

Mayer, R. E., & Gallini, J. K. (1990). When is an illustration worth ten thousand words? *Journal of Educational Psychology, 82*, 715–726.

Mayr, E. (1970). *Populations, species and evolution*. Cambridge, MA: Harvard University Press.

McCloskey, M. (1983). Intuitive physics. *Scientific American, 248*, 122–130.

McCloskey, M., Caramazza, A., & Green, B. (1980). Curvilinear motion in the absence of external forces: Naive beliefs about the motion of objects. *Science, 210*, 1139–1144.

McGonigal, E. (1988). Correlative thinking: Writing analogies about literature. *English Journal, 77*, 66–67.

Medin, D. L., Goldstone, R. L., & Gentner, D. (1993). Respects for similarity. *Psychological Review, 100*, 254–278.

Mendelsohn, E., Gardner, H., & Winner, E. (1981). *A study of children's perception of metaphoric grounds*. Unpublished data.

Merwin, W. S. (1973). *Asian figures*. New York: Atheneum.

Merwin, W. S., & Masson, J. M., translators (1981). *The Peacock's Egg*. San Francisco: North Point Press.

Miller, D. B. (1988). The nature-nurture issue: Lessons from the Pillsbury Doughboy. *Teaching of Psychology, 15*, 147–149.

Miller, G. A. (1974). Towards a third metaphor for psycholinguistics. In W. B. Weimer & D. S. Palermo (eds.), *Cognition and the symbolic processes*. Hillsdale, NJ: Erlbaum.

(1978). Semantic relations among words. In M. Halle, J. Bresnan, & G. A. Miller (eds.), *Linguistic theory and psychological reality*. Cambridge, MA: MIT Press.

Miller, G. A., & Glucksberg, S. (1988). Psycholinguistic aspects of semantics and pragmatics. In D. Luce, R. A. Atkinson, & R. Hernstein (eds.), *Stevens' handbook of experimental psychology* (2d. ed.). New York: Wiley.

Miller, G. A., & Johnson-Laird, P. N. (1976). *Language and perception*. Cambridge, MA: Harvard University Press.

Miller, R. M. (1976). The dubious case for metaphors in educational writing. *Educational Theory, 26*, 174–181.

Miller, S. I. (1987). Some comments on the utility of metaphors for educational theory and practice. *Educational Theory, 37,* 219–227.

Mooij, J. J. A. (1976). *A study of metaphor.* Amsterdam: North-Holland.

Moore, B. (1986). *An example of a young child's use of a physical-psychological metaphor.* Unpublished manuscript, St. Joseph's College, Department of Psychology, Patchogue, NY.

Morgan, J. L. (1978). Two types of convention in indirect speech acts. In P. Cole (ed.), *Syntax and semantics* (vol. 9): *Pragmatics.* New York: Academic Press.

Murry, J. M. (1931). Metaphor. In J. M. Murry, *Countries of the mind.* London: Oxford University Press.

Nayak, N., & Gibbs, R. (1990). Conceptual knowledge in the interpretation of idioms. *Journal of Experimental Psychology: General, 119,* 315–330.

Neisser, U. (1966). Computers as tools and as metaphors. In C. R. Dechert (ed.), *The social impact of cybernetics.* Notre Dame, IN: University of Notre Dame Press.

(1967). *Cognitive psychology.* New York: Appleton-Century-Crofts.

Nelson, K. (1974). Concept, word and sentence: Interrelations in acquisition and development. *Psychological Review, 81,* 267–285.

Nersessian, N. (1984). *Faraday to Einstein: Constructing meaning in scientific theories.* Dordrecht, Holland: Kluwer.

Newell, A., & Simon, H. A. (1972). *Human problem solving.* Englewood Cliffs, NJ: Prentice-Hall.

(1976). Computer science as empirical inquiry: Symbols and search. *Communications of the Association for Computing Machinery, 19,* 113–126.

Newport, E. L., & Bellugi, U. (1978). Linguistic expressions of category levels in a visual-gesture language: A flower is a flower is a flower. In E. Rosch & B. B. Lloyd (eds.), *Cognition and categorization.* Hillsdale, NJ: Erlbaum.

Nicolson, N., & Trautmann, J. (eds.). (1976). *The letters of Virginia Woolf* (vol. 2): *1912–1922.* New York: Harcourt Brace Jovanovich.

Nisbet, R. A. (1969). *Social change and history.* New York: Oxford University Press.

Nisbett, R. E., & Wilson, T. D. (1977). Telling more than we can know: Verbal reports on mental processes. *Psychological Review, 84,* 231–259.

Norman, D. A., Rumelhart, D. E., & the LNR Research Group. (1975). *Explorations in cognition.* San Francisco: Freeman.

Nowottny, W. (1962). *The language poets use.* London: Athlone Press.

Nunberg, G. (1978). *The pragmatics of reference.* Bloomington, IN: Indiana University Linguistics Club.

(1979). The non-uniqueness of semantic solutions: Polysemy. *Linguistics and Philosophy, 3,* 143–184.

Oakeshott, M. (1959). *The voice of poetry in the conversation of mankind.* London: Bowes and Bowes.

Olson, D. R. (1970). Language and thought: Aspects of a cognitive theory of semantics. *Psychological Review, 77,* 257–273.

(1988). On what's a metaphor for? *Metaphor and Symbolic Activity, 3,* 215–222.

Olson, D. R., & Hildyard, A. (1983). Literacy and the comprehension and expression of literal meaning. In F. Coulman & K. Ehrlich (eds.), *Writing in focus.* New York: Mouton.

O'Neill, B. J., & Paivio, A. (1978). Semantic constraints in encoding judgments and free recall of concrete and abstract sentences. *Canadian Journal of Psychology, 32,* 3–18.

Ortony, A. (1975). Why metaphors are necessary and not just nice. *Educational Theory, 25,* 45–53.

   (1976). On the nature and value of metaphor: A reply to my critics. *Educational Theory, 26,* 395–398.

   (1979). Beyond literal similarity. *Psychological Review, 86,* 161–180.

Ortony, A., Reynolds, R. E., & Arter, J. A. (1978). Metaphor: Theoretical and empirical research. *Psychological Bulletin, 85,* 919–943.

Ortony, A., Schallert, D. L., Reynolds, R. E., & Antos, S. J. (1978). Interpreting metaphors and idioms: Some effects of context on comprehension. *Journal of Verbal Learning and Verbal Behavior, 17,* 465–477.

Ortony, A., Vondruska, R. J., Foss, M. A., & Jones, L. E. (1985). Salience, similes, and the asymmetry of similarity. *Journal of Memory and Language, 24,* 569–594.

Osgood, C. E. (1953). *Method and theory in experimental psychology.* New York: Oxford University Press.

   (1963). Language universals and psycholinguistics. In J. Greenberg (ed.), *Universals of language* (2d ed.). Cambridge, MA: MIT Press.

   (1980). The cognitive dynamics of synesthesia and metaphor. In R. P. Honeck & R. R. Hoffman (eds.), *Cognition and figurative language,* Hillsdale, NJ: Erlbaum.

Osgood, C. E., Suci, G. J., & Tannenbaum, P. H. (1957). *The measurement of meaning.* Urbana: University of Illinois Press.

Paige, J. M., & Simon, H. A. (1966). Cognitive processes in solving algebra word problems. In B. Kleinmuntz (ed.), *Problem solving: Research, method, and theory.* New York: Wiley.

Paivio, A. (1963). Learning of adjective-noun paired associates as a function of adjective-noun word order and noun abstractness. *Canadian Journal of Psychology, 17,* 370–379.

   (1971). *Imagery and verbal processes.* New York: Holt, Rinehart, and Winston.

   (1975a). Coding distinctions and repetition effects in memory. In G. H. Bower (ed.), *The psychology of learning and motivation* (vol. 9). New York: Academic Press.

   (1975b). Imagery and synchronic thinking. *Canadian Psychology Review, 16,* 147–163.

   (1986). *Mental representations: A dual-coding approach.* New York: Oxford University Press.

Paivio, A., & Begg, I. (1971). Imagery and comprehension latencies as a function of sentence concreteness and structure. *Perception and Psychophysics, 10,* 408–412.

Paivio, A., & Clark, J. M. (1986). The role of topic and vehicle imagery in metaphor comprehension. *Communication and Cognition, 19,* 367–388.

Paivio, A., & Yarmey, A. D. (1966). Pictures versus words as stimuli and responses in paired-associate learning. *Psychonomic Science, 5,* 235–236.

Pasachoff, J. M., Pasachoff, N., & Cooney, T. M. (1986). *Physical science.* Glenview, IL: Scott, Foresman.

Pepper, S. (1942). *World hypotheses*. Berkeley: University of California Press.

Perner, J., & Wimmer, H. (1985). "John thinks that Mary thinks that . . .": Attribution of second-order beliefs by 5- to 10-year-old children. *Journal of Experimental Child Psychology, 39*, 437–471.

Petrie, H. G. (1976). Metaphorical models of mastery: Or how to learn to do the problems at the end of the chapter in the physics textbook. In R. S. Cohen, C. A. Hooker, A. C. Michalos, & J. W. vanEvra (eds.), *Proceedings of the Philosophy of Science Association, 1974*. Dordrecht, Holland: D. Reidel.

(1981). *The dilemma of enquiry and learning*. Chicago: The University of Chicago Press.

Piaget, J. (1972). *The principles of genetic epistemology*. New York: Basic Books.

(1974). *The language and thought of the child*. New York: New American Library.

Plato. (1937). *Meno*. In B. Jowett (ed. and trans.), *The dialogues of Plato*. New York: Random House.

Polanyi, M. (1966). *The tacit dimension*. Garden City, NY: Doubleday.

Pollio, H. R., & Burns, B. C. (1977). The anomaly of anomaly. *Journal of Psycholinguistic Research, 6*, 247–260.

Pollio, M., & Pollio, H. (1974). The development of figurative language in school children. *Journal of Psycholinguistic Research, 40*, 299–313.

Polya, G. (1954). *Induction and analogy in mathematics* (vol. 1): *Of mathematics and plausible reasoning*. Princeton, NJ: Princeton University Press.

Polyson, J. A., & Blick, K. A. (1985). Basketball game as psychology experiment. *Teaching of Psychology, 12*, 52–53.

Poskozim, P. S., Wazorick, J. W., Tiempetpaisal, P., & Poskozim, J. A. (1986). Analogies for Avogadro's number. *Journal of Chemical Education, 63*, 125–126.

Preminger, A. (1974). *The Princeton encyclopedia of poetry and poetics*. Princeton, NJ: Princeton University Press.

Price, H. H. (1950). *Perception*. London: Methuen.

Putnam, H. (1967). Psychological predicates. In W. H. Capitan & D. D. Merrill (eds.), *Art, mind and religion*. Pittsburgh, PA: University of Pittsburgh Press.

(1975a). The meaning of meaning. In H. Putnam, *Mind, language and reality*. Cambridge University Press.

(1975b). Explanation and reference. In H. Putnam, *Mind, language and reality*. Cambridge University Press.

(1975c). The nature of mental states. In H. Putnam, *Mind, language and reality*. Cambridge University Press.

(1975d). Philosophy and our mental life. In H. Putnam, *Mind, language and reality*. Cambridge University Press.

(1975e). Language and reality. In H. Putnam, *Mind, language and reality*. Cambridge University Press.

(1975f). The mental life of some machines. In H. Putnam, *Mind, language and reality*. Cambridge University Press.

(1977). Realism and reason. *Proceedings and addresses of the American Philosophical Association, 50*, 483–498.

Pylyshyn, Z. W. (1973). What the mind's eye tells the mind's brain: A critique of mental imagery. *Psychological Bulletin, 80*, 1–24.

(1978a). Complexity and the study of human and machine intelligence. In M.

Ringle (ed.), *Philosophical perspectives in artificial intelligence.* New York: Humanities Press.

(1978b). Imagery and artificial intelligence. In C. W. Savage (ed.), *Minnesota studies in the philosophy of science* (vol. 9). Minneapolis: University of Minnesota Press.

(1978c). *On the explanatory adequacy of cognitive process models.* Paper presented at the MIT Workshop on Representation, Massachusetts Institute of Technology.

Quine, W. V., & Ullian, J. S. (1970). *The web of belief.* New York: Random House.

Reddy, M. J. (1969). A semantic approach to metaphor. In *Papers from the fifth regional meeting, Chicago Linguistic Society.* Chicago: University of Chicago, Department of Linguistics.

(1973). Formal referential models of poetic structure. In *Papers from the ninth regional meeting, Chicago Linguistic Society.* Chicago: University of Chicago, Department of Linguistics.

Redgrove, H. S. (1922). *Alchemy: Ancient and modern.* London: William Rider and Son.

Reed, S. K. (1987). A structure-mapping model for word problems. *Journal of Experimental Psychology: Learning, Memory, and Cognition, 13,* 124–139.

Reese, H. W. (1968). *The perception of stimulus relations: Discrimination learning and transposition.* New York: Academic Press.

Reichmann, P., & Coste, E. (1980). Mental imagery and the comprehension of figurative language: Is there a relationship? In R. P. Honeck & R. R. Hoffman (eds.), *Cognition and figurative language.* Hillsdale, NJ: Erlbaum.

Reigeluth, C. M. (1980). *Meaningfulness and instruction: Relating what is being learned to what a student knows.* Syracuse, NY: Syracuse University, School of Education. (ERIC Document Reproduction Service No. ED 195 263.)

Rein, M. (1976). *Social science and public policy.* New York: Penguin.

Rein, M., & Schön, D. (1974). *The design process.* (Mimeo) Massachusetts Institute of Technology.

(1977). Problem-setting in policy research. In C. H. Weiss (ed.), *Using social research in public policy making.* Lexington, MA: D. C. Health.

Reinhart, T. (1976). On understanding poetic metaphor. *Poetics, 5,* 383–402.

Reyna, V. F. (1986). Metaphor and associated phenomena: Specifying the boundaries of psychological inquiry. *Metaphor and Symbolic Activity, 1,* 271–290.

Reynolds, R. E., & Schwartz, R. M. (1983). Relation of metaphoric processing to comprehension and memory. *Journal of Educational Psychology, 75,* 450–459.

Richards, I. A. (1936a). *The philosophy of rhetoric.* London: Oxford University Press.

(1936b). Metaphor. In I. A. Richards, *The philosophy of rhetoric.* London: Oxford University Press.

Ricoeur, P. (1970). *Freud and philosophy: An essay in interpretation.* New Haven, CT: Yale University Press.

Rigg, M. (1937). The relationship between discrimination in music and discrimination in poetry. *Journal of Educational Psychology, 28,* 149–152.

Rorty, R. (1989). *Contingency, irony, and solidarity.* Cambridge University Press.

Rosch, E. (1973). On the internal structure of perceptual and semantic categories.

In T. E. Moore (ed.), *Cognitive development and the acquisition of language.* New York: Academic Press.

(1975a). Cognitive reference points. *Cognitive Psychology, 7,* 532–547.

(1975b). Cognitive representations in semantic categories. *Journal of Experimental Psychology: General, 104,* 192–233.

Rosch, E., Mervis, C. B., Gray, W. D., Johnson, D. M., & Boyes-Braem, P. (1976). Basic objects in natural categories. *Cognitive Psychology, 8,* 382–439.

Ross, B. H. (1984). Remindings and their effects in learning a cognitive skill. *Cognitive Psychology, 16,* 371–416.

(1987). This is like that: The use of earlier problems and the separation of similarity effects. *Journal of Experimental Psychology: Learning, Memory, and Cognition, 13,* 629–639.

Ross, G. (1980). Categorization in 1- to 2-year-olds. *Developmental Psychology, 16,* 391–396.

Rothenberg, A. (1984). Creativity and psychotherapy. *Psychoanalysis and Contemporary Thought, 7,* 233–268.

Rothenberg, J. (ed.), (1985). *Technicians of the sacred.* Berkeley: University of California Press.

Rozin, R., & Fallon, A. E. (1987). A perspective on disgust. *Psychological Review, 94,* 23–41.

Rumelhart, D. E., & Abrahamson, A. A. (1973). A model for analogical reasoning. *Cognitive Psychology, 5,* 1–28.

Rumelhart, D. E., & Norman, D. A. (1981). Analogical processes in learning. In J. R. Anderson (ed.), *Cognitive skills and their acquisition.* Hillsdale, NJ: Erlbaum.

Rumelhart, D. E., & Ortony, A. 1977. The representation of knowledge in memory. In R. C. Anderson, R. J. Spiro, & W. E. Montague (eds.), *Schooling and the acquisition of knowledge.* Hillsdale, NJ: Erlbaum.

Russell, B. (1956). *Logic and knowledge.* Edited by R. C. Marsh. London: Allen & Unwin.

Sadock, J. M. (1976). Methodological problems of linguistic pragmatics. In *Problems in linguistic methatheory.* East Lansing: Michigan State University, Department of Linguistics.

(1978). On testing for conversational implicature. In P. Cole (ed.), *Syntax and semantics* (vol. 9): *Pragmatics.* New York: Academic Press.

Sapir, E. (1921). *Language: An introduction to the study of speech.* New York: Harcourt, Brace and World.

Sapir, J. D. (1977). The anatomy of metaphor. In J. D. Sapir & J. C. Crocker (eds.), *The social use of metaphor: Essays on the anthropology of rhetoric.* Philadelphia: University of Pennsylvania Press.

Schank, R. C., & Abelson, R.P. (1977). *Scripts, plans, goals and understanding.* Hillsdale, NJ: Erlbaum.

Scheffler, I. (1967). *Science and subjectivity.* New York: Bobbs-Merrill.

Schön, D. (1963). *Displacement of concepts.* New York: Humanities Press.

(1971). *Beyond the stable state.* New York: Random House.

Schön, D., & Argyris, C. (1978). *Organizational learning: A theory of action perspective.* Reading, MA: Addison-Wesley.

Schön, D., & Bamberger, J. (1976). *The figural/formal transactions: A parable of generative metaphor.* Cambridge, MA: MIT, Division for Study and Research in Education.

Schumacher, R., & Gentner, D. (1987). *Similarity-based remindings: The effects of similarity and interitem distance.* Paper presented at the Midwestern Psychological Association, 1987.

Searle, J. R. (1969). *Speech acts.* Cambridge University Press.

(1975). Indirect speech acts. In P. Cole & J. L. Morgan (eds.), *Syntax and semantics* (vol. 3): *Speech acts.* New York: Academic Press.

(1978). Literal meaning. *Erkenntnis, 13,* 207–224.

Segal, A. U. (1976). *Verbal and nonverbal encoding and retrieval differences.* Doctoral dissertation, University of Western Ontario.

Sennert, D. (1619). *De chymicorum cum Aristotelicis et Galenicis consensu ac dissensu.* Translated by N. Culpeper & A. Cole.

Sereno, K., & Mortensen, C. (eds.). (1970). *Foundations of communication theory.* New York: Harper & Row.

Shannon, C. E., & Weaver, W. (1949). *The mathematical theory of information.* Urbana: University of Illinois Press.

Shantiris, K. (1983). *Developmental changes in metaphor comprehension: It's not all uphill.* Paper presented at the biennial meeting of the Society for Research in Child Development, Detroit, MI.

Shen, Y. (1987). On the structure and understanding of poetic oxymoron. *Poetics Today, 8,* 105–122.

Shepard, R. N. (1974). Representation of structure in similarity data: Problems and prospects. *Psychometrika, 39,* 373–421.

Shibles, W. A. (1971). *Metaphor: An annotated bibliography and history.* Whitewater, WI: Language Press.

Shinjo, M., & Myers, J. L. (1987). The role of context in metaphor comprehension. *Journal of Memory and Language, 1,* 226–241.

Shinoff, P. (1987). Demjanjuk war-crimes tribunal strikes deep fear among Jews. *San Francisco Examiner,* June 14, p. A8.

Shoemaker, S. (1975a). *Causality and properties.* Unpublished manuscript, Sage School of Philosophy, Cornell University.

(1975b). Functionalism and qualia. *Philosophical Studies, 27,* 291–315.

Shulman, L. S. (1986). Those who understand: Knowledge growth in teaching. *Educational Researcher, 15,* 4–14.

(1987). Knowledge and teaching: Foundations of new reform. *Harvard Educational Review, 57,* 1–22.

Silverman, J., Winner, E., & Gardner, H. (1976). On going beyond the literal: The development of sensitivity to artistic symbols. *Semiotica, 18,* 291–312.

Simon, H. A. (1969). *The sciences of the artificial.* Cambridge, MA: MIT Press.

Simons, P. R. J. (1984). Instructing with analogies. *Journal of Educational Psychology, 76,* 513–527.

Skinner, B. F. (1938). *The behavior of organisms: An experimental analysis.* Englewood Cliffs, NJ: Prentice-Hall.

(1957). *Verbal behavior.* New York: Appleton-Century-Crofts.

Slobin, D. (1971). Developmental psycholinguistics. In W. O. Dingwall (ed.), *Survey of linguistic science.* Stamford, CT: Greylock Publications.

Smart, J. J. C. (1963). *Philosophy and scientific realism*. London: Routledge and Kegan Paul.

Smith, L. B. (1989). From global similarities to kinds of similarities: The construction of dimensions in development. In S. Vosniadou & A. Ortony (eds.), *Similarity and analogical reasoning*. Cambridge University Press.

Smith, T. M. (1970). Some perspectives on the early history of computers. In Z. W. Pylyshyn (ed.), *Perspectives on the computer revolution*. Englewood Cliffs, NJ: Prentice-Hall.

Sperber, D. (1975). *Rethinking symbolism*. Translated by A. L. Morton. Cambridge University Press.

Sperber, D., & Wilson, D. (1981). Irony and the use-mention distinction. In P. Cole (ed.), *Radical pragmatics*. New York: Academic Press.

Spiro, R. J., Coulson, R. L., Feltovich, P. J., & Anderson, D. K. (1988). Cognitive Flexibility Theory: Advanced knowledge acquisition in ill-structured domains. In *Proceedings of the tenth annual conference of the Cognitive Science Society*. Hillsdale, NJ: Erlbaum.

Spiro, R. J., Feltovich, P. J., Coulson, R. L., & Anderson, D. K. (1989). Multiple analogies for complex concepts: Antidotes for analogy-induced misconceptions in advanced knowledge acquisition. In S. Vosniadou & A. Ortony (eds.), *Similarity and analogical reasoning*. Cambridge University Press.

Spiro, R. J., Vispoel, W. P., Schmitz, J. G., Samarapungavan, A., & Boerger, A. E. (1987). Knowledge acquisition for application: Cognitive flexibility and transfer in complex content domains. In B. K. Britton & S. M. Glynn (eds.), *Executive control processes in reading*. Hillsdale, NJ: Erlbaum.

Stalnaker, R. C. (1972). Pragmatics. In D. Davidson & G. Harman (eds.), *Semantics of natural language*. Dordrecht, Holland: D. Reidel.

(1984). *Inquiry*. Cambridge, MA: MIT Press.

Starkey, P., Spelke, E, & Gelman, R. (1983). Detection of intermodal correspondences by human infants. *Science, 222*, 179–181.

Starr, C. A. (1984). Psychological literature: Aphasia. *Psychological Review, 91*, 73–82.

Stepich, D. A., & Newby, T. J. (1988). Analogical instruction within the information processing paradigm: Effective means to facilitate learning. *Instructional Science, 17*, 129–144.

Stern, G. (1965). *Meaning and change of meaning*. Bloomington, IN: Indiana University Press. (Originally published in Sweden 1932.)

Sternberg, R. J. (1977a). Component processes in analogical reasoning. *Psychological Review, 84*, 353–378.

(1977b). *Intelligence, information processing, and analogical reasoning: The componential analysis of human abilities*. Hillsdale, NJ: Erlbaum.

(1978). *Components of inductive reasoning*. Unpublished manuscript, Yale University.

(1985). *Beyond IQ: A triarchic theory of human intelligence*. Cambridge University Press.

(1988). *The triarchic mind: A new theory of human intelligence*. New York: Penguin.

(1990). *Metaphors of mind: Conceptions of the nature of intelligence*. Cambridge University Press.

Sternberg, R. J., & Gardner, M. K. (1978). *A unified theory of inductive reasoning in semantic space.* Unpublished manuscript, Yale University.

Sternberg, R. J., & Nigro, G. (1978). *Component processes in metaphoric comprehension and appreciation.* Unpublished manuscript, Yale University.

Sternberg, R. J., & Rifkin, B. (1979). The development of analogical reasoning processes. *Journal of Experimental Child Psychology, 27,* 195–232.

Stevens, W. (1957). *Opus posthumous.* New York: Knopf.

Sticht, T., Armstrong, W., Hickey, D., & Caylor, J. (1987). *Cast-off youth: policy and training methods from the military experience.* New York: Praeger.

Sticht, T., & Hickey, D. (1991). Functional context theory, literacy, and electronics training. In R. Dillon & J. Pellegrino (eds.), *Instruction: theoretical and applied perspectives.* New York: Praeger.

Stillman, J. M. (1960). *The story of alchemy and early chemistry.* New York: Dover Publications.

Sullivan, K., & Winner, E. (1991). When children understand ignorance, false belief and representational change. *British Journal of Developmental Psychology, 9,* 159–171.

Sunstein, B. S., & Anderson, P. M. (1989). Metaphor, science, and the spectator role: An approach for non-scientists. *Teaching English in the Two-Year College, 16,* 9–16.

Sweetser, E. (1990). *From etymology to pragmatics: The mind-as-body metaphor in semantic structure and semantic change.* Cambridge University Press.

Swift, J. (1971). A modest proposal for preventing the children of poor people from being a burden to their parents or country, and for making them beneficial to the public. In T. Scott (ed.), *The prose works of Jonathan Swift* (vol. 7). New York: AMS Press. (Originally published 1729.)

Talmy, L. (1985). Force dynamics in language and thought. In *Papers from the parasession on causatives and agentivity.* Chicago: Chicago Linguistic Society.

Taylor, F. S. (1949). *The alchemists: Founders of modern chemistry.* New York: Henry Schuman.

Taylor, J. (1989). *Linguistic categorization: Prototypes in linguistic theory.* Oxford: Clarendon Press.

Thoreau, H. D. (1937). *Walden.* In H. S. Canby (ed.), *The works of Thoreau.* Boston: Houghton Mifflin.

Thorndike, E. L. (1927). Reading as reasoning: A study of mistakes in paragraph reading. *Journal of Educational Psychology, 15,* 323–332.

Tourangeau, R., & Sternberg, R. J. (1978). *What makes a good metaphor.* Unpublished manuscript, Yale University.

(1981). Aptness in metaphor. *Cognitive Psychology, 13,* 27–55.

Trager, G. L. (1936–1939). "Cottonwood-Tree," a southwestern linguistic trait. *International Journal of American Linguistics, 9,* 117–118.

Traugott, E. C. (1978). On the expression of spatio-temporal relations in language. In J. H. Greenberg, C. A. Ferguson, & E. A. Moravscik (eds.), *Universals of human language III.* Stanford, CA: Stanford University Press.

(1985). "Conventional" and "dead" metaphors. In W. Paprotte & R. Dirven (eds.), *The ubiquity of metaphor.* Philadelphia, PA: John Benjamin.

Traugott, E. C., & Pratt, M. (1980). *Linguistics for students of literature.* New York: Harcourt Brace Jovanovich.

Tulving, E. (1972). Episodic and semantic memory. In E. Tulving and W. Donaldson (eds.), *Organization of memory*. New York: Academic Press.

Turner, J. F. C. (1976). *Housing by people*. New York: Pantheon.

Turner, J. F. C., & Fichter, R. (eds.). (1972). *Freedom to build*. New York: Macmillan.

Turner, M. (1987). *Death is the mother of beauty: Mind, metaphor, criticism*. Chicago: University of Chicago Press.

(1991). *Reading minds: The study of English in the age of cognitive science*. Princeton, NJ: Princeton University Press.

Turner, V. W. (1974). *Dramas, fields and metaphors: Symbolic action in human society*. Ithaca, NY: Cornell University Press.

Tversky, A. (1977). Features of similarity. *Psychological Review, 84*, 327–352.

Tversky, B., & Hemenway, K. (1984). Objects, parts and categories. *Journal of Experimental Psychology: General, 113*, 169–193.

Tweney, R.D. (1983). *Cognitive psychology and the analysis of science: Michael Faraday and the uses of experiment*. Paper presented at the ninth annual meeting of the Society for Philosophy and Psychology, Wellesley, Wellesley College.

Ullmann, S. (1957). *The principles of semantics* (2d ed.). London: Basil Blackwell.

Underwood, B. J., & Richardson, J. (1956). Some verbal materials for the study of concept formation. *Psychological Bulletin, 53*, 84–95.

Upton, A. (1973). *Design for thinking*. Palo Alto, CA: Pacific Books.

Van Helmont, J. B. (1648). *Ortus Medicinae*. Amsterdam.

Van Lehn, K., & Brown, J. S. (1980). Planning nets: A representation for formalizing analogies and semantic models of procedural skills. In R. E. Snow, P. A. Federico, & W. E. Montague (eds.), *Aptitude, learning and instruction: Cognitive process analyses* (vol. 2). Hillsdale, NJ: Erlbaum.

Van Noppen, J. P., & E. Hols (eds.). (1990). *Metaphor II – A classified bibliography of publications from 1985–1990*. Philadelphia: John Benjamin.

Verbrugge, R. R., & McCarrell, N. S. (1977). Metaphoric comprehension: Studies in reminding and resembling. *Cognitive Psychology, 9*, 494–533.

Vickers, B. (1984). Analogy versus identity: The rejection of occult symbolism, 1580–1680. In B. Vickers (ed.), *Occult and scientific mentalities in the Renaissance*. Cambridge University Press.

Vickers, G. (1973). *Making institutions work*. New York: Wiley.

Vosniadou, S. (1987). Children and metaphors. *Child Development, 58*, 870–885.

(1989). Analogical reasoning as a mechanism in knowledge acquisition: A developmental perspective. In S. Vosniadou & A. Ortony (eds.), *Similarity and analogical reasoning*. Cambridge University Press.

Vosniadou, S., & Brewer, W. F. (1987). Theories of knowledge restructuring in development. *Review of Education Research, 57*, 51–67.

Vosniadou, S., & Ortony, A. (1983). The emergence of the literal-metaphorical-anomalous distinction in young children. *Child Development, 54*, 154–161.

(1989). Similarity and analogical reasoning: A synthesis. In S. Vosniadou & A. Ortony (eds.), *Similarity and analogical reasoning*. Cambridge University Press.

Vosniadou, S., Ortony, A., Reynolds, R., & Wilson, R. (1984). Sources of difficulty in children's understanding of metaphorical language. *Child Development, 55*, 1588–1606.

Vygotsky, L. (1962). *Thought and language*. Cambridge, MA: MIT Press. (Original work published 1934.)

Walsh, M. E. (1988). *A dual coding interpretation of proverb comprehension*. Unpublished doctoral dissertation, University of Western Ontario.

Waltz, D. (1975). Understanding line drawings of scenes with shadows. In P. H. Winston (ed.), *The psychology of computer vision*. New York: McGraw-Hill.

Webb, M. J. (1985). Analogies and their limitations. *School Science and Mathematics, 85,* 645–650.

Wellman, H. (1990). *The child's theory of mind*. Cambridge, MA: Bradford Books.

Werner, H., & Kaplan, B. (1963). *Symbol formation: An organismic developmental approach to the psychology of language and the expression of thought*. New York: Wiley.

Wertheimer, M. (1959). *On productive thinking*. New York: Harper and Row.

Wess, R. C. (1982). *A teacher essay as model for student invention*. Paper presented at the 33rd annual meeting of the conference on College Composition and Communication, San Francisco, CA. (ERIC Document Reproduction Service No. ED 217 478.)

Westfall, R. S. (1977). *The construction of modern science*. Cambridge University Press.

Whatley, J. (1961–1962). 'Like.' *Proceedings of the Aristotelian Society, 62,* 99–116.

White, B. Y. (1984). Designing computer games to help physics students understand Newton's laws of motion. *Cognition and Instruction 1,* 69–108.

White, B. Y., & Frederiksen, J. R. (1987). Qualitative models and intelligent learning environments. In R. W. Lawler & M. Yazdani (eds.), *Artificial intelligence and education* (vol. 1). Norwood, NJ: Ablex.

White, H. (1973). *Metahistory*. Baltimore: Johns Hopkins University Press.
(1978). *Tropics of discourse: Essays in cultural criticism*. Baltimore: Johns Hopkins University Press.

Whitman, N. C. (1975). Chess in the geometry classroom. *Mathematics Teacher, 68,* 71–72.

Whorf, B. L. (1956). *Language, thought, and reality*. Edited by J. B. Carroll. Cambridge, MA: MIT Press.

Wiener, N. (1954). *The human use of human beings: Cybernetics and society* (2d ed.). Garden City, NY: Doubleday Anchor.

Wilensky, R. (1988). Primal content and actual content: An antidote to literal meaning. *Journal of Pragmatics, 13,* 163–186.

Williams, J. (1984). Does mention (or pretense) exhaust the concept of irony? *Journal of Experimental Psychology: General, 113,* 127–129.

Williams, P. S. (1988). Going west to get east: Using metaphors as instructional tools. *Journal of Children in Contemporary Society, 20,* 79–98.

Wilson, D., & Sperber, D. (1989). Representation and relevance. In R. Kempson (ed.), *Mental representations: The interface between language and reality*. Cambridge University Press.
(1990). *Is there a maxim of truthfulness?* Paper presented at the meeting of the International Pragmatics Association, Barcelona, Spain.

Wilson, J. Q. (1975). *In thinking about crime*. New York: Basic Books.

Wilson, S. S. (1981). Sadi Carnot. *Scientific American, 245,* 134–145.

Wimmer, H., & Perner, J. (1983). Beliefs about beliefs: Representation and constraining function of wrong beliefs in young children's understanding of deception. *Cognition, 13,* 103–128.

Winner, E. (1979). New names for old things: The emergence of metaphoric language. *Journal of Child Language, 6,* 469–491.

——— (1988). *The point of words: Children's understanding of metaphor and irony.* Cambridge, MA: Harvard University Press.

Winner, E., & Leekam, S. (1991). Distinguishing irony from deception: Understanding the speaker's second-order intention. *British Journal of Developmental Psychology, 9,* 257–270.

Winner, E., McCarthy, M., & Gardner, H. (1980). The ontogenesis of metaphor. In R. Honeck & R. Hoffman (eds.), *Cognition and figurative language.* Hillsdale, NJ: Erlbaum.

Winner, E., Rosenstiel, A., & Gardner, H. (1976). The development of metaphoric understanding. *Developmental Psychology, 12,* 289–297.

Winner, E., Wapner, W., Cicone, M., & Gardner, H. (1979). Measures of metaphor. *New Directions for Child Development, 6,* 67–75.

Winner, E., Windmueller, G., Rosenblatt, E., Bosco, L., & Best, E. (1987). Making sense of literal and nonliteral falsehood. *Metaphor and Symbolic Activity, 2,* 13–32.

Winokur, S. (1976). *A primer of verbal behavior: An operant view.* Englewood Cliffs, NJ: Prentice-Hall.

Winston, P. H. (1980). Learning and reasoning by analogy. *Communications of the ACM, 23,* 689–703.

——— (1982). Learning new principles from precedents and exercises. *Artificial Intelligence, 19,* 321–350.

Wittgenstein, L. (1953). *Philosophical investigations.* New York: Macmillan.

——— (1961). *Tractatus logico-philosophicus.* Translated by D. F. Pears and B. F. McGuiness. London: Routledge & Kegan Paul. (Originally published 1921.)

Wragg, P. H., & Allen, R. J. (1983). Developing creativity in social studies III: Generating analogies. *Georgia Social Science Journal, 14,* 27–32.

Zegers, D. A. (1983). An urban example for teaching interspecific competition. *The American Biology Teacher, 45,* 276–277.

Zeitoun, H. H. (1984). Teaching scientific analogies: A proposed model. *Research in Science and Technological Education, 2,* 107–125.

Name index

Subject index

abstract representations, 316–20; dual-coding approach to, 321; and integration, 343; memory space use, 323; and salience, 349; and synesthesia, 316–17
abstract words, 321
abstractive seeing, 312–13
accommodation: and anomalous character of metaphor, 587; and assimilation, 544–7, 583–4; in education, 583–4, 587; and schema change, 544–7; in scientific theory change, 483–4, 490–6, 504, 510–11, 517, 541–2
actions, 220–2
activities, in learning, 589, 597–9
actuation, 118–19
adverbial metaphors, 389–90
aesthetics of metaphor, *see* metaphor, aesthetic quality
affective factors: in education, 602–5; in metaphor comprehension, 316–17; and in metaphor production, 607; as salient in metaphors, 134
alchemists, 462–78
algorithms: and computational models, 565; weakness, 219, 249, 565
ambiguity, 127, 130, 496, 525, 530
American Sign Language, 409–10
analogical reasoning: in acquisition of new knowledge, 584; alchemists use of, 462–75; componential theory of, 288; cultural differences in, 475–7; in educational contexts, 627–31; framework for, 296–7, 448–52; historical uses of, 453; and holis-

tic processing, 298; and information processing theory, 287–93, 298; and the Invariance Principle, 235–6; in metaphor definition, 332–4; principles of, 450; process of, 378–9; proportional metaphors as example of, 383–4; in science, 13, 447–80; and structure-mapping, 448–50; and symbols, 467–8
analogical transfer theory, 571–2
analogy (*see also* analogical reasoning): in acquisition of new knowledge, 584; and causal relations, 451; and cognitive change, 601; as comparison statement, 371–3, 378–9; and directionality, 369–70; and generative metaphors, 143, 296–7; historical uses of, 453–75; production of, 606–7; and symbols, 467–8
anger idioms, 273–4
anger metaphors, 228
anomalous character of metaphor, 587, 592–7, 614–18, 624–5
antonyms, 269
apperception; definition, 357; and metaphor, 367, 373; in reading process, 358–68
argument-is-war metaphor, 244
arithmetic story problems, 567–8
arousal, 309
artificial intelligence, 219, 249, 550–1; computer metaphors, 486–7, 493–5, 549–50, 557–58, 565, 626
assimilation–accommodation problem, 544–7, 582–4